Fascism

Series Editor
Darrin McMahon, *Dartmouth College*

After a period of some eclipse, the study of intellectual history has enjoyed a broad resurgence in recent years. The Life of Ideas contributes to this revitalization through the study of ideas as they are produced, disseminated, received, and practiced in different historical contexts. The series aims to embed ideas—those that endured, and those once persuasive but now forgotten—in rich and readable cultural histories. Books in this series draw on the latest methods and theories of intellectual history while being written with elegance and élan for a broad audience of readers.

Fascism

The History of a Word

FEDERICO MARCON

The University of Chicago Press
Chicago and London

The University of Chicago Press, Chicago 60637
The University of Chicago Press, Ltd., London

Published 2025
Printed in the United States of America

34 33 32 31 30 29 28 27 26 25 1 2 3 4 5

ISBN-13: 978-0-226-84130-4 (cloth)
ISBN-13: 978-0-226-84132-8 (paper)
ISBN-13: 978-0-226-84131-1 (e-book)
DOI: https://doi.org/10.7208/chicago/9780226841311.001.0001

Library of Congress Cataloging-in-Publication Data

Names: Marcon, Federico, 1972– author.
Title: Fascism : the history of a word / Federico Marcon.
Description: Chicago : The University of Chicago Press, 2025. |
Series: The life of ideas | Includes bibliographical references and index.
Identifiers: LCCN 2024047696 | ISBN 9780226841304 (cloth) |
ISBN 9780226841328 (paperback) | ISBN 9780226841311 (ebook)
Subjects: LCSH: Fascism—Historiography.
Classification: LCC JC481 .M2845 2025 | DDC 320.53/309—dc23/eng/20250106
LC record available at https://lccn.loc.gov/2024047696

♾ This paper meets the requirements of ANSI/NISO Z39.48-1992 (Permanence of Paper).

To my material teachers, Carol and Massimo,
and to those immaterial ones whom I met only
in texts and through texts,
all of whom taught me that there are no boundaries
to inquisitiveness.
And, it goes without saying, to all those who never stopped
fighting against fascism.

"Ecco, il massimo che si può fare è guardare meglio." ["There: the most we can do is look more closely."]

UMBERTO ECO, *Il nome della rosa*

"Cosa vi terrorizza di più nella purezza?" chiesi. ["What terrifies you most in purity?" I asked.]

"La fretta," rispose Guglielmo. ["Haste," William answered.]

UMBERTO ECO, *Il nome della rosa*

La storia siamo noi, nessuno si senta offeso. . . . La storia siamo noi, attenzione, nessuno si senta escluso. [History is us, no one should feel offended. . . . History is us, pay attention, no one should feel excluded.]

FRANCESCO DE GREGORI, "La storia"

Contents

Preface

> Só existe saber na invenção, na reinvenção, na busca inquieta, impaciente, permanente, que os homens fazem no mundo, com o mundo e com os outros. Busca esperançosa também. [Knowledge emerges only through invention and reinvention, through the restless, impatient, continuing, hopeful inquiry human beings pursue in the world, with the world, and with each other.]
>
> PAULO FREIRE, *Pedagogia do oprimido*

I enjoyed calling this book "my bad idea." After seven years of intensive reading, travel, archival research, discussion, thinking, doubt, writing, erasing, and rewriting, I have not changed my mind a bit: it is a bad idea that breaches every gatekeeping disciplinary rule in academia. But a scorching "fire in the belly," as my former mentor calls it, compelled me to persevere.

This is a history of one word, "fascism," and of its changing political and heuristic agency. It reconstructs and maps the multiplication of its meanings, usages, and referents from its coining in 1919 to the present, by way of its movements around the world, across languages, social groups, and political interests, and through intricate intertextual and intersemiotic networks. It does not just dissect the complex semantic palimpsest of the term, as if the meaning of words were something they naturally contain, simply awaiting conceptual historians' excavation of its orderly structure. Rather, it reconstructs the production of the key semantic markers of "fascism" by different historical actors (Mussolini, Fascist authors, antifascist activists, postwar historians, social and political scientists, artists, philosophers, et al.) and the interpretive habits that these meaning-making acts elicited.

Five wagers led me to embark on this project. The first stemmed from my conviction that a critical analysis of the heuristic affordances of "fascism"—that is, its epistemological efficacy as an analytical category in understanding or classifying movements, ideologies, regimes, attitudes, aesthetics, and so on other than Italian Fascism—must begin from a historical investigation of its meanings. The second implies that this oblique perspective reveals aspects of the counterrevolutionary authoritarianisms of 1919–45 that contribute to the existing scholarship. The third derives from my professional expertise in Japanese history. The history of Japan in the 1930s and early 1940s does not just test the heuristic soundness of "fascism"; it is also a reminder of the global reach of reactionary authoritarianism in the interwar period and its connection to imperialism. Fourth, this study can be read as an investigation into the effects of historians' analytical categories on the cognitive claims that they advance about the past. The nonindexical attribution of the qualifier "fascist" to regimes or ideologies is an operation of inferential labor that historians should account for but rarely do. An analysis of the heuristic legitimacy of "fascism" hence provides us with an opportunity to reflect on historians' practice of knowledge production through the lenses of this case study. The fifth wager stems from my interest in interpretive semiotics—in particular, in its process-based understanding of meaning-making (semiosis) derived from the philosophy of Charles Sanders Peirce and further developed by Roman Jakobson, Juri Lotman, and Umberto Eco—and its application in research of intellectual and conceptual history.

It appears to be quite a timely project. Authoritarianism has become once again a seemingly attractive form of political organization even within traditional democracies in the thoroughly neoliberalized twenty-first century. It would be preposterous to ignore the fact that this project developed in historical circumstances marked by the rise of many extreme right-wing (if not openly fascist) movements and parties around the world. And yet, I programmatically pursued this project in the most untimely fashion.[1] I did not write this book with the purpose of analyzing the present, hypothesizing the causes of today's resurgence of authoritarian ideals; neither is it a practical handbook on how to recognize the early signs of an impending fascist takeover. In presenting Mussolini's rise to power, I had no intention of suggesting to readers that they interpret this volume as an allegorical admonition. But neither can I prohibit readers, who have the sacrosanct right to misread a text as they please insofar as they take responsibility for their interpretations, to adopt it for their presentist agendas.[2] Against the urgency behind so many scholarly efforts today, this book embraces the aversion of William of Baskerville, the detective-monk in Umberto Eco's novel *The Name of the Rose*, to "haste," as quoted in the second epigraph of the book, and advocates taking time for reflection and analysis. And rigorous analysis—what in another passage of the novel Brother William defines simply as "looking more closely"—here takes the form of a reflection on how historians read the historical archives.

My attention to the agency of words is not just a refutation of the naive realism that conceives of historical knowledge as a process of unmediated access to an objectively retrievable past.[3] It is a defense of the idea that the interpretive labor of historians becomes epistemologically more authoritative when its theoretical foundations are explicitly stated and argued for. This is not a capitulation to post-truth or postmodern relativism. Claiming that knowledge is a creative and metabolic process, to borrow some of Freire's words from the epigraph of this preface, does not undermine its truth procedures. It just includes and accounts for the interpretive nature of knowledge itself, and thus of its falsifiability, transiency, contradictoriness, and sociohistorical situatedness, as well as for the coexistence of equally authoritative but divergent truths.

Finally, speaking of the agency of words seems egregiously untimely in a period when many humanistic studies are (rightly) committed to giving agency to the dispossessed and the marginalized, sometimes at the cost of falsifying the sociohistorical conditions that prevented them from having, de facto, any agency at all.[4] Competence in language, the dominant semiotic system (but not the only one) regulating our individual and social lives, contributes to determine the richness or poverty of our ability to make sense of the world we live in, which in turn translates into greater or lesser social agency and greater or lesser chance of emancipation and autonomy. The utopian aspiration at the core of this book is therefore to offer readers some instruments through which they can reflect on how the semiotic environment that sustains our individual and social life works, in order to prevent that environment's being used—as it still is—to create and reproduce inequality and dispossession.

This is why I avoid the rhetoric of persuasion. I do not want to turn readers into proselytes of my own, committedly antifascist views—to the idea that "fascism" refers to a form of counterrevolutionary "democratic" authoritarianism parasitical of the preexisting institutions of capitalist liberalism, and that the term's use as a generic heuristic category should follow a methodological restraint guided by interpretive convenience. Rather, it conceives of the question of the heuristic affordances of "fascism" in terms of interpretive "advantages" and "disadvantages," as well as interpretive "pertinence" and "parsimony," so that the readers can employ this term with a clear and informed understanding of its semiosic capacity, limits, and unintended effects: that is, its agency.

The pedagogic goal that this study pursues is to exorcise the persistent myth that conceives of the meaning of words and of the processes of signification as natural or based on universals.[5] It offers readers some instruments that can help them understand the social conditions leading to the formation and consolidation of the meaning of terms such as "fascism," in an effort to offer a better grasp of (and thus a claim to) the shared ownership of the means of linguistic production.[6] What might appear to be technical questions for initiates are in truth phenomena of meaning-making that we encounter every day and that define every aspect of our daily life. The technical jargon is therefore not a strategy for protecting disciplinary boundaries and social distinction; rather, it is a useful tool kit for enabling the reader to understand how language (semiotic systems in general), society, and the world constantly create one another.

In a sense, the fight against fascism really begins with our emancipation from the spell of its language. If the meanings of words (signs) are not naturally embedded in their signifying vehicles and are not reducible to their referents, neither are they necessarily determined by the will of individuals. The meanings of words are not fixed; they change over time, they have a history: the significance, legitimacy, and fungibility of the words we use in specific historical circumstances to make sense of the world (or to *give* sense to it) derive from the total sum of the collective interventions in communicative acts (monologues, diaries, conversations, drawings, discussions, lectures, articles, books, tweets, symbols, gestures, etc.). In this light, I do not believe that one scholar can impose restrictions, limits, or legitimation on the way we use words. I cannot prescribe (or proscribe) the correct (or incorrect) uses of "fascism" in historical and political analyses. The best I can do is to suggest the heuristic advantages and disadvantages as well as the political consequences of its use.

Introduction

The Advantages and Disadvantages of "Fascism" for History (and for Life)

> Le nostre parole sono spesso prive di significato. Ciò accade perché le abbiamo consumate, estenuate, svuotate con un uso eccessivo e soprattutto inconsapevole. Le abbiamo rese bozzoli vuoti. Per raccontare, dobbiamo rigenerare le nostre parole. Dobbiamo restituire loro senso, consistenza, colore, suono, odore. E per fare questo dobbiamo farle a pezzi e poi ricostruirle. [Our words are often devoid of meaning. This happens because we have consumed them, exhausted them, emptied them with excessive and, above all, unintentional use. We made them empty cocoons. If we want to tell stories, we need to regenerate our words. We have to give them back their sense, consistency, color, sound, smell. And to do this, we have to tear them apart and then putting them back together.]
>
> GIANRICO CAROFIGLIO, *Ragionevoli dubbi*

This book is an investigation into the changes of the meanings, usages, and semiotic functions of the terms *fascio* and *fascismo* (and of their cognate *fascista*) as they transformed from generic words referring to political and cultural associations (and their members), quite common from the second half of the nineteenth to the early twentieth century, into the proper noun that was the name of Mussolini's political movement, regime, and (only later) ideology, to the point that today the earlier uses of the terms are completely forgotten.[1] It traces the transformation of "fascism" into a generic term in the works of antifascist activists and intellectuals, who adopted it as a metaphor to highlight the ideological or structural similarities of different political movements emerging in Europe in the 1920s and 1930s. And it historicizes the quest that engaged postwar historians and political thinkers such as Ernest Nolte, Eugen Weber, Roger Eatwell, Roger Griffin, George Mosse, Stanley Payne, Emilio Gentile, and Robert Paxton, among others, to develop a definition of a "fascist minimum" in an attempt to converting it into the ideal type of a new and potentially universal political form, which could encompass movements and regimes of mass-based reactionary authoritarianism beyond Italy and the transwar period of 1914–45.

This is therefore not a new history of Fascism. It is not, that is, a new synthetic introduction to the rise and fall of Mussolini's regime, although it relies upon and engages with its vast historiography. Neither is it a monograph that introduces new archival findings on the history of Italian Fascism, even though it analyzes a variety of documentary sources—speeches, articles, official documents, letters, treatises, novels, school textbooks, and the like—from archives on different continents. It refuses to propose a new definition of fascism that could encompass, as an ideal type, a variety of political forms in different periods and places, whether or not their adherents adopted or accepted the appellation "fascism" for themselves. In fact, this book originates as a critical inquiry on the epistemological (and political) advantages and disadvantages of postwar historians' attempts to distill a "fascist minimum," a portable definition that aimed to transform fascism into a distinct universal political form alongside democracy, socialism, communism, and liberalism. Furthermore, this book is not a new history of National Socialism: Although it delves into a selection of interwar, postwar, and contemporary authors who wrote on Nazi Germany, it does so only insofar as their works consistently utilized the signifier "fascism" to convey their analyses, thus accruing its genericized meanings and connotations. This book does not, therefore, engage with the most recent historiographical debates on National Socialism and its entanglements with colonialism, scientific racism, big business, mass culture, and so on.

This is simply the history of a word, one of the most infamous in our dictionary—a history of its different meanings and usages and of the epistemological and political consequences of its use as a heuristic category. "Fascism" conjures up meanings, practices, ideals, affects, moods, myths, beliefs, and institutions that contributed to define the history of the twentieth century in the most cruel and repugnant manner. It reverberates once again today as a spectral revenant of past futures, imagined futures of world domination—as in Mussolini's *secolo del Fascismo* or Hitler's *Tausendjähriges Reich*—that were thought to be bygone but seem to have made a comeback, the twenty-first century having thus far showed, *contra* Francis Fukuyama's prediction, that history has hardly ended in the thoroughly neoliberalized world of the post–Cold War era. Fascism—the historical events behind the name—had so great an impact on world history that the term itself has long been used mostly in its figurative rather than literal sense. The *Oxford English Dictionary* records that "fascism" generically refers to "an authoritarian and nationalistic system of government and social organization." Its extended use, denoting "any form of behaviour perceived as autocratic, intolerant, or oppressive," is even more widespread, its earliest usage (in English) dating to 1939 but ubiquitous since the 1960s.[2] Since the Second World War, "fascism" has been loosely mobilized in political propaganda and popular culture as insult or scare word to attack and criticize different forms of perceived authoritarian resurgences. After the Soviet Union coined the term "Velikaya Otechestvennaya voyna protiv fashizma" (Great Patriotic War against Fascism), orthodox Marxists embraced it to rail against any form of perceived reaction, from neo-Nazis to NATO. But the term "fascism" was also mobilized as a critique of Leninism-Stalinism by authors such as Bruno Rizzi, Wilhem Reich, Franz Borkenau, and Otto Rühle in the aftermath of the Molotov-Ribbentrop Pact of 1939.[3] Activists used it to criticize political and police attempts to curb the student, anti-imperialist, and civil rights movements during the global protests of 1968, from Berkeley to Tokyo via Paris, Rome, and Berlin.[4] Antiestablishment commentators used it to condemn the conservative chauvinism of Ronald Reagan's Cold War strategies as well as the friendly dictatorial regimes of Pinochet, Saddam Hussein, George Papadopoulos, and Park Chung Hee.[5] It has roared back to life today in the slogans of both the Left and the Right to denounce Islamofascism and far-right Zionism; Brexiters' isolationism and Trump's MAGA supporters; Turkish, Polish, and Hungarian nationalisms and the *souverainisme* of Matteo Salvini's Lega; and Marine Le Pen's Rassemblement National, Jörg Meuthen's Alternative für Deutschland, and Geert Wilders's Partij voor der Vrijheid, as well as the postfascism of Giorgia Meloni's Fratelli d'Italia.[6] In the United States, appeals to fascism have engaged historians and public intellectuals in an effort to raise people's awareness of the impending authoritarian drift of Donald Trump's presidency.[7] As I write this introduction, it looms behind the rumble of Russian tanks invading Ukraine to pursue Vladimir Putin's imperialistic designs: While Putin claimed that the invasion of Ukraine aimed at a "denazification" of Zelenskyy's government, Western commentators did not hesitate to use "fascism" to define Putin's own regime.[8]

In short, "fascism" continues to be a convenient "boo" word, better used to mobilize consensus by identifying an enemy than to stimulate proper analysis. The words of Gianrico Carofiglio in the epigraph that opens this chapter seem to describe well the predicament of "fascism," emptied by its excessive uses, which have consumed and exhausted it. This book wants to regenerate the significance of "fascism" by tearing apart the history of its usages and meanings and putting it back together with renewed analytical cogency. The risks of the overuse of "fascism" in political analysis were apparent as early as 1926 to the communist Palmiro Togliatti, who warned, "We have become accustomed to use the term 'fascism' in such a general meaning that it serves to designate the most diverse forms of bourgeois reactionary movements. This may be useful for agitation, but it undoubtedly harms the clarity and exact understanding of the facts."[9] The challenge of finding a common ground for what were then perceived as distinct forms of reactionary authoritarian movements and regimes was a common topic of discussion for antifascist intellectuals active in the interwar period, as chapters nine and ten will show. In contrast, the quest for a "fascist minimum" in postwar scholarship was characterized by disputes about which features had to be taken as essential for a working definition of the ideal type of "fascism" that could apply to regimes beyond Italy and the period between the two world wars (chap. 11).

"Fascism," despite its convenience in stirring up militant resistance, hides contradictions, divergencies, and inconsistencies. As Umberto Eco once put it, "'Fascism' has become a synecdoche, a denomination *pars pro toto* for different totalitarian movements." However, "it is pointless to say that Fascism contained in itself all elements of successive totalitarian movements, so to speak 'in a quintessential state.' On the contrary, Fascism contained no quintessence, and not even a single essence. It was a fuzzy form of totalitarianism. It was not a monolithic ideology, but rather a collage of different political and philosophical ideas, a tangle of contradictions."[10] Appeals to fuzziness and complexities may become excuses that allow one to avoid rigorous analysis. Hence the mobilizing power of the word "fascism," which operates as a sort of battle cry that leaves no room for analysis and reflection. As Richard Bosworth put it, "The problem with fascism is that it's a sort of 'boo' word. If you tag somebody with it, then on the one hand you're saying that person is going to murder six million Jews and invade Russia, and on the other hand you feel rather good about using the term and so you don't engage in proper analysis."[11] Bosworth's judgment echoed George Orwell's when in 1946 he noted that "the word Fascism has now no meaning except in so far as it signifies 'something not desirable.'"[12]

Its semantic fuzziness is a consequence of the abuses of "fascism," which seems to have become today the name of any threat to the liberal democratic order, no matter the distinct ontogenesis, ideology, or structure of different regimes it is called to denote.[13] "Fascism" is obviously not the only term marked by such analytical fuzziness; "populism" and "totalitarianism" are similarly fraught with conceptual ambiguities.[14] The main wager of this study is that "fascism" might well be convenient in polemical diatribes, but its abuse and misuse incapacitate its heuristic efficacy and thus its long-term value for the construction of political consciousness. I believe that historical knowledge becomes more advantageous to politics and life precisely when its inquiries do not bend or compromise the rigor of their truth procedures to the necessities of political struggle.

The aim of this book is to tackle the fuzziness, complexities, and contradictions of "fascism." It does not deny that Italian Fascism and German National Socialism were particular instantiations of a new wave of counterrevolutionary authoritarianism in the interwar years. Chapter 5 indeed reckons with the coeval emergence of mass-backed reactionary movements and regimes around the world between the two world wars. Rather, this study questions the epistemological advantages of the term "fascism" as the name of the political form of which these political inventions were instantiations. And it shows the shortcomings of distilling a set of ahistorical essential characteristics (charismatic leadership, populism, nationalism, one-party system, antisemitism, machismo, etc.) from individual cases (Fascism, National Socialism, etc.) removed from the historical context of 1914–45. Japan's authoritarian turn in the 1930s and 1940s does not just question the heuristic affordances of "fascism" but also offers an important non-Eurocentric perspective on the violent consequences of the clash of different imperialistic interests on a global scale in a period of severe economic recession.

Questioning the epistemological limits of the quest for a "fascist minimum" does not mean rejecting decades of excellent scholarship, which has contributed much to our understanding of the political, ideological, cultural, and anthropological impact of Fascism and Nazism in transforming Italian and German societies. It certainly does not intend to side with Gilbert Allardyce, who claims that "only individual things are real; everything abstracted from them, whether concepts or universals, exists solely in the mind. There is no such *thing* as fascism. There are only the men and movements that we call by that name."[15] *Contra* Allardyce, this study conceives of ideas as regulative devices endowed both with the power of directing human actions and decisions (qua historical agents) and with the heuristic capacity of revealing aspects of social reality with cognitive authority and claim to truth. It puts at the center of its analysis the term "fascism" in order both to deconstruct and to reconstruct the ways in which it operated as a historical agent and as a heuristic category of historical interpretation. As an agent, "fascism" was central to the political activity of Mussolini's movement between 1919 and 1945: as the chapters in part I show, its meanings, connotations, and uses changed as the movement it identified by name transformed into a regime and later into an ideology. But "fascism" also operated as a historical agent insofar as it contributed to organizing the theories and practices of intellectuals and activists who opposed Mussolini's regime. It was in the writings of transwar antifascists, the focus of the chapters in part II, that "fascism" first transformed into a generic term that helped mobilize resistance against various forms of mass-based reactionary authoritarianism in Europe and elsewhere. Historicizing the construction of the heuristic category "fascism" will help to shed light not only on the accretions of the meanings of the term between the First and Second World Wars, but also to situate the debates on the creation of the political category of "fascism" and its essentializing definition in the historical context of the Cold War (part III).

Allardyce's approach, which in the late 1970s spurred a legitimate critique of the excessive reductivism of generic "fascism," also seems to ignore the fact that sociocultural phenomena never exist in isolation, as individual atoms, nor are they experienceable in a preconceptual mode; rather, they are imbricated in a web of shared meanings, connotations, and interpretive habits and are subject to transferences, adaptations, and reformulations of the meanings and the practices they elicit. Reconstructing the ways in which the historical agent "fascism" acquired and lost meanings is essential to understanding how the movements legitimately or illegitimately associated with it are related to other coeval political forms, from liberalism to socialism and from monarchism to revolutionary conservatism.

The Semantics of "Fascism" and the Politics of Language

Still, this history of the word "fascism" is not a simple exercise in historical semantics. It is an effort to understand one of the most bewildering paradoxes of modernity: people's voluntary abdication of the modern emancipatory ideals of freedom, equality, and solidarity. Its oblique perspective of inquiry is deliberate. It does not just aim at filling an existing gap in the scholarship of fascism—no empirically detailed systematic history of the meanings and usages of the word "fascism" has been attempted before.[16] It stems from the persuasion that "fascism"—for decades the convenient name given to various forms of political reaction, from Mussolini's to today's populist regimes—ultimately constitutes a heuristic disadvantage for our understanding of what has been (and could still be) alternatively called "democratic authoritarianism" (Antonio Gramsci, Dylan Riley), "revolutionary conservatism" (Ernst Jünger, Armin Mohler), "nationalist totalitarianism" (Giovanni Amendola, Alain Touraine), "totalitarian democracy" (Joseph A. Schumpeter, Jacob L. Talmon, Alessandro Mulieri), or "counterrevolutionary authoritarianism," as this book does.

The name "fascism" represented a semantic break from traditional political ideals and practices. Mussolini indeed insisted on the fact that Fascism was a new form of antipolitical *political* praxis, a revolutionary movement that he intended to be entirely distinct from traditional parties and ideologies. In particular, he wanted it to be different from traditional conservatisms and nationalisms. But he also wanted it to yield a distinct type of social revolution from the one advocated by the socialists and communists. The semantic fuzziness of "fascism"—which, when Mussolini first used it in 1920, could be literally translated into the nondescript "unionism" or "associationism" (chaps. 1 and 2)—was thus a convenient semiotic device that rendered it receptive to being filled with new meanings and connotations. Conversely, the name "fascism" was advantageous for antifascist activists because it allowed them to juxtapose various forms of counterrevolutionary authoritarianism in transwar Europe with the first one that succeeded in taking power, even though the members of these movements (National Socialism, Ustaše, Falangismo, etc.) refused that appellation for themselves.

One disadvantage of "fascism" as a generic word for forms of reactionary political praxis distinct from traditional forms of conservativism lies in its inevitable link with Italian Fascism and its historical unfolding. Because of this link and, even more important, because of the etymological meaninglessness of the term *fascismo* itself, this book contends that it ultimately fails to account for the distinct characteristics and ontogenesis of the different forms of authoritarianism it pretends to identify, especially when used to define movements and regimes that emerged after the end of the Second World War, even if this genericizing practice has become conventional in ordinary language.[17]

Theoretically put, this book conceives of a political dilemma of twentieth-century history in epistemological terms but pursues its analysis through historical investigations. The question it explicitly asks, in its simplest form, is whether "fascism" can function as a generic concept that legitimately collects under the same rubric regimes that have sociohistorically distinct geneses, on the assumption that they share some essential common characteristics. The question is epistemological in nature, as it inquires about the capacity, limits, and legitimacy of "fascism" to operate as a *principium individuationis* (in philosophy, the essential characteristics allowing the identification of a thing as distinct from others) that subsumes within its genericity a heterogeneity of social, political, cultural, and intellectual phenomena.[18] But the investigations it elicits are eminently historical insofar as the meanings of "fascism," a term with no core conceptual meaning, derive from the historical vicissitudes of the regime bearing that name and from the distinct processes of genericization of that proper name into a generic category of analysis. The processes that conventionalized its generic use were themselves situated in different historical contexts (the interwar years of 1918–45 and the postwar years of 1960s to the present) and therefore subjected to different social, political, and intellectual pressures: The historical circumstances that accompanied the formation and consolidation of the different meanings of "fascism" are therefore relevant to the semantic reconstructions this study pursues.

The term "fascism," as we use it today, is an opaque blend of at least four distinct genealogies of meanings and uses. First, it is the proper name of an Italian political movement, ideology, and regime created and led by Benito Mussolini between 1919 and 1945. Second, it is a political category in circulation between the 1920s and the 1940s, which originated among antifascist intellectuals and activists as metonymical generalization (antonomasia) of the proper noun Fascism to refer to other forms of conservative counterrevolution in the interwar period. In both cases, "fascism" operated as a historical agent *qua* actors' category. Third, "fascism" has routinely operated since the 1960s as a metahistorical category that is synecdochically predicated to right-wing regimes, movements, or ideologies beyond the context of Mussolini's Italy—to the extent that Italian Fascism is only one among many others of its instantiation, and often not even the most representative one, as most definitions of the "fascist minimum" were modeled upon German Nazism (chap. 11).

These two processes of generalization operated differently. The first utilized "fascism" to highlight similarities and affinities between coeval movements and regimes: the comparison was *metonymical* insofar as the juxtaposition did not presuppose hierarchical relations but operated horizontally, insisting on their proximity and similarity, so that "fascism" could become a name for them all (as noted earlier, in rhetoric this is a type of metonymy called antonomasia). The second generalization reduced local movements and regimes to instantiations, or tokens, or a general type: the comparison was therefore *synecdochical* insofar as the relation of the genus "fascism" with the individual movements and regimes it subsumed was vertical and, as *totum pro parte*, hierarchical—to the point that Italian Fascism was equally a token of a more generic type of "fascism."[19] In addition to these three semantic genealogies, "fascism" is also an insult or scare word that since the late 1960s has been thrown, with different degrees of efficacy, against political adversaries to emphasize their intolerant, violent, authoritarian, chauvinistic, and racist ideas and actions.[20]

These four usages of "fascism" have distinct geneses, meanings, and *modus operandi*: the first is historical, the third and fourth are ahistorical, and the second is both; one operates as a seemingly rigid designator of a distinct political movement, the other three as a generic category with universalistic aspirations.[21] In singular form with capital "F," it is the name of a distinct movement, regime, and ideology; plural and with small "f," it is an attribution ascribed, with contested legitimacy, to reactionaries who did not necessarily use that term to refer to themselves. When "fascism" is attributed to political movements and ideologies outside the European context of the 1920s–40s, even if simply as an insult, the four meanings get muddled up.

Two things motivated my decision to investigate the epistemological limits of the category "fascism" historically rather than just semantically. First, the term "fascism" has become a political category with universalistic claims only as a consequence of the historical impact of a regime that bore that name, rather than in fidelity to any preexisting meaning, ideology, or utopia it may have signified. This is a distinguishing characteristic of "fascism" when compared to other political categories, such as "democracy," "liberalism," "socialism," or "communism," no matter how fuzzily conceived. In these cases, the name accompanying the concrete instantiations of historically specific movements, parties, and regimes—as, for instance, in Partito Socialista Italiano (Italian Socialist Party, 1892–1994; PSI) or Deutsche Demokratische Partei (German Democratic Party, 1918–30)—maintained a semantic connection, sometimes strong but at other times feeble, with a core conceptual meaning of "socialism," "communism," and "democracy," which gave a sort of indication of the political, social, and economic ideals of the parties they qualified; at the very least, it suggested an affiliation or genealogical derivation from those ideas. "Fascism," on the contrary, was born as the name of a political type only from the genericization of the historical event that was Mussolini's movement and regime. It has no stable semantic core, no inherent meaning, no political orientation except for that which derives from the historical vicissitudes of that regime.[22] If in the case of traditional movements and parties, contingent actualizations follow or derive from an abstract ideal that plays a more or less stringent regulative role, in the case of fascism it is the ideal—differently conceived (and this is of key importance) by Mussolini, by coeval antifascist theorists, and by postwar historians—that follows or derives from the contingent actualization of Mussolini's regime (or Hitler's).[23] The case of "fascism"—a political term without any core meaning—is not unique. "Bolshevism," one of the names for revolutionary socialism in Russia, is similarly a term with no core political meaning; it is derived from the Russian *bolshinstvo* (majority), indicating the majority faction of the Russian Social Democratic Labor Party led by Vladimir Lenin, which formed at its second congress of 1903, but it became the appellation of Marxism-Leninism as a result of the contingent historical unfolding of communism in the Soviet Union after the victory of Lenin's bloc.[24]

The chapters in part I show how Mussolini constantly intervened to institute an orthodox codification of the semantic markers of "fascism," offering new definitions, descriptions, and narratives of what Fascism was and what it meant to be a Fascist in speeches, editorials for *Il popolo d'Italia*, and only in 1932, after ten consecutive years of uncontested power, in *La dottrina del fascismo*.[25] Constant repetitions of the name "Fascismo," self-referential indulgence in new definitions, and conative appeals to the readers (in editorials) and the masses (in rallies and public speeches), who were interpellated to participate in the construction of the Fascist state, were rhetorical strategies aimed at filling a name with meanings it did not have. At times, these definitions bordered on the ridiculous, like the one Mussolini offered in an interview on October 6, 1919 of what it meant to be a fascist: "It is a bit difficult to define fascists. They are republicans, socialists, democrats, conservatives, nationalists. They represent a synthesis of all the negations and of all the affirmations."[26] More often, the ever-shifting definitions of what Fascism or being a Fascist meant were aimed at reflecting a new sociopolitical situation, either domestically or internationally, so that Fascism could better adapt to the circumstances. So, for Mussolini Fascism was "socialist," "democratic," "republican," "anticlerical," and "nationalist" in 1919, but in 1921 it became "antidemocratic" but the only answer to the "hypertrophic democratic demands" of the Italian masses,[27] "antiliberal" but liberalistic in its economic orientation, "monarchical," and the only defender of the Catholic traditions in Italy. In 1922 it continued to claim its revolutionary ambitions while supporting a coalition government of traditional conservatives and moderate centrists. Only "anticommunism" and beliefs in "regenerative violence" remained constant. In 1925 it became "totalitarian" and "corporatist," "populist" and the affirmation of an "aristocracy of command." In 1930 Fascism became "universal" and in 1936 "anti-imperialist" but "imperial." In 1938 it was "antisemitic" and "defender of the Italian race," the Mediterranean Aryans, and in 1943 it returned to its original "antimonarchism" as the genocidal collaborator of the Nazi occupiers.

In other words, the meaning of Fascism, for Mussolini, changed with the changes of his regime, which in turn responded to the changing historical situation—hence the necessity of a historical reconstruction of the moving target that is "fascism." As the socialist historian Angelo Tasca put it, "To define fascism is above all to write its history."[28]

The second motivation for privileging a historical approach lies in the fact that the transformations of the proper noun Fascism into a generic concept are themselves historical events, based on and motivated by the circumstances that produced them. For interwar activists, reaching an understanding of fascism was the necessary condition for organizing their resistance to the dictatorial regime. For most of them, especially Marxist agitators, "fascism" was a convenient name (antonomasia) for the similar socioeconomic circumstances that nurtured the growth and success of different ideologies, organizations, and regimes. Mussolini was keen to rapidly adopt some of his adversaries' definitions. For instance, when the liberal democrat Giovanni Amendola, the Catholic Luigi Sturzo, and the socialist Lelio Basso, one year after the formation of Mussolini's first cabinet in the aftermath of the March on Rome of 1922, accused Mussolini of having turned Italian institutions into a totalitarian regime, Mussolini was quick to appropriate the notion of "totalitarianism" to enthusiastically defend the *feroce volontà totalitaria* (fierce totalitarian will) of the Fascist state, for which "everything in the State, nothing outside the State, nothing against the State."[29]

Similarly, the historiographical quest to develop a generic category of fascism, the subject of part III, was itself situated in the specific historical context of the Cold War. The conservative historian Ernst Nolte was among the first to propose a generic category of fascism not only to reject the *Sonderweg* conception that National Socialism was the inevitable culmination of German history, but also to ideologically exonerate the sociopolitical elites for their support of the violent counterrevolutionary reactions of Hitler's regimes and to sever the link between fascism and capitalist liberalism characteristic of Marxist historiography. Historicizing historians' own interpretations of the past is one of the key methodological wagers of this investigation, stemming from the necessity of distinguishing the opposite semiosic labor behind the two genericizations of "fascism": while for interwar antifascist activists Italian Fascism was the *terminus ab quo* (or that from which their heuristic labor sprang) of their attempts to synthesize an understanding of the new political phenomenon, for postwar scholars fascism was the *terminus ad quem* (or that toward which their heuristic labor was directed) of their investigation.

This book, in short, reconstructs the semiotics of "fascism." It retrieves the ways in which the term "fascism"—the meanings of which fascists, antifascists, historians, and political theorists have all contributed to create—functioned (and still functions) as a meaning-making conceptual device. This is not just an effect of the methodological approach of this investigation, which moves from the traditional methods of intellectual and conceptual history to a semiotically informed history, or a history *sub specie semioticae*.[30] It also follows from the empirical observation that both Mussolini's Fascism and Hitler's National Socialism paid close attention to language and the use of words. Mussolini, a *gladiatore della parola* (word gladiator), self-consciously saw in the state control of language and signification a necessary step toward the anthropological transformation of Italians that his Fascism aimed to achieve.[31]

That rhetoric plays a fundamental role in politics is a truism that is all too often ignored.[32] The role of language is not limited to persuasion and consensus-building. It is constitutive of political praxis and social organization: It creates (and sets the limits to) the possibility of experience and action. "There is no doubt at all," Roland Barthes claimed in *Writing Degree Zero*, "that each regime has its own writing, no history of which has yet been written. Since writing is the spectacular commitment of language, it contains at one and the same time, thanks to a valuable ambiguity, the reality and the appearance of power, what it is, and what it would like to be thought to be: a history of political modes of writing would therefore be the best of social phenomenologies."[33]

Mussolini had been well aware of the power of language ever since his years as a socialist agitator. "Words have their own tremendous magic," he mused.[34] Mussolini modulated his language in both editorials and rallies with unique rhetorical cunning to enhance the "magic" of his words, not only with conative interpellations of the masses (present and imagined) and seemingly redundant phatic anticipations, apophasis, and metalingual expressions (persistently addressing the listeners' or readers' attention to the illocutionary act that they were experiencing),[35] not only with an emphatic use of the body and gesticulation,[36] but especially by exercising tight control over his choice of words. For instance, he made expansive use of mystical, religious, and spiritual terms to convey secular ideas and political actions; he utilized military and war expressions to describe the challenges of everyday life of the common people as well as Fascism's heroic deeds; and he invented hundreds of new words, neologisms whose sole purpose was to give hyperbolic connotations, both positive and negative, to the subjects he discussed.[37] The linguistic strategies of Fascism are the theme of chapter 4.

Global Fascism?

The history of the word "fascism" has local origins but global destiny. The lenses of comparative and transnational history shed light on the development of "fascism" and the ensemble of historical phenomena this word has been recruited to name, legitimately or illegitimately. In the aftermath of the March on Rome and King Vittorio Emanuele III's mandate to Benito Mussolini to form a coalition government, Fascism rapidly transformed from an insignificant local movement to a political phenomenon whose success sent shock waves around the world. News of the Italian political invention traveled rapidly and triggered the interest of governments, commentators, and activists across the globe, from the United States to Japan.

Numerous studies have attempted to locate Fascism within the tradition of the European Right and "revolutionary conservatism."[38] As Enzo Traverso put it, "Italian fascism developed an eclectic and pragmatic synthesis from materials borrowed from different and until then separate traditions of thought. Therein lies its doctrinal originality."[39] But worldwide reactions to the rise of Mussolini's regime have received less attention from historians.[40] While the topic is beyond the scope of this book, a panoramic survey of Fascism's reception worldwide helps account for the semantic growth of the term "fascism" (chap. 5).

Mussolini himself paid close attention to the reactions of other statists around the world. Global responses often affected his own ideological presentations of Fascism. It was ironic that Mussolini's project of internationalizing and universalizing Fascism, through diplomatic missions and intense cultural exchanges, originated specifically in response to the antifascist genericization of "fascism." By the 1930s the rhetorical celebration of the universality of Fascism had become a recurring topic in Mussolini's public speeches and articles. Contrary to Hitler's Nazism, which asserted its "Germanness" (*Volksdeutsche*) both culturally and biologically in open antagonism against any form of internationalism,[41] Mussolini shrewdly capitalized on the worldwide interest in his movement—just as, in the previous decade, he had appropriated the notion of "totalitarianism" from antifascist critics to sustain his ideal of *stato totalitario*.

A Fascist International never formed, despite Mussolini's efforts. Hitler admired Mussolini as "one of the world's great men,"[42] but the relationship between the two dictators was always fraught with tensions, incomprehension, and suspicions throughout the 1930s.[43] Their meetings were arguably more important for enhancing the liturgical and theatrical performance of the two regimes domestically than for achieving pragmatic diplomatic goals internationally.[44] The Stahlpakt or Patto d'Acciaio (Pact of Steel) between Italy and Germany was signed only on May 22, 1939, but despite their vaunted alliance Hitler never informed Mussolini of the invasion of Poland until it was a fait accompli. The Tripartite Pact with Japan would be signed only on September 27, 1940, when the Wehrmacht had already occupied large chunks of continental Europe. Both were defensive military alliances rather than ideological. As Richard Overy has argued, "The Axis states [were] not actually a coherent alliance."[45]

But a history of "fascism" must be global for yet another reason. The invention, dissemination, and success of the ideas and political practices that this term was asked to name as a generic category cannot in fact be understood without reference to the global conjuncture that the traumatic global event of the early twentieth century, the First World War, had created. The ruinous effects of the Great War must be measured not only in terms of human casualties and material destruction, but also in terms of the way it suspended the fundamental norms of civility, both in peace and in war, the consequences of which unfolded in the following three decades. For Antonio Gibelli, the First World War was an *officina* (workshop) that gave birth to new imaginaries and mentalities: unprecedented violence, mass mobilization of civilians, new forms of sociability modeled upon trench camaraderie, and the central role of the state in the organization of the industrial and ideological support for a war which was now really "total."[46] The conflict of 1914–18 was lived by those who survived it as the first instance of modern warfare, which previous conflicts, such as the Russo-Japanese War (1904–5) and the Balkan Wars (1912–13) had only suggested.

Enzo Traverso argued that the First World War brought to an abrupt end the notion of the *bellum justum* (just war), which had at the very least sustained European conflicts ideologically since premodern times. "The law of war," he explained, adopting Carl Schmitt's terminology,[47] "was just one aspect of the *jus publicum europaeum*, marking the advent of a codified system of relations between states possessing the monopoly of legitimate violence within the respective territories. The notion of *bellum justum* allowed for that of sovereignty, which presupposed the inviolability of the power of the state within its frontiers." In this kind of legal context, "war is always legitimate . . . providing it is declared. In other words, a war is now 'just' not because of its aims but because of its conduct."[48] Against that legal consensus, the first global conflict opened a Pandora's box of destruction, both material and spiritual. "People at the time," Jörn Leonhard notes, "were immediately aware that the impact of the war was not just a question of the scale of its casualties; the upshot of it all could not be measured by the millions of dead soldiers and civilians. There was something more fundamentally new in the character of the violence. . . . The war had revealed what was possible in the name of the nation and nation-state, and what was possible had become evident in the widespread breaking of taboos and loss of inhibitions."[49]

Fascism, Nazism, and other forms of counterrevolutionary authoritarianism of the 1920s and 1930s were the offspring of that war, which Fascists and Nazis carried over by other means in their political activities.[50] Moreover, it must be noted that, as Mark Mazower has argued, after the war democratic institutions in most parts of the world were in their infancy and did not constitute a robust protection against illiberal and subversive policies.[51]

The implied premise of this book is that the global conjunction of nationalism, conflicting imperialisms, economic depression, mass politics, and war (both actual and idealized as the purest form of political praxis) that ensued after the Great War is a more persuasive explanation for the coeval emergence of these movements of violent authoritarianism than the presence of an ideologically homogeneous "global fascism." The case of Japan in the late 1930s, which saw its state institutions taking a more marked authoritarian guise but one that was well within the limits of the 1889 Constitution and did not assume the revolutionary characters of Italian Fascism and German Nazism, offers a perspective that helps us to reconsider not only the question of generic "fascism" but especially the global history of authoritarianism of the 1930s in the context of the clash of imperial interests and widespread economic depression.[52]

This study supports the idea that the years 1914–45 should be regarded as one consistent period dominated by war. This is neither a new concept nor one that gathers the consensus of historians.[53] In the Bar-le-Duc speech of July 28, 1946, Charles de Gaulle used the term "Second Thirty Years' War" to refer to this period, an expression that Winston Churchill also adopted in his memoir *The Gathering Storm* and to which such historians as Arno Mayer, Enzo Traverso, Johann Chapoutot, Dan Diner, and Ian Kershaw, among others, gave heuristic legitimacy.[54] This study embraces that idea, but on a global scale. I use the expression not to evoke similarities or convergences with the seventeenth-century European conflict to which de Gaulle referred, but rather to emphasize the dominance of war as idea, praxis, and destiny in the entire period.

The years between the two wars, as Richard Overy persuasively shows, were punctuated by national and imperial conflicts that anticipated the violence soon to erupt in a second global conflict: the Russian Civil War of 1917–23, the Ukrainian-Soviet War of 1917–21, the Polish-Soviet War of 1919–21, the Irish War of Independence of 1918–21, the Chinese Civil War of 1927–37, the Second Italo-Abyssinian War of 1935–37, the Spanish Civil War of 1936–39, and the numerous "incidents" between Japan and China beginning in 1931.[55] Moreover, global political struggles and civilian and labor conflicts between the two world wars often adopted tones and methods of violent upheaval that had the characteristics of a civil war, such as during the widespread social and labor unrest known as the *biennio rosso* (two red years) of 1919–20 in Italy and the socialist upheaval in German towns in the immediate aftermath of the First World War, all violently repressed by the state, often with the collaboration of right-wing paramilitary groups like the Fascist Squadristi and the German Freikorps, which were given free rein and often armed by the police.[56]

Moreover, the experience of trench warfare (*Grabenkrieg*, *Grabenkämpfe*) during the Great War inspired political movements that not only justified the use of violence for political ends but contributed to elevate it as the purest form of political action. In embracing violence, Mussolini anticipated all other ideologues since the early days of the Fasci di Combattimento. On September 20, 1922, in a gathering in Udine, he defended the notion that "violence is not immoral. It is sometimes moral. We contest our enemy the right to lament of our violence. . . . Our violence is the solution for a cancerous situation; it is very moral [*moralissima*], sacrosanct, necessary."[57] While artists such as Otto Dix, Jean-Paul Laurens, Paul Nash, George Grosz, Albin Egger-Lienz, Alberto Martini, Adolf Uzarski, and many others attempted to express the despairs and destructions of the war aesthetically, Futurists such as Mario Carli, Filippo Tommaso Marinetti, and Emilio Settimelli, as well as the public poet (*vate*) Gabriele D'Annunzio, wished to preserve the exalted experience of the war in the form of a political party that would give its support to Mussolini's Fasci di Combattimento.[58] Furthermore, the Bolshevik Revolution of 1917 and its aftershocks in popular upheavals in Germany and Italy in 1919 and 1920 revamped the idea of a *conservative* form of counterrevolutionary revolution, now marked by a strong anticommunist and antiliberal stance, of which Fascism and Nazism became instances.[59]

Historians' Categories

This book reconstructs the development of the systems of signification that different historical actors (Mussolini, other Fascist leaders, transwar antifascist activists and thinkers, postwar historians and political theorists, artists, journalists, et al.) invested in the signifier "fascism" under different historical circumstances and for different purposes.[60] Because historians too participate in this semiotic labor, this investigation would not be complete if it did not turn its analytical gaze to the discipline of history itself. By historicizing the different interpretations of "fascism" in postwar scholarship, the question of "fascism" becomes an invitation to analyze historians' cognitive labor.

That historical knowledge, as a sociohistorically situated and mediated form of knowledge, is interpretive, falsifiable, and often antinomic is a truism that few historians really question today. Yet, the disavowal of theoretical reflection and the emergence of forms of procedural dogmatisms, combined with the erosion of professional historians' authority in the public sphere, invite renewed reflections on historiographical labor.[61] The retellings of the past (history) always change not because of a pernicious effect of postmodernity,[62] nor because the study of the past is necessarily instrumental to the present (presentism).[63] Conceiving of historical knowledge as mediated does not hinder the truth value of historians' labor or the authority of the discipline of history: it is by no means the case that "anything goes," a notion that Carlo Ginzburg, somewhat unfairly, charged Roland Barthes and Hayden White with supporting.[64]

The traces of the past are instructions that guide historians' interpretations, and as such they limit the legitimacy of these interpretations. But to become history, these traces must be embedded in heuristic apparatuses (selecting criteria, terminology, interests, questions, metaphors, analytical tools, theoretical frameworks, instruments, institutions, narratological structures, etc.) that provide them with meaning. These apparatuses need to be accounted for—all the more if they are hidden behind the "reality effect" of a smooth narrative form.[65] The analysis of historians' cognitive practices in this book is not an exercise in disciplinary normativity. It is central to the reconstruction of the meanings of "fascism." In a sense, this book turns Allardyce's method, mentioned above, on its head and claims that we can access "real individual things" of the past only through the mediation of conceptual constructs, which do not exist only in our minds but, as connectors of thoughts, actions, and the material world, contribute in a very real sense to the constitution of the social fabric.[66] The mediatedness of historical knowledge does not hinder the truth value of the discipline of history. It makes knowledge of the past possible.

To avoid the hypostatizing effect of concepts, as in the case of the "fascist minimum," this study assumes that the conceptual apparatus historians adopt to study the past inevitably affects the ways in which the past is constructed as history. It is not just that key heuristic categories present the object of inquiry *in a certain respect*. They have also the reifying effect of *constituting* an "object" of inquiry for an inquiring "subject" out of the heterogeneous material traces that the past has left.[67] It is only through a conceptual apparatus that has both epistemological and institutional legitimacy that this heterogeneity is transformed into a coherent object of study.

The methodological conviction behind this project is that a realist understanding of concepts gives us no choice but to submit its analytical apparatus to the same rigorous analysis and historicization as its object of inquiry. For all these reasons, "fascism" is a word that asks of those who investigate its history that they adopt different interpretive strategies. Like intellectual historians, they must reconstruct genealogies of derivations, convergences, and divergences.[68] Like conceptual historians, they must chronicle the changes and accretions of its semantic values.[69] Like social historians, they must retrieve the social conditions that favored these changes and accretions.[70] Like Bourdieusian analysts, they must self-reflexively examine the epistemological effects of attributing this word to people, movements, regimes, and ideas of the past and of the present.[71] Like semioticians, they must investigate how the system of signification embedded in the signifier "fascism" affects the nature of its relationship with the things, deeds, and ideas it is taken to stand for. The multidisciplinary approach pursued in this study—and of interpretive semiotics in particular—clarifies the process of transference of meaning that ensues when the term "fascism" is used as index that deictically refers to the historical event that was Mussolini's regime and when it is utilized as a generic category for identificatory or epistemological purposes. The interplay of indexicality and symbolicity in the use of the term favors the passage of connotative contents (at once political, ethical, and cognitive) from historical Fascism (e.g., its violence, ultranationalism, chauvinism, statism, imperialism, etc.) to other movements, ideologies, and regimes. The semantic transference of particular connotations from Fascism to other movements deemed fascist that is at the core of the different genericizations of the term reconstructed in parts II and III produced effects of meaning the cognitive impact of which only a semiotic analysis can properly account for.

As a science dedicated to the study of semiosis—that is, of the processes of meaning-making through the production *and* interpretation of signs—semiotics offers an analytical tool kit suited to diachronic reconstruction of the processes that conventionalized the meanings of "fascism" (i.e., its denotations and connotations) in specific historical circumstances and among different social groups: Mussolini and other Fascist authors (part I), antifascist activists (part II), and postwar historians, sociologists, and political thinkers (part III). This book's exploration of the vast archive of interwar Fascist and antifascist authors, as well as of some intertextual conversations in the immense scholarship of postwar historians, political scientists, thinkers, and artists, is not an end in itself. This is not a history of the *discourses* on fascism—whether the term is understood as referring to Italian Fascism or generically to the heterogeneous forms that reactionary authoritarianism can take. It is a history of the processes that produced and conventionalized the semantic palimpsest of the term "fascism," internally fractured into an ensemble of often contradictory denotative and connotative markers and of contested referential uses. Umberto Eco's interpretive semiotics, being a synthesis of structuralism and pragmatism, developed a historical understanding of how phenomena of meaning-making (semiosis) result from acts of sign production and interpretation, and how these acts, once socially registered and conventionalized as interpretive *habiti*, become constitutive parts of the semantic markers of a word.[72] Semiotic analysis reveals how the different denotative and connotative values of "fascism" in the speech acts of Fascists, antifascists, and postwar historians of various political leanings engendered distinct actions, affective responses, discursive practices, and understandings.

Eco's interpretive semiotics offer the historical study of words, ideas, and social practices several analytical advantages. First, it offers a model for understanding the formation of concepts that does not rely on metaphysically suspicious standpoints outside language (universals, referential naturalism, God, etc.). Second, it avoids the tension that conceptual history often leaves unresolved between words (as sign vehicles, or signifiers) and the concepts they convey. Third, it is a model of analysis that is both synchronic and diachronic, insofar as it implies that the compositional structure of the meaning of each term (the ensemble of its denotative and connotative markers) changes over time as a result of the institutionalization and conventionalization of practices of meaning-making. It avoids, in other words, any form of etymological reductionism. Fourth, the polysemy, fuzziness, and aporetic contradictoriness that concepts such as "fascism" generate are conceived of not as a property of those terms, but rather as the result of contrasting uses and conceptions, thus signaling their contested status within a historical society.[73] Fifth, the semantic content of words, conceived as "cultural units" that regulate human interactions with the world in a very real, concrete sense, are not outside history, universal, permanent, or the possession of one specific culture or social group. Rather, the formation and structure of different cultural units (and the way words are used to create different understandings of the world, with real practical effects) are an ever-changing phenomenon, subjected to modifications, transformations, adaptations, and hybridizations.[74] This history of "fascism" is an example of the mutability of words, concepts, and cultural units. Sixth, interpretive semiotics also avoids any hypostatization of semantic structures, as if they constituted an ontological limit to semiosic production. The structuring of semantic markers is not a fact of nature, nor does it "mirror" nature; instead, it is the result of different kinds of semiosic *habitus*. According to this view, the structuring and hence regulative effects of language can be understood without necessarily presupposing either an ontologically conceived semantic system or the intentional intervention of semantic demiurges (be they God, "great historical figures," or white male philosophers), but simply as the total sum of semiosic acts that have acquired a degree of conventionality (and hence stability) within a linguistic community. In producing signs, communicating, producing and interpreting texts of various kind, we all contribute to reinforcing or setting up the conditions for transforming the systems of signification of a historical society. Consequently, interpretive semiotics sheds light on different kinds of cultural practices not simply as cultural events, but as sociopolitical phenomena, the conditions and limits of which are social rather than strictly individual. These include writing, thinking, theorizing, but also leading people, waging war, organizing a political movement, and ruling a state.

Finally, it is from semiotics that the political dimension of every communicative act—including writing a book on the meaning of the word "fascism"—can be formally understood. It is not just that "theoretical research is a form of social practice" with political implications.[75] It derives from the hope that, by reconstructing the formation, consolidation, and uses of terms that, like "fascism," define social life, this book will contribute to enhancing readers' competency regarding our shared encyclopedia, and their capacity to intervene in its structure.

The Advantages and Disadvantages of "Fascism" for Life

This is a work of scholarly analysis. It is not intended as a new promptuary on how to recognize a fascist or how to diagnose the early signs of an imminent fascist takeover. Ever since Donald Trump's presidency, manuals of this kind have occupied a dedicated niche in the publishing market, engaging respectable scholars in the compilation of checklists of warning signs.[76] This book will not offer a new list of essential characteristics of fascism. It is an investigation into the epistemological limits of the heuristic category "fascism," which does not relinquish rigorous analysis for the sake of widespread legibility. Nor does it renounce the duty of critique to respond to the urgency of today's predicament: Like William of Baskerville in Eco's *The Name of the Rose*, quoted in an epigraph to this book, it rejects haste.

Yet, it would be dishonest to pretend that this volume was produced in an ahistorical vacuum, detached from current events. The idea and planning of this project began during my sabbatical leave at Princeton's Institute for Advanced Studies during the 2016 campaign that made the flamboyant businessman and television celebrity Donald Trump president of the United States. The impoverishment of the political language and the progressive affirmation of authoritarian and violent postures that accompanied Trump's presidency (and other political forces around the world) created for scholars a call to action that often trampled careful analysis and proper theorization.

This project was born as a reaction against that frenzy and upholds the importance of critical analysis. Theodor Adorno, in the last essay he published before his untimely death in 1969, called this compulsion to act a "pseudo-activity," an "attempt to rescue enclaves of immediacy in the midst of a thoroughly mediated and rigidified society."[77] Action without reflection, or praxis without theory—what Adorno called "absolutized activism"—is a form of "resignation," for which "the feeling of a new security is purchased with the sacrifice of autonomous thinking. The consolation that thought within the context of collective action is an improvement proves deceptive: thinking, employed only as the instrument of action, is blunted in the same manner as all instrumental reason."[78]

Following Adorno, I believe that scholarship becomes more advantageous to politics and life when it pursues its inquiries with critical ruthlessness. The purpose of this book is to look more closely at the semiotic history of "fascism" as an oblique perspective to understand the rise of mass-based authoritarianisms within liberal democracies. "Looking more closely" is also the ostensibly modest methodology of William of Baskerville. Almost echoing Adorno's worries about pseudoactivity, Eco's hero warns his disciple Adso of Melk that "the most we can do is look more closely."[79] "To look closely" indicates of course "theory," the Greek etymology of which, θεωρία, referred to the action of viewing, contemplation, sight, spectacle.

This study on the consolidation of the different semantic markers of "fascism" and its assessment of the epistemological advantageousness and disadvantageousness for historical knowledge also inevitably generates analytical perspectives on the authoritarian potential inherent in the liberal capitalist order in times of socioeconomic crisis. An authoritarian takeover today would look radically different from the ones that emerged in the interwar period, because the sociohistorical and cultural circumstances of the twenty-first century would elicit different organizational forms, strategies, myths, rhetoric, symbolism, and identitarian ideologies. Would "fascism" be a helpful analytical category for understanding today's predicament, or would it rather hamper it? This book attempts to answer that question.

Italian Fascism, like German Nazism, was symptomatic of the structural weakness of liberal institutions, which made them vulnerable to an authoritarian turn under socioeconomic and political conditions specific to the 1920s and 1930s. A distillation of essential characteristics of those historically specific regimes (a charismatic leader, a single party, paramilitary groups, antisemitism, the glorification of violence and war, etc.) and their transformation into features of an ahistorical typological definition that could be utilized in different sociohistorical circumstances as *principium individuationis* is an epistemological operation that goes beyond simple comparison. It produces an abstract ideal type that, by hypostatizing an ahistorical model, presents a selection of *historical* traits of Italian Fascism and German Nazism as essential properties of an *ahistorical* model assumed to have normative heuristic value. In so doing, it hampers, rather than facilitates, any comparative study of political phenomena emerging in different historical circumstances.

Should we then imagine a more elementary sociopolitical logic or process embedded, almost ghostlike, in liberal capitalist democracies for which "fascism" is a misnomer? This is something that Dylan Riley's idea of "democratic authoritarianism," which he elaborates from Antonio Gramsci, attempts to conceptualize. "Fascist regimes," Riley argues, "are best understood as authoritarian democracies. By this seemingly paradoxical formulation, I mean that fascist political elites claimed a form of democratic legitimacy even as they ruled through authoritarian means. Fascists dismantled parliaments, turned elections into plebiscites, and nullified civil rights, but fully embraced the modern state's claim to represent the people or nation."[80]

Mussolini utilized the term "democracy" ambivalently as well. He was quite keen to distinguish what he called the "liberal" and "social" democracy of the institutional political parties from the political energies of the popular majority that only Fascism could represent in the most authentic way. In an article titled "Democracy" that he published on February 8, 1922, he explicitly drew a distinction between two meanings of "democracy," one ideal and the other actual. When it came to institutional forms, Mussolini wrote, "Italian democracy is a well-organized system of patronages and electoral mafias," a "multitude of egotisms, careerisms, and mafias." The project of conforming political institutions with the "real forces of democracy in the country" was therefore solely "in the hands of Fascism."[81] Fascism could correct the performative failures of liberal democracy without really subverting it. Fascism, he had insisted since 1919, was indeed born as a response to people's "democratic hypertrophy" that the Great War had left in its wake in the dispossessed masses of Italy.[82] Mussolini's solution to the social and political crisis that would unfold in the years after the consolidation of the regime was the invention of a new political form of state rituals that ostensibly realized the democratic spirit of popular will through a totalitarian state that entirely encompassed the lives of its citizens.[83] The "total state," in a sense, became for Mussolini a purer expression and realization of people's sovereignty. "Fascism," if crystallized as an ahistorical ideal type and not simply as an occasion for comparison of the present predicament with that of the interwar years, is instead conceived of as antagonistic, opposite, oxymoronic to the ideals of liberal democracy. Its usage as an ideal type, widespread since the postwar era, hides the parasitic dependency that its historical forms had on the institutions of liberal democracy.[84]

This, I believe, is the greatest political contribution, albeit an indirect one, that this investigation into the meanings of "fascism" can offer today.

PART I

The Invention of "Fascism"

> But names, once they are in common use, quickly become mere sounds, their etymology being buried, like so many of the earth's marvels, beneath the dust of habit.
>
> SALMAN RUSHDIE, *The Satanic Verses*

Parts I and II identify some crucial moments in the determination of the semantic content of the word "fascism" up to the end of the Second World War. Part I specifically analyzes those performative utterances of Benito Mussolini and some of his associates that illustrate the remolding of the signifier *fascio* from a term designating a generic "group" or "association" into the nongeneric name of their new political movement. It reconstructs only partially the historical formation of the semantic markers that constituted the cultural unit denoted by the signifier "fascism" in the interwar period.[1] It must be read in conjunction with the constellation of other terms (e.g., "nation," "revolution," "empire," "race," etc.) that Mussolini and other Fascist ideologues utilized as cooccurrences to further specify the semantic limits of the term "fascism," in conjunction with the political actions that accompanied those expressions and performative utterances (chaps. 2 and 3), with the antagonistic understanding of "fascism" advanced by coeval antifascist thinkers and activists (part II), and with the worldwide reception and apprehension of the rise of Fascism (chap. 5).

Although the exposition takes a chronological approach, the separation of these semantic operations into distinct processes is artificial, motivated only by a mode of presentation that strives for analytical clarity. In fact, many of those semiosic processes happened contemporaneously and were thoroughly imbricated, contaminating one another in a game of semantic integration and cross-fertilization (such as, for instance, when Mussolini reworked the idea of "totalitarianism," originally advanced as a criticism of his illiberal regime, into a positive attribute of Fascism).

The labyrinthine complexity of the network of denotative and connotative markers that the signifier "fascism" organizes in today's semantic encyclopedia is the end result of these historical processes, in addition to the definitions of the term given by historians, philosophers, political theorists, and others since 1945 (part III). The long list of Mussolini's definitions, descriptions, connotations, and metaphors of "fascism" that part I registers is therefore necessary for the understanding of their performative function in molding the sequence of semantic markers of the term.

Methodologically rejecting both a Platonic conception of ideas and their *reductio ad originem* (as well as their *reductio ad etymologiam*), the chapters in part I examine those utterances as a sequence of descriptions that contributed to defining the meaning of the new term "fascism" up to 1945. Mussolini's performative production was, in a sense, *naturaliter semiotica*: it created a string of interpretants with the intent of inducing the formation of heuristic habits among his public that would, in turn, have concrete political effects—what Mussolini referred to as the creation of a "new man," tantamount to an anthropological transformation of Italians.

In the architectonic plan of this book, which reconstructs the formation of what today appears to be an unordered and often antinomic set of semantic markers and interpretive habits regulating the use of the signifier "fascism," part I delineates the foundations which Mussolini and his associates drew in response to world-historical events between the end of the First World War and the dramatic end of the Second. The reader should not expect to find there a thorough introduction to the history of Italian Fascism, nor a comprehensive list of all descriptions, definitions, discourses, and explanations of what Fascists thought Fascism was. Rather, the following chapters isolate significant moments, abrupt turning points, unexpected convergences, and suggestive metaphors among the many interpretants of "fascism" produced by Mussolini and his associates.

1

"Fascism" before Fascism

Fascio as "Union"

Contrary to the complexity of the historiographical debate on the nature of fascism, the origins of its name are quite mundane. That "fascism" became the name of a political doctrine, theory, and praxis seems, in retrospect, serendipitous, almost an accident. Later attempts of Fascist intellectuals to transform its history into hagiography are largely unconvincing. For instance, Emilio Bodrero set the origin of the word *fascista* to the founding of the Fasci di Combattimento in 1919.[1] The Fascist historian Gioacchino Volpe, author of the historical section of the entry "Fascismo" in the *Enciclopedia italiana* of 1932, affirmed, unsupported by any evidence, that the origin of "fascism" should be dated to 1915, when the Fasci d'Azione Rivoluzionaria (League of Revolutionary Action) opened up space for the Fascist movement of 1919 that succeeded it.[2] Carlo Battisti and Giovanni Alessio puzzlingly dated the origin of the term *fascista* in 1918, deriving it from the symbol of the Partito Nazionale Fascista (National Fascist Party; PNF), the *fasces lictoriae*—even though the PNF was not founded until 1921 and the *fasces* would be officially associated with the Fascist movement only in 1920.[3]

Fascista, as an adjective or noun indicating a member of a *fascio* (association, union, or league), is indeed recorded in Italian newspapers as early as 1915.[4] These were references to the activities of members of different *fascio* associations, among them members of the interventionist movement Fascio d'Azione Rivoluzionaria, founded by the socialist syndicalist Alceste de Ambris (1874–1934), Benito Mussolini (1883–1945), and the politician Angelo Oliviero Olivetti (1874–1931) on October 5, 1914 to promote Italy's entrance in the European conflict of 1914. In all instances, the term *fascista* merely indicated membership to an association, without the term's specifying, directly or indirectly, any ideological or doctrinal orientation.[5]

The term *fascio*, indicating a league, union, or association, is a metaphorical derivation from the generic name for a bundle, sheaf, or stack, used in such expressions as *fascio di fiori* (bunch of flowers), *fascio di rami* (bundle of twigs), or *fascio di carte* (stack of paper). This generic use of the term is not uncommon in Italian even today. Less frequently, it is used figuratively to name a group of people (*fascio di persone*) or a group of problems (*fascio di problemi*), but it still appears in the idiomatic phrase *fare di tutta l'erba un fascio*, which literally means "to bundle together all sorts of grasses" and is equivalent to the English "to throw the baby out with the bathwater" or "to paint with a broad brush." In short, *fascio* generically denotes an undetermined and unqualified quantity of objects, originally of elongated form, that could be tied together in a bundle. By extension, it came to mean a set of elements, be these objects, persons, or ideas, grouped together ad hoc for some purpose.[6]

Its figurative use in political symbolism goes back to ancient Rome, where the *fasces lictoriae*—a bundle of straight branches of elm and birch trees—represented the power (*imperium*) of the magistrates and were carried in procession by their bodyguards (*lictores*).[7] Later utilized as ornamental pattern in various courts of early modern Europe—the *faisceaux romains* were decorative devices in palaces of France, Switzerland, Belgium, and other countries[8]—they acquired a new political meaning after the French Revolution, as they came to symbolize the unity and indivisibility of the republic. In France, they continued to be employed well into the nineteenth century, when the *faisceaux* became part of the Great Seal of France of 1848 with the motto *République française démocratique une et indivisible*.[9] As a widespread symbol of republicanism, the *fasces* appear in the iconography of several offices and institutions worldwide: to list but a few examples in the United States, they stand on both sides of the national flag in the House of Representatives; they appear in the seal of the Senate and above the exterior door of the Oval Office; and they decorate the chair where Abraham Lincoln sits in the Lincoln Memorial.[10]

The *fasces lictoriae* are often offered, in dictionaries ranging from the *Oxford English Dictionary* to Wikipedia, as the origin of the name of Mussolini's movement. That is also the explanation given by Carlo Battisti and Giovanni Alessio in the *Dizionario etimologico italiano*, published in 1950. In truth, the association of Fascism with the Roman insignia did not appear until 1920 and was consolidated only after the foundation of the PNF in 1921.[11] When Milan's Fasci di Combattimento, headed by Mussolini himself as the top candidate, ran in the political elections of November 1919, their symbol was a grenade used during the First World War by the Royal Italian Army, the *petardo Thévenot*, made in France and Italy by Sutter & Thévenot since 1916—even though some local Fasci adopted the Roman *fasces* as their symbol before the election.[12] Their electoral coalition, which included, alongside the Fasci, the political groups of the Futurist artist Filippo Tommaso Marinetti and the nationalist poet Gabriele D'Annunzio's Legionari, was dubbed the "Thévenot group."[13] Local sections of the Fasci did not adopt the *fasces* in their insignia until 1920.[14]

There was no ideological proposition behind Mussolini's choice of the term "Fascio" for either the interventionist group of 1914 (disbanded in 1915, as soon as Italy entered the conflict) and the new political group he founded in 1919. He was simply following a common practice of Italian politics. As the Treccani dictionary explains, "In political terminology, the term [*fascio*] (as an extension of its figurative meaning of 'compact group') has been used since the nineteenth century to designate basic organizations and groups of a revolutionary character, especially socialist, syndicalist, and republican."[15] A *fascio* signified a union, a league, an association, formed with the aim of lobbying politicians to push a particular legislative or executive reform (such was the case of Mussolini's own Fasci d'Azione Rivoluzionaria of 1914) or of interest groups (syndicalist, cultural, or educational).[16] The iconic allegory of the *fascio* suggested the strength of union vis-à-vis the weakness of the isolated individual.[17]

The earliest use of *fascio* as the generic name of a group, association, or league goes back to 1871–72, when the first Italian labor unions formed as local sections of the International Workingmen's Association (IWA), founded in St. Martin's Hall, London, in 1864.[18] The term appears in labels such as Fascio Operaio Fiorentino and Fascio Operaio Livornese (1872), local workingmen's unions that aspired to the eventual formation of a unified Fascio Operaio Italiano.[19] "Fascio Operaio" was also the name of a clandestine progressive group founded in Bologna by the former Garibaldian Erminio Pescatori (1836–1905) on November 27, 1871, which the following year would become Emilia-Romagna's section of the IWA. *Fascio operaio* was also the name of the socialist journal of that union, published in 1871–72.[20] The most famous of these workingmen's leagues were perhaps the Fasci Siciliani dei Lavoratori, founded in 1889, the militant and often violent activism of which led Prime Minister Francesco Crispi in 1894 to mobilize the Royal Army to violently suppress them, imposing martial law to defend the property rights of large landowners from the upheaval of dispossessed agricultural laborers.[21] By the early twentieth century, the Fascio Rivoluzionario d'Azione Internazionalista, founded in Milan on October 5, 1914, by the socialist syndicalists Amilcare de Ambris and Filippo Corridoni, had pushed the former members of the Unione Sindacale Italiana to more radical, revolutionary positions.

The term *fascio* had other political uses that were not necessarily revolutionary nor connected to the labor unions. These include the temporary formation of political coalitions gathering members of rival political parties for a common end. In 1883, to give impetus to the democratization of Italian politics, the socialist politician Andrea Costa, the republican philosopher Giovanni Bovio, and the journalist and poet Felice Cavallotti founded the Fascio della Democrazia (Democratic Fascio) to better coordinate and strengthen the political action of different reformist parties. While *fascio* before the First World War tended to be a term in vogue among left-wing politicians and activists, in December 1917 the conservative economist and Freemason Maffeo Pantaleoni—later a supporter of D'Annunzio and his Fiume enterprise—founded a transversal parliamentary group to push for a change in the strategy of war after the defeat at Caporetto (Karfreit, in German): the group was called Fascio Parlamentare per la Difesa Nazionale (Parliamentary Fascio for National Defense). Inspired by Pantaleoni, more groups formed in early 1918, including the Fascio Nazionale Italiano (Italian National Fascio), the Fascio Romano per la Difesa Nazionale (Roman Fascio for National Defense), the Fascio Repubblicano Italiano (Italian Republican Fascio, inspired by Giuseppe Mazzini and the first of these associations to use the *fasces lictoriae* as its official symbol), and the Federazione dei Fasci di Resistenza (Federation of Resistance Fasci).[22] The term *fascio*, in addition to its presence in syndicalist and parliamentary groups, could also be found in the name of nonpolitical organizations, such as the Fascio di Educazione Nazionale (Fascio of National Education), founded in early 1919 by the pedagogue Ernesto Codignola and the philosopher Giovanni Gentile to promote educational reform for the purpose of fighting the Italian population's high rate of illiteracy.

Young Benito Mussolini, a journalist and socialist activist, recorded and commented on the formation of many of these groups. For instance, in an article published in *Avanti!* on June 14, 1914, he criticized the opposition to the Socialist Party of the "so-called 'Fascio Democratico'" and mocked the poor results of what he called the "Fascio Popolare Democratico" in the administrative elections of June 1914.[23] Around the same time, he used the expression "Fascio dell'ordine" (Fascio order) to tease the conservative parties of the bourgeoisie.[24] *Fascio*, in other words, appeared in Mussolini's writings of 1914 in the most generic sense of "group" or "alliance." And that is the use of the term he adopted in December 1914, when he collaborated with Olivetti and Alceste De Ambris to establish the Fascio d'Azione Rivoluzionaria Interventista (Fascio of Revolutionary and Interventionist Action).

The foundation of this Fascio d'Azione came after Mussolini's sudden change from neutralism to interventionism. The turning point was signaled by a long editorial he published in *Avanti!* on October 18, 1914 entitled "Dalla neutralità assoluta alla neutralità attiva ed operante" (From absolute neutrality to active and engaged neutrality). In it, he suggested that the war constituted an advantageous situation for the Socialists to push for a republican revolution.[25] The article provoked a turmoil within the Socialist Party, which embraced a pacifist and neutralist stance. Mussolini was forced to resign as the director of *Avanti!* His expulsion from the party would be formalized on November 29.

Less than two weeks later, Mussolini, along with Corridoni, organized a meeting with fellow interventionists in the Salon of Modern Art of via Lodigiano, in Milan, on the evening of December 11, 1914. The goal was the foundation of a new group, which they called the Fascio d'Azione Rivoluzionaria, whose mission was to support Italy's entry into the European conflict against the Central Empires. *Fascio* was the appropriate term for such a gathering: "We do not intend to establish a new political party," Mussolini declared; "we only need to reach a goal. . . . More than fifty fasci have been constituted in Italy and many others will form after our meeting tonight, which is awaited with solemn and feverish anxiety."[26] To confirm the founders' intention of not constituting a new political movement, he added, "We don't need to spend time on the statutes of the new group," which should only serve the need of mobilizing people toward the war.[27]

Mussolini had no special commitment to the term *fascio*, which he used conventionally to mean a group or union of people with a common purpose. Further confirmation of this technical use of the term can be seen in Mussolini's articles in *Il popolo d'Italia* publicizing the new Fascio. Not only did Mussolini change their name continuously (Fasci Autonomi d'Azione Rivoluzionaria, Fasci Rivoluzionari, Fasci Rivoluzionari d'Azione),[28] but he also called it Gruppo Autonomo d'Azione Rivoluzionaria, dropping the appellation *fascio* altogether.[29]

The semantic umbrella of the term *fascio* was convenient for several reasons. It gave the movement an institutional informality and agility that a political party did not have. It emphasized that the group was temporary and task oriented, its existence ending when the goal of favoring Italy's entry into the war was achieved. It stressed the heterogeneity of its members' political origins and ideological orientations. And as in the case of other *fasci*, it dissociated itself from conventional political parties and distanced itself from parliamentary procedures that Mussolini, De Ambris, and Olivetti deemed responsible for Italy's inability to act.

Mussolini stressed the unconventional character of this Fascio, which in his vitriolic polemic against his former colleagues of the *Avanti!* and of the

Socialist Party assumed the antiestablishment connotations of being against conventional parties, antipolitical and anti-ideological. This antiestablishmentarian and often violent activism of the Fascio d'Azione Rivoluzionaria was its most striking characteristic, such that the early uses of *fascisti* to indicate their members in articles in *Il corriere della sera* and *Avanti!* were mostly derogatory. As Emilio Gentile noted, "The expression 'fascist movement' appears in April 1915 in *Il popolo d'Italia* to define a new kind of association, the *antiparty*, formed by the free spirits of those political militants who refused the doctrinal and organizational restrictions of a political party. The Fasci di Combattimento [of 1919] would be created in the same spirit."[30] Nonetheless, the adjectival use of *fascista* to indicate membership in a union remains generic and not exclusive of Mussolini's Fascio.

Whether the Fascio of 1914 should be considered the origin of Fascism is a question of historiographical interpretation rather than phylogenesis and depends largely on the heuristic value historians embed in the notion of origin.[31] Not only was *fascio* a term for political or cultural associations not unique to Mussolini, but the Fasci d'Azione Rivoluzionaria did not affect its meaning nor its connotations of revolutionary or nonestablishment activism that was typical of the Italian labor movement of the previous half century. It was rather the antiestablishment connotations of the generic uses of *fascio* that would be instrumental for the new movement Mussolini established in 1919.[32]

In semiotic terms, the intertextual occurrences of "fascist" in the documents of the prewar period of 1914–15 unequivocally indicate that the term, grammatically used as either an adjective or a noun, never denoted anything more than membership in a *fascio*, in Mussolini's case the Fascio d'Azione Rivoluzionaria; it did not assume specific ideological connotations. The heuristic presupposition that the occurrences of the term *fascista* in 1914–15 are signs of the origin of the later movement known as Fascism is therefore a fallacy that can be explained in terms of conceptual anachronism, of a teleologically driven *reductio ad originem*, or as prefigured by an interpretive script, the formation of which should be traced in the search for a "fascist minimum" in postwar scholarship.

Mussolini's sudden change of mind in late 1914, when he moved from a vigorous defense of peace—on July 26 he had published an editorial in *Avanti!* entitled "Abbasso la Guerra!" (Down with the war!)[33]—to the most virulent support of war in slightly more than a month, signaled the beginning of frenzied activism. On November 15 he launched a new newspaper under his directorship, *Il popolo d'Italia*, financed by northern Italian and French industrialists that saw in Italy's entrance in the European conflict a potential source of great profits (among them Edison's Carlo Estrelle, Fiat's Giovanni Agnelli, and Ansaldo's Pio Perrone, as well as such heavy-industry entrepreneurs as Emilio Bruzzone and Emanuele Vittorio Parodi).[34] The Fasci d'Azione Rivoluzionaria had a national gathering on January 24 and 25, 1915. In March 1915 Mussolini dueled with his former socialist colleague Claudio Treves, the bloody epilogue of a long battle of pens between the two carried over in the pages of *Avanti!* and *Il popolo d'Italia*. He was then arrested on April 11 during a violent rally in Rome. Mussolini's polemic added a strong antiparliamentary stance to his interventionist rhetoric that the final declaration of war against Austria-Hungary did not moderate: on May 11, 1915 he wrote an editorial ("Abbasso il Parlamento!" [Down with the Parliament!]) in which he argued, "I believe, with ever deeper conviction, that the Italian Parliament is that bubonic plague that poisons the blood of the nation. It must be eradicated."[35]

Conscripted on August 31 into the Twelfth Regiment of Bersaglieri, Mussolini was sent to the front on September 13. It was then that Mussolini began recording his experience of the trench war in the Karst Plateau (Carso) with the Bersaglieri Corps in a diary, serialized in *Il popolo d'Italia*.[36] In March 1916 he was promoted to corporal for merit in battle, but the following year, on February 23, 1917, he suffered severe wounds during a drill, an incident that forced him to witness the end of the war from a hospital bed while concocting the myth of his heroic valor. Not once did the term *fascio* appear in the diary.

The War and the Meeting at San Sepolcro

The First World War had a transformative impact on Mussolini's political trajectory. His interventionist activism of 1915 had acquainted him with public figures like D'Annunzio and Filippo Tommaso Marinetti and with nationalist ideologues like Enrico Corradini, all of whom would have considerable influence on the early development of Fascism in 1919 and 1920.[37]

Most relevant was the intellectual transformation in Mussolini, whose experience in the trenches convinced him that war was the solution for the chronic disease that affected Italy and the Italians. War, for the former socialist, was no longer an occasion for the emancipatory transformation of Italian society (revolution), but rather constituted itself as the foundational myth of a national palingenesis. In a piece published in *Il popolo d'Italia* on February 14, 1915, Mussolini had already insisted that "the war we will fight is a war that should fill Italian souls with pride and trepidation. . . . The war that we want and that we will fight is not a national war because of the objectives we want to achieve at whatever cost, but it is a national war because—for the first time after many centuries of servitude—it will be fought by the nation. It will be the first Italian war. Of the Italian nation, of the Italian people, now united in a solid whole from the Alps to Sicily."[38]

War was the means to achieve what politics and education had failed to build after Italy's unification in 1861: Italians. "The war needs to reveal Italy to the Italians. . . . The war will reveal, perhaps, to ourselves the Italy we ignored."[39] The palingenetic power of war was not specific to Italy but inherent in war itself. In a tone reminiscent of Georges Sorel and Friedrich Nietzsche, Mussolini declared that "war is the test of people. Individuals reveal their inner nature not in the events of daily life, but in facing the unexpected, which threatens his possessions, the people he loves, his own existence."[40] The exaltation of war, struggle, and violence as a purer expression of national politics that surfaced in the 1915 article would continue to be a fundamental ingredient of Mussolini's later political beliefs and rhetoric. His experience of and mythopoeic thinking on war would fuel the creation of a new political experiment in the Fascio of 1919.

The war had a great impact on the young Italian state as well. The "Grande Guerra" had cost Italy about 650,000 dead soldiers and more than one million wounded. Despite its victory, at the end of the war the Italian state was massively indebted, its population marked by starvation, high infant mortality, and expanding unemployment. The state had accumulated 49 billion lire of domestic debt, to which should be added the 15.5 billion lire it owed England and the 8.5 billion due to the United States—about 119 percent of its GDP.[41] The debt not only affected state spending in infrastructural and industrial reconstructions, but also triggered a rampant inflation that further impoverished the population. The artificial burst of productivity during the war years, especially in heavy industry, which was fueled by state spending, could no longer be sustained; it collapsed dramatically after November 1918. Conversion of arms factories into peacetime production was interrupted for lack of domestic and international demand, as well as for the sudden interruption of state funds. As Gaetano Salvemini commented in 1951, "The world war of 1914–18 brought about in Italy, as in all countries, belligerent and neutral, a severe economic crisis. [Some] branches of production . . . had swelled to enormous proportions, while other[s] which had flourished folded up. . . . The reconversion from war economy to peace economy was a painful ordeal—and a noisy one. . . . There were moments when it could be feared that a catastrophe might not be avoided. Yet the breakdown never came. The crisis was one of readjustment and not of disorganization."[42]

The return from the front of four million war veterans—shell-shocked, unemployed, and unemployable, no longer accustomed to normal, peaceful life after years spent in the trenches, disaffected with the military and political elites that had guided them in futile massacres such as Caporetto, and abandoned by political movements (the socialists in particular) that were now striving to organize a proletarian response to the Russian Revolution of the previous year—constituted a problem that was at once economic, political, and social. Malnourished, reluctant to give up their weapons, and alienated from their own land, Italian veterans became the embodiment of a sense of defeat that permeated the Italian victory even before the Treaty of Versailles of 1919.[43] Veterans, in particular the assault corps of the Arditi (elite special forces of the Royal Italian Army), became living symbols of the *vittoria mutilata* (mutilated victory), an expression that D'Annunzio had invented and popularized in an article published in *Il corriere della sera* on October 24, 1918. The international betrayal of the London Pact, the discrimination to which the Great Powers subjected their ally Italy, and a widespread socioeconomic crisis fueled the rhetoric of nationalists like D'Annunzio and Mussolini. The former would soon embark on a military invasion of the city of Fiume, to reclaim it from the Kingdom of Serbs, Croats, and Slovenes. The latter would gather veterans, Arditi, and the disaffected of all sorts in a new movement, which he called Fasci Italiani di Combattimento.

The historical imaginary of the birth of the Fasci Italiani di Combattimento at the gathering of March 23, 1919 is a good example of what in logic is called "genetic fallacy"—that is, confusing the origin of something for its nature, or believing that to understand historical phenomena is sufficient to reconstruct their origins, irrespective of the context and developmental contingencies. Very few of the foundational ideas of the San Sepolcro group survived the rapid transformation of Mussolini's political trajectory. The political form of Fascism, as it consolidated in the course of the 1920s, was certainly not a congruous instantiation of the ideas advanced in the 1919 manifesto. In semiotic terms, the conceptual constellation characterizing the ostensible birth of Fascism at San Sepolcro did not determine the semantic markers of "fascism" in either its common dictionary definition or in the more stringent ones offered by the proponents of the "fascist minimum." March 23, 1919 merely marked the institutional event of the beginning of a movement the forms and ideas of which would slowly take shape in reaction to the challenges it faced during the following decade, to the point of subverting most of the ideals upheld at the meeting.

On the occasion of the celebratory events organized in the early 1930s to commemorate the first decade of Fascist power in Italy, Mussolini actively contributed to the creation of the myth of the origin of Fascism, centered on the two events of San Sepolcro and the March on Rome of 1922, where the second was, however, given far greater importance and relevance.[44] On

March 22, 1932, the thirteenth anniversary of the meeting (and its first public celebration of certain magnitude), Mussolini gave a speech from the balcony of the Palazzo Venezia to remember that "glorious date, already consecrated in the history of the homeland."[45] In fact, no major public celebrations of the meeting of San Sepolcro had been held in the previous years, not even on the occasion of the event's tenth anniversary. It was only in 1932 that Fascism launched a series of large-scale mythopoetic commemorations of its history and legacy. It was in this year that Mussolini and other Fascist authors engaged in an effort to develop a more organic image and coherent definition of "fascism" through exhibitions, celebrations, monographs, and in a long entry for the *Enciclopedia italiana* that Mussolini coauthored, later published in a single volume as *La dottrina del fascismo*.[46] In March 1932 Italy was in the middle of a difficult recovery from the financial crisis of 1929. In his brief speech, Mussolini pointed out that, "despite the economic hardship and the harsh privations imposed by the universally difficult times," the Fascist Party had given ample evidence of its moral and political strength. "This strength," he added, "is perennially nurtured by the idea launched in 1919 and from the men who swore in Piazza San Sepolcro and chose the word 'combat' [*combattimento*] as their motto and insignia."[47]

Little of the San Sepolcro program and few of its protagonists survived the rapid transformation of Fascism between 1919 and 1922. It was a heterogeneous bundle of two hundred people of different social origins and political affiliations who met in the lecture hall of the Alliance for Industry and Commerce in Piazza San Sepolcro, Milan, in March 1919. And just as heterogeneous were the ideas discussed at the meeting, a bundle of mutually contradictory statements on society, the nation, the inalienable rights of property, the free market, and worker solidarity.[48] Revolutionary socialists, union leaders, former interventionists, war veterans, Arditi, members of the unemployed proletariat, liberals, low- and middle-level white-collar workers, Futurist artists and intellectuals, and nationalists, all together averaging the age of thirty, were lured by the violent, antiestablishment rhetoric of Mussolini's articles. He had initially foreseen thousands of adherents, but very few responded to the announcements of *Il popolo d'Italia*.[49]

A few days before the meeting, in the last call to arms in the March 18, 1919, edition of *Il popolo d'Italia*, Mussolini prepared the terrain for the constitution of a political movement distinct and antagonistic to traditional parties. There was a mounting "intolerance toward all the institutions and men that represent the anachronistic past and a deep will for renewal," Mussolini noted.[50] Despite the turmoil of the world conflict and the dramatic social transformations it elicited, only two new political parties had formed: the

Partito Popolare Italiano (Italian People's Party; PPI) and the Partito Liberale Riformatore (Liberal Reform Party; PLR);[51] but, Mussolini continued, "if we examine the programs of both old and new parties, we see that they look alike. Some axioms are the same."[52] The movement he intended to build, on the contrary, was "irreparably different, not only from official socialism, but also from all those groups and people who, perhaps in vain, are looking to reconcile themselves with the big party, in direct or indirect ways and with more or less hidden motives."[53] The new movement, true to the spirit of the prewar experience of interventionism, "claims to itself the right and the duty of transforming Italian life, even with revolutionary methods."[54] It was, Mussolini further explained, neither reactionary nor progressive: it was a movement that, to pursue its political goal of national palingenesis, was ready to use "any necessary means at our disposal: legal and the so-called illegal."[55] Ruthlessness, he concluded, was inevitable: they could not simply wait, like the socialists, for a revolution to come; they were ready to start it themselves, because he believed that "it is opening up in history a period that could be defined as of 'mass politics' [*politica della masse*] or of democratic hypertrophy. We cannot obstruct this movement. We must direct it toward political democracy and toward economic democracy. The first will bring back the masses to the state, the second will reconcile capital and labor."[56] The Fascio di Combattimento was a movement with only one goal: the promotion and guidance of the democratic mobilization of the nation. "Democratic," for Mussolini, pointed not to the procedures and institutions of liberal democracy, but to the direct involvement of the masses.

The March 24, 1919 issue of *Il popolo d'Italia* celebrated the event with a partial publication of the proceedings, but the complete manifesto of the new Fascio would not appear until June 6 of that year, jointly written by Mussolini and Alceste de Ambris. As if to reflect the eclectic orientation of its participants, the manifesto was also a bundle of contradictory and inconsistent ideals. Of socialist inspiration were the proposals to reallocate land to small cultivators and redistribute industrial profits to workers, as well as its open antagonism to the speculations of financial capitalism; it suggested an eight-hour workday and limited working life to fifty-five years of age. Among its democratic aspirations were its antimonarchical republicanism and the proposal to extend suffrage to women. Like prewar pacifists, Mussolini advocated for Italy to join the Society of Nations, noting that it actively supported universal disarmament and the civil conversion of arms industries. Like liberals, Mussolini envisioned the state as an active promoter of private entrepreneurship and proposed to lower taxes on industries. Also important were its nationalist ambitions: it proposed the formation of a national militia and the nationalization of arms factories, condemned the deliberations of the Versailles Peace Conference as a *vittoria mutilata*, and called for the annexation of Dalmatia and of the city of Fiume in particular, six months before D'Annunzio's "Fiume Endeavor."[57]

More than the bundle of ideas discussed at the foundation of the new Fascio, however, it was the rhetorical fashioning of the manifesto that demands a closer reading. The program began with a preamble that reads like a call to arms: "Italians! Here is the national program of a movement that is soundly Italian. Revolutionary, because antidogmatic and antidemagogical; strongly innovative, because against prejudices. We propose the valorization of revolutionary war above everything and above everyone. Other issues—bureaucratic, administrative, juridical, educational, colonial, etc.—we will tackle as soon as we create our leadership."[58] The revolutionary intent of the manifesto is clear not only in its antiestablishment content, but in its formal organization as well. Reproducing the format of socialist declarations, the statement opens with a conative calling to its adherents, only in this case it was not to *lavoratori* (workers) or *compagni* (comrades), but rather "Italians," emphasizing the switch in Mussolini's ideals from a class-based emancipatory politics to a politics that conceived of emancipation in nationalist terms: because of the war, Italians were now emancipated externally from their subordinate position vis-à-vis the established European empires and internally from their subjection to the anachronistic dominance of traditional aristocratic and bourgeois interests. It was through a recodification of the idea of revolution from class to nationhood that Mussolini intended to respond with his new Fascio to the rise of mass politics—or, as he put it, to the rise of people's "hypertrophic" demand for democracy and participation. The switch from class to nation would soon assume strategic importance in establishing a network of alliances between the new movement and traditional forms of conservatism.

In its sense of revolutionary association from below, disconnected from and antagonistic to traditional forms of political organization in the context of representative democracies, *fascio* was the appropriate name for the new movement. To affirm its association with the war that created the "new Italians," the new *fascio* was appropriately qualified as an association of *combattenti* (combatants), which Mussolini intended both literally, thanks to the alliance with the Arditi, and metaphorically, as he conceived of veteran warriors as symbolic representatives of the society of new Italians as those who experimented in the trenches a new form of socialization that should become the template for a national palingenesis.[59]

The foundation of the new Fascio in the early spring of 1919 was an event that did not attract the attention Mussolini expected. As Renzo De Felice noted, the "Fasci di combattimento, in reality, were born in the same way as so many other movements, so many other organizations of the war years and of the immediate postwar period, destined for a wretched existence and a more or less rapid exhaustion."[60] The name adopted for the movement, "Fascio," was far too generic to cause an uproar or even to be noticed at all: it had occupied such a habitual place in Italian political terminology since the 1870s that it did not offer the movement the connotations of novelty that the founders wanted to give it. The Fasci di Combattimento did not have exclusive use of the term: newspapers devoted much more attention to an event of the Fascio Ferroviario (Union of Railway Workers) than to Mussolini's gathering.[61]

Mussolini painstakingly insisted that the new Fascio had connotations of institutional informality that distinguished it from conventional political parties. For him, this was not a simple organizational issue: It realized the antipolitical orientation of the new movement. The movement, he explained on June 25, 1919 in the pages of *Il popolo d'Italia*, "is an antiparty and as such it does not have any prejudices."[62] Aversion toward traditional political organizations and conventional political praxis, Emilio Gentile has noted, was typical of many veteran groups in the immediate post–First World War period, just as a loathing of politics in general characterized syndicalist movements and radical parties even before the war.[63] In the pages of *Il popolo d'Italia* on February 10, 1919, the syndicalist and interventionist Giuseppe Mario Gioda explained that the conception of an antiparty "was clearly born from the failure of the programmatic ideas of all parties [during the war]." The antiparty, once in power, would "determine the end of all cliques, clienteles, devious interests and unspeakable political aims."[64]

The antiestablishment rhetoric of Mussolini and other members of the Fasci di Combattimento, while giving expression to the revolutionary intents of the movement, constituted a strategic weakness with respect to its promotion among the urban electorate of Milan, as the November 1919 elections would soon demonstrate. Although Mussolini wanted to take advantage of the popular dissent regarding the political establishment owing to the weakness it showed at the Paris Conference and its incapacity to solve Italy's widespread social and economic distress, he failed to erase the impression that the Fascio was just another left-wing movement, thus alienating the very urban bourgeoisie he wanted to recruit. The hyperbolic statements of other founding members of the Fascio—like, for instance, the revolutionary syndicalist Agostino Lanzillo, also present at San Sepolcro, who wrote in *Il popolo d'Italia*, "It is the ruling class that must be annihilated"—helped consolidate the idea that the new movement was politically located on the Left, within the revolutionary front.[65]

Mussolini was well aware of the problem. Starting the previous year, he never hesitated in his editorials to criticize the Bolshevik Revolution and its local sympathizers in the Partito Socialist Italiano (Italian Socialist Party; PSI). To give even more visibility to his political conversion away from the Left, on August 1, 1918 he had changed the description in the masthead of *Il popolo d'Italia* from *Quotidiano socialista* (Socialist Newspaper) to *Quotidiano dei combattenti e dei produttori* (Newspaper of Combatants and Producers). As he explained in the opening editorial ("Novità"),

> From now on this newspaper will be the newspaper of combatants and of producers. . . . This newspaper will continue to be the voice of the person who is writing these lines; only in the near future it will take a more noticeable and decisive tendency of being the voice of combatants and producers. The "socialist" in the previous title . . . has become an anachronism. It does not reveal anything anymore. . . . There was rather a comic and ironic element to it, and I clearly noticed it. . . . Words like international, class struggle, and others in the socialist terminology belong to the museum of old clichés. In the most revolutionary period of world history, socialism doesn't do anything, it's dreadfully passive and sterile; and where it was able to get to power [i.e., Lenin's Russia], it has only been capable of producing more chaos and incoherency than the bourgeoisie.[66]

Mussolini believed that the war had concretized the ideal of an organic national community, a symbolic expansion of the experience of trench solidarity that had rendered the Marxist notions of class conflict and proletarian internationalism obsolete. He concluded the op-ed by stating that in the new context of nationalist renewal the war had triggered, socialist internationalism "will be but an imbecilic scribble in this new divine poem."[67]

De Ambris, cofounder of the Fasci and former revolutionary syndicalist, also insisted on separating the new movement from socialism. The Fascio was for him a "third way" that could lead to an "authentic and radical social renewal without destroying the traditional values of European civilization."[68] For De Ambris, "the war has broken the spell of a proletarian universality against a capitalist universality and has summoned us, through bloody demonstrations, to the eternal and immutable reality of the nation and the race."[69] Despite various attempts to direct the main target of the Fascio's political opposition toward the socialists, the antiestablishment rhetoric of the San Sepolcro leaders obfuscated this antagonism and prevented the new movement from gaining the support of the urban bourgeoisie it sought. In short, the first steps of the newborn Fascio were tentative and, despite the bombastic rhetoric of its founder, Mussolini, unremarkable. The Fascio was destined to soon disappear in the political turmoil of postwar Italy.

2

The Advent of "Fascism"

The program of the Fasci Italiani di Combattimento was a mixed bag of ideas and conceptions, inadequate to give the new movement of "combatants" and "producers" the visibility and support that Mussolini aspired to gather from Milan's urban bourgeoisie. It was instead the appeal to violent action and the endorsement of ruthless fight against political enemies (the Socialists, in particular) that became the trademarks of the new movement. Violence was not simply an ideal or a slogan: it was the Fasci Italiani's only practice.

Three weeks after the gathering at San Sepolcro, groups of Arditi, Futurists, and members of Mussolini's Fascio, guided by Marinetti and the Ardito Ferruccio Vecchi, attacked the Milan headquarters of the socialist newspaper *Avanti!* and completely destroyed it. The origin of this "spontaneous mass movement, a movement of fighters and of people tired of the Leninist blackmailing," as Mussolini characterized it in an interview in *Il giornale d'Italia*, was a series of parallel strikes in Rome and Milan to protest the Paris Peace Conference.[1] A general strike in Rome organized by the Socialist Party was interrupted first by a counterstrike of the Associazione Nazionalista Italiana (Italian Nationalist Association) and then by violent repression by police forces. A replica of the strike organized again by the PSI in Milan lasted three days, April 13–15, and was met by even more violent police repression, such that Milan's workers' unions and the socialists dedicated the last day of the strike (April 15) to condemning the repressive actions of the Italian police and of the Royal Army. It was in the context of street fighting between the socialists and the police forces that a group of Arditi and Futurists, Marinetti, and Vecchi led the assault against the Milan headquarters of *Avanti!* in via San Damiano, under the inert supervision and tacit approval of the armed forces.[2]

The attack was more consequential for the symbolic impact it had on the development of Mussolini's Fascio than for its effects against the mounting socialist movement. In fact, the *Avanti!* was back in print only a few days later with an edition printed in Turin on April 23.[3] The quick rebirth of the newspaper was evidence of the strength of the socialist movement in postwar Italy and its ability to mobilize mass support. The election of November 1919 would soon confirm this. But if the violent events of April 15 failed to curb the impetus of the socialist movement in Italy, they gave nationwide exposition to Mussolini's Fascio.

It is true that after March 23 numerous local branches of the Fasci di Combattimento were opened, but it was only after the events of that April that memberships started growing.[4] It is also true that Mussolini had the chance to exploit the nationwide distribution of the newspaper of which he was the editor in chief (thanks to the continuing financial support of heavy-industry entrepreneurs) as a megaphone for his political propaganda. Nonetheless, the movement remained marginal and suffered from the ambiguity of its political orientation: Its radical republicanism alienated it from other conservative and nationalist movements; its anticlericalism set it against those political forces that gravitated around the Vatican; and its antisocialism estranged it from the working classes and progressives in general. Moreover, it failed to unite under its aegis all war veterans, which dispersed in two dozen lists for the political election of November 1919.

The Fasci's violent antisocialism was the beginning of a lasting alliance with the industrialists, middle-class professionals, and artisans of the major urban centers of the industrial north, who increasingly feared the growth of the Socialist Party and the intensification of its revolutionary rhetoric in the wake of the Bolshevik Revolution of 1917. Mussolini did not directly participate in the attack on the *Avanti!*, but he assumed a posteriori the burden of its political responsibility.

For Mussolini, workers' protests and strikes, fueled by the socialists, had hindered economic growth and castrated the energies and inventiveness of the entrepreneurial class, who now "spend their time in coffee houses rather than in workshops" out of fear of the impending revolution. "All this had to stop," Mussolini explained in an interview for the liberal conservative *Il giornale d'Italia*. "It was a climacteric, stormy burst. All that blowing unleashed a hurricane. This was the first episode of a civil war. . . . We Fascists did not organize the attack against the socialist newspaper, but we will bear the moral responsibility of that event."[5] Mussolini, cunning politician that he was, did not hesitate to present his movement to the bourgeois readers of the newspaper as clearly antisocialist and on the side of producers. And he did not miss the chance to promote it: "It [the Fasci di Combattimento] is an antiparty without statute and regulations. . . . We don't have prejudices. We don't have preconditions for Republicans or Monarchists; we don't have Catholic or anti-Catholic prejudices, nor socialist or antisocialist. We are polemicists, we are actualists, we are achievers gathered around a common program."[6]

It was in connection with his struggle to win over the support of a suspicious bourgeoisie that Mussolini began to occasionally adopt the term "fascism" to explain the nature of the new movement.[7] The first time on record that the term appeared was during a public speech he gave at the Teatro Verdi in Fiume on May 22, 1919, when he stated, preposterously, that "Fascism is becoming the soul and conscience of the new national democracy."[8] In a phone interview published in the July 3, 1919 issue of *Il popolo d'Italia* entitled "Il 'Fascismo,'" he claimed that Fascism was "unscrupulous" in its alliances, insofar as the group it associated with "could be utilized for a common goal:"[9] national renewal. But he insisted that Fascism would "cease to be" the moment it transformed into a conventional political party, because "Fascism is antiacademic. It is not a petty political movement [*politicante*]."[10] He concluded: "Fascism is a movement of reality, of truth, of life that adheres to life. It is pragmatist. It does not have a priori. Nor hidden purposes."[11] It was, in other words, temporary, true to the early usages of the term "Fascio": "Once a solution to the fundamental problems that trouble our nation is reached, Fascism won't insist on carrying on . . . but will know how to brilliantly die without solemn grimaces."[12]

These early occurrences of "fascism" should be read with interpretive caution before falling for another *reductio ad originem*. If indeed they record an early appearance of the term, it remains questionable that the nominalizing suffix "-ism" indicated the intention of naming a system of theory or practice, as does "fascism" in today's political terminology.[13] Rather, it seems to simply register "an intent of description of a class of persons, groups, or actions."[14] In support of the latter interpretation, "fascism" never appeared in other newspapers or documents of the period; Mussolini himself used it sporadically until the electoral campaign in the fall of 1919; and the contemporary usages of *fascio* and "fascist" (an adjective denoting membership to a *fascio*) were still not exclusive to the Fasci di Combattimento. Far from marking the foundation of a coherent ideology, Mussolini's adoption of the collectivizing form "fascism" was more or less symptomatic of his frustration with the heterogeneity of his movement; its indexical adoption may be better understood as an attempt of unifying what in reality was not.

The eclecticism of the Fasci was certainly evident at an ideological level, as it gathered together revolutionary socialists and nationalists, veterans and artists, liberals and corporatists. But it was also expressed at an organizational level by the dispersion of its offices and their tenuous connection to the Milan headquarters of Mussolini's Fascio. In the summer of 1919, the movement Mussolini named "Fascism" was still a loose collection of people of different social origins and political inclinations, moved by different political ideals and goals, and organized in a nebula of local *fasci* scattered in dozens of towns in northern Italy. These were internally organized hierarchically around a local representative, who exercised a considerable degree of autonomy of action from the central Fascio. The Fascio Milanese, guided by Mussolini with the collaboration of the revolutionary syndicalists Michele Bianchi and Umberto Pasella, the socialist interventionist Cesare Rossi, and the anarchic interventionist Massimo Rocca, had, at least nominally, governing authority over all local branches. But over the course of 1920–21, leaders such as Italo Balbo (in Ferrara), Roberto Farinacci (in Cremona), Cesare Forni (in Pavia), and Renato Ricci (in Carrara) consolidated such a degree of influence in their territory, built upon personal ties with the local administration, police forces, landowners, industrial entrepreneurs, local banks, and town newspapers, that they intervened in local disputes autonomously from Mussolini's control—a power symbolized by their adoption of the sobriquet "Ras" (an Ethiopian term for a local feudal lord) as their title.[15]

If the internal disunity of the Fasci frustrated Mussolini's attempts to build a unified movement, the Italian political landscape also helped thwart his efforts to create a niche for Fascism. Veterans' associations resisted their incorporation within Fascism and organized themselves in a multiplicity of different political parties. Mussolini's failure to make of his movement an institution that assimilated all war veterans was certainly due to the activities of the Associazione Nazionale dei Combattenti, which was also founded in March 1919, and the successes of the governmental charity organization of the Opera Nazionale Combattenti, established in 1917 but fully operational only beginning in January 1919 under the aegis of the minister of the treasury, Francesco Saverio Nitti. But the event that overshadowed the rise of Mussolini's Fasci in the political scene was Gabriele D'Annunzio's armed occupation of the free city of Fiume, contested by Italian irredentists after the "mutilated victory" at the Paris Conference, on September 12, 1919.

Flocking to D'Annunzio's paramilitary group of "legionaries" were veterans (Arditi and Granatieri), irredentists, nationalists, former interventionists, anarchists, Futurists, and revolutionary syndicalists—in short, members of the same social categories that Mussolini was trying to recruit for his movement. D'Annunzio, one of the most influential public figures in Italy (as the epithets of national *vate* [poet] and *profeta* [prophet] show), invented many of the markers that Mussolini later appropriated for Fascism: the black shirts of the Legionari, the meaningless battle cry "Eia eia alala," the Roman salute, a fanatical desire for national palingenesis, narcissistic supermanism, and a belief in the racial and cultural superiority of Mediterranean civilizations. Even though his relationship with Fascism remained ambiguous for the rest of his life, D'Annunzio inspired many of the symbolic trademarks of mature Fascism.[16]

The day after the occupation, Mussolini saluted with full rhetorical flare the Impresa di Fiume in an editorial published *Il popolo d'Italia*: "Gabriele D'Annunzio's gesture is not only magnificent from the point of view of the nation, but it is eminently revolutionary even from a socialist and proletarian perspective, because it goes against a system that even socialists and proletarians fight."[17] In reality, his public support of D'Annunzio's action was far more ambiguous, and his secret collaboration with the Italian government facilitated the eventual failure of the Fiume enterprise.[18] D'Annunzio was a serious obstacle to Mussolini: his national reputation was unmatched; his political positions anticipated many ideas of Mussolini's Fascio, thus constituting a formidable competitor in recruiting followers; and, unlike Mussolini, D'Annunzio never hesitated to participate directly in the revolutionary and violent acts he advocated. Undoubtedly, the occupation of Fiume presented an additional challenge to Mussolini's attempt to consolidate his leadership of the Fasci di Combattimento, many members of which demanded a more direct and active involvement of the movement.

Mussolini's hesitation was one of the most contested issues in the first National Meeting of the Fasci, organized in Florence on October 9–10, 1919. When he entered the room of the National Theatre to inaugurate the opening of the meeting, he was welcomed by an ovation of cries that, beside the usual "Viva Mussolini!" and "Viva *Il popolo d'Italia*," also saluted "Viva D'Annunzio." Much of his speech was devoted to Fiume and its annexation. And yet, the deliberations at the end of the meeting with representatives of all fifty-six local branches of the Fasci di Combattimento aimed at organizing a united strategy of all local groups for the impending national elections of November 1919.

The meeting discussed the facts that there were no viable political allies and that the Fasci had to limit their support to associations of war volunteers, veterans, Arditi, interventionist socialists, and Futurists.[19] The refusal to participate in any coalition with traditional political parties confirmed Mussolini's antiestablishment position—with violence, the only other distinctive trait of the movement. Within the Fasci, Mussolini had argued, "all those who suffered from the discomfort of old categories and of old mentalities met spontaneously. Although fascism rejects all political parties, it completes them all. In fascism, which has no statutes, there is that surplus of freedom and autonomy that is lacking in rigidly framed and registered organizations."[20]

The general elections of November 16, 1919 were an unmitigated disaster for the Fasci Italiani di Combattimento.[21] The Socialist Party (PSI) of Nicola Bombacci won the elections, earning more than 32 percent of the parliamentary seats and thus constituting a formidable opposition to the second mandate that the King Vittorio Emanuele III gave to Francesco Saverio Nitti to form a center-right coalition government. Nitti, who was prime minister before the election, led a center-right electoral list of Liberals, Democrats, and Radicals that earned only 15.91 percent of the votes, less than either the Socialist Party or the PPI (20.53 percent), the new political party of Luigi Sturzo. Mussolini's Fascio ran as one of twenty-one different lists in the electoral coalition of combatants in the electoral college of Milan, where he collected only 4657 votes (0.08 percent), thus failing to send any representative to Parliament.[22]

In the pages of *Il popolo d'Italia* of November 18, Mussolini remarked that "ours wanted to be and has been a simple affirmation, limited to the electoral district of Milan. It didn't want to be anything more. We write this not to exhibit euphemistic and posthumous justifications and consolations to ourselves and others, but simply because it is the pure, sacred, documentable truth. We took the field to assert ourselves and we succeeded. Ours is neither a victory nor a defeat: it is a political affirmation."[23] "Impudent" words, De Felice commented.[24] Or, more simply, an inevitable rhetorical jugglery of a shrewd politician who saw his movement threatened with completed disappearance. In the aftermath of the election, with the external pressures to solve the Fiume crisis and the internal disturbances of mounting workers' activism, there no longer seemed to be space for Mussolini's political project.

The Rise of Rural Fascism

It was in the turbulent months of social unrest led by workers' unions and the Socialist Party in the year and a half between the spring of 1919 and the fall of 1920 that Mussolini's movement found new impetus and new orientation. The historiographical term *biennio rosso* ("red two years") refers to this period of workers' agitations, strikes, occupations, and violent upheavals that occurred simultaneously in the major urban centers of the north (where most industries were located) and in the rural areas of the Po Valley.[25]

The combination of postwar economic crisis, the electoral victory of the Socialist Party (which acquired a leading role behind the activism of industrial workers thanks to the activities of its most innovative young leaders, including Antonio Gramsci, Amadeo Bordiga, and Umberto Terracini), the renewed dynamism of labor unions, the news of the successful socialist revolution coming from the Soviet Union, and the coeval socialist revolts in German cities were some of the events that motivated and energized the formation of spontaneous movements in the most important areas for Italian economy. These agitations took different forms, and different ideals, practical goals, and strategies motivated the revolts, occupations, and strikes.

Mussolini's movement found in the atmosphere of civil war of the 1919–21 an opportunity he had not foreseen.[26] In July he had prophesied that "Fascism will remain a movement of minorities. *It cannot spread outside the cities.* But soon each of the three hundred main Italian cities will have its Fascio di Combattimento and the forthcoming national meeting will gather this formidable complex of new forces in the harmonious and libertarian unity of action."[27] The electoral debacle had confirmed that the Fasci di Combattimento was a marginal movement; and yet the fifty-six local branches that existed in October 1919 rapidly increased to 120 in May 1920, and by May 1921 there were more than 1001 registered Fasci with a total of 187,098 members.[28] The exponential growth of the movement, however, did not happen, as Mussolini expected, within the major industrial urban centers of the north, but in the provincial towns of the Italian countryside.

The *squadrismo* of the Blackshirts in provincial towns such as Ferrara, Cremona, Lucca, and later Bologna and Florence—towns that were sustained mainly by agricultural capital—embraced the violent guerrilla attitudes of the urban Fasci of 1919 but elevated it to a system of local power. In a sense, the Fascism that would institutionally concretize in the foundation of the PNF on November 9, 1921—so different ideologically, sociologically, and institutionally from the Fascio of 1919—was rooted in the transformation of the anarchic and improvised activism of the early Fasci di Combattimento into the strategically planned violence of rural Fascism.

Local *ras* such as Italo Balbo, Roberto Farinacci, Dino Grandi, Carlo Sforza, and others remodeled improvised bands into well-organized paramilitary groups that acted as vigilante forces in the service of agricultural entrepreneurs and landowners, charged with protecting the rights of property and of labor exploitation against the emancipatory demands of the striking tenant farmers and sharecroppers and of the salaried agricultural proletariat.[29] The *camicie nere* (Blackshirts) that constituted the Fasci's *squadrismo* (vigilantism)—organized in *legioni* (regiments), which were in turn divided into *coorti* (battalions), *centurie* (companies), *manipoli* (platoons), and *squadre* (squads)—soon acquired a reputation of ruthless efficiency in quelling strikes and land occupations in rural areas. Balbo, one of the first of these successful leaders of local Fasci, later recalled that "in the progressive and rapid pressure of destiny, which brought me from my provincial town to lead revolutionary forces in neighboring provinces and later to command national units, I took care, with ever greater passion, of the military formations of the Fascist movement. My vocation was, and still is, that of the soldier. Intuitively I put before every political question the offensive and defensive efficiency of the action squads under my command."[30]

Ruthless violence—targeting principally socialists, unions, and striking laborers—became the most recognizable trait of Fascist Blackshirts. Their repressive violence later moved from the countryside back to the urban areas of Turin, Genoa, and Milan, where local Fasci's squads of "punchers," armed with sticks and old rifles from the First World War, were employed by industrialists to disband protesting workers and liberate factories from union occupation. Despite the attempt of conservative historians to deemphasize the violence of early Fascism,[31] cautious estimates of the casualties in 1920 totaled 288, 172 of whom were socialists and only 4 fascists.[32] Institutional forces—the state police, the royal army, and the governmental offices of the cabinets of Giovanni Giolitti and Ivanoe Bonomi—not only sympathized with the Squadristi, but often gave them logistical and intelligence support.[33] Alcide De Gasperi, member of Parliament and spokesperson of the PPI, wrote on April 7, 1921, "We do not share the opinion of those who condemn every fascist action under the generic condemnation of violence. There are actions in which violence, even if it assumes the appearance of aggression, is actually defensive violence, which is legitimate."[34] In short, even for a self-defined moderate political force like the Catholic PPI, fascist violence was legitimate because it protected the interests of industrialists and landowners.

"By foraging the fascists," wrote the liberal progressive historian Gaetano Salvemini for his Harvard lectures of 1943, "the industrialists, the landowners, and the bankers did not carry out any action that was not in their rights. Capital, like labor, is a social force, and it was natural for capitalists to provide funds to their 'white guards,' just as workers and peasants helped maintain their propagandists and organizers."[35] It happened, after all, in a situation of widespread violence and social unrest, Salvemini acknowledged. "But the Fascists," he concluded, "supported economically by industrialists, landowners, and traders, and politically by the police, judiciary, and military authorities, enjoyed overwhelming strength."[36] And the proportion of the victims of widespread violence during the 1920–21 was crushingly in favor of the fascists.[37] Salvemini, a reformist who ran in the 1919 election in a combatant list, commented in his lectures that, unlike the Fascists, "during the years of their 'tyranny,' the 'Bolsheviks' did not once devastate the office of an association of industrialists, agrarians, or traders; they never coercively forced the resignation of any administration controlled by conservative parties; they didn't even burn a newspaper printing house; they never looted a single house of a political opponent. Such acts of 'heroism' were introduced into Italian life by the 'anti-Bolsheviks.' Furthermore, it should be noted that while the crimes committed by the 'Bolsheviks' in the years 1919–20 were almost always carried out by excited crowds, the 'heroic' exploits of the 'anti-Bolsheviks' were too often prepared and conducted in cold blood by members of those wealthy classes, who claim to be the guardians of civilization."[38]

Despite the national visibility of fascist violence, "fascism" had yet to acquire the denotative value of a systematic political doctrine or recognizable political form it would only in the second half of the 1920s. Mussolini's definitions, explanations, and connotations, in editorials and public speeches, kept repeating the same propagandistic slogan emphasizing the antiparty and antiestablishment nature of the movement: Fascism "adapts to the circumstances" (December 6, 1919);[39] it "has no ideological a priori" (June 12, 1920);[40] it "is action, it does not stagnate . . . it does not want to linger beyond the time strictly necessary to fulfill its goals" (July 3, 1920);[41] it is "not a party, and it leaves complete freedom to individuals and groups within its organization" (August 21, 1920);[42] it is "anti-demagogic" (September 5, 1920);[43] it "means antidemagogy and pragmatism" (September 20, 1920);[44] it is "destined to become the greatest force of national realization" (October 14, 1920);[45] it is "a gathering not of petty politicians, but of warriors" (October 15, 1920);[46] it is "not a political movement in the electoral sense" (October 20, 1920);[47] it is a "typical creation of Italian people, tired of continental metaphysics. . . . Italian Fascism responds to the obscure instinct of the great popular masses. It is not bourgeois, as idiots claim in bad faith, and it is not proletarian in the strictly class sense of the word. It is above the proletariat and the bourgeoisie" (October 20, 1920);[48] "Fascism is above all a mentality and that is why it is difficult to be a fascist;"[49] it is "tendentially republican and not at all monarchical and even less dynastic" (October 29, 1920);[50] it is, "in the field of ideas, a great movement for the revision of all current political values. . . . Fascism only has a history, it does not yet have a doctrine; but it will, when it has had time to elaborate and coordinate its ideas" (November 6, 1920);[51] it is "antimonopolistic" (January 7, 1921);[52] referring to the PSI, "fascism is the eloquent daily documentation that in Italy the introduction of Russian methods is unthinkable except by exasperated and cynical brains" (January 20, 1921);[53] interestingly, an early trace of Fascism's later racism is anticipated in Mussolini's affirmation that "fascism responds to an obscure, inscrutable defense instinct of the lineage, of our Mediterranean and Aryan lineage" (January 27, 1921);[54]

it is "not a church; it is rather a gym. It is not a party; it is a movement; it does not have a program . . . , but it builds day after day the building of its will and passion" (March 23, 1921).[55]

During the *biennio rosso*, and in particular in the early months of 1921, national newspapers began to use the term as the collective name of the organized and systematic violence of Fascist squads. "Fascio" was no longer just an undefined union. But instead of responding to Mussolini's propagandistic slogans, it was now used *exclusively* to denote the nationwide violent and disruptive activities of local Fasci di Combattimento; in short, "fascism" became the name not just of Mussolini's political ideology, but particularly of the violent activism of local (and, in particular, rural) Fasci.[56] The consequences were momentous. First, the association of Mussolini's movement with revolutionary syndicalism and interventionist socialists was completely severed. Second, the participation of Fascist squads in the repression of labor movements in both rural and urban areas created the condition for their transformation into well-armed and organized paramilitary groups.[57] Third, the social composition of the Fasci membership changed quite drastically: while the Sansepolcrists were mostly educated members of the urban bourgeoisie, committed to a revolutionary project often with undisguised socialist sympathies, the rural Fasci collected members from the new rising middle classes of agricultural entrepreneurs, shopkeepers, artisans, white collars, civil servants, midlevel army officers, and professionals (lawyers, journalists, writers, et al.), whose only interest was the defense of class privileges.[58] According to a November 1921 survey of the PNF secretariat, the largest percentage of party members came from the rural middle classes, tenant farmers, and small landowning workers (24.3 percent). It was a remarkable transformation in the social composition of the Fascist movement in the first two years of its life.[59]

The Blackshirts' antisocialist activism not only gave the movement the nationwide visibility Mussolini had aspired but failed to provide; most important, it reconciled it with state institutions, in particular at the local level: their participation in the struggles of the *biennio rosso* on the side of the state forces (police, army, and local administrations) was pivotal to the eventual suppression of agrarian socialism in the Po Valley and the elimination of socialists from most provincial and town councils of northern and central Italy, and it set the foundation of a lasting alliance with the capitalist classes (industrial, agrarian, and financial) that would facilitate the road to power in the coming years.[60] In short, it was Squadrismo, not Mussolini's political scheming, that gave the Fasci movements national visibility and the support of the bourgeoisie.

Mussolini followed the unfolding of the successes of local Fasci from his Milan office almost as a spectator, lauding their initiative on the pages of *Il popolo d'Italia*. On October 17, 1920, he boasted that "Fascism's funeral was held, and the author of these lines was drowned in effigy in the Naviglio's waters. A year has just passed, and fascism, far from being dead, is more alive, more impetuous, more overwhelming than before. Until yesterday there was a specter in Italy: that of communism. Today there is another, more terrible and fearful one: the specter of fascism."[61]

Mussolini could repeatedly boast that "l'ora del Fascismo è arrivata!" (the time of Fascism has come). But in fact, the successes of the local Fasci directly menaced his leadership of the movement. He had hardly any control over the activities of the most powerful *ras*—and most of his interventions to quell local disputes occurred indirectly in the pages of *Il popolo d'Italia*.[62] Mussolini could boast that Fascism's position vis-à-vis the question of land ownership was on the side of those who worked the land.[63] But the fact was that in the Po Valley, the Fascist Blackshirts always sided with landowners to quell any form of protest by agricultural workers.[64] Mussolini's position was harshly contested when, on August 2, 1921, he signed a pacification pact with the PSI and the workers' union Confederazione Generale del Lavoro (General Confederation of Labor; CGL).[65] Soon the tension between Mussolini's ownership claims on the movement and the local interests and political goals of local Fasci turned into an open confrontation.[66] From the counterrevolutionary perspective of rural fascism, Mussolini was indeed betraying the raison d'être of Fascism: he was interrupting a conflict against socialists and labor unions that betrayed the scope of Fasci's action. The strong protests of many *ras* eventually forced Mussolini to rescind the pact.

The normalization of Fascism into an institutional political force was, in a sense, the only path allowing Mussolini to protect his leadership of a movement that was threatening to marginalize or even replace him. It happened in two steps: first, the electoral alliance with traditional conservative parties into a coalition led by Giolitti before the May 1921 general elections; and second, the transformation of the Fasci di Combattimento, a movement founded upon the idea of an antiestablishment antiparty, into an institutional political party in November 1921.

The Foundation of the Fascist Party

The constitution of the Blocchi Nazionali (National Blocs) was, for Giolitti, a necessary step in a context of social turmoil and political weakness. As he would explain in the second volume of his *Memorie della mia vita*, "I advised the formation of blocs in which all forces of the old liberal and democratic parties were gathered." Such coalitions were, for him, inevitable "for the conduct of the electoral struggle, considering that the most serious weakness of the liberal constitutional parties lay in their fragmentation, compared to the unity and compactness of the Socialists and the Popular."[67] The Bloc included Giolitti's Liberal Party, Enrico Corradini's Italian Nationalist Association, the conservative Social Democracy of Giovanni Antonio Colonna, and Mussolini's Fasci di Combattimento.

The participation of the Fasci in a coalition that represented the quintessence of the traditional political-institutional establishment openly contradicted the core idea of being an antiparty, an idea that had characterized Fascist rhetoric since San Sepolcro. Mussolini, responding to the internal opposition in an editorial of April 26, explained that the blocs surely had a "heterogenous composition," as they gathered together "diverse elements."[68] However, he continued, "the aims that fascism set itself by adhering to the blocs have been fully achieved. The sign of the blocs is the *fascio littorio*. In the Bloc lists, a fair share was given to the fascist candidates."[69] Independently of Mussolini's pragmatism, the participation of Fascism in an alliance of conservative political forces contributed to dissipating the revolutionary connotations the movement had in 1919.

Despite Giolitti's hopes, the results of the election of May 15, 1921 were not what he expected, notwithstanding the numerous intimidations and violent coercions organized by the Blackshirts:[70] The Socialist Party won with 24.69 percent of the votes, followed by the PPI (20.39 percent) and the Blocchi Nazionali (19.07 percent). Of the 105 seats earned by Giolitti's coalition, only thirty-five belonged to the Fasci di Combattimento. Mussolini's movement was still a modest party, with slightly more than 6 percent of the overall vote, even though Mussolini was elected to Parliament with the third-highest number of votes ever recorded for an individual deputy.

Following the May election and the entry of thirty-five *fasci* members in the Parliament, the transformation of Fascism into a political party during the third national convention of the Fasci di Combattimento, on November 7–10, 1921, completed its normalization as a constitutional and institutional force. But the growth of Fascism, its arrival on the political scene with the Blocchi Nazionali, and now the project of its institutionalization seemed paradoxically to threaten Mussolini's leadership of the movement.[71] Mussolini had played no prominent role in the strengthening of Fascism during the violent struggles against socialist protests, since it was mostly carried out by local *ras* such as Farinacci, Balbo, Marsich, Grandi, and others. His role as the charismatic leader of postwar combatants and revolutionary nationalists was overshadowed by that of Gabriele D'Annunzio. *Il popolo d'Italia* was not the official voice of the movement, even though it was in its pages that Mussolini conducted a relentless rhetorical refinement of the semantic content of the new term "fascism" for its readers, mostly members of the urban middle classes. In semiotic terms, Mussolini's persistent interventions in offering definitions of Fascism and in expounding its denotations and connotations were illocutionary acts, the intention of which was to consolidate an interpretive frame that could give a coherent political sense of the otherwise scattered Squadristi's actions in the provinces. The meeting of November 1921 was therefore a crucial test for Mussolini to reassert his control of the movement.[72]

That the Fasci were a movement in state of disarray did not go unnoticed. The Jewish intellectual Giorgio Levi Della Vida, commenting on the revolt against Mussolini after the pacification pact, argued that "Fascism does not represent anything positive, it does not respond to any definite tendency, it does not contain any constructive element; . . . it is only the expression of a undefined sense of distress, the manifestation of an undisciplined and reckless action."[73] On the eve of the national meeting of the Fasci, he further added: "In Italy there is no political party or movement in which there coexists, as in Fascism, so many currents that proceed in opposite directions, each one on its own path, without worrying about discipline, about central directive organization, about coordinating the various political attitudes." Della Vida concluded that "there are various regional fascist movements, sometimes even provincial, but there is no national fascism."[74]

Mussolini was certainly aware of the stakes involved in the meeting. The speech he gave on November 8, appropriately titled "Il programma fascista" (The Fascist Program), bears witness that Fascism was at a turning point. The task of Fascism, for him, was to "deal with the problems of the race and its health. . . . So we start from 'the nation' . . . since we are in antithesis with all internationalisms."[75] Mussolini's fundamental axiom was clear: since the essence of the nation is the race (a notion that Mussolini sustained well before the racial laws of 1938), Fascism opposed all forms of internationalism (socialism *in primis*, but also international agreements such as the Paris Peace Conference, as well as international business conglomerates, if hostile to the nation's interests). The state, as the political expression of the nation, must pursue its interests: "Beginning with the nation, we proceed to the state, which is most tangibly expressed by the government. But we are the state." It was therefore necessary for "the state to regain its authority." And that could not be achieved without Fascism.[76]

In terms of political orientation, "Fascism must remain agnostic" vis-à-vis the question of republicanism versus monarchism: "On the economy, we are openly antisocialist. . . . We are liberals, because we believe that the national economy cannot be entrusted to collective and bureaucratic bodies. . . . The ethical State is not the monopolistic State, the bureaucratic State; rather, it is the one that reduces its functions to the strictly necessary. . . . Class struggle is a fairy tale because humanity cannot be divided. Proletariat and bourgeoisie do not exist in history but are both cogs in the same machine."[77] Fascism was, indeed, a response to the "democratic hypertrophy" of the people—as he used to repeat at the time of San Sepolcro. But Mussolini now qualified that response by affirming that the scope of the movement was to show the masses what to do to fulfill their national destiny.

Behind Mussolini's flamboyant rhetoric, the distance of Fascism of 1921 from that of San Sepolcro is significant: Gone were most of the socialist ideas of wealth redistribution and industrial nationalization, in favor of a political economy that fully embraced liberal capitalism. Gone was the radical antimonarchism of Fascism's origins, replaced by a "regime agnosticism." And gone was also the virulent anticlericalism of San Sepolcro, replaced by the recognition that "respect must be accorded to every faith, because for Fascism the religious fact falls within the field of individual conscience. Catholicism can be used for national expansion."[78] In short, the normalization of Fascism from revolutionary force to institutional party was, at least rhetorically and semantically, accomplished.

"The third national fascist meeting was fully successful," Mussolini announced in the pages of *Il popolo d'Italia*. "The National Fascist Party is now a fait accompli. Regulations and statutes remain to be established, and this will be done within a very short time."[79] Mussolini had won the internal battle for the leadership of the movement, now turned into a conventional political party; but it was a truce rather than a victory, as the heterogeneous and polyarchic character of Fascism continued well through the 1920s, even after its political affirmation in October 1922. Mussolini, as Emilio Gentile put it, "managed to get his role as 'Duce' definitely accepted, even if he did not have an officially predominant position in the organization of the new party."[80] On the one hand, Mussolini insisted on continuation: "The Fascist Party is not only a political organization, but . . . also a military organization, in a certain sense."[81] He explicitly assured his people that "immediate consequences of the constitution of the movement as a party are not to be expected," since it "will continue to be a negative force, in the sense that it is always ready to support violent battle against the violent forms of struggle of antinational parties."[82] On the other hand, there were noticeable changes: The movement had now permanently severed its ties with revolutionary syndicalism, and the soon-to-be-published program intended to discipline the function of all local Fascist branches. This was approved and published on December 27, 1921.[83]

The establishment of the PNF was, in a sense, the paradoxical synthesis of irreconcilable opposites: the notion of a "fascist party" juxtaposed the name of an institutionalized organization (the party) with a movement that constitutionally and rhetorically rejected any form of institutionalized politics (*fascio*). The semantic contradiction of a fascist party well expressed both its structural instability and the diverging interests of different historical actors: Giolitti hoped that the institutionalization of Fascism as a political party implied the domestication of its most anarchic tendencies; local *ras* accepted it as a necessary compromise to gain national relevance; and for Mussolini, it was his only chance to maintain his leadership of an increasingly ungovernable political organization.

Despite the ideological and strategic transformations that Fascism underwent in the following decades, many of the constitutive elements of mature Fascism were already explicitly codified in the PNF program. Fascism's priority was to promote the full realization of the nation, as this was "the supreme synthesis of all material and nonmaterial values of a race."[84] At its core lay the foundational belief that the nation was the metaphysical horizon of human destiny, summed up in a conception of international relations conceived of as the "fruitful and peaceful competition among all national societies." At an institutional level, the state was "the juridical embodiment of a nation." The state was therefore "sovereign," and "such sovereignty cannot and ought not be damaged or diminished" by internal and external forces, including the imperialist interest of other nations, organizations that prioritize class interests, internationalist movements, and the Catholic Church. The PNF's attitude and activities depended upon "the moral and material interest of the nation." In other words, the interests and function of the party ostensibly coincided with the interests of the state, conceived of as the institutional realization of the metaphysical a priori that was the nation. Individuals within a state organized in corporations: this was "a historical fact that Fascism cannot oppose," so it aimed at "coordinating corporative development in the pursuit of national objectives." If the affirmation of the nation through the state (at the top) and through corporations (at the bottom) were the axioms that defined the political stance of the party, this implied that "the life of the nation is not characterized by antithetical forms of public and private morality." Instead, the "freedom of individual citizens is subjected to a twofold limit": on the one hand, the liberal principle of "the freedom of other juridical persons" as the limit of individual's actions; on the other, "the sovereign right of the nation to live and develop." In other words, the pursuit of national prosperity was the limit of individual freedom, and hence the importance of the state, which "must favor the nation's growth by promoting (but not monopolizing) all efforts that foster the ethical, intellectual, religious, artistic, judicial, social, economic, and physiological development of the national collective."[85]

The foundation of the PNF gave institutional consolidation to a movement that had been, at the ideological level, a moving target. The Fasci's defense of the interests of the bourgeoisie became clearer with the intensification of workers' struggles in the Po Valley. The growing participations of middle-class activists in local Fasci and, in particular, the violent actions of Squadristi against workers' unions helped dispel the ideological ambiguities of the early Fascism of San Sepolcro. But despite the striking differences between the program of 1919 and that of 1921, Mussolini, in an op-ed of December 28, still insisted, preposterously, that "the program of the PNF was not formulated by the National Council held in Florence on December 19–22. In Florence it was given formulation, to a certain extent definitive, to that varied and complex and collective programmatic elaboration that had begun in March 1919."[86]

The social origins of its members, their ideological orientation, and, above all, their actions during the *biennio rosso* told, however, a completely different story. Emilio Gentile described fascist Squadrism in 1920–21 as "a *maximalism of the middle classes*, and as such it was the real origin of Fascism, as organized force dominating political struggle, consciously oriented toward the conquest of power."[87] As Gentile noted—and a cursory survey of 1921 newspapers confirms—the antiunion, antisocialist violence of the Blackshirts became the most recognizable trait of the Fascists, together with their constant singing of war songs, hymns, and jingles while swinging their clubs.[88]

Before the constitution of the PNF, "fascism" was a term that only Mussolini and few others used, and "fascista" simply indicated the members of a *fascio*-like organization; only in the course of 1920 did the adjectival use come to be exclusive to members of the Fasci di Combattimento, the ideological orientation of which, however, remained far from clear. Its appearance as a qualifying adjective in the name of the new party marked the beginning of its transformation into the name of an identifiable political ideology, however still vague, contradictory, and ambiguous. It would be preposterous to imagine that the PNF program had the performative capacity of functioning as a normative document for all Fasci, which accepted their inclusion in the party but continued to act in quasi-complete autonomy. Powerful *ras* like Balbo, Farinacci, and Grandi continued their Squadristi activities in defense of landowners' and capitalists' property against striking laborers. Vigilante violence was still their most recognizable trademark, but now it was less chaotic and extemporaneous, as it increasingly worked in coordination with local administrations and police forces. It would be even less plausible to assume that the PNF program, as presented in December 1921, had regulative effects in the meanings of Fascism in general. Rather than a normative paradigm, the program could be better conceived of as a standard for measuring the different interpretations, both within and outside the movement, of what the new party stood for, ideologically and pragmatically. Nonetheless, the founding of the PNF and the publication of its political program contributed to give "fascism" and "fascist" a more precise denotation. "Fascista," in semiotic terms, was no longer a generic term referring to various kinds of organizations. It had now acquired a stable *extensional* value insofar as it deictically (indexically) referred to the actions and claims of the PNF. It maintained, however, a degree of semantic (intensional) fuzziness, as it continued to be an unstable ensemble of ideas and practices.

By the end of 1921, the former antiparty movement had become an integral part of a governmental coalition, placing it in open contradiction with its revolutionary intents. Mussolini, a master of ideological fabrications, had the audacity to write in *Il popolo d'Italia*—the same day that the reformist Ivanoe Bonomi, a former member of the Socialist Party, was presenting the king with his new center-right cabinet of ministers—that "civil war cannot and must not become a sort of characteristic of Italian life because, if that were the case, Italy would not have before it the glorious future of greatness that we long for and prepare for, but a future of darkness and blood. On the other hand," he added, since it was evident to all readers that Fascist Blackshirts were the main instigators of the violence he was condemning, "Fascism has carried out what historians will call a real 'national revolution.'"[89] Surely the hyperbolic claim that an electoral gain of 6 percent a few months earlier and the occupation of parliamentary seats within the governing faction could be described as a successful national revolution could not fool anybody, especially those local Fascist leaders who had a hard time accepting Mussolini as their leader. If coexistence with the traditional conservative and nationalist parties of Giolitti and Corradini was sufficient to stir internal dissent within the Fasci di Combattimento, the series of weak and indecisive center-right governments that ensued (Giolitti V until July 1921, Bonomi I until February 1922, and then a succession of two Facta cabinets to October 1922) exacerbated the anti-Mussolini faction within the party.

Mussolini's success in turning the movement into an organized party that recognized the authority of local *ras* quelled, at least temporarily, the internal contrasts within the movement, while giving it legitimacy within the political establishment. Moreover, over the course of 1922, the PNF strengthened its position in all regions of Italy. As Gentile commented, "In 1922, with more than two hundred thousand members, an armed militia, women's and youth associations, and with its own labor unions that counted more than five hundred thousand members, the PNF was the strongest political organization of the country."[90] The PNF was the most successful of all the conservative and moderate parties. Even if fraught with internal disputes, its predicament was not unique compared to the parties of the left, occupied in interminable ideological and strategic conflicts among themselves, especially between the Socialist Party and the newly established Communist Party, led by Amadeo Bordiga.[91]

The *sciopero legalitario*, a general strike launched by the Alleanza del Lavoro (Alliance of Workers' Unions) with the support of the Socialist and Communist Parties on July 31, 1922 against the vigilante violence of Fascist militias, gave Mussolini an unexpected opportunity to demonstrate his resoluteness: on the one hand, he could show the Italian bourgeoisie that the PNF was an organization more efficient than the state when it came to restoring law and order; on the other, he could show local Fascist leaders that he was not an *attendista*, a practitioner of a wait-and-see policy, but that when necessary he was ready to call for decisive action.[92] "We give the state forty-eight hours," Mussolini proclaimed, "to give proof of its authority to all its employees and to all those who are menacing the existence of the Nation. After that, Fascism will claim full liberty of action and will substitute for the state, which once more will have demonstrated its impotence."[93]

Fascist squads acted rapidly, descending with unrestrained violence on striking assemblies in all regions. Within two weeks of violent retaliations, which gave a full demonstration of the military capacities of the black-shirted militias, all workers' unions were destroyed. As Mussolini wrote to the Milan's central directorate of the PNF, "The retaliatory actions you have unleashed have my unconditional approval. . . . No force will ever succeed in overthrowing Fascism."[94] The PNF succeeded where the state had failed. The way to power was now open: "Fascisti!" Mussolini proclaimed on August 9, "the great battle is won on the whole front. The bluff of subversivism, which until yesterday blackmailed the State, . . . was severely and inexorably punished." All militias could demobilize, but they should continue to "assiduously prepare for the greater battle to come."[95]

The participation of fascist militias in quelling the national strike represented a turning point for the movement. As Giulia Albanese has argued, the national workers' upheaval "fueled a vast Fascist and nationalist backlash—serving more as a pretext for it than as an actual cause." In fact, "for the first time,

Fascist mobilisation took the form of a national demonstration and marked the ultimate defeat of left-wing labour organisations and trade unions. But what was at stake for the Fascists on this occasion was not the defence of the State against the latest strike, as claimed by pro-Fascist propaganda and part of the Fascist press, but rather the possibility of determining the orientation of the new government by threatening the country's ruling class."[96] While "the antifascist parties, liberal politicians, public opinion, the state institutions, and the economic forces still underestimated the strength of Fascism and its will to seize power," the movement succeeded in persuading the conservative elites within the government that the PNF constituted an invaluable resource for restoring control of the nation that the progressive forces of the socialist, communist, and labor unions had been threatening since the end of the war.[97]

In the ensuing months, a stalemate dominated the political scene: the indecisive prime minister, Luigi Facta, did nothing, the socialists and communists were counting their losses, and the economic establishment awaited a resolution of the state of disarray. It was in that conjunction that Mussolini made his move. During a PNF gathering in Naples, on October 24, 1922, Mussolini harangued a crowd squeezed into the Teatro di San Carlo: "We Fascists do not intend to go to power through the back door; we Fascists do not intend to give up our formidable ideal birthright for a miserable dish of ministerial lentils! Because we have the vision, which can be called historical, of the problem, compared to the other vision, which can be called political and parliamentary."[98]

Wisely, Mussolini pledged alliance to the monarchy ("There is no doubt that the unitary regime of Italian life is firmly anchored to the Savoy monarchy"), to the royal army ("We, a handful of daring few, have always defended the army"), and the Catholic Church. Fascism, he concluded, was ready to act to defend the nation from its enemy, which he now identified with the burdensome machinery of democratic parliamentarism (since they had already subdued the Bolshevik menace), because "our myth is the nation, our myth is the greatness of the nation. And to this myth, to this greatness that we want to realize, we subordinate everything else."[99] Back on streets of Naples, Mussolini gave the final insurrectionist speech for which he became famous: "Blackshirts from Naples and all over Italy! Today, without a shot being fired, we have conquered the vibrant soul of Naples, the ardent soul of the whole of southern Italy. But I tell you, with all the solemnity that the moment imposes: either they will give us the government, or we will take it by marching on Rome. And I tell you, and I swear to you, that that command, if necessary, will come!"[100]

The performance at Naples was a personal triumph for Mussolini. His speech was attended by the highest-ranking personages of the city: the mayor; the prefect; the president of the University of Naples; Senator Benedetto Croce, one of the most influential and celebrated Italian intellectuals; General Gustavo Fava, and many others. The day after, the internationally acclaimed economist Senator Luigi Einaudi wrote an article for the *Corriere della sera* that praised Mussolini's economic views, concluding with a tone that seemed prophetic of Milton Friedman's shock therapy: "If the [Ministry of] Treasury, I thought, went to a Fascist who was determined to take risks, determined to cut to the heart [of the problem], to say no and then no and again no to everyone, friends as much as enemies! The problem of our finance would be solved. It would be enough if the Fascists demanded this fundamental ministry for one of their own, or for a man they trust; and that they demand that he be provided with all the authority that reasonably belongs to him, so that he could really be in command of the government of the country."[101]

The March on Rome

In the aftermath of the Naples assembly, Mussolini's gamble for power took the form of that theatrical mise-en-scène that was the March on Rome, later celebrated by the regime that it gave birth to as the accomplishment of the "Fascist revolution." Mussolini had suggested the idea of a march on Rome immediately after his successful fight against the national strike, when during an interview he gave to *Il popolo d'Italia* on August 12, 1922 he bluntly admitted in a menacing tone: "The march on Rome is under way." He had then clarified that "it is not yet 'politically' inevitable and fatal. . . . That Fascism wants to become [the] *state* is certain, but it is not equally certain that a coup d'état is required to achieve this objective."[102] It became inevitable two months later, when Mussolini, on October 28, gave the task of organizing a militia of about forty thousand poorly armed Blackshirts to four leaders (the Quadrumvirate), while he planned to stay in Milan, ready to jump on a train bound for Switzerland if the coup failed.[103] The events happened very rapidly: When the march began, Prime Minister Facta asked the king to declare a state of siege in Rome in order to allow the army to be defensively deployed, but the king refused. The king, on October 28, had preferred the opinion of the former chief of staff of the Royal Army, General Armando Diaz (whom Mussolini would soon appoint minister of war), who was against the declaration of the state of siege and the deployment of the army, to that of the current chief of staff, General Pietro Badoglio, who suggested the immediate deployment of the army to quell the illegal uprising of the Blackshirts. On

October 30 Vittorio Emanuele III summoned Mussolini to Rome to give him the mandate of forming a new cabinet as prime minister.[104]

Contemporary chroniclers and postwar historians have long debated on the nature of the events of October 28–31: Was it a revolution, an insurgency, or a coup d'état? During a debate in the Chamber of Deputies, the socialist Filippo Turati accused: "With that revolutionary method, which today is called 'fascistic'—and even though the term means nothing, we also adopt this adjective—the Chamber is not called to discuss and deliberate trust; it is called to give it; and if it does not give it, the government takes it. In short, it is the march on Rome, which for you is a cause of honor, that continues, in impeccable frock coat, inside the Parliament."[105] During the same debate, De Gasperi urged for new elections, since "revolutionary Fascism could have made it [Rome] a bivouac, but the next day, we are convinced, it would have felt that the very majesty of the nation that it intended to restore would have been fatally struck."[106] The liberal intellectual Piero Gobetti commented on November 23 that "the Fascist 'revolution' is not a revolution, but a coup d'état carried out by an oligarchy, through the humiliation of all seriousness and political conscience—with student goliardicism."[107] Ignazio Silone, the former communist activist, commented that "all Fascist literature would like to convince us of the revolutionary character of the march on Rome. . . . But rather than a revolution, the march on Rome turned out to be simply a normal parade."[108] The flamboyant author Curzio Malaparte, in *Technique du coup d'état*, originally published in Paris in 1931, scornfully admitted that the army could have easily quelled the Fascist insurrection.[109] Gaetano Salvemini, in his lectures at Harvard University, called it a "ridiculous demonstration" of "fifty thousand men parading on the streets of Rome to celebrate their victory, after a 'march on Rome' that never happened." For Salvemini, the events of October 28–31 could be summed up as "men that were not in power took over the government with the connivance of the military authorities. . . . To define the march on Rome as a revolution means to absolve the military authorities and the king himself from any accusation of betraying the statute, and to surround Mussolini with an aura of 'revolutionary conqueror.'"[110] Similarly, Angelo Tasca has argued that "a few hundred regular soldiers, a few trucks, a few airplanes, could have easily scared away that crowd, [leaving it] unable to conduct any military operation."[111]

The transformation of the March on Rome in the mythical tale of the Fascist revolution was an operation orchestrated by Mussolini and his collaborators. In a discourse to the Senate, Mussolini affirmed that "Fascism did not come to power by normal means. It got it by marching on Rome *armata manu*, with an exquisitely insurrectionary act."[112] Yearly celebrations of the event punctuated the history of the Fascist regime. Mussolini's participation in the march was invented and staged by his lover, Margherita Sarfatti, who in the hagiographical biography *Dvx* described how "the Duce took up his rifle" and, after inspecting the troops at Civitavecchia, "walked toward Rome."[113] That they were constructing a foundational myth was clear to many Fascist authors. The economist Maffeo Pantaleoni, who inspired the economic measures of the first Mussolini government, argued that "the legend [of the March on Rome] has some use for Fascism in its current phase. It should never be forgotten that our people are imaginative, artistic, emotional, and that they profess a religion full of wonders and miracles." And he added, with quasi-semiotic flair: "Well, every revolution unites the unexpected with something theatrical, like a change of scenery, or it involves something unexplained, which therefore can be explained in many ways, and that cannot be done without heroes, supermen, divinities, and even shivers."[114]

The tenth anniversary of the March on Rome took the form of monumental celebrations of the Fascist revolution. On November 9, 1932, Ottavio Dinale wrote in *Il popolo d'Italia* that the glorious events of 1922 "inaugurated an epoch comparable to Imperial Rome." And he added that "Fascism will fill the century with itself. This is a historical certainty, not a prophecy."[115] Mussolini, too, would contribute to the mythopoesis of the revolution of 1922, and many of his aphorisms adorned the rooms of the "Exhibition of the Fascist Revolution," organized in Rome: "In 1922, I convinced myself since the summer that we had to make a revolution. . . . It is I who wanted it, this March, it was I who set it up, me who cut off all hesitations."[116]

Antonino Repaci's detailed chronicle of the days of the March on Rome offers convincing evidence that the king, Vittorio Emanuele III, before charging Mussolini with the task of organizing a new cabinet, consulted with the president of the General Confederation of Italian Industry, Raimondo Targetti.[117] Moreover, an October 29, 1922 op-ed in the Catholic newspaper *L'osservatore romano* made it absolutely clear that the Vatican too was in favor of a Mussolini government.[118]

Mussolini's rise, one hundred years after the pantomime of the March on Rome, seems in hindsight as resistible as that of the Chicago gangster portrayed in Bertolt Brecht's play.[119] If Mussolini celebrated it as the beginning of the "revolution," most historians present it as a convenient sleight of hand, if not a coup d'état, for the conservative establishment to oppose the formidable electoral rise of the progressive parties, and in particular the PSI. Giulia Albanese has perceptively pointed out that historians "tended to regard the March on Rome as a bluff rather than an event which had a strong political impact and which deserves to be studied as such."[120] Indeed, even admitting that the flamboyant parade of Blackshirts was shrewdly seized on by the king, with the support of industrialist elites and conservative forces, to disentangle the political stalemate that had ensued after the elections of May 1921 and thus safeguard power from the menace of workers' movements and the rise of socialism, the March on Rome was not only the occasion of widespread violence against the headquarters of the PSI, of the newspaper *Avanti!*, and of labor unions—in a sort of dark and murderous carnival comparable to that of the People's Crusade of the eleventh century. It was also, and especially, an "epoch-making event"—as Albanese describes it—even though it unfolded independently of Mussolini's volition (and control) as a coup d'état masked as revolution, because it marked the beginning of his rule over Italian politics, which would last for twenty years.[121] One of the first acts of Mussolini's cabinet that supports the interpretation that the March on Rome—even admitting the fortuity of its success—constituted a turning point in Italian history was the legalization of the Blackshirts into a Milizia Volontaria per la Sicurezza Nazionale (Voluntary Militia for National Security), approved by the Council of Ministers on December 28 and voted for by a large majority of the Parliament on January 12, 1923.[122] The law symbolically and effectively sanctioned the use of violence for political ends and, as Lyttelton put it, it constituted the first step toward dictatorship.[123]

During the first discourse that Mussolini gave at the Chamber of Deputies, on November 16, 1922, with the purpose of presenting his cabinet of ministers, he declared menacingly: "I refused to win big, and I could win big. I have set myself limits. I told myself that the best wisdom is that which does not give up after victory. With 300,000 young men fully armed, determined to do anything and almost mystically ready for my order, I could punish all those who have defamed and tried to tarnish Fascism. I could make of this deaf and gray hall a bivouac of maniples. . . ." The speech was interrupted by the socialist deputy Giuseppe Emanuele Modigliani, older brother of the artist Amedeo, with screams of "Viva il Parlamento!" Mussolini, undisturbed by the protests from the left wing of the chamber, continued: "I could ban the Parliament and set up a government exclusively of Fascists. I could: but I didn't want to, at least for now."[124] Mussolini's claims were exaggerated and preposterous. "Harsh Language of Mussolini at the Chamber" was the title of the opening op-ed of the newspaper *La Stampa* the following day.[125] These words—menacing, hyperbolic, patently false—marked the beginning of what would soon become a ruthless, violent, totalitarian regime.

3

The Semantic Consolidation of "Fascism," 1922–1945

In the first three years since the term was coined in 1919, the semantic markers of "fascism," its connotations, and its nuances had been susceptible to drastic transformations as the movement it named changed political strategy, ideological orientation, membership, and social representativeness.[1] If the semantic pregnancy of "fascism" sprang from the utterances of Mussolini and few other Fasci members, the general use of the adjective "fascist" was limited to signify membership to Fascist organizations (local Fasci and, after 1921, the PNF). Evidence of that is not only the few occasions on which the term "fascism" itself appeared in non-Fascist publications, but also Filippo Turati's words during the parliamentary vote in support of Mussolini's first cabinet, on November 17, 1922, quoted in the previous chapter: "*Even though the term means nothing*, we also adopt this adjective."[2] Turati's remarks were surely polemic and antagonistic; still, they indicate how the meanings of "fascism" at the time were yet to become socially codified beyond the simple indexical use of the term. The main events and dynamics of the movement as it transformed from a noninstitutional association into a political party, introduced in the previous chapter, determined the indexical meaning of "fascism" to 1922. The institutionalization of Fascism as a governmental regime under the aegis of King Vittorio Emanuele III and the Parliament—as well as under legal authorization of the Albertine Statute, the constitutional charter of the kingdom of Italy, in use until 1948—assured in the course of the twenty years of Fascist rule in Italy (the Ventennio, 1922–43) not only a codification of "fascism" as a political term now in general use to denote Mussolini's government and its orientation (and not just membership to the PNF), but also the semantic crystallization of its most important denotative and connotative markers.[3]

As the previous chapter has schematically laid out, Fascism's rise to power was secretly (or opportunistically) choreographed by means of a simulated revolution by King Vittorio Emanuele III with the support of traditional conservative parties (Giolitti), Confindustria (a league of industrialists), and the tacit support of Pope Benedict XV through his secretary of state, the Fascist supporter Cardinal Pietro Gasparri, who would later be the signatory of the Lateran Pacts in 1929.[4] That the widespread violence of Fascist squads throughout the year and their armed insurrection on October 28–29 constituted a sort of blackmailing of the king does not invalidate the interpretation that conceives of Mussolini's rise to power as a legal appointment, with the support of the king and the confirmation of the Parliament.[5]

The consolidation of Mussolini's power happened quickly. In the two sessions held on November 25 and 28, 1922, the Chamber of Deputies and the Chamber of Senators gave the new government full executive powers: The social situation in Italy was in such a state of emergency that Parliament accorded the government the power to operate through executive orders having full legislative force, without the intervention of Parliament.[6] Despite overwhelming parliamentary support (short of the votes from the socialist PSI and the Partito Comunista d'Italia [Communist Party of Italy, PCd'I]), the new government was far from being the result of conventional proceedings. Intellectuals such as Gaetano Salvemini, Giuseppe Prezzolini, Anna Kuliscioff, and Giuseppe Canepa did not hesitate to condemn the illiberal threat of the new "fascist regime" as early as November 1922.[7]

Fascism's grasp of complete political power was confirmed by the general political elections of April 6, 1924, which Mussolini's National List won with the 64.9 percent of the votes.[8] Widespread violence and systematic intimidation contributed a great deal to the result, as did the new electoral law, passed on November 18, 1923, that the Fascist economist Giacomo Acerbo designed to give the majority coalition a premium of two-thirds of the seats in Parliament.[9]

The electoral results were contested in the Parliament. Enrico Presutti, professor of jurisprudence and deputy of the Liberal group, argued during a discussion in the Chamber of Deputies on May 30, 1924 that the elections were illegal.[10] The socialist Giacomo Matteotti accused the Fascists in the same session: "We are contesting the validity of the majority elections here and now. . . . In our opinion, the election is essentially invalid, and we add that it is not valid in all circumscriptions. . . . By your own confirmation, no Italian voter found himself free to decide of his own will. . . . There is an armed militia, made up of citizens of a single party, which has the declared task of supporting a specific government by force, even if it lacks consent."[11] According to Emilio Lussu, as soon as he concluded his speech, after presenting a long list of evidence of violent coercion in many electoral colleges, Matteotti told a fellow party member, "I did my speech. Now it's on you to prepare my funeral eulogy."[12] The majority coalition rejected the motion. On June 10 Matteotti was kidnapped and murdered by a group of five Blackshirts.[13]

The crisis sparked by Matteotti's assassination threatened the survival of the regime.[14] More than a hundred deputies from the Socialist and Communist Parties left Parliament in protest and retreated to the *sala dell'Avventino*; the futility of this protest gave birth to the Italian idiomatic expression "Aventino retreat."[15] Piero Gobetti commented in the pages of his newspaper *La rivoluzione liberale*: "We will not be so naive as to demand justice for the murder of our friend. In some cases, justice becomes the problem of two civilizations, of two principles of struggle. If the opposition has a task, it is to unmask the game of Mussolinism, which tends, by liquidating some high-ranking figures of Fascism, to create another pedestal for the paternal leader, normalizer, and tamer. Instead, it is the entire regime that must be put on trial."[16]

Gobetti's prophesy came only partly true. Mussolini did not fall, in large part because the forces that favored the formation of his government did not act against him. As Bosworth commented, "The King, the Vatican, the army chiefs, business, the academic world, all the old elites, contemplated the crisis and preferred not to swing decisively against the Prime Minister."[17] Mussolini took responsibility for Matteotti's assassination in a speech he gave at the Chamber of Deputies on January 3, 1925:

> I declare here, in the presence of this Assembly and in the presence of all the Italian people, that I alone assume the political, moral, and historical responsibility for everything that has happened. If more or less crippled sentences are enough to hang a man, take out the pole! Take out the rope! If Fascism was nothing more than castor oil and truncheon, and not instead a superb passion of the best Italian youth, it is my fault! If Fascism was a criminal association, I am the head of this criminal association! If all the violence was the result of a specific historical, political, and moral climate, well, I am responsible for this, because I created this historical, political, and moral climate with a propaganda that goes from interventionism to the present.[18]

That speech symbolically marked the beginning of Fascist totalitarian rule.

Matteotti's assassination, far from causing the downfall of Mussolini's regime, strengthened not only the government but, paradoxically, the suppressing activism of Fascist radicals.[19] As Emilio Gentile has commented, "With Mussolini's speech to the Chamber of Deputies, on January 3, 1925, Fascism began a new phase of consolidation and expansion of its power."[20] Home Minister Luigi Federzoni put into motion a series of repressive measures that completely curbed the possibility of political opposition—eventually outlawing the Socialist and Communist Parties (November 1926). Mussolini appointed Roberto Farinacci, the most radical and violent of the *ras*, as secretary of the PNF. The years 1925 and 1926 marked the beginning of a series of reforms nicknamed *leggi fascistissime* (superfascist laws).[21] "The transformation of the Italian political system," Gentile writes, "into a new single-party regime occurred through a sort of 'legal revolution,' that is, with the approval by a Fascist-dominated Parliament of an organic complex of authoritarian laws, elaborated mostly by the jurist Alfredo Rocco, the architect of the Fascist state, which destroyed the parliamentary regime, even though they seemingly left intact the façade of a constitutional monarchy founded on the 1848 statute."[22]

The authoritarian transformation of the state proceeded relentlessly within the confines of previous liberal democratic institutions, with the collaboration (tacit or explicit) of all conservative parties and the economic establishment, and in a language and through procedures that were largely congruent with the Albertine Statute, no matter how deformed its original spirit became.[23] In other words, Fascism's counterrevolutionary revolution did not operate through erasure, substitution, or refoundation. It did not realize a radical regime replacement like the ones that occurred after the big revolutionary events of the previous century and a half in the United States (1776), France (1789), Japan (1868), and Russia (1917). It was, rather, a process of legal denaturing, or internal reconfiguration of the role and meanings of preexisting institutions, rules, and languages. The Albertine Statute, bent and modified but never disavowed or revoked, gave legal legitimacy to those transformations.[24]

The authoritarian transformation of the state began with the Acerbo Law of 1923 and intensified with the subordination of cabinet and Parliament to the authority of the prime minister, the Duce, who responded only to the king (laws of December 24, 1925 and January 31, 1926);[25] the hierarchical reorganization of local administration, with the appointment of a *podestà* (at city level) who responded to a provincial *prefetto* (laws of February 4, 1926 and April 3, 1926);[26] the abolishment of the freedom of association, which led to the dissolution and eventual outlawing of all political parties but the PNF (law of November 26, 1925); the fascistization of all newspapers, resulting from the prohibition on public criticism of the regime (law of November 25, 1926); the institution of a Tribunale Speciale per la Difesa Dello Stato (Special Tribunal for the Defense of the State, law of November 25, 1926), which made any crime against the state a capital offense; the institution of a Gran Consiglio del Fascismo (Grand Council of Fascism, informally founded on January 12, 1923 and fully instituted with the law of December 9, 1928), officially defined as "the supreme organism that coordinates and integrates all the activities of the regime that arose from the revolution of October 1922," which synchronized the PNF to the functioning of the state and operated as the highest legislative and constitutional body;[27] the normalization and stabilization of the state with the Catholic Church (the Pacta Lateranensia, or Lateran Pacts, February 11, 1929);[28] the abolition of all labor unions and the creation of a Confederazione Nazionale delle Corporazioni Sindacali (National Confederation of Trade Union Corporations, January 1922) and, later, of a Confederazione Generale Fascista dell'Industria Italiana (General Fascist Confederation of Italian Industry, with law 563 of April 3, 1926), under the supervision of the Ministero delle Corporazioni (Ministry of Corporations, instituted on July 2, 1926).[29]

Despite the authoritarian transformation of state institutions, the political economy of the new regime essentially pursued the liberal approach of the previous governments, at least until the crisis of 1929, when the state started a plan for financially sustaining industries (via bailouts and stock purchases rather than nationalizations), agricultural reclamations, and infrastructural works. Politicians who served as ministers in economic matters were all from parties of the liberal center right.[30] According to the economic views of the regime, it was not the proletariat that sustained and led economic growth and social prosperity, but rather, and in contradiction with the Marxian conception of class struggle, the synergetic collaboration between the industriousness of the working classes and the leadership and acumen of the entrepreneurial elites. The Carta del Lavoro (Labor Charter), promulgated on April 21, 1927 by the Grand Council of Fascism gave legal status to the corporatist transformation of Italian economy.[31] According to the charter, national prosperity was the final end of economic life, and therefore "the opposing interests of the employers and the workers" had to be subordinated "to the superior interests of production" (Art. 4). But since "the corporative State considers private initiative, in the field of production, to the most efficient and useful instrument of the Nation" (Art. 7), and since the state could intervene only "where private initiative is lacking or insufficient" (Art. 9), Fascism became an instrument that reinforced the interests of the capitalist elites, where the state intervened only to quell class conflict in the name of national development.

Culture, too, became a particularly sensitive domain of Fascist control, crucial to achieving the goal of creating a harmonious community. Mussolini put radios, cinemas, and all other media outlets under strict state control, initially through the Ufficio Stampa della Presidenza del Consiglio (Press Office of the Prime Minister), instituted in 1924, and then, on June 24, 1935, through the Ministero per la Stampa e la Propaganda (Ministry of Press and Propaganda) and, in 1937, the Ministero per la Cultura Popolare (Ministry of Popular Culture). The Istituto Luce (Luce was the acronym for L'Unione Cinematografica Educativa, or the Educational Film Union), founded in 1924 by Mussolini himself via royal decree, became an official organism for the production and distribution of state information and propaganda. It was a nonprofit *istituzione morale* (moral institution), as its constitutional definition explained.[32] Teachers at every level could continue to instruct students in schools and universities only after swearing allegiance to the PNF and its mission.[33]

The transformation of Fascism from movement to regime and its institutionalization as a new form of legally sanctioned authoritarianism constituted the sociohistorical circumstances that favored the consolidation of the semantic markers of the signifier "fascism," which until then had remained unstable and largely served the indexical function of a proper name. The regime, through coercive, suasive, propagandistic, and educational interventions, contributed to the enforcement of interpretive habits that actualized the selection of specific denotations and connotations of the sign vehicle "fascism." These did not exhaust all coeval denotations and connotations of "fascism," which continued to be produced by nonfascist and antifascist authors (see part II) in texts circulating clandestinely or from exile. But the codification of denotative markers in official documents, speeches, and state propaganda resulted in the consolidation of the sanctioned semantic value of "fascism" throughout the period. In short, the institutionalization of Fascism into a regime enforced, through coercion, suasion, indoctrination, and simple repetition, semiosic habits of understanding and use of at least some of the meanings of the sign vehicle "fascism."

A reconstruction of the ways in which the regime forced upon the population a particular set of denotations and connotations of "fascism" should not be read as an argument for Italians' uncritical acceptance or adherence to that semantic usage. It simply registers the explicit production and active enforcement of particular selections of the semantic markers (specific denotations and connotations) of "fascism" (e.g., its denotative synonymity with "state" and "nation," or its connotations of strength, authenticity, and/or virility), and the negation of others (e.g., its original association with socialism and revolutionary syndicalism). Enforcement here stands for different modes of coercion and suasion adopted by the regime. They include forceful and violent interventions, such as censorship, prohibition, imprisonment, book burning, and the like, as well as less invasive means of control (such as denunciation, espionage, indoctrination, participation in state rituals, repetition, etc.).

Censorship legislation was passed in 1924 and started to take full effect after 1925, reaching a more widely diffused effectiveness only in the 1930s. As the historian Scotto di Luzio described it, "Fascist censorship extended over a vast and rugged territory. It subjected to its control the circuits of diffusion of ideas and private conversations, the style of writers and individual conduct; and as such, it functioned as a powerful regulatory mechanism between the public and private spheres in Fascist Italy. At its head were an institutional apparatus, which was gradually perfected over the years, and a plurality of practices and actors."[34] Institutionally, the censoring authorities were the police, the Print and Propaganda Office and, in the 1930s, the Ministry of Popular Culture. But an army of informers among the population as well as the surveilling activities of the OVRA kept dissent against the regime under control.[35]

Education and para-educational activities such as sports, after-work leisure clubs, youth groups, women's associations, and the like also played a fundamental role in regulating the meanings of "fascism," to the point that positive persuasion rather than negative repression was overall a more efficacious means of organizing the consensus of the masses.[36] Prominent intellectuals were recruited in support of the regime, and their publications helped to cement particular meanings and connotations of "fascism." Giovanni Gentile, the idealist philosopher who had served as minister of public education between 1922 and 1924, was an active promoter of Fascism among the intellectual classes and within universities. On April 21, 1925 he published in the main national newspapers a "Manifesto degli intellettuali fascisti" (Manifesto of Fascist Intellectuals), the offspring of a conference organized by the Fascist Institutes of Culture the previous March 29–30, in Bologna. The goal of the manifesto was to recruit academics to the cause of Fascism and give it intellectual authority.

It began with a historical profile of Fascism within Italian history: "Fascism is a recent yet ancient movement of the Italian spirit. It is intimately linked to the history of the Italian nation, yet it is not devoid of meaning and of interest for other nations. Its immediate origins must be sought in 1919, when a handful of veterans from the trenches gathered around Benito Mussolini, determined to combat vigorously the then-dominant democratic socialist politics."[37] The document framed Fascism as a reaction against the political landscape of the immediate postwar period, which only reinforced "an arrogant and menacing opposition of individuals to the state; neglect of the state's authority; a lowering of the prestige enjoyed by the king and the army (symbols of a nation that transcends individuals and individual social categories); the unleashing of base passions and instincts; [and] the fostering of social disintegration, moral degeneration, and a self-centered and mindless spirit of revolt against all forms of discipline and law."[38] But Fascism was also "a political and moral movement" that went beyond immediate necessities because it was pursuing a project, an ideal that transcended historical contingency itself. Indeed, Fascism "understood and championed politics as a training ground for self-denial and sacrifice in the name of the idea. . . . The idea in question is that of the fatherland [*Patria*]. The fatherland is an ideal that is in the process of being historically actualized but that remains inexhaustible. . . . The fatherland is a tradition as well as a sense of mission."[39] Fascism's historical mission was the full realization of the nation: It was the necessary continuation of Giuseppe Mazzini's project of a national Risorgimento. As a movement, Fascism was completely dedicated, with religious zeal, to respond to the appeals of the nation. As a government, it acted on the nation's behalf and in that role was committed to the "reconsecration of all those traditions and institutions that continuously inform a civilization, beyond the flux and perennial recurrence of tradition."[40]

The manifesto, which codified "fascism" in terms of a government in the service of national interests, in line with Mussolini's own conceptions, was undersigned by 250 members of the cultural elite class, among them Gabriele D'Annunzio, Curzio Malaparte, Filippo Tommaso Marinetti, Luigi Pirandello, Margherita Sarfatti, Arrigo Solmi, Ugo Spirito, Giuseppe Ungaretti, Gioacchino Volpe, and many other intellectuals and artists.[41] On May 1, 1925 the Hegelian philosopher Benedetto Croce, a former collaborator of Giovanni Gentile who had also served as minister of public education in 1920–21, published in the pages of *Il Mondo* a "Manifesto degli intellettuali non fascisti" (Manifesto of Nonfascist Intellectuals), in which he criticized Gentile's manifesto and defended the autonomy of culture from politics and the universality of art and science, condemning political violence and the totalitarian state. Luigi Albertini, Sibilla Aleramo, Giovanni Amendola, Piero Calamandrei, Gaetano de Sanctis, Luigi Einaudi, Attilio Momigliano, Eugenio Montale, Gaetano Salvemini, and several hundred politicians, journalists, scholars, jurists, and authors signed the document. Many of these would be ostracized, many recanted their adherence to the manifesto, some were imprisoned, and some emigrated to France, but most of them strove to survive the regime from their places on the margins of society.[42]

Fascism's ideology was, however, more pervasive and suasive in indirect ways, especially through the unrelenting repetition of symbols, slogans, songs, images, faces, and portraits.[43] Repetition of slogans in jingles and popular songs were a ubiquitous soundtrack of the period. Fascist slogans were carved on the walls of the houses in every Italian town and city; many of these can be still seen today, silent companions in the daily lives of Italians. Actively promoted and regulated by the PNF itself since 1930, they turned Italian urban space into a legible repository of Fascist doctrine, each quote a hypertext linking streets, edifices, and bridges with "the fatherland," "the family," "il Duce," "empire."[44] Mussolini's government supported an architectonic policy that monumentalized Fascism, conveying its ideological message in a semiotic system centered in a nonverbal disposition of volumes that constantly reminded Italians of the regime and its Duce.[45] As Emilio Gentile has put it: "The choreographic, liturgical and ludic aspect of the party that absorbed a large part of its activities and of its energies was, in the totalitarian logic of Fascism, one of the principal functions for the Fascist socialization of individuals and masses, a function carried out in full consciousness of its political objectives."[46] Figures of repetition were constitutive of Mussolini's own rhetorical constructions. But repetition was also nonverbal: Italian streets were covered in Fascist symbols. Italo Calvino remembered in his diary, "You could say that I spent the first twenty years of my life with Mussolini's face always in sight, in the sense that his portrait was hung in every classroom, as well as in every public building or office."[47]

Directly or indirectly, coercively or suasively, during the two decades of Fascist power there were constant efforts to stabilize and cement the meaning of "fascism." The aim of this complex operation was clearly ideological, aimed at securing consensus on and support of the regime as well as discouraging opposition and resistance. Whether the regime was successful or not in gathering consensus and which period of the twenty years of Fascist rule should be considered the apex of popular support for Fascism are questions that historians have debated throughout the postwar period, which, however, are beyond the scope of this study.[48] But at the core of these ideological efforts lay the necessity to correct and control the denotations and connotations of what Fascism meant. If in 1922 Turati could insinuate, not without polemical intent, that "fascism" was a meaningless term, during those initial three years of frenetic activity Fascism presented itself mainly in negative terms, as an antiestablishment, antiparty, antiparliamentary, antisocialist, and antiliberal movement. Once in power, Fascism had to reconstruct its denotations and connotations in positive terms, in accordance with its governmental project.

"Fascism" as Government, State, and Nation

As a movement born of an antiestablishment revolt that made violence its preferred mode of political expression, the first challenge of Fascism was to perform its role as the governing authority while maintaining a semblance of its ideological antagonism to traditional parties, institutions, and strategies. It had, that is, to rule without betraying its revolutionary and subversive message of antipolitics. It was a formidable challenge for Mussolini, who led a coalition government that, despite the king's concession and parliamentary authorization of ruling by executive degree, before 1924 was still outnumbered in Parliament and did not yet enjoy the support of the masses.

Moreover, in the early phase of the regime, between late 1922 and through 1925, Fascism was still a largely heterogeneous movement. A multiplicity of ideological positions coexisted, often in open contradiction with one another. On February 15, 1925, in the aftermath of Mussolini's "discourse of the bivouac" to the Italian Parliament, the Futurist author and Fascist sympathizer Volt—the pseudonym of Count Vincenzo Fani Ciotti—published an essay in the journal *Critica fascista* entitled "Le cinque anime del fascismo" (The Five Souls of Fascism). In it, Volt divided the political ideas within the Fascist movement into five groups of differing views and praxes, ranging from "extreme right" to moderate "revisionism." Volt's editorial was a plea for reconciliation, as he saw in this ideological division a threat to the survival of Fascism.[49] Provincial Fascist leaders such as Roberto Farinacci, Mario Carli, and Emilio Settimelli defended the movement's violently authoritarian strategy and condemned Mussolini's renunciation of Fascism's revolutionary goals when he accepted the king's mandate to form a coalition government in late October of 1922. Others saw Fascism as Italy's response to the alienating effects of modernity. Antimodernists such as Malaparte (born Kurt Erich Suckert) conceived of Fascism as a movement that, like Russian Bolshevism, contrasted with the pernicious effects of Nordic modernism with its vision of a society led by the impersonal forces of liberalism, capitalism, free will, and democratic individualism.[50] Mino Maccari proposed that Fascism defended the traditional harmonious social order of the Italian provinces, and that this was the most successful strategy for opposing capitalist modernity.[51] Reactionaries such as Giuseppe Brunati and Giuseppe Attilio Fanelli conceived of Fascism as an effective strategy for transforming Italy into an absolutist monarchy led by the House of Savoy, and they supported that line in their magazine *Il Sabaudo*. Fanelli even proposed to "hand over to the monarchy its full sovereignty."[52] Conservative intellectuals such as Giuseppe Bottai and Massimo Rocca defended Fascism as a form of political modernism and proposed that the *ribellismo* ("rebellism") of its early years had transformed into a governing force that could construct a new culture of national community by embracing technological and economic progress. As Bottai stated in his 1923 book *Il Fascismo e l'Italia nuova*, "Despite some residues of agonizing rebellion, Fascism is on the way to becoming a party of order, in the organic sense of the word. This changes the selective principle of its proselytism, which becomes the moral and intellectual capacity to participate, even in organisms far from the center of government, in the life of the state. The supreme necessity of the state acts in the sense of creating its own men."[53]

The governmental success of Mussolini's Fascism not only came at the expense of local, violent forms of rural activism; it also entailed a transformation of the social composition of its members and the ideal of society they maintained. If the first transformation of Fascism in 1920 required the abandonment of its ties with revolutionary syndicalism, its second transformation into the governing authority necessitated the reduction of its violent militarism in favor of capitalist productivism (which explains the renewed emphasis on "corporativism" in Mussolini's writings and speeches of the period).

It was after Mussolini rose to power that the most noticeable changes in the usage and meanings of "fascism" appeared on a syntactic level. The occurrences of "fascism" in Mussolini's writings and public speeches multiplied exponentially. Frequently, "fascism" appeared as the grammatical subject in sentences that were not simply predicative—aimed at offering a description of the qualities or properties of the subject—but in fact constative. "Fascism" indicated the agent of actions in such sentences as "Fascism decides," "Fascism rules," "Fascism establishes," "Fascism determines," "Fascism acts," "Fascism passes laws," "Fascism solves problems," "Fascism conquers," and so on. This use of the term is ubiquitous in Mussolini's utterances from 1923 onward. In reporting or justifying the government's actions, Mussolini did not use "I" or "the government" as the subject (and thus the actor), but always "Fascism," which stood metonymically for "the Fascist government." As a result, rather than arguing about how Fascism transformed into a governmental force within the institutional and legal framework of parliamentary monarchism that was the kingdom of Italy, Mussolini and other Fascist leaders simply stated how Fascism, as an agent, performed and acted as the government.

The imposed synonymity of "fascism" and "government" was not only reiterated explicitly, such as, for instance, in the founding charter of the PNF, but more often realized through constative speech acts that presented Fascism as de facto acting as the government. To give one example, a meeting report of the Grand Council of Fascism dated July 24, 1924 stated: "The Grand Council of Fascism reminds Italians that Fascism, *guaranteeing* the tranquility and continuity of production with the political order, *made* industrial and agricultural recovery possible, since it *created* the indispensable conditions to ensure the nation an increase in wealth and of prosperity, documented by foreign statistics."[54] Implied in these words is the fact that it was Fascism, as the government, that "guaranteed tranquility," that "made possible," that "created the conditions": as actant of the verb "to guarantee," "to make," and "to create," Fascism became the agent that accomplished and performed those acts. Through prosopopoeia ("fascism" speaks directly rather than being spoken of) and personification ("fascism" acts rather than being acted upon), Fascism not only acquired volition and intentionality, but impersonated the government, which in turn took on the semblance of an identifiable persona. In other words, the relentless repetition of prosopopoeial constative utterances personified Fascism as the body of the state, so that it ceased to be a mere reification of one particular movement or part of it. "Fascism," in these utterances, did not act on behalf of the government or the state—it *was* the government or the state.

In semiotic terms, these ostensibly constative utterances, by virtue of the implied synonymity of "fascism" and "state" via metonymical substitution, had the performative effect of a perlocutionary act, in that the interlocutor was invited to accept the equivalence.[55] Examples of this syntactical use of "fascism" abound in all writings from 1922 on. So, for example, in volume 21 of Benito Mussolini's *Opera omnia* we find that "industrialists had been assured by Fascism that . . ." (19), "Fascism does not have the time . . ." (27), "Fascism establishes that the central committee act . . ." (31), "Fascism suffered a shock but resisted . . ." (48), "Fascism abolished . . ." (51), "Fascism teaches . . ." (56), "Fascism pursues a policy of peace, but with dignity, pride, and discipline" (58), "Fascism intends to advance . . ." (62), "Fascism raises his olive branch" (96), and "Fascism was generous" (111); sometimes the association with the government is stated explicitly: "Fascism, as government and party, intends to energetically protect the interests of the working population" (133).

By identifying Fascism with the government through rhetorical modes of presentation that anthropomorphized it as a human agent, the semantic (intensional) value of "fascism" was resolved extensionally via the actions of Fascism-as-government. The fact that the semantic markers of "fascism" were so indefinite, fuzzy, and mutable during the early years of the movement helped the movement adjust to its new role. Most important, though, the identification of Fascism and government in prosopopoeial utterances in which "fascism" was the actant of the actions connected to "ruling" and "governing" gave the semblance of substance to the ideological notion that, as the government, it was the realization of the state, which in turn fulfilled the metaphysical destiny of the nation it institutionally organized. In short, Fascism was, by a series of syntactical strategies, disguised perlocutionary acts, and numerous connotative implications, identified with the state and the nation itself.

That the denotation of "fascism" as the government formed the basis for the creation of connotations linking it to the nation was also constantly asserted in speeches and public announcements by Mussolini, PNF leaders, and members of the Grand Council of Fascism. Fascism, conceived as governmental doctrine, could not be reduced to abstract and universalistic notions like "democracy" and "socialism" because it pretended to be direct expression of the will of the Italian nation. For instance, on August 4, 1924, during a national congress of the PNF Mussolini declared that "Fascism must, by its very nature, be contrary to any universalistic doctrine, since it must increasingly strengthen the imperial individuality of the Italian nation and not recognize as legitimate any universality other than the Roman and Catholic ones."[56] As the state, Fascism strove to realize the Italian nation: "Today Fascism is a party, a militia, a corporation. It is not enough: it must become something more, it must become a way of life" (June 22, 1925).[57] But Fascism had already succeeded in that, because

> the Fascist government has given back to the Italian people the essential freedoms that were compromised or lost: that of working, that of possessing, that of moving, that of publicly honoring God, that of extolling the victory and sacrifices it imposed, that of having the awareness of itself and its own destiny, that of feeling themselves a strong people, not simply a satellite of the greed and demagogy of others. This is the true national freedom that Fascism has given and guarantees to the Italian people; all the rest is false literature and brazen mystification of the dispossessed and emigrants rejected by life in the limbo of impotence. (July 30, 1925)[58]

Fascism wanted to represent and guide Italians of all social classes, rejecting the socialist ideas of class division and class struggle: "You, above all, know," Mussolini proclaimed at a public rally in Rimini on September 20, 1924, "that Fascism is not, cannot, and does not want to be the bodyguard of the privileges of particular individuals and classes, but it wants to be the great guard that protects the inevitable security and greatness of the Italian people";[59] and again, in the pages of the May 5, 1925 issue of the magazine *La Gerarchia*, he declared that "many workers are rightly convinced that Fascism is not synonymous with slavery, that Fascism [is] the bodyguard not of a particular class, but of the nation."[60] And as he shouted to a worshiping crowd in Vercelli on September 27, 1925, "Fascism is all the people; you are Fascism, the Italian people, and among you the plutocratic bankers, the very rich are certainly a tiny minority."[61] To reinforce that, all sessions of the Parliament concluded with the invocation "Viva il Re! Viva l'Italia! Viva Mussolini! Viva il Fascismo!"

If Fascism was the state, and if the state was the realization of a nation, then Fascism's reach encompassed all spheres of Italian life. It was, by definition, "totalitarian." Mussolini cunningly adopted the notion of totalitarianism from his adversaries. One year after the formation of Mussolini's first cabinet in the aftermath of the March on Rome, the liberal democrat Giovanni Amendola accused Fascism of having a "'totalitarian' spirit."[62] The notion of "totalitarianism" would be soon adopted by other opponents of Mussolini, such as Luigi Sturzo, who believed that Mussolini was forcing upon the Italian state a "totalitarian transformation of any and all moral, cultural, political, and religious forces,"[63] and the socialist Lelio Basso, who, under the pseudonym Prometeo Filodemo, wrote in 1925 that "Fascist totalitarianism has fixed all its principles: suppression of all conflicts for the higher good of the nation, which is identified with the state, which in turn identifies itself with the men who hold all power."[64]

Mussolini never denied but, on the contrary, celebrated the totalitarian mission of Fascism as government and as state.[65] "That goal," he proclaimed in the concluding remarks of the fourth national congress of the PNF, on June 22, 1925, "which defines our ferocious totalitarian will, we will pursue with even greater ferocity, it will truly become the dominant anxiety and preoccupation of our activities. In short, we want to fascisticize [*fascistizzare*] the nation, so much so that tomorrow saying Italian and Fascist will be the same thing as saying Italian and Catholic."[66] On May 26, 1927, in a famous speech in the Chamber of Deputies, he claimed that "the regime is totalitarian, but it is the regime that has the largest consensus of the people in history."[67] And to reiterate the total unification of government, state, and nation under the aegis of Fascism, he explained that participation in state celebrations is "a very important moment of that system of totalitarian and integral education and preparation of the Italian man that the Fascist revolution considers to be one of the fundamental and pre-judicial tasks of the state, indeed the fundamental one" (May 28, 1928).[68]

"Fascism" as Universal, Imperial, and Racist

The ideological labor of Fascist authors consisted of presenting Fascism as the name of that governmental form that strove to transform the state into a full, authentic, and nurturing realization of the nation. If by "ideological labor" we intend, following semiotic terminology, different forms of coercive and suasive attempts to restrict interpretive habits to a limited set of semantic markers (both denotative and connotative) of the signifier "fascism," these practices tended, first, to reinforce the semantic association of "fascism" with the semantic spheres of "government," "state," and "nation" to the ideal point of their co-occurrence, correspondence, and, consequently, mutual synonymity. Second, they tended to exclude, by critique or open censorship, alternative and antagonistic markers, like the ones antifascists were elaborating at the same time (see part II).[69] Third, they pursued their ideological intent via a policy of normative and censoring guidance that targeted cultural production in a variety of modes: from associations (of youths, of women, of workers, of veterans, of labor categories, etc.) to mass liturgies (rallies, festivals, celebrations, commemorations, reenactments, monuments, etc.), from slogans to popular songs, from comics to highbrow literature, from newspapers to radio and cinema programs, from policing of the Italian language itself to philosophical speculation.[70] Alessandra Tarquini distinguishes three aspects of Fascist interventions in cultural production: cultural policies, expressions of knowledge, and ideology. "*Cultural policy*," she explains, "mainly concerns the activity of the Fascist Party and that of the government, and makes it possible to identify the choices of the ruling class, from the creation of new institutions—such as the Istituto Nazionale Fascista di Cultura [Fascist National Institute of Culture; INFC] created in 1925—to the management of traditional government functions, such as school policy. The term *expressions of knowledge*, on the other hand, refers to the contributions that intellectuals and artists made to Fascism," which Tarquini uses as the identification of "a Fascist literature, a Fascist architecture, a Fascist philosophy and so on. And, finally, *ideology*, which was the expression of political myths, that is, of representations composed of images, words and beliefs, capable of giving meaning to the action of a group."[71]

Of all the connotative markers of "fascism" that the regime actively encouraged to enrich the denotation of Fascism as government, state, and nation, three seemed to dominate the ideological language in the 1930s: Fascism as potentially "universal" (1930–34), as "imperial" (1936–40), and as "racist" (1938–45). Of the three, the connotation of "universal" surely appeared to be the least obvious and most surprising one, since Mussolini had previously insisted on the absolute particularity of Fascism, the necessary outcome of Italian history itself.

"UNIVERSAL"

In a speech given on October 4, 1924 Mussolini insisted that "Fascism is a phenomenon of imposing lines. It is an original Italian creation. It cannot be dispersed as the sun disperses the mist in the meadows in the morning. It is a phenomenon that affects the whole world. For two years all over the world there have been discussions of Fascism. A literature in all languages has arisen. Individuals leave Japan, China, and Australia to come here and study. Evidently there too they suffer from the evils we have suffered: the crisis of authority."[72] Worldwide interest in Fascism, Mussolini argued, was a sign that the problems Fascism solved for Italy affected other nations too. But, he clarified on March 3, 1928 in a speech given at the Chamber of Deputies, "Fascism is not an export commodity. If Europe wants to become more and more seriously infected with the evils from which we are cured, this will make us more vigilant in defending ourselves from the most widespread contagion with every weapon."[73]

Two years later, however, Mussolini changed his mind. In a discourse he delivered to the federal directors of the PNF on October 27, 1930 in the Victory Hall of Palazzo Venezia in Rome, which opened a series of celebrations for the eighth anniversary of the March on Rome, he stated: "Today I declare that Fascism, as an idea, a doctrine, and a realization, is universal: Italian in its particular institutions, it is universal in spirit and couldn't be otherwise."[74] In 1932 he boldly declared that "in a decade, Europe will be fascist or fascistized! Contemporary civilization is divided into an antithesis which can be overcome only in one way: with the doctrine and wisdom of Rome."[75]

The universality of Fascism was not merely grounds for rhetorical disputes. As Giulia Albanese has argued, "The Italian choice of adhering to the perspective of a fascist universality and the structuring of a greater organization of propaganda abroad signaled . . . an important landing point for Fascism, not only at the identity level, but also at the political and geopolitical level."[76] The European political landscape, after the wreckage of the economic crisis of 1929–31, had drastically changed, and other forms of counterrevolutionary authoritarianism in France, Spain, Germany, Austria, Hungary, Romania, Norway, and elsewhere had found unprecedented popular support. Fascism had to come to terms with other antiliberal, antidemocratic, and antisocialist forces and possibly assume a leading role on the European continent.

In 1927 the Centre international d'études fascistes (International Center for Fascist Studies; CINEF) was founded. Headquartered in Lausanne, Switzerland, it was financed by the Italian state and directed by the Dutch antisemite Herman de Vries de Heekelingen and the British James Strachey Barnes with the aim of promoting Fascism in Europe.[77] Several texts by Fascist authors such as Mussolini himself, Giuseppe Bottai, and Augusto Turati started to be translated into English, French, and German. In 1933 Mussolini ordered the establishment of the Comitati d'Azione per l'Universalità di Roma (Action Committees for the Universality of Rome; CAUR), which mobilized university students, researchers, and academics to promote Fascism among foreign residents in Italy and globally through lectures and exchange programs in universities around the world.[78] Italian cultural institutions promoted Fascism through events that popularized Italian culture and its patronage by

Mussolini's regime. The Casa Italiana at New York's Columbia University led the organization of events in the United States.[79]

A Fascist International conference was organized in Montreux, Switzerland, on December 16–17, 1934.[80] Thirteen European countries sent representatives of local far-right organizations. These included Eugenio Coselschi, the director of the Fascist CAUR and main organizer of the conference; Vidkun Quisling for the Norwegian Nasjonal Samling (Norwegian National Assembly); Ernesto Giménez Caballero for the Spanish Falange; Marcel Bucard for the French Mouvement Franciste; Ion L. Moța for Romania's Garda de Fier (Iron Guard); and Eoin O'Duffy for the Irish Blueshirts; as well as representatives from Greece, Lithuania, Portugal, Switzerland, Austria, Belgium, and Denmark. The conference was held only a few months after the assassination of the Austrian chancellor, Engelbert Dollfuss, by members of the Austrian Nazi Party, an event that triggered a diplomatic crisis between Italy and Germany.[81] The proceedings were far from friendly, however, as a December 31, 1934 article in *Time* showed. During Coselschi's opening remarks glorifying the universality of Rome, the Quisling was reported to scream in indignation: "Why don't we talk about the universality of Berlin? Adolf Hitler is just as much an exponent of Fascism as Benito Mussolini."[82] The Montreaux meeting failed, largely because of the noticeable absence of representatives from Germany's Nazi Party. Even though a governmental report presented to Mussolini the same year confirmed the presence of fascist movements in thirty-nine countries, "the effort to create a kind of international grouping of extreme nationalist movements was quickly doomed to frustration."[83]

"IMPERIAL"

If the connotation of "universal" fell short of entering the connotative codification that the Fascist leaders aimed to attain, *imperiale* (imperial) was more successful. When Mussolini, in one of his public declamations from the central balcony of the Palazzo Venezia on the evening of May 9, 1936, proclaimed that "Italy finally has its own empire," "imperial" entered the language of Fascism as one of its attributions. "[It is] a Fascist Empire," he continued, "because it bears the indestructible signs of the will and power of the Roman Lictor, because this is the goal toward which the explosive and disciplined energies of the young, vigorous Italian generations were solicited for fourteen years. [It is] an empire of peace, because Italy wants peace for itself and for everyone and decides to go to war only when it is forced there by imperious, incoercible necessities of life. [It is] an empire of civilization and humanity for all the people of Ethiopia."[84]

The imperial ambitions of the Fascist regime, which are usually seen as beginning with the Corfu crisis of 1923 (the first real international crisis during Mussolini's first cabinet), responded to two needs: one geopolitical and economic, the other ideological.[85] Before Fascism's rise to power, the kingdom of Italy had colonies and protectorates in Eritrea, Somalia, Cyrenaica, and Tripolitania (pacified and united as Italian Libya in 1932), and some Greek islands. Even though the expression "Africa romana" circulated among Fascist leaders, and even if in 1926, to commemorate Mussolini's visit to Tripolitania, April 21 became a national holiday known as "Giornata coloniale" (Colonial Day),[86] the idea of a Fascist empire passed into broad national usage only during and after the Italo-Ethiopian War of 1935–36.[87]

Richard Overy has recently argued that the acquisition of an empire was not only the result of a civilizational zeitgeist of progress and modernization, but a necessity to strengthening national autonomy, especially for nation-states like Italy, Japan, and Germany, which were slow to acquire colonial territories. Imperial and national interests were fatally interlocked. If "asserting national interest was regarded as a necessity to protect the home population by guaranteeing its economic future and its demographic development," Italy needed an empire to overcome its economic predicament after the crisis of 1929: "Empire-building was designed to transcend the limitations imposed by the existing global economic and territorial structures by acquiring additional 'living space' to cope with population pressure and land shortages, securing access to resources of raw materials and food, and establishing an economic bloc where trade and investment would be controlled by the imperial center rather than the business community."[88] Italy saw Africa as an opportunity, and control over the Mediterranean, or *mare nostrum* (our sea), an aspiration. As Mussolini stated explicitly: "No doubt can disturb the soul about the further progress in the colonies: The Fascist style is well-known; the Fascist spirit of initiative does not stop, but proceeds forward; it is logical to think that, having passed the period of the crisis that has tormented all peoples, even our colonies, and those that overlook the Mediterranean and the others of the Red Sea and the Indian Ocean, they will move toward an era of wealth and power for them and for the motherland."[89]

The expansion on the Mediterranean, in Libya and the Aegean Sea, was of strategic importance both economically and militarily;[90] but it was also symbolically significant, as the imperial connotations of Fascism played with the idea of restoring dominion over the *mare nostrum* of the Roman Empire. The colonial enterprise of the Fascist state was therefore presented in civilizational terms that were, however, different from the coeval colonial discourse of other empires. The mission of Fascism, for Mussolini, was in fact that of restoring "the unity of the Mediterranean civilization, which was East and West, and created by Rome," which "lasted many centuries. . . . Today, Rome and the Mediterranean, thanks to the Fascist renaissance, which is above all a spiritual rebirth, are turning to resume their unifying function."[91]

The ideological and propagandistic efforts to promote the idea of a Fascist empire were extensive. An anthology of Mussolini's speeches and articles on the imperial enterprise was published in 1936.[92] Other Fascist leaders and intellectuals contributed to the campaign. Filippo Tommaso Marinetti launched an illustrated magazine entitled *Azione imperiale: Rassegna della creazione fascista* (*Imperial Action: Exposés of Fascist Creations*), and Emilio Settimelli founded the monthly *L'impero fascista*, which ran from 1935 to 1941 and collected the heroic deeds of civilizing Italians and racial descriptions of the good savages or the evil Ethiopian satraps. Newspapers like *Il corriere dell'impero* circulated in the empire and the metropole until 1941, as did a number of weekly and monthly publications such as *Eritrea sportiva*, *Il lunedì dell'impero*, and *Impero illustrato*. School textbooks also adhered to the imperial rhetoric, as Giuseppe Bottai also insisted in his preface of *Funzione imperiale della scuola*, edited by the Provincial Education Department of Padua;[93] among the titles adopted in Italian schools were *Storia d'Italia, dal Risorgimento all'Impero* (1936), *Dall'impero dei Cesari all'impero fascista* (1940), and *Storia d'Italia, dal tramontare al sorgere dell'impero* (1940).[94]

The symbolic association between the colonial empire and the Roman Empire had already been suggested in *La dottrina del fascismo*, wherein Mussolini stated that "the Fascist state expresses the will to power and imperium. Here the Roman tradition is embodied in a conception of strength. Imperial power, as understood by Fascist doctrine, is not only territorial, military, and commercial. It is also spiritual and moral." He then explained that "an imperial nation, that is, a nation that directly or indirectly leads other nations, can exist without conquering a single square mile of territory. This said, Fascism considers the imperialistic spirit—that is, the tendency for nations to expand—an expression of their vitality."[95] Meager consolation. Despite all efforts, in fact, the image of a Fascist empire remained largely underwhelming. As Nicola Labanca commented, "The celebrations of the Augustus year (1937) also failed to reconcile the two terms: [on the one hand], the dream of a new Roman empire and [on the other] the reality of a colonial empire larger than the Italian past, but still small compared to those of others. Even the rhetoric of the *mare nostrum*—not entirely abstract, given the military plans of the Fascist navy—could only deal with a Mediterranean of which Italy was anything but master."[96]

The Fascist empire, or, inversely, imperial Fascism had a more lasting impact at the symbolic level within the metropole—since the Fascist empire "reappropriated" African territories that were in antiquity part of the Roman Empire. If the main goal of Fascism, defined as the expression of government, state, and nation, was the creation of a "new man," of a "new Italian," after 1936 the administrative, racial, and cultural relations with colonized Africans became a template for achieving the anthropological revolution of Italians: as Valeria Deplano suggested, the imperial experience helped "reorganize the society of the metropole" along the blueprint of the "racial hierarchies that had formed and had consolidated in the African territories" and helped pushed "toward an autarchical economy that was based, above all from a propagandistic perspective, on the mutual support of African and Italian territories."[97] In other words, it was through the colonial experience that the Fascist empire elevated social hierarchy to metaphysical datum: The modes of socialization of the new Italians concretized the hierarchical (and unequal) structure of the national community, opposing leaders to followers, entrepreneurs to workers, in the name of prosperity and advancement, just as the opposition of colonizer and colonized concretized a hierarchy that ostensibly benefited both.[98]

The imperial outreach of the Fascist state, even though successful more at a symbolic level of national propaganda than economically and geopolitically, was the occasion for a reconciliation between Italy and Nazi Germany: Almost unanimously condemned by all countries, the Italo-Ethiopian War forced Italy in 1937 to leave the League of Nations, to which it had belonged since the beginning as a member of the Security Council. Only Hitler's Germany supported and acknowledged the rightness of Italy's colonial enterprise, marking the beginning of a rapprochement between Mussolini and Hitler.[99] Most important, the Italo-Ethiopian War and the previous colonial experience constituted the background that prepared the racist turn of Fascism, with the racial laws of 1938.[100]

"RACIST"

Only since the 1990s historians have begun to dismantle the historiographical and popular myth that Fascist racism was not as horrible as the Nazis' and that the racial laws were forced upon Mussolini by his alliance with the much stronger Germany.[101] Evidence of Fascist antisemitism well before 1938, of widespread racist practices within the nation and the empire, and the active collaboration of Italian institutions and army in the deportation and extermination of the European Jews has rendered the earlier positive views no longer defendable.[102]

On May 26, 1927, more than ten years before the passing of the racial laws, Mussolini declared in a long discourse in the Chamber of Deputies that Fascism, as the expression of the Italian state and the leading force of the Italian nation, had the duty to protect the "Italian race," which he defined as "the Italian people in their physical expression":[103] After listing the threats to its well-being—coming not only from diseases like malaria and "Oriental maladies" like "yellow fever and Bolshevism,"[104] but also from deviant behaviors like alcoholism and homosexuality—he stated that "we must seriously watch over the destiny of the race, we must take care of the race, starting with motherhood and childhood."[105] Even before that, the opening statement in the PNF program of 1921, "Fundamental Elements," clearly noted that "the nation is the supreme synthesis of all material and nonmaterial values of a race."[106]

It is true that Mussolini often used "race" somewhat ambivalently, almost as a synonym of "nation" or even "population."[107] But he also used it distinctively from what could be understood as the civilizational properties of a community, such as, for instance, when, during a 1926 interview with a journalist from the Associated Press, he described Italy thus: "Our soil is not rich, but we intend to use what it contains by embracing the contribution of science to our arms. Our cultural heritage is among the richest, the vitality of our race is among the most remarkable and our thirst for prosperity is undeniable."[108] Italians of different classes or living in different regions (and thus speaking different dialects) were simply "different branches of the same race," with race being defined as the biological belonging of the people of one nation.[109]

The colonial experience in Africa brought these preexisting elements of Fascist racism to the fore.[110] Racial discrimination and segregation were practiced in the African colonies even before Fascism's rise to power. Mussolini's propaganda that Italian Fascism built an "empire of work" in opposition to the purely exploitative imperialism of the "plutocratic nations" falsified a situation of unequal coexistence and wealth of the colonizer relative to the colonized.[111] Apart from segregationist and discriminatory practices separating the African communities from the Italian colonists, widespread sexual slavery was practiced and even informally promoted in popular culture (as, for instance, in popular songs like "Faccetta nera"),[112] even though the Fascist authorities still believed it necessary to uphold an austere Fascist racism to prevent the "weakening" of the Italian race from sexual intercourse between colonizer and colonized: *meticciato*, or "race mixing," was treated by Fascist authorities as both "a biological attack on the purity of the white race and an insidious conciliation between the two communities."[113]

Prejudices and discrimination against Slavic minorities and Roma communities, often prompted by concerns over public hygiene, intensified during the second half of the 1920s.[114] Antisemitism had a long history in Italy before the advent of Fascism, but it found in its midst fertile ground to grow. The journalist Telesio Interlandi, an antisemite before 1922, as editor in chief of the Roman newspaper *Il Tevere* became a critic from the right of the Fascist regime, openly accusing the Jews of hatching Masonic plots against the interests of the nation and of spreading Bolshevik propaganda. These forms of widespread antisemitism could frequently be found in local newspapers like Farinacci's *Cremona nuova*, Treviso's *La Tribuna*, and the Roman *L'Impero*, and in weekly and biweekly magazines like *La vita italiana*, founded and edited by the Fascist Giovanni Preziosi, who in 1921 translated and published, in collaboration with the Catholic priest Umberto Benigni, the Italian version of the *Protocols of the Elders of Zion*.[115] In 1933 Nicola Pende, an endocrinologist and anthropologist, published an essay titled "Bonifica umana razionale e biologia politica" (Rational Human Reclamation and Political Biology), dedicated to Mussolini, in which he laid the foundation for a scientific defense of racial discrimination on the basis of a natural hierarchy of the development of different human races, as evidenced by the different developments of the endocrinological system.[116] Antisemitism was supported also within currents of "Fascist mysticism," the activities of which were concentrated in the Scuola di mistica fascista (School of Fascist Mysticism), founded in Milan on April 10, 1930, where Fascist intellectuals such as Niccolò Giani, Julius Evola, and Paolo Orano defended an activist antisemitism and the embracing of the mystical traditions of Aryanism, Pagan cults, Templarism, and oriental mysticism such as Tantric and Zen Buddhism.[117]

On July 14, 1938, *Il giornale d'Italia* published an anonymous article titled "Il fascismo e i problemi della razza" (Fascism and Racial Problems), later attributed to Mussolini and the staff of the Ministry of Culture. Reprinted as "The Manifesto of Race" in the first issue of *La difesa della razza*, a biweekly magazine founded by Mussolini and edited by Telesio Interlandi and Giorgio Almirante, with a scientific board that included the philosopher Sabato Visco and Julius Evola, the manifesto defended ten points:[118]

1. Human races exist.
2. There are "large" races and "small" races.
3. Race is a purely biological concept.
4. The population of Italy today is of Aryan origin and its civilization is Aryan.
5. The notion that, during the historical epoch, great hordes of men made a contribution to the formation of Italy is a legend.

6. A pure "Italian race" has by now come into existence.
7. The time has come for Italians to openly declare themselves racist.
8. A clear distinction must be made between Mediterranean Europe (populated by Occidentals), on the one hand, and the Oriental and African Mediterranean, on the other.
9. Jews do not belong to the Italian race.
10. Italians' purely European characteristics, both physical and psychological, must not be altered in any way.[119]

The manifesto anticipated the implementation of the racial laws, announced by Mussolini on September 18, 1938 and added to the penal code as Regio Decreto (Royal Decree) no. 1728 on November 17, 1938. The scope of the laws was extensive, limiting the civil rights of Italian Jews (prohibiting them from attending public schools and from all kinds of higher education, excluding Jews from public offices, banning books written by Jewish authors, severe restrictions on travel, etc.) and the seizure of Jewish assets.[120] Mussolini justified the racial laws by causally linking the defense of the race to colonialism:

> With regard to domestic politics, the burning issue is the racial one. . . . The racial problem did not break out as suddenly as those who are used to abrupt awakenings think, because they are used to long, lazy sleeps. It is related to the conquest of the empire, since history teaches us that empires are conquered with arms, but they are held with prestige. And for prestige a clear, severe racial conscience is needed, which establishes not only differences, but very clear superiorities. The Jewish problem is therefore only one aspect of this phenomenon. Our position was determined by these indisputable facts. For sixteen years world Judaism has been, despite our politics, an irreconcilable enemy of Fascism. In Italy our politics has determined in the Semitic elements what can today be called, one could call, a real rush to attack.[121]

The effects of the racial laws were immediate. If the connotation "racist" was largely marginal and concealed (but never absent) throughout the 1920s and early 1930s in the denotative markers of "fascism" as "governmental force," it became the legitimate and publicly acknowledged connotation of "fascism" during the Italo-Ethiopian War and the legally authorized connotative codification after 1938. "Racist" became the recurrent connotation of "fascism" in all public discourses, with the enthusiastic support of such Fascist leaders as Giuseppe Bottai, then the minister of national education. As Gianluca Gabrielli has commented, "Between September and November 1938 an extremely complex persecutory legal system was launched in Italy, even more severe than the German one regarding the exclusion of Jews from public schools and the expulsion from the country of foreigners of Israelite origin."[122] Mussolini emphatically insisted on the racist contributions of Fascism: "The racial problem is a very important achievement for me," he boasted on October 25, 1938, "and it is very important to have introduced it in the history of Italy. The ancient Romans were racist beyond belief. The great struggle of the Roman Republic was precisely this: to know if the Roman race could join other races."[123]

"Fascism" as (Counterrevolutionary) Revolution

Since its early days in 1919, Fascism had declared itself to be a "revolutionary" movement, and this remained one of its more stable, long-lasting, and recurring self-descriptions. But with its transformation from movement to political party and, finally, to regime, what the word "revolution" indicated changed quite radically from institutional subversion to institutional actualization. Mussolini's own ideological identification, which moved rapidly from the revolutionary faction of the Socialist Party to what has become in the post–Second World War political imaginary the name of the most extreme form of right-wing politics, never relinquished the notion of pursuing a revolution.

A simple dismissal of the notion of revolution in Fascism's political utterances as simply an ideological smokescreen would mask the social transformation that Mussolini's regime engineered, with its painstaking attention to propaganda, education, popular culture, and language. To put it in Gramscian terms, the Fascist counterrevolutionary revolution operated at the level of culture and its representations in order to keep intact the structure of social relations in the economic sphere. A reconstruction of the semantic shifts and turns that Mussolini imposed on the signifier "revolution," which remained until the end, for him, a *parola sublime* (sublime word), mirrors the political trajectory of the Fascist regime.

The semiotic strategies that Mussolini adopted to frame Fascism as a revolutionary project changed over time. Nonetheless, "revolution" stood for Mussolini as a placeholder for different combinations of conceptual concerns that maintained a certain degree of consistency since 1914: revolution for him was national rather than international, emotional rather than rational, and transformative but in the interest of a national community conceived in abstract, cultural, and racial terms rather than in terms of class emancipation. If we simply count the number of times that this term appears in Mussolini's writings in the formative years of his political career, we see that "revolution" was clearly the gravitational center that kept together around its orbit an ensemble of different conceptions, connotations, symbolic associations, and pragmatic strategies.[124]

"Revolution" appeared to have a distinctive Marxian tone when, in an article published on March 23, 1912, the young socialist Mussolini maintained that Marx gave the working classes the *forma mentis*, the analytical tools, to achieve a social revolution.[125] In the pages of *La lotta di classe*, Mussolini sustained the revolutionary character of Marx's political philosophy to criticize the positivist and reformist attitudes of the moderate faction of the PSI. Revolution, for the twenty-eight-year-old Mussolini, was "the element of vitality" that Marx could instill in political philosophy and praxis, a conception that had "rejuvenating" effects.[126] Revolution could not be simply a slogan to pursue an "electoral strategy"—a criticism he leveled at the reformists.[127] It could not be reduced to an ideal, an intellectual game of the bourgeois elites of the PSI, but had to be returned to the working class as their right and prerogative.[128]

Marx inspired Mussolini to believe in mass revolution as the only viable political strategy for socialism. But the French political theorist Georges Sorel's texts taught him that revolution was born from passion rather than reason, from faith rather than intellectual calculations. Sorel, Mussolini wrote on July 18, 1912 in *Avanti!*, "has presented us with a Socialism that was decisively anti-intellectualist, religious. The myth of the general strike in Sorel's terrible, grave, and sublime socialism is a myth, a fairy tale, something we cannot demonstrate, unachievable, which must be an act of faith, the act of faith of the proletariat."[129] Marx taught Mussolini that the social revolution was the inevitable outcome of economic determinism, and that such "rational understanding" should define the strategy of socialism.[130] But it was from Sorel that Mussolini learned that it could only result from the party's ability to produce in the masses an irrational act of faith, a fidelity to a myth: "Social revolution," he wrote on January 15, 1914, "is not a mental schema or calculation, but, first of all, an act of faith."[131]

We see in the writings of young Mussolini that other ideals as well framed his revolutionary aspirations. One of these looked back at the promises of Giuseppe Mazzini's project of spiritual revolution that the Risorgimento—the movement of national unity that spurred the riots of 1848 and, eventually, the unification of 1861 under the Savoy crown—only partially fulfilled. Another component of his revolutionary constellation was the Nietzschean conception of the *Übermensch*, which inspired the construction of Mussolini's political persona. As early as 1908, he saw in the Übermensch "a symbol, exemplar of this anguished and tragic period of crisis of European consciousness. . . . It is the realization of our weakness, but also the hope for our redemption. It is the twilight—it is the dawn. Above all, it is a hymn to life—to a life lived will all energies, in constant tension toward something higher, more refined, more daring. . . ."[132]

Nietzsche completed Mussolini's conceptual template for his revolutionary political project. Marx gave the reasons for its historical inevitability and Sorel suggested a strategy to organize consensus around it, but it was from Nietzsche that Mussolini learned the ruthlessness and courage he needed to become its leader.[133] If Sorel's philosophy helped him connect revolution and nationalism, political strategy and myth, Nietzsche and Marx coexisted in Mussolini's rhetoric as a contradictory but indissoluble whole. The political revolution, he wrote in 1913, was surely the rational unfolding of a progressive social movement;[134] but only violence and war could fulfill that destiny: "Revolutions must be considered the revenge of folly against good sense. Because revolutions are crazy, headless, violent, idiotic, bestial. They are like war."[135]

The outbreak of the First World War in 1914 fulfilled Mussolini's revolutionary aspirations. If until then it was an ideal, more a Sorelian myth than an actual political project that he had mobilized mostly in an internal conflict for factional hegemony within the PSI, the war gave Mussolini a chance to answer the prophetic call for the completion of national unification. As he proclaimed in January 1915, "Today is war, the revolution will be tomorrow."[136] In all his interviews of that year, Mussolini hailed "war" and "revolution" as synonyms. The war, and the sentiments of fear, patriotism, and solidarity it triggered, were for him the emotional conduits through which he would be able to recruit members from all classes for the eventual revolutionary upheaval; but war was also the affirmation of a violent claim upon life that was in itself revolutionary, if only in the form of an existential drive that he had learned from his readings of Nietzsche.

In a sort of irony of fate, Mussolini missed the Bolshevik Revolution of February 1917 because his severe injuries had confined him in a camp hospital. He recorded his reactions only later, but even then the war situation worried him more. *Il popolo d'Italia* initially applauded the revolution, praising the "victorious Russian revolution against Germanophile reactionaries."[137] After the October Revolution in that same year, however, Mussolini's views on Russia changed abruptly: he experienced almost simultaneously the coup that brought to power the Bolshevik faction—"Lenin the traitor" would become a mantra in Mussolini vitriolic articles of that winter in *Il popolo d'Italia*—and the catastrophic defeat of the Italian troops in the Battle of Caporetto later that month. In Mussolini's editorials, the two events were more or less conjoined as one single trauma. Their simultaneity led him to rethink his political identity as a revolutionary socialist. If until then Mussolini's revolution maintained, notwithstanding its Sorelian and Nietzschean connotations, some connections with the working classes (albeit transfigured in the vaguer "popolo"), between the fall of 1917 and the spring of 1918 it would be subjected to a major semantic shift.

The composition of Mussolini's conceptual constellation of "revolution" had changed quite noticeably by then: the national cause supplanted the international impulse of socialism, and class interests was replaced by his support of combatants and producers against the *imbelle* (cowardly) and inept political elites. Workers were no longer the main addressees of his political editorials; they were replaced by the comrades who fought in the trenches and the producers that converted their factories to support the military effort. The targets of Mussolini's spiteful articles were now, above all others, the members of the PSI, who "lost the train of history" by embracing neutrality and also lost sight of their revolutionary goals, too enamored of their status quo within liberal institutions.[138] He attacked the Bolshevik revolutionaries, "a phenomenon of social degeneration," who transformed the war into "a slaughterhouse" and betrayed the progressive alliance against the German enemy.[139]

In the sociopolitical disarray immediately after the Great War, Mussolini reconfigured once more the conceptual constellation of "revolution." On March 18, 1919 he boasted in *Il popolo d'Italia* that "we interventionists are the only ones in Italy who have the right to speak of revolution."[140] The European conflict was the real revolutionary moment, and therefore only the interventionists of 1915 could be acknowledged as its rightful leaders. Consequently, those parties that had defended pacifism and neutrality—above all the PSI—must be understood as the enemies of the revolution and of the working classes.[141] Most important, since they had relinquished their commitment to the revolutionary ideal, they must be understood as "counterrevolutionary."[142] As Mussolini explained on March 18, 1919, "we are openly and proudly fighting . . . against that dark phenomenon of regression, of counterrevolution, and of impotence that is Bolshevism. We are defending our renovating and creative revolution from the assaults of the retrograde and destructive counterrevolution that is Leninism."[143]

In an act of conceptual somersault, Mussolini intended to disconnect revolution from the socialist agenda and to reframe it in terms of national renewal and collaboration among classes. This conception of interclass collaboration stood in stark opposition to the Marxian notion of class struggle and supported a division of labor and consequently a social hierarchy that was based on "competence" rather than equality. Nor was Mussolini's antisocialist turn close to the tradition of revolutionary conservatism, which stressed the natural hierarchy dividing the ruler and the ruled within the national community. Repeating an argument that he had defended in 1915, Mussolini insisted that the war had given Italy the chance of completing once and for all the project of national unification that the Risorgimento had left unfinished, in both the territorial and the spiritual senses.[144]

After the foundation of the Fasci di Combattimento and the recruitment of local Fasci to violent antiunion repression, the Fascist revolution, as Gioacchino Volpe put it in his history of the movement, by "disarming revolutionary socialism, addressed the needs and aspirations of the working classes."[145] In those years, all parties seized the term for different targets: the Great War of 1914–18 was revolutionary, as revolutionary as the interventionist movement Mussolini led in 1915. The social situation that the war had left behind in Italian society was revolutionary. The subversive rhetoric of the PSI, which attempted to seize the impetus of the Bolshevik Revolution, was revolutionary; but for Volpi, who followed Mussolini, the socialists were in fact "counterrevolutionary," because they were against the interests of the Italian nation. It was instead Fascism, concluded Volpi, that was truly revolutionary, because it was a movement rather than a party—"an antiparty or a superparty"—that could "keep together Italians of all creeds and from all productive classes and push them toward new, inevitable battles to complete and valorize the revolutionary great war."[146]

Mussolini's rhetorical insistence on the revolutionary nature of Fascism was a claim to the right of ownership of the term against rival contentions. At a minimum, it meant opposition to the socialists' revolution as well as to the liberal government and the parliamentary system in general. But in practice, it meant constant and ruthless violence: it was a "civil war," as Mussolini defined the urban guerrilla movement of 1919 that opposed workers' unions and the police forces, socialism and nationalist Squadristi, subversion and national renovation for the political future of the nation.

The institutionalization of the movement into a political party in 1921 did not sever its denotation as revolutionary. The day after the founding of the PNF on November 9, 1921, Mussolini hyperbolically saw in his political party a historical force that was having an epochal impact comparable only to that of the constituent assemblies of the French Revolution.[147] It was, for him, the first European example of a "revolution without revolt."[148] Fascism's revolution was nationalist, renovative, always new and therefore youthful, pure energy, and thus inevitably violent, but always because these were attributes of Fascism itself. In other words, "revolution" was meaningful only insofar as it acquired the meaning Fascism projected into it. Once the central aspiration of Mussolini, a star shining its light on his political actions and goals, with the rise of the Fascist regime "revolution" was downgraded to a rocky satellite that only reflected Fascism's light. But Fascism's revolution lacked normativity, as it did not have a vision of social organization like socialism. It was a pure drive to power. Or, more precisely, it did not really have a *revolutionary* idea of social organization, but merely reframed the preexisting power relations between industrialists and workers and between landowners and agricultural laborers.

On October 27, 1932, from the balcony of the Palazzo Venezia, Mussolini opened a season of events that celebrated the tenth anniversary of the "Fascist Revolution"—an expression that by then had been consolidated in the political language and social imaginary of Italians. "The first ten years of the revolution," he proclaimed to an ecstatic crowd that had by then been well trained on how to mark the syntagmatic structure of Mussolini's speeches with cries of rejoicing, "come today to a close with emotional enthusiasm of the people of Italy. . . . On the earth, on the seas, in the skies, everywhere there are signs of our power and our will."[149] In the first ten years of Fascist power, Mussolini had repeated, the regime had "perfected the creation of Risorgimento";[150] the "Fascist Revolution is still very young and very fresh [*giovanissima e freschissima*]";[151] it was not disruptive because it persisted "united, disciplined, and totalitarian";[152] and it was acknowledged everywhere in the world as unique in its transformative power.[153] In *La dottrina del fascismo*, he explained that "the Fascist state is a unique and original creation. It is not reactionary but revolutionary, for it provides solutions to a number of universal problems that have arisen elsewhere."[154]

The consolidation of the idea of a Fascist revolution operated within a complex system of state rituals and monumental symbolism. The obsessive repetition of the expression "rivoluzione fascista" was an essential part of the semiotic strategy of Fascism to favor form over content, presentation over argument, style over substance. In 1933 the Fascist journalist Bruno Spampanato published a long essay entitled "Democrazia fascista" (Fascist Democracy) in which he argued that Fascism was the realization of the popular demand for democracy, as Mussolini himself had been arguing since the 1919. "Fascist democracy," wrote Spampanato, "is healthy, uncorrupted, youthful. The Fascist regime knows freedom, a vital element of life and justice, and it is the guarantor of that freedom; it knows the equality of duties and the right of an inequality that is based on individuals' position within their community; it places the moral law before the legal norm; it knows a way of life, of action, of thought, above all of belief; it knows citizens' solidarity within the state."[155] The expression "Fascist revolution," for Spampanato, reinforced the perception that Fascism was indeed a revolution that broke with the preexisting forms of parliamentarism, and that its ideology and political practice was a continuation of the project that the French Revolution had put in motion in 1789 but that the Bolshevik Revolution (and its socialist advocates in Italy) had perverted.

Of all the Fascist leaders, Giuseppe Bottai was the one who in his writings addressed the issue of Fascism as revolution in a more systematic and consistent way. As one of the regime's philosophers, Bottai, as minister of national education between 1936 and 1943, played an important role in orchestrating Fascist control and recruitment of cultural production for the promotion of Fascism. Like Gentile, Bottai insisted that the Fascist revolution was not in antagonism with the democratic ideals that the "French Revolution rendered . . . historically and ethically concrete," but rather that it made sure to end its most pernicious deviations, in particular "social atomism," "individualism," and "civil liberties": "In Italy," he stated, "we experienced the worse kind of democracy: an ochlocracy defined by the transfer of sovereign power from the law to the mob."[156] The mission of his journal *Critica fascista* was to engage Italian intellectuals in an "open, serene, and responsible discussion" to convince them of the democratic nature of the Fascist regime, a "regime of liberty" that was able to achieve "ideological unity" via dialectical arguments rather than the street violence of the early Squadristi such as Farinacci.[157]

The goal of the 1932 "Mostra della rivoluzione fascista" (Exhibition of the Fascist Revolution) was to consolidating, through the mythologization of the March on Rome and the glorification of the regime's cultural achievements, the revolutionary nature of Fascism by reframing the meaning of "revolution" along the lines of its anti-Bolshevism. As the regime's "first comprehensive effort to represent itself in the mirror of history," the exhibition aimed to become a commemoration and reenactment of the revolutionary impetus of 1922.[158] The result was, however, "a skeleton of paradoxes," as Jeffrey Schnapp argues.[159] On the one hand, the exhibition was in its own presentation revolutionary: "new, ultramodern, audacious, free from the melancholy and mourning that usually accompany the remembrance of things past." By adopting the most sophisticated forms of representational media and technologies, "it strove to reactivate" in the minds of its four million visitors the experience of its revolutionary origins.[160] In this way the exhibition continued the collaboration of Fascism with modernist artists to pursue a "cultural revolution" in Italy that aimed at renovating the eternal national community via forms of artistic experimentalism that intended to break with the past.[161] On the other hand, however, the insistence on the revolutionary nature of Fascism inevitably had to empty the transformative and rebellious connotations of "revolution" because the exhibition was also "committed to build[ing] up and consolidating a monumental state, a dictatorship built around the cult of Mussolini."[162]

Fascism, ten years after its climb to power, *had* to be understood as a revolution. It was a "revolution in form, a revolution in substance, a revolution in methods, a revolution that had not one but many enemies, a revolution that was achieved in many years of sacrifices and blood," stated Giorgio Alberto Chiurco fiercely at the beginning of his five-volume *Storia della rivoluzione fascista*.[163] But for Chiurco, too, what the revolutionary nature of Fascism consisted of was, tautologically, the Fascist totalitarian state, which deprived the idea of "revolution" of its rebellious, subversive, and extremist connotations to sustain instead a regime of discipline, law, and order.

The End of the Fascism (but Not of "Fascism")

The Fascist regime ended as it started: just as, twenty years earlier, it had been King Vittorio Emanuele III who, following a legal procedure, gave Mussolini the task of forming a government, on July 25, 1943, after a vote of the Grand Council of Fascism, it was the king who divested Mussolini of his role of Duce. Italy's entry into the Second World War in 1940 with the Axis Powers was disastrous, and the Allied invasion of Sicily, which had begun on July 9, threatened the political and material survival of the nation itself. Mussolini, deemed solely responsible for Italy's debacle, was arrested the same day.

On September 3 Brigadier General Giuseppe Castellaro, on behalf of the king and of the newly appointed prime minister, General Pietro Badoglio, secretly signed an unconditional armistice with the Allied Major General Walter Bedell.[164] The armistice was publicly announced a few days later, on September 8. Nazi troops invaded the peninsula shortly thereafter. The Fascist regime, which began in violence, maintained its power through violence, and made of violence the purest conception of politics, coherently ended in violence: the Nazi-controlled puppet state that was the Repubblica Sociale Italiana (Italian Social Republic; RSI), founded in the aftermath of the armistice around September 15, unleashed the most brutal form of violent repression, collaborating with the Wehrmacht and SS battalions to massacre the population of central and northern Italy suspected of giving support to bands of antifascist partisans and to deport Italian Jews for extermination in the camps of central and eastern Europe.[165] Mussolini died as violently as he had lived—or, perhaps more appropriately, as he had caused others to live. Captured by a partisan group near the town of Dongo while escaping to Switzerland on April 27, 1945, Mussolini was executed by firing squad the following day. On April 29, the bodies of Mussolini, his lover Claretta Petacci, and the Fascist devotees Nicola Bombacci, Alessandro Pavolini, and Achille Starace were hanged upside down from the roof of a gas station in Milan's Piazzale Loreto.

The semantic markers of "fascism" did not change much in the last years of the regime. The signing of the Pact of Steel between Italy and Germany on May 22, 1939 cemented "the close bonds of friendship and solidarity that exist between Fascist Italy and National Socialist Germany."[166] After the German invasion of Poland and the eruption of a second global conflict, on the evening of June 10, 1940 Mussolini announced to a less cheering than usual crowd that Italy was entering the conflict: "We take the field against the plutocratic and reactionary democracies of the West, which, at all times, have hindered the march, and often undermined the very existence of the Italian people."[167]

Italy was absolutely unprepared for the conflict, yet Mussolini did not hesitate: "This gigantic struggle is only a phase in the logical development of our revolution; it is the struggle of the poor against those who fiercely hold the monopoly of all the riches and all the gold of the earth; it is the struggle of the fruitful and young peoples against the sterile and dying peoples; it is the struggle between two centuries and two ideas."[168] He concluded: "Italy, proletarian and fascist, is standing for the third time, strong, proud, and compact as never before."[169] All semantic elements of "fascism" appeared in the declaration: the identification of Fascism with the state and, by metonymy, the nation; the revolutionary nature of Fascism and its proletarian origins; Italy's victimization by the conspiracy of plutocratic empires; and war and violence as the raison d'être of Fascism.

The war was a disaster on all fronts. The Italian troops, unequipped, insufficiently armed, untrained, and poorly led, faced defeats in France, the Balkans, Greece, Africa, and Russia—a remarkable achievement for a regime that claimed to be led by a fierce military spirit and glorified war as the engine of history.[170] But the collapse of Fascism was slow. After he was deposed and arrested, Mussolini was freed in a Hollywood-style operation led by the German Obersturmbannführer Otto Skorzeny and placed at the head of a puppet regime that was completely submissive to Germany. In his first public communication with the members of the newly established RSI, Mussolini blamed the Italian king for the defeat of Fascism: "I am now more than ever convinced that the House of Savoy wanted to prepare, organize, even in the smallest details, the coup d'état; the accomplice and executor [was] Badoglio, the accomplices [were] some spineless and slacker generals and some cowardly elements of Fascism. There can be no doubt that the king authorized, immediately after my capture, negotiations for the armistice, negotiations which may already have been framed between the dynasties of Rome and London. It was the king who advised his accomplices to deceive Germany in the most miserable way, denying even after the signing that negotiations were in progress. It is the dynastic complex that prepared and carried out the demolition of Fascism."[171]

Fascism had a chance to return to its original, revolutionary and anti-monarchical essence: "The state we want to establish will be national and social in the highest sense of the word, that is, it will be Fascist, thus going back to our origins."[172] It was, however, a pantomime of a state, its nominal capital of Rome and its ministries scattered all over the Po Vally: Salò (which gave the new republic its nickname), Brescia, Gargnano, Toscolano Maderno, Gardone Riviera, San Felice del Benaco, Polpenazze del Garda, Cremona, Verona, Bergamo, Padua, Venice, Treviso, Ponte di Brenta, San Pellegrino Terme, Iseo, Vicenza, Aprica, Asoleo, Monza, Crocetta del Montello, and Milan. Nonetheless, it was organized as a semipresidential republic, with a two-chamber parliament and a juridical apparatus directly voted by the people. It had an army of volunteers and conscripts (the Esercito Nazionale Repubblicano), the operations of which depended almost entirely on German forces under the command of Generalfeldmarschall Albert Kesselring.[173]

As if in response to its reduced sovereignty and actual power, Fascism became leaner and meaner. The Carta di Verona (Verona Charter) declared that it intended to "go back to the premises that first gave life to the Fasci di Combattimento, premises to which we often turned when the revolution's future became clouded due to the seepage of base elements into our ranks, to the bourgeois propensities of many comrades, and to constant bureaucratic obstructionism."[174] It reconfirmed its staunch anticommunism and antiliberalism, and it made the accusation that there was a the plutocratic plot against Italy "controlled by the Jewish international and run with unabashed egotism."[175]

Mussolini kept an open line of communication with the population via press releases, known as "notes" of the *Corrispondenza repubblicana*, dispatched from the Ministry of Popular Culture in Salò. These notes were forcibly published in all northern Italian newspapers. Note no. 13, titled "Rivoluzione sociale: Primi sintomi" (Social Revolution: First Symptoms), reinforced the idea that Fascism had returned to its origins, stating that, "freed from the many trappings that had weighed down its march, and from too many compromises forced by contingencies, it returns to its revolutionary origins in all sectors, but mainly in the social one, which is fundamental in individual and collective life."[176] Regular RSI troops and various sorts of militias, including the brutal Decima Flottiglia Motoscafi Armati Siluranti (Tenth Assault

Vehicle Flotilla; Xª MAS) of the Nazi sympathizer Junio Valerio Borghese, kept the occupied zones in a state of terror, actively collaborating with the German Waffen-SS troops to quell partisan guerrilla activities and massacre the local population of ostensibly rebellious towns, as well as to round up Jews in hiding to be sent to concentration camps.[177]

The fall of the regime on April 25, 1945 marked the end of "really existing" Fascism. But "fascism" did not end in 1945. It has persisted in different forms to the present. The following chapters, while registering the formation of alternative semantic markers for "fascism" by coeval antifascist thinkers and activists and postwar historians and political scientists, will also record the survival of the term as political category. "Fascism" also survived, surreptitiously, in the activities of neofascist political movements. Some of these acknowledged and bent to the Italian democratic system and its alliance with the North Atlantic Treaty Organization (NATO), like the Movimento Sociale Italiano, a postfascist party led by such former Fascist leaders as Pino Romualdi, Giorgio Almirante (who served as editor in chief of the racist magazine *La difesa della razza*), Pino Rauti, Junio Valerio Borghese, and Rodolfo Graziani, the historical transformations of which directly lead to the Fratelli d'Italia, the current majority party of Prime Minister Giorgia Meloni.[178] Other maintained their Fascist beliefs in their roles as civil servants, actively engaging in operations of diversion and disinformation during the period of the *strategia della tensione*, in the turbulent years of 1969–80.[179] Others still operated in groups that organized assassinations and terrorist acts during those years.[180] Junio Valerio Borghese, former head of the Xª MAS brigades, even attempted a coup d'état in December 1970.[181] Others, like Licio Gelli, a former Fascist leader with Nazi sympathies and founder of the secret Masonic society Propaganda 2, which was behind many criminal operations in postwar Italy and among whose members was the TV magnate and former prime minister Silvio Berlusconi, schemed to influence party politics to effectively pursue Fascist ideals. Before his death in 2008, Gelli declared: "Io sono nato sotto il Fascismo, ho studiato col Fascismo, ho combattuto per il Fascismo, sono un fascista e morirò fascista" (I was born under Fascism, I studied with Fascism, I fought for Fascism, I am a Fascist, and I will die Fascist).[182] Often, former Fascist civil servants, economic and financial elites with Fascist sympathies, conservative politicians, and ultranationalist, extraparliamentary groups found support from the US's Central Intelligence Agency (CIA) as a measure to counter the advance of communism in Italy during the Cold War.[183]

Fascism as a regime died on April 25, 1945. But fascism as an ideal survived the turmoil of the Cold War and is now undergoing a revival following the waning of antifascism, the crises of the twenty-first century, and the rise of populist and authoritarian movements and governments all around the world.[184] Since the end of the Fascist regime, the semantic markers of "fascism" have grown, expanded, and formed new conceptual constellations and connotative associations. Parts II and III reconstruct the constitution of two important sets of markers: the definitions of "fascism" given by transwar antifascists, and the postwar attempts to develop it into a new political typology.

4
The Language of Fascism

The previous chapter reconstructed the regime's relentless semiosic interventions, aimed at consolidating and conventionalizing the approved semantic markers of "fascism" in circulation during the mature phase of Fascism. Having disavowed its primitive meanings of *fascio* (i.e., the denotation of "union" and the connotation of "revolutionary syndicalism"), the term was used in official documents, speeches, and communications of the regime as a synonym of "government" and "state." This equivalence operated at both a syntactical and a semantic level, actualizing in speech practices a conception of Fascism that Mussolini and other leaders had presented as the purest institutional expression of a "nation" whose interests and full blossoming it alone could guarantee.

As the previous chapter showed, to fulfill its mission as "state" and "regime," "fascism" embraced the connotations of "totalitarian," "imperial," and "racist." As political ideal and praxis, "fascism" was also "universal" and authentically "revolutionary" (in opposition to socialism and communism, which denied the ontological axioms of nation and race in the name of internationalism), because it intended to subvert the system of liberalism, founded upon representative mediation, in order to impose a new regime that was established upon an unmediated relation between state and people through rituals of communion with the Duce (in rallies, ceremonies, and by acknowledging his omnipresent face and voice) and through the participation of all in Fascism (at school, in sports, at work, within the family, etc.).

The regime imposed a network of denotative and connotative markers through processes of sign production that were ideological, insofar as they negated—violently and coercively through censorship, imprisonment, forced exiles, and the like—alternative interpretations of the Fascist regime while suasively promoting its orthodox meanings. Fascist leaders adopted a variety of illocutionary strategies: public speeches and rallies, public celebrations, and architectonic framing that favored slogans, catchphrases, jingles, and formulae that, in contrast to treatises and essays, were assertive rather than argumentative, performative rather than demonstrative, emotional rather than rational, conative and phatic rather than invitations to reasoning, debate, negotiation, and good arguments. In short, they showed and performed the meaning of "fascism" rather than discursively explaining it.

Form, more than content, played a central role in the conveyance of the ideological meanings of "fascism" because it directly expressed the regime's belief in the directness, unmediatedness, and nonrepresentational bond linking Fascism, incarnated in its leader, Benito Mussolini, and the nation, embodied by the screaming crowds at his rallies. Fascism's mise-en-scène was not just ideological brainwashing: it was an instantiation of participation, opposed to the perception of passivity conveyed by the mediateness at the core of representative politics and institutions. It was surely a simulacrum and a pantomime of participation, but it was nonetheless ideologically powerful: the liturgy of mass chanting of Fascist jingles actualized participation, just as religious ceremonies and sport cheering actualize belonging in a religious or team-support community. Fascism became the vehicle for the realization of the nation insofar as it organized its concretization not just in rallies and state ceremonies, but also through a complete recodification of life practices in communal, national, cultural, and racial senses: going to school, learning, participating in cultural activities, serving in the army or in neighborhood associations, and even just diligently applying oneself to one's job or social role were ways to participate and fulfill the destiny of one's community.

In semiotic terms, the conventionalization of the semantic markers of "fascism" through their redundant repetitions in rallies, rituals, jingles, "petrified ideology," and so on was more effective than its textual and discursive encoding, explaining Mussolini's reluctance to engage in argumentative treatises on Fascism. This does not mean that more scholarly or academic research into the meanings of "fascism" was absent. Quite the contrary: Giuseppe Bottai, Giovanni Gentile, Ugo Spirito, and Mussolini himself, alongside other Fascist intellectuals, persistently engaged in a continuous refinement of the denotative and connotative values of the terms. But while the latter has been extensively studied in postwar scholarship, the former has been at the center of the work of only a handful of scholars. While during the Fascist Ventennio the former operated primarily within the small and more or less closed circle of academia, the latter affected the language of Italians in profound ways.

Philosophies of Fascism

La dottrina del fascismo, which historians have often treated as the foundational text of Fascism, just as Hitler's *Mein Kampf* was that of National Socialism, was not published until 1932, ten years after the establishment of the regime. Concomitantly with the large-scale celebrations of the tenth anniversary of the Fascist revolution, Mussolini and Giovanni Gentile published a systematic account of Fascism, albeit in the underwhelming form of an entry ("Fascism") in the fourteenth volume of the *Enciclopedia italiana di scienze, lettere e arti* (Italian Encyclopedia of Science, Letters, and Arts), edited by Giovanni Treccani between 1929 and 1936.[1] It would later be published as a single volume as *La dottrina del fascismo* in different editions since 1932.[2]

The author(s) explained that although Fascism must be understood as both "action and thought," it certainly privileged the former over the latter, since it was "action in which doctrine is immanent, and doctrine arising from a given system of historical forces in which it inserts itself and works from within." What this meant is that the form Fascism took in Italy in the 1920s and 1930s was "informed by contingencies of time and space," and yet "it retains an ideal content that makes it an expression of truth in the higher region of the history of thought."[3] It concerned, that is, the very essence of human life and its place in the world, which, for Fascism, were not exhausted by those philosophies that concentrated on the individual, because the "Fascist man is not only an individual but also a nation and a country." On the one hand, "Fascism wants man to be active and engaged in action" because "it conceives of life as a struggle."[4] But on the other, "in the Fascist conception of history, man is man only by virtue of the spiritual process to which he contributes as a member of a family, a social group, a nation. . . ." The destiny of the individual was therefore that of the nation, because "outside history man ceases to exist."[5]

From this equation, Mussolini and Gentile drew the following consequences. First, the nation existed *in potentia* as a universal idea, but only the state could bring it about *in acto*, to a concrete reality: "It is the state that creates the nation, granting volition and therefore real existence to a people that has become aware of its moral unity."[6] Second, "a nation, as expressed in the state, is a living, ethical entity to the degree that it is capable of evolving." Third, since "the Fascist state embodies a spiritual force encompassing all manifestation of the moral and intellectual life of a man," it is the agent for the actualization of a nation through the state. This is because, fourth, "the Fascist state is no mere mechanical device for delimiting the sphere within which individuals may exercise their supposed rights," but is instead "a standard and rule of conduct," "the very principle . . . that inspires every man who is member of a civilized society." Fascism was, therefore, the name of a state in which the nation could be fully realized, both materially (institutionally) and spiritually (ethically): "Fascism is not only a law giver and a founder of institutions but also an educator and a promoter of spiritual life."[7] In sum, "Fascism is clearly defined not only as a regime but as a doctrine."[8] As both, it is "against pacifism," "against historical materialism and class-struggle," and "against liberal democracies."[9]

The Doctrine of Fascism was certainly not the only theoretical exposition that attempted to provide a unitary and coherent introduction to the ideological basis of Fascism. Giovanni Gentile published a series of booklets in support of Fascism: *Che cos'è il fascismo* (Florence: Vallecchi, 1925), *Fascismo e cultura* (Milano: Fratelli Treves, 1928), *Origini e dottrina del fascismo* (Roma: Istituto Nazionale Fascista di Cultura, 1929), and *La mia religione* (Florence: Le Lettere, 1943).[10] Alfredo Rocco, the Fascist jurist who reshaped the penal code to accommodate Fascism, published *La dottrina politica del fascismo*, in which he defended the philosophical origins of Fascism, which he conceived of as an "integral doctrine of sociality antithetical to the atomism of liberal, democratic, and socialistic theories."[11] Other Fascist leaders published exegetical treatises on Fascism as state doctrine and philosophy. Giuseppe Bottai argued that Fascism was principally an "intellectual revolution" (1924), while Ugo Spirito defended the notion that only in the Fascist state were the "absolute liberalism" of circulation and the "absolute socialism" of production achieved (1932).

It is worth remembering that Gentile, Bottai, Spirito, and others, while acting as organic intellectuals within the Fascist regime as members of Italian academia and actively involved in different ministerial functions must be considered more than mere state ideologues. Like Martin Heidegger and Carl Schmitt, they were philosophers with international reputations and extensive scholarly publications. Yet, their philosophical production remained ultimately instrumental in the cause of Fascism. Gentile framed the Fascist state within a metaphysics of action that justified its historical mission. Bottai defended Fascism as a political movement that was "decisively intellectual."[12] For him, Fascism derived from the same emancipatory project as the French Revolution, and it had to be understood as "democratic," in the sense of being based on the sovereignty of the people—but not in an "atomistic" sense, as in France, or in the ochlocratic fashion of pre-Fascist Italy.[13] For Bottai, Fascism was not necessarily antiliberal, since it intended to continue liberalism's "historical project" in the "same spirit of freedom, . . . but freedom understood not as individual will but as a higher will, opposed to individual whims, that emerges from the synthesis of freedom and authority."[14] Ugo Spirito, one of the most influential theorists of "corporativism" and a member of the left-wing faction of Fascism (after the war he became a supporter of the Communist Party), gave further philosophical support to Gentile's and Bottai's defenses of Fascism by arguing that Fascist corporativism was the attempt to overcome the antinomies of the individual and the nation that were at the core of both liberalism and socialism. "Corporativism," he claimed, "replies to liberalism by confirming that every person's individual freedom is sacred," but it become antiliberal "only because the individual under liberalism is not a true individual," but a mechanism of capitalist accumulation that ultimately deprived him of his natural belonging to a national community. Similarly, Spirito argued that Fascism conformed to the socialist "desire to seek true liberty and justice within the state," but it was "antisocialist only because the state under socialism is not a true state," since it denies the ultimate solidarity of all members of a national community.[15]

The essays on Fascist philosophy, from Mussolini's own *La dottrina del fascismo* to the ones authored by Gentile, Bottai, Alfredo Rosso, Spirito, and others, had a target audience of intellectuals and members of the educated middle classes. They never enjoyed the far-reaching, almost biblical distribution of *Mein Kampf* in Germany, whether Hitler's book was actually read or not.[16] In terms of content, they presented, in a more organic philosophical language, the principles Mussolini had defended in his speeches and editorials: that Fascism was a praxis of government, and that its goal was the realization of the potential of the nation, which was the concrete, institutionalized expression of one biological group (race).

But as noted above, the association of Fascism and the state was performed, rather than explained or even argued, first and foremost at the formal level of syntax, insofar as "fascism" appeared as the subject and agent of governmental initiatives. A presentation of the contribution of Fascist leaders to the semantic markers of "fascism" would therefore be incomplete without some observations on the formal aspects of their language and style.

The Language of Fascism

Victor Klemperer, that extraordinary chronicler of Nazi Germany, applied his analytical skills as a philologist to analyze the linguistic transformations imposed by the Nazis in *LTI—Lingua Tertii Imperii: Notizbuch eines Philologen*, published in 1947. In it he reported watching the documentary film *Ten Years of Fascism* at a movie theater on October 23, 1932, before Hitler's rise to power, and observed:

> For the first time I hear and see the Duce talking. The film is a great artistic achievement. Mussolini speaks to the crowd from the balcony of the palace in Naples; shots of the masses and close-ups of the speaker, the words of Mussolini alternate with the responses of those he is addressing. You can see clearly how the Duce literally pumps himself up for each sentence, how, following brief moments of deflation, he repeatedly generates the impression of utmost energy and tautness, you hear the passionately sermonizing, ritualistic and ecclesiastical intonation of his terse outbursts, each consisting of only the shortest of sentences, like fragments of a liturgy to which everyone can react emotionally without the least bit of intellectual effort, even if they don't understand the meaning—indeed all the more so if they don't. His mouth is gigantic. Now and then he gesticulates with his fingers in a typically Italian manner. And the howling of the masses, ecstatic interjections or, when an enemy is invoked, shrill whistling. And again and again, accompanying all this, the raised arm of the Fascist salute.[17]

As Klemperer's account suggests, the signifier "fascism" stood for the rhetorical, theatrical, and ritualistic form of presentation of its content. The obsessive self-referentiality of Fascism was functional to the regime's endeavor to conventionalize the new meanings of "fascism," which were constantly reiterated through state rituals (marches, parades, games, etc.) and the constant exposition to the Duce's voice, face, and body.

It would be a mistake, however, to dismiss these rituals of secular religiosity, as Emilio Gentile, following George L. Mosse, called them, as simple tricks to assure and coerce popular consensus. Alongside concrete forms of state intervention in language, education, civic associationism, and propaganda disseminated by the media, Fascism shaped the culture and lives of those who lived through it.[18] Furthermore, the involvement of the people in secular liturgies originated from and consolidated preexisting forms of civic mobilization and associationism at the core of Fascism: the very name "fascism" bore witness of this legacy of people's political activity (see chap. 1). Klemperer attributed a similar character to Hitler's National Socialism: "Nazism permeated the flesh and blood of the people through single words, idioms and sentence structures which were imposed on them in a million repetitions and taken on board mechanically and unconsciously."[19]

Mussolini, that *gladiatore della parola*,[20] self-consciously saw in the state control of language and signification a necessary step toward the anthropological transformation of Italians that Fascism aimed to achieve. Fascism radicalized the "nationalization of the masses" initiated after the unification of 1861 by directly intervening in the language of the Italian people.[21] As Alessandra Tarquini put it, "The linguistic policy of Fascism was expressed through a continuous normative activity aimed at enhancing the use of Italian."[22] The regime interventions in language were both direct and indirect. Linguistic legislation aimed at normatively controlling the public use of words, via censorship and prohibitions. But it was the example of Mussolini's own language as a model to imitate that contributed the most to recruiting the Italian language to the revolutionary transformation of Italians that Fascism planned to achieve.

The linguistic policies of the regime targeted four main areas.[23] As Patrizia Dogliani put it, "This operation must . . . be framed in the more general policy of linguistic unification undertaken since the beginning by Fascism under the valence of 'one nation = one language.' "[24] First, it prohibited the use of dialects, the principal means of communication and socialization in all regions and by all social classes in a country that at the time had one of the lowest literacy rates in all Europe. In this case, Fascism only radicalized a policy that preceded it. Alessandra Tarquini explains that "the real obstacle to the fulfillment of their programs was represented by the dialects, which, in a country where the illiteracy rate reached an average of 78% of the population, were by far the most prevalent form of communication, making Italian a 'language celebrated but not used and, so to speak, foreign at home,' spoken by less than 10% of the subjects of the kingdom."[25] In 1923 the teaching of Italian became a required subject in elementary schools, at first following a gradual passage from dialect to Italian, but, in 1925, prohibiting and censoring altogether the use of dialect in schools.[26] The state also intervened in changing the names of towns, cities, and regions in an effort to reduce "barbarisms" and enhance the "Roman origin" of the Italian state.[27]

Second, a widespread plan for the repression of linguistic minorities was implemented in Aosta (French), Alto Adige (German), and Venezia-Giulia (Slovene). Beginning with the academic year 1923–24, all the alloglot schools in the border provinces of northern Italy had to cancel classes taught in any language other than Italian.[28] Foreign surnames and place-names were forcibly Italianized (for instance, Chatillon was turned into Costiglion Dora and La Thuile into Porta Littoria),[29] the display of bilingual signs and announcements was prohibited,[30] and enrollment in after-school classes in minority languages (e.g., French in Aosta and German in Alto Adige) was not only stigmatized but suspiciously conceived as sign of possible "antifascism."[31]

Third, Fascism censored the use of foreign words, replacing terms of English, French, or German origin with awkward Italian neologisms. These measures were enthusiastically embraced by neopurist linguists such as Bruno Migliorini and Giacomo Devoto, who engaged in a "struggle against any sort of innovation."[32] The Royal Academy of Italy constituted, in 1940, a Commissione per l'Italianità della Lingua (Committee for the Italianness of Language), directed by Migliorini with the assistance of such writers and linguists as Filippo Tommaso Marinetti, Carlo Formichi, Riccardo Bacchelli, Emilio Cecchi, and Enrico Falqui, who were charged with developing lists of Italian equivalents of foreign loanwords: these included terms like *àlcole* (alcohol), *acquavite* (whisky), *sciampagna* (champagne), *autista* (chauffeur) *cornetto* (croissant), *pellicola* (film), *rimessa* (garage), *albergo* (hotel), *lista* (menu), and *fetta di pan tosto* (toast), to name just a few.[33]

Fourth, the regime encouraged replacing the third-person singular *lei* in formal/polite expressions with the second-person singular *tu* and the second-person plural *voi*. The campaign was launched by the author Bruno Cicognani on the pages of *Il corriere della sera* when he stated: "The Fascist Revolution set out to bring the spirit of the race to its ancient origins, freeing it from all pollution. Well, let this purification also be accomplished and return, in this too, as it is in use in Rome, to the 'you' [*tu*] as expression of the Roman and Christian universal. 'You' [*voi*] must be a sign of respect, recognition, and hierarchy. But in any other instance, the form of communication, in writing and speaking, must be 'you' [*tu*]."[34] The directness of *tu* and its polite form, *voi*, claimed Achille Starace, PNF secretary between 1931 and 1939, was the realization of the virility of the "Fascist style."[35]

The linguistic policies of Fascism were not simply a defense of the Italian language. They were, rather, an integral part of the regime's intention of turning the Fascist Italian into a "new man."[36] Antonio Gramsci understood this program: The cultural and linguistic interventions of the Fascist state were aimed at "the formation and expansion of a ruling class, the need to establish more intimate and secure relationships between the ruling groups and the popular-national mass, that is, to reorganize cultural hegemony."[37] The idea that language and its control were fundamental steps in the realization of the totalitarian state was explicitly defended by Giuseppe Bottai, who in 1934 wrote that the task of Fascist politics was to "determine the renewal and creation of the spoken language" of Italians, a fundamental step in the creation of the Fascist *uomo nuovo*.[38]

As the words of Gramsci and Bottai demonstrate, the importance that the regime attributed to language far exceeded its censoring legislations. It defined far more than the linguistic style of the regime: It constituted the foundation for the reconceptualization of an ostensibly unmediated form of popular sovereignty.[39] Fascism realized its revolutionary intents by adopting a performative use of language that instituted, through an excessive use of conative and phatic expressions, a deep emotional bond with the addressees.[40] It was through language that the political communion of the leader and the masses was effected. Fascism, commented the antifascist historian Franco Venturi, was "a kingdom of words that moves in a world of ghosts, which it ends up believing to be real."[41] Fascism realized in Italy a "regime of lies," as Pietro Calamandrei famously described it.[42] Mussolini, suggested Thomas Mann, was like Cavaliere Cipolla, the magician in his 1929 short story "Mario und der Zauberer" (Mario and the Magician), an illusionist and mesmerizer capable of turning the audience of his show in a thoughtless mass of adulators.[43]

But the regime was not just a "factory of emptiness," to use another of Venturi's expressions, a regime without ideology, a smokescreen that hid its systematic use of violence, repression, and ruthless exercise of power, as it was conventionally described by orthodox Marxist historians in the early postwar period.[44] The language of Fascism was constitutive of its (pseudo) revolutionary project and found a model in Mussolini's linguistic style. Mario Isnenghi observes that "the regime speaks and makes people talk about itself continuously. It is largely a creation of words; but of words that have become facts or that are declared facts. Until the very end, . . . the words, the images, the ideology are integral and constitutive parts of Fascism: of Fascism as it is presented and as people live it."[45] It was, in Gramscian terms, an example of effective "normative grammar," which "tended to make the organism learn the whole of the given language, and to create a spiritual attitude that enables one always to orient oneself in the linguistic environment."[46] A normative grammar like the one imposed by the Fascist regime is "always a 'choice,' a cultural direction, it is always an act of national-cultural policy," the aim of which was "to centralize what already exists in a diffused, scattered, but inorganic and incoherent state," in order to create a coordinated and subservient popular mass.[47]

The notion that Mussolini's language became the model for the development of a linguistic style that dominated the linguistic production in Italy during the regime is not just a hypothesis of historical interpretation.[48] It can be traced in the number of publications that explicitly sampled Mussolini's phraseology and style as a model to be imitated in schools and in national newspapers. Not only did he add neologisms to the Italian vocabulary, but he contributed to add semantic markers to words beyond the immediate constellation of Fascist ideology. In a discourse to the PNF directorate of 24 June 1943, two weeks before the Allied invasion of Sicily, Mussolini famously blustered: "The Italian people are now convinced that it is a question of life or death. As soon as the enemy tries to disembark, he must be frozen on that line that sailors call the *bagnasciuga*, the line of sand where the water ends and the land begins."[49] Mussolini referred to the water's edge on the seashore, the portion of the beach that is constantly bathed by waves; but the correct term for it was not *bagnasciuga*, which, in maritime terminology, indicates a ship's boot topping (the part of a ship's hull that is between the load line and the water line when the ship is not loaded), but *battigia*. Mussolini's lexical mistake became the semantic rule: in all Italian dictionaries in use today *bagnasciuga* is defined as both the boot topping and the seawater's edge. The Duce's charisma, in a way, survives today in the fossilized form of numerous semantic modifications of the Italian vocabulary.

Mussolini's influence on the Italian language went beyond the lexicon to create a distinct style of linguistic production. The journalist Bruno Biancini compiled a *Dizionario mussoliniano*, which would be reprinted multiple times as a writing aid for students, journalists, and young authors.[50] Newspapers and periodicals were the most likely to adopt a Mussolinian style, which can be traced as far back as the beginning of the regime, in the formative period of 1923–25.[51] Studies on the language and rhetorical skills of Mussolini abounded, but it is often difficult to separate their analytical and hagiographical approach. Lorenzo Bianchi's *Mussolini scrittore e oratore* was a bestseller (and was translated into German), as were Andrea Gustarelli's *Mussolini, scrittore e oratore* and Carlo Villani's *Stile di Mussolini*.[52] The linguist Hermann Ellwanger wrote his graduation thesis under the guidance of the German philologist Emil Winkler; it was published in the original German as *Studien zur Sprache Benito Mussolinis* and in Italian translation as *Sulla lingua di Mussolini* under the patronage of Giovanni Gentile and the Italian philologist Alfredo Schiaffini.[53] According to Ellwanger, Mussolini rejected Italian political language because it had become as corrupted and meaningless as its parliamentary institutions: "For him, political discourse in particular had lost value through its abuse in parliament, words were often used for their own sake and political discourse had become parliamentary jargon, devoid of force, worn-out."[54] To overcome this impasse, Mussolini developed a new political language, the fundamental characteristics of which were to "limit speeches to a minimum, say only essential things with essential words, few if possible, declare war on traditional speeches of the past, on old-style eloquence in all its manifestations."[55] Studying the language of Mussolini gave Ellwanger the opportunity to experience "up-close the workshop of the speechmaker [*officina dell'oratore*] . . . and it gives us a little guide of Mussolinian style."[56]

Fascism's linguistic policy, in short, had as its goal that all Italians learn to speak like a Fascist, and in that way take part, with the regime leader, in the realization of the full potential of the nation that former political practices had hindered by either speaking an indecipherable political lingo or by allowing the persistence of dialects. The goal of Mussolini's linguistic policies was therefore a realization of the ideological plan of Fascism itself. Outside the confines of the ideology, learning how to speak like a Fascist actually meant accepting the existing social order and one's position within it. The sense of agency that the Fascist linguistic rituals gave the masses of Italians, springing from the emotional responses to the direct interpellations of the Duce, found its impassable limit in the sacrifices (and subjection) that the regime demanded of its subjects for the prosperity of the nation as soldiers, as workers, as mothers, and as students. As Chiara Ferrari puts it, "The rhetoric of sacrifice sutured a fundamental fissure of fascist discourse. The function of a 'voice in unison' that simultaneously suppressed and elicited speech was to provide not only an image of consensus and popular support of the Duce and the regime, but also a blueprint for the role of the individual in fascist society."[57]

Mussolini's language was hyperbolic, enchanting, narrativizing rather than argumentative. It was a verbal instantiation of the Fascist belief in violence. Giorgio Fedel isolated three linguistic ambits where Mussolini intervened to create his own linguistic style: grammatical-syntactical, phonic-rhythmic, and stylistic-rhetorical.[58] At a grammatical-syntactical level, Mussolini privileged a paratactical construction of the periods: the phraseological elements of the sentence were linked by simple coordination, without any apparent logical connectivity:[59] "There are no links; the propositions, almost all main clauses, are placed side by side. . . . Propositions are grammatically 'isolated,' but this lack of formal links in the discourse does not seem to impinge in the least on the 'sense value' of the latter. Indeed, paratactic articulation seems to render that which is enunciated cogent and irrefutable precisely by virtue of the fact that clarifying links are not necessary to reach the evidence."[60] The utterance is not argumentative, but it is rendered almost deictic by the paratactical structure itself. In an example from an article dated March 23, 1921 analyzed by Fedel, the language of the Duce, in its syntagmatic structure, seems to become action: "Due anni! Rapida successione di eventi! Tumulto e passare di uomini! Giornate grigie e giornate di sole. Giornate di lutto e giornate di trionfo. Sordo rintocco di campane funebri; squillare gioioso di fanfare all'attacco. Fra poco il Fascismo dominerà la situazione" (Two years! Rapid succession of events! Tumult and passing of men! Gray days and sunny days! Days of mourning and days of triumph! Dull ringing of funeral bells; joyful sound of fanfare on the attack. Soon Fascism will dominate the situation).[61] The ellipsis of verbs imbues the entire passage with a sense of immediacy: each nominal phrase becomes the indexical pointer to an action and its transformative effects. Mussolini's words, as Erasmo Leso puts it, are themselves charismatic: "Parataxis serves Mussolini, on the one hand, by accentuating in public the impression of a communion between orator and listeners and, on the other, by presenting his own as an essential oratory, voluntaristically free from intellectual complications, yet intelligently organized."[62]

The utterances are immediate, rapid, and instantly intelligible. This character of Mussolini's language turned it into a "stimulus to action," which mirrored, at a formal level, one of the main features of Fascism conceptually sustained in *La dottrina del fascismo*: "Mussolini's discourse is explicitly presented as an agitating discourse [*discorso agitatorio*]."[63] It was therefore nondialogical and refused argumentation, preferring instead slogan and storytelling as modes of presentation, both explicitly addressing the masses rather than the elites. Consequently, Mussolini's discourse became revelatory: on the one hand, its straightforward and legible storytelling disclosed the truth of the matter that complex argumentations only disguised; on the other, it revealed "that which is (and cannot not be) the feeling of every Fascist": "The Fascist listening to the speech of his boss (which is the voice of the nation) is freed from his inessential and brute forms (egotisms, material interests) and led back to his primordial and unconscious truth: his belonging to the ethical state, to the nation."[64] This belonging, through the immediacy of the paratactical form of presentation, is implicit, not explained; it is showed and made it felt, not demonstrated. It was affectively illocutionary rather than syllogistic and argumentative.

The charisma of Mussolini's agitating, deictically revelatory, and ostensibly alethic discourse was strengthened by the phonic and rhythmic effects that its paratactic organization created. Ellwanger, Leso, and Fedel show how Mussolini's utterances, in speeches as well as in published articles, created a ternary rhythm, much like religious hymns or sports-fan choruses, by breaking the periods into three sentences or by listing elements and adjectives in groups of three.[65] The tropes that abounded in his texts—prolepsis (anticipations), polysyndeton (the paratactic repetitions of elements), anaphora (use of pronouns and ellipsis), and paranomasia (puns)—all emphasize rhythm, repetition, listing, with a hypnotic effect that reinforced the deictic, axiomatic nature of the discourse itself.[66] Leso's close analyses of Mussolini's speeches demonstrates how "it happens at every step that one comes across, while reading Mussolini, passages . . . that do not say anything at a specific referential or political level." His utterances, continues Leso, do not proclaim a political program, but rather are "the title of a novel, a slogan, or a battle cry. Which he, it must be said, articulates very skillfully, evoking in a sort of disembodied abstraction the idea of creating, of life, of strength, of beauty."[67]

To disenchant the magic of Mussolini's language, in sum, "we must analyze Mussolini's discourse on the basis of functions that are not those of mere transmission of information."[68] This does not mean that the discourse was vacuous and empty, as Venturi, Calamandrei, and Bobbio suggest. It possessed a powerful semiosic effect, operating through its expressive form rather than through its content, which accomplished the goal of creating an emotional community of shared intent and mission: "Mussolini's discourse does not aim to 'make [it] understood' that the nation, the community, exists based on intellectual reasoning, but rather to make it *heard* through the rhythm of the words, the perceptible characteristics of which are capable of evoking, in a sense, even the heartbeat of this Supreme Being."[69]

The novelty of Mussolini's political invention can be grasped by his use of language in texts and speeches that dramatized politics by transmitting agency to the masses—a simulacrum of agency, however, since it existed only in the rhetorical effect of participating in a national discourse that was produced by the Duce. The frequent use of metaphors that Mussolini adopted from religious and military terminology and the insistence on metonymical aspects of the topics he discussed further enhanced the concrete and agitational meanings of his discourses. Mussolini's metaphors, so numerous in all his texts, for Fedel "aim at sentimentalization and, in turn, to push to action. . . . The ability of metaphor . . . to express, synthetically and peculiarly, the feelings of the speaker and/or to arouse the feelings of the listener lies in the fact that the metaphorical procedure creates an image that underlines those perceptive or expressive elements that the argumentative situation requires."[70] For instance, the League of Nations was a "sort of monstrous miscarriage of plutocratic idealism." To emphasize the participation of all in the project of national palingenesis, he declared that "we must all have the sacred pride of being the servants of the nation: The employee is a soldier." The nation was often described as an organism, and thus Mussolini could claim that he had "the pulse of the nation in my hand, and I measure its heartbeats."

Similarly, Mussolini's use of metonymy and synecdoche, Leso argues, "reduces reality to the particular, to the figurative detail, to color, and the like; on the other hand, it refers not only from the particular to the general, but from the concrete particular to the abstract general. In the first case, it exhibits a precise reality, minutely exact, but incomplete; in the other, a reality of pure forms waiting to be concretely determined: in both cases there is the representation of a diminished reality—either fragmentary or empty—and thoroughly symbolic, and, at the same time, in Mussolini's linguistic context, which is so strongly characterized in a voluntaristic sense, the prefiguration of another reality, which can only be glimpsed in glimmers but which already exists in those glimpses and which in any case must fatally come true."[71] So the Fascists were always "Blackshirts," the younger generation always *la giovinezza italiana* (the Italian youth), the male population *il popolo del lavoro* (the working people).

Mussolini's language was emotional rather than analytical, stimulative rather than cognitive, subjective rather than objective: the abundance of figurative expressions reinforced these qualities by focusing on affective particulars to express either an entire class (i.e., *cappelli piumati* [feathered hats], an endearing expression for the army corps of the Bersaglieri) or a general category ("labor," "army," "lookout" for the Italian population).[72] Metonymy and synecdoche, in particular, conveyed a feeling of belonging and of taking part in the creation of a national community with connotations, mediated from religious discourse, of participation, sacrifice, and a warring spirit.

What Victor Klemperer described in his *LTI* as an impoverishment of the German language under National Socialism should be qualified in the Italian case as an impoverishment not of language itself, but of its semiosic capacity. Mussolini and other Fascist leaders put on full display the poetic and rhetorical potential of the Italian language. Yet, the metaphorical and affective flamboyance of the Fascist style that all Italians were to imitate masked constant interventions to regiment and control the semiosic potential of that bombastic language so that its users could only reiterate through it their membership within the national community conceived in Fascist terms. The identitarian fundamentalism behind the many linguistic policies of the Fascist regime hypostatized an imagined community that strove for authenticity by eliminating any form of deviation, difference, otherness, and foreignness. It was not language itself that was impoverished, but its signifying potential. The rhetorical exuberance of the Fascist language was the mask that repressed the polysemic nature of language itself.

The nationalization of the masses, the final goal of many of the regime's policies, including linguistic regulations, was certainly not unique to Italy in the interwar period. Similar processes were occurring in democracies such as the United States, France, and Weimar Germany, as well as in authoritarian regimes such as Turkey, Japan, Chiang Kai-shek's China, the new socialist experiment that was the Soviet Union, and especially in the many new nation-states created after the fall of the ancien régime empires.[73] In this sense, the linguistic nationalism of Fascism followed political reforms and practices that were ubiquitous in the reconfigurations of states into nations (and nation-empires) that the First World War had triggered. As the next chapter will show, this accounts for the positive reception that Mussolini's regime received worldwide.

What is interesting about Fascist linguistic nationalization is that Mussolini and other ideologues conceived of it in revolutionary terms that resembled those of the Soviet Union, insofar as Mussolini presented the imposition of the Italian language and the participation of the masses in Fascist secular rituals in emancipatory terms.[74] Indeed, the prescription of a state-sanctioned Italian language, purified of dialectical and foreign influences, was one of the means through which Fascism politicized "masses" that had previously been excluded from having political voice and agency. But Fascism's politicization of the masses also implied severe limitations on their agency: first, the amorphous, diverse, and indefinite masses could claim sovereignty and political participation only on the condition that they acknowledged their redefinition as a structured and homogeneous national community (as *il popolo*); second, the political "nation" had by definition to prioritize harmony and collaboration (the principle of Fascist corporatism) over class struggle and class interests; third, just as the natural conditions of different nations (defined by their racial essence) were to be structured in hierarchies of power that justified the imperialistic subjection of others, the national community was inherently hierarchical; fourth, the hierarchical structure of the nation defined social roles (of the worker, the soldier, the entrepreneur, the leader, etc.) that limited social action itself for the sake of collaboration aimed at national prosperity; fifth, this hierarchy included unequal positionalities depending on age, gender, and religion. Finally, the excluded ones, ranging from those who did not belong to the national community (foreigners, migrants, colonized minorities, and religious minorities, as well as those who transgressed gender and sexual norms) to those who chose to place themselves outside that community by rejecting or resisting the palingenetic mission of Fascism-as-state (the antifascists) were excluded from being part of the national community and lost political agency.

The language of Fascism was illocutionary and agitational, assertive rather than constative, and hence conceived of as a form of praxis. It was virile and direct as well as nurturing and healing, engendering a division of men and women symbolically based on the social templates of the frontline trenches and the home front. It was monosemic in its referential and denotative use even when it indulged in metaphorical creativity, because it had to mirror the homogeneity and commonality of intents of the national community. It was a language, in short, the impossible task of which was not only to negate the mediating function of signification, but to deny that there was any separation between words and world.

PART II

Antifascists' "Fascism"

> Sondern der Faschismus ist in der Tat weniger "ideologisch," insoweit er das Prinzip der Herrschaft unmittelbar proklamiert, das anderswo sich versteckt. [Fascism is itself less "ideological," in so far as it openly proclaims the principle of domination that is elsewhere concealed.]
>
> THEODOR W. ADORNO, *Minima Moralia*

The historical processes that lead to the consolidation of the socially accepted meanings of words and concepts are events that can, at least in theory, be reconstructed. The operation of semantic decodification that this book attempts is facilitated by the fact that the birth, development, hybridizations, and transformations of the term "fascism" occurred in historical circumstances recent enough to leave a large volume of occurrences, where textual and circumstantial pathways of sense making can be easily tracked and analyzed. Part I recounted the attempts of Benito Mussolini and other Fascist leaders to codify a set of denotative and connotative markers that intended to regulate the meanings of "fascism" within the Italian linguistic community—that is, the selection and activation in communicative acts of those markers of the term that adhered to a semantic orthodoxy that the regime intended to enforce. That semiotic labor, imposed by coercive and suasive means, aimed at consolidating interpretive habits that were opposed to the ones associated with the activities of the movement before its rise to power (chap. 2) and that routinized the denotative understanding of "fascism" as associated to "state," "nation," and "empire," and with connotations of "totalitarian," unmediated popular participation in the state, "racial purity," "virility," "community," and so on (chap. 3).

From the perspective of interpretive semiotics, the meaning of all kinds of sign vehicles, however, is the sum of different and often contradictory forms of semiosic labor that coexist within a linguistic community.[1] Hence, in different historical circumstances some semantic markers dominate others, new connotations form while others fall into disuse, and new denotative selections circulate at different speeds among different social groups. The regime's efforts to impose an orthodox meaning of "fascism," surveyed in chapter 4, consisted of concerted interventions in the cultural and linguistic habits of Italians that, insofar as they aimed at limiting the permissible denotations (and thus the possible interpretations) of the term and what the term stood for, should be understood as ideological—here intending "ideology" in its elementary, semiotic sense of any form of coercive and suasive erasure, concealment, or negation of alternative meanings.[2]

At the same time, the critical analyses of antifascist thinkers and activists with liberal conservative, liberal progressive, or Marxist leanings developed alternative meanings of "fascism." These antagonistic processes of semiosis proposed alternative denotative and connotative markers that, although they circulated in texts at the margins of the official culture sanctioned by the regime—in underground circles and from exile—contributed both to contemporary resistance against Fascism and to postwar analyses of historians and political thinkers. The chapters in part II follow the formation of the most significant among the antagonistic conceptions of what "fascism" meant and what the Fascist regime stood for in the writings of authors that resisted and fought against it. This is, therefore, not a history of antifascists' *discourses* on "fascism" but rather of the processes that led to the consolidation of new semantic markers of the term in the interwar period. These applied initially to Italian Fascism, but soon, and particularly within Marxist debates, the term "fascism" began to stand as antonomasia for other forms of counterrevolutionary authoritarianism emerging in different countries. The most sophisticated forms of this genericized use of "fascism" attempted to reconcile Mussolini's regime and ideology with Hitler's National Socialism. Chapters 8 and 9, which reconstruct the processes of the genericization of "fascism," are therefore not a comparative analysis of Fascism and National Socialism. Nor do they aim at summarizing or validating interwar theories of fascism as a generic political form. They simply register the consolidation of new semantic markers and new interpretive *habiti* of "fascism" used as antonomasia for National Socialism, thus augmenting its semantic value (and, to an extent, internal contradictoriness).

5

Contexts

The Global Reception of Fascism and the Invention of "Antifascism"

The March on Rome in 1922 and the birth of a Fascist government soon after were closely monitored by state diplomats, politicians, activists, journalists, authors, and thinkers from all around the world. Political reactions, as Giulia Albanese shows, were largely supportive if not admiring of Mussolini's decisive action: "The main concern in diplomatic circles was Mussolini's revisionist attitude in foreign policy and his demand for revisions of the peace treaties. These aspects must not obscure, however, the overall positive judgment of the political movement and its leader coming both from European diplomacy and from the moderate, conservative, and right-wing press, which especially appreciated the image that Fascism succeeded in projecting, of a movement capable of restoring order in a country fraught by social conflict and of stopping the socialist advance."[1]

Mussolini's counterrevolutionary revolution found favorable conditions for its international acceptance in the interwar period. The political landscape of the continent in 1919 was radically different from that of 1914. After the peace conferences of Versailles, the collapse of the empires of Austria-Hungary, of Czarist Russia, and of the Hohenzollern in Germany, as well as the revolutionary upheaval and ensuing civil war in Russia, favored the creation of nine new nation-states: Finland, Austria, Czechoslovakia, Yugoslavia, Poland, Hungary, Latvia, Lithuania, and Estonia. The war had ended the *anciens régimes* that still persisted in the first decade of the twentieth century; the collapse of nations led by aristocracies marked, as Mark Mazower defines it, a "bourgeois triumph."

This triumph took the form of a radical transformation of the institutional structure of many European states. "Before the First World War," explains Mazower, "there had been just three republics in Europe; by the end of 1918 there were thirteen."[2] New constitutions were drafted and adopted in most countries.[3] Parliamentary democracies, forming a belt "stretching from the Baltic Sea down through Germany and Poland to the Balkans," became the dominant institutional form of government in Europe.[4] By 1920 universal male suffrage was common in most European countries (with the exception of Lithuania, which adopted it in 1922; Bulgaria, in 1945; and Malta, in 1947), while women's suffrage was extended after the war in Russia, Austria, Czechoslovakia, Estonia, Hungary, Poland, Germany, Sweden, the Netherlands, Latvia, and Luxemburg, which joined Finland, Norway, and Denmark.[5] Mass politics, which grew steadily through the period 1880–1914, expanded and grew even stronger in the interwar period. Nevertheless, as Aristotle Kallis argues, "the liberal-democratic paradigm was plagued from the outset by minimal or half-hearted elite support and popular legitimacy, as well as by the lack of strong political and institutional foundation. Democracy appeared to become mainstream in the early 1920s, if by mainstream one means the number of countries formally adopting it and the predominant official discourse of political elites at the helm of these experiments. But this popularity was superficial, disguising mounting undercurrents of animus and suppressed desired to reverse it."[6] The First World War effectively put an end to the "authoritarian infection" that had dominated the European political landscape before 1918.[7] This was true not only of political institutions and praxis, but also of popular participation in politics (within or without traditional parties), which the solidarity created by the experience of the trench war had awakened.

The old political establishment of most European countries found in the societies that emerged from the ruins of the First World War a rather different environment than that which obtained before the war.[8] The rules of the political game had changed, but the democratic parliamentarisms that ensued were fragile: first, the political class was still dominated by member of the traditional prewar elites; second, wealth distribution had yet to create the formation of a robust middle class; and third, the energy with which the Bolshevik Revolution had imbued socialist and communist parties and labor movements was now threatening the existence of the new political regimes in their infancies.

Socialist movements and labor unions carried out their activities more enthusiastically than before the conflict. Upheaval and revolutionary attempts took place throughout Europe: the communist uprisings in Germany (1918–19), including the *Spartakusaufstand*, led by Karl Liebknecht and Rosa Luxemburg (1919), and the short-lived Bavarian soviet republic (1918–19); the *biennio rosso* in Italy (1919–20); the Irish War of Independence (1919–21); the Venizelist agitations in Greece (1919–22); widespread strikes in Spain, especially in Catalonia, during the *trienio bolchevique* of 1918–21; and similar revolutionary movements in Portugal, Turkey, Malta, Hungary, the Netherlands,

Belgium, among many others.[9] In this context of growing democratization of politics and of socialist uprisings in western and central Europe that threatened the social privileges of the bourgeoisie, the success of Mussolini in quelling and "pacifying" the Italian peninsula was a welcome reassurance to the political and economic elites. The counterrevolutionary impetus Fascism transmitted did not originate from a traditional, elitist party, but from a new movement that declared itself to be based on mass support, and hence of and for the masses: Fascism was appealing because it constituted a successful anti-socialist bloc ostensibly for those masses that elsewhere upheld a communist revolution.

The political energies that the First World War unleashed extended far beyond Europe. The Turkish War of Independence, which lasted from May 1919 till June 1923, resulted in the dissolution of the Ottoman Empire—the fall of the Turkish monarchy and of the Islamic caliphate, mirroring the fate of European *anciens régimes*—and saw the emergence of a republican nationalism that followed a trajectory of mass-based parties similar to that of interwar Europe. Mustafa Kemal Atatürk, the leader of the revolutionary forces and first president of the Republic of Turkey, set up a series of modernizing reforms, ranging from constitutional rights and representative institutions to the building of infrastructure and industrialization, the creation of an educational system, the establishment of a unified national language, and the employment of nationalist rhetoric, among other things, that mirrored similar developments in Italy and other European countries.[10]

In India, the war gave further impulse to nationalist movements, disappointed with the limited autonomy that the Montagu-Chelmsford reforms and the Government of India Act of 1919 granted Indians, especially after the sacrifices the Indian troops had made in support of the British military efforts during the First World War and the succeeding Anglo-Afghan war of 1919.[11] In China, the nationalist impetus that ensued at Versailles from the unfair compensation for the Chinese contribution to the war against the Central Empires triggered the anti-imperialist May 4th Movement, which fueled a widespread political participation of the masses in nationalist and communist movements. As Rebecca Karl comments, after the turmoil of May 1919, "mass politics was here to stay, and any political movement would require at least lip service to 'the masses.'"[12]

Japan benefited the most from the First World War, despite its comparatively minor engagement. It acquired new territories in China from the dissolution of the German Empire (Shandong), a permanent seat on the Council of the League of Nations, and, for the first time, international recognition as one of the world's major nation-empires.[13] The new international situation affected Japan both in its colonies and domestically. In annexed Korea, Japan was forced to change its colonial policies in response to the widespread anticolonial, independentist rebellions of the March 1st Movement.[14] Domestically, it opened a season of popular participation in party politics and labor unions, which, however, did not alter the authoritarian state institutions set up by the Meiji Constitution of 1889.[15] In short, the combination of mass politics, the rise of revolutionary communist and labor movements, and the nationalistic impetus of the interwar period that fueled the rise to power of Fascism in Italy constituted a global condition that affected the positive reaction toward Mussolini's regime among the traditional political and economic elites as well as the leaders of anticolonial nationalist movements.

Praise and congratulations for Mussolini came from all over. In Great Britain, both Winston Churchill and Austen Chamberlain admired him. As Peter Neville argues, while "foreigners noticed that Mussolini seemed to be more interested in making press statements than engaging in orthodox diplomacy," by the time of the Locarno Conference of 1925 "Mussolini was beginning to win important foreign admirers. Austen Chamberlain, British Foreign Secretary from 1924 to 1929, was one. Winston Churchill was another, while the US Ambassador to Italy, Richard Washburn Child, was one of Mussolini's most uncritical devotees."[16]

In the United States, Mussolini was regarded as the leader who had succeeded better than any of his predecessors in solving the chronic Italian pathologies of social disorder and political inefficacy. "Conservatives," Robert A. Rosenbaum observes, "admired Mussolini far more than liberals did."[17] But across the political spectrum and especially among the most prominent businessmen, the shared belief that "Mussolini had prevented a Communist takeover of Italy" cemented his reputation within the country.[18] There were certainly contrarian views. For example, the day after the appointment of Mussolini as prime minister, against the prevailingly positive reactions of the media and of the economic and political elites, the American journalist Carleton Beals, who at the time was a lecturer at the University of Rome while freelancing for *The Nation*, added a premonitory note in his diary:

> More rain . . . driving over the towers of Rome . . . rattling on my balcony as I type these lines. Giornata triste![19] Grim October in Italy whirls to its grave.
>
> Overhead, just clearing the roofs, circles an aëroplane through the gray mist. Mussolini has come to Rome. By grace of the king and destiny and his own genius, minister of the realm—in all but name, dictator of Italy . . . "La paix est signée, le drame est fini," as Cavour once wrote.
>
> . . . From this day, October 30, 1922, political democracy means as little as it did under the sway of Cromwell. It makes no difference that the herd has bent

> the neck willingly to the new yoke. The present Chamber of Deputies, with its hurried, nervous attestations of loyalty to Fascism, has as little significance (or as much) as the Rump or Praisegod Barebone's Parliament. If necessary, a new Pride's Purge can be invoked to eliminate the anti-Fascist deputies.
>
> But these are trifles to be memorized in textbooks in future centuries. The significant thing: a new era has begun in Italy—as it began in Rome with the dictatorship of Sulla. The events of these last few days are a part of a European tendency that began with the Great War, embraced the Russian revolution, that may not end in our generation.[20]

Nonetheless, positive voices prevailed. In 1931 the president of Columbia University, Nicholas Murray Butler, welcomed the new class of undergraduates with words of praise for Mussolini, admitting, "It is rather startling for convinced believers in democracy to observe that [dictatorship] appears to bring into authority and power men of far greater intelligence, far strong[er] character and far more courage than does [democracy]."[21] In 1933 Edward M. House, who had been an advisor to Woodrow Wilson, reported that there was "considerable sentiment favorable to a Mussolini sort of dictatorship in conservative circles in America."[22] And as late as 1939 General Dwight Eisenhower confessed that he had "some degree of admiration for Mussolini."[23] Italian immigrants had established Fascio branches in New York, Cleveland, Philadelphia, and other, smaller US cities beginning in the early 1920s.[24] Ezra Pound was, notoriously, a great admirer and follower of Mussolini; his authority, for Pound, "comes as Eirugina proclaimed authority comes, 'from right reason' and from the general fascist conviction that he is more likely to be right than anyone else."[25]

In Germany, Adolf Hitler never hid his admiration for Mussolini. The Nazi historian Walter Frank admitted that "in that tempestuous year of 1923, Hitler had hoped to create the Reich of his dreams in one fell swoop, much in the manner of Mussolini's 'March on Rome.' "[26] A few days after the March on Rome, on November 3, 1922, Herman Esser, chief editor of the *Völkischer Beobachter*, proclaimed that "Germany's Mussolini is called Adolf Hitler," which, for Ian Kershaw, "marked the symbolic moment when Hitler's followers invented the Führer cult."[27] Hitler himself admitted in 1941 that one should not "suppose that the events in Italy had no influence on us. The brown shirt would probably not have existed without the black shirt. The march on Rome, in October 1922, was one of the turning points of history. The mere fact that anything of the sort could be attempted, and could succeed, gave us impetus."[28] The history of ideological and stylistic influences, transferences, and hybridizations between Italian Fascism and German National Socialism goes beyond the scope of this book.[29]

Admiration for Mussolini's charisma and his successes as Duce abounded. In November 1923 the king of Spain, Alfonso XIII, during a diplomatic trip to Italy, introduced the new head of state, General Miguel Primo de Rivera, as "my Mussolini."[30] Corneliu Zelea Codreanu, leader of the Romanian League for National Christian Defense, recounted how "I heard the news of the huge Fascist eruption: the March on Rome and Mussolini's victory. I rejoiced as much as if it were my own country's victory. . . . Mussolini, the brave man who trampled the dragon underfoot, was one of us."[31] In Great Britain, Rotha Lintorn-Orman, founder of the British Fascists (1923), the first political movement explicitly dedicated to spreading Fascism in the world, "admired Mussolini as a man who had dealt firmly with the socialist menace."[32] Later, Sir Oswald Mosley, who in 1932 founded the British Union of Fascists, "after a visit to see Mussolini's International Fascist exhibition in the spring . . . organized the first large BUF march in June 1932 when 1,000 Blackshirts marched through London."[33] In Portugal, the professor of economics Antonio de Oliveira Salazar established a regime of dictatorial corporatist authoritarianism (Estado Novo) that shared with Mussolini's Fascism some key features, especially in political economics, but never hesitated to publicly reject the style and ideology of the Duce as "pagan Caesarism."[34] To confirm his opposition to the methods of Italian Fascism, he violently repressed Rolão Preto's *camisas-azuis*, or Blueshirts (Movimento Nacional-Sindicalista), which in 1933 "emerged as a significant political force . . . , advocating an amalgam of native organic nationalism imbued with loyalty to the Church and the monarchy and adapting 'fascist' ideas largely inspired by Mussolini's movement in Italy."[35]

In France, Georges Valois, a journalist and syndicalist friend of Georges Sorel, member of the Action Française and in 1925 founder of the political party Le Faisceau, greatly admired Mussolini, admitting that "we were all won over by the personal prestige of the leader of the Fascist revolution just as one is won over by any powerful personality."[36] His plan of becoming a French Mussolini, as he admitted, failed.[37] But the Duce harvested followers among the creators of what Robert Paxton called French rural Fascism: not only Roger Grand, president of the Union Centrale des Syndicats Agricoles between from 1934 to 1937, "made no secret of his admiration for Mussolini and for his belief that corporatism had been the salvation of other European states in trouble,"[38] but also the nationalist agrarianist Henri Dorgères, who in 1929 founded the Comités de Défense Paysanne (also known as the *chemises vertes* or Greenshirts), claimed that, in order to defend the interests of an agrarian autarchy, the strategies of Fascism had to be pursued in France too: "Only a strong state could bring us out of our predicament. We want the results that Mussolini obtained"; and again, "I believe in the development of a movement similar to Fascism," he claimed. "If you knew, French peasants, what Mussolini accomplished for the Italian peasant, you will all demand a Mussolini for France."[39]

In the Middle East and Mediterranean Africa, Arab nationalism responded positively to Mussolini's propaganda of liberation, targeting in particular those Islamic territories under the colonial control of England and France.[40] As Stanley Payne, put it, "From an early date Mussolini chose to present himself as a promoter of Arab nationalism, above all for the expansion of Italian influence."[41] By 1939 some nationalist groups in Syria, Egypt, Lebanon, and Iraq had adopted the fashion of shirted movements, but they remained at the margin of political life.[42] Their actual support and favorable disposition toward Mussolini, however, rapidly waned with the intensification of Italian colonial expansion in Africa.

In the rest of Asia, Hindu nationalist elites found inspiration in Benito Mussolini's transformative successes in Italy, and such political leaders as Subhas Chandra Bose, Syama Prasad Mookerjee, and Rash Behari Bose, as well as such thinkers and activists as Keshav Ballram Hedgewar and Balakrishna Shivram Moonje, among others, not only wrote positively of Mussolini's charisma and political strategies but sought to meet with him and entertain a lasting relationship with Italian Fascists. Hedgewar's subversive organization Rashtriya Swayamsewak Sangh (RSS) was explicitly modeled upon Blackshirts and Balilla groups in Italy.[43] Moonje, during a meeting with "Signor Mussolini, one of the great men of the European world," who had admitted a "great respect for Gandhi," told the Duce that, in his view, "every aspiring and growing nation needs such organisations [Italy's Blackshirts and Balilla]. India needs them most for her military regeneration. . . . I shall have no hesitation to raise my voice from the public platform both in India and England whenever occasion may arise in praise of your Balilla and Fascist organisations."[44]

In China, the word "fascism" began circulating in the early 1930s in the phonetic rendition of *faxisi zhuyi* (法西斯主义) and found fertile ground within Chiang Kai-shek's Blueshirts Society (Lanyishe [藍衣社]), which found inspiration in Fascist corporatism and violent suppression of socialist and syndicalist activism.[45] Although the relationship between Italy and Nationalist China deteriorated after the colonial war in Ethiopia, in 1935 the Generalissimo addressed the Blueshirts saying: "What China needs today is not an 'ism' that discusses what kind of ideal future China will have, but a method that will save China at the present moment. . . . Fascism is a stimulant for a declining society. Can fascism save China? We answer: yes. Fascism is what China now most needs. . . . At the present stage of China's critical situation, fascism is a wonderful medicine exactly suited to China, and the only spirit that can save it."[46]

In Japan, too, the rise of Fascism stirred the attention not only of the political elites, but of popular news media as well. Defined early on as a prototypical example of an ultranationalist party (*kokusuitō* [国粋党]), Mussolini's regime was scrupulously analyzed in dispatches that the Japanese ambassador to Italy, Ochiai Kentarō, regularly sent to the minister of foreign affairs, Uchida Kōsai, beginning August 25, 1922.[47] Mussolini soon entered the social imaginary thanks to the chronicles of a fanatic follower, Shimoi Harukichi, who had participated in D'Annunzio's Fiume endeavor, was in Rome when Mussolini was given the mandate to form his first cabinet, and engaged in relentless attempts to popularize the Italian brand of nationalism in Japan, with particular emphasis on martial spirit, violent resolution, and faith in the charismatic leadership of the Duce.[48] Mussolini was briefly the object of popular fandom, especially between 1927 and 1931. In a 1927 newspaper article, Mussolini was hailed as the best "among today's world leaders."[49] The hero worship accorded the Duce, portrayed in popular *manga*, theatrical pieces, and musicals, identified in his resoluteness and courage the way to heal all the contradictions of modern society.[50] However, popular enthusiasm soon plummeted, and Italian Fascism was rejected both by right-wing ideologues, who searched within Asian traditions for the roots of a Japanese nationalism,[51] and by state technocrats, who saw in German Nazism a more satisfactory model for the Japanese state apparatus.[52]

It was in Latin America, and more precisely in Argentina, that Italian Fascism gathered favor and established lasting connections. As Federico Finchelstein argues, "Argentina in the first half of the twentieth century was often presented on both sides of the Atlantic as a natural receptacle for fascism. . . . Mussolini himself certainly thought in their terms, and he targeted Argentina as the most important country for fascist imperialism in Latin America."[53] The Argentine ambassador in Rome, Ángel Gallardo, saluted Mussolini's first cabinet as a much-needed "nationalist reaction against the communist and antimilitarist movement."[54] Stanley Payne considered Argentina, even before the presidency of Juan Perón, to have been "the home of the most continuous and the most ideologically developed radical right in Latin America," which was even more receptive toward Italian Fascism than toward German Nazism because of its links with (and more benevolent attitude toward) the Catholic Church. After the Second World War, Perón judged in retrospect that "Mussolini was the greatest man of our century, but he committed certain disastrous errors," allying with Nazi Germany foremost among them.[55] In Brazil, a cluster of extreme right-wing political parties, from the Legião do Cruzeiro do Sul to the Partido Fascista Brasileiro, were receptive toward the ideologies and methods of Italian Fascism and German National Socialism, but they remained largely on the margins of political life.[56]

This brief panoramic view of international reactions to the rise of Fascism in Italy is not meant to cover the transnational reach of the Italian regime. On the one hand, it simply registers the global attention Fascism attracted, to the extent that the number of foreign reporters active in Italy grew during the first decade of the regime.[57] On the other, it highlights the fact that Fascism and, in particular, the charisma of its Duce, Benito Mussolini, met with a largely positive response around the world from both political and economic elites and public opinion in general (at least in the 1920s and early 1930s): From the perspective of the outside observer, Mussolini had solved the chronic problems of the irresoluteness of Italian governments and the immobilism and corruption of its bureaucratic apparatus. Most important, Mussolini was perceived as the only leader capable of stopping the threat of a communist upheaval in Italy and, to a large extent, also helping curb the growth of socialist parties and labor movements, reestablishing the conditions for industrial production and investments that had worried foreign economic agents.[58]

As Martin Blinkhorn notes, Mussolini posited a new model of rulership for the right that took the institutions of liberal democracy as its legitimating and legal ground for the establishment of an authoritarianism that was distinct from the model of the *anciens régimes* or the one proposed by revolutionary conservatives built on a spiritual and cultural aristocracy: "The *fascisant* imitators—[Francisco] Franco, [Ionnis] Metaxas, King Carol [II of Romania], [Antanas] Smetona, even [António de Oliveira] Salazar and [Marshal Philippe] Pétain, and the rest—intuitively grasped an underlying truth that analyses based on fascist theory and elite culture have tended to avoid. This was that more often than not 'fascism,' as ideology and stylistic veneer or as political movement, was something the conservative authoritarian right could use, and when appropriate discard, but which they had serious reason to fear in only rare instances and exceptional circumstances."[59] The Italian case is a perfect example of this tendency. Before October 1922, Fascism had expanded its following to larger chunks of the middle classes, especially in the rural areas, but Mussolini would not have reached power without the active support of traditional conservative forces. In terms of strategies, rhetoric, and only marginally ideology, Italian Fascism had transformative effects on the way worldwide conservative forces organized themselves and adopted some of its corporative solutions, especially after the crisis of 1929.[60]

In a sense, Fascism's "effective collaboration with traditional elites" was less "uneasy" than Paxton asserted.[61] As Aristotle Kallis has argued, "So long as this 'fascism,' in its particular Italian and/or German guise or as a combined force through the Axis alliance, was seen as 'successful' and victorious, others observed it as a critically empowering precedent that had opened up the field of opportunity in an increasingly radical and uncompromising direction. The kaleidoscope of ensuing hybrid ideological-political outcomes were [*sic*] not just different from their sources of inspiration or from one another but also occasionally even more radical in some respects than their prototypes, infused with communicative ingredients that only made sense in their originating particular national-cultural setting."[62]

Mussolini's rise to power did not pass unnoticed. From the March on Rome onward, Fascism occupied the front pages of newspapers around the world. As positive paradigm or, less frequently, cautionary warning, it became, soon after the affirmation of "really existing communism" in the former Russian Empire, evidence of how the fragile world order of liberal democracies established in the wake of the First World War could end in the blink of an eye.

The Invention of Antifascism

It can be argued that not just "fascism" but "antifascism," too, was invented by Mussolini, directly and indirectly. Two clusters of evidence sustain this claim: the first semantic, the second political.

It was Mussolini and, later, other fellow Fascists that first coined the word *antifascismo* (antifascism) as an umbrella term that included all those political forces, no matter their ideological orientation, that opposed the Fasci and the PNF even before the March on Rome. Mussolini used it for the first time in an article in *Il popolo d'Italia* of January 2, 1921 to refer to the Socialist Party, his historical political adversary as a champion of antifascism.[63] Socialists were the main addressees of the accusation of antifascism in most articles of 1921, but occasionally other political forces could be included:[64] Luigi Sturzo's PPI was so labeled on May 31 and June 1;[65] Giolitti's Unione Liberale (Liberal Union) on June 7;[66] the Associazione Nazionale dei Combattenti, also on June 7;[67] and the Republican Party on July 16.[68] Then, in an article dated November 19, 1921, Mussolini included them all: "Because anarchists, republicans, populars [Sturzo's PPI], socialists, communists, *cagoians*,[69] conservatives, revolutionaries, bourgeois, and proletarians all identify themselves in, pair up against, and support each other—*wie Hunde auf freier Gasse*, as Heine would say—in the name of antifascism; a concoction that, deep inside, must be quite disgusting even to those who make it up."[70]

After Mussolini's rise to power, the occurrences of "antifascism" in his parliamentary speeches and at rallies or in interviews to domestic and international newspapers became sporadic. In these cases, with the exception of few references to the former antiwar faction,[71] the term was always vague, undefined, having lost all identifying attributions to former political parties. "Antifascism" was rather used indeterminately as the antithesis of Fascism, in an *ante litteram* Schmittian sense of identifying the "enemies"—such as, for instance, when he declared on March 23, 1924 that "you have to be either for or against. Either for Fascism or for Antifascism. Whoever is not with us is against us. The political struggle in Italy never had a more precise simplification that this one."[72]

Antifascists were all those who not only opposed but actually hindered the mission of Fascism. Since Fascism, in those years, defined itself as coextensive with government, state, and nation (the *patria*, or fatherland), being antifascist meant to be an enemy of the Italian nation, and so it was necessary that antifascists be eliminated: at first, eliminated from public life (such as, for instance, with law no. 1227 of August 28, 1931, which required membership in the PNF of all university professors), then from working life (via mandatory enrollment in the Fascist labor union or membership in the PNF), and ultimately from society by means of forced *confino* (confinement),[73] exile abroad,[74] imprisonment,[75] or death.[76]

The Fascist notion of antifascism had profound political implications: It created the conditions for the formation of alliances between forces as distant as communists, socialists, democrats, members of Sturzo's PPI, and even liberal conservatives such as Benedetto Croce. This transparty and transideological alliance laid the foundation, after the end of the Second World War, for the formation of a new political landscape and the creation of the first Italian republic in 1946–47. Open and organized antagonism to the Fascist regime in the form of antifascism did not, however, take shape for a long time.

The socialists and communists were soon excluded from political life and outlawed after the authoritarian turn of 1925, but these movements had been already severely curtailed by the widespread violence of Squadristi in the weeks after October 31, 1922.[77] The other moderate forces of the center and center right initially voted in support of the Mussolini's first cabinet—voting also in favor of the king's mandate to Mussolini allowing him to discretionally govern via executive orders. The PPI supported Mussolini's first cabinet, and two of their members were offered the positions of ministers of Treasury and of Labor. The following year, however, Sturzo and others condemned the totalitarian policies of Mussolini, determining the collapse of the PPI itself: Sturzo, Alcide De Gasperi, and others were forced to resign (having lost the support of the Vatican, which viewed Mussolini's regime favorably) and eventually into exile; some maintained an ambiguously neutralist position, while others entered the PNF.[78] Croce enthusiastically supported Mussolini's speech in Naples on October 24, 1922 and voted in favor of the Fascist government not only in 1922 but also after the assassination of Giacomo Matteotti in 1924, with the hope, expressed in an interview published in *Il giornale d'Italia*, that Mussolini's government "could not and should not have been anything other than a bridge leading to the restoration of a more severe liberal regime, for a stronger state."[79] When Croce's hopes for state-imposed liberalism were not realized, he became the head of a conservative-liberal opposition to the regime, the first action of which was the publication of the "Manifesto degli intellettuali non fascisti" on May 1, 1925.[80]

As a creation of Fascism—deriving, that is, from the regime's censoring and controlling apparatus—antifascism was not at first an organized movement: it involved members of different political parties and social categories that ranged from army officers, bureaucrats, and intellectuals to the members of the working classes. It was ideologically heterogeneous, unplanned, spontaneous, and unevenly distributed in different regions. The regime operated systematically to curb resistance and maintained close control over potentially subversive activities thanks to a vast network of informants.[81]

Among the early antifascists forced into exile were politicians, journalists, and academics of different political leanings, among them conservative liberals such as Carlo Sforza, Francesco Saverio Nitti, Alcide De Gasperi, and Luigi Sturzo; progressive liberals such as Gaetano Salvemini, Piero Gobetti, Arturo Labriola, Giuseppe Antonio Borgese, Emilio Lussu, Carlo Rosselli, and Max Salvadori; socialists such as Filippo Turati, Pietro Nenni, and Giuseppe Saragat; and communists such as Ignazio Silone, Palmiro Togliatti, and Angelo Tasca.[82] Others were arrested, like Antonio Gramsci. Still others died as a result of repeated beatings by Fascist thugs, like Piero Gobetti, or simply killed by Fascist *sicarios*, like the brothers Carlo and Nello Rosselli. Because of the efficiency of the surveilling apparatus and the popular support for the Fascist regime in the second half of the 1920s and the early 1930s, antifascist activism operated largely outside Italy. Communist opposition to the regime operated from Moscow, while the Socialists had their headquarters in France, like the Liberals and the Republicans; Sturzo escaped to London and, after a brief sojourn in Paris, settled in New York City. Anarchists chose Spain or France. Their writings contributed to the formation of the early interpretations of Fascism.

Antifascist resistance found new energy after the armistice of September 8, 1943 and the formation of the puppet state of the Repubblica Sociale

Italiana.[83] It was the experience of armed resistance against "Nazifascism" that gave unity of organization and intent to movements and individuals that until that moment had operated largely autonomously and separately. Antifascist resistance, loosely guided from Rome by a Comitato di Liberazione Nazionale (Committee for National Liberation; CLN), had members of different political orientations, sometimes grouped in ideologically homogeneous bands (such as, for instance, the communist Brigate Garibaldi [Garibaldi Brigades]; Giustizia e libertà [Justice and Liberty], part of the center-left Partito d'Azione [Action Party]; and the socialist Brigate Matteotti [Matteotti Brigades]), but often in groups that were either mixed or apolitical. Monarchists fought side by side with communists and anarchists, Catholics with atheists, liberals with socialists; intellectuals and illiterates with no previous interest in politics were all bound together by the common goal of the fight against Fascism and the Nazi invaders.[84] The antifascism of the resistance laid the political foundations for the new state that would be built after the war: The spirit of antifascism permeated the constitution of the Italian republic, approved on December 22, 1947 and promulgated a few days later, on December 27.[85] The active antifascism of the 1943–45 Italian Civil War was a workshop where another sort of nationalization of Italians occurred, different from the one Fascism had imposed for twenty years:[86] It laid the foundation for a new kind of democratic participation and a newly felt sense of popular sovereignty.[87]

During the Civil War of 1943–45, antifascism, no longer simply an ideological and political struggle but an actual armed fight against Fascism, often cruel and ruthless, became the laboratory for the realization of a civic ideal of democratic participation, often egalitarian and subject to rules of coexistence and negotiation, which realized in daily experiences a social praxis that Fascism had negated for twenty years in the name of national renewal. The harsh fights in the mountain ranges of northern and central Italy revealed the lie of the pantomime of sovereignty, the simulacrum of participation, that Fascism had enforced in twenty years of totalitarian power. Antifascist resistance involved army soldiers who refused to fight for the RSI, police officers, intellectuals, bourgeois, members of the working classes (often illiterate), women and men working together, often with the collaboration of children; it required a network of logistics, intelligence, and food supplies, and it united people from different political backgrounds and social origins, all equalized by the fight.

The antifascist resistance against Fascism was not just a myth constructed in the immediate postwar period by the Left in order to assure their cultural hegemony, as revisionist journalists-turned-historians and opinion-makers in the last three decades have been maintaining.[88] Francesco De Gregori's

1982 song quoted in the epigraph of this book captures the shared sense of popular agency in the making of history that so many letters, diaries, memoirs, and novels of the antifascist resistance show:[89] "History is us, nobody should feel excluded."

The claim that Italian postwar democracy is rooted in the social and political ground that the antifascist resistance had prepared is not a romantic idealization. The partisans' war had certainly been subjected to processes of celebration and mythicization during the difficult years of reconstruction of the newly birthed Italian Republic.[90] Its effective role in the defeat of Nazifascism should not be overstated and was probably marginal or at least not indispensable from a purely military perspective.[91] But at the social and political levels, its importance was surely critical to the postwar reconstruction of Italian society and its redemption after twenty years of Fascist rule. The sort of horizontal sociability that the antifascist struggle imposed on the partisans—be they fighters or simply supporters—resulted often from the reduction of daily life to its crude essentials: poor food, provisional lodgings, and constant fears of being captured, tortured, and killed by the Black Brigades and their informants.[92] The resistance was violent, often gratuitously so;[93] there were private vendettas and indiscriminate killings. However, far from justifying today's revisionism, it must be remembered that these acts happened not only in a time of war, but also in response of two decades of Fascist violence that was quantitatively and qualitatively incomparable.[94]

That antifascism and antifascist resistance constituted the premises for postwar reconstruction of a democratic order was certainly not exclusive to Italy. Much has been written on the importance of the French Resistance for the construction of the French Fourth Republic.[95] The war against Nazifascism was the basis for the world order built after 1945: Antifascism was a force of union during the war effort, and disunion—grounded in the clash between two different conceptions of antifascism, the liberal and the communist—afterward.[96]

More relevant to the scope of this study, antifascism was the source of new definitions of "fascism" that opposed the ones imposed by the Fascist regime. These were diverse, often mutually contradictory, as they were inspired by different theoretical and political convictions.[97] As Claudio Pavone hypothesized, "It is probably during the Civil War that the word 'fascism' took on, with particular intensity, a meaning that went beyond the concrete and specific historical experience of Fascism, ending up designating a human type negatively connoted under all public and private profiles."[98]

Most if not all interpretations and analyses of Italian Fascism by postwar historians, sociologists, and political scientists derived from—or were at least anticipated by—the writings of antifascist thinkers and activists during the twenty years of Fascist rule. This is no hyperbolic reductionism of an antifascist: it can be easily verified in the language and bibliographical sources of postwar scholarship. Indeed, as even a revisionist historian like Renzo De Felice, who critically dismissed antifascism as a meaningless "state ideology" of the Italian republic,[99] acknowledged, "Books, newsletters, *pamphlets*, correspondence, inquiries, articles, conferences: Between 1919 and 1945 the *literature* on *fascism* was immense. The simple observation of this fact shows how much Ernst Nolte came close to the truth when he spoke of an 'era of fascism.'"[100]

If we extend the appellation of "antifascism" to all those voices that were critical of or at least nonaligned with the regime, what they all shared was a resistance to accepting the ideologically charged self-definitions of "fascism" given by Mussolini and others. Their analyses proposed alternative semantic markers to "fascism" that were antagonistic to the ones imposed by the regime. Contemporary critics developed new definitions on the basis of observations and analyses of what the regime did rather than what it preached, and of the social, economic, institutional, and political impacts of its rule. For these reasons, it is not surprising to discover a conceptual and interpretive affinity between the writings of Mussolini-era antifascists and those of postwar scholars. And just as Mussolini-era antifascists proposed different but equally legitimate interpretations of Fascism on the basis of their different epistemological and political orientations, postwar analyses, too, reproduced many of those differences.

Early Reactions to Fascism

Some critical analyses of Fascism preceded Mussolini's rise to power. To quote three early instances, one from the right, one from the progressive center, and one from the left, the writings of Mario Missiroli, Piero Gobetti, and Antonio Gramsci can be considered precursors of later antifascism. Their analyses, with the hindsight of today's perspective, read like precognitions.

Mario Missiroli, the child prodigy of Italian journalism and close friend of Giovanni Gentile, Benedetto Croce, and Georges Sorel, saw in Fascism as early as 1921 a movement symptomatic of the complex dynamics that the First World War had left in its wake. In the immediate aftermath of the war, he claimed, the Fascist movement, with its connotations of "romanticism and idealism," appealed to the youth of the middle classes: "Disappointed by socialism, abandoned by the bourgeoisie, misunderstood by the world of official culture, these young people looked toward themselves and became passionate about their personal action: individual value was a refuge for the imagination and the heart."[101]

Missiroli considered the members of the younger generation of the middle class to be the ones who, being hit the hardest among all the classes by the war, were turning to nationalist ideals and Fascism for consolation: "The middle classes were the most unfortunate. They gave soldiers and officers to the war, contributed more than any other to resistance and victory, and were the worst rewarded. The war economy favored the big bourgeoisie, the workers, and the peasants, but it has impoverished the middle classes, those classes that in Italy form public opinion."[102] Fascism did more than offer them an excuse to unleash their social and political frustration in the violent actions of its squads against the Socialist headquarters, the offices of the newspaper *Avanti!*, and the urban and rural labor unions: "The economically beaten classes try to redeem themselves through political struggle. . . . It is the time of the conservatives, the time of the reactionaries."[103]

It was not only disillusioned youths from the middle class who participated in this simulacrum of revolution: "Old moderates, high officials who did not want to be discharged, landlords, merchants, shopkeepers, retail speculators, landowners: an incapable old bourgeoisie, who would have traded everything in order not to feel troubled in their privileges and in their own comforts, limps after the Fascists, displays the flags, and shouts, in a nasal voice, 'Viva l'Italia!' "[104] Missiroli concluded that Fascism, which violently revolted against those who wanted to bring a workers' revolution to Italy, ended up becoming the party that united the disaffected middle class with the old bourgeoisie: The latter realized that the Fascist revolutionary "social policies" were the only way to preserve their privileges in a context of social turmoil; the former, that "inert, leaden, opaque mass, without ideals and without faith," found in Fascism the expression of their reactionary, antisocialist tendencies.

Missiroli's criticism of Fascism during the violence of the *biennio rosso* incurred Mussolini's rage, who decried him as a "perfidious Jesuit and most solemn coward."[105] The two even engaged in a duel with swords on May 12, 1922.[106] On the day of the March on Rome, Missiroli wrote an editorial in *Il Secolo* in which he foresaw Mussolini's rise to power, stating that "the power of Fascism is enough for demanding the Government through violent pressure. Unfortunately, violence can give the government, but it is not enough to keep it."[107] Missiroli remained editor in chief of *Il Secolo* until July 1923, when Mussolini had him fired. In 1926, thanks to the intervention of his friend Leandro Arpinati, *podestà* (head of municipal administration) of Bologna, he became a member of the PNF and returned to practice journalism. In contrast to his earlier stance, he was now authoring articles supporting the regime, including its racist laws and the alliance with Nazi Germany.[108] After 1943, in a new feat of political transformism, he collaborated with the Resistance.[109]

Piero Gobetti, another child prodigy of Italian journalism, was one of the most prestigious young voices of progressive liberalism in the transwar period. A student of Luigi Einaudi and a follower of Gaetano Salvemini, as editor in chief of the journal *Energie nove* he engaged in a fierce competition against Gramsci's *L'ordine nuovo* for hegemony over Turin's cultural and political scene. During the *biennio rosso*, Gobetti increasingly sided with the labor movement and, while remaining firm in his liberal, non-Marxist orientation, befriended a number of socialist intellectuals, Gramsci in particular. On February 12, 1922, he founded *La rivoluzione liberale*, a weekly liberal progressive political journal that, after Mussolini's rise to power, gave a voice to those politicians whom the regime had silenced, from Gramsci to Sturzo. It was in its pages that Gobetti launched his critical campaign against Fascism.

The journal itself, as Claudio Panizza observed, made of Fascism a "theoretical countermodel for [Gobetti's] notion of the 'liberal revolution.'"[110] The critical articles were not just polemical pieces for political agitation, but early analyses of the causes and characteristics of Fascism itself, which for Gobetti was an epochal moment in the "autobiography of the nation." In an article he signed as "Antiguelfo" on May 28, 1922, he claimed that Fascism, in its agrarian phase, was "a valid element of the Italian political struggle" because it expressed "the dominant type of political organization" favored by the landowning bourgeoise in the Italian countryside.[111] There, "Fascism was the reaction against the revolution. Legitimate and victorious where the revolution was instead weak, talkative, and hypocritical. It is this undeniable 'legitimacy' of the reaction that fills our soul with sadness."[112] Fascism, a prototypical counterrevolutionary movement, was "the thermometer of our crisis, the measure of the people's powerlessness to create their own state. But precisely for this reason it becomes naive to ask Fascism for a positive program of reconstruction."[113] Fascism could not substitute nor hope to become the state, because "in reality, no party can replace the State."[114]

Fascism, for Gobetti, could never realize itself as state because it was not a political force capable of producing lasting effects on the nation. Fascism's reactive, agitational character prevented it from becoming an authoritative governing agent. Fascists' praise of action, an expression of their political weakness, was a symptom of their social composition: "The movement has gathered all the 'stragglers': the veterans of the scoundrel Futurist experience, the ones who are exasperated by a bilious impotence, the ones exuberant with optimism."[115] It was also sign of the intellectual and ideological poverty of the movement: "The theorist Mussolini has never written a book, his brilliant intuitions never took shape in an expression that was more than contingent. . . . I cannot imagine Mussolini otherwise than in the guise of the most audacious and troubled leader of a brigade of mercenaries; or, better, as the primitive leader of a savage gang possessed of a dogmatic terror that does not permit reflection. His most characteristic posture is itself an anachronism."[116]

Mussolini, a thug disguised as an intellectual, was the perfect man for his times. For Gobetti, "he remains divided and indecisive between moments of coherence so dogmatic that they become clumsy and of anarchically unjustified outbursts of exuberance. He needs a world in which the leader is not asked to be a politician."[117] But that was precisely the world the first global conflict had created. Mussolini's party, caught between the paradigms of insurrection and legality, revolution and the preservation of law, order, and property, reflected not only its substantial ideological and political vacuousness, but also a contradiction inherent in Italian society. On the one hand, Gobetti argued, "Mussolini hides under the dilemma of insurrection v. legality the internal conflict of Fascism, which is no longer able to express its agrarian substance in a frankly reactionary ideology."[118] On the other, that contradiction mirrored "Italy's most tragic weakness," with "its inability to create and feed a reactionary party."[119] In Italy, he continued, nationalism was only pseudonationalism, revolution pseudorevolution, and socialism pseudosocialism. Fascism was simply a symptom of Italy's political immaturity: It "indicate[d] very clearly the uncertainties of our industrialists and agrarians in their political action."[120]

The contradictoriness of the movement paradoxically empowered Mussolini: he, "now aware of the unpreparedness of industrialists, crushe[d] their tendential republicanism and intentions of reaction, exploit[ed] all the strength of his traditional demagogy, and use[d] Fascism as a maneuver for his personal careerism."[121] In that sense, for Gobetti, Fascism aptly expressed the autobiography of the nation: It was the symptom of its immaturity.

In September 1922, on the eve of the March on Rome, Gobetti was still skeptical that Fascism could succeed: "Fascism cannot justify itself with a nonrevolutionary attitude: the only justification can come from its achievements, which we are unable to see for now."[122] Afterward, Gobetti had no choice but to accept it as a surprising fait accompli, which he interpreted: "The secret of Mussolini's success lies in his intuition of the theatrical nature of Italians," who on the Neapolitan stage "childishly applauded Mussolini's clumsy intentions of educating and protecting the masses!"[123] But Gobetti still believed it could not last: "Fascism does not even have the shadow of a program, not even an economic perspective. . . . Born as it is to carry out an activity that is contingently domestic, even though very profound, it is naturally unsuitable, for its own historical destiny, to propose an issue that goes beyond the homeland."[124] Gobetti's view on the events of October 31 were clear: "Mussolini has no political competence," and "the Fascist 'revolution' is not a revolution, but a coup d'état carried out by an oligarchy, through the humiliation of all seriousness and political conscience—with student goliardicism." Mussolini "has no other strength [than the Blackshirts squads] to lean on." Gobetti believed that "universal suffrage is the instrument, imperfect but unique, for the political and moral formation of the masses (in the long term). Mussolini will make it useless by doing the elections with the dealers, plunging back to ten years ago."[125] In short, for Gobetti, writing in the immediate aftermath of the March on Rome, Fascism had no future.

The other early voice of antifascist opposition was Antonio Gramsci, one of the founders of the PCd'I and editor in chief of *L'ordine nuovo*. It was from the pages of that weekly journal of socialist culture that Gramsci prophetically wrote on July 27, 1921, in an article revealingly entitled "Colpo di stato" (Coup d'état), that "today there are two repressive and punitive devices in Italy: Fascism and the bourgeois state. A simple calculation leads us to predict that at some point the ruling class will want to officially amalgamate these two apparatuses and that it will break the opposing resistances of the bureaucracy with a direct blow against the central governing bodies. We will then have the 'coup d'état.'"[126]

Gramsci had already written about the intimate connection between Mussolini's movement and the petty bourgeoisie, and between Fascism and big industry, which had financially supported the movement since its beginning.[127] For him, Fascism was an international phenomenon. In this he anticipated all the other theorists who were linking various forms of violent reaction in Europe: "The phenomenon of 'fascism' is not only Italian, just as the formation of the Communist Party is not only Italian. 'Fascism' is the preparatory phase for the restoration of the state, that is, of a hardening of the capitalist reaction, of an exacerbation of the capitalist struggle against the most vital needs of the proletarian class. Fascism is the illegality of capitalist violence. . . . This development is universal; it has already occurred in part and will continue to develop also in Italy."[128]

Gramsci, like Gobetti, doubted that Fascism could by itself become a governing force: "Fascism, as a national phenomenon, cannot establish its own state, cannot organize itself into central power."[129] But, unlike Gobetti, he did not attribute this to any deficiencies or failings on the part of Mussolini, but rather to the fact that Fascism "is already confused with the state, . . . it already finds its focus in the current Giolitti government; Fascism . . . is a contradiction, it is not an antithesis; it is the face of the Giolitti government itself, it has nothing revolutionary about it, because it is unable to dialectically overcome its apparent opponent, because it is unable to replace him."[130] Fascism, Gramsci argued in a famous essay in *L'ordine nuovo*, was "the last 'representation' offered by the urban petty bourgeoisie in the theater of national political life."[131] In other words, for Gramsci Fascism was by no means a new form of political praxis and thought: It was just a radicalized aspect of the existing institutions of the liberal state which emerged in defense of a bourgeoisie facing a crisis of social and political legitimacy. In the presence of an unprecedented crisis that was at once economic, social, and psychological, "the petty bourgeoisie, which has definitively lost all hopes of regaining a productive function . . . , tries in every way to maintain a position of historical initiative: it apes the working class and takes to the streets. . . . This had happened: the petty bourgeoisie, which had enslaved itself to governmental power through parliamentary corruption, changes the form of its work, becomes antiparliamentary, and tries to corrupt public opinion."[132] Given these circumstances, Fascism became for Gramsci the pure expression of a disoriented petty bourgeoisies:

> *Having corrupted and ruined the parliamentary institution, the petty bourgeoisie also corrupts and ruins the other institutions [which give] fundamental support to the state: the army, the police, the judiciary.* And once the state had been weakened by the corruption of the bourgeoisie, [the class of] owners, in order to defend themselves, finance and sustain a private organization [the Fascist squads], which, to disguise their real nature, must assume "revolutionary" political attitudes and break up the most powerful defense of property, the state. . . . The petty bourgeoisie, even in this latest political incarnation as "Fascism," has definitively shown itself in its true nature of servant of capitalism and land ownership, as an agent of the counterrevolution.[133]

With the expansion of the Fascist movement, Gramsci's fears were confirmed: "Fascism presented itself as the antiparty" and had "thus become a cultural fact; it has identified itself with the barbaric and antisocial psychology of some strata of the Italian people, not yet modified by a new tradition, by the school, by coexistence in a well-ordered and well-administered state."[134] Gramsci agreed with both Missiroli and Gobetti that "Fascism is the name of the profound decomposition of Italian society, which could not fail to accompany the profound decomposition of the state and can only be explained today with reference to the low level of civilization that the Italian nation has been able to achieve in these sixty years of unitary administration."[135] Its strength, Gramsci claimed, was due only to favorable circumstances: Fascism succeeded "only because tens of thousands of state officials, especially from the public security bodies (police, royal guards, carabinieri) and the judiciary, became their moral and material accomplices."[136]

As a result of this alliance between the pseudorevolutionary force of Fascism and the apparatuses of law and order, the state falsely attributed the complete responsibility of the social disorders to the Communist Party: "The state recognizes in the fascists an independent authority and treats with them as equals, and recognizes in them the right, if pacification does not take place, to continue with impunity to burn, to assassinate, to invade cities and villages, to decree exiles and the dissolution of public administrations."[137] It was as a consequence of this analytical reasoning that Gramsci shortly thereafter foresaw the coming coup d'état in the article quoted above, fifteen months before the March on Rome.[138]

Before Mussolini's rise to power and during the early consolidation of the Fascist regime, antifascist thinkers and activists had already dismissed three of the main semantic markers that Mussolini would programmatically impose to "fascism." The conservative Missiroli, the liberal progressive Gobetti, and the Marxist Gramsci rejected the notion that Fascism was an authentic revolutionary movement, that it could speak on behalf of the nation rather than a particular social group, and that it could become a credible and authoritative force of governance and state authority. All three, despite their different conceptions of state and society, concluded that "fascism" was the name of a violent, reactionary movement that gave irrational and emotional expression to a specific class, the petty bourgeoisie (for whom Fascism became a redemptive utopia), while defending the interests of landowners and industrialists, who pragmatically supported the movement and allowed it to grow and take root in a number of northern Italian provinces. All three denied that the March on Rome was a revolutionary act and instead conceived of it as a coup d'état supported by the king and the traditional conservative elites. It is therefore hard to believe that the Fascist takeover of October 1922 was unexpected.

6

Liberals' "Fascism"

Antifascism took as many forms as there were antifascists. It consisted of a nebula of attitudes and conceptions that ranged from the most personal grievances to philosophical critique. Opposition to Fascism was sporadic and liminal during the peak years of popular consensus for the regime. It became more pronounced after the Italo-Ethiopian War, the institution of the racial laws, and the disastrous military intervention during the Second World War. It finally assumed the character of popular upheaval or, as Claudio Pavone put it, civil war during the years of the RSI (1943–45). It was often spontaneous, emotional, and strategically oriented toward an armed opposition. Rarely did it offer a reasoned defense of its antagonism to Fascism, which renders the project of extrapolating some dominant semantic conceptions of "fascism" beyond the conceptualization of intellectuals fragmentary at best.

Antifascist struggle, politically heterodox as it was, was not purely reactive, a pure negation: the fight against Fascism was conceived by all as the precondition for national reconstruction. As Claudio Natoli puts it, "One of the fundamental traits of Italian antifascism was, during the thirties, the belief—shared by all its components, from the forces of democratic orientation to those of socialist and communist inspiration—that the fall of the Fascist regime should not lead to a restoration of the old liberal state, but should instead pave the way for a deeply renewed democracy capable of combining political freedoms with social rights and of carrying out profound structural reforms aimed at severing the political and social roots of the regime."[1] Such an ambitious project, in other words, necessitated the willingness of antifascist activists to negotiate not only a common ground from which the new state and society could emerge after the destruction of Fascism, but also a shared understanding of what constituted the essential nature of Fascism.

This was far from an easy task. Natoli acknowledges that "this acquisition was not a foregone conclusion; it was the result of a long and troubled process of revision that went hand in hand with the formation of an 'anti-fascist conscience' on the Italian and international level."[2] Such conceptual labor rested on mutually irreconcilable understandings of "fascism." It was not only liberals who gave Fascism a radically different interpretation from that of Marxists; even within the larger group of liberals—who identified a general adherence to the political forms of representative democracy and a free-market economy—progressives and conservatives differed in their conception of, and often their relation to, Fascism.

Italian liberalism, in the decades before the rise of Fascism, was a barrel of different ideologies and political practices. Conceptually dependent on traditions that developed in France and England, it never constituted a unitary political front. Its different orientations and styles were realized in distinct political parties. Cavour, one of the leaders of Italian unification, was liberal but also conservative. In the early twentieth century, the conservative-liberal tradition dominated the Italian political scene. Its foremost representative was Giovanni Giolitti, whose Unione Liberale continued to guarantee the political hegemony of the Destra Storica (Historic Right). Strictly monarchical, it represented the interests of the bourgeoisie of northern Italy as well as the aristocracy of absentee landowners of the south and resisted the demands of mass-based politics that arose in the aftermath of the First World War.

Within Italian liberalism, however, was a group of more pronounced democratic ideals, which had its origins in the activism of Giuseppe Mazzini. This progressive form of liberalism distanced itself from the Destra Storica and embraced reformism, universal suffrage for men, and mass politics. In the 1919 elections it was the vehicle for a number of parties that called themselves democratic. Alongside this centrist orientation, Luigi Sturzo's Partito Popolare Italiano was largely a political movement within the confines of conservative liberalism, but it developed into a mass-based party conceived of as the political voice of Italian Catholics, with close ties to the Vatican, characterized by moderate social welfare, a liberal political economy, a firmly antisocialist and anticommunist stance, and based on conservative ethical views. More radical was the "revolutionary" liberalism of Piero Gobetti, who was closer to a political ideal of social progress and emancipation, without, however, compromising with movements of Marxist leaning.[3]

Conservative Liberals' Understanding of Fascism

Despite the explicit rhetoric of antiliberalism that accompanied the rise of Mussolini, from the San Sepolcro program to the performance at the Teatro di San Carlo in Naples on the eve of the March on Rome, the quasi-totality of the elected politicians within the large and eclectic liberal front voted in favor of Mussolini's first cabinet, voted in favor of his rule by executive decree soon after, and voted in support of Mussolini's cabinet after the corrupted elections of 1924 and the assassination of Giacomo Matteotti. Furthermore, most of them voted to confirm Mussolini's leadership after his speech of January 3, 1925. Politically speaking, Italian liberalism not only facilitated the establishment of Fascism but was largely responsible for its success.

Liberals of the caliber of Luigi Einaudi, Giovanni Amendola, and Benedetto Croce enthusiastically supported and welcomed Mussolini in 1922. Amendola, who later became one of the strongest opponents of Fascism among moderate liberals, on the eve of the March on Rome acknowledged the necessity of Fascism to establish social pacification and the reconstitution of legality—thus discharging the Fascist Blackshirts of any responsibility for the widespread violence in the previous years: "We must recognize that Fascism chaperones a firm and radical restoration of the national conscience and a consolidation in the Italian soul of the moral value of our participation in the Great War. Tomorrow, after this period of violent crisis, all political parties will once again have the same right of citizenship in our public life."[4] Fascism, for Amendola, restored national pride and the conditions for the reestablishment of a state of normalcy. The economist Luigi Einaudi welcomed the rise of Fascism with the "benevolent expectation that it would solve the problems of the liberal state in the sense expressed by the liberalists."[5] After October 31, 1922, the large majority of conservative liberals threw their support behind Mussolini's government, and many became de facto members of the PNF and active within state institutions during the Fascist period. Even Benedetto Croce, today remembered as the most famous of antifascists, initially saluted the rise of Fascism.[6] The philosopher, perhaps one of the most influential public intellectuals in the history of modern Italy, enthusiastically acknowledged Mussolini's speech in Naples and voted in favor of his government even after the assassination of Matteotti.

There is no systematic analysis of the rise of Fascism in Croce's writings. A fierce critic of the Hegelian notion of the "ethical state," Croce nonetheless supported the authoritarianism of Fascism as instrumentally useful for the restoration of the primacy of politics against the initiative of the masses.[7] Gioacchino Volpe maintained that, because of his political views, Croce was the foremost Italian representative of European conservative revolutionism.[8] Fascism, for Croce, was the continuation in peacetime of the societal solidarity and self-abnegation for the sake of the nation that the Great War had triggered. In that spirit, if not openly supportive, he was clearly accepting the Blackshirts' violence when it was directed against labor and communist upheavals. Fascist violence was the necessary remedy to the inefficiencies of Italian liberalism. In an interview published in the October 27, 1923 edition of the newspaper *Il giornale d'Italia*, Croce maintained that the Italian predicament required that liberals "keep faith in liberalism and cordially help Fascism," which was an "inevitable necessity" for the nation, since "if the liberals did not have the strength and the virtue to save Italy from the anarchy in which it struggled, they must complain only about themselves, recite the *mea culpa*, and in the meantime accept the good from whatever side it arose."[9]

On February 1, 1924, while Italy was preparing for new elections, Croce admitted in an interview for the *Corriere italiano* that for him "the essence of Fascism is love for the Italian fatherland, it is the feeling for its salvation, of the salvation of the state."[10] And after voting in favor of the cabinet in a motion of confidence on June 24, 1924, only two weeks after the disappearance of the socialist Matteotti and the incarceration of his killers, all of them former Arditi and members of the Fascist militia, Croce again defended Mussolini's government in an interview on June 25, later published on July 10 in the *Giornale d'Italia*: "One could not wait, or even wish, for Fascism to suddenly collapse. It wasn't an infatuation or a game. It responded to serious needs and did a lot of good."[11] Luigi Russo, one of Croce's close friends, later admitted, "I have never seen Croce so gloomy as after . . . Matteotti's murder."[12] Yet, the Neapolitan philosopher did not hesitate to defend Mussolini and his violent regime for the sake of completing the "process of transformation" of state institutions.[13]

After Mussolini's speech on January 3, 1925, in which he assumed responsibility for Matteotti's assassination, Croce halted his support for the regime, initiating a period of critical nonfascism but not provoking any censorship or suppression by the Fascist regime. The most important aspect of his initiative was the publication of his "Manifesto degli intellettuali non fascisti," on May 1, 1925, as a critical response to Gentile's own manifesto. In it, he accused Gentile of "arbitrary historical interpretations and manipulations," of "abuse of the term 'religion,'" and of producing an "incoherent, bizarre mishmash of demagoguery and appeals to authority, vows of reverence for the law, ultramodern concepts, and mildewed old rubbish, absolutist stances and Bolshevik tendencies." The target of Croce's vitriolic rhetoric, however, was not Fascism, but Gentile's manifesto. In fact, he stated, "As for the present government, it has enacted or initiated a number of plausible measures. But, like the manifesto's formulations, they contain nothing original, nothing that points in the direction of a brand-new political system bearing the label 'fascism.'" And he concluded, with naive optimism, that "the present political strife in Italy, thanks to the very nature of these conflicts, will revive in our people a far deeper and more concrete understanding of the virtues of liberal laws and methods. . . . The day will come, perhaps, when one can calmly look back upon the past and conclude that the difficult and painful ordeal that Italy is at present undergoing was a necessary stage. A necessary stage beyond which lies a renewal of national life, the completion of Italy's political education, and a more intense sense of responsibility as a civilized people."[14]

Despite the mildness of its critical tone, the manifesto became the source of the postwar reimagining of Croce as a pillar of Italian antifascism, his active support of the regime going almost unmentioned; even the name of the manifesto changed from "nonfascist" to "antifascist."[15] Yet, the symbolic, if not practical and factual, contribution of Benedetto Croce to the antifascist cause was immense. As Gaetano Salvemini acknowledged, "Every other voice in Italy was muffled in prisons, sequestered in house arrests, forced to stay in exile. His [Croce's] silence itself was a protest. Resistance and silence came from the stratosphere, no doubt. But their effect was powerful."[16]

It was only after the liberation of Naples that Croce attempted a more or less systematic evaluation of Fascism from his perspective of conservative antifascist. In an article published on October 29, 1944 in *Il giornale di Napoli*, Croce reflected on the question in an article titled "Chi è 'fascista'?" (Who Is a Fascist?).[17] The article begins with an apparent rejection of the indiscriminate use of the term: "In daily controversies, the qualification of *fascist* is very often thrown and re-thrown from one opponent to another. . . . But that word, in the ways in which it is now used, risks becoming a simple and generic insult, good for any occurrence, if its historical and logical meaning is not determined and maintained." The use of the term in political debates, he continued, is meaningless and falsifies the broad class-transcending support Mussolini enjoyed: "Anyone who remembers the origins and the first outbreak of Fascism in Italy . . . knows that Fascism found its supporters in all classes and in all economic and intellectual strata, industrialists and agrarians, clericals and old aristocrats, proletarians and petty bourgeois, workers and rural people." He quoted, in support of his thesis on the "nonclassist origins of Fascism," the conservative economist Frank Drucker's study *The End of Economic Man: A Study of the New Totalitarianism*, which rejected the theory of the capitalist origins of Fascism and National Socialism.[18]

For Croce, "Fascism and Nazism were an intellectual and moral disease, not of classist origins but a disease of sentiment, of imagination and generically of human will, a crisis born of lost faith not only in rational liberalism but also in Marxism, which was in its own way rational although materialistic, but which failed in the promised implementation of a free society of equals and gave rise to regimes of absolutism and privileged bureaucratic classism."[19]

Fascism was nothing but a mix of authoritarianism and demagoguery inspired by Bolshevism, a disease, a malady of the mind, an episodic interruption in the rational progress of human societies: "It is naive to believe that we have found its root in the superficial and mechanical concepts of economic classes and their antinomies, but we must go deeper: into the brains of men; and there to discover evil, and there (and it is certainly difficult) to exercise the only cure that has hope of restoring health."[20] In short, liberalist reeducation was for Croce the antidote to that sickness of modernity that was Fascism.

Croce's position on Fascism as a disease, a temporary disruption in the liberal order of morality and society caused by a combination of weak state institutions, the contingent social disorder of the postwar years, and the threat of a communist upheaval, was paradigmatic of the conservative interpretations of Fascism and National Socialism shared by Friedrich Meinecke, Karl Popper, Gerhard Richter, Friedrich von Hayek, and Golo Mann, Thomas Mann's son. All were reluctant to indulge in speculations on "fascism" as a generic typology of political organization and preferred to regard it as an interruption, a parenthesis, a pathology; they conceived of it as closer to Soviet communism than capitalism. Such views had the effect of hiding, if not erasing, the collaboration of the liberal forces and of the economic elites in assuring the success of Mussolini's and Hitler's regimes, while explaining their dictatorial unfolding by affirming their phylogenetic affinity to communism.

Sturzo, the founder and head of the Catholic, liberal conservative PPI, also conceived of Fascism and Bolshevism as phenomena that both emerged from the economic distress of the postwar period. Like all other political parties apart from the Socialists and the Communists, the PPI voted in favor of Mussolini's cabinet in 1922 and supported the Fascist government until the assassination of Giacomo Matteotti, when it joined the oppositions in the Aventino secession. It would be dissolved on November 9, 1926. Sturzo, who had opposed the party decision to sustain the first Mussolini cabinet, was forced to leave its leadership on April 14, 1923, charged with "leftist" sympathies by both Mussolini and Cardinal Pietro Gasparri, the secretary of state for Pope Pius XI. Alcide De Gasperi stepped in as the new leader of the political party, but his relationship with the Vatican elites, from Cardinal Gasparri, who later signed the Lateran Pacts with the regime, and his successor as secretary of state, Cardinal Eugenio Pacelli, who was a sympathizer of both the Fascist and the National Socialist regimes, were fraught. In his diary he asked himself, puzzled: "But how was it possible that Christians, bishops, would close their eyes to Fascism, this antidemocratic, totalitarian, and violent political phenomenon?"[21]

Sturzo and De Gasperi gave voice to the antifascism of those Catholics who still identified themselves with tradition and religious values. Like

Benedetto Croce, they eventually became symbols of conservative bourgeois antifascism. They would provide inspiration and political directionality to the *Resistenza bianca* (white Resistance) during the twenty months of civil war in 1943–45, the resistance of Catholics like Paolo Emilio Taviani, Maria Eletta Martini, Tina Anselmi, and Aurelia Oreglia (Lelletta) d'Isola.[22]

In an article in *La rivoluzione liberale*, Sturzo asked himself why Fascism, the violence of which was "understandable (but not justifiable)" during the disorders of the "Bolshevizing period" of the *biennio rosso*, still resorted to "this system of threats, violence, and oppression."[23] The answer, for Sturzo, lay in Fascism's "prevailing tendency[, which] is that of the totalitarian transformation of every moral, cultural, political, religious force in this new conception: 'the fascist.' And since the minds do not bend, nor are the consciences transformed, it is fatal that it [Fascism] bends their heads and knees with the use of external force."[24] Behind this crude form of political action, there was no plan, no design, no ideology or theory: Fascism was a "convulsive movement," a "sentimental expression of conflicting moods and interests."[25] Behind its façade of a government of "clerical-nationalists and Hegelians" and its "corporatist" political economy, the regime was merely a simulacrum that hid a ruthless and irrational exercise of power. The real beneficiaries of the Fascist practice of power, for Sturzo, were the "parasitical industries and the financial speculations" that fueled the war: "Today Italy is ruled by Po Valley agrarianism and Lombard-Ligurian industrialism." But "the spirit of dictatorship that pervades Italy today is an element of moral and social disorder."[26] For Sturzo, only the restoration of the democratic order could solve the chaotic contradictions of Fascism.

Conservative antifascism, in Italy, did not leave as copious a corpus of documents as that of other political activists and thinkers. Fascism, for conservatives, was essentially a betrayal of the ideals of nationalism for the private interests of Mussolini, his henchmen, and his supporters. Antifascism consisted merely in liberating the traditional sources of authority, the monarchy and the Church, from the spell of Fascism in order to reestablish them as the basis for the restoration of political normalcy. Antifascist conservatives saw in Italian Fascism an aberration, a deviation, or, to use Croce's metaphor, a disease affecting political institutions and morality caused by the threat of a communist upheaval that the First World War and the Bolshevik Revolution had inspired among the working classes. The fight against Fascism had as its final end the restoration and reinvigoration of the prewar liberal order. It was this prognosis, or goal, rather than their diagnosis, that most markedly distinguished conservative liberals from the progressive voices of Italian liberalism.

Progressive Liberals' "Fascism"

Despite their differences, liberal thinkers and activists engaged in robust collaboration. Progressive liberals, while presenting a distinct understanding of Fascism, never hesitated to acknowledge in Benedetto Croce a guiding spirit in the common struggle.[27] And yet, for them Fascism was more than an accident, a temporary deviation, or a disease: It was inherent in the biography of an immature nation (Gobetti), the clinging to power by antidemocratic forces (Amendola, Salvemini), the result of the excesses of nationalist fervor (Salvatorelli). It was the deformed birth of a failed modernization of Italian society after 1861.

The social democrat Giovanni Amendola, journalist and politician, cofounder of the opposition newspaper *Il Mondo*, opposed the rise of Fascism after his initial acceptance of its inevitability. Between 1922 and 1924 he worked to build an alliance of all the liberal forces to oppose Mussolini. He strategically operated to transform his party, Unione Nazionale, into "a modern secular party, liberal and open on economic and social issues, with the scope of overcoming the galaxy of personal positions of individual parliamentarians belonging to a generically liberal area."[28] The year before, in a famous 1923 editorial, Amendola had warned of the danger that Fascism posed to Italian society: "Truly the most salient characteristic of the Fascist movement will remain, for those who study it in the future, its 'totalitarian' spirit, which does not allow the future to have dawns that will not be greeted with the Roman gesture, just as it does not allow the present to feed souls who are not bent on confessions of 'I believe!' This singular 'religious war' that has been raging in Italy for over a year does not offer you a faith . . . , but it does deny you the right to a conscience—yours and not someone else's; it precludes you from the future with a dark mortgage."[29] Amendola, like Croce and other liberals, saw in Fascism an abhorred form of political action, the sole pursuit of which was the preservation of power. It was power that elevated strength and oppression to a system, legitimated by a quasi-religious worship of its mission to preserve the national spirit. Amendola published Croce's manifesto in *Il Mondo* on May 1, 1925. Shortly thereafter, on July 19, 1925, he was severely beaten, which led to his death on April 7, 1926 in France.

For the historian and journalist Luigi Salvatorelli, Amendola's collaborator and fellow member of Unità Nazionale, "National-Fascismo" was a radical continuation of the liberal nationalism of Enrico Corradini, Giovanni Giolitti, and others. But Mussolini's was a much stronger, more ruthless nationalism, which "subjugated the Parliament, suspended the constitution, [and] imposed a military and police dictatorship, with the support of producers."

In his view, the overwhelming parliamentary support that Mussolini received had derived from lingering elements of the ancien régime, which "virtually, theoretically, still existed." The liberal conservative establishment, incapable of a "bourgeois revolution in Gallic style," did not constitute a moral and political force strong enough to oppose the favor that Fascism had received from the industrialists. That is why Salvatorelli preferred the name "National Fascism": Mussolini's regime, taking advantage of the widespread fear among liberals of a socialist revolution in Italy, became the dominant form of nationalism in Italy.[30]

Salvatorelli survived Fascism and became a prolific historian after the war. In 1942 he contributed to the foundation of the Partito d'Azione, which counted among its members such liberal and democratic antifascist thinkers and activists as Leone Ginzburg (a professor of Russian literature and the husband of Natalia Levi, with whom he had Carlo, who would become one of the most famous historians of postwar Italy; he would die in prison, tortured by Nazifascists), Norberto Bobbio (the political philosopher), Vittorio Foa (who would join the Communist Party after the war), Emilio Lussu (a war hero and writer), Gaetano Salvemini (a historian), Ferruccio Parri, Ugo La Malfa, and Carlo Rosselli (assassinated by Fascist *sicarios* in 1937).[31] "The ultimate root of the continuing Fascist illegality," he wrote in his monumental *Storia d'Italia nel periodo fascista*, "was the exceptional position that Fascism and Mussolini claimed in Italian life, whereby anyone who was not with them was against the country, an outlaw, or at least a citizen with inferior rights."[32] In the aftermath of the election of 1924, Salvatorelli claimed, Fascism imposed the narrative that it alone authentically represented Italy's nationalist spirit, since it was thanks to Fascism that the Italian victory in the First World War was morally and materially vindicated.[33] For Salvatorelli, Fascism was, in essence, a National Fascism, a violent and forceful imposition upon Italians of membership in a national community according to the terms and conditions the Fascists imposed. As such, it was the "negation of the law and of liberty."[34]

Gaetano Salvemini, an interventionist in 1914 and elected in 1919 with the Lista Combattenti, was an antifascist from the very beginning of Mussolini's government.[35] He predicted that Fascism's "disgusting and carnivalesque tragedy of brigands" would not last long after Matteotti's assassination.[36] Arrested in 1925 for antifascist subversion, he escaped to France, where with Carlo and Nello Rosselli he founded the resistance movement Giustizia e Libertà (Justice and Liberty), the precursor of the Action Party. In 1929 he moved to the United States, where he joined the faculty of the history department of Harvard University. His extensive writings on Fascism are foundational to postwar scholarship.[37] After the war, he returned in Italy in 1947, where he continued his political activism until his death in 1957.

In *Under the Axe of Fascism*, Salvemini sought the origins of Fascism's success in the support of the industrialists of northern Italy.[38] He described the formal and informal organizations of Fascism: the restructuring of labor relations along corporatist lines, widely disseminated state propaganda, and the legal infrastructure of the Fascist state. For Salvemini, Fascism conducted a "permanent revolution" in the social organization of production, carried on and overseen by Mussolini himself through the Chamber of Corporations.[39] In the last chapter of the book (titled "Is Fascism a Capitalist Dictatorship?"), Salvemini critiqued the view, then dominant among conservative antifascists, that Fascism was a continuation of socialism and Bolshevism. He claimed that "Fascist revolutionary syndicalism is mere humbug. The Fascist 'syndicates' are actually the direct opposite of those 'syndicates' to which Georges Sorel in his clouded imagination entrusted the duty of destroying capitalist society and of laying the foundations of a new society of labour."[40] Instead, "what Fascist doctrine has in common with Sorel is not syndicalism, but the dislike of parliamentary institutions, the advocacy of violent direct action as a means of political action and the method of exciting the emotions of the mob through myths in order to be able to exploit those emotions for ends anything but mythical."[41]

Salvemini rejected also US libertarians' claims that Franklin D. Roosevelt's New Deal state intervention in the economy was similar to Fascist corporatism, stating that

> the policy of intervention in economic life is characteristic neither of free, nor of despotic, nor of oligarchical, nor of democratic Governments. All Governments in all periods have intervened, more or less thoroughly, in the economic life of their countries, if by no other fact than that they have built roads, imposed taxes, and issued currency. Whether capitalists or proletarians, men are not favourable in an absolute sense either to laissez-faire or State intervention. They invoke such intervention when they expect to profit by it, and they repulse it when they foresee no advantage or fear a positive injury from its action.[42]

Did this make Fascism a "capitalist dictatorship?" On the one hand, he claimed, "under the heel of the Fascist dictatorship in Italy to-day are found not only the working classes, but the great majority of the middle and lower middle classes as well, although the latter groups stand a step higher in the social scale than the working classes. On the other hand, the oligarchy of which Mussolini is the supreme chieftain consists not only of capitalists, but of other groups who can be called capitalists only by an arbitrary use of this term. The capitalists proper—big business men, big landowners, and the upper professional classes—would not be able to survive in Italy if the masses of the middle, lower middle, and working classes were not kept in obedience by no less than three bureaucracies: the officers of the regular army, the civil service, and the officials of the Fascist Party."[43] But the class of capitalists, too, was, in a sense, taken hostage by Mussolini and his henchmen: In fact, "the big capitalists are far from exercising an uncontested sway."[44] The Blackshirt militias and the party were no longer financed by industrialists and financiers as in the 1920s, but by taxpayers. Civil servants, the real agents of the Fascist state in daily transactions, were now in control of the economic life in Italy: "When a disagreement arises between a big business man and a high civil servant, Mussolini's spontaneous inclination is to favour the high civil servant."[45] If the economic elites favored and supported Mussolini's rise to power, "to-day the great industrialists, bankers, great landowners, and shipping companies are imploring the Government to save them from ruin."[46] If in the early days of Fascism Mussolini depended on capitalists for funding, now and especially after the crisis of 1929 it was the capitalists who depended on the Fascist state for support—which came with precise indications on how investments had to be directed. If the agents of capitalism still played a role in the economic life of the nation, for Salvemini capitalism survived its crisis of 1929 by denaturing its own foundation in market laissez-faire. But that, he concluded, was suicide.[47]

Salvemini chronicled the rise of Fascism in *Le origini del fascismo in Italia*, a monograph deriving from the course he taught at Harvard. He traced its origins to nationalism: "If Fascism has a coherent doctrine, it is due to the fact that the Fascists bought the nationalist doctrine wholesale."[48] Fascism was ultranationalist from the very beginning: "From the beginning, Italian Fascism and German Nazism were essentially movements composed of impoverished elements of the middle classes who were determined not to sink to the level of the proletariat, and who began to wrest from the hands of the lower classes that part of the national wealth they had won."[49]

In the context of the *biennio rosso*, Fascism was as much an offspring of the socioeconomic crisis that the war had left as Bolshevism. However, "Fascism was by no means a medicine for the Bolshevik disease; it was a new and even more terrifying disease—civil war—which took the place of revolutionary exaltation; or rather a new and even more terrifying phase of that same disease from which, more or less, all countries suffered: postwar neurasthenia."[50] No analysis of its ideological and practical strategies was sufficient to understand the reasons for Fascism's success. Historians, Salvemini insisted, must look at Fascism within the sociopolitical context that sustained it: "The military authorities, the police and the judiciary never interfered in Fascist activities, but they helped and favored them. . . . For a conservative movement to become a fascist movement, there are two conditions. First of all, that the Conservatives take the path of illegality and bloodshed. Secondly, they should be able to find a sufficient number of high-ranking military authorities, members of the police, and the judiciary who have completely lost any sense of right and honor and are willing to employ the impartial power that the law has entrusted to them in favor of the wealthy classes and against the working classes. As long as these two conditions do not exist, speaking of fascism for any conservative movement is meaningless."[51]

That is why Salvemini, too, considered the March on Rome a coup d'état: "Only an anti-parliamentary coup could have prevented the House from forming a coalition of Popular Democrats and Socialists. . . . In conclusion, the March on Rome was designed not because parliamentary paralysis had become intolerable, but because parliamentary paralysis could be overcome by a coalition of democratic groups."[52] Despite later efforts of Fascist authors such as Gioacchino Volpe to construct the myth of a Fascist revolution to explain the events of October 28, 1922, Salvemini dismissed their arguments: Rather than a revolution, it was, for him, an "opera buffa."[53] It was a *coup de main*, if not a full-fledged coup d'état:[54] "Defining the March on Rome as a 'revolution' means absolving the military authorities and the king himself of any lack of fidelity to the Statutes and surrounding Mussolini with the aura of a 'revolutionary conqueror' who reached power after God knows how many battlefields and how many hard trials."[55]

After the coup, the transformation of Italy into a Fascist regime was rapid. The first step, for Salvemini, was the institutionalization of the Blackshirt squads into a national militia, followed by the electoral law that paved the way for the pantomime of plebiscitarian victory in 1924. On January 3, 1925, the day of the actual Fascist coup d'état, Fascism became officially a "totalitarian state":[56] a dictatorship that dismantled all constitutional liberties, imposing a single political party structured in a rigid centralizing hierarchy with Mussolini at its apex;[57] where the executive power of the government no longer depended on the legislative power and local authorities were no longer elected;[58] where all antigovernmental activity was "severely prohibited" and the entire educational and informational system was devoted solely to creating a national spirit that conformed fully to the model of the Fascist party.[59]

Pushing Salvemini's interpretation of Fascism in an even more radical direction, Piero Gobetti, the liberal who was the first to foresee the danger of Mussolini's movement, continued his antifascist activities in the pages of his *La rivoluzione liberale*. For him, "Fascism in Italy is a catastrophe, it is an indication of its [the nation's] decisional childishness, because it marks the triumph of ease, confidence, optimism, enthusiasm."[60] After the elections of 1924, Gobetti acknowledged that "if Fascism were only a dictatorship, it would soon be liquidated with barricades: but its strength is especially garrisoned by the existence of a consensus."[61] The elections, for him, confirmed his claim that the March on Rome was a coup d'état, the sole effect of which was "the abolition of the proportional [electoral system] and thus the strengthening the economic dictatorship of the plutocratic classes."[62]

Gobetti's critical articles against the regime turned him into an enemy of the state. In a telegram of June 1, 1924 to Enrico Palmieri, prefect of Turin, Mussolini ordered: "I am told that Gobetti has recently been in Paris and that today he is in Sicily. Please inform me and be sure to make life difficult for this stupid opponent of the government and Fascism."[63] On June 9 Gobetti was beaten up by a group of Blackshirts. After the even more pressing antifascist campaign that Gobetti launched in the wake of Matteotti's assassination, his fate was sealed: "Ever since June 1924, Italian politics has been dominated by the assassination of Giacomo Matteotti. It was a political assassination, a crime on the part of the regime, in the face of which we, antifascists and anti-Mussolinians, summoned the regime to stand trial. It was clear to us from the first day that we have to make of Matteotti the Dreyfus Affair of the Italians, since it has become the touchstone of our dignity as a modern people."[64] Gobetti's *j'accuse* was clear: "Matteotti was killed because he demonstrated the ineligibility of all current members of the government majority."[65] All attempts of the opposition were futile, and no *political* solution to the scandal was possible, for Gobetti, because "two years of Fascism have distanced us even more irremediably from the mores of the political struggle."[66]

On October 27 the prefect of Turin shut down *La rivoluzione liberale* indefinitely. Gobetti decided to move to France to continue his fight from there. But a few days after his departure, on February 11, 1926, he died, officially of pneumonia, turned fatal by a heart condition caused by the repeated beatings he suffered from the Blackshirts.[67]

Despite the mutual divergencies among individual thinkers, liberal progressives conceived of Fascism as an extreme form of nationalism. Although the question of whether Fascism was a product of capitalism or could at least be regarded as congruent with capitalism had received different answers (Gobetti was more inclined to this view, Salvemini less so, and Amendola and Salvatorelli disagreed altogether), all liberal progressives acknowledged that Mussolini, his movement, and his regime had received vital support from the industrial and financial elites of northern Italy. Also, all of them fiercely denied Mussolini's claim that Fascism was a direct expression of the nation and of its people: rather, its power derived from the ruthless totalitarian means through which it imposed, with the connivance of the armed forces, the police, and the justice system, a transformation of state institutions beyond the legal boundaries of its constitution.

Fascism exploited an ultranationalist ideology (Amendola, Salvatorelli, Salvemini), rendered more persuasive by the political immaturity of the Italians (Croce, Gobetti), with the aim of turning the liberal institutions of the state into an organism of totalitarian repression that some liberals conceived of as similar (Sturzo, De Gasperi), if not phylogenetically linked (Croce), to the Bolshevik dictatorship. Even though it benefited from the support of the king, the pope, and the capitalist elites of northern and central Italy, Fascism betrayed the monarchical and religious institutions and perverted the economic system of market liberalism. For most liberals, then, Fascism could not be reduced to an expression of bourgeois capital. In that they differed from Marxist activists and thinkers, who, in their attempt to demonstrate the continuity of liberal capitalism within Fascism, developed extremely sophisticated analyses of a political phenomenon that, for them, transcended the Italian case.

7

Marxists' "Fascism"

Giacomo Matteotti and the "Fascism" of Italian Socialists

On the afternoon of January 31, 1921, the socialist deputy Giacomo Matteotti launched an accusation against the governing majority's silent support of widespread Fascist violence against socialists and members of the labor unions: "Today in Italy there is an organization of armed gangs—its members, its leaders, its composition, and its headquarters publicly recognized and known— . . . that openly declare that they are ready to execute acts of violence and arson as soon as any deed committed by the workers to the detriment of the capitalists or of the bourgeois class occurs or is pretended to have occurred. It is clearly an organization of private justice; this is an incontrovertible fact."[1]

Ever since the foundation of the Fasci di Combattimento in 1919, the main target of Fascist squads had indeed been the socialists:[2] their party headquarters, the branch offices of the newspaper *Avanti!*, and the private homes of elected socialist administrators in townships and cities of northern Italy. What Matteotti charged the governing parties, the liberal conservatives of the Unione Liberale, the party of Prime Minister Giovanni Giolitti, along with the other moderate liberals, democrats, and members of Sturzo's PPI who made up Giolitti's cabinet, was their hypocritical and self-interested tolerance, if not support, of Fascist violence: "We recognize in Fascism the courage to expose itself, while the hypocrisy of not openly supporting it persists in the vast majority of the country's capitalist society, the hypocrisy of attributing the violence of these days to the most stupid socialist provocations!"[3] Fascism, Matteotti argued, despite its revolutionary rhetoric, was nothing less than a criminal organization perfectly in sync with the interests of the capitalist elites: "The truth is that the violence and illegality of that armed organization corresponds, at this moment, to a supposed interest of the capitalist class."[4]

Giacomo Matteotti—the "Tempest," as his socialist friends called him for his political courage and impetuousness—expressed well Marxist thinkers' and activists' interpretation of Fascism from its earliest years: It was a subversive, armed, and violent movement of the capitalist classes of industrialists, bankers, stakeholders, and landowners that intended to protect their interests against the claims of labor unions and socialists.[5] Matteotti, along with Filippo Turati, was expelled from the Socialist Party in 1922 for his reformist opposition to the revolutionary methods inspired by the Russian Bolsheviks. Nonetheless, he shared with Marxists of different inclinations (orthodox and eclectic, revolutionary hard-liners and reformists) the interpretation that saw in Fascism a movement linked to capitalism.[6]

It is in the texts of Marxist thinkers that we find the most systematic and sociohistorically sophisticated interpretations of Fascism as movement, regime, and ideology of the interwar period. Analyses of Fascism and its sociopolitical affinity with the capitalist classes circulated in Marxist circles at the international level. In the immediate aftermath of the March on Rome, the Russian revolutionary Karl Radek addressed the fourth Comintern congress in November 1922, charging the Italian Left that "I see in the victory of Fascism not merely a mechanical victory for Fascism arms, but the heaviest defeat that socialism and communism had suffered since the start of the period of world revolution."[7] For Radek, the Italian leftist intelligentsia was guilty of indulging in too many debates. The Fascists, Radek claimed, were able to recruit to their nationalist cause those disaffected classes of the lower bourgeoisie that, in "an economically ruined country" like Italy, should have been the natural interlocutors of the Socialist Party.

While Radek's harsh judgment on the failures of Italian socialism rightly pointed to its internal fractures in mutually antagonistic factions, unable to organize a united front against the Fascist attacks, it utterly disregarded the intensity of the Squadristi's violence against the socialists and labor unions, unhindered or even directly supported by the police. Klara Zetkin, a friend of Rosa Luxemburg who had escaped to Italy after the suppression of the Spartacist rebellion (*Spartakusaufstand*), witnessed the March on Rome and was, along with Gramsci, one of the first political theorists to use "fascism" generically to express the common features of the different reactionary movements in Europe. Her speech at the Enlarged Executive of the Comintern, in June 1923, was less condemnatory than Radek's. She claimed, in fact, that "in Fascism the proletariat confronts an exceptionally dangerous and terrible foe."[8] Surely, she noted, "Fascism is the classic expression, the most powerful and concentrated form, of the general offensive of the international bourgeoisie at the present time."[9] Italian Fascism exercised its terroristic violence against the proletariat with the same ruthlessness as did Miklós Horthy's terror squads in Hungary—but with an important difference. Italian Fascism, Zetkin asserted, "is in no sense the revenge of the bourgeoisie against the revolutionary advance of the proletariat. . . . And the 'bearers' of fascism are not a small caste, but broad social strata, popular masses, reaching even into the proletariat. We must be clear about these essential differences if we are to deal with fascism. We will not subdue it by military means alone; we must overcome it on the political and ideological levels as well."[10]

Matteotti and other antifascists of the Left experienced firsthand the strength of Fascism both as a force of violent repression and as a formidable ideological competitor for the recruitment of disaffected members of the lower middle and working classes. He was unquestioningly the most outspoken of the Italian antifascists and probably the only one with the organizational and negotiating abilities to build a united front of leftist forces. However, soon after his accusation that the 1924 elections were illegal, made in the famous speech mentioned above, he was kidnapped and killed by a gang of Blackshirts.[11]

Matteotti was not the only voice critical of the regime, so the reasons behind his assassination—even though the political, if not direct, responsibility of Mussolini is unquestioned—remain unclear.[12] His allegation of electoral illegalities surely would not have brought about the cancellation of the elections and the deposition of Mussolini. More likely, his speech should be interpreted as announcing Matteotti's own candidacy to lead a united opposition of reformist and maximalist socialists, communists, liberal democrats (Amendola), and De Gasperi's PPI. In this scenario, his elimination signified a weakening of parliamentary obstacles for Mussolini, because Matteotti was probably the only member of the opposition capable of building such a cross-ideological alliance.[13]

The opposition parties described their retreat in the Aventino as a gesture of refusal to participate any longer in parliamentary proceedings, which the assassination of Matteotti had for them delegitimated. But if morally and legally meaningful, the withdrawal had no political effect: on the contrary, it de facto prevented the opposition from leaving official records of their accusations in parliamentary proceedings. Soon, without a political leader who, like Matteotti, was capable of effectively negotiating with forces ideologically distant, the alliance broke apart. As Silvio Pons argues, "The sectarianism of the Italian communists and the never-ending diatribes with the socialists reflected an underestimation of Fascism and a tendency to see in the developments of 'reaction' the conditions for a revolutionary opportunity."[14]

Matteotti did not leave a systematic analysis of Fascism. Earlier in 1924, he had succeeded in smuggling out to London a book manuscript, *Un anno di dominazione fascista*, which was published in translation as *The Fascists Exposed: A Year of Fascist Domination* at almost the same time as his assassination.[15] The book is a collection of public declarations by Mussolini and other Fascists, newspaper articles, and detailed statistical data, only sparsely commented on by Matteotti, that demonstrated, first, how Fascism's violence and illegality were not just in reaction to socialist demonstrations during the *biennio rosso* but continued well after Mussolini took power and in the absence of any meaningful provocation; second, that the economic conditions in the postwar years improved independently of Fascist legislative intervention; and, third, that only the financial and industrial elites profited from this economic growth.

After Matteotti's death, the strengthening of the regime was paradoxically favored by the Aventino protest of antifascist parties, which had the effect of an abdication.[16] With their voluntary abandonment of the Parliament, the opposition had lost any ability to intervene politically. It was too late to restore the conditions for parliamentary struggle. Moreover, the labor movements had been crippled by Fascism too severely to encourage any illusion of organizing a broader revolutionary resistance. Antifascists of various leanings withdrew into private life: Some continued to write critical analyses of the regime in newspapers and journals that were subjected to increasingly tighter control by the police; many went in voluntary exile; others were sent to coercive *confino* (confinement); some ended up in prison; many died, assassinated or by disease.[17] In those years of retreat, it was Antonio Gramsci, Palmiro Togliatti, Angelo Tasca, and a few other Marxist activists who in the 1920s and 1930s left the most systematic attempts to understand the rise of Fascism with the sharpest political, sociological, and ideological theorizations.

"Fascism" according to Gramsci

Antonio Gramsci, whose writings on Fascism anticipated all others in predicting the victory of Mussolini's movement, continued his analytical and agitational activities. During the first years of the regime, he consolidated his views on Fascism as the repressive expression of the capitalist class, which had recruited the support of the middle classes with an ideology that stressed nationalism, antipolitics, and government efficiency, and with a rhetorical strategy focused on capturing the affective response of the masses.

In an essay he published in the November 1, 1923 issue of *La voce della gioventù*, the journal of the Federazione Giovanile Comunista Italiana (Italian Communist Youth Federation), Gramsci acknowledged the defeat of the labor movement and of the socialist party in Italy and explained the favors

Fascism collected from the Italian bourgeoisie as resulting from two causes: first, the disarray of Italian society and of its productive infrastructure in the wake of the First World War, which the workers' agitations and widespread Fascist violence had only exacerbated; and second, the chronic weakness and inefficiencies of the Italian state apparatus, made up of a quarrelsome and divided legislative branch, an indecisive executive branch, and an incompetent judiciary.[18] To counteract Fascism, Gramsci encouraged study and education: "We must start from this: from the study of the doctrine that is proper to the working class, which is the philosophy of the working class, which is the sociology of the working class, from the study of historical materialism, from the study of Marxism."[19] Antifascist resistance could not be improvised. It had to be built on the foundations of shared knowledge.

Fascism, for Gramsci, far from being the revolutionary movement it presented itself as and far from being the direct expression of the Italian nation, "tends to give the class dictatorship of the bourgeoisie stability and permanence deriving from the open transformation of the former self-styled liberal state into the organ and form of this dictatorship."[20] The permanence, at least as an empty simulacrum, of the liberal institutions had the dual function of hiding the inherently bourgeois-oriented politics of Fascism and of disarming all those antagonistic parties (the Partito Socialista Unitario [Unitary Socialist Party; PSU] of Turati and Matteotti; the Partito Liberale Democratico [Democratic Liberal Party; PLDI] of Giovanni Amendola; and the PPI of Sturzo and De Gasperi) that limited their political agitation to parliamentary proceduralism. But Fascism did not operate openly. It strategically appealed to the masses at an emotional level: "It is said . . . that Fascism is a romantic movement, that Fascism is even Italian romanticism itself. Although I am convinced that Fascism is a social movement, that is, a political-economic one, which occurred in Italy and was able to triumph due to an exceptional historical situation, I do not feel like rejecting this profound synthetic vision of Fascism."[21] Indeed, he added, "the environment in which the individual Fascists were formed, the ideology with which they were abundantly nourished, can be called romanticism."[22] The romanticism that Gramsci referred to, reminiscent of Missiroli's own linking of Fascism and romanticism, pointed to a sociocultural environment dominated by the feuilleton:

> This is the romantic side of the Fascist movement, of fascists like Mario Gioda, Massimo Rocca, Curzio Suckert, Roberto Farinacci, etc., etc.: an unbalanced fantasy, a thrill of heroic fury, a psychological restlessness that has no other ideal content than the sentiments diffused in the feuilletons of French romanticism of 1848: anarchists thought of the revolution as a chapter of *Les*

> *Misérables*, with its Grantavins, l'Aigle de Meaux and C., with a side dish of Gavroche and Jean Valjean; as for the Fascists, they want to be the "Prince Rudolph" of the good Italian people. The historical conjuncture has allowed this romanticism to become a "ruling class," for the whole of Italy to become a feuilleton.[23]

Gramsci, far from embracing the mechanical reductionism of later orthodox Marxists, was a keen analyst of the cultural bases of Fascist hegemony: alongside its repressive apparatus, its "terroristic" mode of coercively securing consensus, the connivance of traditional conservative parties, and the support of the capitalist classes, Fascism imposed itself in the Italian imaginary through a style that was familiar to the petty-bourgeois readers of feuilletons and operetta-goers. Mussolini, too, seemed carved out of a stereotyped character of these novels:

> We have the Fascist regime in Italy, we have Benito Mussolini at the head of Fascism, we have an official ideology in which the "boss" [*capo*] is deified, is declared infallible, is acknowledged as organizer and inspirer of a reborn Holy Roman Empire. We see printed in the newspapers, every day, dozens, hundreds of telegrams of homage to their "boss" from the numerous local tribes. Let's see the photographs: the hardest mask of a face that we have already seen in socialist rallies. We know that face: We know that rolling of the eyes in their sockets that in the past, with their ferocious mechanics, frightened the bourgeoisie, and today the proletariat. We know that fist, always closed as a threat. We know this mechanism, all these paraphernalia, and we understand that it can impress and move the young people of the bourgeois schools.[24]

Mussolini was not an instantiation of the Nietzschean ideal of the Übermensch, and neither was he the embodiment of the Weberian notion of charismatic authority; rather, for Gramsci Mussolini was modeled upon the characters of adventure novels and romantic feuilletons. Mussolini played a role, and the function of that role in this novelization of life was thoroughly ideological. Indeed, it was at the level of culture that Fascism gathered support. The March on Rome, the rallies, the parliamentary speeches were all acts in a pantomime that masked with romantic flair the fact that "Benito Mussolini conquered the government and is maintaining it with the most violent and arbitrary repression."[25]

The flamboyancy of Mussolini and of the Fascist theatrical paraphernalia should not, Gramsci warned before the election of April 1924, be taken lightly. Fascism would not fall via conventional electoral competition. Rather, "Fascism can only be overthrown by a popular uprising."[26] But in that case, the antifascist forces—he was referring, obviously, to the Communist Party and the working classes here—must "organize propaganda domestically, among workers and peasants, moving them from their torpor, from their passivity, with the example of a party that throws itself into the struggle, that faces dangers, that it is not afraid of Fascism, and is thus helping to dispel this atmosphere of indistinct, apocalyptic panic, this stupid amazement of the masses, [and make them understand] that Fascism has replaced the democratic mists with the oppression and enslavement of the working people."[27] And, he added, Fascism could count on the support of the Vatican and of Pope Pius XI, who, "when he was still called Felice Ratti and was cardinal of Milan, repeatedly expressed his sympathies for Fascism and Mussolini."[28]

The Varieties of "Fascism" within the Partito Comunista d'Italia

The question of "fascism"—its definition, the analysis of its causes, and the plan for its defeat—for Italian communists was not simply a matter of theoretical disputes or parliamentary strategy. It mirrored the complex history of its survival and eventual outlawing in the first years of the Fascist regime. It defined the positionality of the different currents within the party itself: the party leader Amadeo Bordiga, opposed by the "Stalinist" faction of Togliatti and Terracini, on the one hand; and the eclectic internationalism of Gramsci, on the other. It also defined the position of the PCd'I vis-à-vis other European communist movements and its relation to the Soviet-controlled Comintern.[29]

In 1923 Gramsci was appointed liaison between the PCd'I and other European communist parties. This position in the Comintern forced him to travel to Moscow, where he contributed to the ongoing discussion on Fascism. After Bordiga's incarceration in 1923 and Lenin's death in early 1924, the PCd'I divided into factions, often quarreling with one another over party strategy and each expressing different interpretations of Fascism. In Bordiga's writings, the question of Fascism was somewhat marginal. In his 1922 "Rome Thesis," he had maintained that "the present situation in Italy contains in outline all the essential elements of a *coup d'état*. . . . The bourgeois class is fully aware of this situation, but its interest requires that the external appearance of formal democracy should not be subjected to the more profound disturbance of a violent upheaval, which in point of fact would provide no greater protection for its privileges than it currently enjoys."[30] Those being the circumstances in the wake of Mussolini's first cabinet, for Bordiga Italy was nurturing "a further stage of proletarian martyrdom."[31] For Bordiga, the rise of Fascism was not, as both conservative and progressive liberals had at times surmised, the result of lingering feudalistic relations dominating the largely rural economy of Italy. It was rather inherent in advanced societies where the capitalist mode of production prevailed, where Fascist anti-proletarian violence was closely related to the reaction against the labor movement in all European countries, since, he claimed elsewhere, it was nothing less than "the natural continuation of the method applied before and after the war by 'democracy.'"[32]

Against Bordiga, Togliatti, who presented his "Rapporto sul Fascismo" at the Fourth World Congress of the Communist Party held in Petrograd and Moscow in late 1922, asserted that "the Fascist movement as it has developed in Italy in recent years must undoubtedly be considered a particular moment in postwar proletarian history, as a link in the chain of offensive actions carried out by the bourgeoisie to break every possibility and every hope of proletarian recovery; but the forms it assumes and its probable future developments cannot possibly be understood and envisaged if one does not regard Fascism as the last aspect of a crisis of the Italian state and society."[33]

The Fascist reaction, for Togliatti, could be understood only in the context of Italy's flawed modernizing process, the fraught legacy of "that national movement (political and economic at the same time) that takes the name of 'Italian Risorgimento.'"[34] The bourgeoisie, far from maturing a class consciousness, continued to be divided into "heterogeneous social groups":[35] industrialists in the north; agricultural entrepreneurs in the Po Valley; and the traditional landowners in central and southern Italy, who placed great emphasis on the family-centered organization of economic activities, historical ties with the territory, collusion with Mafia organizations, and uninterrupted feudalistic relationship with the labor forces, had all nurtured a reactionary movement that impeded a coordinated development of the working classes in the unevenly developed Italian peninsula. Under these circumstances, "the Italian reactionary movement that takes the name of Fascism, although it arose as early as 1918 and 1919, . . . does not achieve notable development and does not assume decisive importance except when the defeat of the revolutionary movement appears inexorably marked by the miserable end of the 'occupation of factories.'"[36] In other words, for Togliatti the rise of Fascism had to be understood as happening only *after* its defeat of the labor movement. It was a continuation of the patriotic "interventionism" of 1915, which now gathered around itself an eclectic ensemble of social classes, "not well defined and ranging from the disadvantaged professional (lawyers, doctors, engineers) in search of political fortunes to the retired officer who has not yet found a job that guarantees him a social position of prestige equivalent to what he had had in the army; from the restless intellectual eager for novelty to the speculator of politics; from the student to the unscrupulous lowlife, yesterday socialist today reactionary, and beyond that also to semi-proletarian elements who have left the ranks of the labor movement when they saw that it failed to keep its promises and to fulfill the hopes it had first nurtured."[37] Their social disorientation, challenges to integration, nationalist beliefs, and determination to use violence, in the void left by the defeat of the workers' revolutionary upheaval, made of these socially dispossessed groups from different social classes natural allies of the northern industrialists, who cultivated a strong "anti-labor and anti-socialist attitude"; of the Po Valley landowners; and of small businessmen, shopkeepers, and financial speculators.[38] Added to all that was the constant support, logistic and legal, of the police forces for the Fascist squads, designed by Congressman Giolitti, "initiator of the legal protection system of Fascism."[39]

In the middle between Bordiga, who saw in Fascism an automatic development of capitalism, and Togliatti, who saw it as an effect of the imperfect modernization of Italian society, stood Gramsci.[40] As he more systematically maintained in his report to the Central Committee of the PCd'I on August 13–14, 1924, "The radical crisis of the capitalist regime . . . has not been healed by Fascism. Fascism, with its repressive method of government, had made very difficult and in fact almost totally prevented the political manifestations of the general capitalist crisis; however, it did not halt them, much less did it favor the recovery and development of the national economy."[41] Indeed, the crisis of capitalism that followed the First World War had more serious causes in Italy than elsewhere, because its industrial infostructure was less developed.[42] Industries were concentrated in the north, and in particular in the northwestern triangle formed by Milan, Turin, and Genoa. The northeast and the center were mainly agricultural but controlled by a small class of landowning families with the support of a troop of administrators from the middle classes; and the south had an underdeveloped agriculture organized around a clientelist system of absentee large landowners. In that situation, only the north had a substantially large population of proletarians. Fascism therefore found fertile ground to grow in the midst of the disaffected and impoverished middle classes of north, center, and south, to which a largely inefficient state could give no reassurance. "The Italian economic crisis," Gramsci concluded, "can only be resolved by the proletariat. Only by entering a European and world revolution can the Italian people regain the ability to assert their human productive forces and restore the development of the national apparatus of production. Fascism has only delayed the proletarian revolution, it has not made it impossible: indeed, it has contributed to widening and deepening the terrain of the proletarian revolution, which after the Fascist experiment will be truly popular."[43]

Mussolini's success was for Gramsci only temporary: Surely "the originality of Fascism consists in having found the adequate form of organization for a social class that has always been unable to have a unitary structure and ideology,"[44] but "Fascism is unable to achieve any of its ideological premises."[45] This was because "there is no essence of Fascism in Fascism itself."[46] It worked insofar as it unleashed the repressed violence of the petty bourgeoisie that it succeeded in organizing. But as a governing regime, Fascism could not obtain the results it pursued: "Fascism, by the nature of its organization, does not tolerate collaborators with equal rights, it only wants servants in chains."[47] On the one hand, "Fascism will tend to preserve a base of armed organizations to be brought back into the field as soon as a new revolutionary wave emerges."[48] On the other, it might try to recruit within the governing majority portions of the current oppositions, with the risk, however, that "Mussolini's government is placed in a clear minority."[49] For Gramsci, the only viable solution for the PCd'I was to continue the antifascist struggle by mustering the conditions for a real revolutionary movement. To that end, "it is necessary to reorganize the great masses and become a large party, the only party in which the working population sees the expression of its political will, the defense of its immediate and permanent interests in history."[50]

Gramsci's "optimism of the will" coincided with the early governmental phase of Fascism. But Mussolini's speech of January 3, 1925 took Gramsci by surprise. He admitted as much himself in a second report he sent to the Central Committee of the PCd'I on February 6, 1925. The muzzling of the press and the failure of the king to intervene—as all members of the opposition had hoped—meant that the Aventino strategy had failed.

On the eve of the third congress of the PCd'I, organized in Lyon in January 1926, the three leaders of the communist movement in Italy—Bordiga, Gramsci, and Togliatti—were bound together in a knot of contradictory views regarding both Fascism and the Comintern. Bordiga saw in Fascism a stage in the development of capitalism, which posited him tendentially in favor of a genericization of the term into a political category in line with the plan of the Comintern, from which, however, he wanted to keep the PCd'I independent. Togliatti, however, was in favor of coordinating the activity of the PCd'I within a Comintern increasingly under the control of Joseph Stalin, but he was skeptical of abstracting from Italian Fascism a generalized conception of "fascism." Gramsci, who would gather around the "Theses" he presented at Lyon the consensus of the majority of the participants, was inclined to develop a theoretical understanding of Fascism that could be heuristically expanded to other sociopolitical contexts, but he refused to conceive of it in a too rigidly deterministic sense, as Bordiga did; at the same time, as liaison of the PCd'I with other communist parties in Europe, he favored a larger role for the Italian party within the Comintern. With this double move, Gramsci wanted to respond to the criticism of European Marxists to the provincialism of Italian communists' interpretation of Fascism, in particular of Togliatti's.[51] However, while he wished that Italian communism played a more important role within the Comintern, Gramsci did not share Togliatti's enthusiasm for the Stalinist takeover of the institution.

Gramsci's "Theses" gave his new analysis of Fascism a prominent role, both heuristically and strategically. From the very beginning, Gramsci dismissed any "exceptionalist" conception of the phenomenon, including that of Togliatti, by affirming that "as an armed reaction movement that aims to break up and disorganize the working class in order to immobilize it, [Fascism] falls within the framework of the traditional politics of the Italian ruling classes, and in the struggle of capitalism against the working class" in general.[52] Its social basis consisted of "urban petty bourgeoisie" and the "new rural bourgeoisie," both of which were forms of "emergent capitalism" and as such found in it a cohesion of intent. Its ideology emerged from "the tradition of war," which "allow[ed] Fascism, as opposed to the old ruling classes, to conceive and implement a plan to conquer the state."[53] Consequently, it was "absurd" to conceive of the events of 1922 as a "revolution."[54] In essence, "Fascism modifies the conservative and reactionary program that has always dominated Italian politics only in the different ways in which it conceives of the process of unification of the reactionary forces."[55]

Once in power, Fascism was not devoid of inherent contradictions. In fact, if "in the economic field, Fascism acts as an instrument of an industrial and agrarian oligarchy to centralize the control of all the country's wealth in the hands of capitalism," nonetheless it could not avoid "causing discontent among the petty bourgeoisie which, with the advent of Fascism, believed the era of its domination had arrived."[56] Accordingly, the regime operated as a liberal government that "favors a new industrial concentration" and the consolidation of large entrepreneurial "agrarians against small and medium cultivators."[57] To quell its base's dissatisfaction, Fascism coordinated a large-scale propaganda campaign, the purpose of which was to externalize the crisis abroad: "The completion of the ideological propaganda and of the political and economic action of Fascism is its tendency to 'imperialism.' This tendency is the expression of the need felt by the Italian industrial-agrarian ruling classes to find the elements for resolving the crisis in Italian society outside the national sphere. It contains the seeds of a war that will ostensibly be fought for Italian expansion but in which, in reality, Fascist Italy will be an instrument in the hands of one of the imperialist groups competing for world domination."[58]

After Lyon, Gramsci consolidated his leadership of the PCd'I, thanks largely to the consensus his "Theses" was accorded by the party. His relationship with the Stalin-dominated Central Committee of the Comintern, however, rapidly deteriorated.[59] When Mussolini passed the security laws of November 8, 1926, the Communist Party was outlawed, and Gramsci was arrested. He was scheduled for release on April 21, 1937 but was too ill to be moved; he died of a cerebral hemorrhage a few days later, on April 27.

The *Prison Notebooks*, that fragmentary masterpiece of theoretical and intellectual reflections produced in the trying conditions of incarceration, do not add much to what Gramsci had previously theorized about Fascism. The word appears only occasionally, and mostly in the titles of articles Gramsci referred to. This is because he was constantly worried about censorship and the possible repercussions on his life in prison and on his prospects for release.[60] In its place we get reflections on "Caesarism." In Notebook 6 (1930–33), for instance, we read in a discussion on demagogy in political strategy: "Demagogy means several things: in the worst sense, it means using the popular masses, their passions wisely excited and nurtured, for their own particular ends, for their small ambitions (parliamentarism and electionism offer a propitious ground for this particular form of demagogy, which culminates in Caesarism and Bonapartism with their plebiscitary regimes)."[61]

Most important, though, Gramsci's notebooks offered a larger space for cultural and historical reflections, with brilliant excurses on literature, philosophy, linguistics, education, the sociology of intellectuals, popular culture, and anthropology. Indeed, if his analysis of Fascism did not change during his years in prison, for Gramsci the question of how a regime could exist while clearly ruling against the interests of those social classes that most fervently supported it (the petty bourgeoisie, and the lower middle classes in particular) could be answered only through the analysis of forms of cultural hegemony as vehicles of an ideological organization of consensus. It was in that context that the early meditation on the imagination of the "boss" (*capo*), an ironic paraphrasis of Mussolini's title of "Duce," as inspired by the heroes of feuilletons, operettas, and radio comedies were further explored in Notebooks 9, 14, 17, 21, and 27, which added complexity to the Weberian notion of political charisma, while in Notebooks 13, 15, 17, and 18 he reflected on the applicability of Machiavelli's *The Prince* as a heuristic key for decoding the function of the charisma of the *capo* (explicitly taken as a modern translation of "prince") in governance. He dedicated Notebook 25 to the susceptibility and vulnerability of the subaltern classes to ideological propaganda, while Notebooks 11 and 12 turned to the role of intellectuals in constructing worldviews organic to the social classes of their origins or identification.

"Fascism" according to Togliatti

With Bordiga and Gramsci both in prison and Angelo Tasca, in disagreement with the Stalinist turn of the Comintern, playing a marginal role in the Central Committee (until his expulsion in 1929), in 1926 Palmiro Togliatti became the undisputed leader of the PCd'I, now operating largely from abroad. In that role he became the leading Italian contributor to an institutionalization of the definition of "fascism" within the doctrinal guidelines that the Comintern was coordinating with the various national communist parties.

The Comintern, in a "Resolution" published on July 5, 1923, in the *Internationale Presse-Korrespondenz* and in a second one the following year with some amendments to the earlier one, had institutionalized and legitimized a generic use of "fascism" to indicate "one of the classic forms of the counterrevolution in the era of capitalist decay," "an instrument of the big bourgeoisie for fighting the proletariat, when the legal means available to the state proved insufficient to subdue them," and "the extralegal arm of the big bourgeoisie for establishing and consolidating its dictatorship."[62] Togliatti, despite his loyalty to Stalin, was the most critical voice against this generic use of "fascism." He claimed that "we have become accustomed to use the term 'fascism' in such a general meaning that it serves to designate the most diverse forms of bourgeois reactionary movements. This may be useful for agitation, but it undoubtedly harms the clarity and exact understanding of the facts."[63] He added: "Among the movements that in different countries are designated by the name 'fascism,' points of contact can obviously be found, and it is useful to look for them and highlight them to better show a characteristic of the current international situation. However, I believe that when we analyze them, it is more important to look for the particularity of each of these movements, that is, for what differentiates it from all the others. In any case, this analysis must precede any generalization."[64] For Togliatti, this was not just a matter of analytical precision or theoretical orthodoxy, but a question of political efficacy: when they used "fascism" too arbitrarily, "our parties have sometimes made tactical errors because they attributed too general and too abstract a sense to the term 'fascism,' and because they had not bothered to make a social and political analysis to establish what it really was, in a specific country and situation, the movement designated by this name."[65] Togliatti thus preferred to limit his analyses to the case of Italian Fascism.

Sharing the Comintern definition, he stated that "Fascism is a form of bourgeois reaction, a form of defense of the capitalist order against the threat of the proletarian revolution. So far everyone agrees."[66] But a close study of the Italian situation revealed that "Italian Fascism cannot be sociologically defined in reference to a single class," because the Italian "petty bourgeoisie is not a homogeneous class."[67] It was diverse, composed of different and often contradictory interests, and, most important, it occupied an intermediate position between the industrial and the landowning bourgeoisie. The petty bourgeoisie fluctuated between these two wealthier but smaller classes. So, "to understand how Fascism came to power and consolidated in Italy, it is essential to understand these fluctuations together with the maneuvers carried out by the industrial bourgeoisie and the agrarians to derive all possible profit for their reactionary purposes."[68]

Togliatti's critique of the reductionist determinism of the Comintern's definition of "fascism" continued in 1928: "Fascism, its essence, its origins, its development, as an object of study, seem to interest the world of workers and parties that make up the Communist International more and more. However, I do not think that this 'need to know' always corresponds to an exact conception of the Fascist phenomenon, examined under its various aspects. . . . On the contrary, it seems to me that instead we allow ourselves to be substituted for the in-depth study of the phenomenon by exposing completely abstract generalizations that do not completely correspond to reality."[69] In Italy, "Fascism was not just a capitalist reaction. It included many other elements at the same time. It included a movement of the rural petty-bourgeois masses; it was also a political struggle waged by certain representatives of the petty and middle bourgeoisie against a part of the old ruling classes; it was an attempt to create a unified organization, extending throughout the country, grouping a fraction of the petty bourgeois in the cities headed by demoted elements (former officers, unemployed professionals, etc.); and it was, finally, a military organization that could claim to oppose the regular armed forces of the state with some probability of success."[70]

Poverty of analysis was for Togliatti the reason for liberals' and socialists' failure to hinder his rise, because "the complexity of the Fascist phenomenon meant that the evolution of the movement was not determined exclusively by the goals toward which the bourgeoisie and the agrarians were tending; it was also influenced by other reasons, of a different nature, by other impulses, arising from the very heart of the movement and which at certain moments even tried to dominate it."[71] In schematic form, then, Togliatti held that "Fascism is the most consequential system of integrated reaction that has existed up to now in countries where capitalism has reached a certain degree of development."[72] The thoroughness of this sort of reaction cannot be measured simply in quantitative terms but must rather be evaluated qualitatively as a "total systematic suppression of all forms of autonomous organization of the masses," which occurred differently in different societies.

Fascism's "total suppression of democratic freedoms" was necessary in Italy, "a very poor country," where the concentration of wealth and ownership of the means of production in only a few hands meant that the petty bourgeois struggled to contain "growing pressure exerted by the exuberant working population of the cities (proletarians and artisans) and the countryside (agricultural workers, poor peasants)."[73] It was unique to the Italian situation that Fascism developed into "a reactionary regime pushed to its extreme consequences."[74] That said, Togliatti concluded, after a thorough analysis of the complex "social bases" of Fascism, that "there is little chance of seeing a movement analogous to Italian Fascism arise in a completely different historical and social environment, and especially in a country where capitalism is very strong. . . . There is no need to do very thorough research to conclude that, in general, these conditions exist only in states with a weak economic structure, without political equilibrium, and where middle- and petty-bourgeois strata abound."[75]

Gramsci and Togliatti believed that the reasons behind the popular consent for Fascism, which, as a regime, never fulfilled the class interests of the petty bourgeoisie that supported it, could only be understood by unmasking its ideological principle, which united nationalism and imperialism as an indissoluble whole. The imperialistic project of Fascism, in fact, was charged with presenting "the struggle of Italy, a poor country fighting for its expansion, as a sort of class struggle."[76] Imperialism had the function, in other words, of presenting the geopolitical struggle of the Italian state in the arena of international diplomacy using the metaphor of the "class struggle" of the proletariat. In turn, this explained, for Togliatti, the ideological justification of the state's taking precedence over individuals and their "natural rights," because only the state, as an "organism that stands above all classes," would be able to solve the problems of class conflict by developing "an organization within which the various agents of production (proletarian, semiproletarian, and bourgeois) will collaborate directly and organically in order to seek the best structure to be given to production and the most equitable system of distribution of products."[77] And this organization of production would be possible only after Italian Fascism had improved its subordinate status vis-à-vis the other imperial nations.

Togliatti's resistance against a too-generic and deterministic understanding of "fascism" circulating within the Comintern did not prevent him from playing an increasingly influential role within it, owing largely to his political fidelity to Stalin.[78] After the outlawing of the opposition parties in November 1926 and the incarceration of Gramsci, Togliatti moved to Moscow and would not return to Italy until 1944. As chapter 9 will show, Togliatti continued to defend the idea that the socioeconomic analysis of individual movements, parties, and regimes of the extreme Right had to precede any generic theorization of the political form of "fascism," which became more urgent after Hitler's rise to power. It was in his *Corso sugli avversari* (Lectures on the Adversaries) that Togliatti elaborated a more sophisticated analysis of "fascism," which dialectically mediated between particular occurrences and the general logic of the bourgeois counterrevolutionary reaction.

8

The Liberals' Genericizations of "Fascism"

The First Genericizations of "Fascism"

The scholars, theoreticians, and political activists that attempted an analysis of the origins, characteristics, and ideology of Italian Fascism in the 1920s and 1930s with the aim of understanding and more effectively combating this new form of violent political reaction were confronted with the fact that they could observe the rise of similar movements at a global scale. Mark Mazower correctly observed that "every Fascist party worth its salt between the wars highlighted its impeccably nationalist credentials and often believed in them too, making sure they had their own special colour for their shirts and their own national symbols. Sartorially, to be a fascist between the wars meant wearing a brown shirt in Germany, a black one in Italy, green in Romania, blue in Spain, grey in South Africa, and gold in Mexico."[1] Ultranationalist paramilitary groups, engaged in often marginal but always violent political activism, expressing fundamentalist beliefs in Christianity and holding strong racist and antisemitic attitudes, seemed to pop up everywhere in the world, left in the wake of the First World War. Many expressed their nationalism through a sartorial selection of a particular color, as Mazower suggests; others did not. But the fact that groups of this sort were a transnational reality in the 1920s and 1930s explains quite well the urge on the part of contemporary observers to find a synthetic theory that could explain them all. These groups, most of which remained politically irrelevant in their countries, were constantly hybridizing, adapting, and copying styles, mottos, symbols, ideologies, and tactics from one another. "None of this," Mazower clarified, "of course meant there were not substantial ideological affinities with other, older and more prestigious movements. Quite the contrary: the insistence on one's own national credentials went alongside endless copying and borrowing of both content and presentation."[2]

It is not surprising that antifascist thinkers, too, tended to look transnationally and comparatively for similarities and differences, for common ontogenesis and diverging ideological constellations among the various forms of violent reaction emerging in the transwar period. For many, the question remained purely comparative, and thus even when the term "fascism" was used as a shortcut for the movements that were compared, its semantic function was clearly metonymical, emphasizing proximity, sharedness, and horizontal commonality as antonomasia, rather than a *pars pro toto*, or vertical synecdochical logic that signaled belonging to a higher categorical entity in which the compared movements participated.

Only Marxist thinkers, and even among them with varying degrees of reductionist stringency, attempted to derive inductively from the movements they observed a generic category that could express a political form that, as a symptom, denoted a transformation in the relations of production in capitalism during a period of crisis. In these cases, the generic category "fascism" explained the common socioeconomic origins rather than the shared political, institutional, or ideological characteristics of different movements. "Fascism" was thus defined as a counterrevolutionary reaction of the bourgeoisie against the revolutionary claims of the proletariat in a historically contingent condition of economic crisis and monopolistic consolidation in the wake of the First World War; but this reaction took different forms in different countries, depending on the social structures, cultural norms, customs, and tendencies within each nation. In Marxist writings of the transwar period, the taxonomy established by the genericized category "fascism" did not signify, as it did in postwar historiography, the reduction of individual political movements to a higher-level political *type* of which they were conceived as particular *tokens*; rather, it stood for the similar socioeconomic circumstances that gave rise to the formation of different forms of political reaction at the superstructural level. This might surely appear to be a subtle heuristic difference, which tended to disappear in the ideological ossification of "fascism" during the Cold War years, but it is still of great importance, since it suggests a different kind of cognitive labor behind the use of the genericized category "fascism" in the two historical contexts, producing distinct semantic markers associated with the term.

The use of the term "fascism" to identify movements and ideologies outside Italy by virtue of their resemblance to and affinity with Mussolini's occurred early on. Antonio Gramsci was probably the first commentator to advance, as early as 1920, the idea that Italian Fascism was not a political deviation or aberration exclusive of Italy, as Croce and others would later surmise; rather, he maintained, "the phenomenon of 'fascism' is not only Italian, just as the formation of the Communist Party is not only Italian."[3] The Comintern instituted a commission to study Fascism, of which Gramsci and Tasca were appointed members, only two weeks after Mussolini was given the title of prime minister. Karl Radek, Clara Zetkin, Grigory Zinovyev, and many others offered competing definitions and explanations of the fascist phenomenon beyond the Italian case in an attempt to abstract a generic theorization of the new political form.

The fact that the early genericizations of "fascism" occurred among Marxist thinkers and activists, which the following chapter will survey, is not surprising. For Marxism, the political, in its institutional and ideological forms, was an effect of the social relation of production. Thus, the new movements of violent counterrevolutionary reaction emerging in Europe in the wake of the First World War and the Bolshevik Revolution could be explained as new brands of bourgeois reaction to the emancipatory claims of the working classes and, at a structural level, as the political framework that capitalism needed in order to confirm the dominion of the capitalist class over the means and relations of production in a context of economic depression.

According to this explanatory model, the actual forms fascist movements took—whether or not they formed around charismatic leadership, whether or not they assumed the configuration of paramilitary organizations, whether or not they adopted racial or antisemitic ideologies, and so on—were accidental features that grew out of the contingent historical condition of the society in which these movements emerged rather than a necessary requirement of their fascist character (as in the postwar literature of the "fascist minimum"). Despite the attempts of the Comintern to impose an orthodox definition of "fascism," over the course of the 1920s and 1930s a variety of definitions and theorizations of the fascist phenomenon emerged from the Marxist front.

Theorizations of a generic fascism were more sporadic among non-Marxist political thinkers. Conservative liberals dismissed fascism as a contingent aberration, conceding, when they indulged in comparative analyses, that it was a product of politically immature societies or reflective of, if not directly generated by, the Bolshevik Revolution. Progressive liberals conceived of it as either the product of ultranationalist ideologies or the effect of the political preponderance of military elites in economically underdeveloped or immature capitalist nations. Both denied the Marxist allegations that fascism was in some respects an effect of capitalism. The rise of National Socialism in Germany in the second half of the 1920s and especially after Hitler's rise to power in 1933 favored the production of comparative analyses even among the most reluctant of theorists.

Generic Fascism in Conservative Liberals' Analyses

Benedetto Croce, the leader of conservative-liberal antifascists, wrote an article commissioned by the *New York Times* titled "The Fascist Germ Still Lives."[4] Written on October 14, 1943 but not published until six weeks later, it aimed at offering an ideological portrait of Fascism. "Outside Italy," Mussolini claimed, "the word 'fascism' had been interpreted in different ways and the sentiments which accompanied it have ranged from abhorrence to admiration."[5] The situation after the First World War, Croce explained, forgetting to mention that he was among the early supporters of Mussolini's regime, was a mixture of a weak political class, menacing upheavals of revolutionary communists, and an immature public opinion that still awaited a "man of providence." It was in those circumstances that the Fascist germ grew and spread.

From a recently liberated Naples Croce wrote confidently that "now Italy is free of the fascist infection. Although still in grave danger, she can die any kind of death but no longer that death."[6] Far from suggesting any sort of reassurance, he warned that "the germs of fascism" were still in circulation.[7] "Because if fascism has shown itself in a violent form in Italy," he claimed in a rare instance of the generic use of the term, "it is not exclusively an Italian fact, but as tendency, effort, aspiration, expectation, it has spread throughout the world."[8] It fed on the moral "lowering of the consciousness of liberty," a consciousness that, Croce was confident, "in all its brightness and fullness will rise again."[9] But despite the military success of the Allied forces, "the ideological danger of fascism still persists, even though it be latent." Indeed, fascism could spread its virulence beyond Italy and Germany, since the moral disease that predisposes a society to the advancement of fascism, for Croce, was inherent in the suspension of the principles that sustain common life in peacetime.

Peace was a necessary condition for the principles of liberalism, for Croce the standards of a good society, to flourish: "The changing vicissitudes of free competition, and the necessity of submitting to criticism, of holding discussions, of using demonstration and persuasion toward others" constituted the foundations of a peaceful, liberal society. But the protracted war that was necessary to defeat fascism could recreate the conditions for its persistence: "That is why," he warned his American readers, "I permit myself to suggest that fascism be not judged as a 'morbus Italicus' but as a contemporary sickness from which Italy was the first to suffer. It is because of her painful experiences that she can teach other peoples about it."[10] Fascism, for Croce, was the name of a pathological condition—a moral sickness—of modern societies, which, in times of crises produced by war, led them to forsake the liberal morals of individual freedom, the procedures of liberal democracy, and a capitalist free market. War was the ultimate cause of fascism, to which a politically weak and morally immature nation such as Italy easily surrendered, but to which not even mature countries like the United States were immune.

War and its effects on a morally immature nation-state were the ingredients for the rise of fascism also in the works of Helmut Plessner, Friedrich Meinecke, and Hans Kohn. Plessner, a philosophical anthropologist, in a monograph initially published in Switzerland under the title *Das Schicksal deutschen Geistes im Ausgang seiner bürgerlichen Epoche* (The Fate of the German Spirit at the End of Its Bourgeois Epoch), charged that Hitlerism had turned Germany into the enemy of the "political humanism of the Western world."[11] Just like Fascism in Italy, National Socialism could develop in the ruinous conditions left by the First World War, which brought to the fore the unsolved problems of German modernization. Plessner did not explicitly use "fascism" as sign vehicle for the regimes of Mussolini and Hitler. Still, he developed a parallel analysis of Italy and Germany aimed at explaining the coeval rise of Fascism and Nazism as inherent to the imperfect development of young nations: Germany's *Schicksal* (fate) was to inherit from its *Vergangenheitsbewältigung* (a coming to terms with its past) a developmental pathway for a modern state without an "idea" or "true mission," made up of a population that German Lutheranism had rendered "subservient" to authority (thus blunting the "emancipatory impulses" coming from the Enlightenment) while eagerly engaged in economic industriousness.[12] Its intellectuals, divided between a worship of culture and *Lebensphilosophie* (philosophy of life),[13] could not protect it from the rise of the "authoritarian biology" of National Socialism and its belief in *Volk*, race, blood, and soil.[14] Opposing the view that saw in fascism a new phase of capitalist development, as was proposed in the 1930s by the authors of the Frankfurt School, and anticipating, as a precursor, the argument of the *Sonderweg* historians of the 1960s, Plessner, like Croce, saw in the advent of National Socialism a disease similar to Fascism in Italy: a subversion of Enlightenment rationality and the affirmation of irrationalist beliefs that were however inherent in the *besonderer deutscher Weg* (special German path to modernity).

The First World War played a central role in the analyses of fascism of other conservative liberals. Friedrich Meinecke, a nationalist historian who did not hide his sympathies with the antisemitism of the Nazis, saw the rise of National Socialism as a catastrophe for the German nation. In *Die deutsche Katastrophe*, published in the immediate aftermath of the Second World War, Meinecke saw in Hitlerism an unfortunate accident that befell Germany, an aberrant version of nationalism that, in the social and moral disorder left by the First World War, adopted the form of violent rebellion from the Bolshevik movements that erupted in many German cities.[15] Like Croce, Meinecke saw in Nazism a disease that perverted the path toward the realization of a German liberalism, which, for him as for Croce, consisted of individual liberties and a market economy guaranteed by an authoritarian state.

Karl Popper and Friedrich von Hayek, too, postulated a correlation, if not a direct equivalence, between fascism (and Nazism) and socialism. In his 1949 book *The Open Society and Its Enemies*, Popper, a German sociologist and philosopher of science, maintained that "fascism," which for him stood as a proxy for both Italian Fascism and German Nazism, was nothing but the sign of a "perennial revolt against freedom and reason," like all forms of "modern totalitarianism," of which both fascism and socialism were typical examples.[16] As a form of subversion against the rational order of liberal societies, fascism "grew partly out of the spiritual and political breakdown of Marxism."[17] Hayek, a Viennese economist and one of the most influential theorists of conservative liberalism, similarly argued in his 1944 work *The Road to Serfdom* that "fascism" (by which he meant both the Italian and German regimes) derived directly from Marxism: "Few are ready to recognize," he complained, "that the rise of Fascism and Nazism was not a reaction against the socialist trends of the preceding period, but a necessary outcome of those tendencies."[18] Fascism was, in fact, a sort of socialism of the middle classes: "There is a great deal of truth in the often heard statement that Fascism and National Socialism are a sort of middle-class socialism. . . . It was to a large extent a revolt of a new under-privileged class against the labour aristocracy which the industrial labour movement had created."[19]

The US historian Hans Kohn, too, considered fascism—in all the forms it took in Europe—and communism two sides of the same phenomenon, typical of twentieth-century totalitarian dictatorships.[20] What Kohn believed Italian Fascism and German National Socialism shared, however, was an embrace of war as the "normal state of life," effectively "the culmination in which the vital and ethical energies of man reveal themselves at their best."[21] More important than their nationalism and anticommunism, European fascisms emphasized war as the essence of their political message: "Politics," for them, "now becomes a preparation for war, receives its direction and meaning from this extreme 'Ernstfall' [emergency]."[22] For Kohn, "the totalitarian philosophy of war makes wars at present fought by the totalitarian states fundamentally different from the wars of the nineteenth century and even from the first World War."[23] Therefore, while sharing with other conservative liberals the conviction that fascism was a form of antiliberal reaction more similar to communism than to liberalism, for Kohn it was its fanatic attitude toward war that rendered them both catastrophically dangerous.

Generic Fascism as a Loose Transnational Political Category

In the interwar period, liberals' conceptualizations of "fascism" as a generic political phenomenon were mainly found in the writings of émigrés who were able to find asylum from the persecutions of Fascism and Nazism. As Enzo Traverso put it, "Anti-fascist culture was also, to a very great extent, a culture of exile."[24] Scholars including Franz Borkenau, Aurel Kolnai, Gaetano Salvemini, Ernst Toller, Franz Neumann, Sebastian Haffner, and many others contributed with their writings to the formation of a firm antifascism among the British literate and scholarly society.[25] But in the same period, the term "fascism" was often employed, in political speeches and newspapers op-eds, in a vaguely generic sense to identify counterrevolutionary reactions beyond Mussolini's and often independent of it. This sort of genericization was rarely conceptualized and is more difficult to assess with precision from a semiotic perspective. It can be understood as a linguistic practice not unlike antonomasic or eponymic naming, like "hooligan," "aspirin," "diesel," or "quixotic," which genericize a proper noun to a common one on the basis of perceived similarities of aspect, structure, or function, but without thorough theorization or argumentation.[26] It had surely rhetorical aims, appealing to shared values and affective reaction for either sympathizers or antifascists. But it de facto facilitated the transference of denotative connotations attached to the indexical use of "fascism" as a proper noun to other movements and ideologies, with evident cognitive effects.

To give a few examples of this use, in Great Britain conservative liberals who were committed to explicit antifascism were caught in a contradictory position. For most, "antifascism" was really a proxy for anti-Nazism (despite the persistent sympathies for Hitler among the British aristocracy), since Mussolini had gathered among British conservatives a large consensus from the beginning.[27] As Philip Williamson put it, "A number of [British] Conservatives admired fascism in one or more of its British or foreign forms. . . . Yet the party as a whole was, at the very least, the largest 'non-fascist' political organization."[28] The antifascism of British conservatives, in both its passive and active forms, consisted of an "ideological and moral resistance towards dictatorship and totalitarianism," even though they shared with fascist regimes a visceral anticommunism and the conviction that the state had to intervene in coordinating industrial and agricultural production for the sake of national prosperity (especially after the Great Slump of the early 1930s).[29]

The institutional channels where most of the antifascist organizations and propaganda operated were the Labour Party and the unions, even though this antifascism often took the form of a passive resistance that embraced a firm pacifist stance.[30] Antifascism mobilized against what was conceived of as a global phenomenon: internationally, that included Franco's *falangismo* and the growing threat of Hitler's Germany, but also, under the umbrella of "totalitarianism," Stalin's Soviet Union; domestically, they confronted the small but very vocal activism of Oswald Mosley's British Union of Fascists, which united themes from traditional conservatism (a hierarchical view of society, antisemitism, racial and cultural exclusivism, military values, etc.) and socialism (the nationalization of heavy industries, a corporativist conception of macroeconomic organization, and labor unions modeled on the Confederazione Nazionale delle Corporazioni Sindacali [National Confederation of Labor Corporations] of Edmondo Rossoni, Dino Grandi, and Massimo Rocca).[31]

In the France of the 1930s, which "found itself under attack from the new forces of the right,"[32] "fascism" became the sign vehicle through which different extreme-right phenomena could be collectively addressed, thus augmenting its referential capacity. With the exception of Marxist theorizations, which the next chapter analyzes, the use was largely metonymical, "fascism" being used as antonomasia to group together coeval and contiguous movements of extreme nationalism and paramilitarism. While the conservative Fédération Républicaine under the leadership of Louis Marin remained within the confines of liberalism, the Jeunesses Patriotes of Pierre Taittinger defined its program as expressing "a very republican fascism";[33] Georges Valois's Le Faisceau was directly inspired by Mussolini's movement and similarly funded by industrialists (e.g., Eugène Mathon and François Coty), who hoped that its corporative policy could curb the growing labor movement in France. Charles Maurras's Action Française was strongly counterrevolutionary and antiliberal but more monarchist and aristocratic than populist when compared with the various extreme-right leagues.[34] François de La Rocque's Croix-de-Feu, counterrevolutionary, xenophobic, and antisemitic, like many other rightist leagues mixed elements of mass politics (universal suffrage, corporatism, military values, etc.) and attracted the sympathies of Catholic conservatives.[35] Antisemitism, as the Israeli historian Zeev Sternhell has argued, had stronger roots in France than anywhere else in Europe, to the point that he believes that "fascism," for him the name of a new political form that emerged in the late nineteenth century and to which Mussolini's movement contributed only by giving it a name a posteriori, should be regarded as a French invention, starting from Georges Boulanger's Bonapartism and including such varied ideological formulations as Georges Sorel's syndicalism, the cultural circle that formed around Valois's Cercle Proudhon, and others.[36] Liberal antifascism in France also insisted on the close relationship between fascism and communism insofar as both targeted the political and economic institutions of liberalism.[37]

Throughout the 1930s, "fascism" operated as a term that loosely identified both the counterrevolutionary, antigovernmental activism of subversive movements and the authoritarian tendencies within the government. The metonymical association with the regimes of Mussolini and, later, Hitler functioned in those cases as a critique aimed at warning against a perceived decay of liberal institutions. Examples of such use were ubiquitous in Europe. They occurred largely in the writings of antifascists, since only a minority of ultranationalist movements (in the UK, Ireland, France, and Poland) adopted the term "fascism" in their names.[38] But retracing its use outside the European context, where comparisons with Italy (and Germany) were less obvious, gives a sense of the transnational fungibility of this term in the interwar years.[39] While a comprehensive reconstruction of this history goes beyond the scope of this study, the case of Japan is particularly revealing given its later alliance with Italy and Germany.

Welcomed after the First World War within the League of Nation as one of the "Big Four" global powers, during the 1930s Japan was often presented as a country that was undergoing an authoritarian turn. "In the thirties," George Wilson stated, "both Japanese and Western writers were quick to fasten on fascism as a label for the extremist patriotic groups—civilian and military—that were appearing on the scene."[40] In fact, the brief parenthesis of bottom-up political initiatives (political parties, labor unions, socialism, etc.), which in the Taishō era (1912–26) had fostered the development of an active public sphere and the expansion of the suffrage to all of the male population, did not changed the authoritarian structures of the Meiji Constitution of 1889.

In 1930s Japan, the use of "fascism" was not without ambiguities: it negatively connoted paramilitary groups and ultranationalist associations engaged in subversive activities aimed at "restoring" absolute powers to the emperor, as well as the government, especially after the invasion of Manchuria in 1931 and mainland China in 1937 (even though it was the same government that quelled the terrorism of the ultranationalists). For instance, in 1932 the American journalist Thomas Arthur Bisson, a sympathizer of the Chinese Communist movement, reported on "the rise of Fascism in Japan."[41] In 1936 the journalist William Henry Chamberlin described Japan as a "semi-fascist" state and anticipated its "natural alliance" with Germany. In Japan, he wrote, "intellectuals, always responsive to new foreign ideas and influences, were impressed by the sweep of Fascism in Europe."[42] In 1937 E. B. Ashton compared the Japanese political and economic systems to those of fascist states such as Italy and Germany, pointing out the similar collectivization of capitalist economy by monopolistic agents who operated in close collaboration with fascist elites inside the state apparatus.[43] Wilfrid Fleisher, after fleeing Japan in the summer of 1941, declared that the country had entered a fascist stage as a "collective dictatorship." A resident of Japan since his childhood, Fleisher moved back to the United States to work for the Foreign Office and, during the postwar occupation, became an investigator for General Douglas MacArthur. In two texts he published in 1941 and 1942, Fleischer described Japan as "engulfed by the Fascist tide" and explained: "[The] Japanese insistently repudiate the term 'Fascist' as applied to their national movement, contending that it is not a copy of Italian and German methods but a nationalism of Japanese origin, rooted in feudal days. Certainly Japanese Fascism has elements of its own, but in recent years it has looked principally to Germany for guidance in the establishment of a totalitarian state."[44]

"Fascism" circulated also domestically among Japanese liberals. In 1932 Yoshino Sakuzō published in English an article titled "Fascism in Japan."[45] In it, he complained that "the party politicians work under the orders of their paymasters, the plutocrats, and these orders are obviously to serve the interests of big business, while the little man, and particularly the farmer, is progressively impoverished."[46] Like Yoshino, other Japanese liberal thinkers employed "fascism" to qualify specific elements of state ideology. The progressive liberal journalist Hasegawa Nyozekan, author of a critique of Japanese fascism, *Nihon fashizumu hihan* (1932), acknowledged that fascism constituted a serious threat for Japan.[47] He wrote in the immediate aftermath of the invasion of Manchuria and the military intervention in Shanghai, which cost Japan its membership in the League of Nations.[48] Similarly to Marxists, he was convinced that "ultimately, fascism serves to reinforce capitalism and its 'bourgeois dictatorship' by the elimination of all organized legal opposition, especially that of the working class."[49] The economist Kawai Eijirō also employed "fascism" as generic category to criticize the militaristic tendencies of Japanese political and economic elites.[50] Other Japanese liberals, such as Kiryū Yūyū, Yanaihara Tadao, Ishibashi Tanzan, Kiyosawa Kiyoshi, Masaki Hiroshi, Ubukata Toshirō, and Ienaga Saburō, denounced the fascistic or militaristic descent of the Japanese government, but after 1937 they were more or less forced by the authorities to moderate their critiques. The conservative liberal Imanaka Tsugimaro believed that German Nazism and Italian Fascism were not "reactionary" but "revolutionary" movements, the roots of which lay in socialism, and suggested that fascism, as a "third way," "is not a concept that can be completely subsumed under the category of a capitalist reactionary movement."[51] Indeed, for him "the parallel direction in the force of fascism and communism is a fact difficult to ignore";[52] both had to be understood as similarly advocating an anticapitalist revolution. Unlike communism, however, fascism located its redemptive aspirations in constructing an ethnically pure national community.

Opposition to "fascism" came not only from political antagonists, but also from ultranationalists, those whom Reto Hofmann calls the "fascists" who rejected Fascism.[53] Ultranationalists such as Tōyama Mitsuru, Nakano Seigō, Ōkawa Shūmei, Kita Ikki, Araki Sadao, and Hashimoto Kingorō, among many others, organized concerted attacks against the most liberal members of the political class and operated through paramilitary secret societies to plot coups d'état intended to restore absolute power to the emperor. Some of them held positions within big financial-industrial conglomerates (Kita, Ōkawa, and Hashimoto), within the armed forces (Araki, Masaki, and Hashimoto), and within the state bureaucracy (Nakano, Ōkawa, and Araki). For them, "fascism" did not offer anything that could be of ideological use for their dreams of national palingenesis—as a European doctrine, it had nothing to offer their nationalist cause.

Despite an increase in acts of domestic right-wing terrorism beginning in 1931 and culminating in a failed coup d'état on February 26, 1936, which involved many of the ultranationalists mentioned above, the government stood firm under the hegemony of Konoe Fumimaro, who preserved the existing state institutions, until the intensification of the war in China in 1937–38. The National General Mobilization Law was enacted on March 24, 1938, and only after the Tripartite Pact with Italy and Germany, on October 12, 1940, when war had already assumed the connotation of "total," did all political parties voluntarily disband to form the *Taisei yakusankai* (Imperial Rule Assistance Association).[54]

During the war years, and especially after Japan's alliance with Italy and Germany, Japan would be regarded as part of the fascist Axis; and yet, even in propaganda such as Frank Capra's documentary *Know Your Enemy: Japan*, the emphasis was on explaining how Japan's feudal samurai mentality had indoctrinated its population to accept sacrifice for the semidivine emperor, rather than on fascism. Interestingly, when all wartime commentators appealed to "fascism" to clarify the nature of the authoritarianism and aggressive imperialism of Japan, they tended to refer to Nazi Germany, rather than Fascist Italy, as the model upon which Japanese fascism was built. It was only among Japanese Marxists that a generic use of "fascism" as a well-defined political category would consolidate, as the next chapter will show.

"Fascism" as Totalitarianism

A disease, an aberration, or a parenthesis, "fascism" for liberals of conservative and progressive leanings signified a further interruption of the reconstitution of a liberal sociopolitical order from the disruptions of the First World War and of the Bolshevik Revolution. Fascisms, with their excessive nationalism, worship of war and violence, and mass mobilization around a charismatic leader, were not just antithetical to the idea of liberalism but, especially for conservative liberals, directly linked to Bolshevism, for some as a sort of obverse analogy (Croce), for others as virtually equivalent (Hayek and Popper).

The interpretation of generic fascism that received the largest consensus among conservative and progressive liberals was that which conceived of it as a form of "totalitarianism"—a term designating, in Traverso's words, both a *fait* (fact), the "totalitarian regimes as historical realities," and a *concept* (concept), "a model of domination established by the comparative analysis of totalitarian regimes."[55] Although one could find a precursor of the idea of the *totale Staat* (total state) in Hegel's philosophy of right, which conceived of the *sittlicher Staat* (ethical state) as an encompassing unity and culmination of the rational will of all its individual members, the idea of "totalitarianism" derived from the notion of *totale Krieg* (total war) as realized during the First World War and fully conceptualized in the work of Erich Ludendorff.[56]

The "totalitarian state," as Hans Barth defined it, "appeared as a state engaged in war. In the [First] World War, for the first time in the twentieth century, the total reserves of national strength were concentrated in one great effort to destroy the enemy. The war was not the concern of the mobilized armies alone. It engaged the whole nation."[57] Total war was the form war took in the era of democracy and mass politics: as such, it abandoned the norms of the *jus in bello* prevalent during the anciens régimes to become what Immanuel Kant had prefigured as a *bellum internecinum*, a war of extermination.[58] To pursue the complete annihilation of the enemy, total war required the full collaboration of all social, economic, political, cultural, and intellectual resources of the nation.[59] The total war that was the First World War presaged the creation of a new idealization of war, in which heroism, sacrifice, and the methodical calculation of the enemy's complete destruction were sublimated in a new aesthetics by postwar Futurists and the ideologues of the conservative revolution.[60] All these elements merged in the definition of "totalitarian" that the early critics of Fascism (the liberal Amendola, the socialist Basso, and the Catholic Sturzo) proposed as early as 1923 for Mussolini's regime.[61]

War literally and symbolically regulated the political maturation of both Benito Mussolini and Adolf Hitler, whose experiences in the trenches translated into their new ideas of state and society. Fascism and Nazism, as totalitarianisms, were thus "children of modernity and presuppose a mass society, urban and industrial; they arise from the 'nationalization of the masses,' of which the First World War was a powerful accelerator."[62] Fascist totalitarianisms appropriated the experience of the trench war and translated it into a political project that, in contrast with traditional conservativism and its nostalgia for the *anciens régimes*, was grounded, like democracy, in mass support but presented itself as antiliberal, rejecting, that is, the principles of representative government, a market economy, negotiation, rational discussion, and so on that characterized the liberal state. As Enzo Traverso and Peter Reichel have argued, however, the masses that fascist totalitarianisms prefigured were not real "political subjects" but functioned as mere choreography, having no more than an "ornamental function."[63] Hans Kohn had pointed that out as early as 1941: "Modern dictatorships are post-democratic movements" insofar as they turn the model of liberal democracy upside down while conserving some of its features.[64]

Mussolini and other Fascist ideologues skillfully appropriated the notion of "totalitarianism" from their critics and repurposed it to express a new conception of the state, which became "not only a moral and spiritual entity capable of embodying the conscience of the nation, but above all a Moloch capable of completely encompassing the civil society."[65] The idea of the totalitarian state was sustained by an eclectic synthesis of fuzzy ideas and well-orchestrated rituals—a pastiche of myths, moods, emotions, and impressions rather than argument and sound reasoning—the aim of which was to facilitate the identification of the masses with the state through a skillful combination of storytelling, rhetorical manipulation of the language, and a secular state liturgy that offered them a feeling of belonging and participation.[66] "Totalitarianism," observes Traverso, "was the ideology in which the Fascist regime tried to amalgamate a set of values and myths linked to the heterogeneous elements of its culture: vitalism, the will to power, nationalism, *romanità*, the contempt of danger, the cult of virility, of technique, of warrior community, of violence, of conquest, of military expansion."[67] It served as a regulative idea that operated as gravitation pull around which a disparate constellation of creeds, myths, imaginaries, and moods were kept together to sustain the communion of masses and state through its incarnation, the Duce.

"Totalitarianism," in the Fascist ideological strategy, simplified the complexities of social life in a country such as Italy that was marked by irresolvable regional, linguistic, and social differences, reducing them to a communitarian camaraderie inspired by the experience of trench warfare. In Germany, Ernst Jünger developed a similar sense of emotional communion of individual and state in his idea of *totale Mobilmachung* (total mobilization), which turned the experience of the war into an internal awakening to a new conception of the national community, by him conceived as an ensemble of self-abnegating soldier-workers devoted to the protection and nurturing of the state.[68] Carl Schmitt's *totale Staat* also rejected the "degenerate normativism" of the liberal state and wanted to "restore the authentic function of the Hobbesian absolute state, that is to say, in his interpretation, the embodiment of sovereignty without any internal fracture and without any external constraint."[69] Schmitt's total state, like Mussolini's, substituted the praxis, institutions, and conceptions of the liberal state with a national community structured on the template of a secularized religious community.[70] For him, not only was the individual's own existence completely absorbed in and indistinguishable from the national community, but this was conceived of as being perpetually opposed to other national communities in an eschatological opposition of *Freunde und Feinde* (friends and foes), since "the essence of all things is war. The nature of total war determines the nature of the form of the state in its totality."[71]

The totalitarianism of Italian Fascism, for Schmitt, provided a solution to the crisis of the Weimar Republic. Schmitt's student Ernst Forsthoff clearly stated something similar in 1933: "The total state is the antithesis of the liberal state; it is a wholesome state opposed to the liberal state, which is emptied of all content, diminished and annihilated because of its fragmentation, that is to say, because of the juridical guarantees determined by laws which respond to particular interests. The total state is a formula that should serve to announce and clarify in the eyes of a political world still accustomed to the liberal conceptual system the emergence of a new state with the strength of its antithesis to it. The total state is therefore a liberal term indicating something absolutely nonliberal."[72] A total state could realize the historical mission of the nation only through an authoritarian government that repressed individualistic desires for the common struggle against other nations. In turn, "authoritarian government requires a justification that goes beyond the personal. This justification must be metaphysical; it must legitimate authority in addition to leadership."[73] That is the central role of the *Führer* (leader) in guiding a national community in the total state: "The order of domination of the total state must thus have a dual structure. It will remain predictable and bureaucratic in some important areas, but the rest will have to be organized hierarchically, imperatively, in the forms of personal rule. For only a state in which even the lower levels have personal rule, tamed by unlimited responsibility and carried by an initiative that is in principle free but obligated to the will of the Führer, is truly authoritarian and conceivable as a total state. Only such a state can extend its claim to rule to areas that resist all schematization and calculable regimentation."[74] In Forsthoff's conception, the denotations of "total" and "totalitarian" conformed to those of the critics of Fascism (starting from Amendola, Sturzo, and Basso)—that is, the negation of the institutions and values of the liberal state and the corresponding affirmation of authoritarianism and surrender to the leadership of the Duce and the Führer—but its connotations were now turned from negative to positive, thus neutralizing the rhetorical and critical efficacy of the term.

As the ideological polarization of liberal versus authoritarian values intensified in the 1930s, "totalitarian" became a heuristic category applicable not only to Fascist Italy and Nazi Germany, but to the state-centered authoritarianism of the Soviet Union under Joseph Stalin. For instance, Sturzo, in exile in the United States, argued that, while "we must . . . avoid abstract formulae" and understand that "reality refuses to fit into formulae," "since we are obliged, for the sake of convenience of language, to seek the general and the typical, we speak readily of a totalitarianism that may be Bolshevist, Fascist or Nazi."[75] For Sturzo, it was an unfortunate effect of the "changes and upheavals of the [First] World War" which assured the affirmation of a sense of nation antithetical to the democratic principle of the liberal state that the last decades of the nineteenth century had promised to deliver: "Centralization, militarism, state schools and protective tariffs" facilitated a nationalistic centralization that paved the way to the totalitarian state.[76] Its characteristics, in both fascist and Bolshevist articulations, were "administrative centralization . . . carried to extremes," complete "control of the army," the tendency "to militarize the country," a "rigorous monopoly" of "state education," and a "harsher and more strictly controlled economic policy."[77] For the Catholic philosopher Jacques Maritain as for Sturzo, "totalitarianism" identified a similarity between the modernism of Nazism and Italian Fascism, which looked back to paganism and ancient Rome, and the atheist modernism of the Bolshevik state. Both regimes, for Maritain, transformed "hatred into a virtue and dedicated themselves to war," and in so doing bent "man to an inhuman humanism of a sort, one the atheistic humanism of the dictatorship of the proletariat, the other the idolatrous humanism of Caesar, or the zoological humanism of blood and race."[78] As a supporter of religious and philosophical pluralism, Maritain conceived of totalitarianism, in whatever form, as a limitation on the variety and diversity of individuals coexisting within a community.[79] Yet, Fascism was for him "a greater historic power than the Stalinist evil."[80] While Marxism, despite its Stalinist deformation, had at least the potential to realize the ideal of a peaceful coexistence of differences that

Maritain embraced, fascism, in both its Italian and German forms, inevitably subjected the individual to the demands of the state.

The Austrian Franz Borkenau conceived of "totalitarianism" as what Nazi Germany and Stalin's Russia had in common, claiming in 1938 that "the state he [Lenin] created was neither democratic not Soviet, but simply a state of a totalitarian bureaucracy."[81] This extended use of "totalitarianism" was compatible with the idea of "red fascism," first developed by the Italian anarchist Luigi Fabbri, who in his *La controrivoluzione preventiva* (1922) wrote: "Bolshevism, understood in the sense of absolute civil and military power, of power with an iron fist, entrusted to a single class, indeed to a single party, indeed to a few leaders of a party—the dictatorship of the proletariat is an expression that can also mean dictatorship over the proletariat—that would certainly be bad, the worst expression of the revolution of the working class; but very probably the currently dominant classes are preparing its triumph spiritually and materially. The royal guards and the current fascists [are] perhaps prelude to the future red guards and red fascists."[82] Red fascists, Fabbri explained, was the term used to designate "those Bolshevik communists who are more inclined to adopt the methods of fascism toward their adversaries."[83]

Explicit references to the idea of "red fascism" can be found in Franz Borkenau's *The Totalitarian Enemy* (1939),[84] Otto Rühle's *The Struggle against Fascism Begins with the Struggle against Bolshevism* (1939),[85] Wilhelm Reich's *Die Massenpsychologie des Faschismus* (1933),[86] Volin's *Le fascisme rouge* (1934),[87] and others. Reich rooted the origin of "fascism" (which in his book stands as a proxy for National Socialism) in the patriarchal family and the punishing form of socialization it imposes upon the child.[88] In its political form, fascism "is not," for Reich, "as is generally believed, a purely reactionary movement; rather, it is a mixture of *rebellious* emotions and *reactionary* social ideas."[89] As such, it is "*never* revolutionary."[90] Because of its origin in the repressive patriarchal family, "a mechanistic authoritarian civilization only reaps, in the form of fascism, from the little, suppressed man what for hundreds of years it has sown in the masses of little, suppressed individuals in the form of mysticism, top-sergeant mentality, and automatism. This little man has only too well learned the way of the big man and now gives it back, enlarged and distorted."[91] Fascism is therefore irrational, or, as he put it, "the sum total of all *irrational* reactions of the average human character."[92] Consequently, it is an "extreme expression of religious mysticism," which had its fountainhead in Nazi theories of race.[93]

Fascism, for Reich, acted as a totalitarian dictatorship, which was "based on the irrationalism which the masses of people have inevitably acquired as a result of their upbringing."[94] Totalitarian authoritarianism, Reich admitted, was not limited to fascist regimes: "In the Soviet Union, the mixture of longing for freedom and structural fear of responsible self-government created a form of state which corresponded less and less to the original program of the Communists and which finally assumed authoritarian, totalitarian and dictatorial forms."[95] But while Soviet totalitarianism was the result of a degeneration of an emancipatory ideal (Reich here seems to echo Maritain), fascism was more than a political party imposing its governmental authority: It was "a specific Weltanschauung and a specific attitude towards people, towards love and work."[96] This, for Reich, was a point of fundamental importance in qualifying the two distinct totalitarianisms not only for analysis, but also for the political organization of an antifascist resistance: "Clearly, international fascism will never be vanquished by political maneuvers. It can only be vanquished by the natural organization of work, love and knowledge on an international scale."[97]

The Spanish philosopher José Ortega y Gasset, although he never used the term "totalitarianism," saw in both fascism and Bolshevism the birth of a dictatorial state that negated the rights and full development of the individual in the name of their being expressions of the *hombre-masa* (mass man).[98] Similarly, the French historian Élie Halévy conceived of fascism and bolshevism as consequences of the First World War: Germany and Italy, the dictatorial fascist regimes, were for him "direct imitations of Russian governmental methods," which they employed as a "reaction against 'socialist anarchy.' "[99]

Even Leon Trotsky embraced the notion of "totalitarianism" as a critique of the Stalinist transformation of the goals of the 1917 revolution. In 1936 he claimed that "the [Stalinist] regime had become 'totalitarian' in character several years before this word arrived from Germany."[100] He added that "if exploitation [in Russia] is 'ended forever,' if the country is really now on the road from socialism, that is, the lowest stage *of* communism, to its higher stage, then there remains nothing for society to do but to throw off at last the straitjacket *of* the state. In place of this—it is hard even to grasp this contrast with the mind!—the Soviet state has acquired a totalitarian-bureaucratic character."[101]

As Traverso points out, the view that Fascism, Nazism, and Stalinism were three aspects of the same totalitarian tendency remained a minority one before and during the Second World War, the Soviet Union being at the time perceived as a bastion against the advance of Nazism and Fascism in Europe.[102] Indeed, the liberal philosopher and historian Hans Kohn had pointed out in 1935 that if fascism and communism were equally postdemocratic forms of government, they developed opposite regimes: the first nationalist, the second cosmopolitan; the first nihilist, the second humanist; the first antisocialist, the second anticapitalist; the first realizing itself as a "charismatic," "nationalist," and "permanent" dictatorship, the second pursuing a "rationalist," "universalist," and "temporary" dictatorship.[103]

The consolidation of the use of "totalitarianism" for both Nazi Germany (and Fascist Italy) and the Soviet Union is a postwar development, the early formulations of which were in Karl Popper's *The Open Society and Its Enemy* (1945), E. H. Carr's *The Soviet Impact on the Western World* (1947), Hannah Arendt's *The Origins of Totalitarianism* (1951), and Zbigniew Brzezinski and Carl Friedrich's *Totalitarian Dictatorship and Autocracy* (1956). The endurance of this expanded usage of "totalitarianism" to encompass both fascism and communism is a heuristic practice that consolidated in the context of the Cold War and still persists today, for instance in Resolution no. 2819 (2019) of the European Parliament, which de facto equalizes "fascisms" with communism.[104]

The notion of "totalitarianism" as defining the shared character of Fascism and Nazism was particularly appealing to progressive liberals. The liberal anarchist Daniel Guérin, in his 1936 *Fascisme et grand capital*, argued that the totalitarian state Mussolini and Hitler created was necessary to stabilize their regimes, the success of which was possible in part thanks to the support of the revolutionary "plebeians" (Guérin's expression for the working classes). Once power was won, Fascism's "financial backers . . . attained their objectives: the annihilation of parliamentary democracy, the extermination of the proletarian organizations, and the formation of an authoritarian state through which they can impose their will and raise their profits."[105] For Guérin, Fascism's totalitarian state safeguarded the interests of the capitalist groups from the interference of the working classes:

> The capitalist groups in light industry put up no serious resistance to fascism. "They did not want its triumph, its 'totalitarian' dictatorship, but they did nothing effective to block its progress. Why not? First, because fascism was a 'national' movement, that is to say, in the service of the owning class and deserving, by this token, the sympathy, or at least the tolerance, of all property owners. . . . They saw fascism as just one more political movement, which they could manipulate and even make use of. And so in both countries [Italy and Germany], 'liberal' politicians closely connected to the light industry groups temporized with fascism."[106]

What was at first instrumentalist support of the capitalist classes for movements such as Fascism and Nazism that rhetorically presented themselves as being on the side of the "plebeians" became full support for a totalitarian exercise of power that effectively marginalized the "plebeian interests" and guaranteed the continuation of the profits of the capitalists of light industry that were now, de facto if not de jure, integrated with the machinery of state administration.

With the outbreak of the war and, after 1941, with the antifascist alliance between the UK, the United States, and the Soviet Union, "totalitarianism" ceased to play a central terminological role: "From the summer of 1941, with the Nazi aggression against the USSR and the reversal of alliances during the war, the notion of totalitarianism ceased to be used in its comparatist sense. It seemed to have disappeared from the Allied press and antifascist literature."[107] The war was officially and for all intents and purposes a war against fascism, and with the noticeable exceptions of Popper and von Hayek, reference to "totalitarianism" was cautiously avoided, especially when it included the regime of the Allied Power of Joseph Stalin's Soviet Union.

The notion of totalitarianism appealed instead to some Marxist theorists. Trotsky, as mentioned earlier, used it in his polemic against what he perceived to be Stalin's perversion of the October Revolution. Herbert Marcuse employed it to define the common characteristics of both Italian Fascism and German Nazism. In a direct refutation of Popper, Marcuse argued that "the roots of Fascism are traceable to the antagonisms between growing industrial monopolization and the democratic system."[108] In the social and economic disarray that the First World War had left, "the most powerful industrial groups tended to assume direct political power in order to organize monopolistic production, to destroy the socialist opposition, and to resume imperialist expansion."[109] The "totalitarian state" was also central to Franz Neumann's anatomy of the Nazi State, which was the repudiation of "the philosophical, legal, sociological, and economic concepts with which we operate daily and which characterize our society."[110] The "totalitarian ideology" of Nazism, he claimed, "differs from democratic ideologies not only because it is single and exclusive"—it rejected, that is, the possibility of any view other than that of the Führer—"but because it is fused with terror," with the ruthless exercise of violence that disallowed the coexistence of other ideologies.[111] "The idea of the totalitarian state," he elaborated, "grew out of the demand that all power be concentrated in the hands of the president. Immediately after Hitler's accession to power, political theorists began to make much of the totalitarian idea as elaborated by the constitutional lawyers. All power was to be vested in the state; anything less was sabotage of the National Socialist revolution. The totalitarian state was described as an order of domination and a form of people's community. It was anti-democratic because democracy, with its notion of an identity between the ruler and the ruled, undermined the necessary authority of leadership. Leadership, the National Socialists declared, is not delegated by the people."[112] But the *Führerprinzip* (lit., leader principle; the idea that the word of the leader transcends any and all written law), which regulated the entirety of the Nazi totalitarian state, created a situation of chaotic anarchies among different centers of powers, which Neumann effectively represented with the image of the biblical Behemoth. It effectively created a polyarchy engaged in an internecine competition, a sort of *bellum omnium contra omnes* (war of all against all), to better interpret and impersonate Hitler's guiding principles. The resulting state that the Third Reich built became the executor of the will of the German *Volk* that only the Führer could understand, direct, and actualize. The conflicts opposing the armed forces, the paramilitary organization of the SS, the economic elites, the party, the state bureaucracy, and so on to one another were not the result of a failure in governance, but the inevitable result of a polycratic structure and of its ideology, which elevated the principle of survival of the strongest to a system of governance. Hitler's totalitarian state was, in effect, a polyarchy which took the form of a "chaotic, lawless, and amorphous monster."[113]

"After having been theorized for Italian fascism and used in an essentially descriptive way by different groups of exiled intellectuals," concludes Traverso, "the notion of totalitarianism reached, during the outbreak of the Second World War, the status of a keyword in the political vocabulary whose usage is shared by liberals as well as by several Christian antifascists, joined by a minority of Marxists and a few communist intellectuals disappointed with Stalinism."[114] Its heuristic success, however, came to full fruition only after the Second World War and with the beginning of a new, colder one.

9

The Marxists' Genericizations of "Fascism"

The most sophisticated attempts to develop a genericized understanding of "fascism" as a category encompassing a diverse array of political movements in the interwar period came from thinkers and activists in the Marxist camp. This is hardly surprising. Differently from conservative and progressive liberals, who conceived of Fascism and Nazism as essentially derivative and contingent phenomena of specific societies and historical circumstances, Marxists saw in "fascism" a symptom that was structurally embedded in the socioeconomic transformations of capitalism in the 1920s and 1930s. Conservative liberals conceived of the authoritarian turns in Italy and Germany as a disease or an aberration linked more or less directly to the contingent delayed development of those countries and to the international effects of the communist revolution in Russia. Progressive liberals, despite the different interpretations they endorsed, for the most part conceived of it as a radical form of militaristic nationalism sustained by the middle classes, who were left impoverished by the economic crises of the 1920s, and by the veterans of the First World War, who wanted to transfer their war experience into politics. Liberals of different political orientations, that is, similarly saw fascism essentially as a political degeneration resulting from the socioeconomic precarity of the 1920s and mainly affecting delayed, underdeveloped, or structurally uneven nations.

For Marxists, however, Fascism and Nazism were not simply historical accidents, but two different political actualizations of a new developmental stage of capitalism, one that originated as a reaction against the emancipatory claims of the working classes in order to protect the interests of the capitalist classes. Marxists' propensity for generalized structural analyses was methodological. Although conservative and progressive liberals tended to limit their political and socioeconomic analyses to individual national communities, Marxists privileged what might be called a transnationalism *ante litteram*, an approach that looked at dynamics and processes transcending the distinct nation-states and that thus favored analyses that stressed comparison and connectivity. And although liberals conceived of politics as the regulative force that ordered a national community, for Marxists, political institutions and forms of governance were the consequences of capitalism's socially unequal organization of production, the circuits of which operated beyond the border of singular nation-states, involving the development of empires as self-sufficient systems of resources, labor, and market exploitation.

Fascism and National Socialism were, for Marxists, political ideologies that responded to changing relations of production created by the economic crises that ensued after the First World War (in the early 1920s) and the financial crisis of 1929, which, expanding to the entire world in the early 1930s, favored a monopolistic restructuring of industrial production. In that global context, "fascism," a term that Marxists used to generically denote different movements and regimes in the interwar period, was essentially reactionary *and* counterrevolutionary inasmuch as it expressed a violent anticommunism that originated as a response to the revolutionary waves in Europe inspired by the success of the Bolsheviks in Russia. In contrast to traditional forms of reactionary conservatism, fascism took the form of mass-based movements that, like Italian Fascism and German National Socialism, defined themselves as revolutionary, and as such antidemocratic and antiliberal in that they aimed to offer an alternative "third way" to the loss of legitimation and efficacy of traditional liberal democratic institutions.

But for Marxists, Fascists' and Nazis' claims that they were revolutionary movements had to be understood as integral part of their ideological strategies. They were, in fact, mere simulacra of revolution, for at least three reasons: first, both regimes left unchanged social divisions, suppressing the idea of class struggle in the name of national prosperity; second, they both affirmed the naturalness of social hierarchy and the ontological inequality of men within the national community, since they supported a conception of society metaphysically structured by competition and the rights of the strongest to dominate the weakest; and third, they both left substantially unaltered the legal framework of private property and the mechanisms of the market economy, albeit increasingly subjecting them to state control, especially with the intensification of military endeavors in the late 1930s.

The Development of a Comintern Orthodoxy on "Fascism"

Despite the dogmatic reductionism that many of the Marxist definitions of "fascism" assumed in the postwar years, thinkers and activists who operated within the conceptual framework of Marxism in the interwar years developed quite different conceptualizations of generic fascism. By the late 1920s, the international community's growing hostility to communism and the progressive corrosion of diplomatic relations in the years leading up to the Second World War pressured Marxists to consolidate a unified definition of "fascism" that could be tactically and strategically useful for the looming, inevitable conflict with Hitler's Germany and its Italian ally. The demand for a synthetic, unified definition of fascism also arose from internal developments of the communist movement itself, owing largely to Joseph Stalin's struggle for hegemony over the Comintern: the Congresses of 1924, 1928, and 1935 revealed a growing pressure to develop an ecumenical conception of generic fascism that minimized internal discord and put it in line with Stalin's interpretation.

An understanding of fascism as a political movement that is not specific to Italy developed early on among Marxists. To my knowledge, the first to conceive of "fascism" as a transnational phenomenon was Antonio Gramsci, who, as we saw in chapter 5, had theorized as early as the fall of 1920:

> This "reaction" is not only Italian: it is an international phenomenon, because capitalism not only in Italy but throughout the world has become incapable of dominating the productive forces. The phenomenon of "fascism" is not only Italian, just as the formation of the Communist Party is not only Italian. "Fascism" is the preparatory phase for the restoration of the state, that is, of a hardening of the capitalist reaction, of an exacerbation of the capitalist struggle against the most vital needs of the proletarian class. Fascism is the illegality of capitalist violence: the restoration of the state is the legalization of this violence: it is a well-known historical law that praxis precedes the law. . . . Fascism murders the militants of the working class: the restored state will send them "legally" to jail and, once the death penalty has also been restored, will have them "legally" killed by a new government official: the executioner. This development is universal; it has already occurred in part and will continue to develop normally in Italy.[1]

The rise of Fascism in Italy was placed on the agenda of the fourth Comintern Congress, in November 1922, at the last minute, but the reports of Amadeo Bordiga and the harsh reply of Karl Radek confined the debate on Fascism to Italy as a political phenomenon unique to that country. It was shortly thereafter, in June 1923, that Clara Zetkin wrote a report to the Enlarged Executive Committee of the Comintern on fascism defining it as the new enemy of the workers' movement, beyond the specific Italian situation. After analyzing the political landscapes of Italy, Germany, and Hungary, Zetkin concluded that "in fascism the proletariat confronts an exceptionally dangerous and terrible foe. Fascism is the classic expression, the most powerful and concentrated form, of the general offensive of the international bourgeoisie at the present time."[2]

The report was the culmination of the analytical work of a Provisional International Committee for Combating Fascism, of which Zetkin served as chairman since its formation in January 1923. The report was completed after the presentation of an early draft at a conference held in Frankfurt on March 17–20 of the same year, organized by the Rhine-Westphalia factory committees for the purpose of discussing with 250 delegates from different countries the constitution of a united front to combat the rise of fascism.[3] The organization of a unified front with a coordinated strategy and integrated vision was, for Zetkin, of fundamental importance in the fight against fascism, because in her view this new form of reaction was far more than mere "revenge of the bourgeoisie for the revolutionary advance of the proletariat," as was surmised during the fourth Comintern meeting.[4] If fascism was simply a reaction of capitalist elites against the communist revolution, she maintained, its defeat would be simply a matter of military strategy. But in fact, "considered historically and objectively, fascism presents itself much more as a punishment on the proletariat for not having continued and extended the revolution that began in Russia. And the 'bearers' of fascism are not a small caste, but broad social strata, popular masses, reaching even into the proletariat."[5]

Fascism, in other words, was not just a new form of the traditional bourgeois reaction against the claims of the proletariats. It was not just another form of revolutionary conservatism, nor simply a new kind of violent repression. Fascism, being "the result of the decay and disintegration of the capitalist economy, and a symptom of the dissolution of the bourgeois state," had recruited to its ranks the victims of that dissolution, the dispossessed members of the middle classes as well as members of the proletariat.[6] It was, for Zetkin, the failures of the proletarian movements in Europe to bring forth a successful revolution that fueled the emergence of fascisms: "A large part of the petty and middle bourgeoisie," she maintained, with an argument that would be later defended by Walter Benjamin, "were already either proletarianised or threatened by it, and had exchanged their war psychosis for a certain sympathy towards reformist socialism. They expected from it a historical turning point, thanks to 'democracy,' but their expectations have been bitterly disappointed."[7]

From these analytical premises, it was clear to Zetkin that the only way fascism could be successfully resisted was to create a united labor front that operated on multiple levels—organizational, pedagogic, ideological, and military. After the failure of the *biennio rosso*, fascism appealed to the lower classes. Surely "class conflicts are more powerful than all the ideologies which deny them," she claimed.[8] But the possibility of a peaceful reformist solution sustained by other popular parties, such as the PPI and sections of the socialist movement, might undermine the fight against fascism. To overcome this obstacle, it was necessary "to initiate the most energetic campaign for the allegiance not only of those proletarians who have fallen under the influence of fascism, but of the petty and middle bourgeoisie, the peasantry, intellectuals, in short of all those strata whose economic and social situation brings them into increasing opposition to large scale capitalism, and hence into bitter struggle against it."[9]

Zetkin's proposal to form a united front comprising the working classes and all progressive forces (despite the critique advanced against the pernicious effects of reformism in her 1923 report to the Provisional Committee) was rejected at the Fifth Comintern Congress of June–July 1924. In its place, the organizational model of the Soviet Union's Communist Party, now securely under Stalin's control, was imposed as the standard model for communist movements in all countries. As Geoff Eley notes, at the Fifth Comintern Congress of July 1924 "a new policy of 'Bolshevization' was adopted, which dragooned the Communist Parties toward stricter bureaucratic centralism. This flattened out the earlier diversity of radicalisms, welding them into a single approved model of Communist organization."[10]

Grigory Zinovyev, Comintern's chairman, pressured the 504 delegates from forty-six different countries to accept Stalin's conception of fascism as the sole orthodoxy. In Zinovyev's words, fascism was "one of the classic forms of the counter-revolution in the epoch of capitalist decay," and as such it was "the instrument of the big bourgeoisie for fighting the proletariat, when the legal means available to the state have proved insufficient to subdue them."[11] In a critical socioeconomic context, since "the more bourgeois society decays, the more all the bourgeois parties, particularly Social Democracy, take on a more or less fascist character," an extended alliance of all leftist forces such as the one prefigured by Zetkin was not just strategically inadvisable but structurally incompatible with antifascism. Indeed, for him "Fascism and Social Democracy are the two sides of a single instrument of capitalist dictatorship."[12]

The resolution of the Comintern was that communist parties all over the world should adopt a similar organizational structure and strategic resistance plan, following the example of the Communist Party of the Soviet Union. Stalin himself had insisted that same year that "Fascism is not only a military-technical category. Fascism is the bourgeoisie's fighting organization that relies on the active support of Social Democracy."[13] Both short-term tactical and long-term strategic alliances with the reformist Left were therefore impossible, because, according to Stalin, it had already been compromised by fascism, which was simply a political expression of a new mode of capitalist organization (monopoly capital), one that social democrats and progressives in general had no interest in subverting. For Stephen Kotkin, "Stalin's inability to understand fascism was sorely evident. He followed Lenin, who had insisted that the non-Bolshevik left—Mensheviks, SRs [Socialist Revolutionaries], other moderates—were the most dangerous of all counterrevolutionaries, because they hid behind the mask of socialism. This chasm on the left undergirded the misinterpretation of fascism, and was institutionalized globally at the Fifth Comintern Congress."[14]

Whether or not Stalin's views on fascism were tarnished by his "inability to understand" it, the imposition upon the Comintern and its associates of an orthodox understanding of fascism that restricted the strategic activities of all those Marxists who acknowledged the Comintern as the legitimate political institution of communism was politically consequential for asserting Stalin's hegemony over all communist parties. In other words, the imposition of a Comintern orthodoxy on fascism was inherently linked to Stalin's control of the movement itself. As the previous chapters have shown, antifascisms, and interpretations of "fascism," were as numerous and varied as the political orientations of its interpreters. In a sense, the definitions of "fascism" debated in the 1920s had become not a window that revealed a "correct" understanding of it, but a prism that reflected the political commitments and beliefs of those who studied it.

Zinovyev, who would later be sentenced to death for allegedly plotting against Stalin, played a key role in facilitating the progressive bolshevization of the Comintern, a policy that was met with considerable resistance by the Italian delegation, in particular by Bordiga (who would be accused of Trotskyism and later dismissed from the PCd'I), Angelo Tasca (who would be soon expulsed from both the PCd'I and the Comintern), and Gramsci (who, while politically critical of the positions of Filippo Turati's socialists, was nonetheless hostile to Stalin's idea of "social fascism").[15] As a result, any interpretation of "fascism" that diverged from the Comintern's (i.e., Stalin's) orthodoxy encountered greater resistance from Marxist activists.

At the Sixth World Congress of the Communist International of 1928, now chaired by Nikolai Bukharin, the equivalency of fascism, as an openly reactionary ideology, and social democracy, as democratic reformism, was further consolidated under the label "social fascism." The "Theses on the International Situation" by the Enlarged Executive of the Communist International, developed during the 1928 congress, reiterated that "in this situation of growing imperialist contradictions and sharpening of the class struggle, increasingly fascism becomes the dominant method of bourgeois rule."[16] Because the world had allegedly entered a "third phase" of capitalist crisis, paving the way for a new stage of revolutionary upheaval, it was imperative that all communist parties remain faithful to the Comintern plan and resist the temptation of organizing political alliances with other progressive forces. Indeed, the document stated, "in countries where there are strong Social Democratic parties, fascism assumes the particular form of social-fascism, which to an ever-increasing extent serves the bourgeoisie as an instrument for the paralyzing of the activity of the masses in the struggle against the regime of fascist dictatorship."[17]

Since, according to the standard Comintern definition, fascism in all its international variants was a symptom of the collapse of the capitalist order and its inability to reorganize economic production rationally, especially in those countries where capitalism was less mature, a revolutionary movement of the proletarian forces was the only possible form of resistance, since the reformism of liberal progressives and social democrats tended to favor the stabilization of the capitalist productive system rather than its dissolution. As Dmitriy Manuilski, secretary of the Comintern Executive Committee, further argued, "The fascist regime is not just any new type of state; it is one of the forms of bourgeois dictatorship characteristic of the imperialist epoch. Fascism grows organically out of bourgeois democracy. The process whereby bourgeois dictatorship switches to an open form of suppression of the workers thus also represents the essence of the fascisation of bourgeois democracy."[18] For Manuilski, fascism existed in Europe in two forms: it either occupied the totality of the state, as in Italy and Poland, or it constituted a radical element within democratic institutions, as in France and England; but because of the progressive erosion of the relations of production, "Social Democracy intentionally deceives the masses, obscuring from them the fact that the modern capitalist state constitutes a dictatorship of the bourgeoisie, whether this takes the form of a bourgeois democracy in the process of fascisation [as in advanced economies such as France and England] or of open fascism."[19] Fascism, "a product of monopoly capital" that employed an "extreme nationalist ideology" only to mask what in reality was "the open dictatorship of the bourgeoisie over the working class," cannot be defeated by those political forces (from the "Social Democratic apparatus" to the "reformist trade unions, the cooperatives, etc.") that, antifascist in name only, had no intention of dismantling the capitalist system.[20]

The dogmatism of the Comintern definition of fascism had the effect, on the one hand, of strengthening the ideological hegemony of that organization, under Stalin's control, over the international communist movement and of marginalizing any form of heterodoxy within the Marxist field; on the other, it systematically opposed all forms of tactical antifascist alliance between communist parties and other socialist and reformist parties. The most striking outcome of the Comintern views on "social fascism" was visible in Germany, where the anti-Nazi resistance during the Weimar Republic dispersed in a multiplicity of parties that ended up favoring the electoral advances of Hitler's Nationalsozialistische Deutsche Arbeiterpartei (National Socialist German Workers' Party, or Nazi Party; NSDAP).[21] Ernst Thälmann, leader of the Kommunistische Partei Deutschland (Communist Party of Germany; KPD) from 1925 to 1933, argued that the Sozialdemokratische Partei Deutschlands (Social Democratic Party of Germany; SPD) had become increasingly fascistized during the government of Heinrich Brünning, copying from Nazi organizational forms and the utilization of terror squads.[22] Since, for him, the SPD constituted the main conduit for a fascistization of German society that would in the long run favor the rise to power of the NSDAP, "our strategy," he declared, "directs its main thrust against Social Democracy, without thereby diminishing the struggle against Hitler-fascism."[23] In support of his hypothesis, he cited Stalin's *On the Road to October* and maintained that "to defeat Social Democracy is synonymous with winning the majority of the proletariat, and creating the most essential preconditions of the proletarian revolution."[24] As it turned out, the main accomplishment of Stalin's idea of "social fascism" was to favor the affirmation of Hitler's NSDAP.

After Hitler's rise to power in 1933, Palmiro Togliatti, who during the proceedings of the Sixth Comintern Congress of 1928 had timidly criticized the assimilation of fascism (a mass movement of petty and middle bourgeoisie dominated by the industrial and agricultural elites) and social democracy (a mass movement of the working classes and the petty bourgeoisie), nonetheless pledged alliance to Stalin and agreed to purge both Tasca and Bordiga from the PCd'I. To demonstrate his adherence to the Comintern orthodoxy, he argued that Germany's descent into fascism should certainly be attributed to the inevitable crisis of capital accumulation and the unsustainability of the existing relations of production under "the piratical terms of the Versailles Treaty." But these tendencies were aggravated by "the policy pursued for fifteen years by Social Democracy."[25] Togliatti's alignment with Comintern orthodoxy was further confirmed by his idea that "social democracy could not fight against fascism because it penetrated too deeply into the institutions of the capitalist and reactionary state, because it merged with them and with bourgeois society, because it is fascism's *sister*, because it has become *social fascism*."[26]

In 1934, after years of peregrinations all over Europe, Togliatti moved to Moscow, where he consolidated his own views on fascism, now consonant with Stalin's doctrine, in a series of lectures he offered at the Meždunarodnaja leninskaja škola (International Leninist School) in Moscow between January and April of 1935.[27] He presented materials from the lectures at the Seventh World Congress of the Comintern, held in Moscow in August of the same year and chaired by Georgi Dimitrov. The course consisted of fifteen lessons, the first of which presented a preliminary definition of fascism—referring both to Italian Fascism and generically to the "general characters" of fascist movements in Europe. Utilizing this definition, the rest of the classes would treat a variety of subjects: in order, the evolution of the PNF, its organization, the fascist militia, fascist labor unions, *dopolavoro* (after-work activities), corporatism, competitions among corporations, rural fascism, social democracy, Italian social democracy, republican maximalism, and anarchism.

In the first lesson, Togliatti, who had always resisted the transformation of "fascism" into a generic category, pledged his loyalty to the Comintern consensus, admitting that "the most complete definition of fascism was given by the 13th meeting of the Enlarged Executive of the Communist International and is as follows: 'Fascism is the open terrorist dictatorship of the most reactionary, most chauvinistic, most imperialist elements of finance capital.' "[28] He acknowledged that it took a long time to develop that definition, and the process was not without dissent (he mentioned Zetkin's and Bordiga's positions). Indeed, he recognized that many different and often contrasting definitions of "fascism" had been circulating since Mussolini's rise to power in 1922. The fact was, Togliatti explained, that "the movement of the masses isn't the same in every country. Not even the dictatorship is the same in every country. This is why I must forewarn you of an error that is easily made. Do not think that what is true for Italy must also be true, must hold, for every other country. Fascism can take different forms in different countries." But also, "Fascism assumes different aspects at different times in the same country."[29]

Eclectic in its manifestations, fascism pursues for Togliatti a single logic. The logic of fascism was the dictatorship of the bourgeoisie, which took on openly terroristic and reactionary aspects in a period of crisis of capital accumulation in order to counteract the dissatisfaction of the masses and prevent their revolutionary upheaval. That logic, for Togliatti, derived directly from a politicoeconomic context determined by imperialism: "Imperialism is characterized by: 1) the concentration of production and capital, the formation of monopolies which play a decisive role in economic life; 2) the merging of bank capital with industrial capital, and the creation, on the basis of finance capital, of a financial oligarchy; 3) the great importance acquired by the export of capital; 4) the rise of international capitalist monopolies, and, lastly, the repartitioning of the world among the great capitalist powers, which can now be viewed as complete."[30] These tendencies predated the formation of openly fascistic forms of domination, which became necessary when the monopolistic system of production exercised an unprecedented "heavy pressure on the workers," whose resistance required the violent reaction of fascist squads that aimed at "the preservation of capitalist society." In short, with the increased pressured created by the acceleration of empire formation and the expansion of financial capital, "the bourgeoisie must turn reactionary and resort to fascism."[31]

But fascism, Togliatti continued, was not just reaction. In fact, it denoted something new, a process that went beyond the simple exercise of power: "Fascism does not denote only the struggle against bourgeois democracy; we cannot use this expression when we are confronted with that struggle alone." Rather, "we must use it only when the fight against the working class develops on a new mass base with a petty-bourgeois character, as we can see in Germany, Italy, France, England—anywhere a typical fascism exists."[32] To put it differently, in order to contrast itself with the emancipatory struggle of the proletarian masses, fascism mimicked the form of communist revolution, becoming a mass movement of the lower middle classes. Its authoritarian character, in turn, became necessary because a "fascist dictatorship is only a sign of the weakening of the bourgeoisie."[33] It resorted to using democratic institutions to create a totalitarian state because the ideological apparatus of liberalism that justified them was no longer believed to be legitimate.

It is for that reason that "fascist ideology contains a series of heterogeneous ingredients."[34] The differing aspects and ideas it nurtures within one single country and in different nations derive precisely from the different interests, circumstances, and conditions of that inherently diverse social group that was the petty bourgeoisie: "fascism [is] made up of various unhomogeneous groups."[35] Accordingly, Togliatti cautioned his students, "I warn you against the tendency to regard fascist ideology as something that is solidly formed, complete, homogeneous. Nothing more closely resembles a chameleon than fascist ideology. *Don't look at fascist ideology without considering the objectives which fascism proposes to reach at a given moment with a given ideology*."[36] Ultimately, for Togliatti, fascism was just a mechanism the bourgeoisie adopted to allow it to obtain, maintain, and exercise power by any means necessary in socioeconomic circumstances that no longer guaranteed the maintenance of a hierarchical order of society and control over the means of production within liberal democratic institutions.

The Global Effects of Comintern Orthodoxy: The Case of Japan

The Seventh Comintern Congress opened in Moscow on July 25, 1935 and was attended by 512 delegates of affiliated communist parties from sixty-five different countries.[37] That the question of fascism dominated the proceedings was made clear with the opening speech, by Wilhelm Pick: it closed with the invitation to all delegates to overcome any doctrinal division in order to fight against the expanding menace of Fascism.[38] To have a sense of the hegemonic reach of Stalin's consensus regarding the official definition of "fascism," it is worth following the discussion of Japanese Marxists in the 1930s.

In response to Dimitrov's report at the Congress, on August 2, 1935, Marxist thinkers of all countries began investigating the dissemination of fascist movements and ideologies worldwide.[39] Dimitrov's appeal sprang from the admonition, given at the previous Congress of 1928, that "a new fascist offensive was under way and [the Congress] called for a struggle against it."[40] The Comintern elites felt it was necessary to investigate the manifest and disguised forms that fascism could take on the premise that "in a more or less developed form, fascist tendencies and the germs of a fascist movement are to be found almost everywhere."[41] The struggle against fascism, for the movement, was vital for two main reasons: first, "fascism" represented the most sophisticated political form developed by monopoly capitalism in the context of a worldwide crisis of capital accumulation; second, fascism distorted people's understanding of class struggle, thus preventing the emergence of emancipatory revolutionary movements from below: "Fascism aims at the most unbridled exploitation of the masses, but it approaches them with the most artful anti-capitalist demagogy, taking advantage of the deep hatred of the working people against the plundering bourgeoisie, the banks, trusts and financial magnates, and advancing those slogans which at the given moment are most alluring to the politically immature masses."[42]

Fascist elements, Dimitrov argued, were ubiquitous in all industrial societies. But the extent to which they had spread into state institutions was far less obvious. In the cases of Italy and Germany the situation was clear: there, "fascism, appearing as an open terroristic dictatorship of the most reactionary, most chauvinistic, and most imperialistic elements of finance capital, shakes off all the 'democratic' cloaks masking the subordination of the state apparatus to the monopolies."[43] Following the research objective launched by Dimitrov, I. A. Latyshev, a Russian historian and journalist at *Pravda*, argued that Japan was an "openly terroristic fascist regime," the specific character of which lay "in [the fact] that absolute monarchy was its form, while the leaders of the Japanese military came forward in the role of fascist dictators [and were] the most ardent servants of the *zaibatsu* and landlords, the cruelest butchers of the Japanese people. Therefore, in order to set off and underline the specific character of the fascist dictatorship in Japan, [we may] call it monarcho-fascist dictatorship, or military-fascist dictatorship."[44]

If Latyshev's research, together with Yu. I. Avdeyev and V. N. Strunnikov's study of Japanese imperialism, represented orthodox views on Japanese fascism in the postwar Soviet Union and the template for orthodox Marxists worldwide, in the 1930s Marxist theorists held conflicting positions.[45] The famous study of the two Russian orientalists known as O. Tanin and E. Yohan, pseudonyms for the historians O. S. Tarkhanov and Ye. S. Iolk, *Militarism and Fascism in Japan*, published in 1934, rejected the notion that Japan's "reactionary chauvinist regime" could be assimilated to the Western notion of fascism because of the "peculiarities of the social structure and the peculiar historical development of Japanese military-feudal imperialism."[46]

Tanin and Yohan offered two arguments in support of their assertion. First, while Western European fascism was "primarily an instrument of finance capital," in Japan the reactionary regime was an instrument not only of "finance capital but also of the Japanese monarchy which represent[ed] a *bloc* of two class forces: finance capital and semi-feudal landowners."[47] Second, because of the less developed nature of Japanese democracy, the reactionary ruling elites made, on the whole, a "limited use of social demagogy."[48] Furthermore, Tanin and Yohan contended, the Japanese reactionary movement was split into two factions, one grouping together reactionary organizations of the privileged classes, the other consisting of "the reactionary chauvinist organizations among the intermediate social strata, principally small landed proprietors and the urban petty bourgeoisie."[49] This latter was, "in its ideology, closer to West European fascism."[50] But it was to all effects cut off from direct state power and would actually be suppressed by the government after the attempted coup in 1936.[51]

Tanin and Yohan confirmed in their study the thesis that Otto Kuusien, a Finnish historian and politician who had moved to the Soviet Union in 1918, had proposed to the Comintern just a few years earlier, in March 1932, in the immediate aftermath of the Shanghai incident (January 28–March 3, 1932); it has since become known as the "1932 Thesis."[52] Published in the Comintern bulletin in the following May under the title "Extracts from the Theses of the West European Bureau of the ECCI [Executive Committee of the Communist International] on the Situation in Japan and the Tasks of the Japanese Communist Party," the report emphasized the connection between Japan's predatory imperialist expansion abroad and the reactionary politics of the regime at home.[53] Aggressive imperialist expansion and domestic reactionary authoritarianism were two expressions of the same political predicament, the result of an incomplete bourgeois revolution that maintained the hierarchical division of society intact from its feudal past. Rather than a fascist regime—expression of a realized bourgeois form of capitalist domination—Japan, said Kuusinen, should be understood as an expression of "absolutist militaristic-feudalistic imperialism."[54]

Tanin and Yohan's study was introduced by a long essay, authored by the Polish-born Communist leader Karl Radek, who not long afterward would become a victim of one of Stalin's purges and be incarcerated in a Siberian labor camp.[55] In the essay, Radek praised the analysis of the two specialists but highlighted their mistaken understanding of fascism, which led to their failure to recognize its presence in Japan. Fascism, Radek explained, "develops on the economic basis of the domination of monopoly capitalism, which is no longer able to solve the main economic problems facing society, which is feeling the approach of the social revolution and which is experiencing an ever-deepening crisis."[56] It was on account of this sense of impending revolution that fascism developed into a "dictatorship resting upon mass organizations, mostly petty-bourgeois," which "combine[d] the greatest terrorism against workers and revolutionary peasants with an unbridled social demagogy."[57] Following very closely the orthodox interpretation of the Comintern, Radek emphasized that fascism was not "simply a reactionary dictatorship," but a dictatorship that was expression of finance capital and "which has been able . . . to secure for itself the support of the petty bourgeoisie by means of a demagogic policy and mass mobilization."[58] The case of Japan, according to Radek, was not dissimilar, "although the leading role in the fascist movement of that country is played by the landowners and the higher bureaucracy."[59] Japan's imperialism should therefore be understood, according to Radek, in terms of finance capital extending its monopolistic reach in search of resources, cheap labor, and controlled markets.

When these Soviet reports started to circulate in Japan—Matsubara Hiroshi and Mori Kiichi's 1936 translation of Tanin and Yohan's study was distributed by the left-wing publisher Sōbunkaku—they exercised enormous influence upon Japanese Marxists' interpretations of the political situation of the 1930s and 1940s. They also provided theoretical instruments for a controversy regarding Japanese "fascism" among Marxist thinkers in the immediate postwar period. It was certainly a controversy over the interpretation of the origins of Japanese imperialism, but it was also a critique of the Left's failure to avert Japan's descent into total war. As Germaine Hoston puts it, "The controversies on the origins and nature of Japanese imperialism and 'fascism' allowed the Rōnō-ha and Kōza-ha to confront, in theoretical terms, the political events they had tried vainly to avert."[60]

The differing interpretations of Japanese imperialism of the two factions of Japanese Marxism were, in turn, based on divergent understandings of the events of 1868—on whether, that is, the social and political transformation of the Meiji Restoration could be interpreted as tantamount to a bourgeois revolution. The theoretical conflicts that divided these two factions originated in the 1930s. The Kōza (lectures or symposia) *ha* (faction) took its name from the authors of a history of Japanese capitalism published by Iwanami Shoten in 1932–33.[61] The Rōnō (worker-farmer) faction, made up of eclectic Marxists, took its name from the magazine *Rōnō*, published between 1927 and 1932. In the view of the Kōza-ha, Japan did not have a complete bourgeois revolution in 1868, which explained the resilience of feudal privileges among the economic elites. As a result, there were no mature bourgeois institutions that could sustain the development of class consciousness and emancipatory movements, so that the semifeudal power structures inside the modern state were protected by a consciousness that still accepted social hierarchy as a fact of nature. The Rōnō-ha activists argued instead that the Meiji Restoration, incomplete as it might have been in the immediate aftermath of the Boshin War of 1868–69, marked a revolutionary transformation of Japanese society into a full-fledged capitalist state, protected by institutions that could be conceived of as analogous to those of liberal democracies.

The different interpretations of 1868 by the two Marxist factions put a different spin on their respective understandings of the intensification of Japanese military expansion in 1931. In that regard, the Kōza-ha activists adhered more closely to the interpretation of the Japanese state's militaristic character, describe in Kuusinen's 1932 Theses as deriving from a *tennōsei zattaishugi* (imperial absolutism) with lingering feudal values.[62] The differing interpretations of the Meiji Restoration called for different political strategies. Kōza-ha scholar-activists such as Noro Eitarō, Yamada Shōtarō, Hirano Yoshitarō, Hattori Shisō, and Hani Gorō focused on cultural and political analyses and proposed a two-stage political program that aimed at the development of democratic institutions and consciousness, the only basis on which a mature socialist movement could develop. The Rōnō activists Hirabayashi Taiko, Sakai Toshihiko, and Yamakawa Hitoshi, among others, emphasized quantitative economic analyses and insisted on the incidental nature of feudal relics among Japanese society, which was solidly structured around a capitalist mode of production.[63] The split between the two factions continued in the postwar period, when analyses of "Japanese fascism" diverged on the basis of the theoretical stance of the two factions.[64]

In the immediate aftermath of the Second World War, Rōnō thinkers strove to develop an original theory of Japanese fascism. Following the example of

Sakisaka Itsurō and Takahashi Masao, who in 1932 had both published warnings on Japan's growing turn toward fascism, Rōnō-ha activists such as Yamakawa Hitoshi, Ōuchi Hyōe, and Tasuchiya Takao, with the collaboration of Sakisaka and Takahashi themselves, analyzed the transition from a liberal parliamentarism of the 1920s to fascism.[65] Following Dimitrov's interpretive model faithfully, Rōnō activists conceived of fascism as the systematic combination of state power and monopoly capital, which for them was essential if the interests of the capitalist shareholders were to be preserved during a global systematic economic crisis. In the context of Japan, "the Rōnō-ha had willingly acknowledged that semi-feudal 'remnants' existed in the prewar state," but these lingering elements—a mixture of agricultural landowners, patriotic military officials, and the symbolic presence of the emperor—became an integral part of the fascist transformation of the state.[66]

The Kōza faction initially denied that Japan experienced a fascist phase precisely because of the presence of feudal holdovers. Kamiyama Shigeo, in particular, insisted that the "emperor system" was enough to explain the "absolutist reaction" of the war years (which he termed *zettai kunshusei* [absolutist monarchy] or *tennōsei zettaishugi* [emperor-system absolutism]).[67] Soon, however, Kamiyama found himself in the minority relative to his fellow Kōza members. Kōza scholars such as Shiga Yoshio and Inoue Kiyoshi, in fact, criticized Kamiyama's analysis and developed a new conception, according to which in the 1930s Japan had indeed fostered a fascist transformation that was peculiar to Japan, and thus distinct from the cases of Italy and Germany. As Shiga explained, "The development of Japanese finance capital and the intensification of its contradictions by the world economic depression caused fascism to grow dramatically between 1931 and 1945."[68] He concluded that, during the war years in Asia, "the absolutist emperor system came to be made to execute fascist tasks."[69]

Shiga's position was soon endorsed by theorists like Inoue Kiyoshi (who called the wartime regime a *tennōsei fashizumu* [emperor-system fascism]),[70] Hattori Shisō, and Moriya Fumio, who further refined Shiga's analysis. Their views of fascism reduced the doctrinal gap between the two factions of Marxist theorists. Both Rōnō and Kōza Marxists now followed the Stalinist orthodoxy and conceived of fascism as essentially an expression of monopoly capital, which assured its own existence through a form of political dictatorship characterized by internal repression, external aggression, and exasperated nationalism in the form of emperor worship—hence the phrase *tennōsei fashizumu*. As the Kōza member Tanaka Sōgorō put it, "Fascism is one form of dictatorship attempted at the time when capitalist society stands at the brink of disaster."[71]

The "Fascism" of Heterodox Marxists

On the eve of the Seventh Comintern Congress in the summer of 1935, it seemed that all European Marxists who played an active institutional role in their respective communist parties joined together in the Comintern's orthodox view on "fascism." Even Japanese Marxists, whose debates opposed two irreconcilable views of the Japanese regime, by the end of the 1930s came to an agreement on "Japanese fascism" along the line of Stalinist orthodoxy. The reconciliation of diverging views on fascism in different countries worldwide was certainly facilitated by a new sense of urgency. The political situation of 1935 was radically different from that of the previous congress: The growth of ultranationalist and authoritarian movements, which was only a threat in 1928, had become not only a reality after Hitler's appointment as chancellor on January 30, 1933, but a rapidly accelerating process that was now threatening to disrupt the unstable European order. If in the 1920s the Marxist debate on fascism as a stage in capitalist development was centered on a relatively marginal European country such as Italy, by the 1930s it switched its attention to Germany, which had the potential to become the largest economic power in Europe.[72] Fascism ceased to be a mere academic or doctrinal problem: It was now an urgent issue of transnational geopolitics.

It was in the 1930s that discussions on generic "fascism" multiplied. The question of fascism no longer involved the complex social composition of Italian supporters of Mussolini's movement, because it was now Germany that attracted the attention of political analysts. It was in those years, as chapter 3 has shown, that Mussolini and other fascist leaders strove to protect the brand name "fascism" from its Nazification, defending its precedence and authenticity in publications, public celebrations, and cultural activities. Mussolini's defense of the "universality of Fascism" was an attempt to protect the ideological relevance of his movement by demonstrating its distinction from Nazism and the derivative nature of the latter vis-à-vis the former's originality.[73]

Despite the Comintern's success in organizing a communist consensus, at the fringes of the movement activists and thinkers who engaged with the Marxian paradigm—without, however, following local communist parties' political line—developed alternative understandings of transnational "fascism" that were distinct from both liberals' interpretations and the Stalinist orthodoxy. As Leon Trotsky put it, "The Stalinist theory of fascism indubitably represents one of the most tragic examples of the injurious practical consequences that can follow from the substitution of the dialectical analysis of reality . . . by abstract categories formulated upon the basis of a partial and insufficient historical experience (or a narrow and insufficient view of the whole)."[74] Stalin's mistake, for Trotsky, was not in pointing out the strong relationship between monopoly capital and fascism. It was rather a methodological mistake, an inferential fallacy, insofar as "they [the Comintern theorists] draw in a purely deductive, formally logical manner the same conclusions for all the countries and for all stages of development."[75] In truth, for Trotsky capitalist reaction can take many forms, not all of them reducible to "fascism." Capitalism, he claimed, "never accommodated itself to 'pure' democracy"; indeed, "between parliamentary democracy and the fascist regime a series of transitional forms, one after another, inevitably interposes itself, now 'peaceable,' now by civil war."[76] In 1930s Europe, Trotsky insisted, it was essential to develop more efficient forms of political analyses. Fascism, for him, had to be distinguished from Bonapartism and its former appearance as Caesarism.[77] But fascism was not just another form of authoritarianism from above. As a mass movement, it was "a specific means of mobilizing and organizing the petty bourgeoisie in the social interests of finance capital. During the democratic regime, capital inevitably attempted to inoculate the workers with confidence in the reformist and pacifist petty bourgeoisie."[78] Fascism emerged from the clash of these two subordinate social classes, the proletariat and the petty bourgeoisie, which it set in conflict in an attempt to prevent their strategic alliance. A clear understanding of the political forms financial capital endorsed in different sociohistorical contexts, for Trotsky, was of fundamental importance not just for the sake of analysis of the changing relations of capital interest (base) and political organization (superstructure) but for the development of a successful strategy for the revolutionary resistance against it. In fact, "the prolonged domination of finance capital by means of reactionary social demagogy and petty-bourgeois terror is impossible," he declared; "Having arrived in power, the fascist chiefs are forced to muzzle the masses who follow them by means of the state apparatus. By the same token, they lose the support of broad masses of the petty bourgeoisie."[79] That was why, for Trotsky, fascism "regenerated into Bonapartism," which originated from "the destruction, disillusionment and . . . demoralization of the two camps of the masses," that is, the working classes and the petty bourgeoisie.[80] Its rule in the form of a totalitarian state "signifies the beginning of its end."[81]

The optimistic spin in Trotsky's analysis required, in order for it to become effective political action, a strategy that was the exact opposite of the one advocated by the Stalinist Comintern, because it needed to recruit the disaffected petty bourgeoisie to the antifascist cause. If France was, for Trotsky, the battleground for an antifascism that rejected Stalin's orthodoxy (with the support, for instance, of Maritain's Catholic antifascist communitarianism), for the communist activist Andrés Nin, who largely shared his analytical standpoint, it was Spain. Nin attacked the "International's unfortunate theorists," whose attachment to a misconception of fascism led them to endorse a political tactic that failed to respond to Primo de Rivera's fall.[82] A similar position was taken by Ignazio Silone, a writer and former adherent of the PCd'I, who similarly condemned the dogmatic reductionism of the Comintern definition of "fascism," which for him had to be clearly distinguished from "military dictatorships" and from traditional forms of "reactionary conservatisms" that aimed at consolidating the "ancient state-form." For Silone, who would later be unjustly accused of being a secret informant for the Fascist regime, fascism established itself in those countries where capitalism was less socially consolidated than in England and France, and where the labor movement was still in its political infancy.[83] Alienating the petty bourgeoisie, as in Stalin's theorization of fascism, was a disastrous misstep for the antifascist movement. Other Marxist activists, such as the socialists Karl Kautsky and Otto Bauer, opposed the Comintern orthodoxy and proposed an understanding of fascism as a form of capitalist counterrevolutionary reaction, without, however, indulging in the mechanistic reductionism that was hegemonic in the parties that gravitated to the Comintern.[84]

The Hypergenericization of "Fascism"

A complete survey of all theorizations of fascism is an encyclopedic indulgence in doctrinal subtleties that goes beyond the scope of this book. Some of the most interesting conceptualizations of fascism that emerged in the 1930s and early 1940s, however, came from theorists who, while engaging with Marxian terminology and perspective, refused any strict affiliation with the political movement that the Comintern pretended to represent and lead. Some of them, especially the thinkers associated with the Frankfurt Institut für Sozialforschung (Institute for Social Research), would set the terms for the postwar discussion on "fascism," now conceived of as a hypergenericized form of capitalist totalitarianism, without immediate or obvious reference to either Fascist Italy or Nazi Germany. The focus of their analysis was on culture, society, and psychology, rather than politicoeconomic institutions and practices.

Walter Benjamin, only informally associated with the Frankfurt School, did not develop a coherent theory of fascism. He did not care to distinguish whether the term referred to Italian Fascism, to German Nazism, to both, or to a new typology of political ideology; nor did he explicitly defend its generic use, even though this is the connotation the term assumed in most of his writings. Yet, his entire philosophical oeuvre could be read as an attempt to exorcise the spell of fascism from the social, political, and cultural life of 1930s Europe. There is a discernible qualitative progression in Benjamin's engagement with fascism that followed both his own intellectual and political maturation and the expansion of fascist movements in Europe. At first, Benjamin ironically portrayed Italian Fascism as a sort of carnivalesque phenomenon.[85] It was only with the rise of Hitler and the affirmation of "German fascism" that "fascism" came to occupy center stage in Benjamin's political reflections. By then, Benjamin's friendship with Bertolt Brecht had deepened and his Marxist commitment consolidated. Whether the radicalization of his views on "fascism" derived from his adherence to communism and historical materialism, or it was the rapid expansion of fascism in Europe that pushed Benjamin toward Marxism, is a dispute that still divides the scholarly interpretations of his thought today.[86]

In Benjamin's writings, "fascism" took two main semiotic forms. First, it was the name of a particular configuration (or, to use one of his categories, a "constellation") of connotations, moods, and concepts (such as "ideology," "violence," "war," "simulacrum," etc.). Resulting from a particular permutation of a constellation of ideas and forms, it often took the form of a *Bild* (image), the temporary congealment of a conceptual "constellation" conveying a particular understanding of "fascism." In these cases, the meanings of "fascism" were not explicitly explained but rather conveyed by a suggestive "thought-image" (*Denkbild*).[87] For instance, in his 1935 review of Bertolt Brecht's *Dreigroschenroman* (*Threepenny Novel*, 1934), Benjamin describes the character of Macheath in the novel—one "who knows how to parade what the stunted petit bourgeois imagines a personality to be"—as the embodiment of "fascism" and a symbolic representation of the attraction it exercised on the petty bourgeoisies: "Ruled by hundreds of authorities, tossed on the waves of price increases, victimized by crises, this habitué of statistics needs someone to cling to."[88] Just as the success of the highwayman Macheath in Brecht's novel gave a cathartic answer to the need for agency for a castrated bourgeoisie, fascism offered a simulacrum of hope to the dispossessed middle classes for a social resurgence that was impossible to achieve. In fact, it masked new forms of violent repression: "Just as a ballerina is expected not only to dance but also to be pretty, fascism requires not only that there be a savior for capital but also that he be a noble human being."[89] "German fascism," in another thought-image Benjamin conjured up in his critical review of the collection of essays *War and Warriors*, edited by Ernst Jünger, took the form of an entanglement of ideas and myths (sacrifice, heroism, masculinity, etc.) that was capturing the imagination of younger generations of Germans on the redemptive power of war. The "mysticism of the death of the world" that took place in the essays in Jünger's anthology expressed the pathological hope that only through struggle and war could Germany put an end to its state of crisis. But just as "fascism" was an ideological simulacrum of redemption, so Jünger's idealization of war "is only this: the one, fearful, last chance to correct the incapacity of peoples to order their relationships to one another in accord with the relationship they possess to nature through their technology."[90]

In the writings of a politically committed Benjamin in the 1930s, "fascism" was no longer the name of a "thought-image" expressing a particular ideology but the name of the condition of the present, a sort of "signature of the age" he was living in.[91] Fascism was now the "common and undisguised manifestation" of "two of the most important developments of the age:" "the decline of democracy and the preparation for the war."[92] It was a condition that inevitably modified the possibility of culture.[93] It framed, as a sort of theatrical stage, the presentation (and thus the reception) of any form of cultural production.[94] But, as a historical condition, fascism affected all European countries, not just the ones that were openly "fascist," like Italy and Germany. The two works in which Benjamin addressed the question of "fascism" more directly were "Das Kunstwerk im Zeitalter seiner technischen Reproduzierbarkeit" (The Work of Art in the Age of Mechanical Reproducibility), of which he developed three versions between 1935 and 1939, and the manuscript "Über den Begriff der Geschichte" (On the Concept of History, 1940), sketched, presumably, only a few weeks before he committed suicide by overdosing on morphine at Portbou, near the Spanish-French border, while trying to escape the Nazis.[95]

In "The Work of Art in the Age of Mechanical Reproducibility," Benjamin surmised that in the thoroughly industrialized modern world, art had become an article of industrial reproduction as a commodity.[96] The result of this transformation was, however, ambivalent. Artworks were no longer the exclusive possession of the social elites, and, because, thanks to technology, they were reproducible, they had lost the auratic sacredness that surrounded them. Once the exclusive possession of the aristocracy, the Church, and the *haute bourgeoisie*, works of art were now accessible to all—in a sense, they had been democratized. On the one hand, the reproducibility of and accessibility to art had popularized it, rendering it democratic; on the other, the loss of its auratic power made it manipulable, which transformed it into a powerful ideological tool for the organization of consensus. No longer socially exclusive, a democratized art offered the means for the emancipation of the masses but also for a new form of subjection: The work of art in a thoroughly industrialized world became a phantasmagoric phenomenon that furthered people's alienation and rendered them vulnerable to coercion by turning the masses into spectators, so that they voluntarily abdicated their historical agency.[97] That was the secret of fascism's success: By controlling the means of technological reproduction, it assured itself of the support of the masses by reducing them to spectators of themselves acting as political masses. The politicization of the masses, therefore, was itself just a phantasmagoria, a simulacrum of agency. Deprived of any actual political agency by the delusion of being protagonists, the masses were actively engaged in assuring their own submission. Because "fascism," he explained in the conclusion of the essay, "attempts to organize the newly proletarianized masses while leaving intact the property relations which they strive to abolish. It sees its salvation in granting expression to the masses—but on no account granting them rights."[98] For Benjamin, fascism was indeed only a simulacrum of a mass movement, since it could offer only a pantomime of equality and emancipation. It was a theatrical representation that masked the perpetuation of dispossession and of the unequal capitalist relations of production and property. "The logical outcome of fascism," he concluded, "is an aestheticizing of political life." But that was merely a degradation not just of the potentially redemptive power of art for the sake of consensus, but of art itself. The aestheticization of politics, the function of which was to keep the masses trapped in a phantasmagoria of agency that curbed their revolutionary potential, had only one possible, catastrophic outcome: "*All efforts to aestheticize politics culminate in one point. That one point is war.* War, and only war, makes it possible to set a goal for mass movements on the grandest scale while preserving traditional property relations. That is how the situation presents itself in political terms. In technological terms it can be formulated as follows: only war makes it possible to mobilize all of today's technological resources while maintaining property relations."[99]

The democratic potential of industrial technology, in other words, had to be curbed by fascism in order to preserve the capitalist social order; the result was a hijacking of the technological apparatus to wage wars—which, in the world of global empires, for Benjamin, could only take the form of an imperial war. "It goes without saying," he explained, "that the fascist glorification of war does not make use of *these* arguments."[100] Fascism, concluded Benjamin, expected from war "the artistic gratification of a sense perception altered by technology. This is evidently the consummation of *l'art pour l'art*." Rather than the triumph of art, however, the fascist aestheticization of politics meant the final demise of art: "Its self-alienation has reached the point where it can experience its own annihilation as a supreme aesthetic pleasure.

Such is the aestheticizing of politics, as practiced by fascism."[101] The proper response is, for Benjamin, a contrary politicization of art.[102]

As the generic and often fuzzy name of a political *and* cultural praxis that exploited new expressive media (radio, cinema, art) and offered the masses a phantasmagoric sense of participation to the state, "fascism" became in "On the Concept of History" the form that social domination took in the present.[103] The inscription of fascism within a global history of domination reconfigured it as "a further stage in the triumphal procession of the victors, as the head of the Medusa, as the supreme, final face of the recurrent barbarism of the powerful."[104] In the two years separating these essays, the optimism Benjamin expressed in "The Work of Art" had disappeared. There was no longer space for hope or redemption to be found in history, in tradition, in art, or in culture in the form in which they had been transmitted to the present: as the "historical materialist" well knew, "there is no document of culture which is not at the same time a document of barbarism."[105] It was not enough, for Benjamin, to acknowledge that the past was merely a "pile of debris [that] grows toward the sky" before the "Angel of History."[106] It was necessary to renew the faith of the masses in their emancipatory mission. The only chance against Fascism lay in a messianic faith in reconstituting the masses as a revolutionary subject, which could only come from a hope for "a revolutionary chance in the fight for the oppressed past."[107] Benjamin converted late to Marxism, to the chagrin of his friend Gershom Scholem, and with an enthusiasm that was met with skepticism by another friend, Theodor Adorno. From Marxism he inherited the view of fascism as a capitalist reaction against the revolutionary aspiration of the proletariat. But he never really engaged in sociological and class analyses, preferring to indulge in critical readings of the effects of class inequalities and private property in cultural products.

The indistinct notion of generic fascism that ensued from Benjamin's writings would have a massive impact, along that developed by Max Horkheimer, Adorno, and others, in the writings of the post-1968 New Left. A comprehensive survey of the different theories of fascism of the various members of the Frankfurt School deserves its own monograph and cannot possibly be covered in a few paragraphs. Psychologists like Wilhelm Reich and Erich Fromm developed insights from Freud to discuss the mass psychology of fascism, its origins in the authoritarianism of the traditional family, the irrationality of mass movements, and the appeal of charismatic leadership. Political economists such as Franz Neumann and Friedrich Pollock analyzed the governmental and economic structures of Nazi Germany: The former treated the polyarchic exercise of political and economic power within the Nazi state apparatus, while the latter concentrated on the role of the state as the organizer of economic activities and engine of capital accumulation (the thesis of state capitalism).[108]

Adorno and Horkheimer, while sharing the views of Pollock and Neumann, saw in interwar authoritarianism the unleashing of an inherent contradiction that existed within the Enlightenment process. Like their other associates at the Institute, they experienced the repressive violence of National Socialism directly: All had to emigrate to survive, and some, such as Herbert Marcuse, never returned to Europe. For them, the question of fascism was not just theoretical: It defined their lives and research. As Adorno noted in a celebratory letter that he sent Horkheimer on May 9, 1945: "It is a pity that we have not experienced the demise of the Nazis together. Hitler's regime has, after all, been the immediate cause of all the external developments in our lives for the last twenty years, and the expectation that things might change has been one of the decisive forces that have kept us alive. Conversely, the fact that our two lives have become conjoined is inextricably linked to fascism."[109] Adorno's *beschädigtes Leben* (damaged life), Benjamin's suicide, Horkheimer's pessimistic views on the eclipse of reason, and Leo Löwenthal's notion of interrupted experience, among other circumstances and ways of thinking, were individual elaborations that had sprung from a shared experience of rejection, genocidal discrimination, escape, exile, and death. National Socialism—the historical referent of most of their meditations on "fascism"—was the force that defined their experiences of life, politics, modernity, society, culture, critique, and art. For some of them the battle against Nazifascism was not simply a philosophical enterprise: Neumann, Löwenthal, Marcuse and others collaborated during the Second World War with the Office of War Information and the Research and Analysis Branch of the Office of Strategic Services (OSS), and Pollock was a consultant for the Department of Justice.[110] Their collective analyses continued in the postwar period, conceived as an attempt not only to understand philosophically, sociologically, and historically Europe's descent into a new kind of "barbarism," as Horkheimer and Adorno described it, but to lay the foundation for the reconstruction of an authentically democratic order from the ruins of the war.[111]

Adorno's research on the social, psychological, and intellectual basis of fascism was relentless, first in the United States and then in Germany after his return in 1949.[112] In the United States, Adorno participated in a research project on the social and psychological foundation of antisemitism. Published in 1944 as *The Authoritarian Personality*, the qualitative sociological experiments and interviews to the design of which he contributed guided research on the authoritarian disposition behind popular support of antisemitism, which included the development of a progressive "f-scale"—"f" obviously standing for "fascism." The research, conceived with the broader aim of studying different forms of prejudice, conducted interviews and questionnaires with 2,099 women and men (mostly from the region around the University of California, Berkeley, but also from Oregon, Southern California, and Washington, DC) of different social classes in order to establish correlations between certain psychological dispositions (such as aggression, anti-intellectualism, conventionality, cynicism, etc.) and the propensity to support authoritarian movements and ideologies.[113] As Peter E. Gordon notes, "*The Authoritarian Personality* has a density of psychological and statistical detail that distinguishes it as among the largest and most methodologically sophisticated research efforts of its kind."[114] Despite its critical reception[115]—partly motivated by the surprising results showing an unexpected propensity among the American population for antisemitism and authoritarian forms of government—the study "represents one of the most sophisticated attempts to explore the origins of fascism not merely as a political phenomenon, but as the manifestation of dispositions that lie at the very core of the modern psyche."[116]

While the research of the Berkeley team focused on the psychological disposition of individuals, Adorno also researched the effects of ideological propaganda. The first of these works was published as "Democratic Leadership and Mass Manipulation" in Alvin W. Gouldner's *Studies in Leadership*, where Adorno again stressed how antisemitism operated as a "spearhead of fascism."[117] The second, devoted to the demagogical skills of the Christian-right radio host Martin Luther Thomas, consisted of a series of essays developed in the late 1930s and early 1940s but published posthumously in 1975 that sharply dissected the rhetorical and ideological manipulations of Thomas's radio speeches. "Fascism," Adorno argued, "feeds upon the lack of emotional gratification in an industrial society" and "grants to the people that irrational satisfaction which is denied them by today's social and economic setup."[118] However, he continued, "the irrational gratifications which fascism offers are themselves planned and handled in an utterly rational way. Such manipulation results in a kind of psycho-technics, borrowed from the modern factory and applied to the population as a whole."[119] The rhetorical strategies of fascism took full advantage of the technological means of communication of the culture industry: "By the 1940s," observes Gordon, "Adorno came to believe that fascism, too, owed much of its success to techniques first developed in advertising (such as the use of mass-produced logos and carefully crafted appeals to personal satisfaction) along with the 'repetition of designated words' that magically invoked states of personal and collective bliss."[120] The unleashing of irrational energies in a sort of "hypnotic" ritual among the listeners,

Adorno showed, aimed only at the justification of the establishment of an authoritarian society: "Fascism aims at the repressive maintenance of an antagonistic society."[121]

What "fascism" stood for, in both Horkheimer's and Adorno's essays, is a semantic constellation of denotations, connotations, and referents that is hard to disentangle with any precision. It is often undefined, with no explicit references to Italian Fascism, and is seemingly used interchangeably with "National Socialism," "authoritarianism," "antisemitism," and, more rarely, "totalitarianism," without any apparent coherency or consistency. In some texts, "fascism" refers generically to a universal category, but in others it stands simply as a placeholder for National Socialism. "Much as the members of the Frankfurt School and their associates," Lars Fischer remarks, "sought to develop a conceptual understanding of fascism in general and National Socialism in particular—as significant political movements and regimes whose policies and crimes they witnessed—this was a rather different undertaking from subsequent (and current) attempts to develop some sort of definitive, succinct and yet all-encompassing definition of fascism and/or National Socialism."[122] They were not, in short, precursors of the postwar scholars of the "fascist minimum" approach, nor were they trying to contribute to the Marxist analysis of the common socioeconomic conditions behind these new forms of political reaction. Rather, their conception of "fascism" added an undefined series of connotative markers that would become conventional in the most generic sense only during the Cold War.

Both thinkers more or less accepted the Marxist formulation that fascism was not the professed "third way"—the alternative to both liberal capitalism and communism that Mussolini and Hitler alike claimed their movements to be—but somewhat related to and deriving from capitalism. In a much-criticized essay from 1939, Horkheimer boldly stated that "wer aber von Kapitalismus nicht reden will, sollte auch vom Faschismus schweigen" (whoever is not willing to talk about capitalism should also keep silent about fascism).[123] But neither Horkheimer nor Adorno sustained this assertion with elaborated economic analyses: instead, they relied on Pollock's thesis of Nazism as a form of "state capitalism" and Neumann's theory of a polyarchic behemoth.[124] "Fascism" stood for the authoritarian and despotic forms of government of Germany and Italy. But in their writings of exile and war—such as Horkheimer's *Eclipse of Reason*, Adorno's *Minima Moralia*, and the coauthored *Dialectic of Enlightenment*—"fascism" stood also for the catastrophic effects of the dark side of the Enlightenment. Written during the Second World War, these philosophically complex, at time impenetrable, and often contradictory texts are the legacy of Adorno's and Horkheimer's concerted attempts to make sense of the descent into barbarism that National Socialism (the main political referents behind their use of "fascism") forced upon Germany, Europe, and eventually the entire world. In *Eclipse of Reason*, a collection of essays Horkheimer started writing in 1941 and first published in English in 1947 with Oxford University Press, "fascism" was what liberalism tended to "tilt over into" when nationalism became the ideology that a state mobilized to suppress the contradictions created by the social inequalities of capitalism.[125] Far from being simply a form of irrationality, however, "in modern fascism, rationality has reached a point at which it is no longer satisfied with simply repressing nature; rationality now exploits nature by incorporating into its own system the rebellious potentialities of nature."[126] Instrumental reason, the prevailing expression of the Enlightenment project within capitalist modernity, was for Horkheimer the source that unleashed within its ostensibly "rational" appearance the "irrational" drive to domination.[127] Within this perspective, he believed that "we might describe fascism as a satanic synthesis of reason and nature—the very opposite of that reconciliation of the two poles that philosophy has always dreamed of."[128]

The same themes were at the core of *Dialectic of Enlightenment*, a collection of essays Horkheimer coauthored with Adorno in the form of "philosophical fragments," published in a limited edition by the Dutch publisher Querido in 1947 but written between 1942 and 1944. The aim of the essays was, again, to understand why the "Enlightenment, understood in the widest sense as the advance of thought, has always aimed at liberating human beings from fear and installing them as masters. Yet the wholly enlightened earth is radiant with triumphant calamity."[129] In this text, too, "fascism," "German fascism," "totalitarianism," and "monopoly capitalism" seem to have been used as synonyms. Adopting the thesis of state capitalism developed by Pollock, to whom it was dedicated, the book conceived of fascism as the form that capitalism took in order to solve its inherent contradictions after the crisis of 1929.[130]

Insofar as "the market economy it [the Enlightenment] unleashed was at once the prevailing form of reason and the power which ruined reason,"[131] it was the "bourgeois economy," for Horkheimer and Adorno, that concocted fascism so that "violence" could be multiplied "through the mediation of the market."[132] Fascism sprang from the irrationality of instrumental reason, which, normally disguised under the triumphalist banner of progress, became visible in the critical circumstances unleashed by the financial crisis.[133] In that sense, fascism was specific to capitalist modernity. But its irrationality replicated an instinct for domination that was at the core of the entire history of Western civilization and that rational thinking, from Homer's time to today's techno-science via the eighteenth-century Enlightenment, was unable to suppress. In its concrete instantiation as National Socialism, "fascism triumphed under a crassly xenophobic, anticultural, collectivist ideology."[134] It was fully modern and embraced the means that the culture industry put at its disposal.[135]

The most visible character of fascist rationalization of its irrational impulse was antisemitism: "The Jews are today the group which, in practice and in theory, draws to itself the destructive urge which the wrong social order spontaneously produces. They are branded as absolute evil by absolute evil. In this sense they are indeed the chosen people. Now that power is no longer needed for economic reasons, the Jews are designated as its absolute object, existing merely for the exercise of power."[136] For Horkheimer, probably the main author of the chapter,[137] the fate of the Jews was a symbolic placeholder for the crisis of capital, and their extermination as the symptom of fascism's "paranoia";[138] and, as Anson Rabinbach notes, he "ultimately holds the Jews accountable for their own faith."[139] But if, in the chapter titled "Elements of Anti-Semitism," the extermination of the Jews was instrumental for Horkheimer and Adorno's argument on "fascism" as the quintessential expression of the dialectic of reason rather than a theme in itself, it nonetheless acquired the status of a symbolic benchmark for all future history because of the magnitude of its murderous violence. In a sense, the authors were bellwethers in the use of such expressions as "extermination,"[140] "destruction,"[141] "universal murder,"[142] "gas chambers,"[143] "Zyklon gas factory,"[144] and so on, to such an extent that the question of antisemitism, only marginal in other coeval generalizations of "fascism," became an inherent element of all successive discussions of generic fascism.[145]

In *Minima Moralia*, a collection of reflections on "damaged life" that Adorno wrote between 1944 and 1949,[146] he insisted that fascism was simply the most radical instantiation of a *Prinzip der Herrschaft* (principle of domination)—the irrational drive that persisted within rationality, thus denying the emancipatory potential it upheld—that he and Horkheimer had theorized in *Dialectic of Enlightenment*. But unlike the totally administered life within a liberal order dominated by the imperative of competition, Fascism had no need to hide its own system of domination behind the ideological façade of freedom and laissez-faire:[147] "Fascism is itself less 'ideological,' in so far as it openly proclaims the principle of domination that is elsewhere concealed. Whatever humane values the democracies can oppose it with, it can effortlessly refute by pointing out that they represent not the whole of humanity but a mere illusory image that Fascism has had the courage to discard."[148] The violent social Darwinism at the core of Hitler's *Mein Kampf*—the regulative logic behind the *Führerprinzip*, as Neumann had interpreted it in his *Behemoth*—was therefore nothing but the radicalization of an instinct of domination that Enlightenment reason not only had failed to eradicate, but had actually sublimated into the politicoeconomic system of liberalism. It was an instantiation of the same principle of domination that liberal capitalism adhered to in disguise. Adorno adopted the Marxist thesis that fascism constituted the survival of capitalism in a society that had put its existence in crisis, but he reworked it by subsuming *both* politicoeconomic systems into an anthropological theory of domination that focused on the persistence of a violent, irrational instinct in human life and that the Enlightenment project had so far failed to come to terms with.

Philosophical interpretations of generic fascism were not unique to the thinkers of the Frankfurt School, even though it was their writings that reawakened a renewed generalist use of the term during the student movements of the late 1960s and 1970s. In Japan, Tosaka Jun, a student of the Kyoto philosopher Nishida Kitarō, developed a political philosophy that eclectically interpreted the work of Marx and Engels in ways that bear some similarities to the thought of Gramsci and Adorno.[149] For Tosaka, "fascism" was the name of a *seiji kikō* (political mechanism) that ensued when "monopoly capitalism assumed an imperialistic form" and "exploit[ed] the anxieties of the petit bourgeoisie for the domestic and international situation."[150] As such, fascism "exploits the delusions of the middle classes [by claiming] that it shares their interests," whereas in truth it "successfully pursues the expansion of finance capital."[151]

Starting from that general definition, Tosaka acknowledged that there were different sorts of political mechanisms in different countries (Mussolini's Fascism, Nazi fascism, social fascism, etc.).[152] In Japan, for him, it assumed the form of *nihonshugi* (Japanism), of which *ajiashugi* (Pan-Asianism)—imperialism disguised as an anti-imperialist liberation movement of Asia led by Japan—and the *ōdōshugi* (Imperial Way)—the worship of the emperor as *kokutai* (embodiment of the nation)—were mere derivations.[153] Japanism expressed itself in the form of *bunkengakushugi* (classicism), a term that is difficult to render in English because it subsumes denotations of "canonical texts" and their philological study (so that *bunkengaku* is commonly translated as "philology"), but for Tosaka it also connoted an almost religious deference toward texts thought to be foundational to Japanese civilization and thus imbued with an aura of sacredness.[154] As classicism, Japanism was, for Tosaka, tantamount to a culturalist ideology of national identity that was based on an orthodox view of *kokushi* (national history) conceived of in terms of the unfolding of the history of the imperial house directly descending from the gods. This emperor-centered history of Japan involved *kokumin* (nationals) in an organic synergy conceived in terms of *nihonseishinshugi* (Japanese spiritualism), *nihonnōhonshugi* (Japanese agrarianism), and *nihon-ajiashugi* (Japanese Asianism), which viewed Japan as the designated leader of a movement to emancipate Asian nations from Western imperialism.[155] In its concrete institutionalization, Japanism is a form of *zettaishugi* (absolutism). Japanism, with all its idiosyncrasies, must still be conceived as a form of "fascism," and thus as an international phenomenon in the conjuncture of the interwar crisis of capitalism.[156] This is important because, for Tosaka, even though Japanism was a form of spiritual worship of Japanese culture and spirituality, it utilized many of the ideas and strategies of European fascism, like the logic of a *zentaishugiteki shakai* (totalitarian society), which he defined as equivalent to *Gemeinschaft* (community) and "total state."[157] In the circumstances of the 1930s, Tosaka explains, Japanism "takes . . . the appearance of the consciousness of an aggressive, militarist nation, the character of which is defined by the existence and way of thinking of a professional group that in Japan occupies a privileged position: the military. The particular consciousness of a militaristic nation, one of the clearest features of Japanism, is an imperial, fascist, and militaristic antiforeignism. This is the definitive characteristic of Japanism, which is the essence of Japanese fascism."[158]

Although Tosaka accepted the premises of the Marxist interpretation of "fascism" as a superstructural phenomenon of monopoly capitalism, he did not exercise any substantive influence on Japanese Marxian debate until much later in the postwar period. He was fired from his teaching positions in 1933 and imprisoned in 1938, and he died in Nagano Prison on the day the second atomic bomb was dropped on Nagasaki. Yet, the conceptual apparatus of his *Nihon ideorogiron* represents one of the most sophisticated Marxian contributions to political philosophy.

The Legacy of Marxian Antifascism

The global rise of various forms of authoritarianism in the second half of the 1930s and, soon after, the eruption of the Second World War temporarily ended the doctrinarian divisions among Marxists and among communist and liberal antifascists. As Terence Renaud, following Anson Rabinbach and Eric Hobsbawm, puts it, in the antifascism of the years immediately before the war "there were two main currents. The first and by far the largest was the Popular Front. This big-tent coalition brought together liberals, moderate Christians, conservatives, Social Democrats, and Communists."[159] Renaud called the second current that of "alternative antifascisms," which he conceived of as comprising "religious socialists" and "libertarian anarchists."[160]

From a global perspective, the worldwide advances of authoritarianisms in the mid-1930s, in the context of the sociopolitical state of emergency that the economic crisis had produced, rendered the previous doctrinarian divisions on the definition of "fascism" less relevant. Italy and Germany, the two major dictatorships in Europe, stood as examples of an alternative between liberalism and socialism. But extreme right-wing parties were a reality everywhere in Europe. Most of them called themselves "nationalist" or "national-socialist";[161] only a minority used "fascist" in their name;[162] and then there were the Croat Ustaše, the Spanish Falange Española, and the Nationalist Parties of Estonia, Latvia, and Lithuania. Many of these were minority movements, but authoritarian regimes and governments dominated the political scene in Belgium, Estonia, Latvia, Lithuania, Poland, Austria, Hungary, Portugal, Romania, Bulgaria, and Greece, while the civil war in Spain, where the republic was under assault from Francisco Franco, became the battleground where all antifascist forces united.[163]

The Comintern's rejection of any collaboration with moderate forces ("social fascism") led the way to a pragmatic alliance dictated by the advances of fascism worldwide. Indeed, the world that the economic crisis of 1929 left in its wake was one where authoritarianism received more popular support than liberal democracy. It was at this juncture that "fascism" acquired the metonymical capacity of signifying them all. After 1939 the war against fascism favored a wide-spectrum alliance among all antifascist forces, and the question of politically defining "fascism" was replaced by a strategy of defeating it militarily.

Antifascist resistance ultimately defeated Italian Fascism and German National Socialism—the two main referents of the signifier "fascism" between the 1920s and the 1940s, as Japan was only occasionally defined as such during the war—not by the force of arguments, analyses, or popular opposition from within, but after the deadliest conflict in human history. This is a truism that is nonetheless important to explicitly articulate in order to understand the broad consensus that these authoritarian regimes were able to mobilize among different social strata and to appreciate the concrete (if often ineffective) urgency behind the theoretical labor of antifascist analysts. The fraught social, economic, and political circumstances of the interwar years that had favored the affirmation of Nazifascism do not diminish the fundamental fact that it had to be defeated through sheer violence and after almost six years of ruthless total war.

Mussolini was deposed by the king on July 25, 1943 in response to the vote of no confidence from the Grand Council of Fascism, *only after* the disastrous performance of the Italian armed forces in the global conflict that

Italy had joined three years before, on June 10, 1940. The puppet regime of the Salò Republic in northern Italy (the Italian Social Republic, or RSI) collapsed twenty months later, *only after* being defeated by the concerted attacks of the Allied troops and partisan guerrillas. Hitler committed suicide on April 30, 1945, *only after* the city of Berlin had become the battleground of a bloody endgame, the Russian troops only a few blocks away from the bunker where he was hiding.[164] Mussolini had been shot dead two days earlier, on April 28, 1945.

The truism that fascism was defeated by war is a reminder that antifascism too operated in the form of a military-industrial apparatus of unprecedented magnitude and as a pragmatic alliance between radically different political organizations—Anglo-American democratic liberalism and Soviet communism.[165] In other words, while the chapters of part II have mapped, contextualized, and interpreted some of the most significant definitions of "fascism" advanced between 1920 and 1945 by antifascist activists and thinkers, the antifascism that won the war against it took the form of a military alliance internally fraught with difficulties and mutual distrust. The Allies fought and won a war against a common enemy, but they understood fascism in radically different ways. For the Soviet Union, fascism had more in common with the liberalism of its allies than they acknowledged, while for the Anglo-Americans, fascism was a form of totalitarianism just like Stalinism. The ideological contradiction that existed within the antifascist front continued in the postwar years, where the new confrontation between the United States (and its allies) and the Soviet Union (and its allies) in the ensuing Cold War repurposed the concepts of "totalitarianism" and "fascism" to redefine the former ally into a new enemy.

PART III

"Fascism" since 1945

> Das Höchste wäre: zu begreifen, daß alles Faktische schon Theorie ist. [The utmost would be to understand that everything that is factual is already theory.]
>
> JOHANN WOLFGANG VON GOETHE, *Wilhelm Meisters Wanderjahre*

Many of the aporetic definitions of "fascism" that were developed in the interwar years persisted after 1945 in the works of historians, political scientists, philosophers, and literary scholars, whose research aimed at understanding Italian Fascism, German Nazism, and, more generically, the global rise of authoritarianism as a way to explain the violent eruption of the Second World War. This immense scholarly production did not subvert or replace the semantic composition of the signifier "fascism" inherited from the writings of interwar authors, who were typically antifascist. Certainly some of its semantic markers, especially those codified by the Fascist regime (e.g., "fascism" as a synonym of "state"), became outdated or were subjected to repression and forgetting. But in general, postwar historiographical and political-scientific research refined descriptions and definitions that had been in use since the interwar period, thus codifying these denotative and connotative markers in today's encyclopedia. What the definitions of "fascism" in postwar scholarship lost was their interwar political connotations, which became now less evident if not altogether disavowed.

The process of semantic recodification engendered an interesting inversion. The interwar definitions of "fascism" advanced by Fascist leaders and antifascist activists had primarily a political intent, even when produced in the most rigorous scholarly fashion.[1] By contrast, the postwar debate on the nature of Italian Fascism, of National Socialism, and later of generic fascism was primarily the subject of interpretive confrontations between historians, philosophers, and political theorists in a scholarly language and setting, and for an audience of academics. This scholarly enterprise was not immediately or intentionally political, but it nonetheless played an important political function, as it helped lay the foundation for the reconstruction of new democratic orders in Italy, Germany, and Japan. In most cases, scholars' definitions of "fascism" tended to reproduce the political divisions that existed before the Second World War. For instance, in Italy historians of conservative-liberal leanings (such as Benedetto Croce and, later, Renzo De Felice) tended to see in Fascism a tragic parenthesis in the modernizing path of the Italian state, directly or indirectly linked to the communist agitations of 1919–20. Progressive liberal scholars (for instance, Norberto Bobbio and Emilio Gentile) conceived of Fascism as having been caused by the excesses of nationalism and militarism, which found the favor of the disenfranchised petty bourgeoisie and the industrial and landowning elites striving to consolidate their capital, in a social context of widespread economic and political crisis resulting from the First World War, framed by a condition of political immaturity of the masses. For Marxists (for example, Nicola Tranfaglia and Paolo Alatri), fascism was the political-ideological form that monopoly capital took in its counterrevolutionary reaction to the emancipatory upheavals of the working classes.

Scholars' interpretive labor did not occur in a vacuum but under the normative umbrella of a new ideological division of the world into two irreconcilably antagonistic parts. Inevitably, definitions of "fascism" were *also* political claims on the Cold War—implied or simply disguised under the ideological veil of methodological objectivity—whether in defense of the liberal capitalist order, of the socialist utopia (often despite the totalitarian outlook it took in really existing socialism), or of a multitude of "new Lefts" that rejected the binary alternative of exploitative free-market liberalism versus Soviet totalitarianism, especially after the USSR's invasion of Czechoslovakia in 1956 and of Hungary in 1968.[2]

The most noticeable novelty in postwar scholarship was the development of a new genericization of "fascism" into a political ideal type, distinct from the previous abstractions of Marxist thinkers. Historians, philosophers, and social scientists, beginning from the almost coeval proposals of Ernst Nolte and Eugen Weber in the early 1960s, strove to distill a definition of a "fascist minimum" or of an "essential" or "eternal" fascism that logically (and for some, such as Zeev Sternhell, even historically) preceded the individual instantiations of Mussolini's and Hitler's regimes. Because they denied fascism's link to capitalism (in Marxist definitions) and to the institutions of democratic liberalism (in the writings of Antonio Gramsci and the Frankfurt School thinkers), "fascism" for these scholars referred to a distinct form of political organization, governance, and ideology that had to be added to the existing categories of democracy, socialism, and communism. In the context of the Cold War, refusing to acknowledge the link between economic liberalism and fascism served the purpose of reinforcing the political views that free-market and political democracy was the only viable alternative to the totalitarian tendencies of both communism and fascism. In the twenty-first century, in the condition of seemingly endless war and economic instability that have come to dominate the post–Cold War era of globalization, disingenuously defined as "postideological," the scholarship of the "fascist minimum" found new fertile ground for the conceptualization of an interwar era of "global fascism" or for a renewed but contested usage of "fascism" as the name for the populist authoritarianisms that arose.

The following chapters, after sketching the consolidation of the dominant denotative markers of "fascism" in Italian scholarly debate, reconstruct the attempt to distill a typological definition of "fascism" with the aim of turning it into a universal and potentially ahistorical political category. In so doing, they directly confront historians' epistemological dilemma of how rigorous interpretive work can produce diverging and potentially antinomic visions of the past—that is, how authoritative but different interpretations of "fascism" reflect scholars' political positions independently of the quality of their archival research.

10

Contexts

"Fascism" between the Postwar Era and the Cold War

Fascism in Postwar Italy

In the first decade of material, economic, political, legal, and moral reconstruction after the war, discourses on Fascism in Italy were at once pervasive and repressed. The antifascist foundations of the newly born republic were clearly stated in the Constitution of 1947, and in the midst of the ensuing Cold War, the participation in the Resistance of members of the new political parties was affirmed in their electoral campaigns. At the same time, historians and social scientists largely ignored the question of Italian Fascism until the 1960s, while newspapers and radios actively intervened in the construction of a public memory that celebrated the antifascist Resistance but tended to ignore the dictatorial nature of Fascism and its responsibility for the war. Antifascism was affirmed and the Resistance celebrated as a moment of national renewal, but antifascist struggle was conceived of as almost exclusively against the German invader, the political implication of the Fascist past hidden behind a rhetoric of sacrifice and heroism. The more antifascism and the Resistance were celebrated, the more the twenty years of Mussolini's regime were ignored or simply subjected to selective amnesia.[1] As Filippo Focardi shows, the attempt to erase the popular consensus that the Fascist regime had gathered in the 1920s and 1930s and the reframing of the Pact of Steel between Germany and Italy as a personal affair between Hitler and Mussolini—so that the role of Italians could be reconceptualized as both "victims" of Nazism and "victors" against it after 1945 alongside a myth of "the bad Germans and the good Italians"—started even before the war had ended and even enjoyed the support of the Allied press.[2]

In that context of memorialization and selective forgetting, novelists, artists, and filmmakers were often the only dissonant voices opposing this editing of the past. In their works, reflections on Fascism were motivated by a commitment to truth and a willingness to contribute politically to the construction of a new democratic order. Novels, films, paintings, and musical compositions had the urgency of testimony, the explicit aim of which was the preservation of the experience of life under the Fascist dictatorship and the struggle to resist it.[3] Diaries and memoirs of life in the Resistance were also published in large numbers.[4] Women's contribution to the liberation was acknowledged not just in literature and memoirs, but also in the political sphere, where two former partisans, Tina Anselmi and Nilde Iotti, became prominent exponents of the two main political parties, Democrazia Cristiana (Christian Democracy Party; DC) and the Partito Comunista Italiano.[5] The war and antifascist resistance were at the center of neorealist films shot among the ruins of Rome, Naples, and Berlin in the immediate aftermath of their liberation. Renato Guttuso dedicated his pictorial research to the war against fascism; and the early compositions of Luigi Nono joined the memorializing efforts of Krzysztof Penderecki, Dmitri Shostakovich, Arnold Schoenberg, Benjamin Britten, and Olivier Messiaen. These works of art were at once historical documents, political statements, and aesthetic experiments. The search for a new expressive voice coincided with the injunction to contribute to the reconstitution of the national community on new ethical, political, and artistic foundations. Their portrayals of Fascism through the experience of the antifascist struggle had the dual function of offering a truthful representation of life under Mussolini's regime and of defending the legacy of antifascism.

The new republic openly embraced its commitment to antifascism. The years immediately following the end of the war found an Italian society that was not only impoverished and in ruins, but deeply divided vis-à-vis individuals' responsibility during the twenty years of Fascist dictatorship: in the summer of 1945, Italy seemed to be on the brink of a new and larger civil war.[6] The main effort of the first provisional government, composed of the leaders of all forces involved in the Resistance, from the Christian Democrats of De Gasperi to the Communists of Palmiro Togliatti, and of the constituent assembly tasked with the writing of a new constitution, was to transition Italians to a condition of normalcy that would hinder the return of unrest and civil war.

Article 12 of the "Transitory and Final Dispositions" ordered that "the reorganization, in any form, of the dissolved Fascist party is prohibited."[7] The disposition was later turned into Law no. 645 of 20 June 1952, proposed by Home Minister Mario Scelba, a Christian Democrat with conservative leanings. It prohibited any "association or movement [that] pursues goals of antidemocratic practices typical of the Fascist Party, exalting, threatening, or using violence as a method of political struggle, or advocating the suppression of the freedoms guaranteed by the Constitution, or denigrating democracy, its institutions and the values of the Resistance, or carrying out racist propaganda, or directing its activities to the exaltation of exponents, principles, facts and methods of the aforesaid party or performs external demonstrations of a Fascist nature," and mandated a sentence of three to ten years' imprisonment for "anyone who promotes or organizes the reconstitution of the dissolved Fascist party."[8] Although the Constitution and the Scelba law of 1952 consolidated the antifascist nature of the new republic, the application of the law was from the beginning sporadic and contested. The law did not prevent, for instance, Giorgio Almirante, former editor of the racist magazine *La difesa della razza*, former RSI minister of popular culture, and unrepentant Fascist, from continuing his political activities as the head of the postfascist party Movimento Sociale Italiano (Italian Social Movement; MSI).[9]

The political legitimation of a postfascist party like the MSI and the rehabilitation of former Fascist leaders, antisemites, and collaborators in genocide, such as Giorgio Almirante, Pino Romualdi, Junio Valerio Borghese, Pino Rauti, and Rodolfo Graziani were only the most visible signs of a systematic continuation of the Fascist state apparatus within the new republic. Much of the state bureaucracy, of the police forces, of the newly formed secret services, of the judiciary, and of the educational system continued from the Fascist period and were largely unaffected by the process of "democratization" of the state.[10] As Paul Ginsborg notes, the "*epurazione* [purge of Fascist personnel] proved a disastrous failure. The judiciary itself went untouched, and duly proceeded to discharge as many cases as it dared. Other essential sectors of the state's personnel were also unaffected. In 1960 it was calculated that sixty-two out of sixty-four prefects had been functionaries under Fascism. So too had all 135 police chiefs and their 139 deputies. Only five of these last had in any way contributed to the Resistance. Leading Fascists were acquitted on outrageous grounds."[11]

The amnesty that the interim minister of justice in 1945–46, the communist Palmiro Togliatti, had passed on June 22, 1946 intended to be an act of *concordia nazionale* (national pacification), but it actually had far harsher consequences for the partisans than for former Fascists.[12] As Focardi puts it, "The overall effect [of the amnesty of 1946 and successive ones] was significant in every way: the Resistance was impeached and criminalized."[13] Despite the public celebration of liberation from Nazifascism—on April 22, 1946 the government proclaimed a national holiday on April 25, to be called Liberation Day—and of the contribution of the Resistance, the former partisans suffered psychological and legal repercussions far more severe than Fascist Repubblichini (adherents of the RSI) who had actively collaborated with the

Nazis in terrorizing the population of central and northern Italy:[14] "At the end of the day the only effective *epurazione* was that carried out by Christian Democrat ministers against those partisans and anti-Fascists who had entered the state administration immediately after the national insurrection."[15]

Alongside the legal and political rehabilitation of former Fascists, a revisionist campaign offered a more positive evaluation of Fascism as cherished by the population and incomparably less totalitarian than their Nazi allies.[16] The periodical *L'uomo qualunque*, founded in 1944 by Guglielmo Giannini in the immediate aftermath of the liberation of Rome, became the platform for the right-wing populist and monarchist movement Fronte dell'Uomo Qualunque (Common Man's Front), characterized by cynical disengagement, anticommunism, anti–political populism, and nostalgia for the Fascist period. Less revisionist but on just as firm an anticommunist ground were the satirical periodical *Candido*, founded by the journalist Giovanni Mosca and the novelist Giovannino Guareschi, author of the famous serial novels about Don Camillo and Peppone, and the conservative-liberal *Il Borghese*, edited by the former Fascist sympathizer Leo Longanesi.[17] These publications set up a strategic representation of Fascism in benevolent terms, and often in open opposition to a political enemy, communism, that stood for actual totalitarianism.[18]

In Italy, the failure of an effective defascistization of society and politics was actively encouraged by the United States in the context of a rapidly intensifying antagonism toward the Soviet bloc. It was not even unique to Italy. A similar change in strategy and extent of the democratizing effort was pursued at the same time in US-occupied Japan. In what is known as the "reverse course," in Italy, Japan, and Germany former members of the Fascist and Japanese ultramilitarist governments, bureaucracies, and military were rehabilitated, while members of socialist and communist parties were purged from the state bureaucracy and the educational system.[19] A Marshall Plan of massive economic support and industrial reconstruction for the European countries devastated by the war, enacted in 1948, was conditioned by the marginalization of socialist and communist presence in the public life of the beneficiary nations.[20] Finally, former Fascists and National Socialists were also involved in a constellation of clandestine paramilitary groups whose purpose was to prevent possible revolutionary upheavals accompanying eventual electoral victories of local communist parties.[21] Ample evidence suggests an involvement of these groups with conservative politicians and some members of the Italian secret services (and organized crime syndicates such as the Mafia) to organize and maintain a *strategia della tensione* (strategy of tension) that offered legitimacy to stricter police controls on the activities of fringe political movements.[22]

The postwar reconstruction of a democratic order thus progressively corroded the wartime alliance between the different antifascisms and increasingly separated them into antagonistic positions. This antagonism turned into open conflict during the campaign leading to the elections of April 1948, often unleashing intimidation and violence. As Paul Ginsborg puts it, the "conflict of interests and ideology" between a liberal and a socialist front, which was "at first masked in Italy by the continued cooperation of the anti-Fascist parties, reached dramatic and decisive heights by the time of the spring elections of 1948."[23] The opposition did not consist merely of irreconcilable conceptions and definitions of Fascism; rather, these were proxies for the new conflict between political parties ideologically close to the Atlantic and the Soviet blocs.

The Cold War had made of Italy a new battleground, where the DC and the PCI operated as local proxies of the two superpowers. With the ruins of the war still visible in most cities of the peninsula, Italy was now at the center of a new conflict: the Christian Democrats, which struggled to maintain their political hegemony, were the center-right liberal party that represented the interests of NATO; the People's Bloc (the PCI and the Partito Socialista Italiano [PSI]), although it did not openly dispute the Atlantic alliance, had strong ties to the USSR of Joseph Stalin. The DC won the 1948 election by a considerable margin—48.5 percent of the votes against the 30.9 percent of the Fronte Democratico Popolare (Popular Democratic Front, a coalition of the PCI and the PSI). Still, the fact that the DC did not earn an absolute majority and that there was a strong communist sector in the electorate contributed to a climate of political and ideological instability that would last for decades.[24]

The postwar order was explicitly conceptualized in terms of antifascism not just in Italy, but globally. "World War II," the historian Sakamoto Yushikazu noted, "was defined by the United Nations as a war of democracy against 'Nazism' or 'fascism.'"[25] In that context, the definitions of "fascism" operated, at the political, ideological, constitutional, legal, cultural, sociological, historiographical, and philosophical level simultaneously, as the obverse of "democracy," insofar as "defascistization" and *Entnazifizierung* (denazification) were the first necessary steps toward a "democratization" of the Allies' former enemies. The new democratic order that accompanied the reconstruction of the countries devastated by the deadliest and most destructive conflict in human history was based on conceptions of "democracy" that, in turn, responded to what "fascism," as the main cause of the war, had represented for thinkers and activists of a different political orientation. In other words, the meanings of "democracy" were as different and as contradictory as the meanings of "fascism" from which they ensued as antonyms. Hence, for those conservative thinkers who conceived of "fascism" as a pathological descent into irrationalism that the First World War had triggered among the middle classes and that the threat of the impending Bolshevik Revolution had exacerbated, "democracy" stood for the top-down restoration of the legal norms of political-economic liberalism, which alone could guarantee the full realization of a rational society, as philosophers such as Benedetto Croce and Karl Popper and economists such as Friedrich Hayek maintained. For those progressive liberals like Gaetano Salvemini and Norberto Bobbio, for whom "fascism" represented the totalitarian excesses of nationalism in socioeconomically underdeveloped and politically immature nations, "democracy" stood for the responsibility of the state to become the promoter of reforms aimed at rebuilding not only stronger liberal institutions and a regulated market economy, but also a civic consciousness of bottom-up participation in the democratic life of the nation. For Marxists of various leanings, "democracy" stood for either the construction of a social democratic state that realized an equal and solidary society that could prevent future developments of the authoritarian tendencies inherent in unbridled capitalism (as in the writings of the Frankfurt School thinkers), or the initiation of a revolutionary movement that had the long-term aim of bringing socialism to those countries that were devastated by "fascism."

The Question of "Fascism" in Postwar Italy

In the first decade of the postwar period, Fascism had a negligible presence in Italian scholarship.[26] It became a topic of historical research only toward the end of the 1950s, while the problem of giving a synthetic definition of Fascism was largely ignored until the late 1960s. As Emilio Gentile notes, "It is well known that until the beginning of the 1960s Italian historiographers showed minimal interest in the study of fascism."[27] Indeed, Leonardo Rapone argued that "the 1950s were overall a lost decade" in the scholarship of Fascism.[28]

When it slowly started to make its appearance in professional publications, the early investigations into Mussolini's regime paid attention almost exclusively to the decisions and actions of political and military elites, in line with the then-prevailing tendency of academic historiography to focus on local history and on the deeds of great historical figures.[29] Only in the course of the 1960s did new methodologies of historiographical research begin to have a noticeable effect on a discipline that, in Italy, was traditionally reluctant to embrace innovation and experimentation.[30] Marxism had yet to become a theoretical template of historical analysis among professional historians, while the sociological, political, and cultural analyses of Togliatti, Antonio Gramsci, and Angelo Tasca had essentially no influence on historiographical publications in the first two decades after the war, primarily because they remained largely inaccessible.

There were also other reasons, the primary among them being, as Gianpasquale Santomassimo has suggested, "the widespread annoyance (Croce's famous 'repugnance') toward the task of writing the history of the recent past."[31] Indeed, "the reasons for the difficulty of making history of Fascism must be sought in that vast—and to a large extent, inevitable—involvement of Italian intellectuals in the cultural policy and initiatives of the fascist regime, which had its moment of maximum development precisely in the years of World War II."[32] The long duration of Mussolini's regime had either silenced or regimented the contributions of intellectuals to such an extent that at the end of the war it took years for a community of engaged scholars to regain their voices. As Arnaldo Momigliano confessed, "The real harm done by Fascism to historical studies lies not in the nonsense that was said, but in the thoughts that were never thought again. Many of the best, if they didn't say anything that shouldn't be said, didn't say everything they should have said."[33]

If Fascism was an issue that existed (probably) in the minds of all but (certainly) in the pens of few, the question of what went wrong in the process of Italian modernization in the aftermath of the First World War was at first addressed indirectly and moralistically. The moralistic conception of Fascism as a disease that Croce advanced was matched by the essentializing generalization of the economic historian Fabio Cusin that Fascism was the "expression of a tendency innate within the society and in the nature of the Italian spirit," and of such Marxist historians as Paolo Alatri, for whom Mussolini's regime was, as Gramsci and Togliatti had conceptualized in the transwar period, the creation of a backward, reactionary petty bourgeoisie.[34] Neither, however, defended their different conceptions of Fascism before the 1960s. The question of Fascism was also addressed indirectly through a discussion of the nature of the Risorgimento—whether, that is, the new nation-state of Italy, created in 1861, was accompanied by an authentic bourgeois revolution of its society or was still marked by lingering feudalistic relations in parts of its territory, which would explain the success of Mussolini's totalitarian government.[35] This was not unique to Italian historians, as in Japan, too, scholars writing in the immediate aftermath of the Second World War engaged in a reevaluation of the nature and meaning of the Meiji Restoration of 1868 in order to find the causes of the ultramilitarist imperialism of the 1930s.

Marxism began its long courtship of Italian historians only in the postwar period, but it took a while before it affected the methodology of their research. Only in the second half of the 1960s and throughout the 1970s would an explicitly Marxist-inspired historiography engage in analyses of Fascism, reconnecting with the scholarship of the transwar period. A selection of Gramsci's works was published only in the late 1950s, and no complete edition of his *Prison Notebooks* was available until 1964.[36] Togliatti's *Lezioni sul fascismo* were published in 1970, while Tasca's *Nascita e avvento del Fascismo*, originally published in French in 1938, was published only in part, and in very few copies, in 1950; its first complete publication had to wait until 1965. Once historians began producing new research on Fascism in the 1960s, their works displayed two tendencies. First, they all shared a clear conception of Italian Fascism as a "historical negativity," as Emilio Gentile defines it, as did the antifascism of the postwar reconstruction. Second, despite this ethical-political judgment, they distanced themselves from the initial attitude of intellectuals in the immediate postwar period, who conceived of Fascism as "a kind of epiphenomenon lacking an individuality of its own that would justify historiographical interest."[37]

Yet, the representations of Fascism in the work of different historians were as irreconcilable as their political leanings, whether these were clearly expressed or not. Thus, for conservative liberals Fascism tended to be a force of antimodernity, while for Marxists it remained a form of modern counterrevolutionary reaction. That was due in part to the fact that Fascism, as Gentile acknowledges, "could not be studied in the same way as other movements such as liberalism, democracy, and socialism. These had their own ideological, social, and political individuality, since they had arisen from the development of history towards modernity and freedom. By contrast, fascism had been a revival of anti-modern and reactionary forces against these movements; in other words, against the very sense of history itself."[38] So, even when historians intended to "truly understand fascism" and tell "how things really happened," the answers they gave reflected not only their archival analyses and historical reconstructions, but also their metahistorical and political commitments.[39] These reproduced many of the conceptions that had already developed in the transwar period.

Perhaps one of the most significant interpretations of Italian Fascism came from Bobbio, a political philosopher and jurist. A classmate in the early 1920s of Leone Ginzburg, Vittorio Foa, and Cesare Pavese, who from the beginning all played important roles in the antifascist resistance, Bobbio initially supported Fascism and in 1928 became a member of the PNF. He studied law with Luigi Einaudi and took a second degree in philosophy, specializing in the phenomenology of Edmund Husserl. He became a professor of the philosophy of jurisprudence in 1935. Not until October 1942 did he join the antifascist resistance as a member of the clandestine Partito d'Azione. Incarcerated for a few months during the RSI, after the war he returned to his academic career as a professor of the philosophy of law at the University of Turin. A social democrat, Bobbio was one of the most esteemed public intellectuals of the Italian Republic. As Alessandra Tarquini argues, "Bobbio represented those democratic and antifascist intellectuals who, immediately after the war, interpreted their role as scholars as a mission to combat any form of subordination to the directives of a party or a state, be it fascist or Soviet, which, in the midst of the Cold War, was a point of reference for a large part of the Italian Left."[40]

Bobbio's views on Fascism were an idiosyncratic synthesis of the conceptions of Croce and Piero Gobetti. For Bobbio, Mussolini realized a regime that became the exact antithesis of the democratic ideals that the political philosophy of the Enlightenment had developed—in particular that of Jean-Jacques Rousseau. As such, Fascism, while antagonistic and ideologically opposed to socialism and communism, shared with these revolutionary forms a firm denial of the democratic organization of society. Bobbio addressed the question of Fascism in various texts, especially in the 1970s. In "L'ideologia del fascismo" (The Ideology of Fascism), a lecture he gave at the University of Milan in 1975, Bobbio connected the ideology of Fascism to "conceptions of the world and of history, political and social ideas, ethical and juridical modes of thinking, spiritual attitudes, moods and polemical arguments" that had been circulating in Europe since the late nineteenth century—an interpretation later sustained by historians like George L. Mosse, Zeev Sternhell, and Mimmo Cangiano.[41] Fascism was a quintessentially "negative" and "destructive" ideology, insofar as it defined itself as "being 'against' something."[42] But despite the fact that Mussolini declared his movement to be anticommunist, antisocialist, antiliberal, and antidemocratic, for Bobbio "antidemocratism" was the defining characteristic not only of Fascism, but also of all other forms of revolutionary conservatism active in Europe at the turn of the twentieth century.[43] What lay at the origins of Fascism was a reaction against the Enlightenment project productive of various forms of anti-intellectualism that ended up fueling all forms of antidemocratism of the early twentieth century.[44] The denial of reason and historical progress, in turn, produced another characteristic of anti-Enlightenment and antidemocratic reactionary movements: "racism."[45]

Fascism not only inherited the legacy of antidemocratic thought, but also systematically applied it to overcome its ethical norms (e.g., "pacifism," "egalitarianism") and institutions (e.g., "universal suffrage," "Parliament").[46] For this reason, Fascism could not have any definite economic policy because it always affirmed the hegemony of political decision-making over economic necessities: "From this follows the primacy of politics over the economy, the subordination of economic interests to those of the state."[47] As a result, Fascism, in order to respond to the different and often contradictory demands of the classes that sustained it (petty bourgeoisie, landowners, industrialists, financiers, et al.), had to constantly intervene in the economic life of the nation: State intervention in the economy became therefore a necessity.[48] All these elements, for Bobbio, were consistent with Mussolini's ideas about the "primacy of action" vis-à-vis thought.[49] The result was that Fascism, contrary to other political forms such as liberalism, socialism, and democracy, developed not just an ideology, but a doctrine, something closer to religion than philosophy—a principle of power that could not develop into a coherent and systematic political form. Given the ideological vacuity of Fascism as a new system of power, it developed different faces according to the social groups it intended to recruit.

But Fascism was not a monolith. For Bobbio, it took different forms in its twenty years of power. There was a "conservative Fascism," which appealed to and was an expression of "the frightened conservatives, coming from the Historical Right [i.e., Croce and Giovanni Giolitti] and from right-wing nationalists, who demanded above all order, discipline, and firmness of leadership—in short, the reestablishment of state authority":[50] It "presented itself as the antithesis of Bolshevism, and therefore as a continuation and completion, or suppression-overcoming, of classical liberalism, which was now incapable of fighting the monster [of Bolshevism] with its own weapons."[51] This was the movement Mussolini presented to the industrialists of northern Italy, the landowners of the central north, and the aristocracy of the south. Its opposite was "subversive Fascism," an expression of the " 'uprooted,' young people of the new generation, plunged by the intoxication of war and victory into the idealless mediocrity of everyday life, who asked not only for order but for a new order and were the theorists of a subversive fascism, in their own way revolutionary."[52] These were the war veterans of the petty bourgeoisie, the followers of Marinetti's Futurism, the warriors who could not return to a peaceful existence in the aftermath of the First World War, and the legionnaires who embarked on D'Annunzio's Fiume conquest. Subversive Fascism was, "above all, the antithesis of liberal democracy, and therefore a revolutionary competitor of the Soviet revolution (fascism as the 'true' revolution of the 20th century)."[53] Finally, there was a Fascism that attempted to mediate between these two forms: It "presented itself as a negation of both liberal democracy and Bolshevism, setting itself up as a conciliation of opposites, a synthesis, a 'third way.' "[54] This was the Fascism of "the petty bourgeois, crushed between the opposing ranks of antagonists, who sought a mediation, a synthesis between old and new, between conservation and revolution."[55] The philosopher Giovanni Gentile represented the first, conservative form of Fascism: the Fascism of old conservatives, of "university professors," of those who conceived of Mussolini's regime as an attempt to produce a "true liberalism."[56] For the subversives, however, Fascism was a "universal movement," whose "mission" was "ultranational and as such, precisely, a revolutionary mission." The state that the Fascist revolution (the only "authentic revolution") produced had no choice but to become an empire to fulfill its historical mission of domination.[57] But of the three forms of Fascism, "the image that ended up prevailing so as to become one of the dominant motifs of official propaganda was the last one: fascism as a third way."[58] This was the Fascism of the corporations, which were "the bodies destined to reconcile the opposing interests, to obtain the collaboration of the opposing classes, in the name of the higher interest of the nation. The corporate state eliminates the anarchy of the liberal state without falling into the despotism of the communist state."[59]

These three forms of Fascism, mere "images" rather than typologies, for Bobbio helped one also to understand the different interpretations that antifascists gave to it. Thus, the concept of Fascism as totalitarianism derived from the liberals' critique of its false claims to liberalism, since, as totalitarian, Fascism was more similar to communism than to the regimes of liberal democracy. By contrast, for Marxists Fascism was the last, extreme attempt of economic liberalism to resist the egalitarian and emancipatory project of the communist revolution. Bobbio rejected both these interpretations and concluded instead that "it cannot come as a surprise that the interpretation of fascism as an antithesis, not so much of the liberal state with which it shared the defense of capitalism, not so much of the communist state with which it shared some political institutions, starting with the unchallenged domination of a single party, but of democracy, if by democracy we mean a regime that should have accommodated the needs of socialism in the economic field without destroying the conquests of liberalism in the political field, has become the official ideology of the Resistance, albeit one that is increasingly evanescent in the new Italian democracy."[60]

Over the course of the 1970s, Bobbio developed a new, synthetic understanding of Fascism that was in dialogue with the explosion of historical research on Mussolini's regime and across the boundary dividing academia and public opinion.[61] By then Italian historians had overcome the initial "repugnance" toward research on Fascism and since the early 1960s had published on the origins of Mussolini's regime,[62] the state institutions it created,[63] its political economy,[64] its impact on Italian society,[65] Fascism at war,[66] its ideology,[67] its culture,[68] Fascist antisemitism,[69] and Fascism as a metahistorical problem in Italian history.[70] New archives and documents were discovered, thanks especially to the indefatigable work of Renzo De Felice, whose multivolume biography of Mussolini was explicitly presented in terms of an antibiographical socioinstitutional history that rejected the reduction of the twenty years of Fascist regime to Mussolinism.[71]

In that scholarly context, Bobbio's understanding of Fascism as "antidemocratism" attempted to overcome the irreconcilable opposition of differing concepts, the liberal and the Marxian, that divided historians and political theorists just as it had in the political analyses of the transwar period. By positing it as the antithesis primarily to democracy, Bobbio intended to highlight, on the one hand, its affinities with market economy and the support it received from the capitalist elites, without, however, that these affinities resolving the inherent contradictions between the two, such that the "primacy of the political" and the centrality of the state as the means and final end of economic activities prevented the reduction of Fascism to monopoly capitalism (as it did in the orthodox Marxist view). On the other hand, Bobbio pointed out that Mussolini's regime developed into a totalitarian state resembling that of actually existing socialism. He nonetheless rejected, against De Felice's revisionism, the assimilation of Fascism with Soviet communism into the amorphous category of "totalitarianism," arguing that the two political forms were not equidistant from the ideals of a democratic society, primarily because "communism represents the attempt to implement in a distorted form a great universalist ideal, that of human emancipation, of liberation from the slavery of need; it is a powerful idea that runs through the whole history of man, from Plato onward, passing through the Church fathers, while fascism has an opposite aspiration."[72]

Two considerations can be drawn from Bobbio's concept of Fascism. First, despite its attempt to overcome the irreconcilable positions of liberal and Marxist analyses, Bobbio's interpretation also conceived of Fascism as the obverse of the political ideal he upheld, that is, a participatory democratic egalitarianism that aspired to Enlightenment ideals.[73] Second, for Bobbio, as for Croce, Fascism did not seem to possess a political ideology sufficiently well developed to make of it a distinct political form. As a regime, it developed into an authoritarian state-centered power that asserted itself through violence and coercion. It never developed a distinct culture, as he hinted in *Politica e cultura*, in 1955, and argued more systematically in a 1973 essay titled "La cultura e il fascismo."[74]

If Fascism was incapable of asserting itself politically and ideologically, if not as a negation of preexisting political forms,[75] it was also incapable of producing any form of original culture.[76] That view, in a sense coherent with Croce's insistence that Fascism was only a temporary descent into irrationalism, was stoutly held by Italian intellectuals in the 1960s and 1970s, preventing any serious engagement with its ideological and cultural interventions until the studies of Alessandra Tarquini, Pier Giorgio Zunino, and Emilio Gentile in the 1990s and 2000s. It also reflected the pervasive notion, brilliantly portrayed in Federico Fellini's film *Amarcord* (1973), that Fascism was nothing but the obvious result of Italy's "adolescence" as a nation.[77] As Tarquini has convincingly argued, Bobbio's refusal to acknowledge that Fascism had produced an original culture effectively relinquished the possibility of explaining the collaboration and support of Italian intellectuals for the regime if not in terms of convenience and subjection. The effect of this interpretive gesture was an "involuntarily 'defascistization'" of Fascism, "that is, to remove from the regime the attributes that characterize its historical individuality by denying that it had a culture, an ideology, a ruling class, a totalitarian character and, in short, its specificity."[78] If Fascism was nothing but a ruthless exercise of power, then the popular consensus for the regime could not be thought of except as coercive submission, effectively denying any shared responsibility for the Fascist past. Ultimately, for Bobbio, Italians could not be held responsible for the violence, repression, imperial expansion, war, and collaboration in the Holocaust because they possessed neither agency nor political maturity.

The question of consent and responsibility became central to historiographical debates in the 1970s, especially after the publication of the fourth volume of De Felice's biography of Mussolini, subtitled *Gli anni del consenso, 1929–1936* (The Years of Consensus, 1929–1936).[79] His argument that the regime enjoyed great popular support was intended to subvert not only the postwar perception that it had subjected the Italian population to the coercive violence of an efficient repressive apparatus and the conception of a widespread "antifascism" upon which the Republic was founded after 1946, but also Bobbio's conviction that, deprived of authentic ideology and culture, Fascism was inherently incapable of producing consensus but rather enjoyed people's miseducation when it came to democratic participation.[80] As De Felice insists, "The Fascist regime has as an element that distinguishes it from reactionary and conservative regimes, the mobilization and participation of the masses. That this was achieved in demagogic forms is another matter: the principle is that of active participation, not exclusion."[81] As the historian Gianpiero Carocci has aptly commented, De Felice "takes up an affirmation widely diffused in Fascist publications: it is, that is, an affirmation which De Felice comes to on the basis of a literal interpretation of those documents."[82]

From the perspective of historical epistemology, the question cannot be addressed just empirically, especially if gathered from Fascist official archives. Santomassimo has convincingly claimed that "the historiographical debate has paid tribute to the inevitably subjective nature of the reflection on the sources through which the phenomenon can be measured in a dictatorial regime: sources that are to a very large extent police papers, reports from prefects and quaestors, letters from informants and trustees of the many secret polices, i.e., everything that replaces, in the absence of freedom, the registration of a free unfolding of opinions and feelings."[83]

The epistemological uncertainties that the notion of popular consensus triggers when used as heuristic category are not limited to the legitimacy of the documentary sources or the statistical or qualitative methodologies employed to measure it.[84] They are inherent to the notion itself, especially in the context of authoritarian and dictatorial regimes. For historians tackling the question of popular consensus, therefore, it is not enough to report, as chapters 3 and 4 did, that the regime was ruthlessly engaged in its early years in silencing all forms of opposition through intimidation, violence, *confino* (confinement), imprisonment, forced exile, censorship, and murder; or that it soon mobilized, alongside these coercive means, a systematic campaign of suasive indoctrination that affected the language, work, and lifestyles of Italians, with the aim of engineering their anthropological transformation. Heuristic categories such as "consensus" or "approval" imply a claim on the actual *intentions* of the population, which are indeed impossible to sustain with any evidence, and even less if based on a compromised archive like the one used by De Felice.

De Felice's revisionist portrait questions both the historical role of antifascist resistance (which his historical analyses downplayed with respect to its scope, efficacy, and proportion) and the coercive nature of the authoritarian regime.[85] These constitute the bulk of the ideological revisionism of Fascism by the Italian Right from the 1990s to the present.[86] The polemic on De Felice's theses divided establishment historians and political theorists, but it also forced historians to abandon many dogmatic assumptions.[87]

With the end of the Cold War, the ideological opposition that fueled the scholarship on Fascism gave way to research into the most diverse spheres of the Fascist Ventennio. De Felice's student Emilio Gentile established himself at the turn of the twenty-first century as one of the most prolific authors on Italian Fascism as well as, along with Enzo Collotti, one of the most influential.[88] Like his mentor, Gentile rejected any attempt to transform Mussolini's regime in an epiphenomenon or negative reaction to the First World War, in an expression of an irrationalist European zeitgeist, or in the political form of monopoly capital. He rather intended to "give back to Fascism its own individuality, by representing it, without either demonization or excuses, for what it had been historically."[89] For Gentile, Fascism could be defined as "a modern political phenomenon, nationalist and revolutionary, antiliberal and anti-Marxist, organized in a militia party, with a totalitarian conception of politics and the state, with an activist and antitheoretical ideology, mythically based, virile and antihedonistic, sacralized as secular religion, which affirms the absolute primacy of the nation, understood as an ethnically homogeneous organic community, hierarchically organized in a corporate state, with a warlike vocation to the politics of grandeur, power, and conquest, aimed at the creation of a new order and a new civilization."[90] Closer to Bobbio in his defense of the ideals of democracy than to De Felice's revisionist conservatism, Gentile, the main voice of a liberal understanding of "fascism," looked at the legacy of Mosse and Hannah Arendt for theoretical support of his archival research. Also unlike De Felice, Gentile, following the example of Collodi, did not give up on the attempt to genericize the experience of Italian Fascism into a political form that could be applied to other historical situations, as the next chapter will show.

In twenty-first-century Italy, the question of Fascism changed shape once again. The end of the postwar party system (now informally called the "first republic") and the dissolution of the center-right coalition headed by the DC and the PSI after a series of corruption scandals made room for a new party system (the "second republic") that paradoxically reenergized a debate on "fascism" that had been languishing in the waning years of the Cold War. The terms of the debate, in the public sphere and among professional academics, have changed dramatically.

A series of political transformations progressively dismantled the social democratic state apparatus and made of Italy a country fully integrated into the global neoliberal system. These include the political debut in 1994 of the flamboyant television magnate Silvio Berlusconi, with his personality-centered, populist party-enterprise Forza Italia; the dissolution in 1991 of the largest Western European communist party, the PCI, and its transformation into a sequence of political parties (the Partito Democratico della Sinistra until 1998, the Democratici di Sinistra until 2007, and the Partito Democratico since then) that progressively moved toward the center and explicitly embraced economic liberalism; the rise of a territorialist, identitarian, and separatist political party in northern Italy (Lega Nord), the members of which often entertained close ties with other European and Russian extreme right-wing parties, movements, and think tanks; the entrance in the first

Berlusconi's government (1994) of the postfascist party MSI, now renamed Alleanza Nazionale; and in 2022 the election of Prime Minister Giorgia Meloni, the head of a political party explicitly linked to the MSI.[91]

In the context of such tumultuous transformations, the question of "fascism" paradoxically reemerged not from a concerned antifascist front, but from the ideological labor of political figures close to Forza Italia, Lega Nord, Alleanza Nazionale, and Fratelli d'Italia, with the aim of advancing a revisionist and explicitly anti-antifascist reappraisal of Fascism while at the same time launching attacks against the legitimacy and legacy of antifascism. The consequences of this ideological operation of historical falsification through books and television shows are not just cosmetic surgery on the image of Mussolini and his regime. It occurred contemporaneously with the multiplication of neo-Fascist and neo-Nazi groups and an unprecedented increase in their membership, especially among the lower strata of the population, who were more severely affected by the consequences of economic globalization, the precariousness of the job market, and the progressive dismantling of the welfare state. The members of such extreme right-wing groups as CasaPound and Forza Nuova received support and legitimation from mainstream conservative parties by participating with them in local administrations.[92]

Parallel to this operation of historiographical and ideological fabrications, a new generation of academic historians has been pushing the study of Fascism in previously unexplored directions, in conversation with other disciplines and international scholars, and with an unprecedented global reach.[93] Others, such as Mimmo Franzinelli, Carlo Greppi, and Francesco Filippi, devoted their professional expertise in the history and historiography of Fascism to fact-checking and uncovering the falsifications behind today's ideological refashioning of Mussolini and his regime. But the changed social status of intellectuals within the larger society in the last thirty years renders research on Fascism even more heroic.

Scholars, even those few who are striving to keep alive the ideal of the public intellectual of the 1960s and 1970s, have lost much of the traction they used to have to direct or influence public opinion. The figure of the "organic intellectual," as Gramsci called it in the *Prison Notebooks*, seems to have disappeared. And if Pierre Bourdieu in the 1980s and 1990s still classified academics and intellectual producers as a subordinate subgroup within the dominant strata of French society, even that condition seems altogether lost in the indeterminate noise of social-media post-truths and conspiracy theories. As Giorgio Caravare disconsolately observed, Italy seems to have become today a society without intellectuals.[94]

Conclusions

In the scholarly production of postwar Italian academics, the sign vehicle "fascism" operated indexically to refer deictically to Mussolini's movement, regime, and ideology. It functioned essentially as a proper name even when syntactically presented with the lowercase "f" of a common noun. The denotations of an authoritarian and totalitarian regime remained largely undisputed; only the connotative judgments on the degree of its dictatorial ruthlessness, popular support, success, and so on depended on historians' political orientation, independently of the rigor of their archival and historiographical analyses. When the term was used generically in political propaganda, in slogans, and during the protest movements of the long 1970s, the clear reference was to the past experience of Fascism, the regime that connotatively stood for the qualities of authoritarianism, intolerance, oppression, violence, chauvinism, and the like.[95] The attribution of "fascist" thus established a relationship of comparison and similitude (analogy), and when used as an epithet in lieu of the name of an adversarial party, movement, or politician, it operated as a metaphorical substitution. When the attribution was instead predicated, either by the antagonists or by themselves, on political movements that explicitly aspired to Fascism, often with the addition of the prefix "neo-," it operated as a genealogical metonymy, since groups such as Avanguardia Nazionale, Ordine Nuovo, Nuclei Armati Rivoluzionari, and the Fronte Nazionale Rivoluzionario were violent, reactionary, and subversive movements that conceived of themselves as descending from or continuing the struggle of historical Fascism.[96]

With the exception of Enzo Collodi and few others, Italian academics remained largely distant from the attempts to genericize "fascism" into a new political form or ideal type that had engaged historians, philosophers, and political theorists around the world since the early 1960s.[97] The resistance to such genericization derived, in part, from their reluctance to assimilate Fascism to German National Socialism—a differentiation at once political and intellectual that characterized both public and academic discourse since the end of the war. In part, that was also due to the reluctance of De Felice and his numerous students and affiliates to engage in such reductionism. But it was also due to the fact that among Marxist historians, "fascism" already operated somewhat transnationally to identify distinct authoritarian regimes emerging in similar socioeconomic circumstances.

11

The Search for a "Fascist Minimum"

Generic Fascism and the Fight for Democracy during the Cold War

The term "fascism" has circulated since 1945 predominantly in its generic and extended senses rather than as the name of Mussolini's regime. Marxist scholarship certainly played an important role, but it was above all the impact of Nazi Germany (and only secondarily of Japan in the Pacific theater) during the Second World War one of the determining factors that favored the dissociation of "fascism" from Mussolini's regime. Indeed, during the transnational process of reconstruction of a new world order after the Second World War, "fascism" consolidated as a term fuzzily referring to the totalitarian enemy deemed responsible for that war and serving as the obverse upon which to rebuild Europe (and the world) on antifascist (and postcolonial) premises. This loosely generic understanding of "fascism" can be traced, for example, in the political declaration of President Franklin Roosevelt, who on September 23, 1944 stated that "the victory of the American people and their allies will be a victory against Fascism and the blind alley of despotism it represents,"[1] as well as in the Soviet Union terminology of the Velikaya Otechestvennaya voyna protiv fashizma (Great Patriotic War against Fascism).

Originally developed on ideological and pragmatic bases with the goal of organizing the consensus for the war against the Axis countries, these ideals waned rapidly with the intensification of the Cold War.[2] In European countries such as Italy and France, where antifascism defined the armed Resistance against Mussolini's and the Vichy regimes, generic "fascism" stood both as metonymy for the catastrophic war and as antinomy for the invention of a new political community. A similarly undetermined use of "fascism" reappeared in the slogans, propaganda, and slurs identifying behaviors that were judged authoritarian, chauvinistic, intolerant, and so on in the global context of the student and civil rights movements of the late 1960s, loosely inspired by the political ideals of Herbert Marcuse, Erich Fromm, Norberto Bobbio, and Theodor Adorno, among many other thinkers who had made in their texts a similarly fuzzy use of the term.[3]

Adorno's understanding of "fascism" exercised considerable influence in postwar political thought, more extensively than is usually acknowledged in the scholarship on Nazifascism. The relentless interviews he gave on radio shows and in newspaper articles, as well as his numerous public lectures, forced the question of the Holocaust upon the political discourse of postwar Germany.[4] By placing Auschwitz at the center of his philosophical reflections on the catastrophe of modernity, Adorno contributed to make the genocide of the European Jews one of the constituent features of National Socialism and, in turn, of generic fascism—an issue largely ignored in wartime Marxist debate. He was also instrumental in preventing Germans' collective responsibility for their attempted extermination of European Jews from being erased or repressed for the sake of political convenience in the ensuing context of the Cold War. The Holocaust, for Adorno, became the ineludible benchmark that preceded, as a critical precondition, any form of cultural or political intervention: It prevented any artistic attempt to cathartically celebrate the end of the war;[5] it constituted the foundation of people's education to democratic citizenship,[6] and of the possibility of philosophy itself.[7]

After the Second World War, fascism and war constituted the negative standard for any future political praxis. As Adorno stated in 1959, "I consider the survival of National Socialism *within* democracy to be potentially more menacing than the survival of fascist tendencies *against* democracy."[8] It is therefore not surprising that the analyses of the scholars of the Frankfurt School were inspirational for antifascist movements during the Cold War, often despite their intentions. In a sense, the writings of Adorno, Horkheimer, and Marcuse not only posited "fascism" as the central stake in the struggle for democracy, but contributed to the transformation of "fascism" into a generic label that discredited all forms of reactionarianism and authoritarianism.[9] It was that generic use of the term that informed the slogans of the global civil rights and student movements of the 1960s.[10]

Marcuse, who joined the Institute of Social Research after breaking with his PhD advisor, Martin Heidegger, became one of the referent thinkers for students mobilizing in the late 1960s. Like Adorno, he saw in the survival of fascism within democratic institutions the greatest threat to an emancipated society. In a 1970 lecture he gave at Princeton University at the invitation of the historian Arno J. Mayer, later published as "The Left under the Counterrevolution," he clearly stated that "a higher stage of capitalist development in the United States would call for a higher stage of fascism. . . . The relation between liberal democracy and fascism has found its shortest and most striking formulation in the phrase: 'liberal democracy is the face of the propertied classes when they are not afraid, fascism when they are afraid.' "[11]

In Marcuse's political philosophy, "fascism" was the name of the violent reaction of capital for its own survival in times of crisis. Like Adorno, he denied that the historical experience of fascist reaction had concluded with the Second World War: "On the road from laissez-faire to monopoly and state capitalism," he wrote in 1972, "bourgeois democracy in its present form marks the stage where only two alternatives seem possible: neo-fascism on a global scale, or transition to socialism."[12] That was not only a danger for countries where democratic institutions had a shorter history, like West Germany and Italy; it also applied to the oldest modern democracy, the United States: "American fascism," he claimed in a 1970 interview with the German writer Hans Magnus Enzensburger, "will look different than German fascism, and, to be sure, to the extent that American society is different from German society of 1933. A charismatic leader is no longer necessary. I remind you of an excellent formulation by William Shirer who, God knows, is no socialist: this man said recently that American fascism will probably be the first which comes to power by democratic means and with democratic support."[13]

The civil rights, antiwar, and student movements that erupted in different countries in the late 1960s were spurred by different social conditions and had different stakes, depending on the various political situations in the United States, Western Europe, Latin America, and Japan, where activists were inspired by different ideals, terminologies, thinkers, and leaders. The generic use of "fascism" as the name for the authoritarian, illiberal, repressive, and antidemocratic tendencies persisting within the institutions of democratic countries was adopted in the slogans, songs, and speeches of activists everywhere. The connotations of this unqualified generic use of "fascism" were clearly indebted to the Marxian tradition, and yet it seemed to reject the dogmatism of the Comintern definition. The "fascism" of the late-1960s movements did not disavow the socioeconomic premises of the Marxist conception, but like Benjamin, Adorno, Marcuse, Fromm, Reich, and other critical theorists, they preferred to look for fascist tendencies in political discourse, social practices (family structure, gender relations, racial discrimination, sexual orientation, etc.), psychological attitudes, and culture in general.

Toward a Theory of Generic "Fascism"

If the first genericization of "fascism" largely occurred semiotically in Marxist texts, it was also among Marxists that we read early warnings about the loss of its heuristic efficacy and analytical precision. In the conclusion of his *La naissance du Fascisme: L'Italie de 1918 à 1922*, Angelo Tasca acknowledged the inherent contradiction at the core of any attempt to distill a generic definition of "fascism" applicable to different forms of counterrevolutionary authoritarianisms. "Fascism is a dictatorship," he wrote; "this is the starting point of all the definitions of fascism that have been attempted so far. But beyond that point, the consensus is far from settled. . . . We should be careful not to put into circulation a new 'definition' which would, of course, be the good one, a 'portable formula' that anyone can pull out in case of need to dispel any doubts, of him and of others. For us, *defining fascism is above all writing its history*."[14] Rather, he insisted, "a theory of fascism could therefore only emerge from the study of all forms of fascism, hidden or open, repressed or triumphant."[15]

Like Gramsci and the early Togliatti, Tasca believed that any investigation into fascisms had to begin from the sociohistorical study of the conditions that favored the rise to power of each individual movements and regimes. To that aim, he listed the "general conditions" shared by all the different authoritarian regimes: the legacy of the First World War, systemic economic crisis ("*Without economic crisis*," as Tasca put it, "[there is] *no fascism*"),[16] a sense of emergency shared by the middle classes,[17] mass politics,[18] and, finally, the "existence of a given 'climate,' of a special atmosphere of excitement and delirium."[19] In that atmosphere of "delirium," violence took hold and replaced negotiation and institutional representation as preferred form of political intervention. Fascism was the resulting form of governance that elevated violence to a system instead of regarding it for what it really was: a "social pathology."[20] Tasca's analyses operated within the parameters of a Marxian paradigm, despite his break with the PCd'I and his collaboration with the Vichy government. He rejected the mechanistic reductionism of the Comintern orthodoxy. He also rejected the possibility of identifying fundamental attributes that could lead to a synthetic and portable definition of "fascism," like the one that would soon engage the writers of the "fascism minimum."

Before Ernst Nolte and Eugen Weber independently launched the enterprise of turning "fascism" into a new and universal type of political organization, comparative research on Fascism, National Socialism, and other transwar forms of authoritarian regimes took other forms. First, there were Marxist analyses, which were based on a metonymical understanding of "fascism" as referring to the differing political forms that emerged from a similar condition of capitalist development (see chap. 9). Second, there were explicitly comparative analyses, where the cases of Italy, Germany, Spain, Vichy France, and other regimes were juxtaposed with the purpose of highlighting similarities and differences but without any attempt to subsume them into a generic category. An example of this second form was the work of the French literary historian Henri Lemaître, who, in his *Les fascismes dans l'histoire* (1959), compared the regimes of Hitler and Mussolini as distinct "concrete forms of taking and exercising power," tantamount, in their formal diversity, to a similar development of a "technical modernization of imperial totalitarianism."[21] Like Gramsci, Lemaître conceived of these totalitarian regimes as sharing Rousseau's ideal of a general will to which individual freedoms were subordinated; but, unlike in traditional democracies, this general will was embodied in the figure of a *chef* (boss) rather than in representational institutions.[22] Despite their counterrevolutionary genesis, they were "antibourgeois," "antitraditionalist," "antiuniversalist," and prone to militarism.[23] Lemaître's study had a limited impact on subsequent scholarship, but it nonetheless adopted the category of "totalitarianism" as the essence of all fascist regimes he analyzed. In that, it was not alone. Indeed, as Enzo Traverso has pointed out, "The period from 1947 to 1960 was . . . the golden age of the idea of totalitarianism, which reached then a complete theoretical formulation and its widest diffusion."[24]

The text that set the conceptual parameters of the idea of "totalitarianism" in postwar scholarship was Hannah Arendt's *The Origins of Totalitarianism*, first published in English in 1951. Divided into three parts, "Antisemitism," "Imperialism," and "Totalitarianism," her long essay can be best described as an attempt to understand National Socialism in the light of the genocide of the European Jews and in the conjoined contexts of imperialism (for Arendt, the geopolitical condition of the contemporary world) and traditional antisemitism. Rather than attempting to synthesize the historical experiences of Italian Fascism and German Nazism—"fascism," apart from some exceptions, is not used generically—Arendt saw in totalitarianism the political form in which both participated.

The Origins of Totalitarianism adopted an *ante litteram* genealogical approach. In the way it unfolded in the 1920s and 1930s, totalitarianism was a synthesis of ideological conceptions and political dynamics that had originated in the previous century. The first of those, "antisemitism," had a long history in Europe, but it now assumed the character of pseudoscientific racial discrimination, which substituted the ideal of cultural assimilation with that of extirpation, removal, and extermination. "Imperialism," as it developed in the nineteenth century, conceived of the extra-European territories (with the exclusion of the United States) as a reservoir of resources to be colonized, subjected to the political and economic necessities of the metropole in the name of a civilizational mission and a hierarchy of races. Both concepts, "antisemitism" and "imperialism" alike, fueled the development of the modern nation-state, which fused together a sophisticated bureaucratic apparatus aimed at the total administration of society (a concern common also in the philosophy of both her former advisor and lover, Martin Heidegger, and his theoretical adversaries, Adorno and Horkheimer) and a nationalism that was itself the product of the union of mass politics and capitalist economy.

The totalitarian state was the radicalization of these tendencies, which were perfectly symbolized, for Arendt, in the technologically sophisticated and bureaucratically administered extermination camps. Most important, however, the totalitarian state, for Arendt, expressed the perfect machine for total administrative domination: "The true goal of Fascism was only to seize power and establish the Fascist 'elite' as uncontested ruler over the country. Totalitarianism is never content to rule by external means, namely, through the state and a machinery of violence; thanks to its peculiar ideology and the role assigned to it in this apparatus of coercion, totalitarianism has discovered a means of dominating and terrorizing human beings from within."[25] But, Arendt added, it was not simply a new form of authoritarianism, because totalitarianism "eliminates the distance between the rulers and the ruled and achieves a condition in which power and the will to power, as we understand them, play no role, or at best, a secondary role. In substance, the totalitarian leader is nothing more nor less than the functionary of the masses he leads; he is not a power-hungry individual imposing a tyrannical and arbitrary will upon his subjects."[26]

Arendt's argument was far more complex than this and elicited critical responses and charges of reductionism that would be beyond the scope of this chapter to review.[27] Interestingly, for Arendt Mussolini's did not really qualify as a totalitarian state. As Margaret Canovan observes, "Arendt stressed that Italian Fascism should not be thought of as totalitarian, since it was a dictatorial attempt to strengthen the state and the nation."[28] For that reason alone Arendt rejected the genericized use of "fascism" to refer to both the Italian and the German regimes. On the contrary, "totalitarianism" should become the term to define a new political form that placed itself in explicit contradiction with Enlightenment-based ideas of freedom and people's rights: It consisted of "a fusion of Nazism and Stalinism based upon a mass society and involving a totalitarian movement and concentration camps."[29]

The use of "totalitarianism" as a critique of Mussolini's regime went back to 1923 (see chap. 8). The enlargement of its heuristic capacity to include first National Socialism and later Stalin's Soviet Union originated in the 1930s. It was a category privileged by liberal thinkers but also occasionally utilized by socialist and Marxist activists as well. While the term was avoided during the Second World War, it soon became a central political and historiographical category in the early phase of the Cold War: It was a useful conceptual device for changing the previous alliance into a new ideological rivalry by connoting that the fight against illiberalism was now targeting a new enemy, the Soviet Union. As Traverso points out, however, "This canonization took place at the price of a significant change: far more than a critical function toward existing regimes—as in the thirties—the concept of totalitarianism now fulfilled an essentially *apologetic* function of the Western order; in other words, it was transformed into an *ideology*. At the origin of this change there was a *translatio imperii*—the emergence of the American hegemony—with the complete overthrow of alliances that this implied: the old totalitarian enemy, Germany, became, in its western region, an outpost of the 'free world' in Europe, while the former ally, the USSR, was transformed into the main incarnation of totalitarianism. Thus, antitotalitarianism was clothed as anticommunism."[30]

To properly function as ideology for the new era of diplomatic and military Cold War, "totalitarianism" had to lose its former association and synonymity with antifascism.[31] Antitotalitarianism, to become synonymous with anticommunism, had to subsume Fascism and Nazism into the bureaucratic state-centrism of Stalin's Soviet Union. As US President Harry S. Truman declared on May 13, 1947: "There isn't any difference in totalitarian states. I don't care what you call them, Nazi, Communist or Fascist."[32]

Ernst Nolte's Era of Fascism and Its Legacy

The project of developing a generic conception of "fascism" that responded to the geopolitical circumstances of the Cold War was at the core of Ernst Nolte's *Der Faschismus in seiner Epoche* of 1963. A former student of Martin Heidegger, Ernst Nolte was forty years old when he published his *Habilitationsschrift* (dissertation), two years before occupying his first academic position at the University of Marburg. Its English translation, *Three Faces of Fascism*, would change the scholarship on "fascism" in the following decades.[33] Nolte's "fascism" had little to do with Mussolini's movement—even though Nolte acknowledged the genealogy of the term in the entry he wrote for the *Geschichtliche Grundbegriffe*.[34] It was, rather, an attempt to explain the rise of German Nazism within the framing of a political-philosophical movement that was European rather than German. For the purpose of this study, it is less important to understand how Nolte's work affected the study of National Socialism than to record how his theorization of generic fascism contributed to expanding the semantic marker of "fascism." It was in fact his work that launched the project of transforming the term into a universal political category from a non-Marxist standpoint.

For Nolte, the historical phenomenon that the term "fascism" identified exceeded the serendipitous developments of latecomer nations such as Italy and Germany. Like the original German title of the book revealed, fascism was a product of *seiner Epoche* (its age). Although some of the elements of mature fascism developed in the context of late nineteenth-century France—marked by widespread antisemitism, racism, and imperialist hubris (a theme that would later reappear in Zeev Sternhell's work)—it fully developed only in what he called the "era of the world wars," which he dated between August 1, 1914 and May 8, 1945. That period, said Nolte, should be more aptly called the "era of fascism."[35] Born in an epoch marked by total war, fascism, a phenomenon of "political transcendence," distinguished itself from all other form of bourgeois politics: "It was the war that made room for a political phenomenon, which was, so to speak, its very own child, a child which by innate law strove in turn to engender yet another war."[36]

Nolte's historical investigation ensued from a philosophical assumption: that modern politics in all its forms (liberalism, socialism, communism, etc.) was the expression of a bourgeois concept of society that sided with abstract universality rather than concrete particularity. Modern societies, in other words, were for Nolte engineered by a self-aware bourgeoisie that was able to escape "the confines of the everyday world" to conceive of society as the realization of a transcendental universal ideal.[37] Such a "theoretical transcendence," which Nolte identified in the political philosophy of Immanuel Kant, engendered a kind of political thinking that went beyond the confines of the village, the community, the kingdom, and the nation-state, and instead embraced the entire world. Just as the Kantian "transcendental subject" went beyond the contingent limits of the individual human being to become an impersonal subject that was purely formal intellectual possibility (schematism), transcendental politics, for Nolte, conceived of society as the potential instantiation of a rational universal form. The practical consequence of this took the form of a "social process . . . that continually widens human relationships, thereby rendering them in general more subtle and more abstract—the process that disengages the individual from traditional ties and increases the power of the group until it finally assails even the primordial forces of nature and history."[38]

So, in the nineteenth century, capitalism was a practical instantiation of a rational organization of production and exchange that bourgeoise transcendence produced. Karl Marx, Nolte noted, acknowledged its alienating effects and conceptualized an overcoming of that transcendence with a revolution that was itself, however, producing its own form of transcendence: Socialism was but a practical effect of the same political "theoretical transcendence" born in Enlightenment rationality. A paradox thus lay at the core of modern bourgeois societies, according to Nolte: The transcendental drive to subsume within its formalistic grasp all aspects of the material, social, and psychological world (i.e., imperialism, capitalist globalization, the totalitarian state, etc.) created the conditions for its own derailment. Fascism, as quintessentially anti-Marxist, was a new form of resistance against transcendence directly produced by the effects of the Bolshevik Revolution of 1917.

Nolte's comparative analysis of three individual forms that ensued from the resistance to communist transcendentalism—the French Action Française, Italian Fascism, and German National Socialism (logically operating as, respectively, thesis, antithesis, and final synthesis)—had the goal of begetting an understanding of the epochal revolt against the two dominant practical effects of "theoretical transcendence": capitalism and communism. Nolte acknowledged that "fascism" was, strictly speaking, just a name, and he did not hesitate to acknowledge that Italian Fascism, which gave it the name, was an isolated phenomenon and thus *not* epochal at all.[39] The meaning of the signifier "fascism," the use of which had become a semantic habit, therefore could not be grasped in isolation, by analyzing each individual counterrevolutionary authoritarian movement that emerged in the "era of the world wars." Fascism was rather to be understood only as coextensive with its era.[40]

"Fascism," in other words, was for Nolte an imperfect, synecdochical compromise that covered for the absence of an explicit theorization of the nature of the epoch of the world wars, but that had the signifying effects of bringing analytical attention to the common essence of phenotypically different political phenomena of that period. "The aim of this study," he stated, "is to present not a picture of the era, but a concept of it, insofar as this can be derived from the nature of fascism."[41] "Fascism" was simply the name of that concept, which operated as a gravitational pull for all coeval global events. The three case studies that Nolte analyzed in the central part of the book therefore served to confirm the hypothetical definition of "fascism" he gave at the beginning of the book, printed in capital letters: "FASCISM IS ANTI-MARXISM WHICH SEEKS TO DESTROY THE ENEMY BY THE EVOLVEMENT OF A RADICALLY OPPOSED AND YET RELATED IDEOLOGY AND BY THE USE OF ALMOST IDENTICAL AND YET TYPICALLY MODIFIED METHODS, ALWAYS, HOWEVER, WITHIN THE UNYIELDING FRAMEWORK OF NATIONAL SELF-ASSERTION AND AUTONOMY."[42] Nolte admitted that fascism, the "metapolitical form" behind different movements and regimes operating between 1919 and 1945, took the form of a reaction that defined itself only in negative terms:[43] "There is no reason not to suppose that, in the overall relationships of the age, fascism for its part will have to be regarded as being primarily a reaction."[44]

In its various historical forms, fascism was a political force that operated symptomatically as an aberration engendered by its obverse, Marxism. At a sociological level, it generated forms of sociation that antagonized bourgeois values: localism rather than internationalism; fidelity to tradition rather than trust in abstract reason; religion and mysticism rather than Enlightenment values; emphasis on blood ties rather than on humanity in the abstract, and on *Volksgemeinschaft* (racial community) rather than impersonal *Gesellschaft* (society); hierarchy rather than equality; war and conflict rather than the Kantian utopia of *ewiger Frieden* (perpetual peace); and so on. In this sense, fascism operated as a "metapolitical phenomenon" precisely because it represented a form of "resistance to transcendence," and thus resistance to modernity and its alienating forces.[45] For Nolte, the search for a definition of "fascism" was therefore not a search for a definition that could encompass and be applied to the various forms of historical fascism that existed in 1914–45. It was rather the definition of a conceptual possibility inherent in modernity that could realize its own overcoming, its own dissolution.[46] Nolte was quite explicit on that when he stated, "Fascism is at the same time resistance to practical transcendence and struggle against theoretical transcendence. But this struggle must needs be concealed, since the original motivations can never be entirely dispensed with. And insofar as practical transcendence from its most superficial aspect is nothing but the possibility of concentration of power, fascism pursues its resistance to transcendence from within that transcendence and at times in the clear consciousness of a struggle for world hegemony."[47]

The crisis that fascism expressed was, however, reactive rather than foundational. In its mature form (Hitler's National Socialism), fascism produced horrors that exactly mirrored the horror of the transcendental praxis of Soviet communism against which it reacted. The labor and extermination camps were the antitranscendental response to the gulag; the totalitarian state apparatus of Nazi Germany was the obverse of the Stalinist one; and the extermination of the European Jews symbolically represented an attempt to exterminate the embodiment of modernity itself. As Domenico Losurdo put it in his study of historical revisionism, "In Nolte's view, the horror of the Third Reich took the form of a replica of, and prophylactic measure against, the horrors hailing from Soviet Russia," since the October Revolution, for him, was nothing less than "the primordial source of the catastrophe of the twentieth century."[48] Rejecting the transcendental drive of communism, fascism turned its totalitarian state apparatus to reaffirm the national (Italian Fascism) and racial (Nazism) community. Against socialist internationalism and the liberal notions of impersonal humanity and society, it defended the closed space of the traditional community, homogeneous in culture (Fascism) and blood (Nazism). Against the global reach and interconnectedness of market economy and financial capital, fascism idealized an economic autarky centered on the coexistence and synergy of professional corporations. But it was the ruthless violence of the Bolshevik Revolution and the Soviet state that determined the terror that the fascist state apparatuses unleashed.

Nolte's revisionism was predicated on an equivalency between communism and fascism that had already been advanced by conservative liberals since the transwar period, from Benedetto Croce to Friedrich von Hayek, from Karl Popper to Gerhard Ritter and Friedrich Meinecke. Arendt's reconceptualization of the notion of "totalitarianism," one that encompassed both the Nazi and the Stalinist experiences, had facilitated since the 1950s the acceptance of the equivalency paradigm among progressive liberals as well. This idea still attracts a large consensus today.[49]

Even though the complex language and philosophical approach of Nolte's book slowed historians' response to its thesis—a brilliant exception was George L. Mosse's critical review of 1966[50]—*Der Faschismus in seiner Epoche* "stirred up interest in the problem of generic fascism more than any other single work of the 1960s."[51] As Ian Kershaw noted, "Within five years [of its publication in English in 1965] several major international conferences had been held, numerous anthologies were in print containing studies of the nature and manifestation of fascist movements throughout Europe, and a considerable scholarly literature had built up."[52] By refunctioning the sign vehicle "fascism" to name and thus identify a generic form of political ideology that concretized in different instantiations in France, Italy, and Germany in the interwar years, Nolte had effectively set the parameters for the theoretical and empirical problem of isolating, defining, and identifying a new political ideal type. The book de facto baptized a new genre of fascism studies that would engage scholars of different backgrounds (intellectual, political, cultural, and social historians as well as political theorists and sociologists) in the search for a minimum definition of the essential features of the political form that "fascism" had now become. This "new consensus," as Roger Griffin defines it, not only strove to present fascism as a new, self-contained, and coherent form of political organization and ideology;[53] it also distinguished itself from the Marxist genericizations of fascism as a stage of capitalist development. Fascism was now a political form on its own. Its links with the institutions of liberal democracy and capitalism, central to the interpretation of Marxist scholars of different leanings as well as to the work of some liberal progressives such as Salvemini, Gobetti, and Bobbio, were severed for good.

Nolte's anti-Marxist conceptualization of "fascism" appealed to sectors of the German conservative intelligentsia that, in the 1960s, was increasingly ill at ease with the apologetic attitude of German political elites and the dominant consensus among historians that National Socialism was ineluctably linked to the particular historical development of the German nation (the so-called *Sonderweg* thesis).[54] By positing fascism as a force of anticommunist resistance, Nolte exculpated the German social and intellectual elites from their role in facilitating Hitler's rise to power, a position that Reinhart Koselleck had also hinted at in the introduction of his 1959 *Kritik und Krise*, albeit from the radically different perspective of a political crisis that stemmed as early as the Enlightenment reaction against the ancien régime.[55] Nolte's revisionism went beyond the mere conceptualization of Nazism as a "mirror image" of Soviet communism when he morally exonerated the Germans from the extermination of the Jews. As Jürgen Habermas points out, in Nolte's historical relativization of the "Jewish question," "the destruction of the Jews appears then to be only the regrettable result of a nevertheless understandable reaction to that which Hitler must have perceived as a threat of destruction."[56]

Nolte's notion of generic fascism and the apologetic views on German Nazism it triggered continued in his later works. They exploded in open and often aggressive polemic during the so-called *Historikerstreit* (historians' dispute), which Nolte himself started with an article he published in the *Frankfurter Allgemeine Zeitung* on June 6, 1986, titled "Vergangenheit, die nicht vergehen will: Eine Rede, die geschrieben, aber nicht mehr gehalten werden konnte" (The Past That Will Not Pass: A Speech That Could Be Written but Not Delivered).[57] Nolte claimed that unilateral attention on Nazi atrocities and German guilt was nothing but bad faith, a politically motivated distraction, diverting the attention from the actual perpetrator of twentieth-century genocidal barbarity: communism. The argument that Nolte had advanced in *Three Faces* reappeared here in a more direct and polemic guise: Fascism, in its mature expression as National Socialism, was nothing but a defense of Western civilization against the threat of the "Asiatic" communism of Stalin's Soviet Union.

Nolte's radical, unapologetic revisionism found support among other conservative intellectuals, including the journalist Joachim Fest and conservative historians such as Andreas Hillgruber, Klaus Hildebrand, and Michael Stürmer. The reaction against the "Vergangenheit" article was rapid and widespread and included the Frankfurt philosopher Jürgen Habermas's op-ed piece in *Die Zeit*, dated July 11, 1986.[58] Following Habermas, the arguments of the revisionists' camp were subjected to ruthless criticism by such historians as Hans-Ulrich Wehler, Jürgen Kochka, Wolfgang Mommsen, Martin Broszat, and many others.[59]

Nolte's argument, which saw in fascism a theoretical reaction against the violence of the abstract transcendentalism of modernity and in National Socialism a defensive reaction to the brutality of Stalinist communism, has ever since become the central argument of much postfascist revisionism, both in its most radical and abject form of historical denialism (expressed by such pseudo-scholars as Arthur Butz, David Irving, and Robert Faurisson) and in the more cautious forms of revisionism (as, for instance, in Renzo De Felice's apologetic stance toward Italian Fascism and skepticism about the political value of antifascism).[60] It continues today in the public sphere, where charges against fascism—whether generic or Italian—are rebuked by appealing to its coming as a reaction against Soviet communism or comparatively asserting the much deadlier records of communist crimes.[61]

The Search for the Fascist Minimum

Despite Nolte's revisionism, his attempt to conceptualize generic fascism directly inspired the research of historians, sociologists, and political theorists, not all of them necessarily of conservative leanings but no one really sympathetic to the Marxist approach. For Wolfgang Sauer, Ernst Nolte's *Der Faschismus* was "the first serious attempt to develop a workable, non-Marxist concept of fascism."[62] Despite some methodological objections, he believed that it opened the path for new research leading to a "non-Marxist theory of fascism with a socioeconomic dimension,"[63] which would finally demonstrate that "fascism is not, as the Marxist interpretation holds, merely a manipulation by monopoly capitalists."[64] Zeev Sternhell acknowledged that Nolte's work was "an attempt to give a comprehensive explanation of fascism," and as such it was "hailed as a very great book."[65] Other participants in the ensuing search for a "fascism minimum" recognized in Nolte's book their precursor, insofar as it set up the parameters for a new conceptualization of generic fascism. First, it opposed the previous generalization of transwar Marxist thinkers by rejecting their assumption of a causal link between fascism and capitalist liberalism. Second, the process of genericization was conceived differently: Although for Marxists what "fascism" indicated generically was a metonymical affiliation of movements, regimes, and ideologies that could be consistently different, the new generic fascism isolated those distinctive features that all different movements, regimes, and ideologies shared as their essential characteristics, which, once distilled in a synthetic definition, could serve as a synecdochical yardstick for the purposes of identification and classification. Third, and consequently, while for Marxists generic "fascism" identified symptomatically a state of crisis or radicalization of the universal political form of "liberal democracy," for the "minimum" scholars it named a new political form, a new ideal type distinct from but of equal heuristic standing with other political universals such as "democracy," "socialism," "communism," and so on.[66] Fourth, even though the word "fascism" was clearly derived from a genericization of the Italian experience, for most authors involved in the search of a minimum definition of generic fascism it was German National Socialism that expressed it in the most mature potentiality, both in quantitative terms for its impact in world history as the main cause of the Second World War, and in qualitative terms for its more marked distance from preexisting state institutions. Finally, because most if not all exponents of the fascist minimum scholarship were declaredly non-Marxist (and many of them were distinctly anti-Marxist), the new definition of "fascism" as unrelated to capitalist liberalism indirectly served to counterbalance the Cold War rhetoric of the Soviet Union and of the most radical members of the civil rights and student movements in the global 1968, who saw in the NATO alliance and in policies of its member states the shadow of lingering fascism—a view that was not completely unjustified, given the continued presence of former Fascists and Nazis (and ultramilitarists) in the administrative institutions of Italy and Germany (and Japan).

Scholarship on the fascist minimum had a lasting effect on the compositional semantic structure of "fascism." It was on the authority of this scholarship that the term became a key heuristic category for the interpretation of the political, ideological, social, and cultural developments in countries outside Europe and beyond the confines of the interwar period, in particular Latin America and Japan.[67] It had also a momentous impact on the study of German National Socialism.[68] The remainder of this chapter retraces the key contributions of the scholarly search for a fascism minimum, the attempt to instrumentally conceive of the historical study of interwar Fascism and Nazism as a strategy to theorize a new political ideal type. The focus is therefore on the semiotic labor of adding a new and coherent semantic marker to the signifier "fascism" rather than on the effect that this scholarship had in our understanding of interwar authoritarianism.

At almost the same time Nolte wrote his *Der Faschismus*, the American-Romanian historian Eugen Weber published an essay in which he too attempted to demonstrate that Italian Fascism and German National Socialism were instances of a new form of political praxis and ideology.[69] Weber's approach was comparative and intellectual, in that it searched for a common core in the ideologies of various political movements in Italy, France,

Germany, Hungary, Romania, Great Britain, Spain, and Belgium. Weber's methodology was different from Nolte's. While the latter searched for a consistent conceptual understanding of an epoch he believed should be defined by fascism, the former moved within the more traditional parameters of comparative intellectual history. Also, the geographical coverage of the two studies was radically different, Weber adding a larger European platform to Nolte's three paradigmatic cases. As Weber put it, "Although we have been fascinated by Fascist practice in Italy and Nazi practice under Hitler, we have paid relatively little attention to their theory and even less to evidence from other countries where similar movements and similar doctrines flourished."[70]

Weber found the intellectual preconditions for the rise of fascism in the ideologies of nationalism and socialism: Both were a "by-product of disintegrating liberal democracy."[71] It was the failure of the constituted order to withstand the crisis in the aftermath of the First World War that opened up the possibility for fascist movements: "The fascists can only succeed when social circumstances provide a public their appeal attracts or, at least, the resources that will help them win it."[72] Fascist reaction ensued in response to the perceived threat coming from the global economic crisis and the successes of Soviet communist, and it took the form of a revolutionary utopianism of Fascism and National Socialism, the roots of which, according to Weber, could be traced as far back as Rousseau and Hegel as well as the irrationalism of Friedrich Nietzsche, Henri Bergson, and Émile Durkheim. Rousseau, whom Bobbio hailed as the forefather of modern democracy and the enemy of a fascist concept of society, became for Weber (and Nolte) one of the sources of fascist ideology.[73]

That fascism constituted a singular European phenomenon that erupted after the First World War was an idea propounded in 1966 by George L. Mosse as well, who, in the inaugural issue of the *Journal of Contemporary History*, contended that "if we want to get closer to the essence of the fascist revolution we must analyse it on a European-wide scale, taking into account important variations, but first trying to establish what these movements had in common."[74] The most salient of its features was, for him, irrationalism: "Fascism (although of course the word was not used at the time) originated in the attack on positivism and liberalism at the end of the nineteenth century. This was a general European phenomenon, and examples readily spring to mind."[75] Like Bobbio and Nolte, Mosse believed that fascism originated in this revolt against Enlightenment reason. But its success did not merely consist in sharing with other forms of fin-de-siècle irrationalism an inclination to social revolt. It actually claimed to be capable of offering a timely solution to the despair that the war had left on its wake: "The impact of the first world war shows this rhythm of fascism, just as it gave the movement a mass base. The *élan* of the battlefield was transformed into activism at home."[76] The reconfiguration of popular participation elaborated by Mussolini and Hitler engaged the people in "mass meetings" that adopted from the Christian tradition a set of "liturgical elements," including "endless repetition of slogans, choruses, and symbols."[77] In Italy, Germany, Hungary, and France, "Fascism was a movement of youth, not only in the sense that it covered a short span of time, but also in its membership."[78]

It was, indeed, in ideology that all early contributors to the search of a fascist minimum recognized the consistency of this new political form. In 1967 F. L. Carsten concluded his survey of the varieties of Fascism in Italy, Germany, Finland, Hungary, Spain, the Netherlands, Great Britain, and Austria by affirming that "the fascist movements, as has been emphasized by other writers, had much in common in their ideology—so much that they were able to borrow from each other. They were not only strongly nationalist and violently anti-Communist and anti-Marxist: that they had in common with other parties and groups of the extreme Right. . . . The fascists not only hated liberalism and democracy and the political parties, but they wanted to eliminate them and to replace them by a new authoritarian and corporative state."[79]

For Stuart J. Woolf and Wolfgang Schieder, too, ideology was the convenient point from which to grasp what the diverse European movements had in common.[80] And it was only in ideology that the common roots of the various fascist movements in Europe could be identified, according to historian John Weiss, who, however, rejected the irrationalist theses of Carsten, Mosse, and Nolte, and conceived of fascism as a radicalization of the nineteenth-century tradition of revolutionary conservatism. As a generic political form, fascism was a revolutionary embodiment of the ideals of an organic community led by a ruling elite capable of channeling the spiritual and material needs of the population. As a form of radical idealism, it was antidemocratic, anticapitalist, anticommunist, nationalist, and racist.[81] Gilbert Allardyce, before publishing, in 1979, what would become the manifesto against the project of a generic understanding of fascism, edited a collection of essays assessing the trans-European importance of fascism in the twentieth century.[82]

Italian historians were reluctant to embrace a generic or universal understanding of fascism, with the exception of Marxists, who, however, did not participate in the search for a new ideal type. During a conversation with the conservative American historian Michael A. Ledeen, Renzo De Felice insisted: "I am absolutely firm in believing that fascism is a phenomenon that can and must be rigidly circumscribed; otherwise we no longer understand anything."[83] What it shared with other movements—and De Felice referred mainly to Germany—were characteristics so general that they could hardly help a definition of a generic type conducive to a generative understanding of transwar political history. A noteworthy exception was the Catholic political philosopher Augusto Del Noce, who followed Nolte in acknowledging in fascism a transpolitical form of "resistance to transcendence." However, for Del Noce fascism shared with communism a radical antispiritualist instantiation of antireligious secularization. Fascism and communism, for Del Noce, were the two obverse faces of the same epochal tendency toward secular materialism, rending asunder, with tragic consequences in the areas controlled by Nazi Germany and the Soviet Union, their link with the Christian tradition.[84]

Another exception was the work of a historian on the opposite political spectrum from Del Noce. In 1989 Enzo Collotti published a long essay of synthetic analysis that offered one of the most radical contributions to Italian historiography on Mussolini's regime. Collotti first dismissed the tradition that attempted to minimize the importance of Fascism in Italian history (Croce's school) and De Felice's assertion that the popular support of the regime resulted from a spontaneous movement from below, showing instead that it was the result of an orchestrated system of suasion and coercion.[85] Then he interpreted Fascism within a counterrevolutionary trend in European politics, which took various forms but were all pursuing a violent imperialistic expansion and the systematic persecution of the Jews: "Only a historiography pursuing a banal empiricism, which rejected any process of abstraction and reconstruction, could deny acknowledging such an approach."[86] Without reducing the heterogeneous forms of European authoritarian regimes to a universal type, Collotti argued that "interwar Europe experienced a historical process of fascistization."[87]

The focus on ideology did not simply mirror the popularity of this subgenre of history writing in the late 1960s through the 1970s. It also benefited from the methodological rigor it offered to the attempt of distilling a definition of generic fascism. The political theorist (and eugenic apologist) A. James Gregor, who had conservative-liberal leanings, criticized the state of the field in comparative studies of European fascisms in his *Interpretations of Fascism* (1974), where, without denying the cognitive authority of the search for the parameters of a generic fascism, he emphasized the formidable epistemological challenges of that enterprise.[88] Like Nolte and De Felice, Gregor believed that fascism was pragmatically and ideologically the obverse effect of communism, a thesis he had advanced since 1969 in *The Ideology of Fascism* and continued to defend it in later works.[89] In 1979 he claimed that fascism, in both its Italian "developmental" form and its German "radical" form, was nothing more than a "variant of Classical Marxism," and as late as *The Faces of Janus* (2000), he stated that "Fascists were almost all Marxists—serious theorists who had long been identified with Italy's intelligentsia of the Left."[90]

Intellectual histories of fascist ideology certainly provided the comparative analyses of Italian Fascism, German National Socialism, and other European movements with a sense of coherency that a juxtaposition of political strategies and event-based narratives in the different national contexts did not have. It was only in the 1970s that social historians, sociologists, and political scientists contributed to a generic understanding of "fascism." Among the most influential of the early sociological approaches was "Some Notes Toward a Comparative Study of Fascism in Sociological Historical Perspective," by the Spanish sociologist Juan José Linz, which the historian Walter Laqueur placed as the opening essay of his collection *Fascism: A Reader's Guide*.[91] Linz's approach was primarily comparative and aimed at providing a minimum common denominator of fascist movements around the world, including minor extreme right-wing parties in Brazil, Bolivia, Mexico, Turkey, the Arab world, China, and Japan. Ideological constructs were not ignored but rather juxtaposed to a comparative analysis of institutions, organizations, class mobilization, voters' and civic associationism, and the like.

For Linz, all fascist movements were characterized by the copresence of homogeneity and heterogeneity. Linz explained the apparent homogeneity of fascisms by appealing to the First World War and the socioeconomic and political crisis left in its wake. "Fascism," he claimed, "was the novel response to the crisis—profound or temporary—of the pre-war social structure and party system and to the emergence of new institutional arrangements as result of war and post-war dislocation."[92] That was the context that gave birth to the political adversaries all fascist movements identified as their nemesis: socialism and communism primarily, but also parliamentarism (which was given new vigor and importance in the transwar period), liberalism, and so on. All fascisms had therefore a marked "antimovement" character: Everywhere fascism appears, it "defines itself by the things against which it stands but this antithesis in the minds of the ideologists should lead to a new synthesis integrating elements from the political creeds they so violently attack."[93] It was the combination of prewar institutional structures and unprecedented transformations in the economy, social classes, civic participation, and geopolitical landscape that gave all European counterrevolutionary movements their "anti-" character: Thus, fascism, for Linz, was

> anti-Marxist, anti-communist, anti-proletarian, but also anti-liberal, anti-parliamentarian, and in a very special sense, anti-conservative, and anti-bourgeois. Anti-clericalism, perhaps with the exception of the Iron Guard,

> the Ustacha [*sic*], and Brazilian Integralismo, is a more or less central component which in some cases drifts into hostility to established religion. Anti-individualism and anti-democratic authoritarianism and elitism are combined with a strong populist appeal. Anti-Semitism is not originally characteristic of all fascist movements but central to many of them. Anti-urbanism, or at least anti-metropolitanism, is not found in all fascist movements but is often an important element. A distinctive type of anti-capitalism is originally present in many fascist movements. Sometimes anti-feminism appears. Those anti-positions have been summarized as anti-modernism, but that interpretation seems dubious in many cases.[94]

To these, Linz added also anti-internationalism and anticosmopolitanism, best expressed in fascism's violent anti-Marxism.

Parallel to the homologation of all fascisms in an apophatic "anti-" politics, what gave them a distinctive national character was, for Linz, their status as "later-comers."[95] It was only through rigorous comparative sociological-historical analyses that these phenotypical differences could, for Linz, be reconciled in a definition that could synthesize them all.[96] Hence, he defined fascism as "a hypernationalist, often pan-nationalist, anti-parliamentary, anti-liberal, anti-communist, populist and therefore anti-proletarian, partly anti-capitalist and anti-bourgeois, anti-clerical, or at least, non-clerical movement, with the aim of national social integration through a single party and corporative representation not always equally emphasized; with a distinctive style and rhetoric, it relied on activist cadres ready for violent action combined with electoral participation to gain power with totalitarian goals by a combination of legal and violent, tactics."[97] Despite the apparent differences in style, form, rhetorical strategy, and ideological apparatus, all fascisms emerged from a similar social logic, the visible unfolding of which depended on the cultural background of each nation. Similarities deriving from the new historical conditions they all shared forced different movements to adopt similar political tactics.[98]

Linz's conception of generic fascism distinguished itself from other coeval attempts by recounting in its analyses many of the elements of Marxist sociological studies of the transwar period. Ideological consistency was, for him, less important than it was for other scholars. Because they were situated in distinct cultural contexts, the ideological discourses that different movements elaborated were obviously different, despite targeting similar goals in terms of communal cohesion, the downplaying of class struggle, and national prosperity. Ideological ambiguity among movements, for Linz, was not a problem but the result of similar social processes occurring in different cultural contexts. The fact that each fascist program had different strategic aims or emphasized different elements did not undermine the generic homogeneity of the utopian vision they all shared. Linz's comparative study of the structural and sociological aspects of different movements within their respective national contexts therefore favored a new path toward a conceptualization of generic fascism that bypassed some of the obstacles of the previous attempts within the methodology of intellectual history.

The Consolidation of the Fascist Minimum

Apart from Nolte's philosophical history, early studies on generic fascism were essentially comparative analyses of the political structures, social causes, and ideological discourses in the interwar period. The definitions they developed functioned mostly as working hypotheses that helped to identify the common features of disparate movements understood as tokens of a new form of political organization.

The biggest challenge for this enterprise was reconciling the distinctive differences, in terms of sociopolitical causes, development, and institutional form, between Italian Fascism and German National Socialism, unquestionably the two largest and most successful of the transwar counterrevolutionary authoritarianisms. Not only did their alliance develop late and become fraught with misunderstandings and tensions, but the state apparatuses that the two movements built were quite different: Fascism operated *within* the state (in fact conceiving of itself as state), reinforcing its centralizing function, while Nazi Germany functioned as a sort of a dual government, where the Nazi Party's activities occurred parallel and often in antagonism to state institutions, with strong decentralizing tendencies and offices often in a Darwinian competition with one another.[99] Social historians who focused on analyzing the causes of Nazism saw in it the effect of Germany's specific path to modernization.[100] For exponents of the *Sonderweg* theory, Nazism was so quintessentially linked to the specific history of German modernization that its reduction to "fascism" was inconceivable:

> So singular was Hitler's ideological and political contribution to the shaping and direction of the Nazi movement and then the Nazi State that any attempt to label National Socialism as "fascism," thus placing it in comparison with other "similar" movements, is meaningless and implies, moreover, the "trivialization" of Hitler and Nazism. . . . Though excluding vehemently any possibility of regarding "Hitlerism" as a type of fascism, exponents of this interpretation nevertheless attached one important strand of comparison, arguing that the form and nature of Nazi rule made it essential to regard Nazism as a brand of totalitarianism alongside Soviet Communism (in particular Stalinism).[101]

Nonetheless, for Kershaw, "the concept of fascism is more satisfactory and applicable than that of totalitarianism in explaining the character of Nazism, the circumstances of its growth, the nature of its rule, and its place in a European context in the inter-war period. The similarities with other brands of fascism are profound, not peripheral."[102]

The expression "fascist minimum" was used as the name of the project of developing the definitive definition of the new political form only in 1991 by Roger Griffin.[103] Griffin had adopted it from Zeev Sternhell, who in turn had adapted it from Nolte's *Die Krise des liberalen Systems und die faschistischen Bewegungen*.[104] In his 1983 *Ni droite ni gauche*, Sternhell had postulated that "it is up to the researcher to discern the common denominator, the fascist 'minimum,' that is shared not only by the different political movements and ideologies which claim to be fascist, but also by those which reject the description yet nevertheless belong to the same family."[105] In the scholarship of the fascist minimum characteristic of the 1980s through the 2000s, particularly Anglophone scholarship, different methodological strategies were mobilized to develop an understanding of "fascism" that transcended the mere metonymical comparison and rather pursued the development of a definition that could encapsulate the essential nature of an ideal type. In turn, this type would justify a series of identificatory and classificatory synecdochical reductions of different movements that fulfilled the parameter of the posited definition. As Griffin put it, "Hopefully it will be shown that when the elusive 'fascist minimum' is defined strictly in terms of the reborn nation and the post-liberal society which will supposedly underpin it, the resulting ideal type is not only more concise and 'elegant' than those formulated to date but provides new insights into the dynamics of individual fascist movements."[106]

Before Griffin provided methodological consistency to the attempt to find a common denominator of counterrevolutionary authoritarianisms, (non-Marxist) historians and sociologists followed Linz's example to pursue comparative analyses of fascist movements as expressions of latecomer nations, where the middle classes aimed to preserve their upward social mobility and eliminate the social conflicts created by industrialization.[107] Conservative historians and political scientists looked at fascism not as an antimodern force, as did Nolte and the early Mosse, but rather as an attempt to modernize society and politics within the national paradigm and in antagonism to Marxist anticapitalist collectivism.[108]

Mosse linked intellectual and cultural history to social analyses to propose an interpretation of fascism as a European movement that completed the nationalization of the masses that had begun with the First World War. For him, it was only through a "cultural interpretation of fascism" that one could "penetrate fascist self-understanding."[109] Fascism, he maintained, in all its instantiations, recruited the collaboration of the masses to its mission of national revolution through daily rituals of secularized religiosity regarding the symbols of the nation-state (the flag, the national anthem, mass celebrations, etc.): "The nationalization of the masses was a common bond between the French and the fascist revolutions."[110] Unlike Nolte, Mosse saw in fascism not a reaction against the communist revolution in the name of an antimodern resistance. Rather, both fascism and Bolshevism were born of the ideals of democracy and people's sovereignty that had originated in the French Revolution, which both, however, distorted.[111]

In the 1979 essay "Toward a General Theory of Fascism," Mosse argued that "fascism was based upon a strong and unique revolutionary tradition, fired by the emphasis on youth and the war experience; it was able to create a mass consensus that was finally broken only by a lost war."[112] Mussolini, Hitler, and other fascist agitators formed in the midst of the revolutionary culture of European socialism and syndicalism and shared with them organizational modes, mobilizational tactics, and rhetorical strategies, to the extent that "fascists and Bolsheviks integrated various dress codes into their systems." They both "attempted to mobilize masses, to substitute modern mass politics for pluralistic and parliamentary government."[113] Therefore, "fascism was itself a revolution, seizing power by using twentieth-century methods of mass mobilization and control, and replacing an old with a new élite,"[114] the scope of which was the development of a "Third Force" that could become an "alternative revolution to Marxism."[115] Fascism's success was no less the result of its ability of presenting old values as revolutionary: "The traditionalism of the fascist movement coincided with existing society's most basic moral values."[116] This reframing was the result of a transformation of the traditional modus operandi of politics into a secular and nationalist religion.[117]

If in his earlier works Mosse pursued the question of generic fascism from the perspective of intellectual history, it was only in his essays of the 1970s that his studies of various social practices of mass politics led him to think of fascism as a political movement aimed at revolutionizing the life experience of a nation through myths, rituals, symbols, and aesthetic practices that pervaded the daily lives of its citizens. The "new politics" of fascism "cut away the class basis of socialist opposition to the bourgeoisie and substituted the war between generations."[118] It maintained an "anti-bourgeois rhetoric," which, however, did not conceive of the bourgeoisie as "class exploiters," as in Marxist propaganda.[119] It was therefore a sort of "bourgeois anti-bourgeois revolution."[120]

Mosse's scholarship had a great influence on both the study of Nazi Germany and the search for an understanding of a generic fascism. "No other Europeanist historian of the second half of the twentieth century," claimed the editors of a celebratory anthology of Mosse's scholarship, "left [a] greater imprint on the course of historical scholarship, and none worked in a greater number of thematic areas."[121] As Emilio Gentile acknowledged,

> For Mosse, understanding fascism—its origin, its nature, its significance in contemporary history, and above all why it fascinated millions of people—was a cultural, moral, and political challenge that engrossed him both as a man and as a historian. . . . Mosse was a victim of Nazism who wanted to know the fascination of his persecutor by penetrating inside his mind, by studying the ideas, the mentality, the principles, the values, the myths, and the symbols through which he interpreted himself and reality, prefigured the world he wanted to bring into existence, and defined the forms and the methods of action aimed at making it a reality.[122]

The Fascist Minimum as Definitional Orthodoxy

One of Mosse's mentees and colleagues, Stanley G. Payne, further developed the search for a fascist minimum by linking intellectual and political analyses with the sociohistorical research of the previous decade.[123] In *Fascism: Comparison and Definition* (1980), Payne acknowledged that "*fascism* is probably the vaguest of contemporary political terms," but if it is to be studied, "it has first to be identified, and it is doubtful that can be done without some sort of working definition."[124]

The methodological premise of Payne's analysis was that a definition, which "would describe what all fascist movements had in common without trying to describe the unique characteristic of each group," should theoretically be "derived from empirical study of the interwar European movements."[125] The development of such a definition, which for Payne looked like a "general inventory of their distinctive characteristics," had to be pursued "with great care,"[126] since it had to encompass ideological beliefs, orientations in political cultures, and modes of organizations.[127] This could be achieved by identifying three distinct sets of characteristics:[128] a set of "fascist negations," which ostensibly revealed the reactive nature of fascist movements; "common points of ideology and goals"; and "special common features of style and organization."[129] These criteria set up the conditions for the development of a table wherein Payne listed the essential minimum characteristics that offered a "typological description of fascism."[130]

TYPOLOGICAL DESCRIPTION OF FASCISM

A. The Fascist Negations:

Antiliberalism

Anticommunism

Anticonservatism (though with the understanding that fascist groups were willing to undertake temporary alliances with groups from any other sector, most commonly with the right)

B. Ideology and Goals:

Creation of a new nationalist authoritarian state based not merely on traditional principles or models

Organization of some new kind of regulated, multiclass, integrated national economic structure, whether called national corporatist, national socialist, or national syndicalist

The goal of empire or a radical change in the nation's relationship with other powers

Specific espousal of an idealist, voluntarist creed, normally involving the attempt to realize a new form of modern, self-determined secular culture

C. Style and Organization:

Emphasis on esthetic structure of meetings, symbols, and political choreography, stressing romantic and mystical aspects

Attempted mass mobilization with militarization of political relationships and style and with the goal of a mass party militia

Positive evaluation and use of, or willingness to use, violence

Extreme stress on the masculine principle and male dominance, while espousing the organic view of society

Exaltation of youth above other phases of life, emphasizing the conflict of generations, at least in effecting the initial political transformation

Specific tendency toward an authoritarian, charismatic, personal style of command, whether or not the command is to some degree initially elective

The table was a synthetic summa of Payne's own research on the Spanish Revolution and the works of Linz, Nolte, Mosse, Emilio Gentile, and others. It would be reproduced, with only minor changes, in the encyclopedic *A History of Fascism, 1914–1945* (1996),[131] in which Payne specified that "the term *fascist* is used not merely for the sake of convention but because the Italian movement was the first significant force to exhibit those characteristics as a new type and was for a long time the most influential. It constituted the type whose ideas and goals were the most readily generalized, particularly when contrasted with racial National Socialism."[132] The term "fascism," therefore, for him denoted not merely a synecdochical convention originating from chronological precedence, but the genealogical derivation of all other fascist movements, regimes, and ideologies. The novelty of Payne's project was certainly not the specific features he chose to define the fascist minimum.[133] It was rather the subsumption of his long comparative analyses of "fascist" regimes around the world to the identificatory norm he presented at the outset of the volume.

Payne presented the preliminary tripartite definition of fascism as a working hypothesis. It was followed, in both the original 1980 and the expanded 1995 versions, by a historical reconstruction of the rise, ideology, organization, strategies, and so on of the individual fascist movements. In *A History of Fascism*, Payne proceeded in chronological order: He began with from Italian Fascism and the rise of "military-led reaction in southern and eastern Europe,"[134] focusing on minor movements in Hungary, Bulgaria, Romania, Spain, Greece, Poland, Lithuania, Portugal, Yugoslavia, and Turkey.[135] He then moved on to German National Socialism and the changes it forced upon Italian Fascism.[136] Austria, Spain, Hungary, and Romania represented, for Payne, "four major variants of fascism" that expressed distinct differences from Italian and German fascism, somewhat paradigmatic of the ideal type itself, which nonetheless reinforced the initial definitional features of his table rather than compromised them.[137] This was followed by a quick survey of "minor movements" in France, the Low Countries, Great Britain, Ireland, Scandinavia, Switzerland, Czechoslovakia, Finland, Portugal, Greece, Poland, the Baltic states, Yugoslavia, and Bulgaria,[138] as well as a rapid investigation of "fascism around the world," where Payne examined "primary candidates for a non-European fascism" in Japan, South Africa, Latin America, and the Middle East.[139]

The historical examinations of these individual cases, largely based on other secondary sources, served to confirm the definition that Payne provided at the beginning of the book. Rather than offering evidentiary material for the inductive development of a synthetic definition—as Payne himself had declared his own description of a fascist minimum to derive from—the individual cases are presented as a confirmation of that definition for largely identificatory and classificatory aims—that is, mapping which movements or regimes fulfilled the conditions for belonging to the category "fascism" postulated at the beginning of the project.

Payne claimed that the various interpretations of fascism of the interwar years (Marxist, conservative, liberal, etc.) did not "define exactly what they mean by the term or specifically identify which parties or movements they seek to interpret, beyond a primary reference which is normally to National Socialism alone."[140] The fact that no one who embarked on an interpretation of the generic phenomenon of fascism in the interwar period attempted an "empirical definition of what is meant by *fascism* has been an obstacle to conceptual clarification."[141] The implication of this radical judgment was that Payne's own analysis claimed to overcome that impasse. The first of these interpretations, Marxism, was "one of the oldest and most widely disseminated."[142] Payne defined it as an "agent theory" that had "become a part of the very delusion they purported to explain," so that it failed to recognize in "fascism" a new, properly autonomous political form.[143] Similarly flawed, for Payne, were the progressive liberal theories that saw fascism as either the "expression of a unique radicalism of the middle-classes" or a new form of Bonapartism.[144] The theories on "totalitarianism," which "enjoyed [a] considerable vogue during the 1950s," collapsed on themselves, as "by the late 1960s analysts encountered increasing difficulty in defining totalitarianism at all, and many questioned its existence as a continuous, comparable category of political systems."[145] Similarly, the theory of fascism as an "authoritarian polyocracy" was contested and thus abandoned.[146] "One of the clearest, most forceful, and most cogent interpretations of fascism," for Payne, "is George L. Mosse's presentation of fascism as a new form of cultural revolution,"[147] because it rejected "the interpretation advanced by certain Marxists and liberals of a sudden explosion of the irrational" and instead conceived of fascism as "a specific kind of revolution from the right that was based on race and a combination of mystical, semioccult, concepts that were employed to nationalize and mobilize the masses."[148]

Payne's survey of the various theories of fascism paved the way for his own conceptualization of "fascism" as a generic ideal type, which ratified the conceptual core that he had isolated at the opening of the book as a "working hypothesis" and that his review of the historical instantiations confirmed. Acknowledging a set of variations in the ways in which the generic paradigm was instantiated did not, for Payne, repudiate the validity of the paradigm itself, since it took different forms that reflected different social, cultural, and "spiritual" differences.[149] He therefore acknowledged a "paradigmatic form" of the ideal type of "fascism" in Italian Fascism (with derivations in France, England, Belgium, Austria, Hungary, Romania, and Brazil), an "extreme or radical form" in German National Socialism (with derivations in Scandinavia, the Low Countries, the Baltic states, Hungary, and during the Second World War), a "traditionalist form" in Spanish Falangism, a "mystical" and "semireligious form" in the Romanian Legionary and the Iron Guard Movement, and a "moderate form" in the Hungarian Arrow Cross movement.[150]

Payne believed that his conceptualization of the ideal type of fascism could overcome the shortcomings of all previous theories and interpretations of fascism, which lacked "general or even specific validity" because they were based on "monocausal or reductionist" explanations.[151] In his work, "fascism" operated as a modality template, structuring the contingent development of various forms of counterrevolutionary authoritarianisms. Presented as having been derived from his own inductive interpretation of transwar movements and regimes, his tripartite definition operated normatively, guiding the presentation of the individual case studies in the main body of the book. Payne's work represented a synthesis of the various bodies of research on fascism that preceded it, but its cognitive reasoning could not avoid operating in a sort of closed circle in that the empirical cases he presented had the function of confirming a theoretical hypothesis that had regulative effects on the identification and qualification of those cases. Rather than being inductively derived, his definition was the result of a synthesis of previous theorizations of generic fascism; it was not inferred from his empirical sources. That is because the research was not designed to find a conceptual, genealogical, or even purely descriptive common core behind the movements and regimes he compared. Rather, these served to exemplify a generic type, the existence of which had been asserted from the beginning.

In schematic terms, the generic type did not appear to be inductively inferred from the analyzed "tokens" but rather was postulated on the basis of a historiographical (rather than historical) precedence (i.e., the scholarship on generic fascism) and then "tested" on the individual cases; but this test, carried over in the long historical section at the core of the volume, was not performed with the intention of confirming or rejecting the hypothesis of a generic ideal type that opened the book; rather, it had the double function of selecting among the various forms of the extreme Right those that could be identified as "fascist" for classificatory purposes and of determining their degree of "variation" acceptable within the initial theoretical paradigm. In banal terms, Payne's project did not look for, nor did it find, generic or typological fascism in the material it studied because its presence was never really questioned but rather assumed from the beginning.

The most important cognitive effect of Payne's analysis was to hypostasize the conceptual construct of "fascism." By virtue of that semiotic construction, generic fascism, with properly distinct characteristics and genealogically disentangled from any link with the institutions of liberal democracy and the capitalist mode of economic organization, could be talked about, described, analyzed, and mapped as if it had an ontological reality distinct from its local instantiations. It ceased to be a heuristic construct and became an object that could ostensibly be observed. Put differently, generic fascism was assumed to be an "object" or "phenomenon" that could be observed and described through its phenotypical instantiations. Emphasizing that generic fascism was effectively subjected to a process of reification of a theoretical construct through the discursive practices of description and definition does not necessarily negate, *pace* Allardyce's naive realism, the epistemological validity or intellectual value of that research.[152] It simply highlights the fact that being treated as an actually existing object or phenomenon, rather than the end result of an epistemological labor of comparative interpretation, prevented that labor from being properly analyzed, criticized, and justified. Consequently, assuming the existence of generic fascism had the effect of projecting the denotations and connotations conventionally associated with it to individual movements, institutions, events, social and political dynamics, and so on once these were qualified as local symptoms or effects of a globally operating generic fascism, without, however, this semiosic projection's being conceived as the result of interpretive labor and subjected, as such, to proper justification.

The Fascist Minimum after the Cold War

The search for a consistent and coherent definition of "fascism," now conceived as a generic and universal political form, had the normative effect of projecting its denotative and connotative markers onto the historically specific dynamics, structures, and events on which it was predicated. In the historical context of the post–Cold War 1990s, defined by the postideological ideology of the "end of history," the affirmation of generic fascism as a universal and discrete political type confirmed its separation from and antagonism to a liberal model of democratic institutions and capitalist economic organization that had assumed the status of unquestioned paradigmatic normality—a separation that the delegitimation of Marxian analysis in scholarly research has only strengthened.

In post-1990s historiography, historians' synthetic definitions of generic fascism often overshadowed the rigor of the comparative analyses that the heuristic use of the generic category framed. It was the commitment to a normative definition of the ideal type "fascism" that regulated the historical analyses of historians working in extra-European contexts in search of instantiations of generic fascism in Asia and Latin America. Once hypostatized, fascism could be found everywhere in the world.[153]

In *The Nature of Fascism*, Roger Griffin intended to end the "lack of consensus over the term 'fascism'" and propose a "concise definition" that contained the logic shared by many of its distinct instantiations. Hence, for Griffin "fascism is a genus of political ideology whose mythic core in its various permutations is a palingenetic form of populist ultranationalism."[154] As a genus, fascism could be understood as a generic type that subsumes tokens expressing specific variations without betraying a set of core features defining it. These were, for Griffin, a "political ideology" based on a mythic conception of the nation.[155] The aim of this ideology was the construction of a state that could bring a "renewal" or "rebirth" of the nation ("palingenesis"), which implied that a state of crisis imperiled it.[156] It aimed to create an ultranationalist state that did not deny popular sovereignty but rather reconceived it in the form of populism. The fascist state intended to nurture a "new man" that, as *Homo fascistus*, could guarantee the "total support" and the "thorough-going ideological coordination of the national community."[157] For Griffin, fascism was a form of political "idealism" born of a "diffuse sense of cultural pessimism."[158] As a "palingenetic" force, fascism was modernizing, "revolutionary" in nature, the racism of which (although "not intrinsically anti-Semitic or genocidal") was embedded in the mythic character of its ultranationalism.[159]

In a later work, Griffin claimed that, inspired by Mosse's methodological empathy to "penetrate fascist self-understanding," his one-sentence definition was still a good representation of fascists' self-description as pursuing an alternative "third way," antagonistic to both liberalism and Marxism.[160] A good definition, for Griffin, implied a representation of fascism in its own terms. This "third way definition," he claimed, "is the explanatory model that has so far proven to have the greatest heuristic value for researching fascism, as demonstrated by the abundance of articles, chapters, and books produced since the 1990s which apply it, whether explicitly or not."[161] Its cognitive value, in other words, was ostensibly confirmed by its success in contemporary scholarly literature on generic fascism.

Griffin explained that "generic fascism should be treated on a par with other political ideologies which refer to thinkers, movements, regimes, policies or actions motivated by the prospect of realizing a particular vision of the ideal society and set of political and cultural values on which it is based."[162] Empirically, "fascism manifests itself in a wide variety of forms," which should be understood simply as "permutations of the same ideal type."[163] What these variants all shared was a "core utopian myth of an ideal state of society and civilization."[164] This "core utopia myth" was "ideal-typically constructed" and conceived of an "organic 'people' forming an 'ultra-nation,'" which in the historical conjuncture of the transwar period was under threat of "disintegration and decadence."[165] The advantage of his definition, for Griffin, was that it "embraces an ideology, and its related policies and practices, centered on the need to mobilize populist energies of renewal (palingenesis) to bring about the rebirth of the ultra-nation, thereby inaugurating a new, revolutionary national or civilizational order."[166]

Similarly pursuing an understanding of the ideological core of generic fascism on its own terms, the political scientist Roger Eatwell, like Nolte, saw the ideological roots of fascism in the Enlightenment, but unlike Nolte he rejected the characterization of fascism as an antimodern movement.[167] Like Sternhell, he maintained that it developed "a view of human nature that seemed to synthesize common left- and right-wing positions."[168] But unlike Sternhell, whom he criticized for his Francocentric perspective, Nazism was, for him, the prototypical form of fascism. For him, too, the fascist minimum should consist of a single-sentence definition followed by a "core set of annotations."[169] Hence, fascism was "an ideology that strives to forge social rebirth based on a *holistic-national radical Third Way*, though in practice fascism has tended to stress style, especially action and the charismatic leader, more than detailed program, and to engage in a Manichean demonization of its enemies."[170] The central unit of fascism was the nation, which was understood primarily in "cultural terms," although some of its forms (i.e., Nazism) were based on "biological racism."[171] The nation was a "holistic" unit, where "collectivism predominates over individual rights and interests."[172] Hostile to both liberalism and communism, fascism was "not a form of conservatism" either: Its "radicalism" was aimed at creating "an alternative form of modernity."[173]

The importance of ideology as the privileged site for identifying the core nature of fascism in the scholarship on the fascist minimum through the 2000s had such an effect that even a Marxian historian like Mark Neocleous surrendered to a definition focused on ideology: "Fascism is first and foremost an ideology generated by modern industrial capitalism."[174] Similarly, Kevin Passmore defined fascism generically: "Fascism is a set of ideologies and practices that seeks to place the nation, defined in exclusive biological, cultural, and/or historical terms, above all other sources of loyalty, and to create a mobilized national community. Fascist nationalism is reactionary in that it entails implacable hostility to socialism and feminism, for they are seen as prioritizing class or gender rather than nation. This is why fascism is a movement of the *extreme* right."[175]

Obviously there were exceptions to the ideology-centered approach of "minimum" definitions, even though the British sociologist Michael Mann concocted one that similarly reduced the social practices of interwar fascists to a core ideological set of beliefs. Following Griffin, in the beginning of his study he proposed a one-sentence definition that he further elucidated in five points: "I define fascism in terms of the key values, actions, and power organizations of fascists. Most concisely, *fascism is the pursuit of a transcendent and cleansing nation-statism through paramilitarism*. This definition contains five key terms requiring further explanation."[176] The five qualifiers functioned as co-textual anchors that purportedly restricted the semantic extension of "fascism" in the definition. "Nationalism" was for Mann connoted in terms of an "organic" or "integral" national community, racially or culturally defined, violently opposed to its " 'enemies,' both abroad and (especially) at home."[177] He defined "statism," following James Gregor, as the "authoritarian corporate state" that "could supposedly solve crises and bring about social, economic, and moral development," although Mann acknowledged the contradictions, inherent in both fascist and communist regimes, of "movement" versus "bureaucracy" and "permanent revolution" versus "totalitarianism."[178] "Transcendence" pointed to the failure of all fascist regimes to distance themselves from the conservative and liberal democratic orders they wished to replace. Fascism, for Mann, "was partly a response to the crisis of capitalism (as materialists say), but it offered a revolutionary and supposedly achievable solution,"[179] which aimed to transcend social conflict through a corporatist organization of society that rejected both liberal individualism and socialist collectivism. Here Mann explicitly paid tribute to the notion of fascism as a "third way," although for him the expression "seems too weak for this goal of revolutionary transformation."[180] "Cleansing" referred to the action of purification necessary for the realization of an organic society, as "most fascisms entwined both ethnic and political cleansing, though to differing degrees."[181] Finally, "paramilitarism" expressed a "key value and the key organizational form of fascism."[182] It was both an ideological and sociological conception. Mann concluded his definition by admitting that "this combination of qualities obviously made fascists 'revolutionary,' though not in conventional left-right terms. It would be inexact to call them 'revolutionary of the right.' . . . We could in principle plot fascist movements (each one obviously unique) amid a five-dimensional space."[183] This means that Mann, too, like Nolte, Mosse, Sternhell, Griffin, and most contributors to the search for a fascist minimum, conceived of generic fascism as neither traditionally "Right" nor "Left," but rather a synthesis of the pathologies of both.

The search for a fascist minimum in the 1990s and the early 2000s became so pervasive that even a historian like Emilio Gentile, always reluctant to engage in a generic understanding of "fascism," surrendered to the attempt to distill a synthetic definition. Gentile offered a tripartite definition that distinguished an organizational, a cultural, and an institutional dimension. Organizationally, fascism was "a mass movement with inter-class membership in which prevail, among the leaders and militants, the middle classes, in large part new to political activity, organized as a party militia, that bases its identity not on social hierarchy or class origin but on the sense of comradeship, believes itself invested with a mission of national regeneration, considers itself in a state of war against political adversaries and aims at conquering a monopoly of political power by using terror, parliamentary tactics, and deals with leading groups, to create a new regime that destroys parliamentary democracy."[184] In its cultural dimension, fascism strove to develop a "culture founded on mystical thought and on a tragic and activist conception of life," which manifested itself in a "will to power," the "myth of youth as artificer of history," and the "militarization of politics"; an "anti-ideological and pragmatic ideology," self-defined as "anti-materialist," "anti-individualist," "anti-liberal," "anti-democratic," "anti-Marxist," "tendentially populist and anti-capitalist," which expressed itself "aesthetically rather than theoretically"; "a totalitarian conception of the primacy of politics," which was an "integral expression of a continuous revolution" through a "totalitarian state"; and a "civic ethic founded on the absolute subjection of the citizen to the state, on individuals' total dedication to the national community."[185] As for its institutional dimension, the fascist state organized into "a police apparatus that prevents, controls, and represses, even by means of organized terror, dissidence and opposition"; "one single party," the main task of which was to "assure the armed defense of the regime through a private militia"; "a political system founded on the symbiosis of party and state," hierarchically organized around a "leader [*capo*] invested of charismatic sacredness"; a "corporatist organization of the economy," suppressing unions in the name of "principles of technocracy and solidarity"; and a "foreign policy inspired by the search of power and national greatness, with objectives of imperialist expansion with the aim of creating a new civilization."[186] Close to the conceptions he learned from Nolte, Payne, and De Felice, Gentile based his tentative definition of "fascism" principally upon the historical experience of Italian Fascism. He clearly distinguished the character of fascism as movement and as regime, and abandoned the methodology of a single-line definition to highlight ten fundamental features divided into sociological, ideological (or, following Mosse, cultural), and institutional spheres. But unlike Payne, he rejected its utilization for identificatory or classificatory purposes without a previous analysis of the historical unfolding of individual movements and regimes.

One last example of the pervasiveness of the fascist minimum in the historiography of the 1990s and 2000s was *The Anatomy of Fascism*, by the historian of modern France Robert O. Paxton, who engaged with the attempt to distill a generic definition despite his own reservations.[187] The difficulties of studying the phenomenon of fascism comparatively and generically were, for the historian, both structurally connected to the idiosyncratic development of its different instantiations and methodologically ensuing from historians' theoretical biases. These included the exceptional timing of its emergence, that is, the aftermath of the First World War; the widespread "mimicry" of political praxis in that period, whereby not only did fascist movements copy from one another, but "many regimes that were not functionally fascist borrowed elements of fascist décor in order to lend themselves an aura of force, vitality, and mass mobilization";[188] the "dauntingly wide disparity among individual cases in space and time" owing to the local socioeconomic circumstances that favored their emergence;[189] the "ambiguous relationship between doctrine and action," with a heavy preponderance of the latter over the former, which differentiated fascism from all other political forms;[190] and, historiographically, the overuse of the term, whereby "the word 'fascist' has become the most banal of epithets."[191]

Historians have contributed to obfuscating the understanding of generic fascism because they treated it "in a static manner" by looking for "a fixed essence," as in the case of the "famous 'fascist minimum,'" or "in too isolated a manner, without sufficient sustained reference to the political, social, and cultural spaces in which they navigate."[192] The definitional efforts of those scholars pursuing a fascist minimum produced, in Paxton's view, "what we might call 'bestiaries' of fascism," that is, "a catalog of portraits of one beast after another, each one portrayed against a bit of background scenery and identified by its external signs."[193]

Paxton suggested a study of generic fascism that avoided these errors. He emphasized contextualization, comparison, and diachronic development through "five stages": "(1) the initial creation of fascist movements; (2) their rooting as parties in a political system; (3) the acquisition of power; (4) the exercise of power; and, finally, in the longer term, (5) radicalization or entropy."[194] The discrimination of different phases of development, in turn, demanded distinct contextual framing, distinct meters of comparison, and the adoption of different instruments of analysis: intellectual history could be more useful, for instance, in understanding phase (4) and (5), whereas political history was more appropriate for phases (1) and (3), social history for (2) and (5), institutional history for (2) and (4), and so on. In short, Paxton suggested a functionalist and diachronic understanding of fascism as central to the effort to define it.

The Anatomy of Fascism (2004) was his attempt to put into practice the methodology he advocated in the 1998 article.[195] The structure of the book followed closely the five stages he had previously conceptualized: accordingly, chapter 2 compared, through interdisciplinary lenses, the various processes responsible for "creating fascist movements"; chapter 3 their "taking roots"; chapter 4 their "getting power" and chapter 5 their "exercising power"; chapter 6 followed the two distinct roads of "radicalization" and "entropy" of different regimes; chapter 7 explored the possibility of adopting the heuristic category of "fascism" for extra-European experiences; and, finally, after that painstakingly comparative, contextualist, and interdisciplinary analytical labor, chapter 8 attempted a synthetic definition, which is offered at the end rather than at the opening of the essay: "Fascism may be defined as a form of political behavior marked by obsessive preoccupation with community decline, humiliation, or victimhood and by compensatory cults of unity, energy, and purity, in which a mass-based party of committed nationalist militants, working in uneasy but effective collaboration with traditional elites, abandons democratic liberties and pursues with redemptive violence and without ethical or legal restraints goals of internal cleansing and external expansion."[196]

Paxton's brilliant exercise of synthetic analysis hardly fit the synchronic, essentialist project of describing a constant or fixed conceptual core to fascism characteristic of the fascist minimum. In the twenty-first century, the search for the ultimate definition that could capture the essence of fascism beyond the bewildering specificities of its individual instantiations found application in studies of extra-European countries and beyond the limits of the interwar period and the Second World War. The project of isolating a stringent definition of fascism as a distinct political ideal type ceased to be merely an exercise of historical knowledge. It was now important for the identification of a fascist threat in the present and the future.[197] It was not only the various definitions that different historians advanced that could be isolated from their comparative framework and repurposed as normative guidelines for identificatory purposes—and this included Paxton's own definition, despite his own warnings.[198] Rather, the new form that the search for the essence of fascism took was the checklist. One of the earliest of such lists was that compiled by Laurence W. Britt, a "retired international businessperson, writer, and commentator."[199] Derived from his study of Nazi Germany, Fascist Italy, Franco's Spain, Salazar's Portugal, Papadopoulos's Greece, Pinochet's Chile, and Suharto's Indonesia, Britt's list consisted of fourteen "basic characteristics" that could be used to recognize the threat of an impending fascist takeover. These can be summarized as:

1. Powerful and continuing expressions of nationalism.
2. Disdain for the importance of human rights.
3. Identification of enemies/ scapegoats as a unifying cause.
4. Supremacy of the military/avid militarism.

5. Rampant sexism.
6. State-controlled mass media.
7. Obsession with national security.
8. Religion and the ruling elite tied together.
9. Power of corporations protected.
10. Power of labor suppressed or eliminated.
11. Disdain for and suppression of intellectuals and the arts.
12. Obsession with crime and punishment.
13. Rampant cronyism and corruption.
14. Fraudulent elections.

The essay concluded that these symptoms should not ring any "alarm bells," since "historical comparisons like these are just exercises in verbal gymnastics." The last sentence, however, ironically twisted this comforting distancing with a "maybe, maybe not" that questioned the solidity of US democratic institutions given the circumstances of the 2003 Iraq War, justified by the threat of Saddam Hussein's supposed possession of weapons of mass destruction—a proven fabrication that has, thus far, not produced any political or legal consequences for the George W. Bush administration. The appeal of a checklist of symptoms suggesting an imminent fascist takeover found renewed energy after the 2016 election of Donald Trump, now involving in their elaboration academics and scholars as well.[200]

12

Historical Knowledge and the Unbearable Fuzziness of "Fascism"

The scholarly labor of historians, philosophers, and political thinkers that chapters 10 and 11 selectively surveyed has contributed since 1945 to consolidate and conventionalize today's meanings of "fascism." What we today understand by this sign vehicle is clearly not the exclusive result of scholars' research. In fact, their work engaged in a mutual exchange with other forms of semiosic production, including political discourses of various kinds, literary and artistic inventions, and popular movements, as well as a vast repertoire of symbols, images, films, sounds, slogans, songs, myths, objects, places, moods, and atmospheres that have framed social life since 1945.

The signifier "fascism" confronts us today with a complex spectrum of denotative and connotative markers that results from the sediments of all recorded semiosic interventions: that is, uses, interpretations, and disambiguations with varying degrees of conventionalization, recurrence, social fungibility, pertinence, and authority. Some of its markers are but fossils buried in forgotten documents (e.g., *fascio* as "labor union," or "fascism" as a synonym of "state"). Others confront each other as unsolvable contradictions. And new ones strive to find room in scholars' creative reading of archives, in discussions on social media, or in ideological propaganda (i.e., in the anti-antifascism of the Right in twenty-first-century Italy).

We may even suspect it of being the vehicle of more than one semantic unit: the first referring to the system of meanings (the denotations and connotations advanced by Fascist leaders, antifascist activists, and postwar scholars) associated with the name of Mussolini's movement, ideology, and regime; the second with the system of meanings associated with the name of a generic political form, limited to the interwar period for some, transhistorical for others. The separation of the two units would simplify the semantic compound of each. In that case, the use of "fascism" as a sign vehicle of both would be simply a matter of homonymy. But considering "fascism" as referring to a single, albeit very complex, cultural unit comprising a rhizomatic web of denotations and connotations in turn linked to a constellation of co-occurring terms and concepts that favored distinct disambiguations has the advantage of reproducing the historical processes that led to the consolidation of different interpretive habits.

"Fascism" can therefore be disambiguated, in different texts and historical circumstances, as: (1) a proper noun (i.e., name), (2) an antonomasia referring to similar but distinct forms of coeval counterrevolutionary authoritarianisms, (3) a synecdoche identifying a generic and potentially universal political form of which individual movements and regimes (including Mussolini's) are but tokens, (4) a slur, and (5) a hyperbolic expression of political, psychological, or behavioral attitudes. All of these possible interpretive pathways are in turn associated with an ensemble of political, ethical, or aesthetic connotations.

The compositional spectrum of the main interpretants of *fascio*, *fascista*, and *fascismo* that this study has reconstructed can be hence summed up in the following schema:

Fascio:

1. A "bundle," usually of objects of elongated form.
   a. Figuratively, a "sheaf" or "stack" of undefined objects.
      i. In rare circumstances, connoted as burdensome (e.g., *un fascio di problemi*).
   b. Also figuratively, a "ray of light."
2. Symbol of political authority, originally in the form of the *fasces lictoriae*, a symbol of authority with varying connotations during the Roman Republic and Empire.
   a. Mostly in visual form, an undercodified symbol of governmental stability in Renaissance Europe.
   b. After the American and French Revolutions, a symbol of republicanism.
3. Common name of various forms of political, labor, or cultural associations, used in Italy since 1871 and maintaining that generic meaning until the early 1920s.
   a. As the name was predominantly used for labor unions, its connotations evoked socialism, anarchism, subversion, rebellion, the working classes, revolution, etc.
4. Generic appellation of politically transverse associations among individuals normally affiliated to different political parties, groups, or ideologies. That was the meaning, for instance, of the interventionist group Mussolini cofounded in 1914.
   a. Its main connotations evoked transitoriness, informality, unconventionality, task orientation, antipolitics, etc.

5. The name of Mussolini's Fasci Italiani di Combattimento, founded in March 1919. Occupying the political scene over the course of 1920, it rapidly rendered meanings (3) and (4) obsolete in the course of the decade. The term had unstable connotative meanings among their members in the early years of the movement:
    a. 1919: socialist, democratic, republican, anticlerical, anticommunist, nationalist.
    b. 1921: nationalist, monarchical, anticommunist, antibourgeois, antisyndicalist, antiliberal.

Fascista:

1. Pertaining to or designating membership in a *fascio*, understood as in (3), (4), and (5) above.
2. After 1921, exclusively used for members of or pertaining to the PNF.
3. Later 1920s to the present, pertaining to the ideology of Fascism or its adherents.
4. An insult, slur, or political slogan, globally widespread since the late 1960s, aimed at defining a regime, person, psychology, character, etc., as autocratic, intolerant, oppressive, violent, macho, etc.

Fascismo:

1. Ideology and praxis of Mussolini's movement and regime.
    a. Contextually and circumstantially disambiguated within the textual production of Fascist authors, its main denotative markers were used as coextensive with:
        i. Government, state, and nation.
            1. Its denotation as a form of governance favored connotations of totalitarian, nationalistic, traditional, corporatist, revolutionary, defender of social hierarchy and private property, militaristic, defender of the prerogative of the male in social and political life and of the procreative and/or convivial social role of female, authentically democratic, racist, etc.
        ii. Empire.
            1. As empire, it produced connotations of racial superiority of the "Latin Aryans" vis-à-vis inferior races.
            2. "Proletarian" empire vis-à-vis traditional, "plutocratic" empires (British, French, Belgian, Dutch, etc.).
        iii. As both expression of "state" and "empire," the regime was assigned connotations of:
            1. Universality.
            2. Cultural homogeneity and inclusiveness.
            3. Especially after 1938, racial exclusivity.
        iv. Its ideology was connoted in terms that privileged action over reflection, praxis over theory. Also, it was described in apophatic terms: antisocialist, anticommunist, anti-Marxist, antiliberal, antidemocratic, antibourgeois, etc.

b. Contextually and circumstantially disambiguated within antifascist activists:
    i. Among conservative liberals: pathological form of totalitarianism, caused by World War I and/or by the Bolshevik Revolution.
        1. Main connotations were pathological, temporary, irrational, affinity with communism.
    ii. Among progressive liberals: totalitarian form of ultranationalism that grew up after World War I among the middle classes to overcome their growing social domination, which, however, formed alliances with the capitalist elites of industry and agricultural landowners as well as with the forces of law and order (police, military, judiciary).
        1. Main connotations evoked irrationalism, elitism based on superstitious mythologies, violence and coercion, totalitarianism, antiliberalism, derivation from war, symptomatic of the political immaturity of Italy.
    iii. Among Marxists: dictatorial, violent, and repressive regime generated as the counterrevolutionary reaction of monopoly capital against the emancipatory movements that ensued after the successful Bolshevik Revolution.
        1. Main connotations were nationalism and insistence on national community to hide and reinforce forms of social exploitation.
        2. Among its connotative descriptions, while at its base Fascism strengthened capitalist relations of production, in its superstructure it generated ideologies that intended to hide its affinities with capitalism.
        3. Also, it connoted a critical stage of capitalist development, as it compensated the impossibility for capitalism to persist within liberal democratic institutions.
    iv. Postwar historians of Italian Fascism developed a multiplicity of explanations and descriptions of Fascism as movement, regime, and ideology. Its connection with capitalism and the institutions of liberal democracy remained contested, mirroring the different political persuasions of historians just as in the interwar period.
        1. Among the new connotations of Fascism, it is worth noting the insistence, among conservative and revisionist historians, that Fascism was not a thoroughly totalitarian regime like National Socialism; less ruthless than that, and not a participant in its genocidal policies.
        2. Recent historiography attempted to demolish the postwar myth of the "good Italian versus the bad German," and the full and willful collaboration of Fascism in the extermination of the Jews was proven beyond a reasonable doubt.

2. Generic name, originating among Marxist activists in the transwar period, of a new, repressive, counterrevolutionary form of political organization, aimed at

metonymically identifying the similar socioeconomic conditions that favored the emergence of different totalitarian movements and regimes in the world.

   a. The genericization of the term and its connotations remained contested among Marxists, until the Stalin-dominated Comintern was able to exercise hegemonic authority over its use and meanings.
   b. The connotation of its application to the socioeconomic base was that of being derived from "monopoly capitalism" and "financial capital"; at the superstructural level, it included "totalitarian," "counterrevolutionary," "militarist," "ultranationalist," etc.

3. Generic name of a new political ideal type, defined as a heuristic category that is supposed to have cognitive value in a realist-ontological sense, variously defined by historians who wished to distill a "fascist minimum" with synecdochically identificatory and classificatory aims that transcended the limits of the interwar period.
   a. The defining connotation of the "fascist minimum" was that it must be considered an autonomous and distinct political form like "liberalism," "democracy," "socialism," etc.
   b. Unlike the genericization of Marxism, its link with capitalism and liberal democratic institutions was severed.
4. An insult, slur, or political slogan, globally widespread starting from the late 1960s, aiming at defining a regime, person, psychology, character, etc. perceived as autocratic, intolerant, oppressive, violent, macho, etc.
5. Hyperbolic description of a psychological, behavioral, or political attitude, typically autocratic, intolerant, oppressive, etc.

Chapter 1 showed that etymology (*fascio*) is utterly useless when it comes to pinning down a stable semantic core of the term. The survey of the uses and interpretations of "fascism" in the interwar period and since 1945 revealed that its semantic compound consists of denotative and connotative markers that can be mutually contradictory or even antinomic. "Fascism," that is, triggered disambiguating processes that were aporetic not just in the texts of interwar Fascists and antifascist activists, both of which groups obviously bent their interpretations of the term in support of their political persuasions, but also in the research of historians and political theorists since 1945.

This simple observation inevitably invites the following question: If any attempt to produce a synthetic definition or description of fascism, understood as referring to either a discrete regime or a generic political type, seems necessarily to imply a political positionality of the inquirers notwithstanding the methodological rigor of their analyses, does this not compromise the cognitive legitimacy of that labor? Even though any historiographical reconstruction of the past inevitably produces a surplus of political implications, these seem to prejudice discussions on fascism more than others.

The political connotations of the various studies of fascism produced after 1945 are clearly discernible in scholars' interpretations of the documentary archives. Whether fascism, intended specifically as Italian Fascism or generically as a political type, was a form of authoritarianism directly linked to the communist revolution of 1917; a "third way" purporting to be an alternative to both capitalist liberalism and communist socialism; an excess of nationalism and militarism that was a consequence of the social, economic, and political crisis set in motion by the First World War; or the political form capitalism assumes in order to survive in periods of structural crisis, these are aporetic explanations that cannot be disentangled simply with more archival research. They depend directly on a scholar's own political disposition.

This connotative surplus triggers, in turn, a cognitive impasse that seems to contradict the principles of neutrality and objectivity that historians had long embraced as yardsticks of their epistemological authority.[1] It seems, in fact, to confirm Hayden White's claim that "there is an inexpungeable relativity in every representation of historical phenomena," which stirred a fierce diatribe with Carlo Ginzburg during the conference "History, Event, and Discourse," held at UCLA in 1989.[2] Historical knowledge cannot depend solely on historians' ethics, as White seemed to conclude from his reflections on the philosophy of historiography;[3] and yet, the possibility of historiographical objectivity in a realist-ontological sense (rather than in the sense of simply being based on the consensus of the community of professional historians), which Ginzburg seemed to embrace, appears to be either impossible or limited to microhistorical events, thus excluding the possibility of any realist-ontological claim on social dynamics, processes, and changes or any attempt at comparison and synthetic analysis.[4]

In truth, this dilemma might appear less daunting if we approach it from two different perspectives: one that looks at the fuzzy character of the political form that interwar Fascism, National Socialism, and other counterrevolutionary authoritarianisms engendered, and another that defends the cognitive authority of historical knowledge itself without repudiating its interpretive and hence potentially antinomic nature. The question, then, would become whether the semantic fuzziness of "fascism" (and the historical fuzziness of Fascism) impairs its heuristic advantageousness when it is used as a generic category.

The Fuzziness of "Fascism"

In all definitions that Fascists, coeval antifascists, and postwar scholars gave to its political ideology and praxis, fascism was often described in apophatic terms. It was, that is, routinely defined by its opposition to or negation of preexisting ideologies and praxes. For Mussolini and for commentators such as Salvemini, Linz, Bobbio, Griffin, and Gentile, it unfolded as a sort of "anti-" politics: antisocialist, anticommunist, antiliberal, antidemocratic, and so on. In logical terms, such an apophatic definition appears to follow the differential logic of semantic disambiguation.[5] Jerrold Katz classified three kinds of antonymous relations: contradictories (e.g., "mortal" vs. "immortal"), which exclude any mediating middle; contraries (e.g., "superior" vs. "inferior"), which imply intermediary degrees; and converses (e.g., "buy" vs. "sell"), implying mutual relations.[6] In the previous chapters we saw how "fascism" was often defined as contrary or contradictory to preexisting political forms. So, for instance, a progressive liberal like Norberto Bobbio developed an antinomic conception of Italian Fascism that described it as *contrary* to "communism" and *contradictory* to "democracy," whereas for a conservative liberal like Benedetto Croce (or Karl Popper) it was *contradictory* to "liberalism" and the *converse* of "communism," and for a Marxist like Togliatti it was the *converse* of "liberalism," *contradictory* to "communism," and, we may add, *congruent* with "capitalism."

The recurrent apophatic rhetoric in Fascist (and, to some extent, Nazi) self-definitions as well as in antifascist and postwar scholars' descriptions is suggestive of a political ideology that depends on preexisting ones. In the ideological strategy of Fascism, "fascism" did not just participate in a relation of simple antinomy, where the two opposing terms—such as, for instance, "fascism" and "Bolshevism" in Mussolini's texts—collaborated to mutually define each other through their binary opposition as either converses or contradictories. It was positioned in a sort of equidistance from or "equinegation" of a set of established political forms, but without whatever ensued being clarified in positive terms: for instance, Mussolini, like most postwar historians, defined fascism as equally opposed to democracy, liberalism, communism, and other systems.

Before Mussolini's rise to power, this strategy was born out of the necessity to distinguish Fascism not just from other dominant political ideologies, but also from a traditional praxis of party politics that he condemned.[7] After 1922 it helped consolidate the ideological view that fascism, rather than a particular political form or party, was nothing but the state, the purpose of which was to bring to full completion the destiny of the nation it led.[8] In other words, the apophatic or antinomic self-definition of Fascism had the purpose, before its rise to power, of distinguishing it ideologically, sociologically, institutionally, and as praxis from all other parties and movements (especially from socialism); after October 1922 it served to erase its political specificity as one political movement among others, so that its ideological identification with the state could be more successfully achieved.

During its twenty years of power, Fascism developed into a seemingly identifiable political form, as Emilio Gentile argues, despite its reliance on apophatic self-definitions and a doctrine that insisted on action rather than thought (directed by an explicit pragmatism rather than normative doctrinairism). But the inherent contradictoriness of the composite semantic markers of "fascism" complicates the disambiguation of both its ideological self-definitions and the incoherent ensemble of practices and deeds made in its name. This contradictoriness is evident in both fascist archives and in scholarly works published since the end of the Second World War. For instance, fascism was antiliberal, but it did not replace liberal institutions with alternative ones; it often kept them, and slowly repurposed them or emptied them of significance. It was antisocialist, but to a certain degree it shared with interwar socialist movements a tendency toward state-centrism and paramilitary activism. It was antidemocratic, yet it was based upon the reaffirmation of an ostensibly more authentic form of people's sovereignty (*qua* members of a national community defined by culture or race), emerging from the civic activism of syndicalists and former revolutionary socialists (e.g., *fascio* in senses (3) and (4) above). It ranted against bourgeois capitalism, and yet it never really dismantled the institutions of private property, the private ownership of the means of production, and the market economy.

This last point well exemplifies the fuzzy nature of the Fascist regime. Corporatism conceived of the state as directly involved in economic planning and intervention; and yet, and often despite its rhetoric, it failed to subordinate capitalists' private interests to the goal of national prosperity.[9] Fascist corporatism is usually described as unfolding in three phases. The first, lasting from 1922 to 1929 and characterized mainly by the subjection of labor to the needs of industrial production (via the dismantling of all labor unions and the constitution of the Confederazione Nazionale delle Corporazioni Sindacali), was marked by a continuation of the liberal policies of previous governments and was not in contradiction with similar forms of state interventions in other liberal democratic countries such as Great Britain, France, and the United States. The second phase, coinciding with the economic reforms that attempted to cope with the financial crisis of 1929, saw the formation of the corporations (Law no. 163 of February 5, 1934) and the institution of a public holding company, the Istituto per la Ricostruzione Industriale (Institute for Industrial Reconstruction; IRI), in 1933, the purpose of which was to rescue banks and industries at risk of bankruptcy.[10] But even then, no major nationalizations or incorporation of industrial production into the state occurred. That happened only during the third phase, which began with the Italo-Ethiopian War and intensified after 1939; but this restructuring of the economy in a corporatist sense can be understood as the effect of a war economy, which was still pursued by recruiting and involving the major industrial actors in the state rather than by nationalization and expropriation.[11]

During the second and third phases of corporatist transformation, the pursuit of a "pure and integral corporativism," as it was referred to by radical corporatists such as Carlo Costamagna, Ugo Spirito, Arnaldo Volpicelli, among others,[12] essentially took the form of bailouts, whereby the IRI intervened to save the structurally weak heavy-industry sector (e.g., the Ansaldo group) from bankruptcy by purchasing stocks and often becoming itself a majority stockholder.[13] Martin Blinkhorn has argued that state intervention in Italy "greatly surpassed that in Nazi Germany," where big business tended to maintain control of their companies by directly collaborating with the Nazi Party, "giving Italy a public sector second only to that of Stalin's Russia."[14] But state participation in industrial production did not dismantle the structure of the joint-stock company: the state simply became a stockholder by injecting much-needed capital into those industrial and banking sectors that were deemed strategically important but leaving intact the corporate structure of those industries.[15] For instance, Ansaldo, the largest heavy industry of northern Italy, declared bankruptcy in 1932 and was bailed out in 1933 by the IRI, which became a major stockholder of Ansaldo but left its control in the hands of the company's CEO, Agostino Rocca. Rocca was surely a party member, like almost all businessmen at the time, but he always operated as a manager in the private sector rather than as a party man or state bureaucrat.[16] Besides, similar corporatist tendencies were indeed ubiquitous after the crisis of 1929, and not just in authoritarian countries like Italy and Germany.[17] Moreover, a more widely diffused infiltration of the state into private business, via the IRI and other institutions, occurred only after the colonial war of 1935–36 and after Germany's invasion of Poland in 1939.[18]

The corporatist promiscuity of the state and private spheres that structured the Italian system of production after the crisis of 1929 is symptomatic of the inherent ambiguities in design observable in many regimes conventionally identified as fascist. These ambiguities favored the production of mutually contradictory but equally legitimate and empirically sustainable interpretations of fascism by Marxist and liberal historians. Surely a genuinely transnational approach would suggest that in the circumstances of the economic crises of the early 1930s and, especially, of total war in 1939–45, different regimes (liberal democracies, counterrevolutionary authoritarianisms, and Soviet-style communism) tended to develop similar strategies.

Also, one would surely agree with the transhistorical observation that rarely in history did a new regime operate a tabula rasa of previous political forms and institutions; the heuristics of change are always restrained by attention to continuity.[19]

The question of the aporias of "fascism" can be addressed from a different perspective. Historical judgments on how much fascism was imbricated with capitalism (affirmative for Marxist, negative for liberals) are inevitably trapped in an indeterminacy deriving not only from the complex imbrication of fascist institutions and ideology with preexisting conditions, but also from the fuzzy nature of the question itself. The "third way" fascism that its adherents (Mussolini and Hitler) purported to pursue—and that many postwar historians (e.g., Nolte, Mosse, Griffin, Gentile, among others) believed expressive of these regimes on their own terms—appears in fact to be a pastiche or a patchwork of elements from preexisting regimes and ideologies rather than an actual alternative. It surely cannot be persuasively argued that counterrevolutionary authoritarianisms did not have time to create new institutions and practices, since Italian Fascism remained in power for over two decades.

The inherent fuzziness and contradictoriness of "fascism" can be thought of as deriving from the fact that the regimes and ideologies this term is supposed to identify seemed to be made up of bits and pieces of other ideologies and political institutions. Interwar counterrevolutionary authoritarianisms took on the semblance of a political monster, a composite hybrid of different strategies, institutions, and conceptions borrowed from other political forms.

Umberto Eco suggested fascism's fuzzy compositional semantics in a lecture he gave at Columbia University on April 25, 1995, in the immediate aftermath of the Oklahoma City bombing, later published as an article in *The New York Review of Books* on June 22, 1995 as "Ur-Fascism."[20] For him, "the historical precedence does not strike me as sufficient to explain why the word 'fascism' has become a synecdoche," because "it is pointless to say that Fascism contained in itself all the elements of successive totalitarian movements, so to speak, 'in a quintessential state.' On the contrary, Fascism contained no quintessence, and not even a single essence. It was a fuzzy form of totalitarianism. It was not a monolithic ideology, but rather a collage of different political and philosophical ideas, a tangle of contradictions."[21]

"Fuzzy," here, should not be understood in the common sense of "vague" or "ambiguous," but rather in the logical senses of having *degrees* of applicability, truthfulness, or existence, or else as having separations from other conceptual spheres that are not clearly discernible.[22] It is fuzzy logic guiding a judgment that attempts to systematically resolve identificatory, taxonomical, or definitional problems (e.g., is fascism a sort of capitalism? is it a sort of socialism?) through the discrimination of qualities that are, in fact, not distinct but a matter of degree, with no clearly discernible confines. Bluntly put, asking to what degree Italian Fascism had to reproduce the structures, dynamics, or institutions of liberal capitalism in order to be understood as belonging or not belonging to it is a question as logically indeterminate (or fuzzy) as asking how many hairs should one have in order to be called bald. It is on the basis of this logical fuzziness that the political inclinations of the scholars who research fascism conceive of it as closer to liberal capitalism or Soviet communism, *independently of the rigor of their archival investigations.*

Umberto Eco argued that fascism, as an instantiation of "ideological chaos" and "organized confusion," operated with a logic similar to Wittgenstein's notion of game:[23] "The term 'fascism' fits everything because it is possible to eliminate one or more aspects from a fascist regime and it will always be recognizably fascist."[24] Hence, he explained, "Remove the imperialist dimension from Fascism, and you get Franco or Salazar; remove the colonialist dimension, and you get Balkan Fascism. Add to Italian Fascism a dash of radical anti-Capitalism (which never appealed to Mussolini), and you get Ezra Pound. Add the cult of Celtic mythology and the mysticism of the Grail (completely extraneous to official Fascism), and you get one of the most respected gurus of Fascism, Julius Evola."[25] If a combination of fundamental traits was, for Eco, enough to identify "fascism," just as permutations of some traits allowed Wittgenstein to identify a certain social activity as a game, Eco, in an operation that seems to synthesize the literature of the "fascism minimum," listed fourteen characteristics of what he called "Ur-Fascism" or "eternal fascism." These are, schematically:

1. Cult of tradition.
2. Rejection of modernism.
3. Cult of action for action's sake.
4. For Ur-Fascism, disagreement is treason.
5. Natural fear of difference.
6. Appeal to a frustrated middle class.
7. At the root of the Ur-Fascist psychology there is the obsession with a plot, possibly an international one.
8. The followers must feel humiliated by the ostentatious wealth and force of their enemies.
9. For Ur Fascism there is no struggle for life but, rather, life is lived for struggle. Thus pacifism is trafficking with the enemy. It is bad because life is permanent warfare.
10. Ur-Fascism can only advocate a popular elitism.

11. Everybody is educated to become a hero.
12. Machismo.
13. Ur-Fascism is based upon a selective populism, a qualitative populism, one might say. . . . For Ur-Fascism, however, individuals as individuals have no rights, and the People is conceived as a quality, a monolithic entity expressing the Common Will.
14. All the Nazi or Fascist schoolbooks made use of an impoverished vocabulary, and an elementary syntax, in order to limit the instruments for complex and critical reasoning.[26]

Still, even accepting the list of traits in Eco's piece as historically and conceptually pertinent, it is not clear why "fascism" should be an appropriate name for that ensemble apart from heuristic inertia, the continuation of an interpretive habit that began as early as the 1920s.

The malleability and philosophical incoherence of fascist ideology have often been understood as signs of its being a mere pretense, behind which lay a ruthless application of the principle of domination (e.g., Adorno and Horkheimer), the continuation of capitalist relations of production under the false guise of a nationalist revolution (e.g., Marxist definitions, orthodox or not), or the shrewd instrumentalism of power-hungry charismatic leaders (e.g., Ben-Ghiat's "strongmen" theory).[27] But it can also be the effect of inherent political, ideological, and institutional contradictions that so-called fascist regimes were incapable of overcoming.

In this case, fascism's fuzziness offers a more nuanced understanding of Fascists' and Nazis' self-definition of being a third way. The claim of being a third way could be interpreted against the fascist rhetoric (and thus also against its literal adoption by postwar historians), that is, as being neither an affirmation (as in liberal democracies) nor a negation (as in communism) of the capitalist system. Rather, the fuzziness of this third way derived from the impossibility of neatly distinguishing it from the preexisting political forms, institutions, ideologies, terminologies, and legal apparatuses it claimed to oppose and negate, since fascist movements and regimes could exist only by parasitizing them. This would also explain why historians and political thinkers have interpreted fascism as opposing or negating conceptions, institutions, or ideas of society and politics that they implicitly or explicitly upheld as normative or natural: Marxists would regard fascism as an expression of capitalism in critical sociohistorical circumstances, while liberals would conceive of it as an irrational pathology, or an offspring, a reaction against, or a converse (in Katz's sense) of socialism.

This explains why the various conceptions of "fascism" inevitably mirror, in reverse, scholars' own political beliefs. In technical terms, they appear to be etic descriptions of fascist emic structures while these descriptions in truth mirror, in reverse, the interpreters' own emic structures. In short, *the regimes that "fascism" names confronted capitalist democracy as its dark half, just as Stalinism confronted socialism as its perversion.*[28] If fascism and the genocidal violence it produced confront capitalist liberalism as an inerasable possibility within it, evidenced in the fuzziness of the ideologies and praxis it produced, then its hypostatization into a discrete ideal type in the scholarship of the "fascism minimum," which turns that structural fuzziness into the coherence of its normative definitions, has the effect of severing the imbrication of transwar counterrevolutionary authoritarianisms with the political forms of liberal democracy from which they originated and with the Stalinist communism that they antagonized and often mimicked.

The Quest for "Japanese Fascism"

The semantic fuzziness of "fascism," itself mirroring the political fuzziness of the regimes it pretends to identify generically, affects the heuristic efficacy of its use as analytical category. Before proposing an argument about its cautious adoption in historical research, guided by the principles of heuristic advantages (and disadvantages) and of epistemological pertinence and parsimony, it might be worth exploring it at work in an extra-European context.

The case of Japan in the 1930s exemplifies well the limits of its epistemological usefulness. In fact, the idea of "Japanese fascism" is a historiographical construct rather than a historical event.[29] Historically, there were no political parties or movements in Japan between the 1920s and the early 1940s that bore that name or were so dubbed. There was no political ideology that openly declared that it subscribed to the ideas of Mussolini's Fascism. Nor did the political regime of the 1930s and 1940s openly embrace fascism as a governmental model. Fascist ideas, texts, slogans, and agents surely circulated quite broadly in interwar Japan, sparking debates, confrontations, and imitations. But Fascism spread to many other countries before the war, including those that ended up fighting against the Axis Powers in the Second World War.[30] It is certainly possible to write a history of how Fascism attracted, inspired, or repulsed Japanese thinkers, journalists, authors, and political activists in the interwar period.[31] But a history of "Fascism in Japan" is not equivalent to a history of "Fascist Japan." The debates and confrontations that Italian Fascism provoked in Japan is a historical topic distinct from the historiographical interpretation of the nature of Japan's militarist regime between the 1930s and the early 1940s. Whether Japan underwent a "fascist turn" in the course of the 1930s is a question of historical interpretation and political judgment, the legitimacy of which cannot be assumed but must be argued for. Interestingly, the question of "Japanese fascism" unfolded differently in Japan and among Western scholars, especially Anglophones.

The debate over Japanese fascism among Japanese Marxists in the first decades of the postwar period was at the same time a theoretical attempt to come to terms with the catastrophe of the fifteen-year war and a political intervention into the future of Japan in the context of the intensifying Cold War. The debate was carried on using Marxian terminology and on the basis of a Marxist political dialectic of stage development of base-superstructure forms. Throughout the 1950s and 1960s it dominated the intellectual landscape of historical research and provided a political orientation to the majority of Japanese intellectuals. For Marxist theorists, analyses of monopoly capitalism, represented in Japan by the *zaibatsu* conglomerates that the occupying forces had just pretended to dismantle, served as a perspective whereby it was possible to understand the emperor system (*tennōsei*) and the aggressive imperialism in Asia in the 1930s and 1940s, as well as to critically assess the continuation of prewar conservatism after 1945, in the context of the "soft fascism" of Cold War capitalism. The association of armed forces, *zaibatsu*, political parties, and state bureaucracy that constituted the formal structure of Japanese fascism (for the Rōnō-ha) or emperor-centered absolutist fascism (for the Kōza-ha) in the 1930s became, for Marxist theorists, allegories that revealed the corrupted and authoritarian governance of the Liberal Democratic Party.[32] Despite the doctrinal divergences among thinkers of different Marxist factions, "fascism" maintained a clear conceptual consistency in their formulations. It stood for the name of an objective stage of sociopolitical development, characteristic of monopolistic capitalist economies in times of protracted crisis. As such, it signified more than a political form or style of propaganda (superstructure): It was a generic category, the attribution of which depended on scholars' analyses of the socioeconomic development of Japanese society in the interwar period. For Japanese Marxists, Japanese fascism fit the notion of universal fascism that the Comintern had defined in the 1930s.

The only non-Marxist analysis of Japanese imperialism that had great political bearing among postwar Japanese intellectuals was that of Maruyama Masao, one of the most prominent political theorists of postwar Japan.[33] For him, Japan had a defective modernization, the causes of which had to be traced back to the Tokugawa period.[34] Unlike in Italy and Germany, where fascist movements developed from below, in Japan civilian fascism and military-bureaucratic fascism—although neither used the term for itself—were engaged in a complex dialectic of opposition and assimilation that eventually reinforced each other. This characteristic explained, for Maruyama, the marked difference between Japan and its two European allies. On the one hand, the three forms of fascism shared an opposition to liberalism and parliamentarism, a stark antagonism to Marxism and capitalism, and aggressively expansionist policies.[35] On the other hand, the ideology of Japanese fascism had "distinctive characteristics" born of its specific modernizing trajectory.[36]

Maruyama's theorization of fascism had striking similarities with the Marxist interpretation. They both conceived of it in realist terms: It pointed to a distinct and real (in the ontological sense) form of political organization, with both universal characteristics and local specificities. Also like the Marxists, Maruyama's analysis of fascism was propaedeutic to the construction of an authentically democratic consciousness in postwar Japanese society, of which he became one of the most prominent public advocates during the social conflicts of the 1960s. For Maruyama, this analysis of Japanese fascism was indispensable to counteracting what he called a chronic "system of irresponsibility" dominant in the Japanese public sphere.[37] What distinguished Maruyama's "fascism" from the Marxists' was that for him it pointed to a *political* form of power, whereas Marxist theorists ultimately pointed to the socioeconomic condition of monopoly capitalism.

Despite doctrinal disputes and different interpretations, the notion that Japan underwent a fascist phase in the 1930s remained hegemonic among Japanese intellectuals until well into the 1970s. In that context, "fascism," the heuristic legitimacy of which was never questioned, had a twofold function: one was historical, as it gave an interpretive meaning to the wartime experience of Japan that was to be regarded as a negative template against which a new model of democratic citizenship had to evolve in postwar Japan; the other was political, as it stood as a memento of the ever-present danger of political power turning authoritarian, especially as the intensification of the Cold War confrontation with their Communist neighbors required that Japan accede to the demands of the United States.[38]

If the majority of Japanese historians and theorists supported the notion that Japan in the 1930s had indeed turned fascist, quite the opposite interpretation was given by European and American historians, independently of their political orientation. With the exception of Robert A. Scalapino, who coined the term "military-fascism," and Richard Storry, who adopted from Maruyama the notion of a "headless fascism from above," the majority of Anglo-American historians rejected the attribution of "fascism" to Japan.[39] Edwin Reischauer opted for "organized ultranationalist movement" and "military dictatorship with totalitarian tendencies."[40] Delmer Brown rejected "fascism" as well, preferring such locutions as "militarist ultra-nationalism."[41] Albert Craig, too, favored "militarism," although he acknowledged the similarities between Japan and Nazi Germany as an effect of their latecomer modernization.[42] John W. Hall rejected the notion of "fascist Japan" and characterized it instead as a "defensive State" sustained by an "ultranationalist ideology," which mixed the authoritarianism of the Meiji Constitution with the notions of "militarism" and "state socialism."[43] Marius Jansen largely agreed with the interpretation of the first generation of American historians of Japan, who at the time were responding to the predominantly Marxist Japanese academic historians and their consensus regarding Japanese fascism.[44] Opposition to the notion of fascist Japan, however, did not come only from liberal and conservative historians. It was defended and pursued by Marxist historians as well. E. H. Norman, reprising Tanin and Yohan's study, argued that Japan lacked some important distinctive characteristics of fascist dictatorships.[45] Jon Halliday, too, upheld Tanin and Yohan's interpretation and explained the ultramilitarism of the 1930s as an effect of lingering feudal relations.[46]

In continental Europe, where the Marxist historiographical tradition was stronger than in the Anglophone world, historians were less hostile to the notion of Japanese fascism, although they tended to qualify that interpretation by appealing to the distinctive sociocultural context of Japan.[47] But Anglo-American historians of Japan writing from the late 1960s and throughout the 1990s remained suspicious of the qualifier "fascism" to describe transwar and wartime Japan. After rejecting the old developmental interpretations, both Marxist and non-Marxist, and asserting the unfitness of analytical models based on European history, Peter Duus and Daniel I. Okimoto urged that "instead of remaining transfixed by the need to explain the aberrational phenomenon of fascism . . . we need to press beyond the orthodox concerns of the past to formulate new questions, . . . new models, and test these empirically with a broad spectrum of heretofore unexplored perspectives."[48] If there certainly were fascist tendencies among minority movements, especially among military officials, for them the term that best explains the sociopolitical character of transwar Japan is "corporatism."

For Duus and Okimoto, the question of "fascism" ceased to be an eminently ontological problem, as it was in the developmental model of earlier historiography, and became a matter of heuristic accuracy. Accordingly, the research on Japanese fascism in the late 1970s through the 1990s generally relied on structuralist terminology and engaged with the coeval scholarship of typological fascism and its search for a fascist minimum. Although the epistemological approach changed, the overwhelming majority of historians tended to reject the attribution of "fascist" to transwar Japan. Gregory Kasza rejected "fascism" and opted for "military-bureaucratic regime."[49] Relying on Japanese historians who rejected the term—in particular on the work of the revisionist Itō Takashi[50]—Kasza underlined the "conceptual fuzziness" ("fascism" applies to "the entire right wing"), the questionable Marxist "political motivation" behind the uncritical use of the concept, and the fact that "Japan differed from Europe," in that it lacked a charismatic dictator, one-party politics, and grassroots origins.[51] Possible alternative conceptions, for him, were "imperial absolutism," "developmental dictatorship,"[52] "wartime politics," and reliance on "historical nominalism," by which he meant the adoption of "native terms that were prominent in interwar political discourse," such as *kannen uyoku* (idealist right) and *kakushin*, a term he adopted from Itō Takashi. *Kakushin*, Kasza explained, "has no equivalent in the English language. In the interwar context, it is sometimes translated 'renovation.' In the postwar context, it is often translated 'progressive.' . . . Neither translation does it justice. *Kakushin* falls halfway between 'reform,' a modest change within an existing system, and 'revolution,' the replacement of one system by another. *Kakushin* advocates would keep some features of the existing politico-economic system but change others fundamentally. They are selective revolutionaries."[53] The conceptual operation in the interpretations of both Itō and Kasza, however, was that of creating synecdochically a new heuristic category which was supposed to stand—instead of "fascism," but from an epistemological perspective performing the analogous conceptual labor of "fascism"—for the regime that Japan ended up developing in the 1930s and 1940s.

Ben-Amy Shillony emphasized the continuation of political institutions during the war, arguing that labels such as "totalitarian" and "fascist state" "are meaningful only if understood in their broadest and pejorative sense, as nicknames for highlighting the repressive and aggressive character of the state." But upon closer inspection, we see that Japan "possessed neither an official dogma nor an omniscient leader to interpret the truth," and oppression was never comparable "to the concentration camps and wholesale bloodshed of Nazi Germany or Soviet Russia."[54] Similarly, William Miles Fletcher III researched "common themes between European fascist movements and the New Order Movement in Japan," but because "there were few institutional similarities between prewar Japan and fascist Italy or Nazi Germany," he contended that "the Japanese state was not fascist."[55] Interestingly, even though they negated its heuristic accuracy, "fascism" for these historians stood mostly for Nazi Germany rather than Fascist Italy, and the accuracy of such conceptual reductionism was never questioned. Other US historians who, in the 1980s, rejected the attribution of "fascist" to the Japanese state were Mark Peattie, Gordon Berger, and Richard Mitchell.[56] One exception among

Anglophone historians was the Australian Gavan MacCormack, who, while acknowledging the convenience of such labels as *tennōsei* state, quite cautiously defended some advantages that the heuristic category of fascism offered to understanding the socioeconomic developments of transwar Japan.[57]

With the end of the Cold War, the question of Japanese fascism has reappeared in a new form. Today "fascism" no longer harbors the ambition of describing a stage of Japanese sociopolitical development, nor does it define the typology of the Japanese regime in the transwar period. Its target is smaller in size and heuristic ambition. It is rarely called to qualify political institutions, economic organizations, or ideological forms in their entirety, but rather refers to certain cultural and social practices, forms of thoughts, aesthetic tendencies, and patterns of sociability. This change in focus mirrors changes in the writing of history in general that have occurred since the 1990s, especially after the "cultural turn" and the many subturns it triggered. The institutionalization of new genres of historical inquiry, such as postcolonial studies, environmental history, subaltern studies, the history of science and technology, gender history, transnational history, and media studies, among many others, made way for new research questions, new methods, new approaches, and new interpretations of the past.

In Japan, the hegemonic presence of practicing Marxist historians began to wane in the 1980s. Dissenting voices began to emerge: Itō Takashi, for instance, joined forces with the Italian revisionist historian of Fascism Renzo De Felice, contending that the generic use of "fascism" was nothing but a Marxist creation.[58] Among the group of historians that would be later defined as practitioners of *minshūshi* (people's history), politically on the left but no longer committed to Marxism,[59] Yoshimi Yoshiaki in 1984 published a people's history of wartime Japan in which he laid out arguments for the widespread popular support of Japanese militarist expansion after 1937. Yoshimi's groundbreaking study, together with the waning of the institutional predominance of Marxist historians in Japanese research universities, opened up the possibility of the development of new research on wartime Japan. Among the vast bibliographical production, Suzaki Shin'ichi focused on fascism's appeal to state bureaucrats, who looked at Nazi Germany and, to a much lesser extent, Fascist Italy for new forms of administrative and technological solutions to improve the governance of the Japanese empire.[60] In 2012 Fuke Takahiro looked at the cultural and intellectual exchanges of Japanese right-wing activists and ideologues with Italian and German thinkers.[61]

In the United States, as early as 1991 Andrew Gordon broke a decades-long reluctance to employ the concept of "fascism" in Japan and suggested that the notion of "fascism from above," as used by Maruyama Masao and

Yamaguchi Yasushi, was a useful description of the changes in the relations between the state and workers that he analyzed in conjunction with the rise of militarism and imperialist expansion.[62] Harry Harootunian's ambitious *Overcome by Modernity*, a sophisticated intellectual history of Japan in the decades leading up to its involvement in the Second World War, employed "fascism" not as a label of transwar Japan in general but rather to identify a recurring attitude among such intellectuals as Miki Kiyoshi, Hirabayashi Hatsunosuke, Yanagita Kunio, Kon Wajirō, among others, in criticizing the alienating effect of modernization and its technological and economic mechanisms in favor of a return to "authenticity, folkism, and communitarianism."[63] Along similar lines, Julia Adeney Thomas argued that the appeal to "nature," in the ideological constructs of such thinkers as Miki Kiyoshi, Nishida Kitarō, Watsuji Tetsurō, and Tanabe Hajime, among others, supported those concepts of agrarianism, primeval communitarianism, and national character that were constitutive of wartime ultranationalism and analogous to fascism.[64] In the field of cultural history, Alan Tansman scouted the cultural production of the 1920s and 1930s in search of "fascist moments" and found "a wide range of cultural expressions that share an urge for aesthetic wholeness": the aestheticization of violence, militarism, expansionism, a religious attachment to national community, and so on are all elements that echoed similar ones in the European context.[65] In the multiauthor volume *The Culture of Japanese Fascism*, Tansman argues "for the presence of a fascist culture in Japan and for the presence of fascistic ways of healing the crisis of interwar modernity."[66]

Other historians have recently employed "fascism" to speak of political changes in Japanese modernity. Takeshi Fujitani argued that a feminine character distinguished the Japanese nationalist ideology from European fascisms.[67] Kenneth Rouff, in his reconstruction of the wartime celebration of the 2600th anniversary of the founding of Japan, argued that "in political terms, Japan in 1940 shared far more in common with Nazi Germany and Fascist Italy than it did with the United States and Britain."[68] Janis Mimura argued for the heuristic value of "fascism's ideology, expansionist policies, and modern technocratic thrust—all of which Japanese fascism shared with its European counterparts."[69] Aaron Stephen Moore adopted the notion of "techno-fascism," and in his study of the technological and ideological foundations of the Japanese empire he argued that "wartime Japan's technological imaginary represented a form of fascist ideology that employed familiar tropes of modernity and rationality rather than relying primarily on cultural appeals to spiritualism or ultranationalism."[70] Reto Hofmann researched the cultural exchanges between Italy and Japan and the popularity of Fascist ideas in Japan between the 1920s and the end of the war. Hofmann searched in scholarly texts, popular books, political documents, newspaper articles, theatrical pieces, monuments, and artifacts to reconstruct the circulation, understanding, appeal, or refusal of the concept of "fascism" as it was imported in Japan from Italy.[71]

The rediscovery of "fascism" as a heuristic category of choice in the Anglophone historiography of Japan since around 2000—a return with a vengeance, given its ubiquity in the most recent studies of wartime Japan, even when its adoption seems to add little to the issue under investigation[72]—is also evidence of a profound change in its hermeneutic function. Today "fascism" operates in a quite different manner from in the immediate postwar era. It no longer defines a stage of development within an ontologically conceived teleology of modernization, and it no longer operates as an epistemic category capable of capturing the essential nature of the political system and social organization of Japan in the late 1930s. It is rather employed to emphasize the character and quality of *distinct* sociocultural phenomena. It has become, in a sense, less ambitious, more modest and circumscribed in its explicatory labor; but in the process its denotations have become fuzzier. As a qualifier of wartime Japan, "fascism" may stand as a hyperbolic synonym of authoritarianism, statism, totalitarianism, racial ethnocentrism, cultural communitarianism, revolutionary conservatism, or reactionary antimodernism; it can stand for the aestheticization of violence, ultramilitarism, the worship of war and violence, popular support of the war effort, or the demagogic ideology of antimodern modernism. It stands, in other words, for one or several of the characteristics that have been isolated in the definitional quest of fascist-minimum scholarship that support the interpretation of historians of Japan to the extent that its association with Italian Fascism or German National Socialism has become rather tenuous and undefined.

Another effect of the dependence of these studies on the scholarship of the fascist minimum (the works of Payne and Griffin in particular) is that the comparison (or connection) with the Italian or German cases remains vague and general. That is, when "fascism" is adopted to describe or explain certain characteristics of specific social, intellectual, cultural, economic, or political phenomena of interwar Japan (from bureaucratic technocracy and economic planning to political discourses on the national community, philosophical investigations on the alienating effects of industrial modernization, and the aesthetic appreciation of everyday life), its heuristic function hinges on a selection of denotative and connotative markers that are presented as now having a very loose and casual connection with the historical experiences of Fascism and Nazism. It is in the genericity or in the implied (but not demonstrated) global applicability of the ideal type "fascism" that scholars employ it as analytical tool, one step removed from actual historical references to Italy or Germany. In turn, since "fascism" is used as an ideal type with normative affordances, it is no longer required of the historian to argue for its application in extra-European contexts, as was the case for the first generations of postwar historians.

The main effect of this reductive application of the heuristic category of "fascism," now universal, abstract, and largely disconnected from its European instantiations, is its reification into a "global phenomenon." Any form of authoritarianism, no matter the local specificities and ontogenesis, appears to take part in a single political movement. This reductionism might afford historians the opportunity to acknowledge similar patterns (e.g., in propaganda, nationalist rhetoric, archaistic mythologies, bottom-up associationism, militarization of industrial production, etc.) developing coevally in different regions.[73] At the same time, it fails to take into account the fact that prewar Japan was an authoritarian state by design: sovereignty rested in the emperor, and thus the Japanese were subjects rather than citizens; there was no decisive division of powers, nor a system of check and balances; electoral representatives had a marginal role in the legislative and executive branches; the military responded only to the emperor and not to the Diet; industrial and financial conglomerates developed monopolistic tendencies in synergetic alliance with the government and the army since the Meiji period; the development of structural alliances uniting people operating across different sectors (state bureaucracy, political parties, *zaibatsu* conglomerates, and army and navy) in political ties determined a degree of polyarchic contradictoriness of Japan's trajectory in the 1930s; and the political ferment from below of the Taishō era (in the form of labor unions, socialist and communist movements, party politics, the popular struggle for suffrage, cultural associationism, a robust public sphere, etc.) did not produce any changes in the state's constitutional structure. In that context, it is difficult to acknowledge a concrete advantage of the category "fascism" to explain the path to total war in which Japan engaged after 1937. There was no revolutionary change; the masses mobilized in support of an imperialist war only after its intensification; the ideological machine in support of total mobilization geared up only after the war was well under way.[74]

In sum, Japan was not affected by a fascist transformation because it was from the beginning a semi-absolutist constitutional monarchy and an oligarchic "nation-empire" (to return to Richard Overy's expression used in the introduction) that simply reinforced the authoritarianism of its institutions and the pervasiveness of its ideological machine to assure the necessary social conditions to conduct total war. In short, the attribute "fascist" seems to me not particularly useful in the case of Japan. First, it does not help us distinguish the revolutionary intent of Fascism and National Socialism from Japan's traditional and institutional forms of authoritarianism. Second, it does not identify in historical events a breaking point that the advent of "fascism" might have triggered. The "totalitarianism" that developed in Japan in 1937–38 can be more economically understood as an intensification of the preexisting structural authoritarianism deriving from the Meiji Constitution and the ideological appeal of a nationalist ideology that was both pushed from above and endorsed from below for the sake of mobilization for war encoded in terms of the encirclement of Japan by Western empires.[75] In fact, the centralization of power and bottom-up support and collaboration on the home front operated in a similar fashion in Japan, Germany, and the United Kingdom independently of their political affinities.[76] Third, the political, social, and cultural impact of a total war fought with unprecedented human and material resources cannot be ignored in historians' assessment of the advantages or disadvantages of "fascism" as a heuristic category. In the case of Japan, the imbrication of important sectors of the Imperial Army and Navy with the economic powerhouses of the *zaibatsu*, with political parties, and with the state bureaucracy at various levels gave them a degree of autonomy in terms of action and decision-making they did not have in other liberal democracies. Fourth, a more cautious and "localized" use of "fascism," as, for instance, to define aesthetic currents, might have a certain advantage in highlighting and isolating similarities in form and content with other similar movements around the world.[77] This, however, would be more convincing if these "fascistic" or "fascistoid" tendencies were not used to draw inferences about the general nature of Japanese society or to prove the ideological basis for an Axis alliance that grew out of strategic convenience rather than from affinities of political ideals. Indeed, similar aesthetic or philosophical tendencies could be found everywhere in the world in the interwar period, not only in Italy, Germany, and Japan, but also in the United States, Great Britain, France, China, and elsewhere.

"Was Japan fascist?" is therefore a misleading question. We should rather ask whether the metaphorical adoption of "fascism" in understanding the historical development of Japan in the 1930s is heuristically advantageous. And this leads us back to the unbearable fuzziness of the term itself.

On the Interpretive Nature of Historical Knowledge

Fascism appears to be a semantic shape-shifter not only on account of the fuzzy structure of its ideology, praxis, and institutions, but also as result of the interpretive nature of historical knowledge. This is the case in historians' synthetic interpretations of Italian Fascism and even more so in their conceptualizations of generic fascism.[78] The fact that historians' descriptions of the origins, orientations, and affiliations of fascist regimes depend also on their own political persuasions seems to jeopardize the legitimacy of their cognitive claims. The history of the scholarship on fascism discourages the belief that this dilemma can be solved simply with more thorough archival research or philological analyses, because it originates in the theoretical and interpretive apparatus that necessarily frames historians' readings of the documentary sources. It appears to be an empirical confirmation of Hayden White's claim on the relativism of historical knowledge,[79] or of Constantin Fasolt's view that modern historiography has been political by design since its inception in the Renaissance, since it is predicated on the assumed ontological otherness of the past it investigates.[80] Is that really the case, though? Questioning this aporia in historical knowledge is not just an exercise in historiographical theory: It is epistemologically and politically consequential in determining the heuristic capacity of "fascism."

"Fascism," when used generically, does not refer to a "thing," as Gilbert Allardyce correctly pointed out. It is, in fact, a *judgment*. Any nonindexical use of the term beyond the appellation of Mussolini's regime is the result of an evaluative procedure that, implicitly or explicitly, attributes it, as metonymical antonomasia (grounded on similarity) or synecdoche (based on subsumption into a universal type), to an array of historical, political, cultural, and even behavioral phenomena. A we have seen, such attributions are contested and often antinomic. And they presuppose that differing epistemological judgments on "fascism" imply different political and ethical claims, regardless of historians' intentions.

Today it can hardly be disputed that historical knowledge is not an objective and unmediated reproduction of the past as it really happened, or, to use a much-misunderstood expression, *wie es eigentlich gewesen ist*—"as it really was."[81] Hence, attributing the fuzziness of "fascism" to the inclinations of individual historians is as unsatisfactory as pretending that an answer to its indeterminacy can simply come from more archival research.

From a semiotic perspective, history is a mode of sign production that claims to communicate truthful knowledge of the past. What we call "history," however, is not "the past," even though the encyclopedia contradictorily registers this synonymic use.[82] It is rather a possible reconstruction of aspects of the past resulting from investigative labor, or judgment, on the traces (e.g., archaeological remains, documents, witness testimonies, etc.) that the past left, the truth value of which must be socially and epistemologically accounted for.[83] We might then say that historians' texts are tantamount to sign vehicles that convey an ensemble of socially recorded meanings. These meanings are what we call "history": they can be metaphorically imagined as consisting of libraries of often contradictory notions, beliefs, facts, narratives, descriptions, hypotheses, and fabrications on past events, dynamics, and processes.[84] History is the content of historians' work, that is, the "mediating representations" (CP 1.533) or the "proper significate effect" (CP 5.475) of a past that is no more, that cannot be accessed directly or unmediatedly.[85]

The form historians give to their accounts, as Hayden White argued, have semiosic effects in the construction and interpretation of history, just as the form of every sign vehicle produces specific meanings through which an object or event in the world is referred to not in itself, but "in some respect or capacity" (CP 2.228). And yet, it is a mistake to conclude that historians' narratives would be fictitious if not for the ethical or deontological commitment of their authors, as White alleged.[86] Historians' accounts convey a history that attempts to stand for the past in a truthful way. In turn, the truth value of historians' accounts is based on analytical labor that is legitimized by the community of professional historians (producing claims that Alan Megill defines as pertaining to "disciplinary objectivity") but that should also be validated by the soundness of their conjectural labor (producing what Megill calls "procedural objectivity"), hence, in theory, independently of the certification of academic historians—on the condition that historians disclose that labor in their narratives.[87]

The past that historians try to reconstruct by analyzing and interpreting the traces it left is not directly experienceable: archives, a particular kind of trace, are not open windows or time machines. The past is gone, it is absent (a "ghost," to use Ethan Kleinberg's word).[88] It is only through the mediation of historians' conjectures regarding its partial traces that some meaningful images or accounts of the past ("history") can be produced, just as "a sign can *stand for* something else to somebody only because this 'standing for' relation is mediated by an interpretant."[89]

Archival and documentary sources of different sorts constitute the evidentiary apparatus upon which historians tentatively conjecture the reconstruction of a past event or process: "History" can thus stand for the "past" only insofar it is mediated by historians' interpretive labor. On the one hand, these traces are not direct (unmediated) indexical signs of the past events or processes historians want to investigate.[90] What the trace directly indicates as an indexical sign is only the (voluntary or involuntary) act of leaving that trace; the event that historians aim to reconstruct through it is already mediated by it and must therefore be considered a semiotic construct (no longer an indexical sign) that signifies that past event *in some respect and capacity*. On the other hand, historians' accounts ("history") stand for the "past" only as a "possible world," which is taken *as if* it represented the past in a realist-ontological sense only on the basis of a contractual acceptance of historians' interpretive labor.[91]

An indexical trace, pointing either to a past event (in the case of archaeological, geological, or other sorts of material clues) or to the recording of that past event in a text (documentary sources), becomes evidence only when it is embedded, along with other traces, into a process of inferential reasoning, the purpose of which is to conjecture a past state, event, or process.[92] This conjecture follows the logic of what Charles Sanders Peirce called "abduction": hypothesizing a theoretical scenario that can offer a credible explanation for the evidence under scrutiny. It is within the abductive process of inference-making with respect to the archival sources that "fascism" regulates historians' interpretations.[93]

Historians form their inferential reconstructions of the past with a set of clues (documentary traces) far too limited to constitute the basis for inductive reasoning. Like detectives, they operate abductively, conjuring up, consciously or unconsciously, the explanatory paradigm or template that can best make sense of the evidence that confronts them.[94] It is in the construction of a plausible explanatory paradigm that interpretive habits; disciplinary orthodoxies; institutional pressures; philosophical, religious, and political biases; and class, gender, and racial inequalities factor. These paradigms—which tend to operate backstage, often unconsciously, sometimes dogmatically, but always disguised behind the "reality effect" of historians' narrative accounts—are theoretical constructs that turn traces into evidence.[95] This is a way to read Goethe's claim that "everything that is factual is already theory," quoted in the epigraph of part III.

The opposition of empirical versus theoretical approach—a misguided methodological topic of far too many debates and book reviews—falsifies the imbrication of both in the production of historical knowledge. Historians do not produce their accounts of the past out of nothing, but on the basis of a complex assemblage made up of traces (archival documents, archaeological and geological remains, data of various kinds, photographs, paintings, etc.); received notions and competences from national and global historiographical traditions; fashions, concerns, and themes traversing the field in historians' own times; subfield-specific approaches, terminologies, analytical techniques, linguistic competences, and the like; theoretical, philosophical, legal, and methodological beliefs and biases; political, ethical, and religious convictions and prejudices; external and internal compulsions, discriminations, unwritten rules, and commitments grounded on ethnical, racial, sexual, and gender differences; pressures from peers (in individual departments as well as in the field in general); and individual life trajectories (at once personal and social), emotional inclinations, interdisciplinary skills, psychological perversions, creative imaginations, and so on.

Once established as an institutionally sanctioned definition of a generic political form, "fascism" contributes, as an explanatory paradigm, to the reading of the evidentiary traces. But it can also inform the interpretations of its archetypal instantiation, Mussolini's regime, regardless of historians' endorsement of "generic fascism" or Allardycean realism. That is because, as a political form, some of the semantic markers of "fascism" are coextensive with conceptions of society, the individual, the economy, the state, and so on which are not only themselves theoretical constructs, but are also regulated by political connotations that cannot be erased.

In interpreting Mussolini's policies on labor, the economy, the state, and other aspects of government, historians of different persuasions construct their abductive rules on the basis not only of previous scholarship and coeval disciplinary tendencies, but also of conceptions of society, labor relations, ideology, and so on that they hold as normative: accordingly, a left-wing historian can read Blackshirts' violence as a reactionary response aimed at protecting acquired social privileges deemed natural, whereas a liberal-leaning historian might conceive of it as a rightful (though excessive) defense against a perceived socialist threat to the inalienable right of property. Both historians can be outstanding analysts of archival sources, but their diverging interpretations rest on the distinct political prejudices that inform their explanatory paradigms. Neither is "objective" in the sense of politically neutral, and not just because of the inherently political nature of modern historiography, but because there is no natural way of organizing a society. The fact that excellent scholarship from historians of different political leanings can produce divergent judgments on Fascism does not diminish the epistemological validity of that research. Nor does this mean that anything goes—that we must bow down to postmodern relativism, embrace historical research as a form of political advocacy, or, conversely, that we must assume that our interpretations have realist-ontological value in order to be truthful.

The unbearable fuzziness of "fascism" is the sign of both the aporetic structure of its semantic markers and of the compound nature of transwar counterrevolutionary authoritarianisms. It also reflects the conflicting interpretations of historians and political scientists since 1945. The contradictions of "fascism" are inherent in the structure of its semantic compound and cannot simply be erased or disregarded by individual historians. Independently of their epistemological and political intentions, the generic use of "fascism" as a universal and ahistorical ideal type (e.g., in the cases of the Comintern orthodoxy and the scholarship of the fascist minimum) has reifying effects that flatten out the different forms of ultraconservative authoritarianism, their specific ontogenesis, and their imbrications with preexisting social, political, and economic institutions. Paradoxically, it hinders the heuristic possibility of a comparative and transnational study of different forms of coeval authoritarianism: Its epistemological (and political) advantages are immediately erased by the disadvantages of its undefined and unrestricted use.

Conclusions

On the Advantages and Disadvantages of "Fascism," Again

> Die Sprache ist so alt wie das Bewußtsein—die Sprache ist das praktische . . . Bewußtsein. [Language is as old as consciousness—language is practical consciousness.]
>
> KARL MARX AND FRIEDRICH ENGELS, *Die deutsche Ideologie*

This study has reconstructed the historical formation, consolidation, transformation, and obsolescence of some of the most important semantic markers of the term "fascism" as well as of the rules and habits for its disambiguation and use by different historical agents (from Mussolini to postwar historians and political scientists) in different texts, semiotic contexts, and historical circumstances. "Fascism" refers to a political form the meaning of which has expanded since its early use in 1920, producing contradictory semantic markers that encompass denotations and connotations pertinent to (1) Mussolini's regime properly, (2) a variously conceived ensemble of counterrevolutionary authoritarianisms around the world in the interwar period, and, with contested legitimacy, (3) a generic ideal type of political ideology and praxis.

To close the hermeneutic circle, I must address one last time the questions that opened this historical-semiotic investigation. What are the heuristic affordances of "fascism"? Can it operate as a *principium individuationis* of seemingly distinct political phenomena, like "democracy," "socialism," liberalism," and "communism"? What are the epistemological conditions necessary for it to function as a generic concept that legitimately and authoritatively collects under the same rubric regimes that have sociohistorically distinct genesis, on the assumption that they share some essential common characteristics?

Advantages and Disadvantages

Despite the fact that "fascism" has a long history of legitimate use as a heuristic category in the works of historians, social and political scientists, and philosophers, it seems nonetheless condemned to an irresolvable epistemological inconsistency and interpretive fuzziness. I have argued that these heuristic uncertainties derive in part from the historical unfolding of the counterrevolutionary authoritarianisms of the interwar period that it purports to identify; in part from the historical vicissitudes of the semantic markers of the term "fascism" itself; and in part from the irreconcilable contradictions of different interpretations of fascism in the work of historians and political theorists since 1945.

With appropriate adjustments, Italian Fascism and German National Socialism, the two most important forms of authoritarianism that the signifier "fascism" is asked to signify, developed institutions, politicoeconomic forms of governance, practices, and ideologies that fed off preexisting liberal democratic ones, while adopting, in obverse form, organizational strategies, such as paramilitary groups, totalitarian conceptions of the state, and the like from Bolshevik Russia. Despite various attempts to define it as a third way, an alternative to both liberalism and socialism, fascist activists and ideologues could not describe it theoretically nor transform its praxis into a political form that did not parasitize the preexisting ones.

The fuzziness of the denotative and connotative markers of "fascism" does not only mirror the historical indeterminacy of counterrevolutionary authoritarianisms and the oppositional definitions of fascist and antifascist commentators in the interwar period. It is also reproduced in the post-1945 scholarship on fascism. Conservative liberals saw in fascism a momentary descent into irrationalism that, in reaction to or alignment with the Bolshevik Revolution, negated the ideals and forms of liberal capitalism. Progressive liberals saw in it a form of autocratic ultranationalism that emerged in politically immature societies as the combined effect of the First World War and the economic crisis. For Marxists, it was the counterrevolutionary, dictatorial response of a monopolistically oriented capitalist class, engaged in a complicated alliance with the petty bourgeoise in the name of national prosperity against the emancipatory claims of the working classes, in a global context of economic crisis.[1]

Fuzziness, inconsistency, and contradictoriness are not ideal ingredients for any cognitive endeavor. Yet, the fact that the signifier "fascism" has been used for more than a century as a generic term for interwar forms of mass-based counterrevolutionary authoritarianism cannot be dismissed. Indeed, historical semantics demonstrates that the rise and fall of words, concepts, and denotative-connotative markers are never ultimately the effect of individuals, but of the linguistic practices of the entire community. No matter how well intended, any sort of censorial dogmatism seems to me preposterous and futile, especially today, when the authority of academia seems to be lost in the deafening noise of post-truth.

Nonetheless, I think that, in light of the political indeterminacy of the regimes it intends to identify, of the fuzziness of its semantic markers, and of the interpretive nature of historical knowledge itself, the generic use of "fascism" as heuristic category *cannot be conceived except in terms of the cognitive advantages and disadvantages it affords*. On the one hand, if not used as a universal ideal type, it may favor comparative and transnational analyses that can shed light on analogous sociopolitical ontogenesis as well as similarities *and* dissimilarities in strategies, organizations, and ideological constructs. Despite Samuel Moyn's hesitations, it seems to me that when performed in unambiguously comparative terms—and thus making explicit the interpretive labor that the proposed comparison implements in different historical contexts—it may be advantageous for the generation of new and creative perspectives on the interwar period, and maybe even on today's predicament.[2] On the other hand, the reifying effects of its determinist and reductionist genericizations—and I refer here to the most formulaic cases, such as Stalinist orthodoxy and the literature of the fascist minimum examined in chapters 9 and 11, as well as to its uncritical use in the most recent scholarship on global fascism—may lead to falsifications that veil or obscure the specificity of certain authoritarian forms, especially in historical contexts outside Europe and beyond the transwar period of 1914–45. In other words, I accept its generic use as antonomasia but cannot endorse its use as synecdoche. The debate on "fascism" may, in fact, be a distraction hindering recognition of how new forms of authoritarianism find nourishment within today's neoliberal world order.

My modest proposal is that, rather than surrender to disciplinary inertia, institutional dogmatism, and factional doctrinairism, and rather than bend one's analyses to political or ideological convenience, we employ "fascism" explicitly as a heuristic device by following two guiding rules: "pertinency," that is, arguing for its relevance in the context under investigation; and "parsimony," that is, discouraging its use when not heuristically necessary or advantageous.[3] The pragmatic recommendation for pertinency and parsimony in the use of generic "fascism" skirts the unbearable fuzziness of "fascism" and its contradictory meanings.

For instance, the case of wartime Japan suggests—to me, at least—that the qualification of that regime as "fascist" does not add much to our knowledge of a nation-empire that was legally and institutionally authoritarian from its inception; it actually implies a sudden authoritarian transformation of those institutions that falsifies the history of Japanese modernization, the capitalism of which developed along corporatist lines and was characterized by a promiscuous imbrication of public and private as well as civilian and military interests. Moreover, transnational and comparative analyses seem to me heuristically more efficacious than a generic "global fascism" to emphasize how the clash of competing imperialist interests, the worldwide effects of the economic crisis of the early 1930s, and total war favored the emergence and affirmation of different sorts of counterrevolutionary authoritarianisms to fend off the emancipatory claims of the working classes or to support radical forms of nationalism. The use of "fascism" may well be advantageous to point out similarities between different regimes in the 1930s—for instance, in its localized use to highlight parallel developments in labor relations, bureaucratic organization, or corporate strategies. I wonder, however, whether an enlargement of the comparison to include nonfascist regimes would not reveal similar tendencies in labor relations, propaganda, and the organization of the home front across the world and even among the Allies, which would render the use of "fascism" heuristically superfluous if not misguiding.

If the reductionism of the Stalinist definition distinguished fascist regimes from liberal ones only in quantitative rather than qualitative terms, an equally pernicious effect of using "fascism" as an ideal type along the model of the fascist minimum is the severance of its link with liberal institutions and capitalist interests. As abstract and universal ideal type such as "democracy," "socialism," "communism," and the like, "fascism" reinforces the idea that counterrevolutionary authoritarianisms such as Mussolini's and Hitler's developed outside of and in opposition to established liberal democracies, whereas the history of their rise to power showed strong support of and considerable connections with political and economic elites until their demise.

Fascism was not an invading pathogen but a neoplastic condition that developed *within* capitalist liberalism. Thus, new forms of authoritarianisms may well develop today within our own politicoeconomic institutions without assuming the recognizable form of interwar Fascism or Nazism. This approach to fascism might prove interpretively felicitous to understand how democratic ideals could be perverted to support new forms of authoritarianism, thus dispelling, as Philippe Lacoue-Labarthe and Jean-Luc Nancy have argued, the "comfortable security in the certitudes of morality and of democracy," which, however, "not only guarantees nothing, but exposes one to the risk of not seeing the arrival, or the return, of that whose possibility is not due to any simple accident of history."[4]

A New Semiotic Guerrilla

This investigation into the history of the word "fascism" and its changing meanings had the further aim of showing the degree to which social life is defined by the semiotic systems that mediate individuals' cognitive, affective, political, and ethical judgments.[5] As a "primary modeling system," language constitutes a meta-model for the development of other regulative structures to which both power and knowledge adhere.[6] Italian Fascism and German National Socialism paid particular attention to policing language, for them central to the formation of the "new man" as much as to organize consensus.[7] I do not believe that we are less vulnerable, today, from the spell of language than in the interwar period.

The ability to understand the signifying effects of words, concepts, and signs in general, especially those that play a normative role in defining individuals' choices, trajectories, and modes of sociability, is as important to encouraging citizens' agency as is the satisfaction of basic material needs. If social media—privately owned, structurally unequal, and ideologically skewed—have become the new space for political confrontation (a new "public sphere" that is, sadly, not public at all), and if the voices of public intellectuals and academics have lost much of their social leverage in today's post-truth era, scholars should be careful to promote their research in styles, language, and rhetoric analogous to the forces that regulate that space.[8] I believe that favoring legibility and smooth narratives, even when these are sustained by rigorous (but often invisible) research, will not be enough to protect scholarship from its complete submission to the flattening logic of the market. Defending the importance of truth procedures requires that scholars disclose their empirical and theoretical labor of interpretation (e.g., their mode of employment of the heuristic category "fascism"), and in so doing offer readers some instruments for learning how it works.

On January 7, 1977, in his inaugural lecture at the Collège de France, Roland Barthes shocked the audience with the absurd claim that "language—the performance of a language system—is neither reactionary nor progressive; it is quite simply *fascist*; for *fascism* does not prevent speech, it compels speech."[9] His remark might have been a hyperbolic strategy to simply assert that "the sign is a follower, gregarious; in each sign sleeps that monster: a stereotype. I can speak only by picking up what *loiters* around in speech. Once I speak, these two categories unite in me; I am both master and slave. I am not content to repeat what has been said, to settle comfortably in the servitude of signs: I speak, I affirm, I assert *tellingly* what I repeat."[10] But if language, by modeling our experience of the world, is coextensive of power and therefore fascist, there is no escape from it at all. As Umberto Eco critically put it, "more than a *boutade*," Barthes's assertion was "an invitation to confusion. Because in that case fascism, being everywhere, in every situation of power, and in every language, since the beginning of time, would no longer be anywhere.

If the human condition is placed under the banner of fascism, everyone and no-one is a fascist."[11]

Eco admitted that "language is certainly coercive . . . , but its coerciveness does not depend on an individual decision, nor on a center from which all rules radiate; it is a social product, [and] it originates as a constrictive apparatus precisely because of everyone's consensus."[12] Like Barthes, he contended that, as a primary modeling system, language serves as a model for power insofar as it is "a model for those other semiotic systems which, in various cultures, establish themselves as devices of power and knowledge."[13] But this implies that within the semiotic system of language lies the possibility of resisting against its own coercive power.

Barthes, in truth, proposed a way out of language's totalitarianism, which was "to cheat with speech, to cheat speech. This salutary trickery, this evasion, this grand imposture which allows us to understand speech *outside the bounds of power* in the splendor of a permanent revolution of language, I for one call *literature*."[14] But this implies, inevitably, that only the poets have a chance to escape from the spell of language.

Eco, on the other hand, proposed a form of active resistance he called "semiotic guerrilla."[15] It consisted of developing new, creative, and even aberrant interpretations of political or informational statements, the scope of which was to reveal the ideological labor of language. That made sense in the Italian context of the 1970s, where the then "new media" (radio and television) were firmly under the control of the leading political parties. In today's world, however, deafened by the ceaseless noise of excessive information, a new sort of semiotic guerrilla might be necessary, premised, like Eco's, on revealing how signification works, how it is the result of social labor, and how meaning is never natural, despite all attempts at naturalizing it.[16]

A new semiotic guerrilla would be grounded on the notion that "the labor of sign production releases social forces and itself represents a social force. It can produce both ideologies and criticism of ideologies. Thus semiotics (in its double guise as a theory of codes and a theory of sign production) is also a form of *social criticism*, and therefore one among the many forms of *social practice*."[17] That is, only by disclosing to readers how signification works, how it is produced, how it becomes conventionalized, how ideology always attempts to restrict it or naturalize it, and how it contributes to create and maintain societies—in short, how language, as Karl Marx put it in *The German Ideology*, is "practical consciousness"—can the spell of language be resisted.

Accordingly, the procedure I followed in my historical reconstruction of the semiosis of "fascism" is similar to reverse engineering, a breaking apart of this meaning-making device in order to understand how its semiosic function works. At the root of this word was a political form that resulted from the aftermath of the Great War of 1914–18 and developed into a violent and totalitarian regime that claimed to be both the response of the democratic demands of the Italian population and its destiny as the governmental form of the nation-empire. It defined itself as an antipolitical political force that was equally opposed to socialism (and communism) and liberalism (and capitalism). It pursued a sociopolitical revolution that in truth was only a simulacrum that reinforced preexisting social hierarchies, divisions, and systems of domination and ownership, and that reconfigured the democratic ideal of sovereignty in an ostensibly unmediated communion between the masses and the state through its leader. Like other forms of counterrevolutionary authoritarianism, Fascism was an instantiation of participation that offered Italians a semblance of agency that was opposed to the passivity and sense of impotence conveyed by the mediateness at the core of representative politics (especially the top-down liberalism of Giolitti's Destra Storica). But its ideological traction was grounded on a liturgical mise-en-scène that afforded only a pantomime of agency and a simulacrum of participation. It was, in short, a perversion of preexisting liberal democratic institutions and ideas with the aim of preserving the status quo, which was threatened by war and economic crisis.

A history of "fascism" is ultimately an exercise in understanding political ideology in action in terms of a meaning-making apparatus, which operates contemporaneously in a multiplicity of semiotic systems (linguistic, visual, auditory, corporeal, ritual, practical, etc.). The emancipatory potential of language lies in the unveiling of the different processes of meaning-making and the social practices they elicit. Scholars' role, today, is to help all to take care of semiosis and its proper functioning (the goal of a new semiotic guerrilla): to care for its capacity for truth-telling as well its polysemic potential, universal accessibility, and effects in society and the world. This exploration of the historical conditions of meaning-making in the political discourse of fascism (as well as in the scholarly analyses of that discourse) will ultimately be useful if it helps the reader to realize that the means of linguistic production must ultimately be collectively owned by all.

Acknowledgments

A small army of friends, mentors, and colleagues helped me as accomplices, critics, and inspiration. I jokingly admit that the sheer amount of sources and archival competences I needed to acquire to pursue this project is tantamount to getting a second PhD, though without exams and certifications, the completion of which would not have been possible without the help of these guides.

I start by thanking the institutions that funded this project in different stages: Princeton's Institute for Advanced Studies, where I began to conceive of this "bad idea" while enjoying enriching conversations during unforgettably long and delicious lunches with the colleagues of the School of Historical Studies, then directed by Nicola di Cosmo; and the University Center for Human Values, the University Committee on Research in the Humanities and Social Sciences, and the Department of East Asian Studies of Princeton University for awarding me grants that allowed me to visit archives in Europe and Asia. An army of really kind people helped me navigate the labyrinthine secrets of different archives in Rome, Milan, Venice, Treviso, Bologna, Florence, Salò, and Turin, as well as in Paris, Berlin, Washington, DC, and Tokyo. It was an endless source of amusement for me that I learned to use Italian archives only after I became an expat.

Friends and colleagues invited me to present my project in different venues and to different audiences. At Princeton, the Department of History's Works in Progress series and Shelby Cullom Davis Center Seminars; the Department of East Asian Studies' Weekly Lunch Colloquium; the Behrman Faculty Fellows lunch lectures; the Department of Politics workshop on fascism, organized by Martin Conway and Jan-Werner Mueller; the Society of Fellows; and the Global History Lab in Berlin. Thanks also to Laura Cerasi at the Università Ca' Foscari di Venezia; to Michael Bourdaghs at the University of Chicago; to Joshua Seufert and Fabio Lanza at the University of Arizona, in

Tucson; to Sonia Favi and Rosa Caroli at the Università di Torino; and to Zvi Ben-Dor Benite and Stephanos Geroulanos for inviting me to the Remarque Institute annual workshop in Switzerland. My sincerest gratitude goes to the graduate students of my 2018 seminar "Fascism": A Global History (HIS541) and to the students I tormented with my obsession for historiography and the philosophy of history in my version of the introductory seminar HIS 500, which I taught in the fall semesters of 2018, 2019, and 2020 with Yaacob Dweck, Rosina A. Lozano, and Erika L. Milam.

It has been thanks to conversations with so many inspirational friends and colleagues, including some who were (and probably still are) skeptical about this project, which breaches the sacred rule of disciplinary divisions, that I persevered in it. Shel Garon was the first who enthusiastically encouraged me to pursue this "bad idea"; along with Jeremy Adelman, he lured me to inconstant attendance in discussions on global and transnational history, the effects of which are clearly apparent in this study. My Department of East Asian Studies chairs, Anna M. Shields and Martin Kern, were supportive of this project both in their institutional role and as dear friends; and so were my Department of History chairs, Angela N. H. Creager and Keith A. Wailoo. At Princeton I must also thank for their suggestions, critiques, and support, in alphabetical order: David A. Bell, He Bian, D. Graham Burnett, Andrea Capra, Jonathon Catlin, Linda Colley, Tom Conlan, Zahid Daudjee, Phil Decker, Joseph Fronczak, Filippo Gradi, Tony Grafton, Dirk Hartog, Joseph Henares, Harold James, Matthew Jones, Paize Keulemans, Michael Laffan, Melissa Lane, Nino Luraghi, Gaetana Marrone-Puglia, Alison McManus, Phil Nord, Andy Rabinbach, Christy Wampole, Natasha Wheatley, and Trenton Wilson.

While working on this project, I was very fortunate to enjoy the inspiring guidance of mentors and friends, with whom I engaged in conversations on fascism, the philosophy of history, and semiotics. Without them, this book could never have been written. My gratitude goes to my friend Fabio Lanza, my personal Virgil of US academia since 2001, and to Stefanos Geroulanos, Helge Jordheim, Ethan Kleinberg, Gary Shaw, Dagmar Herzog, Massimiliano Tomba, Simon Levis Sullam, Valentina Pisanty, Anna Maria Lorusso, Victoria De Grazia, Nadia Urbinati, Ruth Ben-Ghiat, Robert Stolz, Alessandra Tarquini, Enzo Traverso, and Carlo Ginzburg. The invaluable suggestions of the three anonymous peer reviewers have helped me turn this long manuscript into a readable book. Dylan Montanari, my editor at the University of Chicago Press, has been the best any writer can hope to meet. My thanks to Barbara Norton for polishing my prose, to Malcolm Thompson for indexing this book (and for the many laughs on Facebook), and to all the editorial and marketing staff of Chicago.

This project is for me a sort of love letter to Italy, the country where I was born and raised, the modern history of which is a constant source of marvel, hope, and despair.

Special thanks to my family, Elisa, Sofia, and Leo, for enduring my political rantings and philosophical obsessions; to my parents, Giuseppe and Serafina, for having believed in me and supported my crazy idea of becoming an academic; and to my mother-in-law, Piera.

I dedicate this book, with gratitude and love, to the two teachers who helped me become the scholar that I am: Carol Gluck and Massimo Raveri.

Notes

Book Epigraphs

Eco, *The Name of the Rose*, trans. William Weaver. Unless explicitly stated otherwise, all translations are mine.

Preface

Epigraph: Freire, *Pedagogy of the Oppressed*, trans. Myra Bergman.

1. Friedrich Nietzsche, *Untimely Meditations*, trans. R. J. Hollingdale (Cambridge: Cambridge University Press, 1997).

2. I am skeptical of presentism, even when it is defended with such sophistication in François Hartog's works, but I endorse the project of a history of the present, an example of which is Stefanos Geroulanos, *Transparency in Postwar France: A Critical History of the Present* (Stanford, CA: Stanford University Press, 2017).

3. For an argument against the historiographical claims of unmediatedness, see Ethan Kleinberg, *Haunting History: For a Deconstructive Approach to the Past* (Stanford, CA: Stanford University Press, 2017).

4. Still pertinent in this regard are the reflections of Gayatri C. Spivak, "Can the Subaltern Speak?," in *Marxism and the Interpretation of Culture*, ed. Cary Nelson and Lawrence Grossberg (Urbana: University of Illinois Press, 1988), 271–313.

5. Roland Barthes, *Mythologies*, trans. Annette Lavers (New York: Hill & Wang, 1972), 217–74.

6. Ferruccio Rossi-Landi, *Language as Work and Trade: A Semiotic Homology for Linguistics and Economics*, trans. Martha Adams et al. (South Hadley, MA: Bergin & Garvey, 1983).

Introduction

1. This book distinguishes graphically when the term is used as signifier ("fascism" standing for "the word 'fascism' "), when it refers as proper name to Mussolini's regime (Fascism), and when it refers to a generic concept (fascism).

2. *OED Online*, s.v. "fascism, n.," accessed June 15, 2022, https://www.oed.com/dictionary/fascism_n?tab=meaning_and_use#4791876.

3. The description of Stalinism as "red fascism" appears in Franz Borkenau, *The Totalitarian Enemy* (London: Faber & Faber, 1940), and in Otto Rühle, "The Struggle against Fascism Begins with the Struggle against Bolshevism," *Living Marxism* 4, no. 8 (1939): 245–55. For a historical

overview, see Les K. Adler and Thomas G. Paterson, "Red Fascism: The Merger of Nazi Germany and Soviet Russia in the America Image of Totalitarianism, 1930s–1950s," *American Historical Review* 75, no. 4 (April 1970): 1046–64.

4. Gerald J. DeGroot, *The Sixties Unplugged: A Kaleidoscopic History of a Disorderly Decade* (Cambridge, MA: Harvard University Press, 2008); Michael Seidman, *The Imaginary Revolution: Parisian Students and Workers in 1968* (Oxford: Berghahn, 2004); and George Katsiaficas, *The Global Imagination of 1968: Revolution and Counterrevolution* (Oakland, CA: PM Press, 2018).

5. Ruth Blakeley, *State Terrorism and Neoliberalism: The North in the South* (London: Routledge, 2009).

6. Enzo Traverso, *The New Faces of Fascism: Populism and the Far Right* (New York: Verso, 2019).

7. The list of articles is extensive. A selection of impactful pieces would include Peter Baker, "Rise of Trump Tracks Debate over Fascism," *New York Times*, May 29, 2016, 1; Chauncey Devega, interview with Timothy Snyder, *Salon*, May 1, 2017, https://www.salon.com/2017/05/01/historian-timothy-snyder-its-pretty-much-inevitable-that-trump-will-try-to-stage-a-coup-and-overthrow-democracy/, accessed September 13, 2024; Samuel Moyn, "The Trouble with Comparisons," *New York Review of Books*, May 19, 2020, https://www.nybooks.com/daily/2020/05/19/the-trouble-with-comparisons/, accessed September 13, 2024; Jennifer Szalai, "The Debate over the Word 'Fascism' Takes a New Turn," *New York Times*, June 11, 2020, https://www.nytimes.com/2020/06/10/books/fascism-debate-donald-trump.html, accessed September 13, 2024; Spencer Bokat-Lindell, "Fascism: A Concern," *New York Times*, July 30, 2020, https://www.nytimes.com/2020/07/30/opinion/fascism-us.html, accessed September 13, 2024; Dylan Matthews, "The F Word," *Vox*, January 14, 2021, https://www.vox.com/22225472/fascism-definition-trump-fascist-examples, accessed September 13, 2024; Corey Robin, "A Show about Nothing," in Robin, *The Reactionary Mind: Conservatism from Edmund Burke to Donald Trump*, 2nd ed. (Oxford: Oxford University Press, 2018), 239–72; Ruth Ben-Ghiat, *Strongmen: Mussolini to the Present* (New York: W. W. Norton, 2020); and Daniel Bessner, "Does American Fascism Exist?," *The New Republic*, March 6, 2023, https://newrepublic.com/article/170890/does-american-fascism-exist?fbclid=IwAR3m_YCDUuk2R1bSBg8YkmEJanN0hYJZ01oUzgnwGhvzCGVjJ1ErYWoPJgI, accessed September 13, 2024. For an overview of the debate, see Udi Greenberg, "What Was the Fascism Debate?" *Dissent* (Summer 2021), https://www.dissentmagazine.org/article/what-was-the-fascism-debate, accessed September 13, 2024; Paul Nicholas Jackson, "Debate: Donald Trump and Fascism Studies," *Fascism: Journal of Comparative Fascist Studies* 10, no. 1 (2021): 1–15; and Dagmar Herzog and Stefanos Geroulanos, "Fascisms and Their Afterli(v)es: An Introduction," *Journal of the History of Ideas* 82, no. 1 (2021):73–83. For an anthology, see Daniel Steinmetz-Jenkins, ed., *Did It Happen Here? Perspectives on Fascism and America* (New York: W. W. Norton, 2024).

8. In an op-ed in the *New York Times*, the historian Timothy Snyder has claimed that fascism "is back—and this time the country fighting a fascist war of destruction is Russia. Should Russia win, fascists around the world will be comforted." Timothy Snyder, "We Should Say It. Russia Is Fascist," *New York Times*, May 19, 2022, https://www.nytimes.com/2022/05/19/opinion/russia-fascism-ukraine-putin.html, accessed September 13, 2024.

9. Palmiro Togliatti, "Le basi sociali del fascismo," contemporarily published in *L'internationale communiste* 7, no. 11 (May 1926): 426–33 and *Die Kommunistische Internationale* 7, no. 4 (1926): 28–38. Reprinted in Togliatti, *La politica nel pensiero e nell'azione*, ed. Michele Ciliberto and Giuseppe Vacca (Milan: Bompiani, 2014), 79.

10. Umberto Eco, "Ur-Fascism," in *Five Moral Pieces*, trans. Alastair McEwan (Orlando, FL: Harcourt, 2001), 72–73.

11. *The Guardian*, December 1, 2016, https://www.theguardian.com/us-news/2016/dec/01/comparing-fascism-donald-trump-historians-trumpism, accessed September 13, 2024.

12. Sonia Orwell and Ian Angus, eds., *The Collected Essays, Journalism and Letters of George Orwell*, vol. 4, *In Front of Your Nose, 1945–1950* (London: Secker & Warburg, 1968), 132.

13. In this book, unless explicitly qualified otherwise, the adjective "liberal" and the noun "liberalism" are used to signify adherence to classical liberalism, politically realized in different sorts of representational democratic regimes and supporting an economic order of private enterprise and more or less regulated market transactions. This usage, typical in Europe and Latin America, includes different political orientations ranging from leftist social democracy to rightist conservatism. This is different from the use in the United States, where liberalism typically refers to what elsewhere would be called left-liberalism. So, for example, Giovanni Giolitti's liberal party in the first quarter of the twentieth century should be understood as a conservative party; in its European sense, with the exception of the extreme fringes of the Republican Party, both Democrats and Republicans are considered liberals, the former center left and the latter center right. For a terminological guideline, see Hans Slomp, *Europe, a Political Profile: An American Companion to European Politics* (Santa Barbara, CA: ABC-Clio, 2011), 1:101–24.

14. Jan-Werner Müller, *What Is Populism?* (Philadelphia: University of Pennsylvania Press, 2016), and Enzo Traverso, *Le totalitarisme: Le XXe siècle en débat* (Paris: Éditions Points, 2001).

15. Gilbert Allardyce, "What Fascism Is Not: Thoughts on the Deflation of a Concept," *The American Historical Review* 84, no. 2 (1979): 368.

16. Other works on the word "fascism," of course, exist, but to the best of my knowledge, there is no book-length analysis of the historical development of its semantic markers. The conservative historian Paul Gottfried gave a somewhat revisionist introduction to Fascism by severing its equation with (and thus reduction to) Nazism in the literature of the "fascist minimum" on the basis of an intellectual history of Fascist ideology; see Gottfried, *Fascism: The Career of a Concept* (DeKalb: Northern Illinois University Press, 2015). Ernst Nolte also gave a partial semantic history of "fascism" in "Faschismus," in *Geschichtliche Grundbegriffe*, ed. Werner Conze, Otto Brunner, and Reinhart Koselleck (Stuttgart: Ernst Klett Verlag, 1975), 2:329–36.

17. The postwar development of neofascist and neo-Nazi movements is a distinct issue that this study deals with only in passing. These fringe groups of political extremism, active from the 1960s through the present, pledge fidelity to a conception of Fascism and Nazism that is highly abstract and ideological, a product of the postwar period. In that regard, three processes should be kept distinct: first, the survival of former Fascists and Nazis (bureaucrats, administrators, jurists, intellectuals, industrialists, et al.) in postwar Italy and Germany, thanks to pardons, leniency, and strategic choices of the Allied powers in the context of the ensuing Cold War; second, the survival of fascist themes and ideals in disguise, in post- and crypto-fascist political parties, the best example of which was the Italian Movimento Sociale Italiano (Italian Social Movement; MSI), founded by Giorgio Almirante, the former editor of the racist magazine *La difesa della razza*, on November 12, 1946, which became the fourth party during the First Republic, giving external support to Christian Democrat governments throughout the 1950s; third, new political movements, circles, or parties that explicitly associated themselves to the memory and ideals of Fascism and Nazism. For an overview, see Andrea Mammone, Emmanuel Godin, and Brian Jenkins, eds., *Mapping the Extreme Right in Contemporary Europe: From Local to Transnational* (London: Routledge, 2012); Andrea Mammone, Emmanuel Godin, and Brian Jenkins, eds.,

Varieties of Right-Wing Extremism in Europe (London: Routledge, 2013); and Jean-Yves Camus and Nicolas Lebourg, *Far-Right Politics in Europe*, trans. Jane Marie Todd (Cambridge, MA: Harvard University Press, 2017). See also Traverso, *The New Faces of Fascism*.

18. My main contention is that as *principium individuationis*, the scholarship of the "fascist minimum" uses "fascism" with the assumption that it operates at the ontological level, as their recognition or, more precisely, *individuation* of movements and regimes fulfilling the parameters of the presupposed definition of "fascism" has the purpose of revealing their true nature beyond their own self-presentation. My strategy of framing the analysis in terms of the heuristic advantages and disadvantages of "fascism" has instead the goal of proposing that it should at least operate *explicitly* at an epistemological rather than ontological level, emphasizing therefore the interpretive labor of historians and political theorists adopting it as an attribute or metaphorical descriptor.

19. Metonymy and synecdoche, here, are used not simply to express a rhetorical mode of presentation; rather, they reveal the different logics behind the two processes of genericization, the first of horizontal juxtaposition, the second of vertical implication and reduction. On the logico-epistemological function of rhetorical tropes, see Group μ, *A General Rhetoric*, trans. Paul B. Burrell and Edgar M. Slotkin (Baltimore, MD: Johns Hopkins University Press, 1981), 25–45; George Lakoff and Mark Johnson, *Metaphors We Live By* (Chicago: University of Chicago Press, 1980); and Anna Maria Lorusso, *La trama del testo: Problemi, analisi, prospettive semiotiche* (Milan: Bompiani, 2006).

20. A possible fifth genealogy, here disregarded, is constituted by the myriads of fringe movements of neofascists and neo-Nazis. They are not treated here because they each conceived of themselves as a return to an authentic form of Fascism—though in actuality an invention rather than a return, like all forms of purist primitivism. "Fascism" (and "Nazism") in these cases are not intended to be "generic" but are used by these groups as the proper name of historical Fascism (or National Socialism) that they aim to restore. See the two edited volumes of Mammone, Godin, and Jenkins, cited in n. 17 above. On neofascist and neo-Nazi groups in contemporary Italy, see Paolo Berizzi, *NazItalia: Viaggio in un paese che si è riscoperto fascista* (Milan: Baldini & Castoldi, 2018).

21. On the notion of "rigid designator," see Saul Kripke, *Naming and Necessity* (Cambridge, MA: Harvard University Press, 1980), and Joseph LaPorte, *Rigid Designation and Theoretical Identities* (Oxford: Oxford University Press, 2013). Kripke's conception of rigid designator is grounded on a hard ontology, whereby a proper name functions as rigid designator insofar as it rigidly (i.e., consistently, stably) refers to an entity in an extensional (or referential) sense when all its necessary attributes appear in all possible worlds. I here use the expression in a contractualist sense, implying a much weaker ontology, as defined in Umberto Eco, *Kant and the Platypus: Essays on Language and Cognition*, trans. Alastair McEwen (New York: Harcourt, 2000), 280–336. In the case of "fascism," the definition of which rests on necessary attributes that remain contractually contested, the term would produce a series of circular redundancies if conceived as a rigid designator in a Kripkean sense. Proper names are hence treated here, as Umberto Eco put it in *Sugli specchi e altri saggi* (Milan: Bompiani, 1985), 22, as *designator*[*i*] "*flosc*[*i*]" ("flaccid" designators), insofar as the identification of such necessary properties is itself historically constitutive of the cultural unit that the signifier "fascism" names, and thus regarding it as "rigid designator" in a Kripkean sense would inevitably lead to tautology.

22. This is certainly an oversimplification of a complex issue in political terminology. It is true that political ideals have historically showed a tendency to become indefinite or imprecise

in direct proportion to the multiplication of their particular instantiations. Ernesto Laclau famously described this phenomenon in terms of an emptying of signification, resulting from the failure of a political concept to give representational inclusivity to the ideas and people it aims to signify. "An empty signifier," he claimed, "can only emerge if there is a structural impossibility in signification as such, and only if this impossibility can signify itself as an interruption (subversion, distortion, etc.) of the structure of the sign"; Laclau, *Emancipation(s)* (London: Verso, 1996), 36. An important consequence of empty signifiers in political discourse occurs when the same signifier is called on to express dissimilar or even opposite meanings. "Democratic," for instance, can qualify regimes of liberal parliamentarism and either center-left or center-right political parties, but also communist regimes such as North Korea and the former East Germany. In the case of political representation, Laclau argued, "the non-transparency of the representative to the represented, the irreducible autonomy of the signifier vis-à-vis the signified, is the condition of a hegemony which structures the social from its very ground and is not the epiphenomenal expression of a transcendental signified which would submit the signifier to its own predetermined movements." In Judith Butler, Slavoj Žižek, and Ernesto Laclau, *Contingency, Hegemony, Universality: Contemporary Dialogues on the Left* (London: Springer, 2000), 66. The case of "democracy," the emptying of which allows a refilling of hegemonic meanings in particular sociohistorical situations that exclude social groups, conceptions, or forms of economic organization, is opposite, I suspect, to the case of "fascism," which, rather, than an "empty signifier" is one filled with an exorbitant excess of meaning, precisely because of its empty semantic core.

23. Federico Finchelstein, while willing to understand the relation between fascism and populism historically, assumes, rather than arguing, that fascism is a "globalized form of political ideology, like Marxism and liberalism"; Finchelstein, *From Fascism to Populism in History* (Oakland: University of California Press, 2017), 45.

24. See Orlando Figes and Boris Kolonitskii, *Interpreting the Russian Revolution: The Language and Symbols of 1917* (New Haven, CT: Yale University Press, 1999).

25. The notion of "semantic marker" is preferred to the common but unprecise "meaning" in order to emphasize the active process of meaning-making behind all semiosic practices. This approach has the advantage of avoiding presuppositions of the universality and naturality of meaning, and of emphasizing the *sociohistorical* nature of the processes of meaning-making (semiosis) itself. See Umberto Eco, *A Theory of Semiotics* (Bloomington: Indiana University Press, 1976).

26. Benito Mussolini, "La prima adunata fascista," *Il popolo d'Italia*, October 6, 1919, 6, reprinted in Edoardo and Duilio Susmel, *Opera omnia di Benito Mussolini*, vol. 14, *Dalla Marcia di Ronchi al secondo congress dei Fasci (14 settembre 1919–25 maggio 1919)* (Florence: La Fenice, 1954), 44. Hereafter the *Opera omnia di Benito Mussolini* will be abbreviated as OOBM, followed by the volume number, a colon, and the page number.

27. OOBM, 12:311.

28. Angelo Tasca, *Nascita e avvento del fascismo* (Rome: Laterza, 1965), 553.

29. Mussolini's quotes come from a public speech given on June 22, 1925 at the Mausoleum of Augustus, in Rome, at the end of the fourth national congress of the Partito Nazionale Fascista. The text of the speech was later published in *Il popolo d'Italia*, June 23, 1925, 12, and is reprinted in OOBM, 21:362.

30. B. A. Uspenskii, "Historia sub specie semioticae," *Soviet Studies in Literature* 12, no. 2 (1976): 53–64; Taras Boyko, "Describing the Past: Tartu-Moscow School Ideas on History, Historiography, and the Historian's Craft," *Sign Systems Studies* 43, nos. 2–3 (2015): 269–80; and

Valentina Pisanty, "L'alternativa nella storia," in "Re-Thinking Juri Lotman in the Twenty-First Century," ed. Laura Gherlone, Remo Gramigna, and Massimo Leone, special issue, *Lexia* 39–40 (2022): 231–44.

31. The expression was used in *La folla*, September 29, 1914, 3, reprinted in OOBM, 7:453.

32. George Lakoff, *Women, Fire, and Dangerous Things: What Categories Reveal about the Mind* (Chicago: University of Chicago Press, 1987); David Beaver and Jason Stanley, *The Politics of Language* (Princeton, NJ: Princeton University Press, 2023); Giovanna Cosenza, *Semiotica e comunicazione politica* (Rome: Laterza, 2018); and Laura Clemenzi, *Il discorso politico* (Florence: Franco Cesati, 2023).

33. Roland Barthes, *Writing Degree Zero*, trans. Annette Lavers and Colin Smith (New York: Hill & Wang, 1968), 25.

34. Mussolini first uttered that sentence in a speech he gave at the Costanzi Theatre in Rome on March 23, 1924, in the occasion of the fifth anniversary of the San Sepolcro meeting. The context was his insistence that the March on Rome ought to be understood as a "revolution." The full context is: "And why do I insist on proclaiming that the one in October was historically a revolution? Because words have their own tremendous magic, because it is grotesque to try and have people believe that it was merely a ministerial crisis." It would be later published in *Il popolo d'Italia*, March 25, 1924, 11, and is reprinted in OOBM, 20:207.

35. An analysis of the rhetorical structure of his oratorial performances suggests Mussolini's instinctual understanding and utilization of the six functions of language that Roman Jakobson would formalize only in the 1950s; see Roman Jakobson, "Linguistics and Poetics," in *Style in Language*, ed. Thomas A. Sebeok (New York: Wiley, 1960), 350–77. Jakobson called "conative" the use of language to trigger a response from the addressee; "phatic" expressions are instead used to establish a connection with the addressee, without any substantial communicative content. "Apophasis" is the rhetorical strategy of mentioning a topic by saying that one will not talk about it. "Metalingual expressions" occur when the speaker directs the addressee's attention to the language in use, such as when Mussolini explained that "words have a tremendous power."

36. Sergio Luzzatto, *L'immagine del duce: Mussolini nelle fotografie dell'Istituto Luce* (Rome: Editori Riuniti, 2001) and Luzzatto, *Il corpo del duce* (Turin: Einaudi, 1998).

37. Erasmo Leso, "Osservazioni sulla lingua di Mussolini," in *Credere, obbedire, combattere: Il regime linguistico nel Ventennio*, ed. Fabio Foresti (Bologna: Edizioni Pendragon), 83–126; and Leso, "Aspetti della lingua del fascismo: Prime line di una ricerca," in *Storia linguistica dell'Italia nel Novecento: Atti del quinto convegno internazionale di studi, Roma 1–2 giugno 1971*, ed. Maurizio Gnerre, Mario Medici, and Raffaele Simone (Rome: Bulzoni, 1973), 139–58.

38. For instance, Zeev Sternhell famously dated the birth of fascism to well before the rise of Mussolini's movements, which gave it only the name. See Sternhell, *The Birth of Fascist Ideology: From Cultural Rebellion to Political Revolution*, trans. David Maisel (Princeton, NJ: Princeton University Press, 1994), 3–35. "Revolutionary conservatism" is an expression that can be found in the writings of such authors as Georges Sorel, Hugo von Hofmannsthal, Edgar Julius Jung, Arthur Moeller van der Bruch, Michael Freund, and Walter Benjamin. See George L. Mosse, *The Corporate State and the Conservative Revolution in Weimar Germany* (Brussels: Éditions de la librairie encyclopédique, 1965); and Stefan Breuer, *Anatomie der konservativen Revolution* (Darmstadt: Wissenschaftliche Buchgesellschaft, 1993).

39. Traverso, *Le totalitarisme*, 22.

40. Exceptions are Renzo De Felice, *Il fascismo: Le interpretazioni dei contemporanei e degli storici* (Rome: Laterza, 1970); Emilio Gentile, *In Italia ai tempi di Mussolini: Viaggio in compagnia*

di osservatori stranieri (Milan: Mondadori, 2014); and Giulia Albanese, "Non solo propaganda: Il modello fascista all'estero (1922–35)," in *Il fascismo italiano: Storia e interpretazioni*, ed. Giulia Albanese (Rome: Carocci, 2021), 309–30.

41. Doris L. Bergen, "The Nazi Concept of 'Volksdeutsche' and the Exacerbation of Anti-Semitism in Eastern Europe, 1939–45," *Journal of Contemporary History* 29, no. 4 (1994): 569–82.

42. Adolf Hitler, *Mein Kampf: Zwei Bände in einem Band, ungekürzte Ausgabe* (Munich: Zentralverlag der NSDAP, 1943), 774.

43. See Renzo De Felice, *Mussolini e Hitler: I rapporti segreti, 1922–1933; Con documenti inediti* (Florence: Le Monnier, 1975); Monica Fioravanzo, *Mussolini e Hitler: La Repubblica sociale e il Terzo Reich* (Rome: Donzelli, 2009); Pierre Milza, *Conversations Hitler-Mussolini* (Paris: Librairie Arthème Fayard, 2013); and Christian Goeschel, *Mussolini and Hitler: The Forging of the Fascist Alliance* (New Haven, CT: Yale University Press, 2018).

44. The notion of diplomacy as theater comes from Naoko Shimazu, "Diplomacy as Theatre: Staging the Bandung Conference of 1955," *Modern Asian Studies* 48 (2014): 225–52. See also Goeschel, *Mussolini and Hitler*, 11–16.

45. Richard Overy, *Blood and Ruins: The Last Imperial War, 1931–1945* (London: Viking, 2022), xix and 32–124.

46. Antonio Gibelli, *L'officina della guerra: La grande guerra e le trasformazioni del mondo mentale* (Turin: Bollati Boringhieri, 1991). This is not a claim that the First World War was the *first* "total war" in the chronological sense, but rather that it was the first to be fought as a total war on such a scale. See also David A. Bell, *The First Total War: Napoleon's Europe and the Birth of Warfare as We Know It* (Boston: Mariner Books, 2008).

47. In Carl Schmitt, *The Nomos of the Earth in the International Law of the "Jus Publicum Europaeum,"* trans. G. L. Ulmen (New York: Telos Press, 2003), esp. 142–43 and 165–68.

48. Enzo Traverso, *Fire and Blood: The European Civil War, 1914–1945*, trans. David Fernbach (London: Verso, 2017), 65. Traverso argues that the legal-philosophical discourse on war in the interwar period reflected this state of affairs: the notion of the law of war (*jus in bello*), or acceptable conduct in wartime—which traditionally derived, according to the Geneva and Hague Conventions, from a more general and conditional right to war (*jus ad bellum*), or acceptable reasons to engage in war—gave way to the idea of a war of extermination (*bellum internecinum*) reminiscent of the Hobbesian war of all against all (*bellum omnium contra omnes*) and was conceived of as peculiar to civil wars (*Bürgerkrieg*). See ibid., 64–100.

49. Jörn Leonhard, *Pandora's Box: A History of the First World War*, trans. Patrick Camiller (Cambridge, MA: Harvard University Press, 2018), 892.

50. This is a reversal of Carl von Clausewitz's famous motto "War is a mere continuation of policy by other means"; see Clausewitz, *On War*, trans. J. J. Graham (London: Kegan Paul, Trench, Trubner, 1918), 1:24.

51. Mark Mazower, *Dark Continent: Europe's Twentieth Century* (London: Penguin: 1998), 3–40.

52. The conception of the Second World War as a conflict of different forms of imperialism, formerly sustained by Marxist theorists such as Ernest Mandel, as in, for instance, his *The Meaning of the Second World War* (London: Verso, 1986), has reappeared in recent transnational studies of the war, among them Overy, *Blood and Ruins*.

53. For a critical view, see Philip M. H. Bell, *The Origins of the Second World War in Europe* (London: Longman, 1986), 15–33; and the classic work by A. J. P. Taylor, *The Origins of the Second World War* (New York: Atheneum, 1964).

54. Winston Churchill, *The Second World War*, vol. 1 (Boston: Houghton Mifflin, 1948); Ian Kershaw, "Europe's Second Thirty Years War," *History Today* 55, no. 9 (2005): 10–17; Arno Mayer, *Why Did the Heavens Not Darken? The "Final Solution" in History* (New York: Pantheon Books, 1988), esp. xiv; Dan Diner, *Cataclysms: A History of the Twentieth Century from Europe's Edge*, trans. William Templer and Joel Golb (Madison: University of Wisconsin Press, 2008); Johann Chapoutot, *Fascisme, nazisme et régimes autoritaires en Europe (1918–1945)* (Paris: Presses Universitaires de France, 2013); and Traverso, *Fire and Blood*.

55. Overy, *Blood and Ruins*, 2–31.

56. On state violence during the *biennio rosso*, see Giuseppe Maione, *Il biennio rosso: Autonomia e spontaneità operaia nel 1919–1920* (Bologna: Il Mulino, 1975); Fabio Fabbri, *Le origini della guerra civile: L'Italia dalla Grande Guerra al fascismo, 1918–1921* (Turin: UTET, 2009); and John Foot, *Blood and Power: The Rise and Fall of Italian Fascism* (London: Bloomsbury, 2022). On the Fascist Squadristi, see Mimmo Franzinelli, *Squadristi: Protagonisti e tecniche della violenza fascista, 1919–1922* (Milan: Mondadori, 2003). Sven Reichardt, *Faschistische Kampfbünde: Gewalt und Gemeinschaft im Italienischen Squadrismus und in der deutschen SA* (Cologne: Böhlau, 2002), compares the Italian Squadristi and the German Freikorps. See also Geoff Eley, "Conservatives and Radical Nationalists in Germany: The Production of Fascist Potential, 1912–28," in *Fascists and Conservatives: The Radical Right and the Establishment in Twentieth-Century Europe*, ed. Martin Blinkhorn (New York: Routledge, 1990), 50–70; and Mimmo Cangiano, *Cultura di destra e società di massa: Europa, 1870–1939* (Rome: Nottetempo, 2022).

57. OOBM, 19:413.

58. Emilio Gentile, *Le origini dell'ideologia fascista, 1918–1925* (Bologna: Il Mulino, 2011), 153–90. See also Joanna Bourke, ed., *War and Art: A Visual History of Modern Conflict* (London: Reaktion, 2017). For a comparative view of Japanese artists and war, see Asato Ikeda, *The Politics of Painting: Fascism and Japanese Art During the Second World War* (Honolulu: University of Hawai'i Press, 2018).

59. See Jeffrey Herf, *Reactionary Modernism: Technology, Culture, and the Politics in Weimar and the Third Reich* (Cambridge: Cambridge University Press, 1984); and Enzo Traverso, *The Origins of Nazi Violence*, trans. Janet Lloyd (New York: New Press, 2001).

60. On "system of signification," see Eco, *A Theory of Semiotics*, 32–47; and Patrizia Violi, *Meaning and Experience*, trans. Jeremy Carden (Bloomington: Indiana University Press, 2001), 141–241.

61. I here take an opposite stance to Bruno Latour in "Why Has Critique Run out of Steam? From Matters of Fact to Matters of Concern," *Critical Inquiry* 30, no. 2 (2004): 225–48.

62. *Pace* Peter Novick, *That Noble Dream: The "Objectivity Question" and the American Historical Profession* (Cambridge: Cambridge University Press, 1988).

63. As in François Hartog, *Régimes d'historicité: Présentisme et expériences du temps* (Paris: Le Seuil, 2003).

64. Carlo Ginzburg, *History, Rhetoric, and Proof: The Menahem Stern Jerusalem Lectures* (Hanover, NH: University Press of New England, 1999), 37–38. For a response, see Hayden White, *Figural Realism: Studies in the Mimesis Effect* (Baltimore, MD: Johns Hopkins University Press, 1999), 1–42.

65. Roland Barthes, "From History to Reality," in Barthes, *The Rustle of Language*, trans. Richard Howard (Berkeley: University of California Press, 1989), 127–54.

66. As Hilary Putnam elegantly put it, "The mind and the world jointly make up the mind and the world"; Putnam, *Reason, Truth, and History* (Cambridge: Cambridge University Press, 1981), xi.

67. For a philosophical analysis of the epistemological premises of a distinction of "subject" and "object," see Theodor W. Adorno, "On Subject and Object," in *Critical Models: Interventions and Catchwords*, trans Henry W. Pickford (New York: Columbia University Press, 1998), 245–58.

68. Mark Bevir, "What is Genealogy?," *Journal of the Philosophy of History* 2, no. 3 (2008): 263–75.

69. Reinhart Koselleck, *Begriffsgeschichten: Studien zur Semantik und Pragmatik der politischen und sozialen Sprache* (Frankfurt am Main: Suhrkamp, 2006).

70. Quentin Skinner, "Meaning and Understanding in the History of Ideas," *History and Theory* 8, no. 1 (1969): 3–53.

71. Pierre Bourdieu, *Outline of a Theory of Practice*, trans. Richard Nice (Cambridge: Cambridge University Press, 1977).

72. Umberto Eco developed his methodology in *A Theory of Semiotics* and further refined it in *The Role of the Reader: Explorations in the Semiotics of Texts* (Bloomington: Indiana University Press, 1979), *Semiotics and Philosophy of Language* (Bloomington: Indiana University Press, 1984), and *Kant and the Platypus*. See also Valentina Pisanty and Roberto Pellerey, *Semiotica e interpretazione* (Milan: Bompiani, 2004), and Claudio Paolucci, ed., *Studi di semiotica interpretativa* (Milan: Bompiani, 2007).

73. These four points distinguish the sort of semiotic history I pursue here from any semantic history that postulates meaning as based on referential iconicity, on universals, or on nature. In other words, it directly tackles a question largely disregarded in traditional *Begriffsgeschichte* (whereby historians register variations in meanings in texts from different epochs), intellectual history (which describes the use of terms in individual thinkers, schools, and texts), and Foucauldian archaeology (whereby an ontologically ambiguous episteme is the condition for the structuring of meaning across disciplines).

74. Eco adopted the expression "cultural unit" from David M. Schneider, who defined it as "simply anything that is culturally defined and distinguished as an entity"; Schneider, *American Kinship: A Cultural Account* (New York: Prentice-Hall, 1968), 2.

75. Eco, *A Theory of Semiotics*, 29.

76. Eco's essay "Ur-Fascism" can be regarded as a precursor of the genre. Among the bestsellers, see Timothy Snyder, *On Tyranny: Twenty Lessons from the Twentieth Century* (New York: Crown, 2017); Jason Stanley, *How Fascism Works: The Politics of Us and Them* (New York: Random House, 2018); and Madeleine Albright, *Fascism: A Warning* (New York: Harper Perennial, 2018).

77. In Theodor W. Adorno, "Resignation," trans. Wes Blomster, *Telos* 35 (March 1978): 168.

78. Ibid.

79. Umberto Eco, *The Name of the Rose*, trans. William Weaver (New York: Harcourt Brace Jovanovich, 1983), 205.

80. Dylan Riley, *The Civic Foundations of Fascism in Europe: Italy, Spain, and Romania, 1870–1945*, 2nd ed. (London: Verso, 2019), 3.

81. OOBM, 19:43–45.

82. OOBM, 12:311.

83. Nadia Urbinati, "A Revolt against Intermediary Bodies," *Constellations* 22, no. 4 (2015): 477–86.

84. Alessandro Mulieri, *Democrazia totalitaria: Una storia controversa del governo popolare* (Rome: Donzelli, 2019).

Part I Introduction

1. A "cultural unit" is that abstract entity that, by virtue of historically specific conventions, organizes the intensional (semantic) value of a term, which takes the form of an ever-expanding encyclopedia entry; consequently, the "object" it refers to extensionally (referent) is "not necessarily a thing or a state of the world," but rather "a rule, a law, a prescription" that regulates the interpretation of the sign referring to a certain state of the world on the basis of the interpretive habits and possibilities given by the cultural unit within the semantic encyclopedia of a historical society. See Umberto Eco, *Lector in fabula: La cooperazione interpretativa nei testi narrativi* (Milan: Bompiani, 1993), 29.

Chapter One

1. Emilio Bodrero, "La terminologia politica," *Lingua nostra* 1, no. 1 (1939): 79–80.

2. *Enciclopedia italiana di scienze, lettere ed arti*, s.v. "fascismo," accessed September 15, 2024, http://www.treccani.it/vocabolario/fascismo.

3. Carlo Battisti and Giovanni Alessio, *Dizionario etimologico italiano* (Florence: Barbèra, 1950). See also Erasmo Leso, "Storia di parole politiche: Fascista (fascio, fascismo)," *Lingua nostra* 32, no. 2 (1971): 54–55, and Paola Desideri, "Origini e sviluppo delle analisi e delle teorie sul linguaggio politico (1920–1960)," *Linguistica—Demetrio Skubic octogenario* 49, no. 2 (2009): 41–53.

4. The linguist Bruno Migliorini, who served as chief editor of the *Enciclopedia italiana* between 1930 and 1933, had incorrectly recorded the earliest uses of "fascista" in March 1918. Migliorini, *Saggi sulla lingua del Novecento* (Florence: Sansoni, 1963), 132.

5. The leading Italian newspaper *Il corriere della sera* records the use of the adjective "fascista" to identify members of the interventionist movement Fascio d'Azione Rivoluzionaria in articles dated May 3, 1915; July 8, 1915; and May 22, 1916. The archive of *Il corriere della sera* is available at https://archivio.corriere.it/Archivio/interface/landing.html, accessed September 15, 2024. Mussolini confirms this usage in his articles in *Il popolo d'Italia*, in particular those of January 24, January 31, February 22, February 23, February 28, March 12, April 6, April 9, April 13, April 15, and May 12 (all 1916). See OOBM, 7:141, 211, 219, 222–23, 250, 308, 317, 326, 333, 379, and 425. Renzo De Felice also records the same generic use in a document from the Ministry of War dated October 6, 1915, and in a police report dated December 2, 1917: see De Felice, *Mussolini il rivoluzionario, 1883–1920* (Turin: Einaudi, 1965), 319 and 355. It is worth remembering, however, that the adjective was not at the time used specifically or exclusively for the members of the Fascio d'Azione Rivoluzionaria.

6. In its figurative meaning, it can have connotations of a "burden," an "obligation," or an "encumbrance." For a complete definition, see the *Enciclopedia italiana di scienze, lettere ed arti*, s.v. "fascio," accessed September 15, 2024, http://www.treccani.it/vocabolario/fascio.

7. T. Corey Brennan, *The Fasces: A History of Ancient Rome's Most Dangerous Symbol* (Oxford: Oxford University Press, 2023), 1–108.

8. See, for instance, the illustrations of the Château de Fontainebleau in Louis Dimier, *Les grands palais de France, Fontainebleau, de la Renaissance a Louis XVI* (Paris: Éditions Albert Morance, 1921). See also Brennan, *The Fasces*, 109–35.

9. See the definition given for "Le faisceau de licteur" in the official website of the Élisée, https://www.elysee.fr/la-presidence/le-faisceau-de-licteur, accessed September 15, 2024. Brennan, *The Fasces*, 136–55.

10. Brennan, *The Fasces*, 156–77.

11. On the adoption of Roman symbolism during the Fascist regime, see Emilio Gentile, *Il culto del littorio: La sacralizzazione della politica nell'Italia fascista* (Rome: Laterza, 1993).

12. See *Il popolo d'Italia*, October 25, 1919, 1, where stylized *fasces* are presented as a symbol of unity and strength.

13. Mimmo Franzinelli, *Fascismo anno zero: 1919; La nascita dei Fasci italiani di combattimento* (Milan: Mondadori, 2019), 118–47. See also Angelo L. Pirocchi, *Italian Arditi: Elite Assault Troops, 1917–20* (Oxford: Osprey, 2004), 29–41.

14. Fausto Sparacino, *23 marzo 1919: Piazza San Sepolcro; Centenario della Fondazione a Milano dei Fasci italiani di combattimento* (Milan: Ritter, 2019), 41–66.

15. *Enciclopedia italiana di scienze, lettere ed arti*, s.v. "fascio," accessed on September 15, 2024, http://www.treccani.it/vocabolario/fascio.

16. Brennan, *The Fasces*, 178–79.

17. Ezio Mauro, *La dannazione: 1921; La sinistra divisa all'alba del fascismo* (Milan: Feltrinelli, 2022), 20.

18. Henryk Katz, *The Emancipation of Labor: A History of the First International, 1864–1872* (Westport, CT: Greenwood Press, 1992). On the Italian participation in the First International, see Pier Carlo Masini, *La Federazione Italiana dell'Associazione Internazionale dei Lavoratori: Atti ufficiali 1871–1880* (Milan: Edizioni Avanti!, 1963).

19. See Elio Conti, *Carte della Polizia nell'Archivio di Stato di Firenze, 1871–1898* (Milan: Quaderni di Movimento Operaio, 1953). See also Leso, "Storia di parole politiche," 58.

20. Paolo Favilli, *Storia del marxismo italiano: Dalle origini alla grande Guerra* (Milan: Angeli, 1996), 17–66.

21. Francesco Renda, *I fasci siciliani* (Turin: Einaudi, 1977).

22. For a longer list, see Sparacino, *23 marzo 1919*, 16–21.

23. OOBM, 6:222–25.

24. OOBM, 6:256.

25. OOBM, 6:393–403.

26. OOBM, 7:70–71.

27. Ibid.

28. OOBM, 7:45 and 57.

29. OOBM, 7:64.

30. Emilio Gentile, *Fascismo: Storia e interpretazioni* (Rome: Laterza, 2002), 9; emphasis in the original.

31. See, e.g., Alexander De Grand, *Italian Fascism: Its Origins and Development*, 3rd ed. (Lincoln: University of Nebraska Press, 2000), 3–21.

32. A quick glance at vols. 7 and 8 of the *Opera omnia*, where Mussolini's writings from the year 1915 are collected, reveals that the term appears almost exclusively in expressions indicating membership in the Fasci d'Azione Rivoluzionaria. The term does not appear in Mussolini's writings between 1916 and 1919.

33. OOBM, 6:287–88.

34. De Felice, *Mussolini il rivoluzionario*, 277. On French and Belgian financial support, see ibid., 302–3. See also Roland Sarti, "Fascism and the Industrial Leadership in Italy before the March on Rome," *ILR Review* 21, no. 3 (1968): 400–417.

35. OOBM, 7:376–77.

36. OOBM, 34:3–115.

37. Mussolini was not able to actually meet D'Annunzio, the great inspiration of much of later Fascism's rhetoric and symbolism, until June 23, 1919, and then thanks only to the involvement of Mussolini's lover, the wealthy Jewish intellectual Margherita Sarfatti.

38. OOBM, 7:196.

39. OOBM, 7:197–98.

40. Ibid.

41. Francesco L. Galassi, "Italy at War, 1915–1918," in *The Economics of World War I*, ed. Stephen Broadberry and Mark Harrison (Cambridge: Cambridge University Press, 2005), 276–309.

42. Gaetano Salvemini, "Economic Conditions in Italy, 1919–1922," *Journal of Modern History* 23, no. 1 (1951): 29.

43. Angelo Ventrone, *Grande Guerra e Novecento: La storia che ha cambiato il mondo* (Rome: Donzelli, 2015), esp. chap. 5.

44. The myth of San Sepolcro reappeared only during the turbulent years of the Salò Republic, which Mussolini conceived of as a return of Fascism to its original roots.

45. The speech was published in the following day, in *Il popolo d'Italia*, March 23, 1922, 19; reprinted in OOBM, 25:292–93.

46. Jeffrey T. Schnapp, "Epic Demonstration: Fascist Modernity and the 1932 Exhibition of the Fascist Revolution," in *Fascism, Aesthetics, and Culture*, ed. Richard J. Golsan (Hanover, NH: University Press of New England, 1992), 1–37.

47. OOBM, 25:292.

48. On the Meeting of San Sepolcro and early Fascism, see Franzinelli, *Fascismo anno zero*; De Felice, *Mussolini il rivoluzionario*, 419–543; Angelo Tasca, *Nascita e avvento del fascismo: L'Italia dall'armistizio alla marcia su Roma* (Vicenza: Neri Pozza, 2021), 97–115; Emilio Gentile, *E fu subito regime: Il fascismo e la marcia su Roma* (Rome: Laterza, 2012), 7–21; Roberto Vivarelli, *Storia delle origini del fascismo*, vol. 1, *L'Italia dalla grande guerra alla marcia su Roma* (Bologna: Il Mulino, 1991), 259–336; Cristina Baldassini, *Autobiografia del primo fascismo: Ideologia politica, mentalità, memoria* (Soveria Mannelli: Rubbettino, 2013); Enzo Sereni, *Le origini del fascismo* (Florence: La Nuova Italia, 1998), 161–248; Salvatore Lupo, *Il fascismo: La politica di un regime totalitario* (Rome: Donzelli, 2000), 31–113; Ugo Mancini, *Il fascismo dallo Stato liberale al regime* (Soveria Mennelli: Rubbettino, 2007); Gaetano Salvemini, *Le origini del fascismo in Italia: Lezioni di Harvard*, ed. Roberto Vivarelli (Milan: Feltrinelli, 2015), 122–40; De Grand, *Italian Fascism*, 22–40; Adrian Lyttelton, *The Seizure of Power: Fascism in Italy, 1919–1929* (London: Weidenfeld & Nicolson, 1973), 13–63; and Patrizia Dogliani, *L'Italia fascista, 1922–1940* (Milan: Sansoni, 1999), 13–128.

49. The names and basic biographical information of the 206 participants of the San Sepolcro meeting are in Franzinelli, *Fascismo anno zero*, 171–256. On the age of the early Fascist supporters and on Fascism as a youthful movement, see Maurizio Degl'Innocenti, *L'epoca giovane: Generazioni, fascismo e antifascismo* (Rome: Piero Lacaita, 2002), and Catia Papa, *L'Italia giovane dall'Unità al fascismo* (Rome: Laterza, 2013), 345–94.

50. "23 marzo," *Il popolo d'Italia*, March 18, 1919, 6, reprinted in OOBM, 12:309.

51. The Italian People's Party, founded on January 18, 1919 by the Sicilian Catholic priest Luigi Sturzo, was intended to become the political expression of the Vatican to quell the popular support of the Socialist Party among Italy's lower socioeconomic classes; see Francesco Malgeri, "Il Partito popolare italiano," in *Storia del movimento cattolico in Italia*, ed. Francesco Malgeri (Rome: Il Poligono, 1980), 3:3–201. The Reformist Liberal Party would consolidate within the Partito Liberale in 1922, restructured to counteract the growth of mass politics around the

leadership of Giovanni Giolitti, Antonio Salandra and Vittorio Emanuele Orlando. See Domenico Zanichelli, *Il partito liberale storico in Italia* (Bologna: Forni, 1973).

52. OOBM, 12:309.

53. Ibid.

54. Ibid.

55. Ibid., 12:310.

56. Ibid., 12:310–11.

57. For a complete English translation of the manifesto, see Jeffrey T. Schnapp, ed., *A Primer of Italian Fascism* (Lincoln: University of Nebraska Press, 2000), 3–6.

58. There is a different English translation in ibid., 5.

59. In fact, Mussolini's Fascio struggled to become a movement that unified and represented all war veterans. First, veterans dispersed their vote in a multiplicity of directions. Second, almost contemporaneously with the foundation of the Fasci, in March 1919 and also in Milan, the Associazione Nazionale dei Combattenti (National Veterans Association; ANC) was founded, taking political form as the Partito dei Combattenti, among whose candidates Gaetano Salvemini was later elected to Parliament. On the variety of the political associations and activism of war veterans, see Emilio Gentile, *Le origini dell'ideologia fascista, 1918–1925* (Bologna: Il Mulino, 1996), 153–90.

60. De Felice, *Mussolini il rivoluzionario*, 460.

61. *Il corriere della sera*, March 24, 1919, p. 8 of the local news section, gave a very brief report of the meeting, only twenty-two short lines, mentioning that "prof. [*sic*] Mussolini explained the cornerstones of Fasci's actions, that are: valorization of war and of those who fought it" and "opposition against all those parties that opposed the war." The news occupied the same space given to a meeting of the Fascio Ferroviario and much less than another celebratory meeting of war veterans, both of which occurred the same day in Milan. News of the San Sepolcro meeting did not appear in the editions of *Avanti!* and *La Stampa*. The term "fascista/i" appears in *Il corriere della sera* of 1919 more than a hundred times to signify only membership in a "fascio," and not necessarily the Fascio di Combattimento.

62. OOBM, 13:209.

63. Gentile, *Le origini dell'ideologia fascista*, 128–31.

64. Quoted in ibid., 132.

65. Agostino Lanzillo, "Quel che dovrebbe significare il congresso dei combattenti," *Il popolo d'Italia*, June 21, 1919.

66. OOBM, 11:241–42.

67. Ibid., 11:242.

68. Gentile, *Le origini dell'ideologia fascista*, 143.

69. Alceste De Ambris, "I nuovi orizzonti della vita operaia italiana," *Il Rinnovamento*, June 6, 1918; also quoted in Gentile, *Le origini dell'ideologia fascista*, 147.

Chapter Two

1. The interview is collected in OOBM, 13:61–63.

2. Roberto Vivarelli, *Storia delle origini del fascismo*, vol. 1, *L'Italia dalla grande guerra alla marcia su Roma* (Bologna: Il Mulino, 1991), 372ff.; Mimmo Franzinelli, *Squadristi: Protagonisti e tecniche della violenza fascista, 1919–1922* (Milan: Mondadori, 2003), 21–27, and Franzinelli, *Fascismo anno zero*, 81–90. Franzinelli, in *Squadristi*, refers to the results of an internal investigation

by the inspector general, Giovanni Gasti, into the behavior of the police and the armed forces, which eventually justified the police's decision not intervene in defense of the *Avanti!* because the members of the Fascio consisted of members of the Milanese bourgeoisie and were, like many policemen, fellow veterans of the First World War.

3. "Perché l'Avanti! risorga più grande, più forte, più rosso," *Avanti!*, April 23, 1919, 1. The newspaper also launched a crowdsourcing event to sponsor the reopening of a new office in Milan, which would happen only a few weeks after its destruction in a provisional facility, and, later, on the symbolic date of May 1, 1920, when the Festa del Lavoro (Italian Labor Day) is celebrated, in a new and larger headquarters.

4. Fasci opened local headquarters in Genoa, Turin, and Verona on March 25; in Bergamo and Treviso on March 26; and then in Padua (March 28), Naples (March 30), Pavia (April 1), Stradella (April 2), Trieste (April 3), San Remo (April 6), Mestre (April 7), Brescia (April 8), and Recco (April 9); in Bologna, Parma, Rome, and Vigevano (April 10); and in Feltre (April 13) and Forlì (April 14). After the events of April 15, new headquarters of the Fasci di Combattimento were set up in Savona (April 18); Cremona, Camerino, La Spezia, Trani, and Varese (April 20); Venezia and Zara (April 23); Florence (May 1); Ciriè (May 10); Saronno, Brinzio, Cabiglio, Tradate, Venegono, and Conegliano (May 17); Belluno, Feltre, Pordenone, Udine, and Vicenza (June 4); and Modena (June 30). See Sparacino, *23 marzo 1919*, 118–29, for a complete list.

5. All quotes from the interview are in OOBM, 13:62.

6. OOBM, 13:63.

7. It appears fewer than a dozen times (and these in only three articles) between March and September 1919; see OOBM, 13. Mentions of "fascism" increased exponentially in the month before and immediately after the election of November 16, 1919: there are more than a hundred appearances of the term between October and November, though they became sporadic again in the following months; see OOBM, 14.

8. OOBM, 13:145.

9. He referred specifically to the Associazione dei Volontari di Guerra (Association of War Volunteers, one of the many combatants' groups that formed after the end of the war), the Fascio Popolare di Educazione Sociale (People's Union for Social Education), and "other minor veterans' associations." OOBM, 12:219.

10. Ibid.

11. Ibid.

12. Ibid., 12:220.

13. Questions of intentionality—understood not textually, as *intentio operis*, but referring to the ostensible psychological volition of Benito Mussolini—are not relevant to the analyses in this book.

14. *OED Online*, s.v. "-ism, suffix," accessed September 19, 2022, https://www.oed.com/dictionary/ism_suffix?tab=meaning_and_use#40472123.

15. See Franzinelli, *Squadristi*, 45–86; Paul Corner, *The Fascist Party and Popular Opinion in Mussolini's Italy* (Oxford: Oxford University Press, 2012), 13–72; and Luigi Ponziani, "Fascismo e autonomie locali," in *Lo stato fascista*, ed. Marco Palla (Florence: La Nuova Italia, 2001), 315–56.

16. Raffaella Canovi, *D'Annunzio e il fascismo: Eutanasia di un'icona* (Rome: Bibliotheka, 2019).

17. "Gesto di rivolta," *Il popolo d'Italia*, September 14, 1919, 6, reprinted in OOBM, 14:5.

18. See Renzo De Felice, *Mussolini il rivoluzionario, 1883–1920* (Turin: Einaudi, 1965), 545–98.

19. OOBM, 14:55.

20. "La prima adunata fascista," *Il popolo d'Italia*, October 6, 1919, reprinted in OOBM, 14:44.

21. These were the first general elections since the end of the First World War on the basis of a new electoral law passed only the previous August, determining a propositional system of universal male suffrage.

22. Other lists of combatants were able to have twenty representatives elected. See *Statistica delle Elezioni Generali Politiche*, 25th Legislature, November 16, 1919 (Rome: Ufficio Centrale di Statistica, 1920), LVI–LX and 75–78.

23. "L'affermazione fascista," *Il popolo d'Italia*, November 18, 1919, reprinted in OOBM, 14:136.

24. De Felice, *Mussolini il rivoluzionario*, 573.

25. The bibliography on the *biennio rosso* is extensive. Fundamental scholarly works are Paolo Spriano, *L'occupazione delle fabbriche: Settembre 1920* (Turin: Einaudi, 1964); Giuseppe Maione, *Il biennio rosso: Autonomia e spontaneità operaia nel 1919–1920* (Bologna: Il Mulino, 1975); and Andrea Ventura, *Italia ribelle: Sommosse popolari e rivolte militari nel 1920* (Rome: Carocci, 2020).

26. Gioacchino Volpe, the regime historian and a Fascist from the very beginning, would use the expression "civil war" to describe the period of 1919–21 in his "Storia del Fascismo," originally published in 1932 as a section of the entry "fascism" of the *Enciclopedia italiana*. English translation in Jeffrey T. Schnapp, ed., *A Primer of Italian Fascism* (Lincoln: University of Nebraska Press, 2000), 19–45.

27. "Il 'Fascismo,'" *Il popolo d'Italia*, July 3, 1919, reprinted in OOBM, 13:220; emphasis mine.

28. Data of the General Administrative Office of the State Police, quoted in Franzinelli, *Squadristi*, 46.

29. Franzinelli, *Squadristi*, 57–75; Renato Pallavitini, *Fascismo o fascismi? Storia dell'Italia Mussoliniana (1912–1945)* (Parma: Edizioni all'insegna del Veltro, 2013), 59–94; Sven Reichardt, "Fascismo e teoria delle pratiche sociali: Violenza e comunità come elementi di un concetto praxeologico di fascismo," *Storiografia*, no. 12 (2008): 1–18; Reichardt, *Faschistische Kampfbünde: Gewalt und Gemeinschaft im italienischen Squadrismus und in der deutschen SA* (Cologne: Böhlau, 2002); Matteo Millan, "The Institutionalisation of 'Squadrismo': Disciplining Paramilitary Violence in the Italian Fascist Dictatorship," *Contemporary European History* 22, no. 4 (2013): 551–73; and Millan, "Squadrismo e repressione: Una via italiana alla violenza?," in *Il fascismo italiano: Storia e interpretazioni*, ed. Giulia Albanese (Rome: Carocci, 2021), 25–44.

30. Italo Balbo, *Diario, 1922* (Milan: Mondadori, 1932), 9.

31. See, e.g., Giordano Bruno Guerri, *Fascisti: Gli italiani di Mussolini; Il regime degli italiani* (Milan: Mondadori, 1995), chap. 3.

32. Franzinelli, *Squadristi*, 46.

33. Ibid., 87–119; and Millan, "The Institutionalization of 'Squadrismo.'"

34. Quoted in Guerri, *Fascisti*, 77.

35. Gaetano Salvemini, *Le origini del fascismo in Italia* (Milan: Feltrinelli, 2015), 309.

36. Ibid., 310.

37. According to the conservative estimates of the historian Giorgio Caledoro, in just the first six months of 1921 Fascist groups were involved in 726 destructive acts in the Po Valley alone: 17 printing presses, 59 People's Houses, 119 trade unions' headquarters, 107 cooperatives, the headquarters of 83 agricultural workers' unions, 8 benefit societies, 141 offices of the PSI, 100 cultural circles, 10 libraries, and 53 workers' sport clubs. Caledoro, *Storia dell'Italia moderna*, vol. 8, *La prima guerra mondiale, il dopoguerra, l'avvento del fascismo* (Milan: Feltrinelli, 1996), 353.

38. Salvemini, *Le origini del fascismo in Italia*, 303.

39. OOBM, 14:182.

40. Ibid., 15:31.

41. Ibid., 15:76.

42. Ibid., 15:152.

43. Ibid., 15:189.

44. Ibid., 15:219.

45. Ibid., 15:259.

46. Ibid., 15:263.

47. Ibid., 15:260.

48. Ibid., 15:273.

49. Ibid., 15:284.

50. Ibid., 15:285.

51. Ibid., 15:299.

52. Ibid., 16:101.

53. Ibid., 16:125.

54. Ibid., 16:131.

55. Ibid., 16:212.

56. The archive of *Il corriere della sera*, for instance, records one hundred occurrences of "fascism" during the period April 1920–April 1921, most of them related to Blackshirts' acts of violence.

57. Giulia Albanese, "Violence and Political Participation during the Rise of Fascism (1919–1926)," in *In the Society of Fascists: Acclamation, Acquiescence, and Agency in Mussolini's Italy*, ed. Giulia Albanese and Roberta Pergher (Basingstoke: Palgrave Macmillan, 2012), 49–68.

58. See Emilio Gentile, *Il fascismo in tre capitoli* (Rome: Laterza, 2004), 22; Juan J. Linz, "Some Notes Toward a Comparative Study of Fascism in Sociological Perspective," in *Fascism: A Reader's Guide; Analyses, Interpretations, Bibliography*, ed. Walter Laqueur (Berkeley: University of California Press, 1976), 60–81; and Tommaso Baris, "Consent, Mobilization, and Participation: The Rise of the Middle Class and Its Support for the Fascist Regime," in Albanese and Pergher, *In the Society of Fascists*, 69–86. See also Pietro Grifone, *Il capitale finanziario in Italia: La politica economica del fascismo* (Turin: Einaudi, 1971), 32–43.

59. They were followed by industrial workers (15.5 percent), civil servants and white-collar workers (14.6 percent), students (13 percent), larger landowning entrepreneurs (11.9 percent), businessmen and merchants (9.2 percent), and professionals such as lawyers, physicians, and pharmacists (6.6 percent), industrialists (2.8 percent), and teachers (1 percent). See Gentile, *Il fascismo in tre capitoli*, 22.

60. Alessio Gagliardi, "The Entrepreneurial Bourgeoisie and Fascism," in Albanese and Pergher, *In the Society of Fascists*, 109–30.

61. "La misura è colma . . . ," *Il popolo d'Italia*, October 17, 1920, reprinted in OOBM, 15:264.

62. "Disciplina," *Il popolo d'Italia*, July 24, 1921, reprinted in OOBM, 17:67–68.

63. See, e.g., Mussolini's intervention in "Fascismo e terra," *Il popolo d'Italia*, February 19, 1921, reprinted in OOBM, 16:170–73.

64. Franzinelli, *Squadristi*, 57–86; Angelo Tasca, *La nascita del fascismo* (Turin: Bollati Boringhieri, 2006), 139–200; and Millan, "Squadrismo e repressione," 27–32.

65. Franzinelli, *Squadristi*, 87–96.

66. Roberto Farinacci, *ras* of Cremona, and D'Annunzio's follower Pietro Marsich led an open revolt against the leader of Fascism, organizing demonstrations in the streets of Bologna.

Dino Grandi and Italo Balbo, *ras* of Bologna and Ferrara, secretly met with D'Annunzio to discuss replacing Mussolini as the leader of the movement. See Renzo De Felice, *Mussolini il fascista: La conquista del potere* (Turin: Einaudi, 1966), 143–60. See also Dahlia S. Elazar, *The Making of Fascism: Class, State, and Counter-Revolution* (Westport, CT: Praeger, 2001), 141–43.

67. Giovanni Giolitti, *Memorie della mia vita* (Milan: Fratelli Treves, 1922), 2:608–9.

68. "I blocchi e Giolitti," *Il popolo d'Italia*, April 26, 1921, reprinted in OOBM, 16:283.

69. Ibid., 16:284.

70. More than a hundred deaths resulted from fascist violence preceding the elections. See Maria Serena Piretti, *Le elezioni politiche in Italia dal 1848 a oggi* (Rome: Laterza, 1995), 232–43.

71. Emilio Gentile persuasively demonstrates that Mussolini's role was far from central. The administrative transformation of the Fascio into a nationwide party was largely the labor of Umberto Pisella, a Sansepolcrist and the general secretary of the Fasci di Combattimento since 1919, and the former syndicalist Cesare Rossi, secretary of Milan's Fascio and editor in chief of the movement's official newspaper, *Il Fascio*. See Gentile, *Storia del Partito fascista: Movimento e milizia, 1919–1922*, new rev. ed. (Rome: Laterza, 2021), 94–271.

72. Control encompassing not just executive authority, but also the semantic value of "fascism." See also Gentile, *Storia del Partito fascista*, 401–16.

73. Levi Della Vida, "Idealisti sperduti," *Il Paese*, October 4, 1921, quoted in Gentile, *Storia del Partito fascista*, 402.

74. Levi Della Vida, "Due tendenze irriducibili," *Il Secolo*, November 3, 1921, quoted in Gentile, *Storia del Partito fascista*, 403.

75. OOBM, 17:218.

76. Ibid., 17:219.

77. Ibid., 17:220.

78. Ibid., 17:221.

79. Benito Mussolini, "Il partito fascista," *Il popolo d'Italia*, November 12, 1921, reprinted in OOBM, 17:229.

80. Emilio Gentile, *Fascismo: Storia e interpretazione* (Rome: Laterza, 2002), 13. The role of secretary general of the party was given to Michele Bianchi.

81. OOBM, 17:230.

82. In *Il popolo d'Italia*, December 27, 1921, reprinted in OOBM, 17:334–50.

83. Ibid.

84. All the following quotes from "Il programma fascista" are translated by Maria G. Stampino and Jeffrey T. Schnapp in Schnapp, *A Primer of Italian Fascism*, 10–18.

85. Implicit in the parenthetical addendum was a distinction from the socialist ideals.

86. "Prefazione al programma," *Il popolo d'Italia*, December 28, 1921, reprinted in OOBM, 17:351.

87. Gentile, *Fascismo*, 12; emphasis in original.

88. A brief article in the Milan edition of *Il corriere della sera*, November 7, 1921, 1, chronicled the Fasci Meeting of Rome, noting three times in twenty lines how the audience was constantly intoning chants, implying the goliardic nature of the new party.

89. "In tema di pace," *Il popolo d'Italia*, July 2, 1921, reprinted in OOBM, 17:20.

90. Gentile, *Fascismo*, 14.

91. Ezio Mauro, *La dannazione: 1921; La sinistra divisi all'alba del fascismo* (Milan: Feltrinelli, 2020); and Marcello Flores and Giovanni Gozzini, *Il vento della rivoluzione: La nascita del Partito comunista italiano* (Rome: Laterza, 2021), 48–56.

92. Franzinelli, *Squadristi*, 139–55; and Mimmo Franzinelli, *L'insurrezione fascista: Storia e mito della marcia su Roma* (Milan: Mondadori, 2022), 56–90.

93. Quoted in Giorgio Alberto Chiurco, *Storia della rivoluzione fascista* (Florence: Vallecchi, 1929), 4:193.

94. Undated letter, probably written on August 4, 1922, later published in *Il popolo d'Italia*, August 6, 1922, reprinted in OOBM, 18:486.

95. "Manifesto della smobilitazione fascista," *Il popolo d'Italia*, August 9, 1922, reprinted in OOBM, 18:341–42.

96. Giulia Albanese, *The March on Rome: Violence and the Rise of Italian Fascism*, trans. Sergio Knipe (London: Routledge, 2019), 34.

97. Gentile, *Fascismo*, 15.

98. "Il discorso di Napoli," uttered the morning of October 24, 1922 and published in *Il popolo d'Italia*, October 25, 1922, reprinted in OOBM, 18:455.

99. Ibid., 18:457.

100. Quoted in Franzinelli, *L'insurrezione fascista*, 123.

101. Luigi Einaudi, "Alla radice del male," *Il corriere della sera*, October 26, 1922. For an analysis of the convergency between economists' view on austerity and Fascist economic policies, see Clara E. Mattei, *The Capital Order: How Economists Invented Austerity and Paved the Way to Fascism* (Chicago: University of Chicago Press, 2022), 53–73 and 205–45.

102. In OOBM, 18:349; emphasis in the original.

103. That is at least what Emilio Lussu insinuates; Lussu, *Marcia su Roma e dintorni* (1945; Turin: Einaudi, 2014). The Quadrumvirate included Michele Bianchi (general secretary of the PNF), Italo Balbo (one of the more trustworthy of the *ras*), Cesare Maria De Vecchi (*ras* of Turin, former officer of the royal army and close to the Savoy house), and Emilio De Bono (war hero and army general on active duty).

104. For a chronicle of the events, see Antonino Repaci, *La marcia su Roma* (Milan: Rizzoli, 1972); Albanese, *The March on Rome*; and Franzinelli, *L'insurrezione fascista*. On the role of the king, see Paolo Colombo, *La monarchia fascista, 1922–1940* (Bologna: Il Mulino, 2010), 17–53; on the role of the royal army, see Marco Mondini, *La politica delle armi: Il ruolo dell'esercito nell'avvento del fascismo* (Rome: Laterza, 2006).

105. "Tornata di venerdì 17 novembre 1922," *Atti parlamentari: Camera dei Deputati*, 26th Legislature, session 1a, November 17, 1922 (Rome: Tipografia Camera dei Deputati, 1923), 8421.

106. Ibid., 8443.

107. Pietro Gobetti, "La tirannide," *La rivoluzione liberale*, November 23, 1922, http://liberale.erasmo.it/testi/0452.htm, accessed September 15, 2024.

108. Ignazio Silone, *Il fascismo: Origini e sviluppo*, ed. Mimmo Franzinelli (Milan: Mondadori, 2002), 129. The work was originally published in German as *Der Faschismus: seine Entstehung und seine Entwicklung* (Zurich: Europa-Verlag, 1934).

109. Curzio Malaparte, *Tecnica del colpo di stato* (Milan: Bompiani, 1948), 180.

110. Salvemini, *Le origini del fascismo in Italia*, 391–92.

111. Tasca, *La nascita del fascismo*, 59.

112. Benito Mussolini, *Marcia su Roma*, ed. Asvevo Gravelli (Rome: Nuova Europa, 1934), 14.

113. Margherita Sarfatti, *Dvx* (Milan: Mondadori, 1932), 276.

114. Maffeo Pantaleoni, "Finanza fascista," *Politica* (May–June 1923): 169–70.

115. Ottavio Dinale, "Dieci anni di dittatura," *Il popolo d'Italia*, November 3, 1932, quoted in Franzinelli, *L'insurrezione fascista*, 272.

116. These aphorisms were known as the plaques of the Fascist Revolution and today collected in the Archivio Centrale di Stato in Rome, "Mostra della Rivoluzione Fascista," box no. 72, no. 7. Also quoted in Franzinelli, *L'insurrezione fascista*, 275. See also the online archival inventory at https://search.acs.beniculturali.it/OpacACS/guida/IT-ACS-AS0001-0003706, accessed July 19, 2021.

117. Repaci, *La marcia su Roma*, 306. Repaci published two letters sent by Alfredo Lusignoli, prefect of Milan, to Giolitti and Facta confirming the support of Confindustria to a Mussolini cabinet (ibid., 750 and 769). On the support for Mussolini from northern Italian industrialists and Confindustria, see also Piero Melograni, *Gli industriali e Mussolini: Rapporti tra Confindustria e fascismo dal 1919 al 1929* (Milan: Longanesi, 1972).

118. On the Vatican's support for a Mussolini cabinet, see Repaci, *La marcia su Roma*, 272–74.

119. Bertolt Brecht, *Der aufhaltsame Aufstieg des Arturo Ui* (1941), English trans. John Willet in Brecht, *The Resistible Rise of Arturo Ui* (New York: Arcade, 1981).

120. Albanese, *The March on Rome*, xii.

121. This is also the thesis of such historians as Adrian Lyttelton, *The Seizure of Power: Fascism in Italy, 1919–1929* (1973; London: Routledge, 2004); Mario Isnenghi, *L'Italia in piazza: I luoghi della vita pubblica dal 1848 ai giorni nostri* (1994; Bologna: Il Mulino, 2004); Emilio Gentile, *E fu subito regime: Il fascismo e la marcia su Roma* (Rome: Laterza, 2012); Albanese, *The March on Rome*; and Franzinelli, *L'insurrezione fascista*, among others.

122. With the exception of the PSI and PCd'I. See Albanese, *The March on Rome*, xiii; and Salvatore Lupo, *Il fascismo: La politica in un regime totalitario* (Rome: Donizelli, 2000), 119–37.

123. Lyttelton, *The Seizure of Power*, 85–87. On the importance of the normalization of violence in political thought and praxis after the first world war, see George Mosse, *Fallen Soldiers: Reshaping the Memory of World Wars* (Oxford: Oxford University Press, 1990) and, most recently, Robert Gerhart, *The Vanquished: Why the First World War Failed to End, 1917–1923* (London: Penguin, 2016). See also Patrizia Dogliani, *Il fascismo degli italiani: Una storia sociale* (Turin: UTET, 2008), 15–50.

124. "Tornata di giovedì 16 november 1922," *Atti parlamentari: Camera dei Deputati*, 26th Legislature, session 1a (Rome: Tipografia Camera dei Deputati, 1923), 8390–91.

125. "Il 'duro' linguaggio di Mussolini alla Camera," *La Stampa*, November 17, 1922, 1.

Chapter Three

1. On Fascist political praxis, see Giulia Albanese, "La costruzione delle pratiche fasciste e la nuova politica," in Giulia Albanese, David Bidussa, and Jacopo Perazzoli, *Siamo stati fascisti: Il laboratorio dell'antidemocrazia; Italia, 1900–1922* (Milan: Feltrinelli, 2020), 15–47.

2. Emphasis mine.

3. On the elasticity of the statute and its adjustability to the dictatorial transformation imposed by the Fascist regime, see Roberto Martucci, *Storia costituzionale italiana: Dallo Statuto albertino alla repubblica (1848–2001)* (Rome: Carocci, 2002), esp. 150–253; and Mario Perini, "Il capo dello stato dall'Italia liberale al fascismo: Il re (non) è nudo," *Diritto e questioni pubbliche* 13 (2013): 621–96. See also Sabino Cassese, *Lo stato fascista* (Bologna: Il Mulino, 2016), 15–16 and 33–45; and Paolo Colombo, *La monarchia fascista, 1922–1940* (Bologna: Il Mulino, 2010), 83–133.

4. Three days after the March on Rome, Confindustria released the following public statement: "The new regime is formed. We took to it with great hopes. We will support the program of this regime with all our strength, for in it, for the first time after long years, a protection of

property rights, the general obligation to work, a full valuation of the energy of the individual and of national sentiment are proclaimed energetically"; *L'organizzazione industriale*, November 1, 1922, 1, quoted in William Elwin, *Fascism at Work* (London: M. Hopkinson, 1934), 46. On the relationship between Fascism and the Vatican, see Ernesto Rossi, *Il manganello e l'aspersorio: La collusione fra il Vaticano e il regime fascista nel Ventennio* (Milan: Kaos, 2000); and David I. Kertzer, *The Pope and Mussolini: The Secret History of Pius XI and the Rise of Fascism in Europe* (Oxford: Oxford University Press, 2014), esp. 27–38 on the role of Gasparri in the events of October 1922.

5. Emilio Gentile, *Storia del fascismo* (Rome: Laterza, 2022), 282–333.

6. This would soon became law no. 1601 of December 2, 1922, in *Gazzetta ufficiale* 293, December 15, 1922, 1. See also Emilio Gentile, *E fu subito regime: Il fascismo e la marcia su Roma* (Rome: Laterza, 2012), 249–52.

7. Gentile, *E fu subito regime*, 252–54.

8. Maria Serena Piretti, *Le elezioni politiche in Italia dal 1848 a oggi* (Rome: Laterza, 1995), 289–300; and Gentile, *Storia del fascismo*, 426–53.

9. The passing of the Acerbo electoral law was strongly contested. Filippo Turati commented on July 15, 1923 that "under intimidation there is no law; one does not legislate with guns drawn and with the looming threat of machine guns"; in "Tornata di domenica 15 luglio 1923," *Atti Parlamentari: Camera dei Deputati*, 26th Legislature, session 1a (Rome: Tipografia Camera dei Deputati, 1924), 10657. See Alessandro Visani, *La conquista della maggioranza: Mussolini, il PNF e le elezioni del 1924* (Genova: F.lli Frilli, 2004). The text of the Acerbo law are in *Raccolta ufficiale delle Leggi e dei Decreti del Regno d'Italia*, vol. 8 (Rome: Libreria dello Stato, 1924), 7428–61.

10. "Tornata di venerdi 30 maggio 1924," *Atti Parlamentari: Camera dei Deputati*, 27th Legislature, session 1a (Rome: Tipografia Camera dei Deputati, 1925), 53–54.

11. Ibid., 57–58.

12. Emilio Lussu, *Marcia su Roma e dintorni* (1945; Turin: Einaudi, 2014), 155.

13. Giovanni Borgognone, *Come nasce una dittatura: L'Italia del delitto Matteotti* (Rome: Laterza, 2012).

14. Gentile, *Storia del fascismo*, 467–80.

15. See Giovanni Amendola's memorial, *L'Avventino contro il fascismo: Scritti politici (1924–1926)* (Milan: Ricciardi, 1976).

16. Piero Gobetti, "Ho conosciuto Matteotti," *La rivoluzione liberale* 1, no. 17, June 17, 1924, quoted in Giacomo Matteotti, *Questo è il fascismo: I discorsi del 31 gennaio 1921 e del 30 maggio 1924*, ed. Pietro Polito (Rome: edizioni e/o, 2022), 17.

17. R. J. B. Bosworth, *Mussolini's Italy: Life under the Fascist Dictatorship, 1915–1945* (London: Penguin, 2005), 211–12.

18. "Tornata di sabato 3 gennaio 1925," *Atti Parlamentari: Camera dei Deputati*, 27th Legislature, Session 1a (Rome: Tipografia Camera dei Deputati, 1925), 2030–31.

19. Gentile, *Storia del fascismo*, 509–36.

20. Emilio Gentile, *Fascismo: Storia e interpretazioni* (Rome: Laterza, 2002), 19.

21. On the king's responsibility for allowing this to happen, see Colombo, *La monarchia fascista*, 55–79.

22. Gentile, *Fascismo*, 19–20.

23. For an overview of state institutions during the fascist regime, see Alberto Aquarone, *L'organizzazione dello stato totalitario* (Turin: Einaudi, 1995), 169–288; Cassese, *Lo stato fascista*, esp. 13–85; Paul Corner, *The Fascist Party and Popular Opinion in Mussolini's Italy* (Oxford:

Oxford University Press, 2011), 13–167; Alexander De Grand, *Italian Fascism: Its Origins and Development* (Lincoln: University of Nebraska Press, 2000), 41–91; Gentile, *E fu subito regime*, 230–77; Emilio Gentile, *Il fascismo in tre capitoli* (Rome: Laterza, 2004), 11–55; Salvatore Lupo, *Il fascismo: La politica in un regime totalitario* (Rome: Donizelli, 2000), 185–265; and Guido Melis, *La macchina imperfetta: Immagine e realtà dello Stato fascista* (Bologna: Il Mulino, 2018).

24. Patrizia Dogliani, *Il fascismo degli italiani: Una storia sociale* (Turin: UTET, 2008), 125–65.

25. Gentile, *Storia del fascismo*, 554–73.

26. Ibid., 603–16.

27. Aquarone, *L'organizzazione dello stato totalitario*, 493.

28. Gentile, *Storia del fascismo*, 617–45.

29. Confindustria, which supported the Fascist regime and its dismantling of labor unions, initially resisted the corporatist transformation of economic life by the Fascist regime but then joined in and collaborated with the Ministry of Corporations. On Fascist corporatism, see Alessio Gagliardi, *Il corporativismo fascista* (Rome: Laterza, 2010); Louis Franck, *Il corporativismo e l'economia dell'Italia fascista* (Turin: Bollati Boringhieri, 1990); Gianpasquale Santomassimo, *La terza via fascista: Il mito del corporativismo* (Rome: Carocci, 2006); Bruno Settis, "Economia e fascismo: poteri privati e intervento pubblico," in *Il fascismo italiano: Storia e interpretazioni*, ed. Giulia Albanese (Rome: Carocci, 2021), 113–38; and Clara E. Mattei, *The Capital Order: How Economists Invented Austerity and Paved the Way to Fascism* (Chicago: University of Chicago Press, 2022), 205–45. See also Carl T. Schmitt, *The Corporate State in Action: Italy under Fascism* (Oxford: Oxford University Press, 1939).

30. Corbino was a liberal democrat, Nava with the PPI, Teofilo Rossi a liberal democrat, and Cavazzoni with the PPI.

31. English translation of the Charter in Jeffrey T. Schnapp, ed., *A Primer of Italian Fascism* (Lincoln: University of Nebraska Press, 2000), 308–13. It stated that, since "the Italian Nation is an organism having ends, life, and means of action superior to those of individuals, singly or in groups" (Art. 1), "work, in all its intellectual, technical, and manual forms, is a social obligation" (Art. 2). The "well-being of the producers and the development of national strength" were inseparable, and thus professional and union organizations were directly regulated by the state (Art. 3). Since national prosperity was the ultimate end of economic life, "the opposing interests of the employers and the workers" had to be subordinated "to the superior interests of production" (Art. 4).

32. Daniela Manetti, *Un'arma poderosissima: Industria cinematografica e Stato durante il fascismo, 1922–1943* (Milan: Franco Angeli, 2012).

33. See Ruth Ben-Ghiat, *Fascist Modernities: Italy, 1922–1945* (Berkeley: University of California Press, 2001); Alessio Gagliardi, "'Educare' o intrattenere? Propaganda, mass media e cultura di massa," in Albanese, *Il fascismo italiano*, 255–79; Emilio Gentile, *Fascismo di pietra* (Rome: Laterza, 2007); Francesca Billiani and Laura Pennacchietti, *Architecture and the Novel under the Italian Fascist Regime* (Cham: Palgrave MacMillan, 2019); Gentile, *La via italiana al totalitarismo: Il partito e lo stato nel regime fascista* (Rome: Carocci, 2008); Mario Isnenghi, *L'educazione dell'italiano: Il fascismo e l'organizzazione della cultura* (Bologna: Cappelli, 1979); Alessandra Tarquini, *Storia della cultura fascista* (Bologna: Il Mulino, 2011); and Gentile, *Storia del fascismo*, 539–53 and 886–908.

34. Luca Scotto di Luzio, "Censura," in *Dizionario del fascismo*, ed. Victoria De Grazia e Sergio Luzzatto (Turin: Einaudi, 2002), 1:262.

35. Mimmo Franzinelli, *I tentacoli dell'Ovra: Agenti, collaboratori e vittime della polizia politica fascista* (Turin: Bollati Boringhieri, 1999), is the best introduction to the structure and

activities of the secret political police of the regime. OVRA is ostensibly an initialism, the expansion of which is perhaps Organizzazione Volontaria di Repressione Antifascista (Voluntary Organization of Antifascist Repression), but there is no confirmation of that in any official documentation. On the importance and volume of police informants, see also Franzinelli, *Delatori: Spie e confidenti anonimi; L'arma segreta del regime fascista* (Milan: Mondadori, 2001). On censorship, see Ben-Ghiat, *Fascist Modernity*; Guido Bonsaver, *Censorship and Literature in Fascist Italy* (Toronto: University of Toronto Press, 2007); and Giorgio Fabre, *L'elenco: Censura fascista, editori e autori ebrei* (Turin: Zamorani, 1998).

36. See Joshua Arthurs, "Vivere il fascismo: Politica e vita quotidiana durante il regime," in Albanese, *Il fascismo italiano*, 237–53; Gagliardi, " 'Educare' o intrattenere?"; Alessio Ponzio, *Shaping the New Man: Youth Training Regimes in Fascist Italy and Nazi Germany* (Madison: University of Wisconsin Press, 2015), esp. 25–98; Isnenghi, *L'educazione dell'italiano*, on the educational reforms of the regime; and Tarquini, *Storia della cultura fascista*.

37. English translation of Gentile's Manifesto by Maria Stampino and Jeffrey Schnapp in Schnapp, *A Primer of Italian Fascism*, 297. Gentile's neologism "Demosocialista" was used as a derogatory term for all parties of the center left, not only the socialist but also all the liberal democratic parties that opposed Fascism, including the PPI, which initially supported Mussolini's government.

38. Ibid.

39. Ibid., 298.

40. Ibid., 309.

41. See Emilio Raffaele Papa, *Fascismo e cultura* (Venice: Marsilio, 1975), 159–94 and 211–85; Alberto Asor Rosa, "I 'manifesti degli intellettuali,' " *Storia d'Italia* 4, no. 2 (1975): 1464–70; Emilio Gentile, *Le origini dell'ideologia fascista, 1918–1925* (Bologna: Il Mulino, 1996), 459–66; and Tarquini, *Storia della cultura fascista*, 67–68. In the summer of 1926 Gentile's Manifesto would be translated in French under the title "Manifeste des intellectuels italiens du parti fasciste aux intelllectuels de toutes les nations." See Rosario Gennaro, "Il *Manifesto degli intellettuali fascisti* e l'espansione culturale all'estero," *Nuova storia contemporanea* 17, no. 1 (2013): 79–95.

42. Giuseppe Giordano, "La denuncia di un tradimento: Il 'Manifesto degli intellettuali antifascisti,' " *Il pensiero italiano: Rivista di studi filosofici* 1, no. 1 (2017): 37–50. Interestingly, the original title of the manifesto had "non-fascist" and would be only later renamed "antifascist." More on this in chap. 6.

43. Simonetta Falasca-Zamponi, *Fascist Spectacle: The Aesthetic of Power in Mussolini's Italy* (Berkeley: University of California Press, 1997).

44. Ariberto Segàla, *I muri del duce* (Gardolo: Arca, 2000).

45. Gentile, *Fascismo di pietra*. Gentile shows how Fascist ideology produced a "vast stream of petrified ideology" (vi), which found its main stage in Rome. See also Paolo Nicoloso, "Traces of Fascist Architecture in Republican Italy," in *Rethinking Fascism: The Italian and German Dictatorships*, ed. Andrea Di Michele and Filippo Focardi (Berlin: de Gruyter, 2022), 225–46.

46. Gentile, *La via italiana al totalitarismo*, 187.

47. Italo Calvino, *Hermit in Paris: Autobiographical Writings*, trans. Jonathan Cape (New York: Random House, 2003), 207.

48. Renzo De Felice argued that the years of maximum support for the Fascist regime were those of the economic crisis of 1929–31, while Adrian Lyttelton supported the view that the years immediately after the crisis, between 1931 and 1934, should be regarded as the heyday of Fascism. Historians seem, however, to agree that the beginning of the decline of popular support for

Mussolini and his regime coincided with the Second Italo-Abyssinian War in Ethiopia (1935–37), which descended to resistance during the Second World War. See Gianpasquale Santomassimo, "Consenso," in De Grazia and Luzzatto, *Dizionario del fascismo*, 347–52; Renzo De Felice, *Mussolini il Duce*, vol. 1, *Gli anni del consenso (1929–1936)* (Turin: Einaudi, 1974); Philip V. Cannistraro, *La fabbrica del consenso: Fascismo e mass media* (Rome: Laterza, 1975); Victoria De Grazia, *The Culture of Consent: Mass Organization of Leisure in Fascist Italy* (Cambridge: Cambridge University Press, 1981); Tommaso Baris, "Consent, Mobilization, and Participation: The Rise of the Middle Class and Its Support for the Fascist Regime," in *In the Society of Fascists: Acclamation, Acquiescence, and Agency in Mussolini's Italy*, ed. Giulia Albanese and Roberta Pergher (Basingstoke: Palgrave Macmillan, 2012), 69–86; Paul Corner, "Beyond Consensus: Rethinking Italian Fascism," in De Michele and Focardi, *Rethinking Fascism*, 73–83; Corner, "Fascist Italy in the 1930s: Popular Opinion in the Provinces," in *Popular Opinion in Totalitarian Regimes: Fascism, Nazism, Communism*, ed. Paul Corner (Oxford: Oxford University Press, 2009), 122–47; and Corner, *La dittatura fascista: Consenso e controllo durante il Ventennio* (Rome: Carocci, 2018).

49. Volt [Count Vincenzo Fani Ciotti], "Le cinque anime del fascismo," *Critica fascista*, February 15, 1925, 64–65. Volt was not the only voice within Fascism that warned of the dangers of divisiveness within the PNF. In the same period, political thinkers such as Antonio Goglia and Gerardo Casini had similarly argued for the necessity of unifying the diverging branch of Fascism. See Gentile, *Le origini dell'ideologia fascista*, 323–96.

50. Curzio Malaparte, *Tecnica del colpo di stato* (Milan: Bompiani, 1948).

51. Gentile, *Le origini dell'ideologia fascista*, 360.

52. G. A. Fanelli, "Fascismo e monarchia," *Il Veltro*, September 9, 1922, 1.

53. Giuseppe Bottai, *Il fascismo e l'Italia nuova* (Rome: Berlutti, 1923), 52.

54. Published in *Il popolo d'Italia*, July 25, 1924; reprinted in OOBM, 21:31; emphasis mine.

55. John L. Austin, *How to Do Things with Words* (Oxford: Oxford University Press, 1962), 101.

56. In OOBM, 21:44.

57. Ibid., 21:362.

58. Ibid., 21:377.

59. Ibid., 21:74.

60. Ibid., 21:335.

61. Ibid., 21:392.

62. Giovanni Amendola, "Un anno dopo," *Il Mondo*, November 2, 1923, 1.

63. Luigi Sturzo, "Spirito e realtà," *La rivoluzione liberale* 3, no. 3, January 15, 1924, 9.

64. Prometeo Filodemo, "L'antistato," *La rivoluzione liberale* 4, no. 1, January 2, 1925, 1.

65. See Gentile, *Storia del fascismo*, 509–53.

66. In OOBM, 21:362.

67. Ibid., 22:384.

68. Ibid., 23:126.

69. See Umberto Eco, *A Theory of Semiotics* (Bloomington: Indiana University Press, 1976), 289–98, for a semiotic definition of "ideology."

70. A survey of the modes of Fascism's cultural policies goes beyond the scope and possibilities of this study. A vast literature has uncovered different aspects of Fascist culture. It includes the pioneering works of Gentile, *Le origini dell'ideologia fascista*; Isnenghi, *L'educazione dell'italiano*; Pier Giorgio Zunino, *L'ideologia del fascismo: Miti, credenze, valori* (Bologna: Il Mulino, 1995); and Tarquini, *Storia della cultura fascista*. To these, we must include Dogliani,

Il fascismo degli italiani, 167–246; Mabel Berezin, *Making the Fascist Self: The Political Culture of Interwar Italy* (Ithaca, NY: Cornell University Press, 1997); Richard J. Golsan, ed., *Fascism, Aesthetics, and Culture* (Hanover, NH: University Press of New England, 1992); Gisella Longo, *L'Istituto nazionale fascista di cultura: Da Giovanni Gentile a Camillo Pellizzi (1925–1943)* (Rome: Pellicani, 2000); Luca La Rovere, *Storia dei GUF: Organizzazione, politica e miti della gioventù universitaria fascista, 1919–1943* (Turin: Bollati Boringhieri, 2003); Angelo Ventura, *Intellettuali, cultura e politica tra fascismo e antifascismo* (Rome: Donzelli, 2017); Giorgio Boatti, *Preferirei di no: Le storie dei dodici professori che si opposero a Mussolini* (Turin: Einaudi, 2017); and Claudio Carabba, *Il fascismo a fumetti* (Milan: Bompiani, 2024).

71. Tarquini, *Storia della cultura fascista*, 9.

72. OOBM, 21:96.

73. Speech given at the Chamber of Deputies; reprinted in OOBM, 23:122.

74. In OOBM, 24:283.

75. In OOBM, 25:148.

76. Giulia Albanese, "Non solo propaganda: Il modello fascista all'estero (1922–1935)," in Albanese, *Il fascismo italiano*, 321.

77. See Michael Arthur Ledeen, *Universal Fascism: The Theory and Practice of the Fascist International, 1928–1936* (New York: Howard Fertig, 1972), 86–90; and Marco Cuzzi, *Antieuropa: Il fascismo universale* (Milan: M&B, 2006).

78. Marco Cuzzi, *L'internazionale delle camicie nere: I CAUR di Roma, 1933–1939* (Milan: Mursia, 2005).

79. See Daria Frezza Bicocchi, "Propaganda fascista e comunità italiane in USA: La Casa Italiana della Columbia University." *Studi storici* 11, no. 4 (1970): 661–97; and Giuseppe Prezzolini and Daria Frezza Bicocchi, "A proposito di Casa Italiana alla Columbia University e di fascismo," *Studi storici* 12, no. 2 (1971): 396–418.

80. See Ledeen, *Universal Fascism*, 114–29; and Cuzzi, *L'internazionale delle camicie nere*, 130–66; and Gentile, *Storia del fascismo*, 1041–42.

81. On the extensive literature on the relations between Mussolini and Hitler, see Christian Goeschel, *Mussolini and Hitler: The Forging of the Fascist Alliance* (New Haven, CT: Yale University Press, 2018), esp. 53–59 on the 1934 crisis.

82. See https://web.archive.org/web/20101125075603/http://www.time.com/time/magazine/article/0,9171,754480,00.html, accessed September 15, 2024.

83. Stanley Payne, *A History of Fascism, 1914–1945* (London: Routledge, 1995), 229. A copy of the 1934 report, titled "I movimenti fascisti nel mondo" (Fascist Movements in the World) is reprinted in De Felice, *Mussolini il Duce: Gli anni del consenso*, 872–919.

84. Published in *Il popolo d'Italia*, May 10, 1936, 23, and reprinted in OOBM, 27:268–69.

85. Gentile, *Storia del fascismo*, 1024–42.

86. See, e.g., OOBM, 22:213–27 and 23:213; Valentino Piccoli, *Orizzonti imperiali* (Milan: Scuola di mistica fascista, 1932); and Carlo Scorza, *Fascismo, idea imperiale* (Rome: De Gasperis, 1933). On the celebration of April 21—a symbolic date because, according to legend, Rome was founded on April 21, 753 BCE—see Valeria Deplano, "Dalle colonie all'impero: L'Africa e il progetto nazionale fascista," in Albanese, *Il fascismo italiano*, 45–46.

87. See Nicholas Doumanis, *Myth and Memory in the Mediterranean: Remembering Fascism's Empire* (London: Macmillan, 1997); Riccardo Bottoni, *L'impero fascista: Italia ed Etiopia (1935–1941)* (Bologna: Il Mulino, 2008); Angelo Del Boca, *I gas di Mussolini: Il fascismo e la Guerra d'Etiopia* (Rome: Editori Riuniti, 1996); and De Felice, *Mussolini il Duce: Gli anni del consenso*, 597–808.

88. Richard Overy, *Blood and Ruins: The Last Imperial War, 1931–1945* (London: Viking, 2022), 34–35.

89. OOBM, 26:31.

90. See Davide Rodogno, *Il nuovo ordine mediterraneo: Le politiche di occupazione dell'Italia fascista in Europa (1940–1943)* (Turin: Bollati Boringhieri, 2003).

91. OOBM, 26:127–28.

92. Benito Mussolini, *Scritti e discorsi dell'impero* (Milan: Hoepli, 1936).

93. Provveditorato agli studi di Padova, ed., *Funzione imperiale della scuola* (Padua: Società cooperative tipografica, 1937).

94. Nicola Labanca, "Impero," in De Grazia and Luzzatto, *Dizionario del fascismo*, 1:661.

95. Modified translation from Schnapp, *A Primer of Italian Fascism*, 60.

96. Labanca, "Impero," 661.

97. Deplano, "Dalle colonie all'impero," 47.

98. Alessio Gagliardi, "The Entrepreneurial Bourgeoisie and Fascism," and Chiara Giorgi, "The Allure of the Welfare State," in Albanese and Pergher, *In the Society of Fascists*, 109–30 and 31–48, respectively.

99. See De Felice, *Mussolini il Duce: Gli anni del consenso*, 729–48.

100. Dogliani, *Il fascismo degli italiani*, 281–318; and Gentile, *Storia del fascismo*, 1057–76.

101. See the reconstruction of this myth in David Bidussa, *Il mito del bravo italiano* (Milan: Il Saggiatore, 1994); Angelo Del Boca, *Italiani, brava gente? Un mito duro a morire* (Vicenza: Neri Pozza, 2005); and Filippo Focardi, *Il cattivo tedesco e il bravo italiano: La rimozione delle colpe della seconda Guerra mondiale* (Rome: Laterza, 2013).

102. The literature on Fascism and the Jews has become quite extensive. See Enzo Collotti, *Il fascismo e gli ebrei: Le leggi razziali in Italia* (Rome: Laterza, 2006); Marie-Anne Matard-Bonucci, *L'Italie fasciste et la persécution des Juifs* (Paris: Perrin, 2007); Aaron Gillette, *Racial Theories in Fascist Italy* (London: Routledge, 2002); Giorgio Israel and Pietro Nastasi, *Scienza e razza nell'Italia fascista* (Bologna: Il Mulino, 1998); Francesco Cassata, *"La difesa della razza": Politica, ideologia e imagine del razzismo fascista* (Turin: Einaudi, 2008); Simon Levis Sullam, *I carnefici italiani: Scene dal genocidio degli ebrei, 1943–1945* (Milan: Feltrinelli, 2015); Franco Giustolisi, *L'armadio della vergogna* (Rome: Nutrimenti, 2004); and Valentina Pisanty, *L'irritante questione delle camere a gas: Logica del negazionismo*, new ed. (Milan: Bompiani, 2014).

103. OOBM, 22:361.

104. Ibid., 22:362.

105. Ibid., 22:363–64.

106. Schnapp, *A Primer of Italian Fascism*, 10.

107. OOBM, 22:138.

108. Ibid., 22:190.

109. Ibid., 22:208.

110. Gentile, *Storia del fascismo*, 1093–1115.

111. Deplano, "Dalle colonie all'impero," 62–63.

112. "Faccetta nera" (Pretty Black Face), written by Renato Micheli and Mario Ruccione, was released in 1935 during the invasion of Ethiopia. The song celebrated the Italian colonial war as liberating the Abyssinians from the slavery imposed by Emperor Haile Selassie I. This is also the interpretation of the song given by the journalist and playwriter Marco Ramperti in the article announcing its release: "Faccetta nera," *La Stampa* 14, November 22, 1935, 3. In truth, the song popularized the idea of the sexual enslavement of Ethiopian women. See Igiaba Scego, "La vera

storia di Faccetta nera," *Internazionale*, August 6, 2015, https://www.internazionale.it/opinione/igiaba-scego/2015/08/06/faccetta-nera-razzismo. See also Valentina Pisanty, *La risata fascista: Quando si rideva per ristabilire l'ordine* (Milan: Feltrinelli, 2022).

113. Gianluca Gabrielli, "Razzismo," in De Grazia and Luzzatto, *Dizionario del fascismo*, 473.

114. Giovanna Boursier, "La persecuzione degli zingari nell'Italia fascista," *Studi storici* 37, no. 4 (1996): 1065–82.

115. On the history of the *Protocols* in Italy, see Cesare De Michelis, *Il manoscritto inesistente: I "Protocolli dei savi di Sion"* (Venice: Marsilio, 2004), and Carlo Ginzburg, *Il filo e le tracce* (Milan: Feltrinelli, 2006), 189–204. On the role of Preziosi and Benigni in supporting antisemitism as integral part of Fascism since the 1920s, see Maria Teresa Pichetto, *Alle radici dell'odio: Preziosi e Benigni antisemiti* (Milan: Franco Angeli, 1983).

116. Tarquini, *Storia della cultura fascista*, 195–98; and Cassata, *"La difesa della razza,"* 42–44 and 61–69.

117. Noteworthy is the output of Julius Evola, whose texts have acquired a new readership in the last twenty years among the supporters of extreme right-wing movements in Europe, the United States, and India. Of Evola, see in particular *Tre aspetti del problema ebraico* (Rome: Edizioni Mediterranee, 1936), *Il mito del sangue* (Milan: Hoepli, 1937), and *Sintesi di dottrina della razza* (Milan: Hoepli, 1941). Of the works of Giani, see *Perché siamo antisemiti* (Milan: SMF, 1939). See also Paolo Orano, *Gli ebrei in Italia* (Rome: Pinciana, 1937).

118. On the periodical *La difesa della razza*, see Cassata, *"La difesa della razza"*; Valentina Pisanty, *"La difesa della razza": Antologia, 1938–1943* (Milan: Bompiani, 2006); and Michele Loré, *Antisemitismo e razzismo ne "La difesa della razza"* (Catanzaro: Rubettino, 2008).

119. English translation by Olivia E. Sears in Schnapp, *A Primer of Italian Fascism*, 173–75.

120. Marina Beer, Anna Foa, and Isabella Iannuzzi, eds., *Leggi del 1938 e cultura del razzismo: Storia, memoria, rimozione* (Rome: Viella, 2010); Sullam, *I carnefici italiani*; and Gentile, *Storia del fascismo*, 1116–30.

121. "Discorso di Trieste," *Il popolo d'Italia*, September 19, 1938, 25; reprinted in OOBM, 29:146.

122. Gabrielli, "Razzismo," 475.

123. OOBM, 29:190.

124. On the revolutionary politics of early Mussolini, see Marco Gervasoni, "Mussolini and Revolutionary Syndicalism," in *Mussolini 1883–1915: Triumph and Transformation of a Revolutionary Socialist*, ed. Spencer M. Di Scala and Emilio Gentile (New York: Palgrave Macmillan, 2016), 131–56.

125. The article appeared in the newspaper *La lotta di classe*; reprinted in OOBM, 4:116–19.

126. OOBM, 4:154.

127. Ibid., 5:87.

128. Ibid., 5:91.

129. Ibid., 4:173.

130. Ibid., 4:76.

131. Ibid., 6:51.

132. Ibid., 1:184; suspension points in the original.

133. Antonio Gramsci, in the cultural section of his *Prison Notebooks*, suggested that the idea of the Übermensch derived, rather than from Friedrich Nietzsche, from the hero figure in popular French *feuilletons*, such as Edmund Dantès, D'Artagnan, and other such characters. Mussolini himself published a serialized novel in the style of the *feuilleton*, entitled *Claudia*

Particella: L'amante del cardinale, in installments in Trento's newspaper *Il popolo* in 1910. See, in English, Antonio Gramsci, "Popular Origin of the 'Superman,'" in *Gramsci: Selections from Cultural Writings*, ed. David Forgacs and Geoffrey Nowell-Smiths, trans. William Boelhower (London: Lawrence and Wishart, 1985), 355–59.

134. OOBM, 5:121.

135. Ibid., 5:142.

136. Ibid., 7:141.

137. Renzo De Felice, *Mussolini il rivoluzionario, 1883–1920* (Turin: Einaudi, 1965), 346. Mussolini, in an aphoristic editorial of May 24, considered the Russian Revolution of the previous February the direct result of the experience at the front of Russian comrades rather than the final surge of the masses in an emancipatory movement: it was evidence that his equation of war and revolution had been proven correct. What excited him, however, was not the possible realization of a socialist revolution, but its effect on the war: the February Revolution, argued Mussolini, was the main reason the czar did not sign a separate peace treaty with Germany, thus leaving a window of hope for the war against the central empires. In OOBM, 8:277–79.

138. See, e.g., the articles in OOBM, 12:52–55, 104–6, and 114–16.

139. OOBM, 12:29 and 12:201 respectively. After the war, he continued attacking the Italian political class: it was inept, unpatriotic, without vision and energy. "The Italian victory," he wrote in a letter of January 1, 1919 to D'Annunzio, "must not be mutilated, not even in the name of democracy and Wilsonism. . . . We must use this victory to profoundly renew our national life. We must stop all war saboteurs, all priests of procrastination, all Giolitti's followers and rascals." In OOBM, 12:332.

140. OOBM, 12:310.

141. Ibid., 12:15.

142. Ibid.

143. Ibid., 12:65.

144. Ibid., 13:15.

145. Gioacchino Volpe, "Storia del Fascismo," https://www.polyarchy.org/basta/documenti/storia.fascismo.1932.html, accessed September 16, 2024.

146. Ibid. Volpe here paraphrased Mussolini's words from an interview of June 1, 1921, in OOBM, 16:391–95. See also Gioacchino Volpe, *L'Italia tra le due guerre*, ed. Gennaro Malgieri (Milan: Oaks, 2018).

147. OOBM, 17:233.

148. Ibid., 18:466.

149. Ibid., 25:295.

150. Ibid., 25:294.

151. Ibid., 25:173.

152. Ibid., 25:174.

153. Ibid., 25:154.

154. Ibid., 34:130. English translation in Schnapp, *A Primer of Italian Fascism*, 59.

155. Bruno Spampanato, *Democrazia fascista* (Rome: Edizioni di "Politica Nuova," 1933), 12–13.

156. From a March 17, 1924 speech translated in Schnapp, *A Primer of Italian Fascism*, 82–83.

157. Ben-Ghiat, *Fascist Modernities*, 22, who also translated these excerpts from, in order, Giuseppe Bottai, "Il problema delle riviste al convegno della stampa fascista," *Critica fascista*, June 15, 1924, 30; and Bottai, "Totalità, perennità, universalità della rivoluzione fascista," *Quadrante* 1, no. 8 (1933): 1–2.

158. Jeffrey T. Schnapp, "Epic Demonstration: Fascist Modernity and the 1932 Exhibition of the Fascist Revolution," in Golsan, *Fascism, Aesthetics, and Culture*, 31. See also Maddalena Carli, *Vedere il Fascismo: Arte e politica nelle esposizioni del regime (1928–1942)* (Rome: Carocci, 2020).

159. Schnapp, "Epic Demonstration," 2.

160. Ibid., 31.

161. Ben-Ghiat, *Fascist Modernities*, 56.

162. Ibid.

163. Giorgio Alberto Chiurco, *Storia della rivoluzione fascista* (Florence: Vallecchi, 1929), 1:3.

164. Giorgio Rochat, *Le guerre italiane, 1935–1943: Dall'impero d'Etiopia alla disfatta* (Turin: Einaudi, 2008), 403–36; and Renzo De Felice, *Mussolini l'alleato, 1940–1945*, vol. 2, *La guerra civile, 1943–1945* (Turin: Einaudi, 1997), 72–100.

165. The scholarship on the RSI is vast. On the Salò republic and the puppet role of Mussolini, see De Felice, *Mussolini l'alleato*, vol. 2, *La guerra civile*, 343–555; Amedeo Osti Guerrazzi, *Storia della Repubblica sociale italiana* (Rome: Carocci, 2012); Roberto Chiarini, *L'ultimo fascismo* (Venice: Marsilio, 2009); Mimmo Franzinelli, *Il prigioniero di Salò* (Milan: Mondadori, 2012); Franzinelli, *La repubblica del duce: RSI, 1943–1945, una storia illustrata* (Gorizia: Leg, 2022); Goeschel, *Mussolini and Hitler*, 254–90; and R. J. B. Bosworth, *Mussolini* (London: Arnold, 2002), 382–409. On the regime of terror, jointly administered by RSI's Brigate Nere and the German Wehrmacht, see Lutz Klinkhammer, *L'occupazione tedesca in Italia, 1943–1945* (Turin: Bollati Boringhieri, 1993); Dianella Gagliani, *Brigate nere: Mussolini e la militarizzazione del Partito fascista repubblicano* (Turin: Bollati Boringhieri, 1999); Mimmo Franzinelli, *Tortura: Storie dell'occupazione nazista e della Guerra civile (1943–45)* (Milan: Mondadori, 2018); Marco Cuzzi, *Seicento giorni di terrore a Milano: Vita quotidiana ai tempo di Salò* (Vicenza: Neri Pozza, 2022); and Enrico Cernigoi, *Le SS in Italia* (Florence and Milan: Giunti, 2022).

166. OOBM, 29:527. The text of the pact was published in *Il popolo d'Italia*, May 23, 1939.

167. OOBM, 29:403.

168. Ibid., 29:404.

169. Ibid., 29:405.

170. Rochat, *Le guerre italiane*, 239–399.

171. OOBM, 32:3.

172. Ibid., 32:4.

173. On the RSI Black Brigades, see Gagliani, *Brigate nere*. On the German occupation of Italy, see Lutz Klinkhammer, *Zwischen Bündnis und Besatzung: Das nationalsozialistische Deutschland und die Republik von Salò, 1943–1945* (Tübingen: Niemeyer, 1993), and Carlo Gentile, *I crimini di guerra tedeschi in Italia, 1943–1945* (Turin: Einaudi, 2015).

174. English translation in Schnapp, *A Primer of Italian Fascism*, 202.

175. Ibid., 203.

176. OOBM, 32:267.

177. Police ordinance no. 5 of November 30, 1943. See Matard-Bonucci, *L'Italie fasciste et la persécution des Juifs*, 402–30, and Sullam, *I carnefici italiani*, 9–14. On the Italian Civil War of 1943–45, the literature is vast. For an introduction, Claudio Pavone, *Una guerra civile: Saggio storico sulla moralità nella Resistenza* (1991; Turin: Bollati Boringhieri, 2006); Santo Peli, *Storia della Resistenza in Italia* (Turin: Einaudi, 2006); and Marcello Flores and Mimmo Franzinelli, *Storia della Resistenza* (Rome: Laterza, 2019).

178. Mimmo Franzinelli, *Il fascismo è finito il 25 aprile 1945* (Rome: Laterza, 2022), 101–26.

179. Ibid., 79–94; Paul Ginsborg, *A History of Contemporary Italy: Society and Politics, 1943–1988* (London: Penguin, 1990), 298–404; and Miguel Gotor, *Generazione Settanta: Storia del decennio più lungo del secolo breve, 1966–1982* (Turin: Einaudi, 2022).

180. Franco Ferraresi, *Minacce alla democrazia: La Destra radicale e la strategia della tensione in Italia nel dopoguerra* (Milan: Feltrinelli, 1995), esp. 31–105; Anna Cento Bull, *Italian Neofascism: The Strategy of Tension and the Politics of Nonreconciliation* (New York: Berghahn, 2007); Paolo Morando, *Prima di Piazza Fontana: La prova generale* (Rome: Laterza, 2019); Gianni Oliva, *Anni di piombo e di tritolo, 1969–1980: Il terrorismo nero e il terrorismo rosso da Piazza Fontana alla strage di Bologna* (Milan: Mondadori, 2019); Angelo Ventrone, *La strategia della paura: Eversione e stragismo nell'Italia del Novecento* (Milan: Mondadori, 2019); and Benedetta Tobagi, *Le stragi sono tutte un mistero* (Bari: GLF editori Laterza, 2024).

181. Camillo Arcuri, *Colpo di stato: Storia vera di una inchiesta censurata* (Milan: Rizzoli, 2004).

182. Giorgio Galli, *La venerabile trama: La vera storia di Licio Gelli e della P2* (Turin: Lindau, 2007). See the video of his declaration of Fascism during a television news show of November 3, 2008 at https://video.corriere.it/gelli-sono-fascista-moriro-fascista/8473b9aa-a3cd-11e5-900d-2dd5b80ea9fe, accessed September 16, 2024.

183. Daniele Ganser, *NATO's Secret Armies: Operation Gladio and Terrorism in Western Europe* (London: Routledge, 2005).

184. Sergio Luzzatto, *La crisi dell'antifascismo* (Turin: Einaudi, 2004); and Enzo Traverso, *The New Faces of Fascism: Populism and the Far Right* (New York: Verso, 2019).

Chapter Four

1. *Enciclopedia italiana di scienze, lettere e arti*, 39 vols. (Rome: Istituto Giovanni Treccani, 1929–61).

2. Benito Mussolini, *La dottrina del fascismo: Con una storia del movimento fascista di Gioacchino Volpe* (Milan: Treves-Treccani-Tumminelli, 1932). The short text was published in English by Leonard and Virginia Woolf as *The Political and Social Doctrine of Fascism*, trans. Jane Soames (London: Leonard and Virginia Woolf at the Hogarth Press, 1933). A different English translation was also published by I. S. Munro as *Fundamental Ideas* (London: Alexander Maclehose, 1933), and another one by E. Cope as *The Doctrine of Fascism* (Florence: Vallecchi, 1937). A German translation, *Der Faschismus: Philosophische, politische und gesellschaftliche Grundlehren* (Munich: Beck, 1933), was published the same year and later republished as *Der Geist des Faschismus: Ein Quellenwerk* (Munich: Beck, 1940). Two years later a Polish translation by Stanisław Gniadek was published as *Doktryna faszysmu* (Lviv: Nakładem Filomaty, 1935), and a Russian one was published by the émigré and Fascist sympathizer Vyachelslav N. Novikov as *Doktrinaa fashizma s prilozheniem Khartii truda* (Paris: Vozrozhdenie, 1938). A complete French translation, *La doctrine du fascisme*, was not published until 1938, edited by Charles Belin, for Vallecchi (Florence), although a partial translation was circulated in 1933 by Denoël et Steele as *Le fascisme: Doctrine; Institutions* (Paris: Denoël & Steele, 1933). A partial Japanese translation appeared as *Waga tōseisaku*, ed. Satomi Kōichirō (Tokyo: Sanshūsha, 1938). Translations in Spanish and Portuguese appeared in 1935, both published in Florence for Vallecchi.

3. All of the following English translations are from Jeffrey T. Schnapp, ed., *A Primer of Italian Fascism* (Lincoln: University of Nebraska Press, 2000), 46.

4. Ibid., 47.

5. Ibid., 48.

6. Ibid., 49.

7. Ibid., 50.

8. Ibid., 52.

9. Ibid., 53, 54, and 55.

10. On Gentile, see Alessandra Tarquini, *Il Gentile dei fascisti: Gentiliani e antigentiliani nel regime fascista* (Bologna: Il Mulino, 2009), and Mimmo Franzinelli, *Il filosofo in camicia nera: Giovanni Gentile e gli intellettuali di Mussolini* (Milan: Mondadori, 2021).

11. In Schnapp, *A Primer of Italian Fascism*, 109.

12. Giuseppe Bottai, "Fascism as Intellectual Revolution (1924)," trans. Maria G. Stampino and Jeffrey T. Schnapp, in Schnapp, *A Primer of Italian Fascism*, 76.

13. Ibid., 83.

14. Ibid., 84.

15. Ugo Spirito, "Corporativism and Absolute Liberalism and Absolute Socialism" (1932), in Schnapp, *A Primer of Italian Fascism*, 150.

16. Sven Felix Kellerhoff, *Mein Kampf: Die Karriere eines deutschen Buches* (Stuttgart: Klett-Cotta, 2015).

17. Viktor Klemperer, *The Language of the Third Reich: LTI—Lingua Tertii Imperii; A Philologist's Notebook*, trans. Martin Brady (London: Bloomsbury, 2013), 51–52.

18. Alessandra Tarquini, *Storia della cultura fascista* (Bologna: Il Mulino, 2011).

19. Klemperer, *The Language of the Third Reich*, 15.

20. The expression was used in *La folla* 47, September 29, 1914, 3, reprinted in OOBM, vol. 7, 453.

21. The linguist Tullio de Mauro and the historian George L. Mosse contemporaneously developed the conception of a "nationalization of the masses" in the early 1970s. De Mauro used it to introduce the linguistic politics of Fascism in *Storia linguistica dell'Italia unita* (Bari: Laterza, 1972), 36–51; and Mosse, in *The Nationalization of the Masses: Political Symbolism and Mass Movements in Germany, from the Napoleonic Wars to the Third Reich* (New York: H. Fertig, 1975).

22. Alessandra Tarquini, "Le parole e I discorsi del fascismo: Riflessioni sulla lingua di un regime totalitario," in *Il primate della politica nell'Italia del Novecento: Studi in onore di Emilio Gentile*, ed. Alessandra Tarquini (Rome: Laterza, 2016), 69.

23. See Tarquini, "Le parole e i discorsi del fascismo," 69–73; Patrizia Dogliani, *Il fascismo degli italiani: Una storia sociale* (Turin: UTET, 2008), 259–63; Gabriella Klein, *La politica linguistica del Fascismo* (Bologna: Il Mulino, 1986); Sergio Raffaelli, *Le parole proibite: Purismo di Stato e la regolamentazione della pubblicità in Italia, 1812–1945* (Bologna: Il Mulino, 1983); and Fabio Foresti, ed., *Credere, obbedire, combattere: Il regime linguistico nel Ventennio* (Bologna: Pendragon, 2003). See also Jean Pierre Faye, *Langages totalitaires: Critique de la raison / l'économie narrative* (Paris: Hermann, 1972); and Enzo Golino, *Parola di duce: Il linguaggio totalitario del fascismo e del nazismo*, 2nd ed. (Milan: Bur, 2010).

24. Dogliani, *Il fascismo degli italiani*, 259.

25. Tarquini, "Le parole e i discorsi del fascismo," 69–70.

26. Klein, *La politica linguistica del fascismo*, 56–59.

27. For example, the region of Basilicata was renamed Lucania (1932), the city of Girgenti became Agrigento (1927), and Intra-Pallanza was rechristened Verbania (1939). Dogliani, *Il fascismo degli italiani*, 259–60.

28. Klein, *La politica linguistica del fascismo*, 72–83.

29. Dogliani, *Il fascismo degli italiani*, 260.

30. Klein, *La politica linguistica del fascismo*, 92–93.

31. Gaetano Salvemini, *Mussolini diplomatico (1922–1932)* (Bari: Laterza, 1952), 445.

32. Migliorini's words are quoted in Patrizia Dogliani, "Lingua/Dialetti," in *Dizionario del fascismo*, ed. Victoria De Grazia e Sergio Luzzatto (Turin: Einaudi, 2002), 2:54. The self-described "neopurist[a]" intended to distinguish their activities, addressing *all* linguistic manifestations, from those of "purists," who limited their interventions to literary language alone. Ibid.

33. Fabio Foresti, "Proposte interpretative e di ricerca su lingua e fascismo: la 'politica linguistica,'" in Erasmo Leso, Michele A. Cortelazzo, Ivano Paccagnella, and Fabio Foresti, *La lingua italiana e il fascismo* (Bologna: Consorzio provincial pubblica lettura, 1978), 111–48; and Raffaelli, *Le parole proibite*, 203–25.

34. Bruno Cicognani, "L'abolizione del Lei," *Il corriere della sera*, January 15, 1938, 3, quoted in Tarquini, "Le parole e i discorsi del fascismo," 80.

35. Achille Starace, *Vademecum dello stile fascista*, ed. Asvero Gravelli (Rome: Nuova Europa, 1939), 10.

36. Chiara Ferrari, *The Rhetoric of Violence and Sacrifice in Fascist Italy: Mussolini, Gadda, Vittorini* (Toronto: University of Toronto Press, 2013), 49–76.

37. Quoted in Tarquini, "Le parole e i discorsi del fascismo," 74. See Giancarlo Schirru, "Per la storia e la teoria della linguistica educative: Il Quaderno 29 di Antonio Gramsci," in *Linguistica educativa*, ed. Silvana Ferreri (Rome: Bulzoni, 2012), 77–91. Notebook 29 is collected in Antonio Gramsci, *Quaderni del carcere*, vol. 3, *Quaderni 12–29*, ed. Valentino Gerratana (Turin: Einaudi, 1977), 2339–58.

38. Giuseppe Bottai, "Appunti sui rapport fra lingua e rivoluzione," *L'orto* 4, no. 3 (May–June 1934): 14. On Bottai and Fascist linguistic policy, see Claudio Marazzini, "Bottai e la lingua italiana," *Lingua nostra* 58, nos. 1–2 (1997): 1–12; and Tarquini, "Le parole e i discorsi del fascismo," 75–77.

39. Giovanni Lazzari, *Le parole del fascismo* (Rome: Argileto, 1975).

40. For an overview of the studies on the language of Fascism, see Fabio Foresti, "Le varietà linguistiche e il 'language planning' durante il fascismo: Un bilancio degli studi (1977–2001), in Foresti *Credere, obbedire, combattere*, 11–26.

41. Franco Venturi, "Il regime fascista," in *Trent'anni di storia italiana (1915–1945): Lezioni con testimonianze*, ed. Domenico Zucàro (Turin: Einaudi, 1961), 186.

42. Pietro Calamandrei, *Il fascismo come regime della menzogna* (Rome: Laterza, 2014).

43. English translation in Thomas Mann, "Mario and the Magician," in *Collected Stories*, trans. H. T. Lowe Porter (London: Everyman's Library, 2001), 603–50.

44. For a reevaluation of the importance of ideological discourse for the organization of popular consensus of the Fascist regime, see Pier Giorgio Zunino, *L'ideologia del fascismo: Miti, credenze, valori* (Bologna: Il Mulino, 1995), esp. 11–62; and Emilio Gentile, *Le origini dell'ideologia fascista, 1918–1925* (Bologna: Il Mulino, 1996).

45. Mario Isnenghi, *L'educazione dell'italiano: Il fascismo e l'organizzazione della cultura* (Bologna: Cappelli, 1979), 8.

46. Gramsci, "Quaderno 29," in *Quaderni del carcere*, vol. 3, *Quaderni 12–29*, 2349.

47. Ibid., 2344. The apparatuses that the state mobilizes to impose or realize a "national linguistic conformism within the national masses," for Gramsci, who anticipated Louis Althusser, were "1) the schools; 2) newspapers; 3) artistic writers and popular writers; 4) the theater and the sound cinema; 5) the radio; 6) public meetings of all kinds, including religious ones; 7) the

relations of 'conversation' between the various strata of the population, more educated and less educated." Ibid., 2345.

48. Ferrari, *The Rhetoric of Violence and Sacrifice in Fascist Italy*, 13–48.

49. OOBM, 31:196.

50. Bruno Biancini, ed., *Dizionario mussoliniano: Mille affermazioni e definizioni del DUCE* (Milan: Hoepli, 1939).

51. Erasmo Leso, "Aspetti della lingua del fascismo: Prime line di una ricerca," in *Storia linguistica dell'Italia del Novecento*, ed. Maurizio Gnerre, Mario Medici, and Raffaele Simone (Rome: Bulzoni, 1973), 141–42.

52. Lorenzo Bianchi, *Mussolini scrittore e oratore* (Bologna: Zanichelli, 1937); Andrea Gustarelli, *Mussolini, scrittore e oratore* (Milan: Vallardi, 1935); and Carlo Villani, *Stile di Mussolini* (Turin: SEI, 1937).

53. Hermann Ellwanger, *Studien zur Sprache Benito Mussolinis* (Florence: Sansoni, 1939); translated into Italian as Ellwanger, *Sulla lingua di Mussolini* (Milan: Mondadori, 1941).

54. Ellwanger, *Sulla lingua di Mussolini*, 30; English translation in Ferrari, *The Rhetoric of Violence and Sacrifice in Fascist Italy*, 51.

55. Ellwanger, *Sulla lingua di Mussolini*, 24; English translation in Ferrari, *The Rhetoric of Violence and Sacrifice in Fascist Italy*, 51.

56. Ellwanger, *Sulla lingua di Mussolini*, 27; English translation in Ferrari, *The Rhetoric of Violence and Sacrifice in Fascist Italy*, 56.

57. Ferrari, *The Rhetoric of Violence and Sacrifice in Fascist Italy*, 74.

58. Giorgio Fedel, "Per uno studio del linguaggio di Mussolini," *Il Politico* 43, no. 3 (1978): 468.

59. Michele Cortelazzo, "Mussolini socialista e gli antecedenti della retorica fascista," in Foresti, *Credere, obbedire, combattere*, 67–82, showed how parataxis had been characteristic of Mussolini's rhetoric since his early writings during the Socialist period.

60. Fedel, "Per uno studio del linguaggio di Mussolini," 471.

61. Quoted in ibid.

62. Erasmo Leso, "Osservazioni sulla lingua di Mussolini," in Leso, Cortelazzo, Paccagnella, and Foresti, *La lingua italiana e il fascismo*, 45–46.

63. Fedel, "Per uno studio del linguaggio di Mussolini," 472.

64. Ibid., 475.

65. Ellwanger, *Sulla lingua di Mussolini*, 71–90; Leso, "Osservazioni sulla lingua di Mussolini," 61; and Fedel, "Per uno studio del linguaggio di Mussolini," 476–77.

66. Fedel, "Per uno studio del linguaggio di Mussolini," 478–79.

67. Leso, "Osservazioni sulla lingua di Mussolini," 34–35.

68. Fedel, "Per uno studio del linguaggio di Mussolini," 483.

69. Ibid.

70. Fedel, "Per uno studio della lingua di Mussolini," 488.

71. Leso, "Osservazioni sulla lingua di Mussolini," 38.

72. See Fedel, "Per uno studio della lingua di Mussolini," 487–92, for more examples.

73. The bibliography on nationalism, language and the nationalization of the masses is immense, starting from the essays of Eric Hobsbawm, George L. Mosse, and the now classic Benedict Anderson's *Imagined Communities: Reflections on the Origin and Spread of Nationalism* (London: Verso, 1991). For a historical-conceptual overview, see Mark Mazower, *Dark Continent: Europe's Twentieth Century* (New York: Vintage, 2000); Francesco Tuccari, *La nazione*

(Rome: Laterza, 2000); Aviel Roshwald, *Ethnic Nationalism and the Fall of Empires: Central Europe, Russia, and the Middle East, 1914–1923* (London: Routledge, 2001), and Natasha Wheatley, *The Life and Death of States: Central Europe and the Transformation of Modern Sovereignty* (Princeton, NJ: Princeton University Press, 2023), esp. 103–39. On language and nationalism, see Lenore A. Grenoble, *Language Policy in the Soviet Union* (New York: Springer, 2003); İlker Aytürk, "Turkish Linguists against the West: The Origins of Linguistic Nationalism in Atatürk's Turkey," *Middle Eastern Studies* 40, no. 6 (2004): 1–15; Pieter Judson, *Guardians of the Nation: Activists on the Language Frontiers of Imperial Austria* (Cambridge, MA: Harvard University Press, 2007); Terry Martin, *The Affirmative Action Empire: Nation and Nationalisms in the Soviet Union, 1923–1939* (Ithaca, NY: Cornell University Press, 2011); Atsuko Ueda, *Language, Nation, Race: Linguistic Reform in Meiji Japan, 1868–1912* (Berkeley: University of California Press, 2021); and Janet Y. Chen, *The Sounds of Mandarin: Learning to Speak a National Language in China and Taiwan, 1913–1960* (New York: Columbia University Press, 2023).

74. This is evident when compared to Stalin's understanding of language in terms of constitutive base rather than superstructure in *Marxism and Problems of Linguistics* (Moscow: Foreign Languages Publishing House, 1950), excerpts at https://www.marxists.org/reference/archive/stalin/works/1950/jun/20.htm, accessed September 16, 2024.

Part II Introduction

Epigraph: Adorno, *Minima Moralia*, trans. E. F. N. Jephcott.

1. Umberto Eco, *A Theory of Semiotics* (Bloomington: Indiana University Press, 1976), 76–84.

2. Ibid., 289–98.

Chapter Five

1. Giulia Albanese, "Non solo propaganda: Il modello fascista all'estero (1922–35)," in *Il fascismo italiano: Storia e interpretazioni*, ed. Giulia Albanese (Rome: Carocci, 2021), 311.

2. Mark Mazower, *Dark Continent: Europe's Twentieth Century* (New York: Alfred A. Knopf, 1999), 3.

3. Linda Colley, *The Gun, the Ship, and the Pen: Warfare, Constitutions, and the Making of the Modern World* (New York: Liveright, 2021), 401–12.

4. Mazower, *Dark Continent*, 4.

5. Kevin Duong, "What Was Universal Suffrage?," *Theory and Event* 23, no. 1 (2020): 29–65.

6. Aristotle Kallis, "Fascism and the Right in Interwar Europe: Interaction, Entanglement, Hybridity," in *The Oxford Handbook of European History, 1914–1945*, ed. Nicholas Doumanis (Oxford: Oxford University Press, 2014), 305.

7. The expression is from Martin Blinkhorn, "Allies, Rivals, or Antagonists? Fascists and Conservatives in Modern Europe," in *Fascists and Conservatives: The Radical Right and the Establishment in Twentieth-Century Europe*, ed. Martin Blinkhorn (London: Routledge, 1990), 4.

8. See Jörn Leonhard, *Pandora's Box: A History of the First World War*, trans. Patrick Camiller (Cambridge, MA: Harvard University Press, 2018), 837–73; and Antonio Gibelli, *L'officina della Guerra: La Grande Guerra e le trasformazioni del mondo mentale* (1991; Turin: Bollati Boringhieri, 2007), 164–209.

9. See Stephen C. MacDonald, "Crisis, War, and Revolution in Europe, 1917–23," in *Neutral Europe between War and Revolution, 1917–23*, ed. Hans A. Schmitt (Charlottesville: University

Press of Virginia, 1988), 235–52; and Robert Gerwarth, "The Central European Counter-Revolution: Paramilitary Violence in Germany, Austria, and Hungary after the Great War," *Past and Present* 200, no. 1 (2008): 175–209.

10. Patrick Kinross, *Atatürk: The Rebirth of a Nation* (London: Phoenix Press, 2003); and Erik J. Zurcher, *Turkey: A Modern History* (London: I. B. Tauris, 1997). Stanley Payne commented that Atatürk's regime "constituted probably the most positive example of a developmental dictatorship in the process of creating a sort of 'guided democracy' "; Payne, *A History of Fascism, 1814–1945* (London: Routledge, 1995), 145.

11. Upendra Narayan Chakravorty, *Indian Nationalism and the First World War, 1914–1918* (Ann Arbor: University of Michigan Press, 1997).

12. Rebecca E. Karl, *China's Revolutions in the Modern World: A Brief Interpretive History* (London: Verso, 2020), 65.

13. Frederick R. Dickinson, *War and National Reinvention: Japan in the Great War, 1914–1919* (Cambridge, MA: Harvard University Asia Center, 1999).

14. Jun Uchida, *Brokers of Empire: Japanese Settler Colonialism in Korea, 1876–1945* (Cambridge, MA: Harvard University Asia Center, 2011), 143–226.

15. See the classic study of Peter Duus, *Party Rivalry and Political Change in Taishō Japan* (Cambridge, MA: Harvard University Press, 1968).

16. Peter Neville, *Mussolini*, 2nd ed. (London: Routledge, 2015), 99.

17. Robert A. Rosenbaum, *Waking to Danger: Americans and Nazi Germany, 1933–1941* (Santa Barbara, CA: Praeger, 2010), 58.

18. Ibid.

19. "Sad day!"; in Italian in the original.

20. Carleton Beals, *Rome or Death: The Story of Fascism* (New York: Century,1923), 297–98.

21. *New York Times*, September 24, 1931, 11, quoted in Rosenbaum, *Waking to Danger*, 58.

22. Rosenbaum, *Waking to Danger*, 59.

23. Ibid., 146.

24. Philip V. Cannistraro, *Blackshirts in Little Italy: Italian-Americans and Fascism, 1921–1929* (West Lafayette, IN: Bordighera, 1999); and Joseph Fronczak, *Everything Is Possible: Antifascism and the Left in the Age of Fascism* (New Haven, CT: Yale University Press, 2023).

25. Ezra Pound, *Jefferson and/or Mussolini* (1935; New York: Liveright, 1970), 110.

26. Walter Frank, *Zur Geschichte des Nationalsozialismus* (Hamburg: Hanseatische Verlagsanstalt, 1939), 20, English translation in *The Third Reich Sourcebook*, ed. Anson Rabinbach and Sander L. Gilman (Berkeley: University of California Press, 2013), 40.

27. Ian Kershaw, *Hitler: 1889–1936, Hubris* (New York: W. W. Norton, 1998), 180.

28. Quoted in Hugh Trevor-Roper, *Hitler's Table Talk, 1941–1945* (New York: Enigma, 1996), 10.

29. Probably the best study of Mussolini's influence on Hitler is Wolfgang Schieder, *Adolf Hitler: Politischer Zauberlehrling Mussolinis* (Berlin: de Gruyter, 2017).

30. In Albanese, "Non solo propaganda," 309.

31. Quote in Kallis, "Fascism and the Right in Interwar Europe," 308.

32. Richard Thurlow, *Fascism in Britain: From Oswald Mosley's Blackshirts to the National Front* (London: I. B. Tauris, 1998), 34.

33. Ibid., 68.

34. Payne, *A History of Fascism*, 315.

35. Kallis, "Fascism and the Right in Interwar Europe," 311. On the links between Preto's Blueshirts and Fascism, see António Costa Pinto, " 'Chaos' and 'Order': Preto, Salazar and

Charismatic Appeal in Inter-war Portugal," in *Charisma and Fascism in Interwar Europe*, ed. António Costa Pinto, Roger Eatwell, and Stein Ugelvik Larsen (London: Routledge, 2007), 65–76.

36. Georges Valois, *La revolution nationale: Philosophie de la Victoire* (Paris: La Nouvelle Libraire, 1924), 50; English trans. in Jules Levey, "Georges Valois and the Faisceau: The Making and Breaking of a Fascist," *French Historical Studies* 8, no. 2 (1973): 285.

37. Valois, *La revolution nationale*, 182. See also Robert O. Paxton, *The Anatomy of Fascism* (New York: Alfred A. Knopf, 2004), 48.

38. Robert O. Paxton, *French Peasant Fascism: Henry Dorgères's Greenshirts and the Crises of French Agriculture, 1929–1939* (Oxford: Oxford University Press, 1997), 130.

39. Quoted in Pascal Ory, "Le dorgérisme, institution et discours d'une colère paysanne (1929–1939)," *Revue d'histoire modern et contemporaine* 22, no. 2 (1975): 185.

40. Callum A. MacDonald, "Radio Bari: Italian Wireless Propaganda in the Middle East and British Countermeasures, 1934–38," *Middle Eastern Studies* 13, no. 2 (1977): 195–207.

41. Payne, *A History of Fascism*, 352.

42. Ibid.

43. See Marzia Casolari, *In the Shadow of the Swastika: The Relationship between Indian Radical Nationalism, Italian Fascism and Nazism* (London: Routledge, 2020), 1–56.

44. Quoted in ibid., 43–44.

45. See Orazio Coco, "The Penetration of Italian Fascism in Nationalist China: Political Influence and Economic Legacy," *The International History Review* 43, no. 2 (2021): 264–80.

46. Quoted in Lloyd E. Eastman, *The Abortive Revolution: China under Nationalist Rule, 1927–1937* (Cambridge, MA: Harvard University Asia Center, 1974), 40.

47. *Ikoku "Fashisuchii" tō* 1, in *Kakkoku ni okeru seitō chōsa*, item 1, vol. 3, no. 9, JASCAR no. B03051103900.

48. Reto Hofmann, *The Fascist Effect: Japan and Italy, 1915–1952* (Ithaca, NY: Cornell University Press, 2015), 8–37.

49. Ibid., 38.

50. Ibid, 38–61.

51. Ibid., 68–88.

52. Aaron Stephen Moore, *Constructing East Asia: Technology, Ideology, and Empire in Japan's Wartime Era, 1931–1945* (Stanford, CA: Stanford University Press, 2015).

53. Federico Finchelstein, *Transatlantic Fascism: Ideology, Violence, and the Sacred in Argentina and Italy, 1919–1945* (Durham, NC: Duke University Press, 2010), 8.

54. Quoted in ibid., 51.

55. Quoted in George I. Blankstein, *Perón's Argentina* (Chicago: University of Chicago Press, 1953), 279.

56. Payne, *A History of Fascism*, 345.

57. Emilio Gentile, *In Italia ai tempi di Mussolini: Viaggio in compagnia di osservatori stranieri* (Milan: Mondadori, 2014).

58. On the importance of charismatic leadership in preserving the capitalist order in the interwar period, see the essays Roger Eatwell, "The Concept and Theory of Charismatic Leadership"; Emilio Gentile, "Mussolini as the Prototypical Charismatic Dictator"; and António Costa Pinto and Stein Ugelvik Larse, "Fascism, Dictators, and Charisma" in Costa Pinto, Eatwell, and Larse, *Charisma and Fascism in Interwar Europe*, 3–18, 113–29, and 131–38, respectively. See also Ruth Ben-Ghiat, *Strongmen: Mussolini to the Present* (New York: W. W. Norton, 2020), esp. 19–26 and 119–29.

59. Martin Blinkhorn, *Fascism and the Right in Europe, 1919–1945* (London: Routledge, 2000), 110.

60. Clara E. Mattei, *The Capital Order: How Economists Invented Austerity and Paved the Way to Fascism* (Chicago: University of Chicago Press, 2022), 246–87.

61. Paxton, *The Anatomy of Fascism*, 218.

62. Kallis, "Fascism and the Right in Interwar Europe," 313.

63. "Rinunciatarismo" was Mussolini's interpretation of the antiwar and neutralist positions sustained by the Socialist Party since 1914. Mussolini, "Un ordine del giorno: Partiti e politica," *Il popolo d'Italia*, January 2, 1921, 8; reprinted in OOBM, 16:94.

64. "Antifascismo," referring to the PSI, reappears in sixteen articles of *Il popolo d'Italia* in 1921.

65. The first occurrence was in an editorial for *Il popolo d'Italia*, reprinted in OOBM, 16:390; the second, in an interview for *Il giornale di Sicilia*, reprinted in OOBM, 16:393.

66. OOBM, 16:410.

67. Ibid., 16:411.

68. Ibid., 17:51.

69. Followers of "Cagoia," or, "the Shitter," a depreciative nickname Gabriele D'Annunzio had coined for the prime minister Francesco Saverio Nitti of the Radical Party.

70. Benito Mussolini, "Nel bosco della merlata," *Il popolo d'Italia*, November 19, 1921, 8; reprinted in OOBM, 17:256. The motto "like dogs on the loose" appeared in German in the original.

71. For instance, in a speech at the Chamber of Senators during the presentation of a proposed reform of the army on April 2, 1925, reprinted in OOBM, 21:270–79.

72. OOBM, 20:216. Mussolini's conception of antifascism echoed what Carl Schmitt would conceptualize in 1932 as "the specific political distinction to which political actions and motives can be reduced is that between friend and enemy." See Schmitt, *The Concept of the Political*, trans. George Schwab, expanded ed. (Chicago: University of Chicago Press, 2007), 26.

73. Celso Ghini, *Gli antifascisti al confino, 1926–1943* (Rome: Editori Riuniti, 1971).

74. Aldo Garosci, *Storia dei fuorusciti* (Bari: Laterza, 1953).

75. Adriano Dal Pont, *I lager di Mussolini: L'altra faccia del confino nei documenti della polizia fascista* (Milan: La Pietra, 1975); and Carlo Spartaco Capogreco, *Mussolini's Camps: Civilian Internment in Fascist Italy (1940–1943)*, trans. Norma Bouchard and Valerio Ferme (London: Routledge, 2019).

76. Lorenzo Pompeo D'Alessandro, *Giustizia fascista: Storia del tribunale speciale (1926–1943)* (Bologna: Il Mulino, 2020).

77. Mimmo Franzinelli, *Squadristi: Protagonisti e tecniche della violenza fascista, 1919–1922* (Milan: Mondadori, 2003), 167–72; Franzinelli, *Il tribunale del Duce: La giustizia fascista e le sue vittime (1927–1943)* (Milan: Mondadori, 2017); and Emilio Gentile, *Storia del fascismo* (Rome: Laterza, 2022), 282–301.

78. See Sturzo's antifascist manifesto, published by the liberal journalist Piero Gobetti, in Luigi Struzo, *Pensiero antifascista* (Turin: Gobetti, 1925). See also Gabriele De Rosa, *Storia del partito liberale italiano* (Bari: Laterza, 1966).

79. *Il giornale d'Italia*, July 9, 1924, quoted in Antonella Randazzo, *L'Africa del Duce: I crimini fascisti in Africa* (Varese: Arterigere, 2008), 45.

80. Giuseppe Giordano, "La denuncia di un tradimento: Il 'Manifesto degli intellettuali antifascisti'," *Il pensiero italiano: Rivista di studi filosofici* 1, no. 1 (2017): 37–50.

81. Mimmo Franzinelli, *Delatori: Spie e confidenti anonimi; L'arma segreta del regime fascista* (Milan: Mondadori, 2001).

82. For a longer list, see Michele Cantarella, "Guida bibliografica degli scrittori italiani in esilio (1925–1945)," *Belfagor* 4, no. 3 (May 31, 1949): 338–50. See Charles F. Delzell, "Il fuoruscitismo italiano dal 1922 al 1943," in *Il movimento di liberazione in Italia* (1953), 3–37; Delzell, *I nemici di Mussolini* (Turin: Einaudi, 1966), 43–81; John Tedeschi, *Intellettuali in esilio: Dall'Inquisizione al fascismo* (Rome: Edizioni di Storia e Letteratura, 2012), 253–416; and Santi Fedele, *Il retaggio dell'esilio: Saggi sul fuoruscitismo antifascista* (Soveria Mannelli: Rubbettino, 2000), esp. 5–45.

83. The literature on the Italian resistance and the civil war is vast. For an introductory overview, see Max Salvadori, *Breve storia della Resistenza* (1974; Vicenza: Neri Pozza, 2016); Claudio Pavone, *Una guerra civile: Saggio storico sulla moralità nella Resistenza* (1991; Turin: Bollati Boringhieri, 2006); Santo Peli, *La Resistenza in Italia: Storia e critica* (Turin: Einaudi, 2004); Claudio Pavone, *Storia della Resistenza in Italia* (Turin: Einaudi, 2006); and Marcello Flores and Mimmo Franzinelli, *Storia della Resistenza* (Rome: Laterza, 2019). The best single volume on Italian antifascism is Simona Colarizi, *La resistenza lunga: Storia dell'antifascismo, 1919–1945* (Rome: Laterza, 2023). For comparative views on the resistance in Europe, see Olivier Wieviorka, *The Resistance in Western Europe, 1940–1945*, trans. Jane Marie Todd (New York: Columbia University Press, 2019); and Halik Kochanski, *Resistance: The Underground War against Hitler, 1939–1945* (New York: Liveright, 2022).

84. Giuseppe Filippetta, *L'estate che imparammo a sparare: Storia partigiana della Costituzione* (Milan: Feltrinelli, 2018), 87–142.

85. Leonardo Paggi, *Il "popolo dei morti": La repubblica italiana nata dalla guerra (1940–1946)* (Bologna: Il Mulino, 2009), 145–76; and Filippetta, *L'estate che imparammo a sparare*, 201–29.

86. Pavone, *Una guerra civile*, 169–219.

87. Filippetta, *L'estate che imparammo a sparare*, 11–34 and 230–59.

88. The conservative journalist Gianpaolo Pansa, in *Il sangue dei vinti* (Milan: Sperling & Kupfer, 2003), accusing the communist partisans of widespread and gratuitous violence after April 25, 1945, argued that the mythicization of the resistance had hidden the suffering of those who adhered to the Salò republic. The publication of the book was the occasion for a political campaign of historical revisionism of center-right parties in twenty-first-century Italy that subverted not only the importance of the partisan war but questioned the very legitimacy of antifascism. See Sergio Luzzatto, *La crisi dell'antifascismo* (Turin: Einaudi, 2004), 33. For a history of the delegitimation of antifascism and its lack of foundation in historical evidence, see Carlo Greppi, *L'antifascismo non serve più a niente* (Rome: Laterza, 2020).

89. See, e.g., Giovanni Pirelli, ed., *Lettere della Resistenza europea* (Turin: Einaudi, 1969); Giovanni Pirelli and Piero Malvezzi, eds., *Lettere dei condannati a morte della Resistenza italiana* (Turin: Einaudi, 1973); Giovanni Falaschi, *La resistenza armata nella narrativa italiana* (Turin: Einaudi, 1976); and Giovanni De Luna, *La Resistenza perfetta* (Milan: Feltrinelli, 2015).

90. For a historical overview of the importance and changing view on the Resistance in postwar Italy, see Filippo Focardi, *La guerra della memoria: La Resistenza nel dibattito politico italiano dal 1945 a oggi* (Rome: Laterza, 2020), esp. 3–55.

91. Gianni Oliva, *La grande storia della resistenza, 1943–1948* (Turin: UTET, 2018); and Luca Baldissara, *Italia 1943: La guerra continua* (Bologna: Il Mulino, 2023).

92. Mimmo Franzinelli, *Tortura: Storie dell'occupazione nazista e della guerra civile (1943–45)* (Milan: Mondadori, 2018).

93. Pavone, *Una guerra civile*, 413–513.

94. For an assessment of partisans' violence that critically dismisses the argument of Pansa and others, see Chiara Colombini, *Anche i partigiani però* (Rome: Laterza, 2021).

95. See Philip Nord, *France's New Deal: From the Thirties to the Postwar Era* (Princeton, NJ: Princeton University Press, 2010), 145–213. On the French resistance, see the introductory survey Olivier Wieviorka, *The French Resistance* (Cambridge, MA: Harvard University Press, 2016).

96. Anson Rabinbach, "Legacies of Antifascism," *New German Critique* 67 (Winter 1996): 3–17; and Michael Seidman, *Transatlantic Antifascisms: From the Spanish Civil War to the End of World War II* (Cambridge: Cambridge University Press, 2018), 160–250. Fronczak, in *Everything Is Possible*, argues for the importance of antifascism for the construction of the American Left.

97. Seidman, *Transatlantic Antifascisms*, 2–3.

98. Pavone, *Una guerra civile*, 259–60.

99. De Felice's dismissal of "antifascism" as the foundational ideal of the Italian republic can be read in Giuliano Ferrara, "'Le norme contro il fascismo? Sono grottesche, aboliamole': A colloquio con Renzo De Felice, lo storico del ventennio nero," *Il corriere della sera*, December 27, 1987, 2. The interview marked a polemical distancing of De Felice from other Italian historians of Fascism. The revisionist judgment he defended in the interview that "I know that Italian fascism is safe from the accusation of genocide, it is outside the shadow cone of the Holocaust. In many respects, Italian fascism was 'better' than French or Dutch fascism" was condemned by the majority of historians and later dismissed by archival research; see Enzo Collotti, *Il fascismo e gli ebrei: Le leggi razziali in Italia* (Rome: Laterza, 2003); Angelo Ventura, *Il fascismo e gli ebrei: Il razzismo antisemita nell'ideologia e nella politica del regime* (Rome: Donzelli, 2013); and Simon Levis Sullam, *I carnefici italiani: Scene dal genocidio degli ebrei, 1943–1945* (Milan: Feltrinelli, 2016).

100. Renzo De Felice, *Il fascismo: Le interpretazioni dei contemporanei e degli storici* (Bari: Laterza, 1970), 3. Emphasis in the original. The reference is obviously to Nolte's *Der Faschismus in seiner Epoche* (1963), more on which in chap. 11.

101. Mario Missiroli, *Il fascismo e la crisi italiana* (Bologna: Cappelli, 1921), 15–16.

102. Ibid., 18.

103. Ibid., 19.

104. Ibid.

105. Benito Mussolini, "Pietose illusioni," *Il popolo d'Italia*, May 10, 1922, 9, reprinted in OOBM, 18:184.

106. Gaetano Afeltra, *Missiroli e i suoi tempi* (Milan: Bompiani, 1985), 19.

107. The article would be republished as "Le illusioni di un conservatore" in *La rivoluzione liberale* 1, no. 34, November 23, 1922, 129.

108. Afeltra, *Missiroli e i suoi tempi*, 21. His name appeared among the signatories of the Manifesto della razza of 1938. In support of Nazi Germany, he published *Romanità e germanesimo* (Rome: Tiberino, 1942) and *Die kulturellen Beziehungen zwischen Italien und Deutschland* (Rome: F. Canella, 1942). He participated in the promotion of Fascism abroad, authoring the volume in English titled *What Italy Owes Mussolini* (Rome: Edizioni di Novissima, 1937), published also in Croat (1941), Spanish (1942), and French (1942) translations, all with Edizioni di Novissima.

109. Afeltra, *Missiroli e i suoi tempi*, 24–25.

110. Claudio Panizza, "Piero Gobetti e il fascismo come autobiografia della nazione," in Piero Gobetti, *L'autobiografia della nazione* (Fano: Aras, 2016), 25.

111. Antiguelfo [Piero Gobetti], "Esperienza liberale," *La rivoluzione liberale* 1, no. 15, May 28, 1922, 56.

112. Ibid.

113. Ibid.

114. Ibid.

115. Il Critico [Piero Gobetti], "Uomini e idee," *La rivoluzione liberale* 1, no. 15, May 28, 1922, 56. Excerpt reprinted in Piero Gobetti, "Mussolini," *La rivoluzione liberale* 1, no. 34, November 23, 1922, 130.

116. Ibid.

117. Ibid.

118. Piero Gobetti, "Note di politica interna," *La rivoluzione liberale* 1, no. 23, July 30, 1922, 86.

119. Ibid.

120. Ibid.

121. Ibid.

122. Piero Gobetti, "Note di politica interna II," *La rivoluzione liberale* 1, no. 26, September 10, 1922, 98.

123. Piero Gobetti, "Delizie indigene," *La rivoluzione liberale* 1, no. 32, November 2, 1922, 122.

124. Ibid.

125. Piero Gobetti, "La tirannide," *La rivoluzione liberale* 1, no. 33, November 23 [*sic*; November 9], 1922, 123.

126. Antonio Gramsci, "Colpo di stato," *L'ordine nuovo*, July 21, 1921; reprinted in Gramsci, *Il popolo delle scimmie: Scritti sul fascismo*, ed. Marco Revelli (Turin: Einaudi, 2022), 65.

127. Antonio Gramsci, "Previsioni," *Avanti!* (Piedmontese ed.) 24, no. 268, October 19, 1920, 1.

128. Antonio Gramsci, "Cos'è la reazione?," *Avanti!* (Piedmontese ed.) 24, no. 300, November 20, 1920, 2.

129. Antonio Gramsci, "La forza dello stato," *Avanti!* (Piedmontese ed.) 24, no. 321, December 11, 1920, 1.

130. Ibid.

131. Antonio Gramsci, "Il popolo delle scimmie," *L'ordine nuovo*, January 2, 1921, reprinted in Gramsci, *Il popolo delle scimmie*, 36; emphasis in the original.

132. Ibid., 37.

133. Ibid., 38–39; emphasis in the original.

134. Antonio Gramsci, "Forze elementari," *L'ordine nuovo*, April 26, 1921, reprinted in Gramsci, *Il popolo delle scimmie*, 47.

135. Ibid., 48.

136. Antonio Gramsci, "Socialisti e fascisti," *L'ordine nuovo*, June 11, 1921, reprinted in Gramsci, *Il popolo delle scimmie*, 50.

137. Antonio Gramsci, "Il carnefice e la vittima," *L'ordine nuovo*, July 17, 1921, reprinted in Gramsci, *Il popolo delle scimmie*, 58.

138. Gramsci, "Colpo di stato," *L'ordine nuovo*, July 21, 1921, reprinted in Gramsci, *Il popolo delle scimmie*, 65.

Chapter Six

1. Claudio Natoli, "Il confronto sulla 'nuova democrazia' nell'antifascismo italiano degli anni Trenta," in *Antifascismi e resistenze*, ed. Franco De Felice (Rome: La Nuova Italia Scientifica, 1997), 119.

2. Ibid.

3. On Italian liberalism, see Manlio Di Lalla, *Storia del liberalismo italiano: Dal Risorgimento al fascismo* (Florence: Sansoni, 1976); Antonio Jannazzo, *Il liberalismo italiano del Novecento: Da*

Giolitti a Malagodi (Soveria Mannelli: Rubbettino, 2003); and Massimo L. Salvadori, *Liberalismo italiano: I dilemmi della libertà* (Rome: Donzelli, 2011).

4. Giovanni Amendola, *Il mezzogiorno e la crisi politica italiana* (1922; Turin: Piero Gobetti Editore, 1924), 167.

5. Quoted in Antonio Cardini, *Il grande centro: I liberali in una nazione senza stato; Il problema storico dell'"arretratezza politica" (1796–1996)* (Manduria: Laicata, 1996), 225. On Luigi Einaudi's initial support of Fascism, see Einaudi, *Cronache economiche e politiche di un trentennio (1893–1925)* (Turin: Einaudi, 1965–66), 7:234ff and 8:360ff; and Renzo De Felice, *Mussolini il fascista: La conquista del potere, 1921–1925* (Turin: Einaudi, 1966), 399–401.

6. On Croce and Fascism, see Fabio Fernando Rizi, *Benedetto Croce and Italian Fascism* (Toronto: University of Toronto Press, 2003); and Eugenio Di Rienzo, *Benedetto Croce: Gli anni del fascismo* (Soveria Mannelli: Rubbettino, 2020).

7. Di Rienzo, *Benedetto Croce*, 83–84.

8. Eugenio Di Rienzo, "Volpe e Croce, origini di una lunga amicizia. Stima e consuetudine scientifica nel carteggio fra lo storico e il filosofo," *Nuova storia contemporanea* 9, no. 1 (2007): 53–74.

9. The interview was later edited by Croce and published as "Liberalismo e fascismo" in *Pagine sparse* (Naples: Ricciardi, 1942), 2:371–73. The title of the interview was removed, as well as the judgment on the "inevitable necessity of Fascism."

10. Quoted in De Felice, *Mussolini il fascista*, 653.

11. Ibid.

12. Quoted in Rizi, *Benedetto Croce and Italian Fascism*, 67. In his memoirs of 1944, Croce excused himself, stating, "I was persuaded that he [Mussolini] was not the author of the murder, and that the bad people around him had perpetrated it without his knowledge. And, truly, it seemed folly even against his style that he could have ordered it." Quoted in ibid.

13. In De Felice, *Mussolini il fascista*, 653.

14. English translation in Jeffrey T. Schnapp, ed., *A Primer of Italian Fascism* (Lincoln: University of Nebraska Press, 2000), 304–7.

15. See, e.g., the chronicle of the uncritical, if not falsifying, defense of Croce in the early postwar period in Chester McArthur Destler, "Benedetto Croce and Italian Fascism: A Note on Historical Reliability," *The Journal of Modern History* 24, no. 4 (1952): 382–90.

16. Gaetano Salvemini, "Che cosa è un 'liberale' italiano nel 1946," in Gaetano Salvemini, *Scritti sul Fascismo III*, ed. Roberto Vivarelli (Milan: Feltrinelli, 1974), 363.

17. Benedetto Croce, "Chi è 'fascista'?," *Il giornale di Napoli*, October 29, 1944, 1, later collected in *Scritti e discorsi politici (1943–1947)* (Bari: Laterza, 1963), reprinted in *Scritti e discorsi politici* (Naples: Bibliopolis, 1993), 2:48–52.

18. Peter F. Drucker, *The End of Economic Man: A Study of the New Totalitarianism* (New York: John Day, 1939).

19. Croce, "Chi è 'fascista'?"

20. Ibid.

21. Quoted in Giovanni Pallanti, "I Diari di De Gasperi, 1930–1943: La compromissione della chiesa col fascismo e col nazismo," *Il mantello della giustizia* (February 2020), https://www.ilmantellodellagiustizia.it/febbraio-2020/i-diari-di-de-gasperi-1930-1943-la-compromissione-della-chiesa-col-fascismo-e-col-nazismo?print=pdf. See also Alcide De Gasperi, *Diario, 1930–1943*, ed. Marialuisa Lucia Sergio (Bologna: Il Mulino, 2018), 132 and 193.

22. Giovanni De Luna, *La resistenza perfetta* (Milan: Feltrinelli, 2015); and Raimondo Luraghi, *Eravamo partigiani: Ricordi del tempo di Guerra* (Milan: Bur, 2005).

23. Luigi Sturzo, "Spirito e realtà," *La rivoluzione liberale* 3, no. 3, January 15, 1924, 9.

24. Ibid.

25. Ibid.

26. Ibid., 10.

27. See Paolo Bagnoli, *Il liberalsocialismo* (Florence: Polistampa, 1997); Franco Sbarberi, *L'utopia della libertà eguale: Il liberalismo sociale da Rosselli a Bobbio* (Turin: Bollati Boringhieri, 1999); and Mario Giovana, *Giustizia e Libertà in Italia: Storia di una cospirazione antifascista, 1929–1937* (Turin: Bollati Boringhieri, 2005).

28. Quoted in Massimo Rendina, "Giovanni Amendola, vittima dello squadrismo fascista," *Patria indipendente*, May 21, 2006, 14.

29. Giovanni Amendola, "Un anno dopo," *Il Mondo*, November 2, 1923, 1.

30. All quotes from Luigi Salvatorelli, "Lineamenti del nazionalsocialismo," *La rivoluzione liberale* 2, no. 12, May 1, 1923, 49–50.

31. Giovanni De Luna, *Storia del Partito d'azione* (Turin: UTET, 2006).

32. Luigi Salvatorelli and Giovanni Mira, *Storia d'Italia nel periodo fascista* (Turin: Einaudi, 1956), 320.

33. Ibid., 322.

34. Ibid., 337.

35. On Salvemini, see Gaetano Quagliarello, *Gaetano Salvemini* (Bologna: Il Mulino, 2007).

36. Quoted in Cosimo Ceccuti, *Mussolini nel giudizio dei primi antifascisti (1921–1925)* (Milan: Mondadori, 1983), 67.

37. Gaetano Salvemini contributed to *The Fascist Dictatorship*, ed. International Committee for Political Prisoners (New York: International Committee for Political Prisoners, 1926); he published in French *Mussolini diplomate* (Paris: B. Grasset, 1932), and in English *Under the Axe of Fascism* (London: V. Gollancz, 1936), *Italian Fascism* (London: V. Gollancz, 1938), *Italian Fascist Activities in the US* (Washington, DC: American Council on Public Affairs, 1940), *What to Do with Italy* (New York: Duell, Sloan & Pearce, 1943), and, after the war, *The Fascist Dictatorship in Italy* (New York: H. Fertig, 1967) and the English translation of his Harvard lectures, *The Origins of Fascism in Italy* (New York: Harper & Row, 1973).

38. Salvemini, *Under the Axe of Fascism*, 27.

39. Ibid., 116–25.

40. Ibid., 373.

41. Ibid., 375.

42. Ibid., 378–79.

43. Ibid., 383.

44. Ibid.

45. Ibid., 385–86.

46. Ibid., 389.

47. Ibid., 392.

48. Gaetano Salvemini, *Le origini del fascismo in Italia: Le lezioni di Harvard* (Milan: Feltrinelli, 1961), 79.

49. Ibid., 187–88.

50. Ibid., 313.

51. Ibid., 314.

52. Ibid., 374–75.

53. Ibid., 390.

54. Ibid., 390–91.

55. Ibid., 392.

56. Ibid., 417.

57. Ibid., 418.

58. Ibid., 419–20.

59. Ibid., 420.

60. Piero Gobetti, "Elogio della ghigliottina," *La rivoluzione liberale* 1, no. 34, November 23, 1922, 130.

61. Piero Gobetti, "Dopo le elezioni," *La rivoluzione liberale* 3, no. 16, April 15, 1924, 61.

62. Ibid.

63. Reprinted in OOBM, 20:384. Previously, on April 2, 1924, in the pages of *Il popolo d'Italia*, Mussolini had characterized Gobetti as "a very ferocious, if very powerless enemy of Fascism. Piero Gobetti is a rotten wretch, made malignant by solitary exercises with ink." Benito Mussolini, "Medaglioncini al cromo," *Il popolo d'Italia*, April 2, 1924, 11; reprinted in OOBM 20:221.

64. Piero Gobetti, "Processo al trasformismo," *La rivoluzione liberale* 3, no. 39, October 21, 1924, 158.

65. Ibid.

66. Ibid.

67. Flavio Aliquò Mazzei, *Piero Gobetti: Profilo di un rivoluzionario liberale* (Florence: Pugliese, 2008).

Chapter Seven

1. Giacomo Matteotti, *Contro il fascismo* (Milan: Garzanti, 2019), 24.

2. See chaps. 1 and 2.

3. Matteotti, *Contro il fascismo*, 25.

4. Ibid., 29.

5. For an introduction to the interpretation of Fascism by Italian Marxists, see Giuseppe Vacca, *La tragica modernità del fascismo: Le analisi di Antonio Gramsci, Palmiro Togliatti e Angelo Tasca* (Rome: Carocci, 2002).

6. On Matteotti, see Mirko Grasso, *L'oppositore: Matteotti contro il fascismo* (Rome: Carocci, 2024), and Federico Fornaro, *Giacomo Matteotti: L'Italia migliore* (Turin: Bollati Boringhieri, 2024).

7. Karl Radek, "Capital's Offensive," in *Marxists in the Face of Fascism: Writings by Marxists on Fascism from the Inter-War Period*, ed. David Beetham (Manchester: Manchester University Press, 1983), 99–101.

8. Klara Zetkin, "The Struggle against Fascism," in Beetham, *Marxists in the Face of Fascism*, 102.

9. Ibid.

10. Ibid., 102–3.

11. Giovanni Borgognone, *Come nasce una dittatura: L'Italia del delitto Matteotti* (Bologna: Il Mulino, 2012); and Emilio Gentile, *Storia del fascismo* (Rome: Laterza, 2022), 467–80.

12. The hypothesis that Matteotti had uncovered a series of illegal transactions between the Fascist regime and US oil companies has not found wide acceptance among historians. See Mauro Canali, *Il delitto Matteotti: Affarismo e politica nel primo governo Mussolini* (Bologna: Il Mulino, 1997).

13. Giovanni Sabbatucci, *1924: Il delitto Matteotti* (Rome: Laterza, 2007).

14. Silvio Pons, *I comunisti italiani e gli altri: Visioni e legami internazionali nel mondo del Novecento* (Turin: Einaudi, 2021), 37.

15. The trip to London was brief, and Matteotti's agenda was filled with meetings with leaders of the Labour Party and the trade unions. See Gino Bianco, "Matteotti a Londra," *Una città* 200 (February 2013), https://web.archive.org/web/20151222105854/http://www.unacitta.it/newsite/articolo.asp?id=810, accessed September 18, 2024. See Giacomo Matteotti, *The Fascisti Exposed: A Year of Fascist Domination*, trans. E. W. Dickes (London: Independent Labour Party Publication Dept., 1924). The book was published in Germany as *Faschismus in Italien: Grundlagen, Aufstieg, Niedergang*, trans. H.-E. Kaminski (Berlin: Verlag für Sozialwissenschaft, 1925). The most recent reprint of the work is *Un anno e mezzo di dominazione fascista*, ed. Stefano Caretti (Pisa: Pisa University Press, 2020).

16. Gentile, *Storia del fascismo*, 481–508.

17. Marco Bresciani, "Diventare antifascisti: incertezze, dilemmi, contraddizioni di fronte al fascismo," in *Il fascismo italiano: Storia e interpretazioni*, ed. Giulia Albanese (Rome: Carocci, 2021), 281–308; Simona Colarizi, "La percezione del totalitarismo nell'antifascismo italiano," in *Modernità totalitaria: Il fascismo italiano*, ed. Emilio Gentile (Rome: Laterza, 2008), 23–55; and Claudio Natoli, "Il confronto sulla 'nuova democrazia' nell'antifascismo italiano degli anni Trenta," in *Antifascismi e Resistenze*, ed. Franco De Felice (Rome: La Nuova Italia Scientifica, 1997), 117–147.

18. Giovanni Masci [Antonio Gramsci], "Che fare?," *La voce della gioventù*, November 1, 1923; reprinted in Gramsci, *Il popolo delle scimmie: Scritti sul fascismo*, ed. Marco Revelli (Turin: Einaudi, 2022), 87.

19. Ibid., 88.

20. Antonio Gramsci, "Il partito popolare," *L'Unità*, February 22, 1924, 1.

21. Manalive [Antonio Gramsci], "Gioda o del romanticismo," *L'Unità*, February 28, 1924, 1; reprinted in Gramsci, *Il popolo delle scimmie*, 99.

22. Ibid.

23. Ibid., 100.

24. Published unsigned as "Capo," *L'ordine nuovo*, March 1, 1924, then republished as Antonio Gramsci, "Lenin capo rivoluzionario," *L'Unità*, November 6, 1924, 1; reprinted in Gramsci, *Il popolo delle scimmie*, 104–5.

25. Ibid.

26. Unsigned, "Le elezioni," *L'ordine nuovo*, March 1, 1924; reprinted in Gramsci, *Il popolo delle scimmie*, 108.

27. Ibid.

28. G. Masci [Antonio Gramsci], "Il Vaticano," *La correspondance internationale*, March 12, 1924, 1.

29. Silvio Pons, *The Global Revolution: A History of International Communism, 1917–1991* (Oxford: Oxford University Press, 2014), 24–53; and Marcello Flores, *Il vento della rivoluzione: La nascita del Partito comunista italiano* (Rome: Laterza, 2021), 139–73.

30. English translation in Beetham, *Marxists in Face of Fascism*, 97–99.

31. Ibid.

32. Amadeo Bordiga, "I rapporti delle forze sociali e politiche in Italia," *Rassegna comunista* 29 (September 30, 1922): 1409.

33. Palmiro Togliatti, "Rapporto sul fascismo per il IV Congresso dell'Internazionale," in Togliatti, *La politica nel pensiero e nell'azione: Scritti e discorsi, 1917–1964*, ed. Giuseppe Vacca (Milan: Bompiani, 2014), 43.

34. Ibid., 45.

35. Ibid., 46.

36. Ibid., 54.

37. Ibid., 55–56.

38. Ibid.

39. Ibid., 61.

40. For a synthetic analysis of Gramsci's development of a theory of Fascism during the Matteotti crisis, see Benedetta Garzarelli, "Il fascismo e la crisi italiana negli scritti di Antonio Gramsci, 1924–1926," *Studi storici* 48, no. 4 (2007): 1059–90.

41. Antonio Gramsci, "La crisi italiana," Relazione a Comitato centrale del Partito comunista d'Itala, August 13–14, 1924; later published as "La crisi delle classi medie," *Unità*, August 26, 1924, 1–2; reprinted in Gramsci, *Il popolo delle scimmie*, 128.

42. Gramsci, *Il popolo delle scimmie*, 129.

43. Ibid., 130.

44. Ibid., 133.

45. Ibid., 134.

46. Ibid., 133.

47. Ibid., 136.

48. Ibid., 137.

49. Ibid.

50. Ibid., 139.

51. The Hungarian Gyula Šaš, a longtime resident of Italy living under the name Giulio Aquila, was very critical of the analyses of Fascism by Italian Marxists. In his *Faschismus in Italien* (Hamburg, 1923) he insisted that "Fascism itself is not peculiar to Italy, but is realized most fully on the international level. Its roots are embedded in the general economic and political situation of the present time." English trans. in Beetham, *Marxists in Face of Fascism*, 115. See also Pons, *I comunisti italiani e gli altri*, 35–39.

52. Antonio Gramsci, *La costruzione del partito comunista, 1923–1926* (Turin: Einaudi, 1971), 481–88. For a complete copy of the "Theses," see https://www.marxists.org/italiano/gramsci/26/tesidilione.pdf, accessed September 18, 2024. The section titled "Fascism" is also reprinted in Gramsci, *Il popolo delle scimmie*, 155.

53. Ibid.

54. Ibid.

55. Ibid., 156.

56. Ibid., 157.

57. Ibid.

58. Ibid., 158.

59. Gramsci, the historian Giuseppe Fiori demonstrated, was concerned with the concentration of powers solely in the hands of Joseph Stalin and with the possibility of a fracture between Stalin and the factions of Trotsky, Zinovyev, and Kamenev. Gramsci expressed his concerns in an undated letter sent to the Comintern around mid-October 1926—published as "Lettera al Comitato centrale del Partito comunista sovietico" in Gramsci, *Scritti politici* (Rome: Editori Riuniti, 1971), 713–19. Togliatti decided not to pass the letter on to Stalin. See Aldo Agosti, *Togliatti negli anni del Comintern, 1926–1943: Documenti inediti dagli archive russi* (Rome: Carocci, 2000), 86–90. Gramsci also expressed worry about Stalin's increased power in a *New York Times* article published on October 18, 1926. Gramsci's opposition to Stalin was severely criticized by

Togliatti, causing a rupture between the two and the progressive estrangement of Gramsci, by then in prison, from the Communist movement. Gramsci's fate was, in a sense, prophetic: A fracture within the Comintern did not occur, largely because Stalin eliminated all his political opponents one by one. Trotsky, whom Gramsci never liked, Zinovyev, and Kamenev would be all killed. See Giuseppe Fiori, *Vita di Antonio Gramsci* (Bari: Laterza, 1966), 246–54; and Angelo D'Orsi, *Gramsci: Una nuova biografia* (Milan: Feltrinelli, 2017), 248–54.

60. D'Orsi, *Gramsci*, 313–434.

61. Antonio Gramsci, *Quaderni del carcere*, ed. Valentino Gerratana (Turin: Einaudi, 1975), 2:772. See also para. 27 of Notebook 13 in Gramsci, *Quaderni del carcere*, 3:1619–22, and para. 23 of Notebook 14 in Gramsci, *Quaderni del carcere*, 3:1680–81. On Gramsci's reflections on Caesarism and Bonapartism, see Francesca Antonini, *Caesarism and Bonapartism in Gramsci: Hegemony and the Crisis of Modernity* (Leiden: Brill, 2021).

62. Translated into English in Beetham, *Marxists in the Face of Fascism*, 112.

63. Palmiro Togliatti, "Le basi sociali del fascismo," published in *L'internationale communiste* 7, no. 11 (1926): 426–33, and *Die kommunistische Internationale* 7, no. 4 (1926): 28–38. Reprinted in Togliatti, *La politica nel pensiero e nell'azione*, 79.

64. Togliatti, *La politica nel pensiero e nell'azione*.

65. Ibid.

66. Ibid.

67. Ibid., 80.

68. Ibid.

69. Palmiro Togliatti, "A proposito del fascismo," in Togliatti, *La politica nel pensiero e nell'azione*, 112–15. The essay was originally published in *Kommunisti Českij Internacional* 9, nos. 27–28 (July 13, 1928): 11–21; and reprinted in *Die kommunistische Internationale* 9, nos. 29–30 (July 25, 1928): 1677–92, and in *L'internationale communiste* 9, no. 16 (August 1, 1928): 1124–40.

70. Togliatti, "A proposito del fascismo," 115–16.

71. Ibid.

72. Ibid., 117.

73. Ibid., 120.

74. Ibid., 121.

75. Ibid., 124.

76. Ibid.

77. Ibid., 128.

78. As Giuseppe Vacca argued, Togliatti's "alignment with Stalin's policy stemmed from a double conviction. The first, which surfaced in 1923, was that for a weak party banned by Fascism, such as the PCd'I, there could be no prospect outside of a total loyalty to the Comintern (and therefore to the USSR). . . . The second, which matured in Moscow in 1926, was that the strategy of 'socialism in one country' had no alternatives even if its operative translation was open to several options." Vacca, *La tragica modernità del fascismo*, 77.

Chapter Eight

1. Mark Mazower, "Fascism and Democracy Today: What Use Is the Study of History in the Current Crisis?," *European Law Journal* 22, no. 3 (May 2016): 375. We might add to Mazower's list the Greenshirts of France's Comités de Défense Paysanne of Henri Dorgères, of Plínio Salgado's Ação Integralista Brasileira in Brazil, of Eoin O'Duffy's Cumann Corpruiteac Náisiúnta

(National Corporate Party) in Ireland, of the Hungarian National Socialist Party (Magyar Nemzeti Szocialista Párt) before its merge into the Arrow Cross Party, of José María Valiente Soriano's Juventudes de Acción Popular in Spain, of the Young Egypt Party, and of the Yugoslav Radical Union; the Blueshirts of Ireland's Army Comrades Association (also led by Eoin O'Duffy), of Rotha Lintorn-Orman's British Fascists, of Adrien Arcand's National Unity Party of Canada, of the Kuomintang's Blueshirts Society, of Marcel Bucard's Mouvement Franciste and François Coty's Solidarité Française in France, of Francisco Rolão Preto's Movimento Nacional-Sindicalista in Portugal, and of Sven Olov Londholm's Nationalsocialistika Arbetarepartiet in Sweden; the American Redshirts of Benjamin Tillman, Ellison D. Smith, Josephus Daniels, and Claude Kitchin before they merged into the Ku Klux Klan; and the Whiteshirts of the Silver Legion of America, founded by William Dudley Pelley, also in the United States.

2. Mazower, "Fascism and Democracy Today," 375–76.

3. Antonio Gramsci, "Cos'è la reazione?," *Avanti!* (Piedmontese ed.), November 20, 1920, 2.

4. Benedetto Croce, "The Fascist Germ Still Lives," *New York Times*, November 28, 1943, 43–45. The Italian original was collected in Croce, *Per la nuova vita dell'Italia: Scritti e discorsi, 1943–1944* (Naples: Ricciardi, 1944), 13–20.

5. Croce, "The Fascist Germ Still Lives," *New York Times*, November 28, 1943, 43.

6. Ibid., 44.

7. Ibid., 44–45.

8. Ibid., 45.

9. Ibid.

10. Ibid.

11. Helmuth Plessner, *Das Schicksal deutschen Geistes im Ausgang seiner bürgerlichen Epoche* (Zurich: Max Niehans, 1935), later reprinted as *Die verspätete Nation: Über die Verführbarkeit bürgerlichen Geistes* (Stuttgart: W. Kohlhammer, 1959), collected in Plessner, *Gesammelte Schriften* (Frankfurt am Main: Suhrkamp, 1982), 6:10–223. See also Joachim Whaley, "Helmuth Plessner and *The Delayed Nation*," *Journal of European Studies* 50, no. 1 (2020): 128–40.

12. Whaley, "Helmuth Plessner and *The Delayed Nation*," 134–35.

13. Plessner, *Die verspätete Nation*, in *Gesammelte Schriften*, 6:185–97.

14. Ibid., 162–84; and Whaley, "Helmuth Plessner and *The Delayed Nation*," 136.

15. Friedrich Meinecke, *Die deutsche Katastrophe: Betrachtungen und Erinnerungen* (Wiesbaden: E. Brockhaus Verlag, 1946); English translation in Meinecke, *The German Catastrophe: Reflections and Recollections*, trans. Sidney B. Fay (Boston: Beacon Press, 1950).

16. Karl Popper, *The Open Society and Its Enemies* (Princeton, NJ: Princeton University Press, 2013), 272.

17. Ibid.

18. Friedrich von Hayek, *The Road to Serfdom* (New York: Routledge Classics, 2001), 4.

19. Ibid., 120.

20. Hans Kohn, *The Twentieth Century* (New York: Macmillan, 1949), 75.

21. Hans Kohn, "The Totalitarian Philosophy of War," *Proceedings of the American Philosophical Society* 82, no. 1 (1940): 57.

22. Ibid., 71.

23. Ibid., 72.

24. Enzo Traverso, "Intellectuals and Anti-Fascism: For a Critical Historicization," *New Politics* 9, no. 4 (2004); https://newpol.org/issue_post/intellectuals-and-anti-fascism-critical-historization/, accessed September 18, 2024.

25. Dan Stone, "Anti-Fascism Europe Comes to Britain: Theorising Fascism as a Contribution to Defeating It," in *Varieties of Anti-Fascism: Britain in the Inter-War Period*, ed. Nigel Copsey and Andrzej Olechnowicz (London: Palgrave Macmillan, 2010), 183–201.

26. See Kenneth Holmqvist and Jarosław Płuciennik, "Princess Antonomasia and the Truth: Two Types of Metonymic Relations," in *Tropical Truth(s): The Epistemology of Metaphor and Other Tropes*, ed. Armin Burkhardt and Brigitte Nerlich (Berlin: de Gruyter, 2010), 373–81; and Shawn M. Clankie, *A Theory of Genericization on Brand Name Change* (Lewiston, NY: Edwin Mellen Press, 2002).

27. Jacques Droz, *Histoire de l'antifascisme en Europe, 1923–1939* (Paris: Éditions de Découverte, 1985), 231–35.

28. Philip Williamson, "The Conservative Party, Fascism and Anti-Fascism 1918–1939," in Copsey and Olechnowicz, *Varieties of Anti-Fascism*, 73.

29. Richard Overy, *The Twilight Years: The Paradox of Britain between the Wars* (London: Penguin, 2009); and Daniel Ritschel, *The Politics of Planning: The Debate on Economic Planning in Britain in the 1930s* (Oxford: Oxford University Press, 1997), 183–231.

30. More precisely, these were the National Executive Council, the Trade Unions Congress, the Parliamentary Labour Party, and the newly instituted National Council of Labour. For an overview, see Droz, *Histoire de l'antifascisme en Europe*, 213–35.

31. Stephen Dorril, *Blackshirt: Sir Oswald Mosley and British Fascism* (London: Viking, 2006).

32. William D. Irvine, "French Conservatives and the 'New Right' During the 1930s," *French Historical Studies* 8, no. 4 (1974): 534.

33. Ibid., 536.

34. See Shlomo Sand, "A Flirt or a Love Affair? French Intellectuals between Fascism and Nazism," and Jeannine Verdès-Leroux, "The Intellectual Extreme Right in the Thirties," in *The Development of the Radical Right in France: From Boulanger to le Pen*, ed. Edward J. Arnold (New York: St. Martin's Press, 2000), 83–99 and 119–31 respectively. See also the classic by Pierre Milza, *Fascisme français: Passé et present* (Paris: Flammarion, 1987).

35. William D. Irvine, "Fascism in France and the Strange Case of the *Croix de Feu*," *Journal of Modern History* 63, no. 2 (1991): 271–95.

36. Zeev Sternhell, *Neither Right nor Left: Fascist Ideology in France*, trans. David Maisel (Princeton, NJ: Princeton University Press, 1986), esp. 90–118.

37. Droz, *Histoire de l'antifascisme en Europe*, 179–87 and 203–11.

38. Stanley Payne, *A History of Fascism, 1914–1945* (London: Routledge, 1995), 3–4 and 245–327.

39. Ibid., 328–54.

40. George M. Wilson, "A New Look at the Problem of 'Japanese Fascism,'" *Comparative Studies in Society and History* 10, no. 4 (1968): 408.

41. T. A. Bisson, "The Rise of Fascism in Japan," *Foreign Policy Reports* 8, no. 17 (1932): 196–206.

42. William Henry Chamberlin, *Japan over Asia* (Boston: Little, Brown, 1937), 143.

43. E. B. Ashton, *The Fascist: His State and His Mind* (London: Putnam, 1937), 42–43.

44. Wilfrid Fleisher, *Volcanic Isle* (London: Jonathan Cape, 1941), 62. See also Fleisher, *Our Enemy Japan* (New York: Doubleday, Doran, 1942).

45. Yoshino Sakuzō, "Fascism in Japan," *Contemporary Japan* 1, no. 2 (1932): 185–97.

46. Ibid., 194.

47. Nyozekan Hasegawa, *Nihon fashizumu hihan* (Tokyo: Ōhata Shoten, 1932). On Hasegawa, see Andrew E. Barshay, *State and Intellectual in Imperial Japan: The Public Man in Crisis* (Berkeley: University of California Press, 1988), 123–220.

48. Louise Young, *Japan's Total Empire: Manchuria and the Culture of Wartime Imperialism* (Berkeley: University of California Press, 1998), 55–181.

49. Barshay, *State and Intellectual in Imperial Japan*, 193.

50. Atsuko Hirai, *Individualism and Socialism: The Life and Thought of Kawai Eijirō* (Cambridge, MA: Harvard East Asian Monographs, 1988).

51. Imanaka Tsugimaro, *Fashizumu undōron* (1932), reprinted in *Imanaka Tsugimaro seijigaku ronshū* (Tokyo: Ochanomizu Shobō, 1981), 3:74. Translated into English in Kevin Doak, "Fascism Seen and Unseen: Fascism as a Problem in Cultural Representation," in Alan Tansman, ed., *The Culture of Japanese Fascism* (Durham, NC: Duke University Press, 2009), 36.

52. Doak, "Fascism Seen and Unseen," 36.

53. Reto Hofmann, *The Fascist Effect: Japan and Italy, 1915–1952* (Ithaca, NY: Cornell University Press, 2015), 80–88. See also George Wilson, *Radical Nationalist in Japan: Kita Ikki, 1863–1937* (Cambridge, MA: Harvard University Press, 1969); Ben-Ami Shillony, *Politics and Culture in Wartime Japan* (Oxford: Clarendon Press, 1981); William Miles Fletcher III, *The Search for a New Order: Intellectuals and Fascism in Prewar Japan* (Chapel Hill: University of North Carolina Press, 1982); and Walter Skya, *Japan's Holy War* (Durham, NC: Duke University Press, 2009).

54. Mark Berger, *Parties Out of Power in Japan, 1931–1941* (Princeton, NJ: Princeton University Press, 1977).

55. Enzo Traverso, "Avant-propos," in *Le totalitarisme: The XXe siècle en débat*, ed. Enzo Traverso (Paris: Éditions du Seuil, 2001), 5.

56. Erich Ludendorff, *Der totale Krieg* (Munich: Ludendorff Verlag, 1936). See Hans Barth, "Reality and Ideology of the Totalitarian State," *Review of Politics* 1, no. 3 (July 1939): 275–306; Hans-Ulrich Wehler, "'Absoluter' und 'totaler' Krieg: Von Clausewitz zu Ludendorff," *Politische Vierteljahresschrift* 10, nos. 2–3 (1969): 220–48; and Enzo Traverso, "Le totalitarisme: Jalons pour l'histoire d'un débat," in Traverso, *Le totalitarisme*, 9–19. The view that saw Hegel's "ethical state" as the root of the "total state" originated in Karl Popper's misreading of Hegel's theory of the state in *The Open Society and Its Enemies*, 242–89. For a contemporary rebuttal, see Ernst Cassirer, *The Myth of the State* (New Haven, CT: Yale University Press, 1946); and Herbert Marcuse, *Reason and Revolution* (Oxford: Oxford University Press, 1941). Martin Jay, *Marxism and Totality: The Adventure of a Concept from Lukács to Habermas* (Berkeley: University of California Press, 1986) explores the semantic shifts in the Marxist conception of "totality."

57. Barth, "Reality and Ideology of the Totalitarian State," 275.

58. Traverso, "Le totalitarisme," 9. See also Enzo Traverso, *Fire and Blood: The European Civil War, 1914–1945* (New York: Verso, 2016), 64–100.

59. Antonio Gibelli, *L'officina della Guerra: La grande guerra e le trasformazioni del mondo mentale* (Turin: Bollati Boringhieri, 1991), 76–121; and Jörn Leonhard, *Pandora's Box: A History of the First World War*, trans. Patrick Camiller (Cambridge, MA: Harvard University Press, 2018), 891–907.

60. Simona Forti, *Totalitarianism: A Borderline Idea in Political Philosophy*, trans. Simone Ghelli (Stanford, CA: Stanford University Press, 2024), 13–17.

61. Ibid., 8–13.

62. Traverso, "Le totalitarisme," 14.

63. Ibid., 13–15; and Peter Reichel, *Der schöne Schein des Dritten Reiches: Faszination und Gewalt des Faschismus* (Munich: Hanser, 1991), 157–207.

64. Hans Kohn, "Communist and Fascist Dictatorship: A Comparative Study," in *Revolutions and Dictatorships: Essays in Contemporary History* (Cambridge, MA: Harvard University Press, 1941), 183.

65. Traverso, "Le totalitarisme," 21.

66. See chap. 4.

67. Traverso, "Le totalitarisme," 23.

68. Ernst Jünger, "Die totale Mobilmachung," in *Krieg und Krieger* (Berlin: Junker und Dünnhaupt, 1930), 9–30.

69. Traverso, "Le totalitarisme," 25.

70. Carl Schmitt, *Political Theology: Four Chapters on the Concept of Sovereignty*, trans. George Schwab (Chicago: University of Chicago Press, 2005); originally published in German as *Politische Theologie* (1922).

71. Carl Schmitt, "Totaler Feind, totaler Krieg, totaler Staat" (1937), reprinted in Schmitt, *Positionen und Begriffe im Kampf mit Weimar, Genf, Versailles 1923–1939* (Berlin: Dunker & Humbolt, 1988), 236.

72. Ernst Forsthoff, *Der totale Staat* (Hamburg: Hanseatische Verlagsanstalt, 1933), 7.

73. Ibid., 32; passage translated into English in Arthur J. Jacobson and Bernhard Schlink, eds., *Weimar: A Jurisprudence of Crisis*, trans. Belinda Cooper (Berkeley: University of California Press, 2000), 321.

74. Ibid., 38; translated into English in Jacobson and Schlink, *Weimar*, 322. Forsthoff's notion of the dual state were soon echoed, in critical guise, in Ernst Fraenkel, *The Dual State: A Contribution to the Theory of Dictatorship* (1941; Oxford: Oxford University Press, 2006).

75. Luigi Sturzo, "The Totalitarian State," *Social Research* 3, no. 2 (1936): 222.

76. Ibid., 230.

77. Ibid., 231–33.

78. Traverso points this out as a central theme in Maritain's 1936 *Humanisme intégral*, which he quotes in *Le totalitarisme*, 32.

79. James Chappel, *Catholic Modern: The Challenge of Totalitarianism and the Remaking of the Church* (Cambridge, MA: Harvard University Press, 2018), 113–15 and 134–43.

80. Jacques Maritain, "Europe and the Federal Idea," *Commonweal* 31 (1940): 545.

81. Reprinted in Franz Borkenau, *World Communism: A History of the Communist International* (Ann Arbor: University of Michigan Press, 1961), 56.

82. Luigi Fabbri, *La contro-rivoluzione preventiva: Riflessioni sul fascismo* (Bologna: L. Cappelli, 1922), 92.

83. Ibid. See also Bruno Rizzi, *La lezione dello stalinismo* (Rome: Opere Nuove, 1962), 46.

84. Franz Borkenau, *The Totalitarian Enemy* (London: Faber & Faber, 1940), 13 and 20.

85. Originally published as a long essay in *Living Marxism* 4, no. 8 (1939), later reprinted as a monograph (London: Bratach Dubh, 1981); https://archive.org/details/sparrowsnest-157/page/5/mode/2up?q=%22red+fascist%22, accessed September 19, 2024.

86. Wilhelm Reich, *Die Massenpsychologie des Faschismus* (Cologne: Kiepenheuer & Witsch, 1971), 236; published in English as Reich, *The Mass Psychology of Fascism*, trans. Theodore P. Wolfe (New York: Orgone Institute Press, 1946).

87. Volin (Vsevolod Mikhailovich Eikhenbaum), *Le fascism rouge* (Brussels: Pensée et action, 1934). See Paul Avrich, *Anarchist Portraits* (Princeton, NJ: Princeton University Press, 1988), 125–34.

88. The family, he claimed, was the "central *reactionary germ cell*, the most important place of reproduction of the reactionary and conservative individual. Being itself caused by the authoritarian system, the family becomes the most important institution for its conservation"; Reich, *The Mass Psychology of Fascism*, 88; emphasis in the original. Reich admitted that German National Socialism could be understood through an analysis of Italian Fascism, which equally claimed to be an "anti-capitalist and revolutionary" and yet acted as the "extreme defender of imperialism and the capitalist economic order"; ibid., 35.

89. Ibid., x.

90. Ibid.; emphasis in the original.

91. Ibid., xii.

92. Ibid., x.

93. Ibid.

94. Ibid., 266.

95. Ibid., 193.

96. Ibid., xx.

97. Ibid., xii.

98. José Ortega y Gasset, *La rebelión de las masas* (Madrid: Revista di Occidente, 1930); published in English as Ortega y Gasset, *The Revolt of the Masses* (New York: W. W. Norton, 1932).

99. Élie Halévy, *L'ère des tyrannies* (Paris: TEL-Gallimard, 1936), 215.

100. Leon Trotsky, *The Revolution Betrayed: What Is the Soviet Union and Where Is It Going?*, trans. Max Eastman (New York: Pathfinder, 1937), 100.

101. Ibid., 108.

102. Traverso, "Le totalitarisme," 31.

103. Kohn, "Communist and Fascist Dictatorship," 192.

104. See the text of the resolution at https://www.europarl.europa.eu/doceo/document/B-9-2019-0100_EN.html, accessed September 19, 2024.

105. Published in English as Daniel Guérin, *Fascism and Big Business*, trans. Frances Merr and Mason Merr (New York: Pathfinder, 1973), 187.

106. Ibid., 32.

107. Traverso, "Le totalitarisme," 38.

108. Marcuse, *Reason and Revolution*, 410.

109. Ibid.

110. Franz Neumann, *Behemoth: The Structure and Practice of National Socialism, 1933–1944* (1944; Chicago: Ivan R. Dee, 2009), 38.

111. Ibid., 48.

112. Ibid.

113. Ibid., vii.

114. Traverso, "Le totalitarisme," 37–38.

Chapter Nine

1. Antonio Gramsci, "Cos'è la reazione?," *Avanti!* (Piedmontese ed.), November 20, 1920, 2.

2. Translated into English in David Beetham, ed., *Marxists in the Face of Fascism: Writings by Marxists on Fascism from the Inter-War Period*, (Manchester: Manchester University Press, 1983), 102–3. There is a new translation in Clara Zetkin, *Fighting Fascism: How to Struggle and How to Win*, ed. Mike Taber and John Riddell (Chicago: Haymarket Books, 2017), 23.

3. See Zetkin's call to arms in Clara Zetkin, "Fight Fascism!," *International Press Correspondence* 3, no. 28 (March 22, 1923): 221, https://www.marxists.org/archive/zetkin/1923/03/fascism.htm, accessed September 19, 2024.

4. In Beetham, *Marxists in the Face of Fascism*, 103. See also Zetkin, *Fighting Fascism*, 24.

5. Ibid.

6. Ibid., 104.

7. Ibid., 105.

8. Ibid., 108.

9. Ibid., 110.

10. Geoff Eley, *Forging Democracy: The History of the Left in Europe, 1850–2000* (Oxford: Oxford University Press, 2002), 228.

11. "Resolution on Fascism," *Fifth Comintern Congress*, in Beetham, *Marxists in the Face of Fascism*, 152.

12. Ibid.

13. Joseph Stalin, "On the International Situation," *International Press Correspondence* 4, no. 72 (1924): 792; here quoted from Beetham, *Marxists in the Face of Fascism*, 153.

14. Stephen Kotkin, *Stalin: Paradoxes of Power, 1878–1928* (London: Penguin, 2014), 550.

15. According to the socialist Sandro Pertini, who was incarcerated with Gramsci in the prison of Turi, near Bari, Gramsci opposed the notion of "social fascism" as a "pitiful polemics." See Mario Oppedisano, *La vita di Sandro Pertini*, by Centro Culturale Sandro Pertini (undated), https://web.archive.org/web/20070930103728/http://www.centropertini.org/biografia.htm, accessed September 20, 2024.

16. Tenth Plenum of the Executive Committee of the Comintern, "Thesis on the International Situation and the Current Tasks of the Comintern," *Daily Worker* (New York ed.), August 9, 1929, 2. Also in Beetham, *Marxists in the Face of Fascism*, 155.

17. Ibid.

18. Quoted in Beetham, *Marxists in the Face of Fascism*, 157.

19. Ibid., 158.

20. Ibid., 160.

21. See Lea Haro, "Entering a Theoretical Void: The Theory of Social Fascism and Stalinism in the German Communist Party," *Critique: Journal of Socialist Theory* 39, no. 4 (2011): 563–82.

22. In Beetham, *Marxists in the Face of Fascism*, 163.

23. Ibid., 165.

24. Ibid.

25. Palmiro Togliatti, "Sulla situazione tedesca," *Stato operaio* 7, no. 3 (March 1933): 84–93; reprinted in Togliatti, *La politica nel pensiero e nell'azione: Scritti e discorsi, 1917–1964*, ed. Giuseppe Vacca (Milan: Bompiani, 2014), 169–77; English translation in Beetham, *Marxists in the Face of Fascism*, 168.

26. Togliatti, "Sulla situazione tedesca," 172; emphasis in the original. A different English translation is in Beetham, *Marxists in the Face of Fascism*, 169.

27. The text was first published by Einaudi in 1970, edited by Ernesto Ragionieri, as *Lezioni sul fascismo* on the basis of original transcriptions and notes from his students. It was preserved in the archives of the Soviet Union until 1969, when Ragionieri, on behalf of the Gramsci Institute, requested a copy. The complete edition of the lectures is now in Palmiro Togliatti, *Corso sugli avversari: Le lezioni sul fascismo*, ed. Francesco M. Biscione (Turin: Einaudi, 2010). An

English translation based on Ragionieri's 1970 edition appeared as Palmiro Togliatti, *Lectures on Fascism*, ed. Daniel Dichter (New York: International, 1976).

28. Togliatti, *Lectures on Fascism*, 1. Italian original in Togliatti, *Corso sugli avversari*, 3.

29. Togliatti, *Lectures on Fascism*, 4.

30. Ibid.

31. Ibid.

32. Ibid., 5.

33. Ibid., 7.

34. Ibid., 9.

35. Ibid., 11.

36. Ibid., 10; emphasis in the original.

37. E. H. Carr, *Twilight of the Comintern, 1930–1935* (New York: Pantheon Books, 1982), 403–27.

38. In *Rundschau* 37 (August 14, 1935): 1774; English translation in Carr, *Twilight of the Comintern*, 404.

39. The speech was first published in *Rundschau* 39 (August 18, 1935): 1825–47, and later reprinted in Georgi Dimitrov, *The Fascist Offensive and the Tasks of the Communist International* (Moscow: Foreign Language Publishing House, 1935), https://www.marxists.org/reference/archive/dimitrov/works/1935/08_02.htm, accessed September 20, 2024.

40. Ibid.

41. Ibid.

42. Ibid.

43. Ibid.

44. Igor' Aleksandrovich Latyshev, *Vnutrenniaia politika iaponskogo imperializma nakanune voiny na Tikhom okeane, 1931–1941* (Moscow: Gespolitizdat, 1955), 215–16; English translation in George Macklin Wilson, "A New Look at the Problem of 'Japanese Fascism,'" *Comparative Studies in Society and History* 10, no. 4 (1968): 402. See also E. Stuart Kirby, *Russian Studies of Japan: An Exploratory Survey* (New York: St. Martin's Press, 1981), 51–52.

45. Y. I. Avdeyev and V. N. Strunnikov, *Burzhuaznoe gosudarstvo v period 1919–1939gg* (Moscow: Izdatel'stvo Instituta mezhdunarodnykh otnoshenii, 1962). See also Kirby, *Russian Studies of Japan*, 50–51.

46. O. Tanin and E. Yohan, *Militarism and Fascism in Japan: With an Introduction by Karl Radek* (New York: International, 1934), 266. According to Kirby, "Ye. S. Oil (1900–42) is listed as an historian dealing primarily with China but also working on Japan. In common with others whose activities date back to the generation of Old Bolsheviks, he used various pseudonyms. One was Ye. Iogan, a name also used by O. S. Tarkhanov. Others were Ye. Iogason, Iota and Ye. Barsukov." Kirby, *Russian Studies of Japan*, 20.

47. Tanin and Yohan, *Militarism and Fascism in Japan*, 267.

48. Ibid.

49. Ibid., 272.

50. Ibid.

51. The historical reference here is to the terroristic and paramilitary groups active in Japan in the 1920s and 1930s. For an overview, see the classic Delmer Brown, *Nationalism in Japan* (Berkeley: University of California Press, 1955); and Ben-Amy Shillony, *Revolt in Japan: The Young Officers and the February 26, 1936 Incident* (Princeton, NJ: Princeton University Press, 1973).

52. Also influential on Tanin and Yohan was the study of the Japanese economic situation by the Soviet historian Kh. T. Eidus (1896–1972). See Kirby, *Russian Studies of Japan*, 39–42.

53. Jane Degras, ed., *The Communist International, 1919–1943: Documents* (London: Routledge, 1971), 3:192–203.

54. Ibid.

55. John Dower believes that O. S. Tarkhanov and Ye. S. Iolk were also killed during Stalin's purges. See Dower, "E. H. Norman, Japan, and the Uses of History," in *Origins of the Modern Japanese State: Selected Writings of E. H. Norman*, ed. John Dower (New York: Pantheon Books, 1975), 37.

56. Tanin and Yohan, *Militarism and Fascism in Japan*, 14.

57. Ibid.

58. Ibid.

59. Ibid., 22.

60. Germaine A. Hoston, *Marxism and the Crisis of Development in Prewar Japan* (Princeton, NJ: Princeton University Press, 1986), 256.

61. Ōtsuka Kin'nosuke, Noro Eitarō, Hirano Yoshitarō, Yamada Moritarō, et al., eds., *Nihon shihonshugi hattatsushi kōza*, 7 vols. (Tokyo: Iwanami Shoten, 1932–33).

62. Gavan McCormack, "1930s Japan: Fascist?," *Social Analysis: The International Journal of Social and Cultural Practice* 5, no. 6 (1980): 134.

63. For an overview, see Andrew Barshay, *The Social Sciences in Modern Japan: The Marxian and Modernist Traditions* (Berkeley: University of California Press, 2004), 72–91; and Hoston, *Marxism and the Crisis of Development in Prewar Japan*.

64. Satō Masaru, *Marukusu to Nihonjin: Shakai undo kara mita sengo Nihon* (Tokyo: Akashi, 2015).

65. See Itsurō Sakisaka, "'Nihon shihonshugi bunseki ni okeru hōhōron," in *Nihon shihonshugi no shomondai*, new ed. (Tokyo: Kōdosha, 1947), 3–36.

66. Ibid., 262.

67. Kamiyama Shigeo, *Ten'nōsei ni kansuru rironteki shomondai* (Tokyo: Minshu Hyōronsha, 1956).

68. Shiga Yoshio, *Sekai to Nihon* (Tokyo: Gyōmeisha, 1949), 47–48; English translation in Hoston, *Marxism and the Crisis of Development in Prewar Japan*, 262.

69. English translation in Hoston, *Marxism and the Crisis of Development in Prewar Japan*, 262.

70. Inoue Kiyoshi, *Nihon no rekishi* (Tokyo: Iwanami Shoten, 1966), 3:188.

71. Tanaka Sōgorō, *Nihon fashizumu shi* (Tokyo: Kawade Shobō Shinsha, 1960), 3; English translation in Wilson, "A New Look at the Problem of 'Japanese Fascism,'" 403.

72. After the Great Depression of 1929, Germany registered the fastest and largest growth in terms of GDP than any other European country (except the Soviet Union). Adam Tooze, *The Wages of Destruction* (London: Penguin, 2006), 37–201.

73. See chap. 3.

74. Leon Trotsky, "Bonapartism and Fascism" (1934), in Beetham, *Marxists in the Face of Fascism*, 214–15.

75. Ibid.

76. Ibid.

77. Ibid., 217.

78. Ibid., 218–19.

79. Ibid., 219.

80. Ibid., 219–20.

81. Ibid., 221.

82. Andrés Nin, "The Spanish Revolution, the Communist Party and the Opposition" (1932), in Beetham, *Marxists in the Face of Fascism*, 225–29.

83. Ignazio Silone, *Der Faschismus: Seine Entstehung und seine Entwicklung* (Zürich: Europa Verlag, 1934); English translation (excerpt) in Beetham, *Marxists in the Face of Fascism*, 237–44. On the unfounded collaborationist activities of Silone, see Giuseppe Tamburrano, *Il "caso" Silone* (Turin: UTET, 2006).

84. For an anthology of the different positions, see Beetham, *Marxists in the face of Fascism*, 187–308.

85. *The Correspondence of Walter Benjamin, 1910–1940*, ed. Gershom Scholem and Theodor W. Adorno, trans. Manfred R. Jacobson and Evelyn M. Jacobson (Chicago: University of Chicago Press, 1994), 246.

86. Particularly useful as introductions to Benjamin's life and philosophy are Howard Eiland and Michael W. Jennings, *Walter Benjamin: A Critical Life* (Cambridge, MA: Harvard University Press, 2014); Eli Friedlander, *Walter Benjamin: A Philosophical Portrait* (Cambridge, MA: Harvard University Press, 2012); Giuseppe Buondonno, *Il soggetto rivoluzionario: Attualità di Walter Benjamin* (Verona: Ombre Corte, 2017); and Massimiliano Tomba, *Attraverso la piccolo porta: Quattro studi su Walter Benjamin* (Milan: Mimesis, 2017).

87. Gerhard Richter translates this expression as "thinking image," "image of reflection," or "thought-image," referring more specifically to an essayistic genre of "philosophical miniatures," "a poetic form of condensed, epigrammatic writing in textual snapshots," the only possible genre of philosophical engagement in a social-psychological situation of "damaged life" (*aus dem beschädigten Leben*, as the subtitle of Adorno's *Minima Moralia* suggested). Richter, *Thought-Images: Frankfurt School Writers' Reflections from Damaged Life* (Stanford, CA: Stanford University Press, 2007), 2. See also Susan Buck-Morss, *The Dialectic of Seeing: Walter Benjamin and the Arcades Project* (Cambridge, MA: MIT Press, 1991); and Alison Ross, *Walter Benjamin's Concept of the Image* (London: Routledge, 2015).

88. Walter Benjamin, "Brecht's *Threepenny Novel*," in *Selected Writings*, vol. 3, *1935–1938*, ed. Howard Eiland and Michael W. Jennings (Cambridge, MA: Harvard University Press, 2002), 6.

89. Ibid.

90. Walter Benjamin, "Theories of German Fascism: On the Collection of Essays *War and Warriors*, edited by Ernst Jünger," in *Selected Writings*, vol. 2, *1927–1930*, ed. Michael W. Jennings, Howard Eiland, and Gary Smith (Cambridge, MA: Harvard University Press, 1999), pt. 1, 320–21. The anthology was published as Ernst Jünger, ed., *Krieg und Krieger* (Berlin: Junker & Dünnhaupt, 1930). See also Ansgar Hilliach, "The Aesthetics of Politics: Walter Benjamin's 'Theories of German Fascism,'" *New German Critique* 17 (Spring 1979): 99–119; and Martin Jay, "'The Aesthetic Ideology' as Ideology; or, What Does It Mean to Aestheticize Politics?," *Cultural Critique* 21 (Spring 1992): 41–61.

91. Walter Benjamin, "The Signature of the Age," in *Selected Writings*, vol. 3, *1935–1938*, 139.

92. Ibid.

93. Its most direct philosophical expression being, for Benjamin, the vitalism of Carl Jung and Ludwig Klages, but also, indirectly, that of Henri Bergson. See Friedlander, *Walter Benjamin*, 146–47.

94. As, for instance, on the occasion of the international art conference held in Venice in 1936, whereupon he could claim, "We can see that fascism spoke openly at the Venice conference." Walter Benjamin, "Letter from Paris (2)," in *Selected Writings*, vol. 3, *1935–1938*, 237.

95. The two essays have been the object of thorough analyses and will not be introduced here except for their contribution to shedding light on Benjamin's understanding of "fascism." On the two essays "Work of Art" and "Theses," see Uwe Steiner, *Walter Benjamin: An Introduction to His Work and Thought*, trans. Michael Winkler (Chicago: University of Chicago Press, 2010), 115–26 and 138–73; the essays in Michael P. Steinberg, ed., *Walter Benjamin and the Demands of History* (Ithaca, NY: Cornell University Press, 1996); Michael Löwy, *Fire Alarm: "On the Concept of History,"* trans. Chris Turner (London: Verso, 2005); and Fredric Jameson, *The Benjamin Files* (London: Verso, 2020).

96. Walter Benjamin, "The Work of Art in the Age of Its Technological Reproducibility," trans. Harry Zohn and Edmund Jephcott, in Benjamin, *Selected Writings*, vol. 4, *1938–1940*, ed. Howard Eiland and Michael W. Jennings (Cambridge, MA: Harvard University Press, 2003), 251–83. The first version of the "Kunstwerk" article was written in German in 1935, followed in 1936 by a French version, "L'œuvre d'art à l'époque de sa reproduction mécanisée," written between December 1935 and February 1936 but never published, and by a third version in German, also unpublished during his lifetime and finished in March or April of 1939. All quotes are from the final, third version, since a more philologically pertinent analysis of the three versions is beyond the scope of this book.

97. On Benjamin's notion of "phantasmagoria," see Margaret Cohen, "Walter Benjamin's Phantasmagoria," *New German Critique* 48 (Autumn 1989): 87–101; and Gyorgy Markus, "Walter Benjamin or: The Commodity as Phantasmagoria," *New German Critique* 83 (Spring–Summer 2001): 3–42.

98. Benjamin, "The Work of Art in the Age of Its Technological Reproducibility," 269.

99. Ibid.; emphasis in the original.

100. Ibid.; emphasis in the original.

101. Ibid.

102. Ibid.

103. Benjamin had mailed a copy of the "Theses" to Hannah Arendt for her to pass it on to his friend Theodor Adorno before fleeing Paris on June 13, 1940, headed to the south of France and eventually to the United States, where he was supposed to join the Institute for Social Research in exile. Eiland and Jennings, *Walter Benjamin*, 647–75.

104. Löwy, *Fire Alarm*, 58.

105. Walter Benjamin, "On the Concept of History," in *Selected Writings*, vol. 4, *1938–1940*, 392.

106. Ibid.

107. Ibid., 396.

108. To their studies we should add the work of an external affiliate to the School, Alfred Sohn-Rethel, who in 1973 published one of the most sophisticated Marxist analyses of the economic and labor policies elaborated by the Nazis. See Sohn-Rethel, *The Economy and Class Structure of German Fascism*, trans. Martin Sohn-Rethel (London: Free Association Books, 1987).

109. Theodor W. Adorno and Max Horkheimer, *Briefwechsel* (Frankfurt: Suhrkamp, 2005), 3:100. Translated into English in Lars Fischer, "The Frankfurt School and Fascism," in *The SAGE Handbook of Frankfurt School Critical Theory*, ed. Beverly Best, Werner Bonefeld, and Chris O'Kane (London: SAGE Publications, 2023), 2:799.

110. Franz Neumann, Herbert Marcuse, and Otto Kirchheimer, *Secret Reports on Nazi Germany: The Frankfurt School Contribution to the War Effort*, ed. Raffaele Laudani (Princeton, NJ: Princeton University Press, 2013).

111. See Eric Oberle, *Theodor Adorno and the Century of Negative Identity* (Stanford, CA: Stanford University Press, 2018), 131–206.

112. On Adorno's political philosophy, see Espen Hammer, *Adorno and the Political* (London: Routledge, 2006); on "fascism," see esp. 49–71.

113. Rolf Wiggershaus, *The Frankfurt School: Its History, Theories, and Political Significance*, trans. Michael Robertson (Cambridge, MA: MIT Press, 1995), 414. See also Peter E. Gordon, "Realism and Utopia in *The Authoritarian Personality*," *Polity* 54, no. 1 (2022): 8–28.

114. Peter E. Gordon, "Introduction to *The Authoritarian Personality*," in Theodor W. Adorno, Else Frenkel-Brunswik, Daniel J. Levinson, and R. Nevitt Sanford, *The Authoritarian Personality*, new. ed. (London: Verso, 2019), xxviii.

115. For instance, by the psychologist Peter R. Hofstätter.

116. Gordon, "Introduction," xxiii. Stanley Milgram's 1960s experiments at Yale University on voluntary submission to authority largely confirmed the theories of *The Authoritarian Personality*. See Milgram, *Obedience to Authority: An Experimental View* (New York: Harper, 1974), 204–5.

117. Theodor W. Adorno, "Democratic Leadership and Mass Manipulation," in *Studies in Leadership: Leadership and Democratic Action*, ed. Alvin W. Gouldner (New York: Harper, 1950), 418–38. See also the coeval essays "Anti-Semitism and Fascist Propaganda" and "Freudian Theory and the Pattern of Fascist Propaganda," posthumously published in Adorno, *Gesammelte Schriften* (Frankfurt: Suhrkamp, 1972), 8:397–407 and 408–33.

118. Theodor W. Adorno, *The Psychological Technique of Martin Luther Thomas' Radio Addresses* (Stanford, CA: Stanford University Press, 2000), 7.

119. Ibid., 8.

120. Peter E. Gordon, *Adorno and Existence* (Cambridge, MA: Harvard University Press, 2016), 97.

121. Adorno, *The Psychological Technique of Martin Luther Thomas' Radio Addresses*, 15.

122. Fischer, "The Frankfurt School and Fascism," 799.

123. Max Horkheimer, "Die Juden und Europa," *Zeitschrift für Sozialforschung* 8, nos. 1–2 (1939): 115. Among the first critics of the essay was Gershom Scholem, who in a letter to his friend Walter Benjamin wrote: "After repeated readings I do not find it difficult to give it an easily understood formulation: this is an entirely useless product about which, astonishingly enough, *nothing* beneficial and new can be discovered. The author has neither any knowledge of nor any interest in the Jewish problem"; Gershom Scholem, *Walter Benjamin: The Story of a Friendship*, trans. Harry Zohn (New York: Schocken Books, 1981), 222. Scholem's criticism was shared by later historians: for instance, Martin Jay and Anson Rabinbach correctly remarked that rather than the situation of the Jews in Nazi Germany, the main interest of Horkheimer's article was rather the crisis of capitalism in Europe. See Martin Jay, "The Jews and the Frankfurt School: Critical Theory's Analysis of Anti-Semitism," *New German Critique* 19 (Winter 1980): 137–49; and Anson Rabinbach, "'Why Were the Jews Sacrificed?' The Place of Anti-Semitism in Adorno and Horkheimer's *Dialectic of Enlightenment*," in *Adorno: A Critical Reader*, ed. Nigel C. Gibson and Andrew Rubin (Oxford: Blackwell, 2002), 132–47. Horkheimer, too, later disavowed the article and decided not to include it in his three-volume anthology of essays *Kritische Theorie*, published in 1968. The quote from the essay, however, lived on independently from the core

argument of the article. That aphorism too was subject to criticism by a variety of postwar historians. For instance, Roger Griffin, one of the champions of the "fascist minimum" approach, would take it as an example of Marxist reductionism and commented that: "By assuming fascism to be an essentially anti-proletarian force, they play down its antagonism to the ethos of *laissez-faire* economics, consumerist materialism and the bourgeoisie, and are unable to take seriously its claim to be the negation of nineteenth-century liberalism rather than its perpetuation in a different guise. More seriously, they are reluctant to grant it any autonomous revolutionary thrust as a new ideological force." Griffin, *The Nature of Fascism* (Milton Park: Routledge, 1991), 20. In *Modernism and Fascism*, however, Griffin appropriated the quote to pun upon it that "anyone not prepared to talk about modernity or modernism may by all means speak of fascism, but risks remaining oblivious of important aspects of its dynamics, and incapable of resolving the many paradoxes posed by its relationship to liberal capitalist modernity." Roger Griffin, *Modernism and Fascism: The Sense of a Beginning under Mussolini and Hitler* (Houndmill: Palgrave MacMillan, 2007), 344. In general, the favor or disfavor toward Horkheimer's quote depends exclusively on whether or not a historian accepts or denies the link between fascism and capitalism, a divide that continued in postwar historiography, as the next chapter explains, depending on the political leanings of a given historian rather than on the soundness or legitimacy of their interpretations. It is worth noting, however, that neither Horkheimer nor Adorno conceived of fascism as a mere "epiphenomenon of capitalism," as Adrian Lyttelton surmised in "Concluding Remarks," in *Rethinking the Nature of Fascism: Comparative Perspectives*, ed. António Costa Pinto (London: Palgrave Macmillan, 2011), 276.

124. According to Peter Uwe Hohendahl, "For Adorno, Pollock's theory of state capitalism was more important than Neumann's analysis in *Behemoth* or Kirchheimer's essays. Adorno and Horkheimer followed Pollock's interpretation that state capitalism in Nazi Germany reversed the traditional causal connection between the political system and the economy. The priority of the economy vanishes. This means that the state has taken over the basic functions of capitalist enterprise." Hohendahl, *Prismatic Thought: Theodor W. Adorno* (Lincoln: University of Nebraska Press, 1995), 35. In a public lecture of May 9, 1968, however, Adorno admitted that it was Neumann's *Behemoth* that had developed "the most apposite socioeconomic account of fascism that has yet been produced." Theodor W. Adorno, *Introduction to Sociology*, ed. Christoph Göde, trans. Edmund Jephcott (Stanford, CA: Stanford University Press, 2000), 44. On Horkheimer's response to the analyses of Pollock and Neumann, see also Fischer, "The Frankfurt School and Fascism," 804–7.

125. Max Horkheimer, *Eclipse of Reason* (London: Continuum, 2004), 14.

126. Ibid., 82.

127. For a critical analysis of the uses of "instrumental reason" in Horkheimer, Adorno, and Marcuse, see Martin Jay, "The Critique of Instrumental Reason: Horkheimer, Marcuse, and Adorno," in Jay, *Reason after Its Eclipse: On Late Critical Theory* (Madison: University of Wisconsin Press, 2016), 97–113.

128. Horkheimer, *Eclipse of Reason*, 83.

129. Max Horkheimer and Theodor Adorno, *Dialectic of Enlightenment: Philosophical Fragments*, trans. Edmund Jephcott (Stanford, CA: Stanford University Press, 2002), 1.

130. However, as Robert Hullot-Kentor has pointed out, the "Marxist" tone of the text changed between the original manuscripts and the 1947 printed edition: "In 1947 this manuscript appeared in book form, bearing its present title and significantly revised. Obscurities were edited out; capitalism and totalitarianism, previously conflated with fascism, were differentiated.

But, very importantly, Marxist terminology was replaced by more neutral economic and sociological expressions: *proletariat* became *worker*, *capitalist* became *employer*, and *exploitation* became *suffering*. This hedging, the immigrant authors hoped, would speed the manuscript past federal authorities whose anticommunism they had every reason to fear." Hullot-Kentor, *Things Beyond Resemblance: Collected Essays on Theodor Adorno* (New York: Columbia University Press, 2006), 24.

131. Horkheimer and Adorno, *Dialectic of Enlightenment*, 70.

132. Ibid., 33.

133. Ibid., 174.

134. Ibid., 183.

135. Ibid., 129.

136. Ibid., 137. As Anson Rabinbach has pointed out, in *Dialectic of Enlightenment*'s conception of Nazi antisemitism, "Jews represent, at once, power and abjection, property and impotence. . . . The very torment that the Jews experience as a result of their lack of security and membership in the community, the image of the Jew as powerful, intellectual, wealthy, but also as suffering and powerless, evokes the unfulfilled promises of civilization." Rabinbach, *In the Shadow of Catastrophe: German Intellectuals between Apocalypse and Enlightenment* (Berkeley: University of California Press, 1997), 189.

137. Stefano Petrucciani, *Introduzione a Adorno* (Rome: Laterza, 2007), 48.

138. See Horkheimer and Adorno, *Dialectic of Enlightenment*, 156–58.

139. Rabinbach, *In the Shadow of Catastrophe*, 190.

140. Horkheimer and Adorno, *Dialectic of Enlightenment*, 137, 157, and 171.

141. Ibid., 156 and 165.

142. Ibid., 171.

143. Ibid., 167.

144. Ibid., 171.

145. Orietta Ombrosi, *Il crepuscolo della ragione: Benjamin, Adorno, Horkheimer, e Levinas di fronte alla Catastrofe* (Florence: Giuntina, 2014), 42–47. See also Hammer, *Adorno and the Political*, 64–71, for a revision of Jay's and Rabinbach's charges against Horkheimer and Adorno.

146. First published in Germany as *Minima Moralia: Reflexionen aus dem beschädigten Leben* (Frankfurt: Suhrkamp Verlag, 1951).

147. "With the dissolution of liberalism," after the rise to power of National Socialism, "the truly bourgeois principle, that of competition, far from being overcome, has passed from the objectivity of the social process into the composition of its colliding and jostling atoms, and therewith as if into anthropology"; Theodor W. Adorno, *Minima Moralia: Reflections from Damaged Life*, trans. E. F. N. Jephcott (London: Verso, 2005), 27.

148. Ibid., 108.

149. For an introduction and an anthology of his work in English, see Ken C. Kawashima, Fabian Schaefer, and Robert Stolz, eds., *Tosaka Jun: A Critical Reader* (Ithaca, NY: Cornell University Press, 2013). On Tosaka's view of fascism, see Harry Harootunian, *Archaism and Actuality: Japan and the Global Fascist Imaginary* (Durham, NC: Duke University Press, 2023), esp. 170–222.

150. Tosaka Jun, *Nihon ideorogiron [On Japanese Ideology]* (1936), chap. 10, no. 2. Quotations from the online version of *Nihon ideorogiron* will take the form of, e.g., 10.2, where the first number refers to the chapter and the successive numbers to further hierarchical subdivisions within that chapter; https://www.marxists.org/nihon/tosaka/1936/criticism.htm, accessed September 20, 2024. For a different English translation, see Tosaka Jun, *The Japanese Ideology: A*

Marxist Critique of Liberalism and Fascism, trans. Robert Stolz (New York: Columbia University Press, 2024), 136.

151. Ibid.

152. Ibid., 1.20. For an English translation, see Tosaka, *The Japanese Ideology*, 14.

153. Ibid.

154. These included earlier histories such as the *Kojiki*, collections of imperial poetry (the *Man'yōshū* and the *Kokinshū*), and prose works such as *The Tale of Genji* and *Heike monogatari*—in short, texts that were canonized as Japanese classics in the Meiji period. See Haruo Shirane and Tomi Suzuki, eds., *Inventing the Classics: Modernity, National Identity, and Japanese Literature* (Stanford, CA: Stanford University Press, 2000). Robert Stolz translates *bunkengakushugi* as "philology" and "philologism" in Tosaka, *The Japanese Ideology*, 14–15.

155. Tosaka, *Nihon ideorogiron*, 1.20. English translation in Tosaka, *The Japanese Ideology*, 14.

156. Ibid., 1.21.

157. Ibid.

158. Ibid., 10.4. A different English translation can be found in Tosaka, *The Japanese Ideology*, 137.

159. Terence Renaud, *New Lefts: The Making of a Radical Tradition* (Princeton, NJ: Princeton University Press, 2021), 53.

160. Ibid. See ibid., 53–86, for Renaud's analysis of these two forms of antifascism in the year immediately before the war.

161. Such as, e.g., Austria's Deutsche Nationalsozialistische Arbeiterpartei, which replaced Dollfuss's Vaterländische Front; Belgium's Vlaams Nationaal Verbond alongside Rex; the Bulgarian Narodno sotsialno dvizhenie; the Czechoslovakian Národni souru Partidul Național Creștincenství of Emil Hácha; Denmark's Nationalsocialistiske Arbejderparti; in Hungary, a constellation of Nemzeti Szocialista parties, groups, or associations surrounding the strong Arrow Cross party; the Finnish Flokkur Þjóðernissinna; the Greek National Socialist Party and the Ethniki Enosis Eliados contending with the authoritarian Metaxtas Regime; the Dutch Nationaal-Socialistische Nederlandsche; in Norway, the Nasjonal Samling of Vidkun Quisling; in Portugal, Salazar's own National Union; in Romania, alongside the Romanian Iron Guard, the strong Partidul Național Creștin; the Swedish Nationalsocialistiska partiet; and the Swiss National Front.

162. Czechoslovakia's Národní obec fašistická; France's Le Faisceau; in the United Kingdom, Rotha Lintorn-Orman's British Fascists, Oswald Mosley's British Union of Fascists, and Arnold Leese's Imperial Fascist League; the Russian Fascist Party, founded by a former official of the White Army, Konstantin Rodzaevsku, and active mainly in Manchuria and the United States.

163. For an encyclopedic introduction to ultranationalist (national-socialist and fascist) movements, see Stanley Payne, *A History of Fascism, 1914–1945* (London: Routledge, 1995); and Cyprian P. Blamires, ed., *World Fascism: A Historical Encyclopedia* (Santa Barbara, CA: ABC-CLIO, 2006).

164. Nicholas Startgardt, *The German War: A Nation under Arms, 1939–1945* (New York: Basic Books, 2015), 1–21.

165. See Michael Seidman, *Transatlantic Antifascisms: From the Spanish Civil War to the End of World War II* (Cambridge: Cambridge University Press, 2018).

Part III Introduction

1. It suffices to think about the defenses of Fascism by intellectuals such Giovanni Gentile and Giuseppe Bottai, and, in the German context, the defenses of National Socialism by such

philosophers as Martin Heidegger and Carl Schmitt. Or, among antifascists, the rigorous sociopolitical analyses of Gaetano Salvemini, Antonio Gramsci, or the scholars of the Frankfurt School.

2. These "new left" movements included the historians who grouped around the *New Left Review*; French and Italian intellectuals who became alienated from their communist parties, such as, e.g., Louis Althusser and his students Étienne Balibar, Jacques Rancière, and Alain Badiou in France, or Antonio Negri, Franco "Bifo" Berardi, Adriano Sofri, and many others in Italy; student movements all around the world, which found inspiration in the antifascism of the Frankfurt School and Herbert Marcuse; the various libertarian socialists, civil rights advocates, and Cold War liberals in the United States; and Japanese activists of the heterogeneous anti-Anpō movements, of student movements like the Zengakuren, and of concerned citizen-student movements such as the Beiheiren and Zenkyōtō. See Carl Oglesby, ed., *The New Left Reader* (New York: Grove Press, 1969); and Terence Renaud, *New Lefts: The Making of a Radical Tradition* (Princeton, NJ: Princeton University Press, 2021). On Japan, see William Andrews, *Dissenting Japan: A History of Japanese Radicalism and Counterculture, from 1945 to Fukushima* (London: Hurst, 2016); and Nick Kapur, *Japan at the Crossroads: Conflict and Compromise after Anpo* (Cambridge, MA: Harvard University Press, 2018).

Chapter Ten

1. Michele Battini, *The Missing Italian Nuremberg: Cultural Amnesia and Postwar Politics* (London: Palgrave Macmillan, 2007), 31–42.

2. Filippo Focardi, *Il cattivo tedesco e il bravo italiano: La rimozione delle colpe della seconda guerra mondiale* (Rome: Laterza, 2013), 77–106.

3. Examples of these interventions are the novels of the Resistance, most of which were published in the short period between 1944 and 1954, coinciding with the period of historians' silence on the Fascist past. The first scholarly synthesis of these works appeared as early as 1956: Angelo Paoluzi, *La letteratura della Resistenza* (Florence: Edizioni 5 Lune, 1956). See Andrea Bianchini and Francesca Lolli, eds., *Letteratura e Resistenza* (Bologna: CLUEB, 1997); and Giorgio Luti, ed., *Bella Ciao: Resistenza e letteratura* (Arezzo: Helicon, 2009).

4. Piero Malvezzi and Giovanni Pirelli, eds., *Lettere dei condannati a morte della Resistenza italiana* (Turin: Einaudi, 1955); and Ada Gobetti, *Diario partigiano* (Turin: Einaudi, 1956).

5. Benedetta Tobagi, *La Resistenza delle donne* (Turin: Einaudi, 2022).

6. Giovanni De Luna, *La Repubblica inquieta: L'Italia della Costituzione, 1946–1948* (Milan: Feltrinelli, 2017), 19–57.

7. "Disposizioni transitorie e finali," *Costituzione della repubblica italiana*, https://www.governo.it/it/costituzione-italiana/parte-seconda-ordinamento-della-repubblica/disposizioni-transitorie-e-finali, accessed September 22, 2024.

8. In *Gazzetta ufficiale* 143, June 23, 1952, 1.

9. Davide Conti, *Fascisti contro la democrazia: Almirante e Rauti alle radici della destra italiana, 1946–1976* (Turin: Einaudi, 2023).

10. See Hans Woller, *Die Abrechnung mit dem Faschismus in Italien, 1943 bis 1948* (Munich: Oldenbourg, 1996); and Battini, *The Missing Italian Nuremberg*, 125–44.

11. Paul Ginsborg, *A History of Contemporary Italy: Society and Politics, 1943–1988* (London: Penguin, 1990), 92.

12. Mimmo Franzinelli, *L'amnistia Togliatti: Colpo di spugna sui crimini fascisti* (Milan: Mondadori, 2006).

13. Filippo Focardi, *La guerra della memoria: La Resistenza nel dibattito politico italiano dal 1945 a oggi* (Rome: Laterza, 2005), 28.

14. Lutz Klinkhammer, *Stragi naziste in Italia: La guerra contro i civili (1943–44)* (Rome: Donzelli, 1997); Mimmo Franzinelli, *Le stragi nascoste: L'armadio della vergogna; Impunità e rimozione dei crimini di Guerra nazifascisti, 1943–2001* (Milan: Mondadori, 2002), 17–184; and Donatella Gagliani, *Brigate nere: Mussolini e la militarizzazione del Partito fascista repubblicano* (Turin: Bollati Boringhieri, 2017).

15. Ginsborg, *A History of Contemporary Italy*, 92–93.

16. Focardi, *Il cattivo tedesco e il bravo italiano*, 52–76; and Focardi, *La guerra della memoria*, 19–32.

17. See Luca La Rovere, *L'eredità del fascismo: Gli intellettuali, I giovani e la transizione al postfascismo, 1943–1948* (Turin: Bollati Boringhieri, 2008); and Bianca Maria Dematteis, "La banalisation du fascisms dans l'Italie d'après-guerre," *Politika*, June 13, 2019, https://www.politika.io/fr/article/banalisation-du-fascisme-litalie-dapresguerre, accessed September 22, 2024.

18. Dematteis, "La banalisation du fascismes dans l'Italie d'après-guerre"; and La Rovere, *L'eredità del fascismo*, 9.

19. Manfred Görtemaker, *Die Akte Rosenburg: Das Bundesministerium der Justiz und die NS-Zeit* (Munich: C. H. Beck, 2016); Sugita Yoneyuki, *Pitfall or Panacea: The Irony of US Power in Occupied Japan* (New York: Routledge, 2003), 29–48; and Kapur, *Japan at the Crossroads*, 35–74.

20. Michael J. Hogan, *The Marshall Plan: America, Britain, and the Reconstruction of Western Europe, 1947–1952* (Cambridge: Cambridge University Press, 1987), 1–53.

21. Daniele Ganser, *NATO's Secret Armies: Operation GLADIO and Terrorism in Western Europe* (London: Routledge, 2005).

22. Anna Cento Bull, *Italian Neofascism: The Strategy of Tension and the Politics of Nonreconciliation* (New York: Berghahn, 2012); Mirco Dondi, *L'eco del boato: La strategia della tensione, 1965–1974* (Rome: Laterza, 2015); Aldo Giannuli, *La strategia della tensione: Servizi segreti, partiti, golpe falliti, terrore fascista, politica internazionale: Un bilancio definitive* (Milan: Ponte alle Grazie, 2018); and Benedetta Tobagi, *Le stragi sono tutte un mistero* (Rome: Laterza, 2024).

23. Ginsborg, *A History of Contemporary Italy*, 72.

24. Ibid., 98–120; and Edoardo Novelli, *Le elezioni del Quarantotto: Storia, strategie e immagini della prima campagna elettorale repubblicana* (Rome: Donzelli, 2008).

25. Sakamoto Yoshikazu, "The International Context of the Occupation of Japan," in *Democratizing Japan: The Allied Occupation*, ed. Robert E. Ward and Sakamoto Yoshikazu (Honolulu: University of Hawai'i Press, 1987), 44.

26. See Gianpasquale Santomassimo, "Gli storici italiani tra fascismo e repubblica," *Italia contemporanea* 198 (March 1995): 77–89. A quick perusal of the first ten years after the war of the *Rivista storica italiana*, the most prestigious professional historiographical publication in Italy, from 1948 to 1958 (coinciding with the editorial leadership of Federico Chabod), would reveal that in forty five volumes published, "fascism" appeared only tangentially in two articles, whereas twenty-six focused on nineteenth-century history, forty-nine on the early modern period, thirty on the Middle Ages, eleven on antiquity, and only four on nonfascist twentieth-century history. Furthermore, historiographical and methodological essays did not treat "fascism," but largely philology, archaeology, and historical sources (mostly penned by Arnaldo Momigliano), as well as biographical notes on prominent historians of the past.

27. Emilio Gentile, "Fascism in Italian Historiography: In Search of an Individual Historical Identity," *Journal of Contemporary History* 21, no. 2 (1986): 179.

28. Leonardo Rapone, "*Nascita e avvento del fascismo* e la storiografia italiana," in *Il fascismo in tempo reale: Studi e ricerca di Angelo Tasca sulla genesis e l'evoluzione del regime fascista, 1926–1938*, ed. Giuseppe Vacca and David Bidussa (Milan: Feltrinelli, 2014), 78.

29. Franco De Felice, "La storiografia delle élites nel secondo dopoguerra," *Mélanges des l'école française de Rome* 95, no. 2 (1983): 127–43; and Eugenio Di Rienzo, *Un dopoguerra storiografico: Storici italiani tra Guerra civile e Repubblica* (Florence: Le Lettere, 2004), for two different surveys of the discipline of history in the immediate postwar era. On Di Rienzo's revisionist perspective, see also the review article by Riccardo Fubini, "Dopoguerra e crisi della storiografia italiana: A proposito di un libro recente," *Archivio storico Italiano* 162, no. 4 (2004): 743–62.

30. Santomassimo, "Gli storici italiani tra fascismo e repubblica."

31. Ibid., 79. *Repugnanza* (repugnance) is the term Benedetto Croce employed to describe the instinctual rejection of particular forms of historical inquiry and objects (such as "natural history"); Benedetto Croce, *Teoria e storia della storiografia: Teoria e storia* (Bari: Laterza, 1920), https://www.nilalienum.com/gramsci/0_Croce/TeoriaStoriast.html.

32. Ibid., 80.

33. Arnaldo Momigliano, "Gli studi italiani di storia greca e romana dal 1859 al 1939," in *Cinquant'anni di vita intellettuale italiana, 1896–1946: Scritti in onore di Benedetto Croce per il suo ottantesimo compleanno*, ed. Carlo Antoni and Raffaele Mattioli (Napoli: Edizioni scientifiche italiane, 1950), 1:105–6.

34. Quoted in Gentile, "Fascism in Italian Historiography," 180, from Fabio Cusin, *Antistoria d'Italia* (1948; Milan: Mondadori, 1972), xx.

35. Santomassimo, "Gli storici italiani tra fascismo e repubblica," 84–86.

36. In 1949 the *Rivista storica italiana* published a historiographical article by Carlo Morandi that addressed Antonio Gramsci's essay on intellectuals and the organization of culture; Morandi, "Appunti e documenti per una storia degli italiani fuori d'Italia (A proposito di alcune note di Antonio Gramsci)," *Rivista storica italiana* 61, no. 3 (1949): 379–84. The *Lettere dal carcere* (*Prison Letters*) appeared in 1947 for Einaudi, and the first anthology of Gramsci's writings was published in 1952. A complete publication of his articles in *L'ordine nuovo* appeared only in 1967, also for Einaudi.

37. Gentile, "Fascism in Italian Historiography," 180.

38. Ibid.

39. Nino Valeri, "Cosa fu il fascismo," *Il resto del Carlino*, September 20, 1962.

40. Alessandra Tarquini, *Storia della cultura fascista* (Bologna: Il Mulino, 2011), 12.

41. Norberto Bobbio, *L'ideologia del fascismo*, Quaderni della F.I.A.P. (Rome: Federazione italiana delle associazioni partigiane, 1975), 3, https://www.fiapitalia.it/pubblicazioni/i-quaderni-della-fiap/bobbio-ideologia-del-fascismo-1, accessed September 22, 2024.

42. Ibid.

43. Ibid., 4.

44. Ibid., 9.

45. Ibid., 10.

46. Ibid.

47. Ibid., 16.

48. Ibid., 17.

49. Ibid., 19.

50. Ibid., 20.

51. Ibid., 21.

52. Ibid., 20–21.

53. Ibid., 21.

54. Ibid.

55. Ibid.

56. Ibid., 23.

57. Ibid.

58. Ibid., 26.

59. Ibid.

60. Ibid., 29.

61. See, e.g., Norberto Bobbio, *Maestri e compagni* (Florence: Passigli, 1984). See also Gustavo Zagrebelsky, Massimo L. Salvadori, Riccardo Guastini, et al., *Norberto Bobbio tra diritto e politica* (Rome: Laterza, 2005).

62. E.g., the works of Roberto Vivarelli, *Storia delle origini del fascismo*, vol. 1, *L'Italia dalla grande guerra alla marcia su Roma* (Bologna: Il Mulino, 1991); Gaetano Salvemini, *Le origini del fascismo in Italia: Lezioni di Harvard*, ed. Roberto Vivarelli (Milan: Feltrinelli, 1966); Enzo Santarelli, *Origini del fascismo, 1911–1919* (Urbino: Argalia, 1963); Mario Missiroli, *Il fascismo e il colpo di stato dell'ottobre 1922* (Bologna: Cappelli, 1966); Paolo Alatri, *L'antifascismo italiano* (Rome: Editori Riuniti, 1961); Federico Chabod, *A History of Italian Fascism* (London: Weidenfeld & Nicolson, 1963); Danilo Veneruso, *La vigilia del fascismo: Il primo ministero Facta nella crisi dello stato liberale in Italia* (Bologna: Il Mulino, 1968); Francesco Perfetti, *Il nazionalismo italiano* (Milano: Edizioni del Borghese, 1969); Claudio Giovannini, *L'Italia da Vittorio Veneto all'Avventino: Storia politica delle origini del fascismo (1918–1925)* (Bologna: Pàtron, 1972); Alessandro Giovannini, *Dal sindacalismo rivoluzionario al fascismo: Capitalismo agrario nel Ferrarese (1870–1920)* (Florence: La Nuova Italia, 1972); Domenico Settembrini, *Fascismo, controrivoluzione imperfetta: Movimento al servizio del capitale o primo esperimento di compromesso storico?* (Florence: Sansoni, 1978); Marco Francini, *Primo dopoguerra e origini del fascismo a Pistoia* (Milan: Feltrinelli, 1976); Rolando Cavandoli, *Le origini del fascismo a Reggio Emilia, 1919–1923* (Rome: Editori Riuniti, 1972); Antonino Répaci, *La marcia su Roma* (Milan: Rizzoli, 1972); Gian Franco Venè, *Il golpe fascista del 1922: Cronaca e storia della marcia su Roma* (Milan: Garzanti, 1975); and Paolo Nello, *L'avanguardismo giovanile alle origini del fascismo* (Rome: Laterza, 1978).

63. E.g., Alberto Aquarone, *L'organizzazione dello stato totalitario* (Turin: Einaudi, 1965), and *Il regime fascista* (Bologna: Il Mulino, 1974); Isabella Zanni Rosiello, *Gli apparati statali dall'Unità al fascismo* (Bologna: Il Mulino, 1976); and Sabino Cassese, *Corporazioni e intervento pubblico nell'economia* (Milan: Giuffrè, 1969).

64. E.g., Giulio Sapelli, *Fascismo, grande industria e sindacato: Il caso di Torino, 1929–1935* (Milan: Feltrinelli, 1975), and *Organizzazione, lavoro e innovazione industrial nell'Italia tra le due guerre* (Turin: Rosenberg & Sellier, 1978); Gualberto Gualerni, *Industria e fascismo: Per una interpretazione dello sviluppo economico italiano tra le due guerre* (Milan: Vita e pensiero, 1976); Nicola Tranfaglia, ed., *Fascismo e capitalismo* (Milan: Feltrinelli, 1976), and Tranfaglia, *Dallo Stato liberale al regime fascista: Problemi e ricerche* (Milan: Feltrinelli, 1973); Franco Catalano, *Potere economico e fascismo* (Milan: Bompiani, 1974); and Piero Melograni, *Gli industriali e Mussolini: Rapporti tra Confindustria e fascismo dal 1919 al 1929* (Milan: Longanesi, 1972).

65. E.g., Guido Quazza, ed., *Fascismo e società italiana* (Turin: Einaudi, 1973); Carmen Betti, *L'opera nazionale Balilla e l'educazione fascista* (Florence: La Nuova Italia, 1984); and Simona Colarizi, *L'Italia antifascista dal 1922 aal 1940: La lotta dei protagonisti* (Rome: Laterza, 1976).

66. E.g., Franco Catalano, *Aspetti dell'Italia sotto il Fascismo e Resistenza* (Milan: La goliardica, 1967); and Giorgio Rochat, *Le guerre italiane, 1935–1943: Dall'impero d'Etiopia alla disfatta* (Turin: Einaudi, 2008).

67. E.g., Pier Giorgio Zunino, *L'ideologia del fascismo: Miti, credenze, valori* (Bologna: Il Mulino, 1985); and Emilio Gentile, *Le origini dell'ideologia fascista (1918–1925)* (Bologna: Il Mulino, 1996).

68. E.g., Gabriele Turi, *Fascismo e il consenso degli intellettuali* (Bologna: Il Mulino, 1980); Eugenio Garin, *Cronache di filosofia italiana, 1900–1943* (Bari: Laterza, 1975), and *La filosofia italiana di fronte al fascismo* (Florence: Sansoni, 1983); Alberto Asor Rosa, "I 'manifesti degli intellettuali,'" *Storia d'Italia* 4, no. 2 (1975): 1464–70; Nino Valeri, *Dalla "belle époque" al fascismo: Momenti e personaggi* (Bari: Laterza, 1975), and *Cinema italiano tra le due guerre: Fascismo e politica cinematografica* (Milan: Mursia, 1975); Gian Piero Brunetta, *Intellettuali, cinema e propaganda tra le due guerre* (Bologna: Pàtron, 1972); Roberto Esposito, *Il Sistema dell'in/differenza: Moravia e il fascismo* (Bari: Dedalo, 1978); Luisa Mangoni, *Aspetti della cultura Cattolica sotto il fascismo: La rivista, il frontespizio* (Bologna: Il Mulino, 1972), and *L'interventismo della cultura: Intellettuali e riviste del fascismo* (Rome and Bari; Laterza, 1974); Guido Armellini, *Le immagini del fascismo nelle arti figurative* (Milan: Fabbri, 1980); Michele Ciliberto, *Intellettuali e fascismo: Saggio su Delio Cantimori* (Bari: De Donato, 1977); Oreste Del Buono, *Eia, eia, eia, alalà! La stampa italiana sotto il fascismo, 1919–1943* (Milan: Feltrinelli, 1971); Giuseppe Pagano, *Architettura e città durante il fascismo* (Rome: Laterza, 1976); and Mario Isnenghi, *L'educazione dell'italiano: Il fascismo e l'organizzazione della cultura* (Bologna: Cappelli, 1979), *Intellettuali militanti e intellettuali funzionari: Appunti sulla cultura fascista* (Turin: Einaudi, 1979), and *Storia e autocoscienza del giornalismo fascista: Problemi, strumenti, fonti* (Bologna: Il Mulino, 1979).

69. E.g., Renzo De Felice, *Storia degli ebrei italiani sotto il fascismo* (Turin: Einaudi, 1961); Ugo Caffaz, *L'antisemitismo italiano sotto il fascismo* (Florence: La Nuova Italia, 1975); and Luigi Preti, *I miti dell'impero e della razza nell'Italia degli anni '30* (Rome: Opere Nuove, 1965), and *Impero fascista: Africani ed ebrei* (Milan: Mursia, 1968).

70. E.g., Enzo Erra, *L'interpretazione del fascismo nel problema storico italiano* (Rome: G. Volpe, 1971); Enzo Santarelli, *Ricerche sul fascismo* (Urbino: Argalia, 1971), and *Fascismo e neofascismo: Studi e problemi di ricerca* (Rome: Ed. Riuniti, 1974); Renzo De Felice, *Il fascismo: Le interpretazioni dei contemporanei e degli storici* (Rome: Laterza, 1970); and Ruggero Zangrandi, *Il lungo viaggio attraverso il fascismo: Contributo alla storia di una generazione* (Milan: Feltrinelli, 1962). WorldCat records 4215 book titles published in Italy between 1960 and 1980 containing the word "Fascismo." For a historiographical overview, see Gentile, "Fascism in Italian Historiography"; Niccolò Zapponi, "Fascism in Italian Historiography," *Journal of Contemporary History* 29, no. 4 (1994): 547–68; Danilo Breschi, "Recent Italian Historiography on Italian Fascism," *Telos* 133 (Winter 2005): 15–44; Giovanni Belardelli, "La storiografia italiana di fronte al fascismo: Interpretazioni e rimozioni," in *Vom Umgang mit der Vergangenheit: Ein deutsch-italienischer Dialog*, ed. Christiane Liermann, Marta Margotti, Bernd Sösemann, and Francesco Traniello (Tübingen: Max Niemeyer Verlag, 2007), 121–27; and Gregorio Sorgonà, "Storiografia del fascismo e dibattito sull'antifascismo," *Studi storici* 55, no. 1 (2014): 213–25.

71. By the 1980s Emilio Gentile admitted that "dozens of pages would be required merely to list the books and articles on fascism published by Italian historians in the last twenty years"; Gentile, "Fascism in Italian Historiography," 179.

72. Norberto Bobbio, Renzo De Felice, and Gian Enrico Rusconi, *Italiani, amici nemici* (Milan: Reset, 1996), 11.

73. Norberto Bobbio, *De senectute* (Turin: Einaudi, 1996), 151. See also Bobbio, *Destra e sinistra: Ragioni e significati di una distinzione politica* (Rome: Donzelli, 1994).

74. Norberto Bobbio, *Politica e cultura* (Turin: Einaudi, 1955); and Bobbio, "La cultura e il fascismo," in *Fascismo e società italiane*, ed. Guido Quazza (Turin: Einaudi, 1973), 209–46.

75. Fascism, for Bobbio, was an "antidemocratic, antisocialist, anti-Bolshevik, antiparliamentary, antiliberal, anti-everything movement"; Norberto Bobbio, *Profilo ideologico del Novecento* (Milan: Garzanti, 1990), 153. A different English translation can be found in Norberto Bobbio, *Ideological Profile of Twentieth-Century Italy*, trans. Lydia G. Cochrane (Princeton, NJ: Princeton University Press, 2014), 122.

76. Bobbio, "La cultura e il fascismo," 231.

77. "Fascism and adolescence continue to be, to a certain extent, permanent historical seasons of our life. Adolescence, of our individual life; Fascism, of the national one: in short, this remaining eternally a child, unloading responsibilities onto others, living with the comforting feeling that there is someone who thinks for you." Federico Fellini, *Fare un film* (Turin: Einaudi, 1980), 155.

78. Ibid., 14.

79. Gianpasquale Santomassimo, "Consenso," in *Dizionario del fascismo*, ed. Victoria De Grazia and Sergio Luzzatto (Turin: Einaudi, 2002), 1:347–52.

80. It goes beyond the scope of this investigation to report on the harsh debate on De Felice's conservative revisionism. For an analysis sympathetic to De Felice, see Giovanni Belardelli, "L'intervista pericolosa: De Felice e l'uso dell'antifascismo come arma impropria," *Storia contemporanea* 3, no. 2 (1999): 25–36. For a different view, see Sergio Luzzatto, *La crisi dell'antifascismo* (Turin: Einaudi, 2004); and Donatello Aramini, "Renzo De Felice e la recente storiografia italiana," *Studi storici* 55, no. 1 (2014): 335–48.

81. Renzo De Felice, *Intervista sul fascismo*, ed. Michael A. Ledeen (Rome: Laterza, 1975), 40–41.

82. Gianpiero Carocci, "Postilla all''Intervista sul fascismo,'" in *Fascismo e capitalismo*, ed. Nicola Tranfaglia (Milan: Feltrinelli, 1976), 209.

83. Santomassimo, "Consenso," 347.

84. As, for instance, in the case of R. J. B. Bosworth, for whom the apex of popular consent for the regime should be postponed to the mid-1930s. Bosworth, *Mussolini's Italy: Life under the Fascist Dictatorship, 1915–1945* (London: Penguin, 2005), 327–28.

85. A group of historians associated to the professional journal *Italia contemporanea* (the editorial board of which then included historians of the caliber of Guido Quazza, Enzo Collotti, Claudio Pavone, and Giorgio Rochat) published a refutation of De Felice's volume, questioning both his use of the archival sources and the historiographical *qualunquismo* of its argument, by attacking his vision of a regime that, "if it had not been for its excesses and clownish aspects, . . . would still represent a model of political order and mediation of social conflicts (corporatism) that historians of non-fascist (even more than post-fascist) historiography, after all, do not dislike." Editorial Board [unsigned], "Una storiografia afascista per la 'maggioranza silenziosa,'" *Italia contemporanea* 26, no. 2 (1975): 3. The accusations against De Felice's revisionism found a new basis in 1987 when he declared that "Italian fascism is safe from the accusation of genocide, it is out of the shadow of the Holocaust"; Giuliano Ferrara, "'Le norme contro il fascismo? Sono grottesche, aboliamole': A colloquio con Renzo De Felice, lo storico del ventennio nero," *Il corriere della sera*, December 17, 1987, 2.

86. Luzzatto, *La crisi dell'antifascismo*.

87. See Focardi, *La guerra della memoria*, 252–58.

88. Gentile's most recent work, *Storia del fascismo* (Rome: Laterza, 2022), is a 1376-page summa of his life work.

89. Emilio Gentile, *Fascismo: Storia e interpretazione* (Rome: Laterza, 2002), viii.

90. Ibid., x.

91. Mimmo Franzinelli, *Il fascismo è finito il 25 aprile 1945* (Rome: Laterza, 2022).

92. Paolo Berizzi, *NazItalia: Viaggio in un paese che si è riscoperto fascista* (Milan: Baldini + Castoldi, 2018).

93. See, e.g., Giulia Albanese, *The March on Rome: Violence and the Rise of Italian Fascism*, trans. Sergio Knipe (London: Routledge, 2019), and *Il fascismo italiano: Storia e interpretazioni* (Rome: Carocci, 2021); Lorenzo Benadussi, *The Enemy of the New Man: Homosexuality in Fascist Italy* (Madison: University of Wisconsin Press, 2012); David Bidussa, *Il mito del bravo italiano* (Milan: Il Saggiatore, 1994), and *La misura del potere: Pio XII e i totalitarismi tra il 1932 e il 1948* (Milan: Solferino, 2020); Maddalena Carli, *Vedere il fascismo: Arte e politica nelle esposizioni del regime (1928–1942)* (Rome: Carocci, 2020); Francesco Cassata, *"La Difesa della razza": Politica, ideologia e imagine del razzismo fascista* (Turin: Einaudi, 2008); Laura Cerasi, *Genealogie e geografie dell'anti-democrazia nella crisi europea degli anni Trenta: Fascismi, corporativismi, laburismi* (Venice: Edizioni Ca' Foscari, 2019); Matteo Di Figlia, *Farinacci: Il radicalismo fascista al potere* (Rome: Donzelli, 2007); Focardi, *Il cattivo tedesco e il bravo italiano* and *La guerra della memoria*; Valeria Galimi, *Sotto gli occhi di tutti: La società italiana e le persecuzioni contro gli ebrei* (Florence: Le Monnier, 2018); Luca La Rovere, *Storia dei GUF: Organizzazione, politica e miti della gioventù universitaria fascista, 1919–1943* (Turin: Bollati Boringhieri, 2003), and *L'eredità del fascismo*; Roberta Pergher, *Mussolini's Nation-Empire: Sovereignty and Settlement in Italy's Borderlands, 1922–1943* (Cambridge: Cambridge University Press, 2018); Simon Levis Sullam, *I carnefici italiani: Scene dal genocidio degli ebrei, 1943–1945* (Milan: Feltrinelli, 2015), and *I fantasmi del fascismo: Le metamorfosi degli intellettuali italiani nel dopoguerra* (Milan: Feltrinelli, 2021); and Tarquini, *Storia della cultura fascista*.

94. See Giorgio Caravale, *Senza intellettuali: Politica e cultura in Italia negli ultimi trent'anni* (Rome: Laterza, 2023).

95. Giovanni De Luna, *Le ragioni di un decennio, 1969–1979: Militanza, violenza, sconfitta, memoria* (Milan: Feltrinelli, 2009), 81–95; and Miguel Gotor, *Generazione Settanta: Storia del decennio più lungo del secolo breve, 1966–1982* (Turin: Einaudi, 2022), 101–41.

96. Petra Rosenbaum, *Il nuovo fascismo* (Milan: Feltrinelli, 1975); Mario Caprara and Gianluca Semprini, *Destra estrema e criminale* (Rome: Newton Compton, 2007); and Nicola Antonini, *Fuori dal cerchio: Viaggio nella destra radicale italiana* (Rome: Elliot, 2010).

97. Enzo Collotti, *Fascismo, fascismi* (Milan: Sansoni, 1989).

Chapter Eleven

1. Quoted in Umberto Eco, *Five Moral Pieces*, trans. Alastair McEwen (New York: Harcourt, 2001), 70. See also James MacGregor Burns, *Roosevelt: The Soldier of Freedom* (New York: Harcourt, 1970), 381–88, for other examples.

2. Clayton D. Laurie, *The Propaganda Warriors: America's Crusade against Nazi Germany* (Lawrence: University Press of Kansas, 1996).

3. As the conservative historian Paul E. Gottfried put it, "Fascism's greatest recognition value since its high-water mark has been as a slur—or as an indiscriminately used synonym for Nazi

genocide"; Gottfried, *Fascism: The Career of a Concept* (DeKalb: Northern Illinois University Press, 2016), 150. See also Gottfried, *Antifascism: The Course of a Crusade* (Ithaca, NY: Cornell University Press, 2021), 75–88. For a reflection on slurs in political discourse, see Chang Liu, "Slurs and the Type-Token Distinction of Their Derogatory Force," *Rivista italiana di filosofia del linguaggio* 13, no. 2 (2019): 63–72.

4. See Fabian Freyenhagen, *Adorno's Practical Philosophy: Living Less Wrongly* (Cambridge: Cambridge University Press, 2013), 27–30; and Martin Shuster, *Autonomy after Auschwitz: Adorno, German Idealism, and Modernity* (Chicago: University of Chicago Press, 2014).

5. This is a reference to Adorno's famous injunction, originally leveled against the attempt of Richard Strauss to propose a lyric catharsis that avoided the shared responsibility for the war and the Jewish genocide, whereby "cultural criticism finds itself faced with the final stage of the dialectic of culture and barbarism. To write poetry after Auschwitz is barbaric." Theodor Adorno, *Prisms*, trans. Samuel and Shierry Weber (Cambridge, MA: MIT Press, 1981), 34.

6. Theodor W. Adorno, "Education after Auschwitz," in *Critical Models: Interventions and Catchwords*, trans Henry W. Pickford (New York: Columbia University Press, 1998), 191–204.

7. Theodor W. Adorno, "The Meaning of Working Through the Past," in *Critical Models*, 89–104.

8. Adorno, "The Meaning of Working Through the Past," 90. His critique was directed against Konrad Adenauer's regime (1949–63), which restored West Germany's economy (the *Wirtschaftswunder* of the late 1950s–1960s) at the cost of reinstating former Nazi officials in positions of power. See Fabian Freyenhagen, "Adorno's Politics: Theory and Praxis in Germany's 1960s," *Philosophy & Social Criticism* 40, no. 9 (2014): 867–93.

9. Philipp Felsch, *The Summer of Theory: History of a Rebellion, 1960–1990*, trans. Tony Crawford (Cambridge: Polity, 2022), 11–48.

10. See Andrew T. Lamas, Todd Wolfson, and Peter N. Funke, eds., *The Great Refusal: Herbert Marcuse and Contemporary Social Movements* (Philadelphia: Temple University Press, 2016); Ruggero D'Alessandro, *La teoria critica in Italia: Letture italiane della Scuola di Francoforte* (Rome: Manifestolibri, 2003), 143–220; and Gerhard Richter, ed., "Who's Afraid of the Ivory Tower? A Conversation with Theodor W. Adorno," *Monatshefte* 94, no. 1 (2002): 10–23.

11. Herbert Marcuse, "The Left under the Counterrevolution," in *Counterrevolution and Revolt* (Boston: Beacon Press, 1972), 25. The quote in Marcuse's text was taken from Leo Guiliani, "Les révolutionnaires sont seuls," *Le Monde*, July 23, 1971.

12. Herbert Marcuse, "The Historical Fate of Bourgeois Democracy," in *Towards a Critical Theory of Society: Collected Papers of Herbert Marcuse*, vol. 2, ed. Douglas Kellner (London: Routledge, 2001), 165.

13. Translated into English in Herbert Marcuse, *The New Left and the 1960s: Collected Papers of Herbert Marcuse*, vol. 3, ed. Douglas Kellner (London: Routledge, 2005), 138.

14. Angelo Tasca, *Nascita e avvento del fascismo: L'Italia dall'armistizio alla marcia su Roma* (Vicenza: Neri Pozza, 2021), 391; emphasis in the original. The first edition of Tasca's study was *La naissance du fascisme: L'Italie de 1918 à 1922* (Paris: Gallimard, 1938). The first Italian translation, *Nascita e avvento del fascismo* (Florence: La Nuova Italia, 1950), in limited edition, went mostly unnoticed. It was its reprint by Laterza in 1965, with a preface by Renzo De Felice, that brought to the study the attention it deserved. Tasca published an early English translation under the pseudonym Angelo Rossi, *The Rise of Italian Fascism, 1918–1922*, trans. Peter and Dorothy Wait (London: Methuen, 1938), reprinted by Routledge in 2013. The translation from the Italian here is mine. On Angelo Tasca's analyses of Fascism, see Giuseppe Vacca, *La tragica*

modernità del fascismo: Le analisi di Antonio Gramsci, Palmiro Togliatti e Angelo Tasca (Rome: Carocci, 2022), 171–206.

15. Tasca, *Nascita e avvento del fascismo*, 391.

16. Ibid.; emphasis in the original.

17. Ibid., 393.

18. Ibid., 394.

19. Ibid.

20. Ibid.

21. Henri Lemaître, *Les fascismes dans l'histoire* (Paris: Éditions du Cerf, 1959), 8 and 15.

22. Ibid., 17–26.

23. Ibid., 29–34 and 47–54.

24. Enzo Traverso, "Le totalitarisme: Jalons pour l'histoire d'un débat," in *Le totalitarisme: Le XXe siècle en débat*, ed. Enzo Traverso (Paris: Éditions du Seuil, 2001), 51.

25. Hannah Arendt, *The Origins of Totalitarianism*, new ed. (New York: Harcourt, 1973), 325.

26. Ibid.

27. For two surveys of the reception of Arendt's conception of totalitarianism, see Margaret Canovan, *Hannah Arendt: A Reinterpretation of Her Political Thought* (Cambridge: Cambridge University Press, 1992), 17–98; and Marina Cedronio, *La democrazia in pericolo: Politica e storia del pensiero di Hannah Arendt* (Bologna: Il Mulino, 1994).

28. Canovan, *Hannah Arendt*, 36.

29. Ibid., 18.

30. Traverso, "Le totalitarisme," 51; emphasis in the original.

31. Ibid., 52.

32. Quoted in Les K. Adler and Thomas G. Paterson, "Red Fascism: The Merger of Nazi Germany and Soviet Russia in the American Image of Totalitarianism, 1930's–1950's," *The American Historical Review* 75, no. 4 (1970): 1046. As the authors further elaborated, "The American failure to note distinctions between military fascism and revolutionary Marxism has contributed to a simplistic view of revolutionary and anticolonial movements in the post–World War II era and has led to the establishment of world-wide alliances and permanent military containment policies in Europe and Asia" (1062).

33. First published in English as Ernst Nolte, *Three Faces of Fascism: Action Française, Italian Fascism, National Socialism*, trans. Leila Vennewitz (London: Weidenfeld & Nicolson, 1965).

34. Ernst Nolte, "Faschismus," in *Geschichtliche Grundbegriffe*, ed. Werner Conze, Otto Brunner, and Reinhart Koselleck (Stuttgart: Ernst Klett Verlag, 1975), 2:329–36.

35. Nolte, *Three Faces of Fascism*, 18.

36. Ibid., 19.

37. Ibid., 542.

38. Ibid.

39. Ibid., 18.

40. Ibid.

41. Ibid., 25.

42. Ibid., 40.

43. Ibid., 543.

44. Ibid., 24.

45. Ibid., 537.

46. Nolte's conception of fascism was close to the idea of an "overcoming of modernity" (*kindai no chōkoku*) developed in Japan in 1942. See the anthology *Overcoming Modernity: Cultural Identity in Wartime Japan*, ed. and trans. Richard Calichman (New York: Columbia University Press, 2008), and Harry D. Harootunian, *Overcome by Modernity: History, Culture, and Community in Interwar Japan* (Princeton, NJ: Princeton University Press, 2000).

47. Nolte, *Three Faces of Fascism*, 566–67.

48. Domenico Losurdo, *War and Revolution: Rethinking the Twentieth Century* (London: Verso, 2015), 174.

49. See, e.g., Timothy Snyder, *Bloodlands: Europe between Hitler and Stalin* (New York: Basic Books, 2010), 392, and Anne Applebaum, *Gulag: A History* (London: Penguin, 2004), xxxiii–xxiv.

50. Published in the *Journal of the History of Ideas* 27, no. 4 (1966):621–25.

51. Ian Kershaw, *The Nazi Dictatorship: Problems and Perspectives of Interpretation* (London: Bloomsbury, 2000), 35.

52. Ibid., 30.

53. Roger Griffin, "The Search for the Fascist Minimum: Presentation," in *International Fascism: Theories, Causes and the New Consensus*, ed. Roger Griffin (London: Arnold, 1998), 54.

54. On the question of German responsibility in the early postwar period, see Anson Rabinbach, "The Jewish Question in the German Question," in *Reworking the Past: Hitler, the Holocaust, and the Historians' Debate*, ed. Peter Baldwin (Boston: Beacon Press, 1990), esp. 46–57.

55. Reinhart Koselleck, *Critique and Crisis: Enlightenment and the Pathogenesis of Modern Society* (Cambridge, MA: MIT Press, 1988), 6.

56. Jürgen Habermas, "Eine Art Schadensabwicklung," *Die Zeit*, July 11, 1986; English translation quoted in Rabinbach, "The Jewish Question in the German Question," 64.

57. Translated into English in James Knowlton and Truett Cates, eds. and trans., *Forever in the Shadow of Hitler? Original Documents of the "Historikerstreit," the Controversy Concerning the Singularity of the Holocaust* (Atlantic Highlands, NJ: Humanities Press, 1993), 18–23. *Forever in the Shadow of Hitler?* translates the most important contributions of the participants in the quarrel. For an overview of the debate, see also the essays in Baldwin, *Reworking the Past*; Kershaw, *The Nazi Dictatorship*; Charles S. Maier, *The Unmasterable Past: History, Holocaust, and German National Identity* (Cambridge, MA: Harvard University Press, 1988); Richard J. Evans, *In Hitler's Shadow: West German Historians and the Attempt to Escape from the Nazi Past* (London: I. B. Tauris, 1989); and Siobhan Kattago, *Ambiguous Memory: The Nazi Past and German National Identity* (London: Praeger, 2001). The blog page of the *Journal of the History of Ideas* hosted a conversation between Sultan Doughan, A. Dirk Moses, and Michael Rothberg on the possibility of a "historians' debate" in the 2020s. See Jonathon Catlin, ed., "A New German Historians' Debate? A Conversation with Sultan Doughan, A. Dirk Moses, and Michael Rothberg," JHI Blog, February 2–4, 2022, "Part I," https://jhiblog.org/2022/02/02/a-new-german-historians-debate-a-conversation-with-sultan-doughan-a-dirk-moses-and-michael-rothberg-part-i/?fbclid=IwAR0kyRCrTvKp5RrSVoJNc-jxn375ICADk3RZ_BzCJ_uzPStO9WCZJqQYIyU, accessed September 22, 2024; "Part II," https://www.jhiblog.org/2022/02/04/a-new-german-historians-debate-a-conversation-with-sultan-doughan-a-dirk-moses-and-michael-rothberg-part-ii/, accessed September 22, 2024.

58. Jürgen Habermas, "A Kind of Settlement of Damages: The Apologetic Tendencies in German History Writing," in Knowlton and Cates, *Forever in the Shadow of Hitler?*, 41–42.

59. For an anthology of their texts, see Knowlton and Cates, *Forever in the Shadow of Hitler?*

60. On revisionist negationism, see Deborah Lipstadt, *Denying the Holocaust: The Growing Assault on Truth and Memory* (New York: Penguin, 1994); and Richard J. Evans, *Lying about Hitler: History, Holocaust, and the David Irving Trial* (New York: Basic Books 2002).

61. See, e.g., the analyses of revisionists' rhetoric and arguments in Carlo Greppi, *L'antifascismo non serve più a niente* (Rome: Laterza, 2020); Chiara Colombini, *Anche i partigiani però* . . . (Rome: Laterza, 2021); and Gianluca Falanga, *Non si parla mai dei crimini del comunismo* (Rome: Laterza, 2022).

62. Wolfgang Sauer, "National Socialism: Totalitarianism or Fascism?," *The American Historical Review* 73, no. 2 (1967): 409.

63. Ibid., 415.

64. Ibid., 410.

65. Zeev Sternhell, "Fascist Ideology," in *Fascism: A Reader's Guide; Analyses, Interpretations, Bibliography*, ed. Walter Laqueur (Berkeley: University of California Press, 1976), 368.

66. As Stanley Payne acknowledged, the "term ['fascism'] has probably been used more by its opponents than by its proponents, the former having been responsible for the generalization of the adjective on an international level, as early as 1923." Payne, *A History of Fascism, 1914–1945* (London: Routledge, 1995), 3.

67. See chap. 12.

68. See, e.g., Geoff Eley, *Nazism as Fascism: Violence, Ideology, and the Ground of Consent in Germany, 1930–1945* (London: Routledge, 2013), 198–225.

69. Eugen Weber, *Varieties of Fascism: Doctrines of Revolution in the Twentieth Century* (New York: Van Nostrand Reinhold, 1964), 3.

70. Ibid., 10.

71. Ibid., 139.

72. Ibid., 141.

73. On the ambivalent legacy of Rousseau's political philosophy, see the Robert Nisbet, "Rousseau and Totalitarianism," *Journal of Politics* 5, no. 2 (1943): 93–114; and Lucio Colletti, *From Rousseau to Lenin: Studies in Ideology and Society*, trans. John Merrington and Judith White (New York: Monthly Review Press, 1973).

74. George L. Mosse, "Introduction: The Genesis of Fascism," *Journal of Contemporary History* 1, no. 1 (1966): 14.

75. Ibid.

76. Ibid., 16–17.

77. Ibid., 17.

78. Ibid., 18.

79. F. L. Carsten, *The Rise of Fascism* (London: B. T. Batsford, 1967), 230–31.

80. Stuart J. Woolf, ed., *European Fascism* (London: Weidenfeld & Nicolson, 1968); and Wolfgang Schieder, "Faschismus," in *Sowjetsystem und demokratische Gesellschaft: Eine vergleichende Enzyklopädie*, ed. Claus Dieter Kerning (Freiburg: Herder, 1968), 2:438–77.

81. John Weiss, *The Fascist Tradition: Radical Right-Wing Extremism in Modern Europe* (New York: Harper & Row, 1967), 1–30.

82. See Gilbert Allardyce, ed., *The Place of Fascism in European History* (Englewood Cliffs, NJ: Prentice-Hall, 1971).

83. Renzo De Felice, *Intervista sul fascismo*, ed. Michael A. Ledeen (Bari and Rome: Laterza, 1974), 82.

84. Augusto Del Noce, "Appunti per una definizione storica del fascismo," in *L'epoca della secolarizzazione* (Milan: Giuffrè, 1970), 111–34.

85. Enzo Collotti, *Fascismo, fascismi* (Milan: Sansoni, 1989), 37–63.

86. Ibid., 167.

87. Ibid., 25.

88. A. James Gregor, "Fascism and Modernization: Some Addenda," *World Politics* 26, no. 3 (1974): 384, and *The Fascist Persuasion in Radical Politics* (Princeton, NJ: Princeton University Press, 1974). Gregor attributed the fact that Anglophone scholars had not yet produced a satisfactory understanding of and explanation for the generic phenomenon of "fascism" comparable to Nolte's to their lack of theoretical sophistication: "Historians pursue their narratives with minimal concern for unearthing the empirical generalizations upon which their accounts ultimately rests. At best, historians will weave their accounts together with commonsense generalizations and the logic of ordinary language"; Gregor, *Interpretations of Fascism* (Morristown, NJ: General Learning Press, 1974), 417.

89. A. James Gregor, *The Ideology of Fascism: The Rationale of Totalitarianism* (New York: Free Press, 1969).

90. Respectively in A. James Gregor, *Young Mussolini and the Intellectual Origins of Fascism* (Berkeley: University of California Press, 1979), xi, and *The Faces of Janus: Marxism and Fascism in the Twentieth Century* (New Haven, CT: Yale University Press, 2000), 20.

91. Juan J. Linz, "Some Notes Toward a Comparative Study of Fascism in Sociological Historical Perspective," in Laqueur, *Fascism: A Reader's Guide*, 3–121.

92. Ibid., 7.

93. Ibid., 15–16.

94. Ibid., 16.

95. Ibid., 8.

96. Ibid., 12.

97. Ibid., 12–13.

98. Ibid., 12.

99. For a comparative analysis of Fascist and Nazi state institutions, see Collotti, *Fascismo, fascismi*; Emilio Gentile, *La via italiana al totalitarismo: Il partito e lo stato nel regime fascista* (Rome: Carocci, 2008); Guido Melis, *La macchina imperfetta: Immagine e realtà dello Stato fascista* (Bologna: Il Mulino, 2018); Richard J. Evans, *The Third Reich in Power, 1933–1939* (New York: Penguin, 2005); and Thomas Childers, *The Third Reich: A History of Nazi Germany* (New York: Simon & Schuster, 2017).

100. Kershaw, *The Nazi Dictatorship*, 23–54.

101. Ibid., 26. Historians defending the theory of the "uniqueness" of Germany's "partial modernization" in the 1960s through the 1980s were Fritz Fischer, Hand-Ulrich Wehler, Hans Mommsen, Jürgen Kocka, and others. For a survey, see Kershaw, *The Nazi Dictatorship*, 23–54 and 275–314; Hans-Ulrich Wehler, "'Deutscher Sonderweg' oder allgemeine Probleme des westlichen Kapitalismus," *Merkur* 5 (1981): 478–87; and Marcel Tambarin, "De la misère allemande au *Sonderweg*: L'échec de la révolution bourgeoise en Allemagne," *Chroniques allemandes* 7 (1998–99): 101–13.

102. Kershaw, *The Nazi Dictatorship*, 52. Even though Kershaw never engaged in the attempt to reduce the various extreme right-wing movements to a single paradigm, he admitted as recently as 2015 that "some common ideological features of the extreme Right, whether or

not a movement called itself 'fascist', nonetheless existed." These were "hypernationalism," racial exclusiveness, the annihilation of political enemies, and emphasis on militarism and manliness. Ian Kershaw, *To Hell and Back: Europe, 1914–1949* (New York: Viking, 2015), 228–32.

103. Roger Griffin, *The Nature of Fascism* (London: Routledge, 1991), viii.

104. In that study Nolte isolated six characteristics that constituted a common denominator of the various revolutionary Right movements in Europe: anti-Marxism, antiliberalism, anticonservatism, the *Führerprinzip*, the constitution of a party-army, and totalitarianism. Ernst Nolte, *Die Krise des liberalen Systems und die faschistischen Bewegungen* (Munich: Piper, 1968), 385.

105. Zeev Sternhell, *Neither Right nor Left: Fascist Ideology in France*, trans. David Maisel (Berkeley: University of California Press, 1986), 18.

106. Griffin, *The Nature of Fascism*, viii.

107. See, e.g., Richard F. Hamilton, *Who Voted for Hitler?* (Princeton, NJ: Princeton University Press, 1982); and William Sheridan Allen, *The Nazi Seizure of Power: The Experience of a Single German Town, 1922–1945* (New York: F. Watts, 1984).

108. Examples are the later works of A. James Gregor, as well as Anthony James Joes, *The Rise of Fascism in the Contemporary World: Ideology, Evolution, Resurgence* (Boulder, CO: Westview Press, 1978), and the former-Marxist-turned-conservative Domenico Settembrini, *Fascismo: Controrivoluzione imperfetta* (Florence: Sansoni, 1978). For an overview, see Marco Tarchi, *Fascismo: Teorie, interpretazioni e modelli* (Rome: Laterza, 2003), 97–115.

109. George L. Mosse, *The Fascist Revolution: Toward a General Theory of Fascism* (New York: Howard Fertig, 1999), x.

110. Mosse, "Fascism and the French Revolution," in *The Fascist Revolution*, 72.

111. Ibid., 2.

112. Ibid., 13.

113. Ibid., 5.

114. Ibid., 6.

115. Ibid., 8.

116. Ibid., 20.

117. Ibid., 34.

118. Ibid., 26.

119. Ibid.

120. Mosse, "Fascism and the Avant Garde," in *The Fascist Revolution*, 149.

121. Stanley G. Payne, David J. Sorkin, and John S. Tortorice, eds., *What History Tells: George L. Mosse and the Culture of Modern Europe* (Madison: University of Wisconsin Press, 2004), xiii.

122. Emilio Gentile, "A Provisional Dwelling: The Origin and Development of the Concept of Fascism in Mosse's Historiography," in Payne, Sorkin, and Tortorice, *What History Tells*, 44.

123. See esp. the concluding chapter of Gregor, *Interpretations of Fascism*, 238–61.

124. Stanley G. Payne, *Fascism: Comparison and Definition* (Madison: University of Wisconsin Press, 1980), 4.

125. Ibid., 4–5.

126. Ibid.

127. Ibid., 6.

128. Ibid., a tripartite division that Payne acknowledged in a note as having been suggested to him by Juan Linz.

129. Ibid.

130. Ibid., 7.

131. Payne, *A History of Fascism*, 7.

132. Ibid.

133. His tripartite schema reproduced elements of former definitional attempts: the negation of liberalism, communism, and conservatism; nationalism; authoritarian state apparatus; regulated and integrated control over economic production; expansionist foreign policy; endorsement at once pragmatic, ethical, and aesthetical of violence, militarism, and war; exaltation of youth and masculinity; and mass-based organization sustained and coerced by a party-militia.

134. Payne, *A History of Fascism*, 80–128.

135. Ibid., 131–46.

136. Ibid., 147–211 and 212–44.

137. Ibid., 245–89.

138. Ibid., 290–327.

139. Ibid., 328–53.

140. Ibid., 442.

141. Ibid.

142. Ibid., 443.

143. Ibid., 445.

144. Ibid., 446.

145. Ibid., 448.

146. Ibid., 450.

147. Ibid.

148. Ibid., 451.

149. Ibid., 466.

150. Ibid.

151. Ibid., 487.

152. Gilbert Allardyce, at first involved in the comparative project of generic fascism, claimed in a 1979 forum in *The American Historical Review* that "few concepts are more in need of Ockham's razor than fascism. Only individual things are real; everything abstracted from them, whether concepts or universals, exists solely in the mind. There is no such *thing* as fascism. There are only the men and movements that we call by that name"; Allardyce, "What Fascism Is Not: Thoughts on the Deflation of a Concept," *The American Historical Review* 84, no. 2 (1979): 368. Alas, Allardyce seemed to ignore not only that concepts and ideas are real enough to affect people's behavior and modify the surrounding world; he also ignored that there is no possible way to experience "things" in the world without grasping them within a semiotic and conceptual apparatus of names, denotations, connotations, affects, etc. Perception is imbricated in a semiotic apparatus that makes the percept intelligible and experienceable. See Claudine Tiercelin, "Abduction and the Semiotics of Perception," *Semiotica* 153, no. 1/4 (2005): 389–412; Felice Cimatti, *Cose: Per una filosofia del reale* (Turin: Bollati Boringhieri, 2018); Umberto Eco, *Kant and the Platypus: Essays on Language and Cognition*, trans. Alastair McEwen (New York: Harcourt, 2000), 57–122; Gerald M. Edelman, *Bright Air, Brilliant Fire: On the Matter of the Mind* (New York: Basic Books, 1992), 73–80; and Giorgio Prodi, *Le basi materiali della significazione* (Milan: Bompiani, 1977). Besides, what Allardyce sustained in his piece is exactly the opposite of Ockham's razor, for which *entia non sunt multiplicanda praeter necessitatem*, as "fascism," regardless of the epistemological soundness of its predication, de facto reduced the number of concepts involved in the description of different regimes by subsuming them all.

153. It suffices to register the importance of the definitions of fascism taken from the works of Payne, Griffin, Eatwell, and Mosse with the aim of confirming the presence of "fascism" in the political vicissitudes of Japan, China, Argentina, or India in the 1930s and 1940s. For instance, Alan Tansman, in *The Aesthetics of Japanese Fascism* (Berkeley: University of California Press, 2009), 3 and 282, bases its application in Japan on Griffin's definition of "fascism"; Federico Finchelstein, in *Transatlantic Fascism: Ideology, Violence, and the Sacred in Argentina and Italy, 1919–1945* (Durham, NC: Duke University Press, 2010), 19, 182, 183, bases his definition on Payne, Sternhell, and Paxton; Janis Mimura, in *Planning for Empire: Reform Bureaucrats and the Japanese Wartime State* (Ithaca, NY: Cornell University Press, 2011), 5, bases hers on Payne, Griffin, and Paxton; and Reto Hofmann, in *The Fascist Effect: Japan and Italy, 1915–1952* (Ithaca, NY: Cornell University Press 2015), 1–3, 143 and 145, bases his largely on Payne.

154. Griffin, *The Nature of Fascism*, 26.

155. Ibid., 30.

156. Ibid., 32–36.

157. Ibid., 42–43.

158. Ibid., 47.

159. Ibid., 47–49.

160. Roger Griffin, ed., *Fascism: An Introduction to Comparative Fascist Studies* (London: Polity Press, 2018), 37. For a succinct explanation of his understanding of Mosse's "methodological empathy," see ibid., 37–40.

161. Ibid.

162. Ibid., 46.

163. Ibid.

164. Ibid.

165. Ibid.

166. Ibid.

167. Roger Eatwell, "On Defining the 'Fascist Minimum': The Centrality of Ideology," *Journal of Political Ideologies* 1, no. 3 (1996): 304.

168. Roger Eatwell, *Fascism: A History* (New York: Penguin, 1996), 15.

169. Eatwell, "On Defining the 'Fascist Minimum,'" 313.

170. Ibid.

171. Ibid.

172. Ibid.

173. Ibid., 314.

174. Mark Neocleous, *Fascism* (Buckingham: Open University Press, 1997), xi.

175. Kevin Passmore, *Fascism: A Very Short Introduction* (Oxford: Oxford University Press, 2002), 31.

176. Michael Mann, *Fascists* (Cambridge: Cambridge University Press, 2004), 13; emphasis in the original.

177. Ibid.

178. Ibid., 14. On the contradictions of the totalitarian state, see also Michael Mann, "The Contradictions of Continuous Revolution," in *Stalinism and Nazism: Dictatorship in Comparison*, ed. Ian Kershaw and Moshe Lewin (Cambridge: Cambridge University Press, 1997), 135–57.

179. Mann, *Fascists*, 15.

180. Ibid., 14.

181. Ibid., 16.

182. Ibid.

183. Ibid., 17.

184. Emilio Gentile, *Fascismo: Storia e interpretazione* (Rome: Laterza, 2002), 71. A different English translation can be found in Payne, *A History of Fascism*, 5–6.

185. Gentile, *Fascismo*, 72.

186. Ibid., 72–73.

187. Cogently expressed in Robert O. Paxton, "The Five Stages of Fascism," *The Journal of Modern History* 70, no. 1 (1998): 1–23, esp. 1–9.

188. Ibid., 3.

189. Ibid.

190. Ibid., 4.

191. Ibid., 8.

192. Ibid., 9–10.

193. Ibid., 10.

194. Ibid., 11.

195. Robert O. Paxton, *The Anatomy of Fascism* (New York: Random House, 2004).

196. Ibid., 2018.

197. One of the earliest attempts in that direction was Walter Laqueur, *Fascism: Past, Present, Future* (Oxford: Oxford University Press, 1996), which Paxton defined as dealing "more fully with the present and future than with the past," in Paxton, "The Five Stages of Fascism," 1 n. 1.

198. See, e.g., the definitions extracted from the literature of the fascist minimum in the articles quoted in n. 7 of the introduction.

199. Laurence W. Britt, "Fascism Anyone?," *Free Inquiry* 23, no. 2 (Spring 2003), https://secularhumanism.org/2003/03/fascism-anyone/, accessed September 22, 2024. For a history of Britt's essay, see Daniel Malmer, "The Long, Complicated History of the '14 Defining Characteristics of Fascism': The Origin, History, and Criticism of Laurence W. Britt's Widely-Shared List," published in Malmer's blog on August 19, 2022, https://danielmalmer.medium.com/the-long-complicated-history-of-the-14-defining-characteristics-of-fascism-e366412932f, accessed September 22, 2024.

200. Daniel Steinmetz-Jenkins, ed., *Did It Happen Here? Perspectives on Fascism and America* (New York: W. W. Norton, 2024).

Chapter Twelve

1. Peter Novick, *That Noble Dream: The "Objectivity Question" and the American Historical Profession* (Cambridge: Cambridge University Press, 1988).

2. Hayden White, "Historical Emplotment and the Problem of Truth," in *Probing the Limits of Representation: Nazism and the "Final Solution"*, ed. Saul Friedlander (Cambridge, MA: Harvard University Press, 1992), 37. See also Seamus O'Malley, *Making History New: Modernism and Historical Narrative* (Oxford: Oxford University Press, 2015), 1–47.

3. On White's defense of historians' ethic, see Hayden White, *The Practical Past* (Evanston, IL: Northwestern University Press, 2014).

4. On Ginzburg's defense of the possibility of history as producing truths in a realist-ontological sense, see Carlo Ginzburg, "Just One Witness," in Friedlander, *Probing the Limits of Representation*, 82–96; Ginzburg, *History, Rhetoric, and Proof* (Hanover, NH: Brandeis University Press, 1999), esp. 38–53; and Ginzburg, *Thread and Traces: True, False, Fictive*, trans. Anne C.

Tedeschi and John Tedeschi (Berkeley: University of California Press, 2012), esp. 65–66 and 169–77.

5. It is a recurring theme in linguistics and semantics, from Ferdinand de Saussure to Algirdas Julien Greimas, that sememes are defined oppositionally to contiguous ones, following relations that can be divided into synonymity, antinomy, complementarity, and symmetry. See Umberto Eco, *A Theory of Semiotics* (Bloomington: Indiana University Press, 1975), 80–83; Algirdas-Julien Greimas, *Structural Semantics: An Attempt at a Method*, trans. Daniele McDowell, Ronald Schleifer, and Alan Velie (Lincoln: University of Nebraska Press, 1983), 19–26; and Raffaele Simone, *Fondamenti di linguistica* (Rome: Laterza, 2005), 491–93.

6. Jerrold Kats, *Semantic Theory* (New York: Harper & Row, 1972), 157–71.

7. See chap. 2.

8. See chap. 3.

9. It should be added that the anticapitalist rhetoric of fascism operated differently in the countryside, where it was more marked, than in the industrialized urban centers. See Alberto Acquarone, *L'organizzazione dello Stato totalitario* (Turin: Einaudi, 1978).

10. Chiara E. Mattei argued how austerity was the link between laissez-faire and corporativism; see Mattei, *The Capital Order: How Economists Invented Austerity and Paved the Way to Fascism* (Chicago: University of Chicago Press, 2022), 233–38. On the IRI, see Bruno Amoroso and Ole Jess Olsen, *Lo stato imprenditore* (Rome: Laterza, 1978).

11. Similarly to what occurred in Germany (see Adam Tooze, *The Wages of Destruction* [London: Penguin, 2006], 99–165; and Richard J. Evans, *The Third Reich in Power* [London: Penguin, 2006], 322–413), in Japan (see Sheldon Gardon, *The State and Labor in Modern Japan* [Berkeley: University of California Press, 1987], 187–227; and Andrew Gordon, *Labor and Imperial Democracy in Prewar Japan* [Berkeley: University of California Press, 1991], 237–329), and elsewhere in the world in the second half of the 1930s (see Theda Skocpol and Kenneth Finegold, "State Capacity and Economic Intervention in the Early New Deal," *Political Science Quarterly* 97, no. 2 [1982]: 255–78; Mike Hawkins, "Corporatism and Third Way Discourses in Interwar France," *Journal of Political Ideologies* 7, no. 3 [2002]: 301–14; and Patrick K. O'Brien, "Britain's Economy between the Wars: A Survey of a Counterrevolution in Economic History," *Past & Present* 115, no. 1 [1987]: 107–30).

12. See, for instance, Ugo Spirito, *Capitalismo e corporativismo* (Florence: Sansoni, 1933).

13. Daniel Guerin, *Fascism and Big Business*, trans. Frances Merrill and Mason Merrill (New York: A Monad Press Book, 1973), 191–97; and Pietro Grifone, *Il capitale finanziario in Italia: La politica economica del fascismo* (Turin: Einaudi, 1971), 111–47.

14. Martin Blinkhorn, *Mussolini and Fascist Italy* (New York: Routledge, 1994), 35. The hybrid case of Nazi Germany, where the Nazi Party operated in collaboration with capitalist forces, has been conceptualized as "state capitalism" by Frederick Pollock and as capitalist polyarchy by Franz Neumann. See also Tooze, *The Wages of Destruction*, esp. chap. 4, on the integration of state and capital.

15. As Mattei puts it, "Traditional historiography envisages a discontinuity between Fascism's initial laissez-faire period (1922–25) and the corporativist epoch that followed in Italy (usually understood as the 'real' expression of Fascism). By viewing this same period through a lens of austerity, in terms of both economic policies and economic ideology, one can observe greater coherence across these two different phases. Austerity, in fact, is the thing that ties the two together. It embodied the active intervention of the state to reinforce capital accumulation through privatizations, bailouts of financial-industrial complexes, monetary deflation, and especially coercive control of labor." Mattei, *The Capital Order*, 311.

16. Carolina Lussana, "Agostino Rocca (1895–1978)," *Fondazione Ansaldo* (n.d.), https://www.fondazioneansaldo.it/index.php/i-grandi-dell-ansaldo/128-storiedaraccontare/i-grandi-dell-ansaldo/501-agostino-rocca-1895-1978, accessed September 20, 2024.

17. Traute Rafalski and Michel Vale, "Social Planning and Corporatism: Modernization Tendencies in Italian Fascism," *International Journal of Political Economy* 18, no. 1 (1988): 10–64.

18. Pietro Grifone, *Capitalismo di stato e imperialismo fascista* (Milan: Gabriele Mazzotta, 1975), 88–143; and Giorgio Rochat, *Le guerre italiane, 1935–1943: Dall'impero d'Etiopia alla disfatta* (Turin: Einaudi, 2008), 127–41.

19. On this issue, see Reinhart Koselleck's argument on the advantages and limits of these approaches in Reinhart Koselleck, Javiér Fernández Sebastián, and Juan Francisco Fuentes, "Conceptual History, Memory, and Identity: An Interview with Reinhard Koselleck," *Contributions to the History of Concepts* 2, no. 1 (2006): 99–127. See also Helge Jordheim, "Against Periodization: Koselleck's Theory of Multiple Temporalities," *History and Theory* 51, no. 2 (2012): 151–71.

20. It was later republished as "Ur-Fascism" in Umberto Eco, *Five Moral Pieces*, trans. Alastair McEwan (Orlando, FL: Harcourt, 2001), 65–88. The first Italian edition, with the title "Totalitarismo *fuzzy* e Ur-Fascismo," was published in the June–July 1995 issue of the journal *La rivista dei libri*. The revised version, published as "Il fascismo eterno," was included in *Cinque scritti morali* (Milan: Bompiani, 1997) and published in a new English translation by Alastair McEwen in *Five Moral Pieces*. It has since been republished in a single volume as *Il fascismo eterno* (Milan: La nave di Teseo, 2018) and *How to Spot a Fascist* (London: Harvill Secker, 2020). For a critical assessment, see Francesco Germinario, *"Fascismo eterno" e fascismo storico: Umberto Eco, la destra e la tradizione antifascista* (Trieste: Asterios, 2024).

21. Eco, "Ur-Fascism," 72–73.

22. On the use of "fuzzy" in a logical sense, see Petr Cintula, Christian G. Fermüller, and Carles Noguera, "Fuzzy Logic," *Stanford Encyclopedia of Philosophy*, ed. Edward N. Zalta and Uri Nodelman (Summer 2023), https://plato.stanford.edu/entries/logic-fuzzy/, accessed September 23, 2024. See also Ludwig Wittgenstein, *Philosophical Investigations*, trans. G. E. M. Anscombe (Oxford: Basil Blackwell, 1958), §71; George Lakoff, "Hedges: A Study in Meaning Criteria and the Logic of Fuzzy Concepts," *Journal of Philosophical Logic* 2 (1973), 458–508; and Nicholas J. J. Smith, *Vagueness and Degrees of Truth* (Oxford: Oxford University Press, 2005), 277–315.

23. Eco, "Ur-Fascism," 76; and Wittgenstein, *Philosophical Investigations*, §§562–68.

24. Wittgenstein, *Philosophical Investigations*, 77.

25. Ibid.

26. Ibid., 78–87.

27. Ruth Ben-Ghiat, *Strongmen: Mussolini to the Present* (New York: W. W. Norton, 2020).

28. This would be my corrective to the view that conceives of fascism and communism as equivalent, from Hannah Arendt and Karl Popper to the recent EU equivalency motion.

29. Parts of this section were previously published in Federico Marcon, "The Quest for Japanese Fascism: A Historiographical Overview," in *Itineraries of an Anthropologist: Studies in Honour of Massimo Raveri*, ed. Giovanni Bulian and Silvia Rivadossi (Venice: Edizioni Ca' Foscari, 2021), 53–86.

30. Stanley Payne, *A History of Fascism, 1914–1945* (London: Routledge, 1995), 129–354. See also Michael A. Ledeen, *Universal Fascism: The Theory and Practice of the Fascist International, 1928–1936* (New York: H. Fertig, 1972); Federico Finchelstein, *Transatlantic Fascism: Ideology, Violence, and the Sacred in Argentina and Italy, 1919–1945* (Durham, NC: Duke University Press, 2010); Bradley W. Hart, *Hitler's American Friends: The Third Reich's Supporters in the United*

States (New York: Thomas Dunne Books, 2018); and Joseph Fronczak, *Everything Is Possible: Antifascism and the Left in the Age of Fascism* (New Haven, CT: Yale University Press, 2023).

31. Reto Hofmann, *The Fascist Effect: Japan and Italy, 1915–1952* (Ithaca, NY: Cornell University Press, 2015); Fuke Takahiro, *Senkanki Nihon no shakai shisō: "Chōkokka" he no furontia* (Kyoto: Jinbun Shoin, 2010); and Fuke, *Nihon fashizumu ronsō: Taisen zen'ya no shisōkatachi* (Tokyo: Kawade Shobō, 2012).

32. Michael Schaller, "America's Favorite War Criminal: Kishi Nobusuke and the Transformation of U.S.-Japan Relations," *Japan Policy Research Institute Working Paper*, no 11 (July 1995), http://mailman.lbo-talk.org/2000/2000-July/012577.html, accessed September 23, 2024.

33. On Masao Maruyama, see Andrew Barshay, *The Social Sciences in Modern Japan: The Marxian and Modernist Traditions* (Berkeley: University of California Press, 2004), 197–239; Tadashi Karube, *Maruyama Masao and the Fate of Liberalism in Twentieth-Century Japan* (Tokyo: International House of Japan, 2008); Nick Kapur, *Japan at the Crossroads: Conflict and Compromise after Anpo* (Cambridge, MA: Harvard University Press, 2018), 163–68; and Julia Adeney Thomas, "The Cage of Nature: Modernity's History in Japan," *History and Theory* 40, no. 1 (2001): 16–36.

34. Maruyama Masao, *Nihon seiji shisōshi kenkyū* (Tokyo: Tokyo Daigaku Shuppankai, 1952); translated into English by Mikiso Hane as *Studies in the Intellectual History of Tokugawa Japan* (Princeton, NJ: Princeton University Press, 1974).

35. Maruyama Masao, *Gendai seiji no shisō to kōdō* (Tokyo: Miraisha, 1956); translated into English by Ian Morris as Masao Maruyama, *Thought and Behavior in Modern Japanese Politics* (Oxford: Oxford University Press, 1963), 25–83.

36. For Maruyama, these characteristics were an organicist nationalism (conveyed through the metaphors of *kazoku kokka* [family-state] and *kokutai* [national-body]), in Maruyama, *Thought and Behavior in Modern Japanese Politics*, 36–37; *nōhonshugi* (agrarianism), in ibid., 37–50; and *daiajiashugi* (Pan-Asianism), in ibid., 51. See Marcon, "The Quest for Japanese Fascism," 62–65.

37. Maruyama, *Thought and Behavior in Modern Japanese Politics*, 288.

38. Gavan McCormack, *Client State: Japan in the American Embrace* (London: Verso, 2007).

39. Richard Storry, "Japan in the Thirties: Headless Fascism 'From Below' and 'From Above,'" in *Collected Writings of Richard Storry*, ed. Ian Nish (Tokyo: Japan Library, 2002), 113–24; and Robert A. Scalapino, *Reflections on American Relations with Japan* (New York: American Institute of Pacific Relations, 1953), 391.

40. Edwin O. Reischauer, *Japan, Past and Present* (New York: Alfred A. Knopf, 1946).

41. Delmer M. Brown, *Nationalism in Japan: An Introductory Historical Analysis* (Berkeley: University of California Press, 1955).

42. Edwin O. Reischauer, John K. Fairbank, and Albert M. Craig, *A History of East Asian Civilization*, vol. 2, *East Asia: The Modern Transformation* (Boston: Houghton Mifflin, 1964), 682–725 and 813.

43. John Whitney Hall, *Japan: From Prehistory to Modern Times* (New York: Dell, 1970), 326–29.

44. Marius Jansen, *The Making of Modern Japan* (Cambridge, MA: Belknap Press, 2000), 576.

45. E. Herbert Norman, *Japan's Emergence as a Modern State: Political and Economic Problems of the Meiji Period* (New York: Institute of Pacific Relations, 1940).

46. Jon Halliday, *A Political History of Japanese Capitalism* (New York: Pantheon Books, 1975), 134.

47. See, e.g., Franco Mazzei, *Il capitalismo giapponese: Gli stadi di sviluppo* (Napoli: Liguori, 1979), 108; Alessandro Valota, "Imperialismo e fascismo in Giappone," in *Storia dell'Asia orientale*, ed. Enrica Collotti Pischel (Florence: La Nuova Italia, 1980), 238–78; and, above all, Franco Gatti, *Il fascismo giapponese* (Milan: Franco Angeli, 1983), 256–64.

48. Peter Duus and Daniel I. Okimoto, "Fascism and the History of Pre-War Japan: The Failure of a Concept," *The Journal of Asian Studies* 39, no. 1 (1979): 76. For a critical view on Duus and Okimoto, see Gavan McCormack, "1930s Japan: Fascist?," *Social Analysis: The International Journal of Social and Cultural Practice* 5, no. 6 (1980): 140–41.

49. Gregory J. Kasza, "Fascism from Below? A Comparative Perspective on the Japanese Right, 1931–1936," *Journal of Contemporary History* 19, no. 4 (1984): 607–29.

50. The reference is to Itō Takashi, *Jūgonen sensō* (Tokyo: Shōgakukan, 1976); and Itō, *Taishōki "kakushin"-ha no seiritsu* (Tokyo: Hanawa Shobō, 1978).

51. As in the essay by Yamaguchi Yasushi, "Fashizumu rongi no keken'na sokumen: Nihon ni 'fashizumu' wa nakatta no ka," *Economisuto*, July 29, 1980, 38–45. Quotes from Gregory J. Kasza, "Fascism from Above? Japan's *Kakushin* Right in Comparative Perspective," in *Fascism outside Europe: The European Impulse Against Domestic Conditions in the Diffusion of Global Fascism*, ed. Stein Ugelvik Larsen (Boulder, CO: Social Science Monographs, 2001), 186.

52. As used in George Macklin Wilson, "A New Look at the Problem of 'Japanese Fascism,'" *Comparative Studies in Society and History* 10, no. 4 (1968): 401–12; and Takabatake Michitoshi, "Taishū undo no tayōka to henshitsu," in *Nenpō seijigaku 1977: 55-nen taisei no keisei to hōkai*, ed. Nihon Seiji Gakkai (Tokyo: Iwanami Shoten, 1979), 323–59.

53. Kasza, "Fascism from Above?," 199.

54. Ben-Ami Shillony, *Politics and Culture in Wartime Japan* (Oxford: Oxford University Press, 1981), 15–16.

55. William Miles Fletcher III, *The Search for a New Order: Intellectuals and Fascism in Prewar Japan* (Chapel Hill: University of North Carolina Press, 1982), 163–64.

56. Richard H. Mitchell, *Thought Control in Prewar Japan* (Ithaca, NY: Cornell University Press, 1976); Gordon Mark Berger, *Parties Out of Power in Japan, 1931–1941* (Princeton, NJ: Princeton University Press, 1977); and Mark R. Peattie, *Nan'yō: The Rise and Fall of the Japanese in Micronesia, 1885–1945* (Honolulu: University of Hawai'i Press, 1988).

57. McCormack, "1930s Japan," 142.

58. Itō, *Jūgonen sensō*.

59. Carol Gluck, "The People in History. Recent Trends in Japanese Historiography," *The Journal of Asian Studies* 38, no. 1 (1978): 25–50.

60. Yoshimi Yoshiaki, *Kusa no ne no fashizumu: Nihon minshū no sensō taiken* (Tokyo: Tokyo Daigaku Shuppankai, 1987), translated by Ethan Mark as *Grassroots Fascism: The War Experience of the Japanese People* (New York: Columbia University Press, 2015); Suzaki Shin'ichi, *Nihon fashizumu to sono jidai: Ten'nōsei, gunbu, sensō, minshū* (Tokyo: Ōtsuki Shoten, 1998).

61. Fuke, *Senkanki Nihon no shakai shisō*.

62. Andrew Gordon, *Labor and Imperial Democracy in Prewar Japan* (Berkeley: University of California Press, 1991), 334–35. Gordon's references were Maruyama, *Thought and Behavior in Modern Japanese Politics*, and Yamaguchi Yasushi, *Fashizumu: Sono hikaku kenkyū no tame ni* (Tokyo: Yūhikaku, 1979).

63. Harry D. Harootunian, *Overcome by Modernity: History, Culture, and Community in Interwar Japan* (Princeton, NJ: Princeton University Press, 2000), xxvii–xxxi. Harootunian's *Archaism and Actuality: Japan and the Global Fascist Imaginary* (Durham, NC: Duke University

Press, 2023) expands this argument to connect Japanese ultranationalist and antifascist conceptual terms with the global discourse on fascism in the 1930s.

64. Julia Adeney Thomas, *Reconfiguring Modernity: Concepts of Nature in Japanese Political Ideology* (Berkeley: University of California Press, 2001), 181–88.

65. Alan Tansman, *The Aesthetics of Japanese Fascism* (Berkeley: University of California Press, 2009).

66. Alan Tansman, ed., *The Culture of Japanese Fascism* (Durham, NC: Duke University Press, 2009), 1.

67. Takashi Fujitani, *Splendid Monarchy: Power and Pageantry in Modern Japan* (Berkeley: University of California Press, 1998), 172.

68. Kenneth J. Ruoff, *Imperial Japan at Its Zenith: The Wartime Celebration of the Empire's 2600th Anniversary* (Ithaca, NY: Cornell University Press, 2010), 19.

69. Janis A. Mimura, *Planning for Empire: Reform Bureaucrats and the Japanese Wartime State* (Ithaca, NY: Cornell University Press, 2011), 5.

70. Aaron Stephen Moore, *Constructing East Asia: Technology, Ideology, and Empire in Japan's Wartime Era, 1931–1945* (Stanford, CA: Stanford University Press, 2013), 7.

71. Hofmann, *The Fascist Effect.*

72. Sheldon Garon, "'Total War' or 'Fascism'? Reflections on *Grassroots Fascism*," *Verge: Studies in Global Asia* 2, no. 2 (2016): 25–28.

73. Harootunian, *Archaism and Actuality*, 99–144.

74. Conversely, the intensification of the ideological and institutional authoritarianism of the Japanese government, mostly under the leadership of the prime ministers Konoe Fumimaro and Tōjō Hideki, followed the eruption of wide-scale military activities in China. To offer some examples, the official document *Kokutai no hongi* (*Cardinal Principles of the National Body*), developed by a team of Japanese intellectuals under the guidance of Konoe and introducing a new phase of government aimed at enhancing national strength around the ideological pillars of *kokutai* and *Lebensraum*, was issued in 1937. See Skya, *Japan's Holy War*) 262–96. The imperial policy of a New Order in East Asia (*Tōa shin chitsujō*), which promoted such vague ideals as "Asia for Asians," "Asian autocracy," "anti-communism," and "world peace," all emphasizing an anticolonial project of liberation led by Japan that nonetheless maintained its imperialist prerogatives, was launched by Konoe in November 1938. See Jeremy Yellen, *The Greater East Asia Co-Prosperity Sphere: When Total Empire Met Total War* (Ithaca, NY: Cornell University Press, 2019). The imperialist ideal of *hakkō ichiu*, loosely meaning "all the world under one roof," was the theme of a speech given by Konoe on January 8, 1940. The end of party politics occurred only later that autumn. The Tripartite Pact with Italy and Germany was signed on September 27, 1940. In other words, the militaristic authoritarianism of 1937–45 can be explained more economically by the necessity of fighting a total war with limited resources and within a governmental apparatus that was constitutionally authoritarian by design from the beginning, rather than appealing to notions such as global fascism.

75. Edward Miller, *Bankrupting the Enemy: The US Financial Siege of Japan before Pearl Harbor* (Annapolis, MD: United States Naval Institute, 2007).

76. Sheldon Garon, "Japon: La guerre des autres?," in *Une histoire de la guerre: Du XIXe siècle à nos jours*, ed. Bruno Cabanes (Paris: Seuil, 2018), 538–51.

77. Tansman, *The Aesthetics of Japanese Fascism.*

78. The need to specify the use of "fascism" in this sentence as referring to a specific or generic use of the term is further evidence of its semantic fuzziness. This claim finds further confirmation in the fact that the system of semantic markers constituting the cultural unit signified

by the sign vehicle "fascism" is the result of *historical* processes of meaning-making, as it derives from the history of its uses in different contexts and circumstances by different historical actors for different purposes and in ways that elicited different interpretive habits.

79. The historiographical debate that Friedlander anthologized in *Probing the Limits of Representation*, and in particular the clash between Hayden White and Carlo Ginzburg, attempted to address this epistemological question and its effect on our understanding of the Holocaust. Held after a decade marked by revisionisms and denialisms, the debate was aimed at defending the epistemological value of historical research. The *Historikerstreit* polemic had just ended, but its echoes still reverberated all over the world, including in Italy, with De Felice's contentious positions on antifascism and the noninvolvement of Fascism in the Holocaust. During those years, Holocaust denialism found new supporters—sometimes implicit, as in Ernst Nolte's *Der europäische Bürgerkrieg, 1917–1945: Nationalsozialismus und Bolschewismus* (Berlin: Propyläen Verlag, 1987); sometimes explicit, as in the activism of the Californian Institute for Historical Review and in David Irving's *Hitler's War* (New York: Viking Press, 1977); and sometimes unintentionally, as in the case of Arno J. Mayer's *Why Did the Heavens Not Darken? The "Final Solution" in History* (New York: Pantheon Books, 1988). On the right-wing Institute for Historical Review, see Richard J. Evans, *Telling Lies about Hitler: The Holocaust, History and the David Irving Trial* (London: Verso, 2002), 149–56.

80. Constantin Fasolt, *The Limits of History* (Chicago: University of Chicago Press, 2004), xiii–xxi and 3–45.

81. In Leopold Ranke, *Geschichte der romanischen und germanischen Völker von 1494–1514*, in *Sämtliche Werke* (Leipzig: Duncker & Humblot, 1867–90), 33:v–viii. It is important to note that Ranke's sentence has become the slogan of positivist historiography, though this violates Ranke's own understanding of it. As Frederick C. Beiser clearly put it, "Ranke was perfectly aware of the limits upon historical objectivity. Never did he think that the historian could completely escape his own culture, and never did he assume that he could avoid all concepts and assumptions; still less was he asking for a pure knowledge of reality in itself, as if we could know a reality that existed apart from and prior to any human perspective." Frederick C. Beiser, "Hegel and Ranke: A Re-examination," in *A Companion to Hegel*, ed. Stephen Houlgate and Michael Baur (Chichester: Wiley-Blackwell, 2011), 334. See also Leonard Krieger, *Ranke: The Meaning of History* (Chicago: University of Chicago Press, 1977), esp. 10–20. On the question of historiographical objectivity, see Alan Megill, "Objectivity for Historians," in *Historical Knowledge, Historical Error: A Contemporary Guide to Practice* (Chicago: University of Chicago Press, 2007), 107–24.

82. The English word "history" comes from the Greek *ιστορία*, "an account of one's inquiry," from the verb *ἱστορέω*, "to witness," "to give testimony," "to recount," "to inquire," which in turn comes from the noun *ἵστωρ*, "the wise one," "the one who knows." The semantic ambiguities of the English "history," which can be traced back to its Greek etymology, are the source of epistemological embarrassment. In everyday language, "history" can signify (1) the "texts" (lectures, articles, monographs, videos, etc.) that historians produce, (2) a particular "style" or "genre" of texts, (3) the "meaning" or "content" of these texts, (4) the "referent" of that content of historians' texts (i.e., the past), or (5) the institutional practice or discipline historians belong to. To avoid confusion, I use "the past" to mean (4), "historiography" or "the discipline of history" for (5), and "(historiographical) texts" for (1) and (2), reserving "history" exclusively for (3).

83. For the sake of semiotic punctiliousness, the image of the past leaving traces, in rhetoric, is a prosopopoeia, itself an anthropomorphization of a concept producing reifying effects. The

traces that historians use as evidence are left, voluntarily or involuntarily, by someone or something that existed in the past in circumstances that it is not always possible to ascertain.

84. It is important to also consider history as potentially a fabrication of the past, under which rubric we can include mistakes and misreadings, but also ideologically motivated falsifications and mystifications as well as historical novels and films, so important in the construction of the public memory of the past.

85. The bibliographical reference to Peirce's work in the main body of the text refers to the *Collected Papers of Charles Sanders Peirce*, ed. Charles Hartshorne and Paul Weiss, 8 vols. (Cambridge, MA: Harvard University Press, 1931–66). For example, "CP 1.553" refers to vol. 1, section 553 in the *Collected Papers.*

86. For White, even when confronted by a catastrophe of unprecedented magnitude such as the Holocaust, the only possible intervention of the historian is that pertaining to ethical responsibility, what he called the "practical past," that is, "the ethical and utilitarian aspects of our desire for the past without a basis in being, without an *ontos* and an *ousia* in life"; White, *The Practical Past*, x–xi.

87. Megill, "Objectivity for Historians." It is worth observing that both forms of objectivity (disciplinary and procedural), by not being examples of "absolute objectivity" (possible only, perhaps, to a godlike entity), produce cognitive claims that remain temporary (i.e., historical) and potentially fallible, and thus these two epistemological objectivities translate in the very modest ontological realism of a contingent "as if," in the sense that the procedural or disciplinary certification permits a conjectural claim to be understood *as if* it were matter of fact, but that ultimately is not and cannot be. In other words, its alethic modality remains purely contingent.

88. Ethan Kleinberg, *Haunting History: For a Deconstructive Approach to the Past* (Stanford, CA: Stanford University Press, 2017).

89. Eco, *A Theory of Semiotics*, 15.

90. An indexical sign, "like a pointing finger, exercises a real physiological force over the attention . . . and directs it to a particular object" (CP 8.41). In semiotics, indexical signs are supposed to be based on direct connection, either physical or causal, to that which had produced them and is through them signified.

91. The notion of the "possible world" is a construct of modal epistemology. For an introduction, see Christopher Menzel, "Possible Worlds," in *The Stanford Encyclopedia of Philosophy*, ed. Edward N. Zaita and Uri Nodelman (Fall 2023), https://plato.stanford.edu/entries/possible-worlds/, accessed September 23, 2024. For its application in the truth-value of narrative texts, see Umberto Eco, "*Lector in Fabula*: Pragmatic Strategy in a Metanarrative Text," in *The Role of the Reader: Explorations in the Semiotics of Texts* (Bloomington: Indiana University Press, 1984), 200–260; David Lewis, *On the Plurality of Worlds* (Oxford: Blackwell, 1986); and Takashi Yagisawa, *Worlds and Individuals, Possible and Otherwise* (Oxford: Oxford University Press, 2010).

92. Carlo Ginzburg, "Clues: Roots of an Evidential Paradigm," in *Clues, Myths, and the Historical Methods*, trans. John and Anne C. Tedeschi (Baltimore, MD: John Hopkins University Press, 1989), 96–125.

93. Peirce introduced the logic of abduction in CP 2.623: "Suppose I enter a room and there find a number of bags, containing different kinds of beans. On the table there is a handful of white beans; and, after some searching, I find one of the bags contains white beans only. I at once infer as a probability, or as a fair guess, that this handful was taken out of that bag. This sort of inference is called *making a hypothesis*. It is the inference of a *case* from a *rule* and a *result*." If in a deduction we deduce the "result" of a "case" on the basis of a "rule" we know (if Rule: "all the

beans from this bag are white," and Case: "these beans are from this bag," then, certainly, Result: "these beans are white"), and in an induction we infer, with a varying degree of probability, a "rule" from a "case" and a "result" (given the Case: "these beans are from this bag" and the Result: "these beans are white," then, probably, Rule: "all the beans from this bag are white"), in the abduction we try to infer a "case" by *imagining* a "rule" that can account for a "result" (given Result: "these beans are white," and if, hypothetically, Rule: "all the beans from this bag are white," then, probably, Case: "these beans are from this bag"). See Peirce, "Pragmatism as the Logic of Abduction," 7th Harvard lecture on pragmatism, May 13, 1903, in *The Essential Peirce*, vol. 2, *Selected Philosophical Writings (1893–1913)*, ed. Peirce Edition Project (Bloomington: Indiana University Press, 1998), 226–41. See also Umberto Eco, "Horn, Hooves, Insteps: Some Hypotheses on Three Types of Abduction," in *The Sign of Three: Dupin, Holmes, Peirce*, ed. Umberto Eco and Thomas Sebeok (Bloomington: Indiana University Press, 1983), 198–220; and Massimo A. Bonfantini, *La semiosi e l'abduzione* (Milan: Bompiani, 1987).

94. See also R. G. Collingwood, "Historical Evidence," in *The Idea of History* (Oxford: Oxford University Press, 1946), 249–82; and Carlo Ginzburg, "Morelli, Freud, and Sherlock Holmes," in Eco and Sebeok, *The Sign of Three*, 81–118.

95. Roland Barthes, *The Rustle of Language*, trans. Richard Howard (Berkeley: University of California Press, 1989), 148.

Conclusions

1. The inerasable political connotations of historians' interpretations of fascism—which, as demonstrated in chap. 12, are a constitutive part of the explanatory paradigms at work in their abductive interpretations of archival materials—in turn affect their implicit endorsement of different political views, independently of their intentions as empirical authors. Thus, the definitions, conceptions, and descriptions of fascism in the work of conservative liberals are premised on a paradigmatic conception of society wherein the state should not interfere with the hierarchical structuring of society produced by laissez-faire economic models, often conceived in a naturalistic sense. Progressive liberals, instead, indirectly or subliminally uphold a conception of society organized by a dialectic of capitalist market economy and state intervention to smooth its most dispossessing and alienating effects. While liberals of different inclinations maintain the belief in the interconnection of democracy and capitalism, Marxists envision an ideal society wherein the production and circulation of services and commodities are mediated by the state, the purpose of which is ideally to preserve the emancipated equality of its members until its waning away.

2. Samuel Moyn, "The Trouble with Comparisons," *New York Review of Books*, May 19, 2020, https://www.nybooks.com/daily/2020/05/19/the-trouble-with-comparisons/, accessed on September 13, 2024.

3. For a formal understanding of cognitive pertinence, see Robyn Carston and George Powell, "Relevance Theory—New Directions and Developments," in *The Oxford Handbook of Philosophy of Language*, ed. Ernest Lepore and Barry C. Smith (Oxford: Oxford University Press, 2006), 341–60.

4. Philippe Lacoue-Labarthe and Jean-Luc Nancy, "The Nazi Myth," trans. Brian Holmes, *Critical Inquiry* 16, no. 2 (1990): 312.

5. There is an extensive literature on the mediating role that language exercises in all aspects of human life and in its reifying and falsifying effects. It was a fundamental aspect in the

meditations of "continental" philosophers such as Husserl and Heidegger, but also Benjamin, Adorno, as well as Foucault in *Les mots et les choses* (1966) and Jacques Derrida in *De la grammatologie* (1967). But language models and delimits our capacity of experience for analytical philosophers, too. See, e.g., Ernst Cassirer, *The Philosophy of Symbolic Forms*, trans. Ralph Manheim (New Haven, CT: Yale University Press, 1970); and Hilary Putnam, *Reason, Truth and History* (Cambridge: Cambridge University Press, 1981). See also Charles Taylor, *The Language Animal: The Full Shape of the Human Linguistic Capacity* (Cambridge, MA: Harvard University Press, 2016).

6. Juri M. Lotman, *Universe of the Mind: A Semiotic Theory of Culture*, trans. Ann Shukman (London. I. B. Tauris, 2001); Thomas A. Sebeok and Marcel Danesi, *The Forms of Meaning: Modeling Systems Theory and Semiotic Analysis* (Berlin: Mouton de Gruyer, 2000); Émile Benveniste, "Sémiologie de la langue," *Semiotica* 1, no. 1 (1969): 1–12 and 1, no. 2 (1969): 127–35; and Han-liang Chang, "Is Language a Primary Modelling System? On Juri Lotman's Concept of Semiosphere," *Sign System Studies* 31, no. 2 (2003): 1–15.

7. See chap. 4 and Viktor Klemperer, *The Language of the Third Reich: LTI—Lingua Tertii Imperii; A Philologist's Notebook*, trans. Martin Brady (London: Bloomsbury, 2013).

8. Safiya Umoja Noble, *Algorithms of Oppression: How Search Engines Reinforce Racism* (New York: NYU Press, 2018).

9. Roland Barthes, "Inaugural Lecture, Collège de France," trans. Richard Howard, in *A Barthes Reader*, ed. Susan Sontag (New York: Hill & Wang, 1983), 461; emphasis added.

10. Ibid.; emphasis in the original.

11. Umberto Eco, "La lingua, il potere, la forza" (originally pub. *Alfabeta*, May 1, 1979), *Sette anni di desiderio* (Milan: Bompiani, 1983), 187.

12. Ibid., 186.

13. Ibid., 187.

14. Barthes, "Inaugural Lecture," 462; emphasis in the original.

15. Umberto Eco, "Per una guerriglia semiotica," in *Il costume di casa: Evidenze e misteri dell'ideologia italiana negli anni Sessanta* (Milan: Bompiani, 1973), 290–98. See Paolo Desogus, "La teoria critica di Umberto Eco: La critica dell'ideologia e la guerriglia semiotica," *Enthymema* 7 (2012): 322–34.

16. As the anthropologist Emmanuel Yewah put it, ideological naturalization is "the process of unconscious internalization and expression of beliefs, values, ideas, perceptions and modes of thinking of a given society and class at a given period of time"; Yewah, "Ideology and the De/Naturalization of Meaning in the Cameroonian Novel," *Afrika Focus* 9, nos. 3–4 (1993): 181–82.

17. Umberto Eco, *A Theory of Semiotics* (Bloomington: Indiana University Press, 1976), 298; emphasis in the original.

Index